A WORLD BANK COUNTRY STUDY

Panama Poverty Assessment

*Priorities and Strategies
for Poverty Reduction*

*The World Bank
Washington, D.C.*

PANAMA POVERTY ASSESSMENT:
Priorities and Strategies for Poverty Reduction

TABLE OF CONTENTS

ANNEXES

ABSTRACT

Despite Panama's relatively high income per capita, poverty remains pervasive. Over one million people (37 percent of the population) live below the poverty line, and, of these, over half a million live in extreme poverty. The distribution and magnitude of poverty in Panama varies significantly by geographic area, with a bias towards rural areas. Poverty in indigenous areas can only be described as abysmal: over 95 percent of residents of indigenous areas fall below the poverty line and 86 percent live in extreme poverty. Although poverty is not as widespread or deep in urban areas, a significant share of the poor and near-poor live in Panama's cities. One half of all children are poor and there is a strong correlation between poverty and child malnutrition. Panama is also one of the most unequal countries in the world, with a consumption Gini of 49 and an income Gini of 60.

The problems of poverty, malnutrition, and inequality are symptomatic of underlying disparities in opportunity. The distribution of key productive assets – labor, human capital, physical assets, financial assets, and social capital – is highly unequal. These disparities are most prevalent between the poor and non-poor, but also manifest themselves differently by geographic area.

Such disparities largely reflect a legacy of distortions in Panama's economy and it's uniquely dualistic pattern of development. Factor markets have been segmented by policies that drive up the cost of labor – the poor's most abundant asset – to capital. These interventions not only hamper growth, but they also have a direct link to poverty. Policy-induced rigidities and low productivity have also characterized the traditional sector (primarily agriculture and industry), that is juxtaposed with a dynamic, modern services sector.

Disparities in key assets – notably human capital – also reflect a lack of targeting and efficiency of social policy and social spending. Despite high spending on the social sectors, inefficiencies and inequities have prevented improved outcomes for the poor. Total public spending on education is regressive, with the non-poor benefiting more than the poor. Geographic inequities in public education spending are also apparent, with biases in favor of urban areas and against rural and indigenous areas. Inequities in public spending on health care also abound, with the poorest quintile benefiting the least due to low levels of use and access to these services. While several social assistance programs appear to be effective at reaching the poor, lack of targeting, inefficiencies in program delivery, and possible duplication of functions reduces the effectiveness of the social safety net.

Poverty reduction is the top priority of the new Government. In order to strengthen the key assets of the poor, the Government should take a number of key actions, including: prioritizing among poverty groups, reallocating public spending towards areas that benefit the poor, decentralize and promote community participation in service delivery, implement key policy reforms to reduce disparities in assets, improve targeting mechanisms, and allocate sufficient resources to monitor poverty and poverty reduction interventions.

ACKNOWLEDGMENTS

This report is the outcome of a highly collaborative process by the Government of Panama and the World Bank. The process involved continuous cooperation and numerous missions by World Bank staff to Panama and MIPPE staff to Washington.

The World Bank's task team included: Ana-Maria Arriagada (Sector Leader), Kathy Lindert (Task Manager), Kinnon Scott, Carlos Sobrado, Renos Vakis, Maria-Valeria Junho Pena, Hector Lindo-Fuentes, Tom Wiens, Nobuhiko Fuwa, and Rafael Yrarrazaval. Carlos Becerra and Enriqueta Davis provided invaluable inputs in Panama. Judy McGuire, Tilahun Temesgen, Amit Dar, and Saji Thomas also contributed. Lerick Kebeck edited, was in charge of the presentation, coordinated and managed the production of the report. Norman Hicks and Jose Sokol were the Peer Reviewers. The team also benefited from the guidance of Ian Bannon (Lead Economist).

The task team in the Ministry of Economics and Finance (MEF, formerly the Ministry of Planning and Economic Policy, MIPPE) included: Nuvia Z. de Jarpa (Director of Social Policy), Rosa Elena de De la Cruz (National Coordinator of the LSMS and Poverty Study), Cecilio Gadpaille, Maria Cristina de Pastor, Edith de Kowalczyk, Zuleika de Bustos, Ida de García, Agustín García, Armando Villarreal, Gabriela Montoya, Miguel Achurra, Eudemia Pérez, Tatiana Lombardo, Roberto González, and Julio Diégez H. Pedro Contreras, Gloriela de Gordón and Gloria Rivera of the Ministry of Health also participated in the study. Nuvia Z. de Jarpa and Cecilio Gadpaille also participated in the final revision of the Report.

Funding for the study was generously provided by the Government of Panama (GOP), the World Bank (including funding from the Institutional Development Fund (IDF) and the Strategic Compact), the United Nations Development Programme, the Government of Japan, and the Swiss Agency for Development and Cooperation.

CURRENCY EQUIVALENTS
US1$ = 1 Balboa

FISCAL YEAR
January 1 – December 31

ACCRONYMS AND ABBREVIATIONS

BHN	National Mortgage Bank
CAS	Country Assistance Strategy
CBN	Cost of Basic Needs method for calculating poverty
CEFACEI	Community and Family Centers for Initial Education
CSS	Social Security Institute
DEC	Directorate of Statistics and the Census
FDI	Institutional Development Fund (Fondo de Desarrollo Institucional)
FES	Emergency Social Fund
GDP	Gross Domestic Product
GOP	Government of Panama
HFA	Height for age
IDDAN	National Institute of Aqueducts and Sewers (Instituto de Acueductos y Alcantarillados Nacionales)
IDB	Inter-American Development Bank
ILO	International Labor Organization
LAC	Latin America and the Caribbean
LSMS	Living Standards Measurement Survey
MEF	Ministry of Economy and Finance (formerly MIPPE and Hacienda)
MIDA	Ministry of Agricultural Development
MINEDUC	Ministry of Education
MINSA	Ministry of Health
MINTRAB	Ministry of Labor
MIPPE	Ministry of Planning and Economic Policy (now Ministry of Economics and Finance)
MIVI	Ministry of Housing
MJMNF	Ministry of Youth, Women, Children and Family
NFPS	Non-financial public sector
NGOs	Non-Governmental Organizations
PARVIS	Program for Rapid Support of Social Housing
PM	Poverty Map
PROINLO	Local Investment Program
SCQS	Social Capital Qualitative Survey
WFA	Weight for age
WFH	Weight for height
UNDP	United Nations Development Program

PANAMA POVERTY ASSESSMENT:
Priorities and Strategies for Poverty Reduction

EXECUTIVE SUMMARY

1.   This report has three main objectives. The first is to assess the extent and determinants of poverty, malnutrition and inequality in Panama. The second involves examining the impact of government spending and policies on the poor in key sectors. The third is to outline priorities and steps for translating broad principles for poverty reduction into action.

2.   This study is primarily based on the first nationally-representative Living Standards Measurement Survey (LSMS), which was conducted by the Ministry of Planning and Economic Policy (MIPPE, now the Ministry of Economy and Finance, MEF), with funding from the Government of Panama, the World Bank, the Inter-American Development Bank, the Swiss Agency for Development and Cooperation, Japan's Policy and Human Resource Development Fund, and the United Nations Development Program. The study also draws on results from a Social Capital Qualitative Survey, which was designed to complement the LSMS with in-depth community-level information on perceptions, social organization, and social capital.

3.   The process by which this report was prepared is as important as the document itself. It is based on a highly collaborative process between the Government and the World Bank designed to build local capacity for, and ownership of, the analysis of poverty. The process involved continuous cooperation and numerous missions by Bank staff to Panama and MIPPE/MEF staff to Washington. MIPPE/MEF has also actively disseminated preliminary results, regularly publishing the findings in various bulletins and papers and holding numerous seminars and workshops. The process has already served as an important input for policy making and the development of the Bank's Assistance Strategy for Panama. The LSMS and the Poverty Assessment have provided the empirical underpinnings for the new Government's Social Agenda, which

emphasizes poverty reduction as its top priority. The former Government's Poverty Strategy, which was approved as a Cabinet Resolution in September 1998, was also a direct outcome of this on-going effort. With the technical support of the Bank's Poverty Assessment team, the Government also constructed a new and improved Poverty Map that combines data from the LSMS with the National Census to serve as a policy tool for targeting public spending and interventions.

THE PROBLEMS OF POVERTY, MALNUTRITION AND INEQUALITY...

4.   **Despite Panama's relatively high-income per capita (US$3,080 in 1997), poverty remains pervasive.** Over one million people (37% of the population) live below the poverty line, and of these, over half a million (19%) live in extreme poverty. One half of all Panamanian children are poor. The distribution and magnitude of poverty in Panama varies significantly by geographic area:

- **Rural poverty bias.** Poverty and extreme poverty are concentrated in the countryside. Rural poverty is higher in relative terms (with 65% and 39% of the rural population living in poverty and extreme poverty, respectively) and in absolute terms, with over 788,000 rural residents living in poverty (close to three-quarters of the nation's poor population).

- **Destitution among the indigenous.** Poverty in indigenous areas can only be described as abysmal. Over 95% of residents of indigenous areas (197,003 people) fall below the poverty line and 86% live in extreme poverty. Although indigenous residents represent only 8% of the total population, they account for 19% and 35% of the nation's poor and extreme poor. With higher rates of fertility, indigenous areas are the most rapidly growing segment of the population. As such, Panama's poverty rate will increase in the absence of an aggressive poverty reduction strategy. Poverty and extreme poverty are highest among the Ngobe-Buglé, Panama's largest ethnic indigenous group, followed by the Embera-Wounan. Poverty is lower among the Kuna overall, though it is still quite high among those living in indigenous areas. Geography appears to be a more powerful determinant of poverty than ethnicity, with a higher incidence among ethnic indigenous people living within indigenous areas than those living outside these areas.

- **Urban vulnerability.** Although poverty is not as widespread or deep in urban areas (15% of the urban population), Panama's cities account for an important share of the poor (23% or over 232,000 poor urban residents). Close to 40% of the urban poor (over 90,000 people) live in the Panama City – San Miguelito area. Moreover, a significant share of city-dwellers live just above the poverty line and could be considered vulnerable.

5. **Poverty is a national problem, with several key regional pressure points.** Panama's poor are spread across the country. Although poverty rates are significantly higher further away from the capital area, some 315,000 poor residents are concentrated in the Provinces of Panama and Colón. The new Poverty Map recently constructed by MIPPE/MEF using data from the LSMS and the Population Census confirms this tendency: poverty rates are highest in San Blas, Darién, Bocas del Toro, Coclé, and Chiriquí, and lowest in the Provinces of Panama and Colón. Nonetheless, these latter two provinces account for roughly one third of Panama's poor. Within each region, poverty rates are highest in the rural, indigenous, and remote areas and lowest in the central urban districts.

6. **There is a strong correlation between poverty and child malnutrition in Panama.** Over 16% of all children under five (close to 50,000) suffer from any form of malnutrition. About 85% of these are poor. Close to one quarter of poor children and one third of extreme poor under five are malnourished, compared to 4% among the non-poor. The incidence of malnutrition mirrors the geographic and ethnic patterns of poverty, with one-half of all children in indigenous areas suffering from malnutrition and the highest incidence among the Ngobe-Buglé.

7. **Panama is among the more unequal countries in the world.** With a consumption Gini of 49 and an income Gini of 60, Panama's inequality ranks among the highest – on par with Brazil and just below South Africa, two of the world's most unequal countries in the world. Panama's poorest are very poor and the richest are very rich. Although inequality is higher in rural areas, it is more obvious in urban areas, such as the city of Colón, where the close physical juxtaposition of the modern, dynamic, wealthy sector with poor city slums accentuates the perceived gap between rich and poor.

...REFLECT UNDERLYING DISPARITIES IN ASSETS.

8. **The problems of poverty, malnutrition, and inequality in Panama largely reflect disparities in opportunity.** The distribution of key productive assets – labor, human capital, physical assets, financial assets, and social capital – is highly unequal. These disparities are most prevalent between the poor and non-poor, but also manifest themselves differently by geographic area.

9. **Labor, the poor's most abundant asset, accounts for 77% of their total income** (69% for the non-poor). Nonetheless, the poor are constrained in their use of this key asset in a number of ways:

- **High rates of unemployment for the urban poor.** Though poverty and unemployment are not correlated for the nation as a whole, the poor are twice as likely to be unemployed as the non-poor in Panama's cities. The difference is even higher when taking into account seasonal and discouraged job seekers. Unemployment is particularly high for poor urban women and youths.

- **Potential underemployment among the poor in all areas.** The poor work fewer total hours than the non-poor in all areas – a likely sign of underemployment and low productivity.

- **A strong correlation between informal-sector employment and poverty.** Close to three-quarters of the poor work in the informal sector (40% of the non-poor). Low levels of household consumption are significantly correlated with informal sector employment even after other factors (such as human capital) are taken into account. Earnings in the informal sector are significantly lower than those in the formal sector: informal workers earn 60% and 43% of what those in the private and public formal sector earn. These differences are not explained by differences in human capital, area of residence, or job characteristics.

- **Indigenous workers face probable wage discrimination.** The LSMS shows[1] that the differences in the salaries received by indigenous and non-indigenous workers cannot be explained by factors such as education, experience, type of work, etc. In addition, indigenous workers have few opportunities for employment in the formal sector.

10. **Human capital – education and health – is an important complement to labor, boosting its productivity and potential for income generation.** The LSMS reveals that schooling pays off in terms of higher incomes: each year of schooling yields about a 5% increase in hourly earnings. These returns vary significantly by education level, with primary school (which has fairly equitable coverage) generating much lower returns than secondary or higher education (to which the poor have much less access). Access to health care also generates productivity gains and contributes directly to well-being. The distribution of human capital assets, however, is highly unequal.

11. **Disparities in education are key causes of poverty, malnutrition, and inequality in Panama.** Education is also a crucial elevator for the poor to lift themselves out of poverty. Higher educational attainment for a household head or his/her companion significantly reduces the probability of being poor. Mothers' education significantly affects child nutritional status. Disparities in education

constitute the single most important determinant of inequality, accounting for about 40% of Panama's consumption inequality. Inequities are apparent for achievement, coverage, internal efficiency and the quality of education:

- Although progress has been made in expanding **literacy** and increasing **educational attainment** over time, gaps remain for the poor and the indigenous (particularly indigenous women).

- The main gaps in **access** include the indigenous at all levels, and the rural and urban poor at the pre-primary and secondary levels. Moreover, very few students of higher education are poor (5%). Key obstacles to higher enrollment for the poor include (i) the direct costs of schooling (fees, books, etc.) at the primary and secondary levels; (ii) a lack of "interest" among some poor children (particularly poor urban boys) at the secondary level, which could reflect social pressures as well as quality issues in the educational system; and (iii) a lack of programs at the pre-primary level.

- **Internal efficiency** is also lower among the poor and indigenous, who tend to repeat grades and drop out more frequently than the non-poor.

- Lower **quality** education for the poor is evident from the higher share of poor students without textbooks, a lack of bilingual materials and instruction for indigenous primary students, the high share of the poor in communities reporting insufficient teachers, and dilapidated school facilities in communities with higher concentrations of the poor.

12. **Inequities in health status and health care also abound.** Relatively strong health indicators for the nation as a whole mask large disparities and poor health status among those living in poorer areas. The poor (particularly the indigenous) have lower life expectancy, higher rates of infant mortality and malnutrition, and continue to die from infectious and communicable diseases despite Panama's epidemiological transitioning. The poor and indigenous have less access to health care, and are less likely to seek medical treatment in case

---

[1] The analysis is based on salary regressions that do not include income from self-employment. See Annex 6, Appendix A6.3.

of illness than the non-poor. Low access to health services bears a significant link to child malnutrition in Panama.

13. **Physical assets – such as housing and land – also contribute to income-generating potential and help households avert risk.** The poor commonly use housing and land as a base for productive activities and enterprises. Property also generates rent – through earnings charged to renters or via the savings from "imputed" rent. Households can also use property as collateral for leveraging credit. Emergency income can likewise be generated through sales of property or borrowing against it (equity loans). Finally, housing can be used as a tool for extending personal relationships, building trust, and generating social capital.

14. **The ability of households to use property as an asset depends largely on the security of tenure and the flexibility of land and housing markets.** In Panama, the distribution of housing and land is highly unequal, as is access to the titling of available property.

- **Housing.** The poor tend to live in much lower quality housing than the non-poor. Moreover, while the majority of the population lacks proof of ownership (registered or unregistered titles) for their homes, the gap in titling of housing assets is much worse for the poor. Not owning a house increases a household's probability of being poor, as does the lack of a registered title.

- **Land.** The distribution of land is highly unequal in Panama. The poor, who account for two-thirds of the rural population, own one third of land. Among those who own any land, the Gini coefficient for total land owned is 77. Disparities in land ownership account for 11% of total consumption inequality in Panama. The poor have even less access to *titled* land: only one third of all owned agricultural land is fully titled, and the non-poor own 84% of it.

- **Titling and Income Generation.** The lack of property titles reduces the ability of the poor to obtain credit (since titles are often required as collateral). The lack of guarantees (property titles or other assets)

was the main reason poor households were refused credit. Without formal claim, the poor also lack the possibility of selling or borrowing against these assets for emergency income.

15. **Basic infrastructure services contribute to higher welfare and productivity.** Some services, such as potable water and sanitation, contribute directly to overall welfare and health status. Others, such as electricity and telephones, help households use their homes productively for income generation. The LSMS reveals that access to basic services is highly correlated with a lower probability of being poor. Inequities in access to such services abound in Panama, both between the poor and non-poor and by geographic area (especially among disperse populations in rural and indigenous areas). Key gaps in coverage include: the indigenous for all services and the rural poor for energy and sanitation services and to a lesser extent, potable water. While the urban poor have much greater access to all types of services than their rural counterparts, a lack of sanitation services for an important share of poor city-dwellers raises public health concerns.

16. **Financial assets – savings and credit – allow households to smooth their consumption and invest for future earnings potential.** The poor are much less likely to save than the non-poor; when they do, they tend to put their savings in public institutions (whereas the non-poor are more likely to use private banks). The overall volume of lending to the poor is much smaller than their contribution to the economy. Whereas poor households receive 3% of total credit, they account for 10% of total consumption and income in the economy. Information constraints, physical distance, lack of formal guarantees, and high costs-per-dollar borrowed present obstacles to lending to the poor.

17. **Social capital[2] is one of the assets of the poor.** The poor and extreme poor account for a disproportionate share of those living in communities with high social capital. The LSMS reveals that the poor tend to associate for

---

[2] Social capital – defined as norms, trust, and reciprocity networks that facilitate mutually beneficial cooperation in a community – is an important asset that can reduce vulnerability and increase opportunities.

"public goods" purposes (e.g., in community associations), whereas the non-poor join associations that yield higher private gains (e.g., cooperatives). These patterns suggest that the poor rely on community action (social capital) to compensate for a lack of other assets created by public services. Social capital also helps communities leverage assistance. Communities with high social capital report a higher frequency of assistance from the Government and NGOs. This correlation is observed in all three geographic areas, and is particularly strong in rural and indigenous areas. Interventions should work with communities to build on this important avenue for public action.

SUCH DISPARITIES LARGELY REFLECT A LEGACY OF DISTORTIONS IN PANAMA'S ECONOMY...

18.   **The disparities in the distribution of assets and economic opportunity reflect Panama's uniquely dualistic pattern of development.** Panama's privileged geographic location and its monetary regime anchored in the use of the US dollar as legal tender have fostered its comparative advantage in services, which contribute over three quarters of GDP and generate two-thirds of employment in Panama. These strategic factors have also spurred the rapid development of internationally-oriented, modern, dynamic service enclaves, including the Canal Zone, the Colón Free Zone, and the International Banking Center. While these enclaves generate large shares of GDP, they create little employment (3% of the labor force) or fiscal revenue. Moreover, they inject negative spillovers into the economy due to the huge differentials between wages paid in the enclaves, particularly the Canal Zone (which is subject to the U.S. labor code) and the rest of the economy.

19.   **Indeed, factor markets have been segmented by policies that drive up the cost of labor relative to capital.** Panama's labor market is characterized by a multiplicity of policy regimes, with separate regimes for the private sector, the public sector, the Panama Canal Commission, and the Export Processing Zones. These regimes have created large wage differentials between workers in the Panama Canal Commission, public sector employees, and those employed in the rest of the economy.

20.   **Labor-market interventions not only hamper growth, but also have a direct link to poverty.** By increasing the relative price of labor – and thus reducing demand for the poor's most abundant asset – these distortions have swelled the ranks of the unemployed and encouraged informality. Moreover, while they benefit those who work in formal sector jobs, the resulting segmentation of the labor market can put a heavy toll on informal sector workers by reducing their wages, making it difficult for the working poor to grow out of poverty through their own labor. Indeed, the LSMS reveals that the poor in Panama do not benefit from such distortions, but may be hurt by them: (i) the majority of the working poor receive wages that are below the official minimum wage; (ii) they do not receive the "mandated" fringe benefits; (iii) the majority are employed in the informal sector, where wages are lower and employment terms less favorable; and (iv) the urban poor are hurt by high rates of open unemployment and the rural working poor appear to be underemployed.

21.   **The modern services sector is juxtaposed with a traditional sector (primarily agriculture and industry), that has been constrained by policy-induced rigidities and low productivity for decades.** Until recently, a highly distorted trade regime (one of the most protectionist in Latin America) combined with a complex web of price controls, had the result of protecting inefficient sectors, distorting resource allocation, generating rents for certain groups, and raising the cost of basic staples. Simulations using the LSMS suggest that the net redistributive effects of such protection was regressive, effectively taxing the poor and increasing poverty and inequality.

22.   **A number of fundamental reforms have been adopted since the early 1990s in an attempt to stimulate higher and more inclusive growth and reduce poverty and inequality.** These reforms include: dismantling the labyrinth of trade barriers and price controls, launching a far-reaching privatization program, issuing anti-trust legislation, unifying fiscal incentives for manufacturing firms, and adopting modest but important reforms in the Labor Code. After several years of little growth, the economy began to respond in 1997, with strong growth and some decline in unemployment for

the first time in years. Even more important for the long-term, employment has apparently become more responsive to changes in growth. Despite these reforms, an important policy agenda remains, with several key additional reforms needed to reduce poverty.

...AND BIASES AND INEFFICIENCIES IN PUBLIC SPENDING.

23. **Disparities in key assets – notably human capital – also reflect a lack of targeting of social policy and public spending.** Despite high spending on the social sectors (21% of GDP overall, 6% for education, and 7% for health in 1997), inefficiencies and inequities have prevented improved outcomes for the poor:

- **Total public spending on education is regressive**, with the non-poor benefiting more than the poor. This inequity largely reflects the large share of public spending allocated to higher education (close to one-third of the public education budget), virtually all of which (95%) benefits the non-poor. It also reflects the gaps in coverage of the poor at the pre-primary and secondary levels. Geographic inequities in public spending on education are also apparent, with biases in favor of urban areas and against rural (indigenous and non-indigenous) areas. Furthermore, the poor quality of public education stems from functional inefficiencies in the delivery of education, including over-centralized decision-making, weak policy-making and planning capacity in the Ministry of Education, lack of management information tools, and a disconnect between teacher salaries and performance.

- **Inequities in public spending on health care also abound.** The poorest quintile of the population benefits the least from public spending on health care due to low levels of use and access to these services. Inefficiencies in the health sector – including the fragmentation of the sector by three major providers (the Ministry of Health, the Social Security Institute, and the private sector), few incentives for efficiency and performance, and weak policy-making, financing, and regulation capabilities in the Ministry of Health – have also prevented improved health outcomes among the poor.

- **Since the early 1990s, the Government has attempted to compensate for some of these biases by developing a number of social assistance programs.** While several programs appear to be quite effective at reaching the poor, lack of targeting of some of the larger programs, inefficiencies in program delivery, and possible duplication of functions reduces the effectiveness of these transfers.

SOCIAL AGENDA AND A STRATEGY FOR POVERTY REDUCTION: MAIN PRINCIPLES

24. **Poverty reduction is the top priority of the new Government, as emphasized in the Social Agenda.** This agenda outlines broad strategic principles for reducing poverty, seeking to strengthen the key assets of the poor, taking into account geographic differences in the poverty situation and priorities. The main underlying principles for this strategy include:

- Improved efficiency in social spending to improve its investment impact on human capital;

- Targeting of resources to the poor to improve the likelihood of impact on poverty;

- Decentralization and "de-bureaucratization" of services for improved efficiency and quality of interventions;

- Increased community participation for improved effectiveness; and

- Monitoring of the poverty situation and of the implementation of actions to reduce poverty.

TRANSLATING THESE PRINCIPLES INTO PRIORITIES AND ACTION

25. To translate these principles into action, the Government should:

- **Prioritize among poverty groups.** Given the distribution of poverty, first priority should be given to: the rural poor, the indigenous (particularly the Ngobe-Buglé), poor children and youths, and under-nourished children and pregnant and lactating women. Second priority should be assigned to combating urban poverty. Third priority should be given to programs that target the poor elderly, poor child laborers, poor informal-sector workers and the poor unemployed.

- **Reallocate public expenditures.** The top priority for effective action to reduce poverty should involve reallocating public expenditures. Given the high level of social spending, it is unlikely that a large amount of additional resources will be forthcoming. As such, the Government needs to reallocate existing spending toward areas that benefit the poor, boost cost recovery for services used by the non-poor, and improve efficiency in service delivery. A thorough review of public spending should be conducted to provide guidance on such reallocations. This review should emphasize both the functional aspects of the budget (including the distributional incidence of spending in key sectors) as well as the management of public expenditures. Clear candidates for reallocation of **education** spending include: (i) enforcing higher cost recovery for higher education and shifting freed resources toward basic education; (ii) focusing spending on demand side education schemes to reduce economic barriers faced by poor households to increase enrollment by the poor. Although a thorough analysis of the incidence of **health** spending remains to be done, some candidates for reallocation include: (i) enforcing higher cost recovery for curative and hospital care (disproportionately benefit the non-poor) and (ii) shifting resources to cost-effective primary interventions in poor areas. Spending on **social insurance and assistance** should also be streamlined to ensure a comprehensive, efficient, well-targeted safety net. An inventory of service coverage should be overlayed with the new poverty map to guide spending allocations on **basic services** so as to target key gaps among the poor. In broad terms, transportation, electricity, telephones and potable water have been identified by *rural* communities as priority; potable water is top priority in *indigenous* communities; and transportation and sanitation are key for *urban* communities.

- **Decentralize and promote community participation in service delivery** to improve the effectiveness and efficiency of poverty interventions. Examples include: (i) decentralizing personnel decisions to regional education boards and expanding innovative participatory pre-school programs; (ii) decentralizing food purchases in remote areas under school feeding programs; (iii) expanding use of NGOs and communities as intermediaries in social programs; and (iv) responding to community preferences for service delivery.

- **Implement key policy reforms to reduce disparities in assets.** While maintaining existing reforms is critical, the agenda for the second-generation of economic reforms designed to promote growth is large. Special efforts should be made to ensure that key reforms to reduce disparities in assets, and hence poverty, are undertaken, including: (i) deepening reforms to the labor code; (ii) expanding property titling (both of housing and land), which will also help improve the poor's access to credit; (iii) continuing trade reforms; and (iv) reducing distortions in public and freight transport.

- **Improve targeting mechanisms.** The Government should apply the new poverty map (combining data from the LSMS and the census) to the allocation of expenditures as soon as possible. It should also seek to develop additional mechanisms for targeting, including means-testing and self-targeting.

- **Allocate sufficient resources to monitor poverty and the implementation poverty reduction interventions.** The Government is developing a poverty monitoring system to track living conditions and provide data for impact evaluation of interventions. This system includes LSMS-type surveys to be conducted every three years. The Government should also seek to develop a key set of indicators for monitoring actions to reduce poverty. Program-specific questions should also be included in the next LSMS for additional impact and implementation analysis.

26. **Some key steps for immediate implementation** should include:

- Conducting a thorough review of public expenditure allocations and developing proposals for reallocating expenditures such that they better reach the poor starting with the next fiscal budget;

- Developing a set of indicators to monitor implementation of poverty reduction interventions (including key budget categories) and agreeing on an inter-institutional process for reporting on such indicators and implementation. Funds from the on-going IDF grant could be used to contract technical assistance to help MEF staff developing and monitoring such indicators;

- Applying the new Poverty Map as a tool for targeting and resource allocation; and

- Continuing dissemination efforts for both the Poverty Assessment and the Poverty Map in both Government circles and public forums.

27.   **Areas for further research** include: public expenditure analysis (incidence and management), the links between poverty and the environment, a thorough analysis of the impact of existing legislation on labor markets including the informal sector, an analysis of the distributional incidence of social security, impact evaluations of social assistance programs, participatory research on the obstacles to increased school enrollment among indigenous children, and participatory research on poverty, crime and violence.

INTRODUCTION

1.   **Objectives.** This report has three main objectives. The first is to assess the extent and determinants of poverty, malnutrition and inequality in Panama. The second involves examining the impact of government policies and spending on the poor in key sectors. The third is to outline priorities and steps for translating broad principles for poverty reduction into action.

2.   **Quantitative and Qualitative Data Sources.** This study is primarily based on the first nationally-representative **Living Standards Measurement Survey** (LSMS),[1] which was conducted with funding from the Government, the World Bank (which also provided technical support), the Inter-American Development Bank, the Swiss Agency for Development and Cooperation, Japan's Policy and Human Resource Development Fund, and the United Nations Development Program. The World Bank's Institutional Development Fund (IDF) also provided funds for building the capacity of staff in the Ministry of Economy and Finance (MEF, formerly known as MIPPE)[2] in social policy analysis and formulation. MIPPE carried out the survey in 1997 with active collaboration of an inter-institutional committee consisting of the Ministry of Health, the Ministry of Education, the Ministry of Agriculture, the Directorate of the Census and Statistics, the Social Fund (FES), and MEF/MIPPE. The LSMS household questionnaire includes quantitative data on various aspects of living conditions, including household structure, housing, infrastructure, health, nutrition, education and training, economic activity (labor), migration, spending and consumption, income, savings, credit, independent business activities, and agriculture.[3] The LSMS community questionnaire, covering 436 communities, involved focus-group discussions to collect quantitative and qualitative information from community members on their priorities, perceptions, social problems, and social capital.

3.   The study also draws on results from the joint MIPPE-World **Bank Social Capital Qualitative Survey** (SCQS), which was designed to complement the LSMS with in-depth community-level information on perceptions, social organization, and social capital. Qualitative focus-group discussions for the SCQS were carried out in 16 communities in urban, rural and indigenous areas in November 1997.

4.   **Collaborative Process.** The process by which this report was prepared is as important as the document itself. The objectives of this process were to build capacity for, and ownership of, the analysis in the Government. It is based on a highly collaborative process between the Government and the World Bank, involving continuous cooperation and numerous missions by Bank staff to Panama and MEF staff to Washington. As a result, MEF staff, as well as representatives of several other line ministries and agencies, have been intimately involved in generating and understanding the results. MEF has also actively disseminated results, regularly publishing the findings in various bulletins and papers and holding numerous seminars, workshops and discussions both within the Government and in public forums.

5.   **Policy Impact of the Poverty Assessment and LSMS.** The process has already served as an important input for policy making. **First,** MEF with the FES and technical support from the Bank's Poverty Assessment team constructed an improved Poverty Map that combines data from the LSMS with data from the National Census. This new Poverty Map will serve as an important policy tool for targeting public spending and specific programs (including the FES). **Second,** the LSMS is being used to conduct policy analysis in a number of sectors, including *inter-alia* a demand-and-supply study of health care

---

[1] *Encuesta de Niveles de Vida.* LSMS interviews were fielded from June to September 1997. Data are available for public use on the World Wide Web at: http://ispace.worldbank.org/cgi-bin/frameit.fcg?http://www.worldbank.org/html/prdph/lsms/lsmshome.html
[2] In January 1999, the Ministry of Planning and Economic Policy (MIPPE) merged with Hacienda creating a new ministry called the Ministry of Economics and Finance.
[3] The final sample includes 4,938 households, of the 650,726 households at the national level, and 21,410 individuals of the 2,732,316 individuals in the national population.

services and incidence, and cost-benefit analysis in the education sector. **Third,** the analysis substantially contributed to the development of the Bank's Assistance Strategy for Panama.[4] **Fourth,** the former Government's "New Strategy for Reducing Poverty,"[5] which was passed as a Cabinet Resolution in September 1998, was a direct outcome of the Poverty Assessment process, the analysis of the LSMS (including community focus-group discussions), and several high-level inter-ministerial poverty seminars. **Finally,** the LSMS and Poverty Assessment have also provided the empirical underpinnings for the new Government's Social Agenda, which places poverty reduction as the number one priority for the new administration.[6]

6.   **Road Map for the Report.** This report is divided in two sections. The **first section** presents the main body of the report and is organized as follows. **Chapter 1** examines the extent and distribution of poverty in Panama answering the question Who are the Poor in Panama? It also assesses the extent of malnutrition and inequality. The problems of poverty, malnutrition, and inequality in Panama largely reflect underlying disparities in key assets (labor, human capital, physical assets, financial assets, and social capital), as shown in **Chapters 2 and 3.** Such disparities can largely be traced to a legacy of distortions in Panama's economy, as discussed in **Chapter 4**, and biases in public spending, as discussed in **Chapter 5.** **Chapter 6** outlines priority actions for translating broad principles for poverty reduction into action.

7.   In addition to providing additional details in technical and statistical appendices, **the second section** includes a number of in-depth background papers that were prepared during the Poverty Assessment process. These include papers on: Rural Poverty, Indigenous Poverty, Urban Poverty, the Determinants of Poverty, Malnutrition, Inequality, Poverty and Labor Markets, Poverty and Trade Reforms, Pre-School Programs, Health Care Use and the Incidence of Health Care Spending, School and Health Feeding Programs, Social Capital, and Female Headed Households.

Chapter 1 - Poverty, Malnutrition and Inequality in Panama

1.1.   This chapter identifies the magnitudes of the problems of poverty, malnutrition and inequality in Panama. It starts with a definition and measure of poverty and a description of its extent and distribution. It then examines the magnitude and distribution of malnutrition, which is highly correlated with poverty. Finally, it reviews indicators of inequality in Panama, with geographic comparisons within the country and with other nations.

MEASURING POVERTY AND WELFARE

1.2.   Assessing poverty requires some measure of welfare. Typical measures include consumption, income, and basic-needs indicators. For the first time in Panama, this study uses consumption to measure poverty and welfare. Consumption data tend to be more reliable than income data and consumption tends to fluctuate less than income, making it a better indicator of living standards. Consumption is also less subjective than basic-needs indices and is more responsive to changes in economic circumstances. Using data from the LSMS, two poverty lines were calculated using consumption as a measure of welfare: an extreme poverty line and a full poverty line.

1.3.   The **extreme poverty line** is defined as the level of per capita annual consumption required to satisfy the minimum average daily caloric requirement of 2,280.[7] The annual cost of this minimum caloric requirement yields an extreme poverty line of B./519. Below this level of expenditures,

---

[4] World Bank Report No. 18421-PAN (October 1998).
[5] *Nuevo Enfoque Estratégico Frente a la Pobreza*, Cabinet Resolution No. 134 of September 17, 1998.
[6] *Agenda Social*, 5 volumes, August 1999.
[7] Estimated by the *Instituto de Nutrición de Centro América y Panamá* (INCAP) and MINSA, this minimum represents a weighted average based on the assumption of moderate activity, taking into account the actual age and gender distribution of the Panamanian population in accordance with official population projections for 1997.

individuals cannot maintain the minimum level of caloric consumption even if all resources were allocated to food.

1.4.   The **full poverty line** is defined as the extreme poverty line (the cost of the minimum caloric requirement) plus an allowance for non-food items. This allowance is calculated as the non-food budget share of those individuals with total consumption that is close to the extreme poverty line.[8] It is assumed that, since these individuals would barely meet the minimum caloric requirements even if they spent all of their resources on food, whatever share of total consumption they actually allocate to non-food consumption must constitute true necessities. The analysis found that the non-food share for individuals near the extreme poverty line was 43 percent. This method yields a full poverty line of B./905, below which individuals would be considered poor.[9]

POVERTY IN PANAMA

1.5.   **Despite Panama's relatively high level of GDP per capita (US$3,080 in 1997), over one million people (37 percent of the population) live below the poverty line and over half a million (19 percent of the population) live in extreme poverty** (Table 1.1). Overall poverty is in line with the LAC Regional average (37 percent) but extreme poverty in Panama is higher (16 percent in LAC).[10]

1.6.   **The costs of reducing poverty in Panama are not high.** Given average consumption levels of the poor, it is estimated that the minimum annual cost to bring all poor Panamanians to the poverty line represents roughly five percent of GDP and ten percent of total government spending.[11] For extreme poverty it would cost about one percent of GDP and six percent of total government spending. Although these minimum costs exclude the inevitable administrative costs or leakages to the non-poor associated with virtually all poverty-alleviation schemes, the amounts are quite low. To put this in context, this minimum annual cost of eradicating extreme poverty roughly equals the share of public spending on higher education in 1996, virtually none of which went to the poor.

Table 1.1 – Distribution and Incidence of Poverty in 1997, By Geographic Area					
	% of National Population[a]	Incidence of Poverty Headcount Index[b] (%)		Contribution to National Poverty (% of:)	
		All Poor[c]	Extreme Poor	All Poor	Extreme Poor
Total Panama	100	37.3	18.8	100	100
By Geographic Area					
Urban	55.6	15.3	3.1	22.7	9.2
All Rural[d]	44.4	64.9	38.5	77.3	90.8
Rural (non-indigenous)	36.9	58.7	28.7	57.9	56.2
Indigenous[e]	7.6	95.4	86.4	19.3	34.6

Source: Panama LSMS 1997. (a) The distribution of the national population (2,732,316) is derived from the LSMS sample using the sample weights (expansion factors) from the National Census. It closely reproduces the figures from the National Census. (b) The Headcount Index is the share of the population whose total consumption falls below the poverty line. (c) Throughout this study, "all poor" includes the extreme poor. (d) The "all rural" area category includes: rural (non-indigenous) and indigenous areas. (e) Indigenous in this table refers to geographic area not ethnicity (see Box 1.2).

1.7.   **Poverty appears to have fallen over time.** Comparing estimates of poverty over time in Panama is risky due to large differences in sampling and methodology (Box 1.1 below). Estimates using income data from the 1983 Socioeconomic Survey calculate poverty at 39 percent of the population and

---

[8] In other words, individuals whose total consumption is more or less (+/-10 percent) equal to the extreme poverty line (Annex 2). This is known as the Cost of Basic Needs (CBN) method.

[9] An advantage of the above method for calculating the extreme and full poverty lines over the cost of a pre-determined basket of food and non-food items is that it does not impose assumptions about the consumption preferences and patterns of the population. These patterns are observed – representing the true consumption patterns of the poor in Panama – rather than imposed.

[10] Sources: Hicks and Peeters (World Bank, 1998) and Wodon (World Bank, 1999). These figures are based on household survey data for Latin American countries and similar poverty measurement methodologies.

[11] As a percent of spending by the non-financial public sector (NFPS).

extreme poverty at 20 percent. Adjusting these figures to include indigenous and remote populations[12] yields rough estimates of 46% of the population living in poverty and 28% living in extreme poverty in 1983, suggesting a fall in poverty of roughly nine percentage points over the past 14 years. Trends in social indicators support this apparent improvement in living standards: life expectancy has risen (from 70 years in 1980 to 74 in 1997), infant mortality is down (from 31 per thousand live births in 1980 to 22 in 1997), and educational indicators, such as literacy and secondary school enrollment, have improved.[13]

Box 1.1 – Past Studies of Poverty and Inequality in Panama

Concern with poverty increased in Panama during the 1970s and 1980s, and a number of studies of poverty and inequality were conducted during that time (many of which were commissioned by the Government). A number of agencies (including MIPPE, ECLAC, and ILO) have also tracked poverty on an annual basis using household labor surveys since the late 1980s. Inferring conclusions regarding the trends in poverty and inequality from these studies is risky due to large differences in data coverage (none were nationally representative), methodology, and the definition of welfare variables (most used incomplete measures of income) and poverty lines (most set the extreme poverty line equal the cost of a basic food basket in Panama City and doubled it to obtain the full poverty line).

Some Past Findings on Poverty (poverty figures reported on an individual basis).
- **Molina (1982)** estimated poverty at 39% in **1970** and 37% in **1980** using Census data on incomes.
- **Sahota (1990)** estimated *extreme* poverty at 20% in **1980** using Census data on incomes
- **Sahota (1990)** estimated *extreme* poverty at 20% and *full* poverty at 39% using a fairly complete measure of income from the **1983** Socioeconomic Survey (incomplete sampling of indigenous and remote areas).
- **MIPPE (1996)** tracked poverty using data on cash incomes from the SIAL/ILO Household Survey database (excludes indigenous areas) on an annual basis from **1991-1995**. These estimates suggest a fall in poverty from 55% in 1991 to 47% in 1995 and in extreme poverty from 27% in 1991 to 22% in 1995. This drop mainly comes from a reduction in the share of urban residents living in poverty (from 47% in 1991 to 35% in 1995); rural poverty remained fairly stable during that period (at 71% in 1991 and 72% in 1995).

Some Past Findings on Income Inequality (all Ginis calculated on a per person basis).
- **McLure (1974)** calculated a Gini coefficient of 55.7 using wage data from the **1969** Household Survey
- **Sahota (1972)** calculated a Gini coefficient of 59.7 for **1970** using wage and non-wage income data from the Population Census and Agricultural Census combined with data from the Household Survey for 1969.
- The **DEC (1975)** used income data from the **1971** Income Survey to calculate a Gini coefficient of 56.3.
- **Sahota (1990)** derived a complete measure of income using data from the **1983** Socioeconomic Survey to calculate Gini coefficients of 55 for the nation as a whole (excluding indigenous and remote areas), 47 for urban areas and 56 for rural areas.

1.8.   **One-half of all Panamanian children live in poverty.** Due to higher fertility rates among the poor, a large share of children live in poverty. In fact, 53 percent of children under five (over 160,000) and 48 percent of all children under 18 (over 500,000) live below the poverty line. Close to one third live in extreme poverty. In contrast, 27 percent of senior citizens over age 60 live in poverty, with 12 percent in extreme poverty. This lower share of the elderly in poverty (compared with 37 percent of the overall national population) suggests lower life expectancy among the poor than the average population.

1.9.   **Contrary to conventional wisdom, poverty is not higher among households headed by women than those headed by men.** Overall, female-headed households are not over-represented among the poor in Panama, regardless of the method used to define household headship.[14] Some exceptions do emerge, however: (i) in urban areas, the poverty rate among female-headed households with unmarried partners (*unida*) is significantly higher than households headed by males with common-law partners; and (ii) in indigenous areas, poverty is more prevalent among households headed by widows than by widowers. These exceptions represent a very small percentage of total households however, and as such, female headship is not likely to be a useful proxy for targeting poverty interventions.

---

[12] Which currently represent 23 percent of the poor population in Panama and 36 percent of the extreme poor population. This adjustment also takes into consideration the fact that indigenous and remote populations represent about nine percent of the total population.
[13] Hicks and Peeters (September 1998).
[14] Definitions of headship include self-reported, economic and demographic (Annex 19).

1.10. **Poverty and extreme poverty are concentrated in the countryside** (Figure 1.1). A disproportionate share of the poor and extreme poor live in rural areas in comparison with the share of rural residents in the national population. Three-quarters of the poor and 91 percent of the extreme poor live in the countryside. Two thirds of all rural residents fall below the full poverty line and close to 40 percent live in extreme poverty.

Figure 1.1

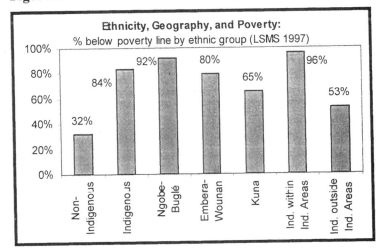

Geographic Distribution of Poverty
(LSMS 1997)

Indigenous 19% Urban 23% Rural 58%

Table 1.2 – Depth and Severity of Poverty in 1997, By Geographic Area					
	% of Pop. below Pov. Line	# Individuals below Pov. Line	Average Total Consumption (B./)[a]	Minimum Cost (mn. B./)[b]	Depth Index[c]	Severity Index[d]
Full Poverty Line (B./905), including those below the extreme poverty line						
Total	37.3	1,020,158	506	406	16.4	9.7
By Area:						
Urban	15.3	232,006	674	53	3.9	1.5
All Rural:	64.9	788,152	457	353	32.1	20.0
Rural Non-Ind.	58.7	591,148	517	229	25.2	14.0
Indigenous[e]	95.4	197,003	276	124	66.1	49.2
Extreme Poverty Line (B./519)						
Total	18.8	514,839	306	109	7.7	4.2
By Area:						
Urban	3.1	47,283	406	5	0.7	0.2
All Rural:	38.5	467,557	297	104	16.5	9.2
Rural Non-Ind.	28.7	289,236	334	53	10.2	5.0
Indigenous[e]	86.4	178,321	236	50	47.0	29.7

Source: Panama LSMS 1997. (a) Represents total annual per capita consumption for those below the poverty line. Figures have been adjusted to national prices using a price index to take into account spatial variation in prices. (b) Represents the minimum cost to bring the total per capita consumption of all individuals below the poverty line up to the line. It is the absolute poverty gap. (c) The Poverty Depth Index (P_1) represents the amount needed to bring all poor individuals up to the poverty line (full or extreme), expressed as a percent of the poverty line taking into account the share of the poor population in the national population. (d) The Poverty Severity Index (P_2) is a derivation of the Poverty Depth Index that takes into account the distribution of total consumption among the poor. In other words, it measures degree of inequality among the population below the poverty line. (e) Indigenous in this table refers to geographic area not ethnicity (see Box 1.2).

1.11. **Poverty in indigenous areas can only be described as abysmal.** Over 95 percent of residents in indigenous areas (close to 200,000 people) fall below the poverty line. Some 86 percent live in extreme poverty. Poverty is also deepest and most severe in indigenous areas (Table 1.2). On average, the indigenous poor would have to more than double their annual consumption to reach the poverty line. Although residents of indigenous areas represent only eight percent of the national population, one fifth of

the poor population and one third of the extreme poor live in indigenous areas. With higher rates of fertility, indigenous areas are the most rapidly growing segment of the population (5.4 percent per year). As such, in the absence of an aggressive poverty reduction strategy for indigenous areas, the share of the poor in the national population will increase.

1.12. **While poverty is high among all ethnic indigenous groups, there is substantial variation in the prevalence of**

Figure 1.2

Ethnicity, Geography, and Poverty:
% below poverty line by ethnic group (LSMS 1997)

Non-Indigenous 32%
Indigenous 84%
Ngobe-Buglé 92%
Embera-Wounan 80%
Kuna 65%
Ind. within Ind. Areas 96%
Ind. outside Ind. Areas 53%

poverty between them.[15] Using language indicators of ethnicity (as opposed to geographic, see Box 1.2), some 84 percent of ethnic indigenous people live below the poverty line. This compares with one third of the ethnically non-indigenous population. Poverty is most widespread among the Ngobe-Buglé, Panama's largest ethnic indigenous group,[16] followed by the Embera-Wounan,[17] and the Kuna (Figure 1.2).[18]

1.13. **Geography appears to be a powerful determinant of indigenous poverty.** Poverty is much higher among ethnic indigenous people living within indigenous areas than those living outside these areas, which makes it easier to target interventions on a geographic basis. Whereas virtually all indigenous people living within indigenous areas are poor, about half of indigenous people residing outside these areas live in poverty (Figure 1.2). The incidence of Kuna living outside indigenous areas is particularly low (34 percent) – slightly lower than the prevalence of poverty for the nation as a whole. This is particularly significant, given that roughly *half* of all ethnic Kuna live outside indigenous areas. Poverty among the Embera-Wounan and the Ngobe-Buglé living outside indigenous areas is still high, though lower than among their counterparts living within these areas.

Box 1.2 – Geography and Ethnicity in the LSMS

Geography. The LSMS is representative nationally and for four mutually-exclusive geographic areas based on demarcations from the National Census, including: urban, "rural" (non-indigenous and not remote), indigenous, and remote access. Previous household surveys have excluded indigenous and remote access areas (for cost and logistical reasons). These four groups are used for this poverty profile in order to examine geographic differences in the incidence of poverty. To simplify presentation, however, remote access areas are combined with "rural" (leaving two non-urban groups: "rural" and indigenous) for the remainder of the study. Urban areas have a population density greater than or equal to 1,500 persons per kilometer.

Ethnicity. As discussed below, indigenous poverty is abysmal. In addition to geographic indicators that provide a demarcation of "indigenous areas," the LSMS included several language indicators to allow for the classification of people and households according to their ethnicity. This is important because not all indigenous people live in the official indigenous *areas* (as demarcated in the census). These indicators also allow for the analysis of the poverty profile of specific ethnic indigenous groups, including the three largest groups: the Ngobe-Buglé, the Kuna, and the Embera-Wounan.

Geography and Ethnicity. Crossing these indicators of ethnicity and the geographic areas reveals that only 7% of people living in indigenous areas are not ethnically indigenous. About 70% of ethnic indigenous live within indigenous areas, while 19% live in urban areas and 10% live in other rural areas. The Ngobe-Buglé (the largest indigenous group) are largely concentrated in indigenous areas (84% reside in indigenous areas), whereas about half of the Kuna and Embera-Wounan live outside indigenous areas (mainly in urban areas).

1.14. **Poverty is not as deep or severe in urban areas, though an important share of the poor are city-dwellers.** Approximately 15 percent of the urban population (over 230,000 people) fall below the poverty line, accounting for one quarter of Panama's poor (Table 1.1). Close to 40 percent of these (over 90,000 people) live in the Panama City – San Miguelito area. Urban poverty is not very deep, and only three percent of city-dwellers live below the extreme poverty line. Nonetheless, a significant share of city-dwellers live just above the poverty line and could be considered vulnerable or at risk. In fact, raising the poverty line (or alternatively, reducing total consumption) by ten percent would increase the incidence of urban poverty by over 20 percent (from 230 to over 280 thousand people). Moreover, given demographic trends and urban migration,[19] a higher share of the poor could be concentrated in urban areas in the future.

---

[15] See Annex 6.

[16] The Ngobe-Buglé live primarily in the western Provinces of Chiriquí and Bocas del Toro. Poverty is probably also quite high among the Naso-Teribe and live in the similar geographic areas as the Ngobe-Buglé. However, their small population size (roughly 2,200) prevents a separate analysis of the Naso-Teribe in the survey.

[17] The Embera-Wounan reside largely in the eastern province of Darien, though about half live outside indigenous areas (largely in urban areas in the Panama Province).

[18] The Kuna traditionally live in the Province of San Blas (the autonomous Comarca Kuna Yala), though about half live outside this area (largely in urban areas in the Panama Province).

[19] The most recent census shows that the growth rate for urban areas averaged 3.7 percent p.a. as compared with 2.0 percent in rural areas and 2.9 percent for the nation as a whole from 1980 to 1990.

1.15. **Poverty is a national problem, with several key regional pressure points.** The poor are spread across the country (Table 1.3). Although poverty rates are significantly higher further away from the capital area, an important share of Panama's poor (about 315,000 people) are concentrated in the Provinces of Panama and Colón. The new Poverty Map, recently constructed by MEF/FES officials using data from the LSMS and the Census confirms this tendency: poverty rates are highest in the Provinces of San Blas, Darien, Bocas del Toro, Coclé and Chiriquí, and lowest in the Provinces of Panama and Colón.[20] Nonetheless, the latter two provinces account for roughly one third of Panama's poor. Within each province, poverty rates are higher in the rural, indigenous, and remote areas, and lowest in the central urban districts.

Table 1.3 – Regional Distribution of Poverty in Panama					
Region	Incidence of Poverty (% of Pop.)	Number of Poor People	Contribution to National Poverty (% of poor)	Region as % of National Population	Provinces included in Region
Panama City & San Miguelito	12%	90,064	9%	28%	Panama
Metropolitan Region[a]	32%	224,749	22%	26%	Panama (excluding PCSM), Colon
Urban	14%	54,169	5%	14%	
Rural[b]	54%	170,580	17%	12%	
Central Region[b]	48%	268,679	26%	20%	Veraguas, Coclé, Herrera, Los Santos
Urban	19%	34,288	3%	6%	
Rural	61%	234,390	23%	14%	
Occidental Region[b]	44%	181,364	18%	15%	Chiriquí, Bocas del Toro
Urban	29%	53,484	5%	7%	
Rural[b]	56%	127,880	13%	8%	
Indigenous	95%	197,003	19%	8%	Indig. areas in Bocas del Toro, Chiriquí, Veraguas, Darién, San Blas
Remote Areas	78%	58,299	6%	3%	Remote areas in Darién, Veraguas, Coclé, Herrera, Chiriqui
Total	37%	1,020,158	100%	100%	All

Source: Panama LSMS 1997. The LSMS is representative at the regional level for the above regions. (a) Excluding Panama City and San Miguelito (PCSM). (b) Excluding indigenous and remote areas.

MALNUTRITION IN PANAMA

1.16. **Over 16 percent of all children under five (close to 50,000) in Panama suffer from some form of malnutrition,**[21] with 14 percent who are chronically malnourished, seven percent who are underweight, and one percent suffering from acute malnutrition.[22] Malnutrition is slightly – but significantly – higher among boys than girls, which is quite common in an absence of discriminatory practices.[23] It is quite low among children aged 0-11 months (indicating that low birth weight is a rare problem), but then rises rapidly during the weaning transition (12-17months), when solids and water are introduced.[24]

1.17. **There is a strong correlation between poverty and child malnutrition.** As such, anthropometric measures appear to be good objective indicators of living standards. About 86 percent of

---

[20] MEF, Poverty Map (the Probability of Being Poor by District and Province), January 1999.

[21] The LSMS collected anthropometric data for children under age five. Three malnutrition indicators were estimated: (i) height-for-age (HFA), an indicator of chronic malnutrition or "stunting;" (ii) weight-for-age (WFA), an indicator of underweight children; and (iii) weight-for-height, an indicator of acute malnutrition or "wasting." A fourth composite measure was created to calculate the number of children from any of these three forms of malnutrition.

[22] This compares with 24 percent in Peru (weight-for-age, 1997), 28 percent in Nicaragua (any form of malnutrition), 1993, and 34 percent in Ecuador (weight-for-age, 1994).

[23] World Health Organization (1997) "Global Database on Child Growth and Malnutrition."

[24] Time series data on malnutrition are not available for children under 5. However, a height-for-age census of primary-school children is conducted periodically in Panama. The share of primary-school children who were malnourished in 1982 was 23%, 19% in 1985, 24% in 1988, and 24% in 1994. Source: World Health Organization (1997): Global Database on Child Growth and Malnutrition.

malnourished children in Panama are poor. Close to one quarter of poor children and one third of extreme poor under five are malnourished, compared to four percent among non-poor children.

1.18.   **The incidence of malnutrition mirrors the geographic and ethnic patterns of poverty.** Geographically, malnutrition is highest in children living in indigenous areas and lowest in urban areas (Figure 1.3). The children of Ngobe-Buglé (the poorest group) have the highest incidence of malnutrition (over 50 percent as compared with about one-third of Kuna and Embera-Wounan children).

Figure 1.3

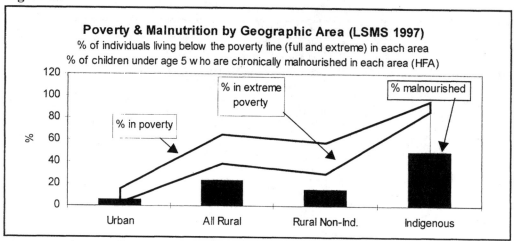

INEQUALITY IN PANAMA

1.19.   International evidence indicates that inequality is a handicap to longer-term poverty reduction for two reasons.[25] First, greater income inequality leads to lower investment in physical and human capital, and hence slower economic growth – which translates into higher poverty. Second, cross-country evidence suggests that, at any given growth rate, higher inequality results in a lower rate of poverty reduction.

1.20.   **Panama is among the more unequal countries in the world.** The Gini index using consumption for Panama as a whole is 49. This is more unequal than most other Latin American countries, and indeed the world (Table 1.4). The Gini index based on income is even higher – measured at 60 for 1997.[26] This puts the degree of inequality in Panama on par with that of Brazil and just below that of South Africa, two of the most unequal countries in the world.

---

[25] See Deininger and Squire (1997), Ravallion and Chen (1997), and Ravallion (mimeo, February 12, 1998) for a survey of cross-country evidence.
[26] Income Ginis are generally higher than Ginis based on consumption due to larger fluctuations in annual income (which exacerbate the dispersion between the extremes), whereas households tend to smooth consumption by drawing on or adding to savings (in kind and in cash). Income is also notoriously difficult to measure.

1.21.   **The poorest are very poor and the richest are very rich in Panama.**   The largest jumps in consumption and income occur at the two extremes of the spectrum: at the bottom, between the first and second quintiles, and the top, between the fourth and fifth quintiles.   While the bottom quintile consumes 3.5 percent of total consumption, the top quintile consumes 53 percent (Figure 1.4).   The poorest quintile receives 1.5 percent of total income, whereas the richest receives 63 percent.

Figure 1.4

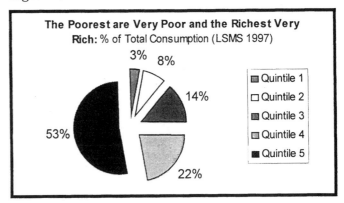

1.22.   **Inequality is highest in rural areas.**   The consumption Gini is 45 in rural areas, as compared with 41 in urban areas.[27]   Nonetheless, inequality is more obvious in urban areas, such as Colón, where the close physical juxtaposition of the modern, dynamic, wealthy sector with poor city slums accentuates the perceived gap between rich and poor.

Table 1.4 – International Comparison of Inequality using the Gini Index		
	Consumption Gini	**Income Gini**
Latin America: median	**45**	**57**
Brazil	55 (1974)	60 (1989)
Panama	**49 (1997)**	**60 (1997)**
Guatemala	n.a.	59 (1989)
Chile	n.a	58 (1989)
Mexico	50 (1992)	55 (1989)
Honduras	n.a	54 (1993)
Colombia	43 (1972)	51 (1991)
Peru	45 (1994)	49 (1981)
El Salvador	n.a	48 (1977)
Costa Rica	n.a	46 (1977)
Bolivia	42 (1990)	n.a
Ecuador	43 (1994)	n.a
Jamaica	38 (1993)	n.a
Nicaragua	50 (1993)	n.a
Africa: median (various countries/years)	48	n.a
Middle East/North Africa: median (various countries/years)	39	n.a
Eastern Europe: median (various countries/years)	36	33
Asia: median (various countries/years)	32	39
Western Europe: median (various countries/years)	32	33
Sources: Panama: 1997 LSMS; Other: World Bank Poverty Assessments, Deininger & Squire (1996). All for national populations.		

---

[27] It is entirely consistent for total inequality in a given country to be higher than inequality in geographic areas (urban, rural) because total inequality captures inequality between the areas as well as within them.

Chapter 2 – Unequal Opportunities: The Assets of the Poor

2.1.   The problems of poverty, malnutrition, and inequality in Panama largely reflect underlying disparities in economic opportunity. The distribution of key assets – labor, human capital, physical assets, financial assets, and social capital – is highly unequal. These disparities are most prevalent between the poor and non-poor, but also manifest themselves differently by geographic area. This chapter reviews the disparities in each of these key assets. The next chapter puts them together to examine their relationship to poverty, malnutrition and inequality using a multi-variate approach so as to provide insights on their relative importance.

LABOR

2.2.   Labor is the poor's most abundant asset. Although poverty is measured by total consumption rather than income (see Chapter 1), income is key in determining consumption levels, and hence poverty status. Moreover, labor is the poor's primary means of generating income. Indeed, it generates 77 percent of the total income of the poor as compared with 69 percent for the non-poor. Nonetheless, the poor are constrained in their use of this key asset, as reflected in:

- **Lower labor force participation among the poor than the non-poor, primarily due to a smaller share of poor women in the workforce.** Although male labor-force participation does not vary much by poverty group, poor women are less likely to enter the labor force than their non-poor counterparts. While one third of poor women join the labor force in Panama, half of non-poor women participate. This result is somewhat surprising, given that the mobilization of female workers is a common household response to poverty and vulnerability.[1] It could result from the higher fertility rates among the poor, and hence larger domestic responsibilities (combined with a general lack of daycare services and access to other basic services).

- **High rates of unemployment among the urban poor.** The poor are more likely to be unemployed than the non-poor[2] in urban areas (Figure 2.1). Unemployment is largely an urban phenomenon in Panama, with unemployment rates almost twice those of rural and indigenous areas, probably because the rural poor are too poor to afford unemployment (Box 2.1). Unemployment among poor city-dwellers is almost twice as high as the rate for non-poor urban residents.[3] The difference is even higher when taking into account seasonal and discouraged job seekers, indicating an important contingent of poor unemployed and discouraged urban workers.

Figure 2.1

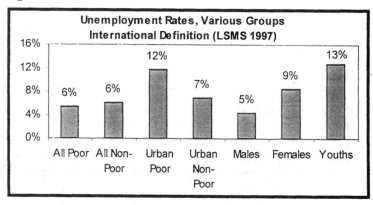

- **Potential underemployment among the poor in all areas.** The poor work fewer total hours than the non-poor (the non-poor work an average of 1.3 times more hours than the poor) – a likely sign of underemployment and low productivity among the poor.

---

[1] Moser (1996).

[2] This correlation between poverty and unemployment does not hold true for the nation overall largely because of low open unemployment in rural and indigenous areas, where poverty rates are higher. In these areas, however, the poor appear to be underemployed.

[3] Lower levels of household consumption are significantly correlated with higher levels of unemployment for both men and women in urban areas even after other factors have been taken into account. See Annex 11.

- **A strong correlation between poverty and informal-sector employment,[4] particularly for women.** One half of the workforce in Panama is employed in the informal sector (largely as blue-collar day laborers, domestic employees, or self-employed workers).[5] Close to 80 percent of the extreme poor and 70 percent of all poor workers are employed in the informal sector (primarily in informal jobs in agriculture, commerce, and services). Indeed, controlling for other factors (such as differences in human capital), lower household consumption increases the probability of being employed in the informal sector. Three-quarters of indigenous workers work in the informal sector. Almost all poor and extremely poor women work in the informal sector.

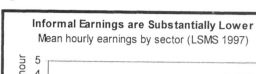

Figure 2.2

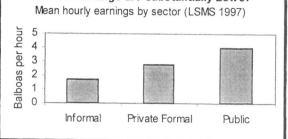

- **Significantly lower earnings in the informal sector – where a large share of the poor are employed.[6]** Lower earnings in the informal sector, as compared with the formal sector (Figure 2.2), are not explained by differences in human capital (education, experience), area of residence, or other job characteristics. These results suggest that employment in the informal sector may serve as an alternative to unemployment in a segmented labor market, but this is a hypothesis that needs additional investigation.[7]

Box 2.1 – Unemployment in Panama: Definitions and Overall Trends

Differences in definitions and sample coverage cloud comparisons of unemployment in Panama (See Annex 11 for details).

- The **national definition** historically used to measure unemployment differs from international standards in many ways, most notably the inclusion of seasonal and discouraged workers and the reference period (counting people as unemployed if they looked for work in the past three months). Moreover, the **sample** for the annual household surveys used to measure unemployment exclude residents of indigenous areas (which tend to have lower rates of unemployment). These data reveal the following historical trends in unemployment in Panama:
    - High levels of unemployment over the past few decades. Indeed, following the introduction of the Labor Code in 1972, unemployment climbed from an average of 6.5% in the preceding decade to an average of 7.3 in the 1970s and 11.9 in the 1980s. By 1994, the national unemployment rate hovered around 14%.
    - A decline in unemployment in recent years, falling to 13.2% in 1997, which can be attributed both to stronger growth in that year and to an improvement in the responsiveness of unemployment to changes in growth resulting from modest but important reforms in the Labor Code in 1995.[8]
- The **international definition** counts an individual as unemployed if he/she did not work at least one hour but actively sought employment in the past week. It excludes seasonal and discouraged workers. An analysis of the nationally-representative **sample** from LSMS data using the **international definition** suggests that:
    - Unemployment in Panama is much lower than previously thought: 5.9% for the nation as a whole in 1997.
    - It is much higher in urban areas (7.4%) than in rural (3.9%) or indigenous (1.3%) areas.
    - Unemployment is strongly correlated with poverty in urban areas.
    - Unemployment is highest among women and youths, as well as among those with secondary and vocational education.

2.3. **Other traditionally vulnerable groups also face adverse conditions in Panama's labor markets** (see Annex 11 for details):

- **Indigenous workers** fare poorly in Panama's labor markets. They face linguistic obstacles to labor force participation and few opportunities for employment in the formal sector (which generates higher

---

[4] Firm characteristics (type, size, field) are used to classify work as formal or informal (Annex 11).

[5] This compares with 70 percent in Nicaragua (1993), 47 percent in Argentina (1993), and 41 percent in Ecuador (1994). Maloney (October 1998) finds that self-employment in Panama is less common than would be expected for a country of its level of development, which could suggest that the degree of informality is not excessive (though self-employment and informality are not synonymous in the definition used here).

[6] Multivariate analysis of the determinants of hourly earnings was conducted separately and jointly for males and females using LSMS data (See Annex 11).

[7] Maloney (February 1998) found the contrary in Mexico, where under certain circumstances, there are reasons for workers to prefer informal employment due to both lower levels of human capital and distortions in the labor code. Likewise, in Nicaragua, informal sector employment is not a good predictor of poverty and monthly earnings in the informal sector are higher than the poverty line; World Bank (1995).

[8] Gonzalez (1998). See also Annex 11.

earnings). They also face apparent wage discrimination (that is not explained by other factors, such as human capital, area of residence, sector of employment, etc.

- **Women** do not appear to suffer discrimination in terms of wages and benefits in Panama. However, a number of factors suggest that Panamanian women have fewer employment opportunities than their male counterparts (lower labor force participation rates, higher unemployment, limited or no employment of women in certain sectors, fewer total hours worked, etc.).

- Unemployment is quite high among **youths** in Panama (Figure 2.1), particularly urban youths, young women, and those with secondary education, suggesting difficulties in the transition from school to work. The possible segmentation arising from a multiplicity of generous labor regimes in both the public and private sector may also raise young peoples' expectations about their potential wages (abnormally high reservation wages).

- Although **child labor** does not appear to be a widespread problem in Panama, child laborers tend to be poor and complete fewer years of schooling than their non-working counterparts. Most are boys and live in rural and indigenous areas.

EDUCATION

2.4.   **Disparities in education are the key causes of poverty, malnutrition, and inequality in Panama.** Education is an important complement to labor, boosting its productivity and potential for income generation. Indeed, the LSMS reveals that schooling pays off in terms of higher incomes: each year of schooling yields about a five percent increase in hourly earnings.[9] The returns to primary school (which has the most equitable and complete coverage) are much lower than those to secondary and higher education (to which the poor have much less access) due to large wage differentials by level of education.[10] Disparities in educational stock (literacy and attainment), current coverage, internal efficiency and quality (Box 2.2) are thus directly translated into inequities in earnings.

Disparities in Literacy and Attainment

2.5.   **Panama has achieved a high degree of literacy, creating an important base for promoting equitable economic development, though important gaps exist among the indigenous.** Literacy in Panama is quite high compared with other Central American countries, even among the poor.[11] In indigenous areas, however, however, less than two-thirds of those over age nine can read and write. Illiteracy is particularly high among women living in indigenous areas, suggesting at least historical biases against girl's education in indigenous areas. Among the ethnic indigenous, literacy is highest among the Kuna (80 percent), followed by the Embera-Wounan (75 percent) and the Ngobe-Buglé (64 percent), the poorest ethnic group in Panama (Box 2.3).

2.6.   **Although progress has been made, the poor have less schooling than the non-poor, and educational attainment is quite low among the indigenous (particularly girls).** The educational attainment of all groups has increased in recent years. The gap between poverty groups has also narrowed slightly among younger generations, suggesting some improvement in both the equity and internal efficiency of the educational system. Indigenous children, however, still leave school much earlier than their urban and rural counterparts. While Panamanian girls tend to complete more years of schooling than boys, the reverse is true in indigenous areas, though this gender gap has narrowed in recent years.[12]

---

[9] Based on regression analysis that controls for the impact of other variables on earnings. Annex 11.

[10] Taking into account the private (household) costs of schooling, the returns to primary schooling average ten percent, as compared with 15 and 24 percent for secondary and higher education respectively. Interestingly, while the returns to primary and secondary education are higher for girls, the reverse is true at the university level. See Annex 14.

[11] Panama's overall literacy rate is 92 percent, which compares with 95 percent in Costa Rica, 73 percent in Honduras, 72 percent in El Salvador; 66 percent in Nicaragua; and 56 percent in Guatemala. Figures from other Central American countries are for 1994 (World Bank/UNICEF EdStats database). The median for Latin America in 1994 was 90 percent.

[12] See Annex 4.

Among *ethnic* indigenous groups, the Kuna have the highest levels of educational attainment (averaging six years), while the Ngobe-Buglé – the poorest group – have the lowest (averaging less than three years).

Box 2.2 – Disparities in Education: Key Gaps Facing the Poor in Panama, by Geographic Area					
	Non-Poor	All Poor	Urban Poor	Rural Poor	Indigenous Poor
Educational Stock:					
Literacy (a)	✓ 97%	❖ 83%	✓ 94%	❖ 86%	!! 62% (d)
Educational Attainment (b)	✓ 9.5	❖ 5.2	❖ 7.0	❖ 5.1	!! 3.3 (d)
Current Coverage: (c)					
Pre-Primary	❖ 68%	!! 26%	!! 46%	!! 23%	!! 14%
Primary	✓ 95%	✓ 90%	✓ 92%	✓ 91%	!! 83%
Secondary	✓ 82%	!! 37%	!! 60%	!! 37%	!! 16%
Higher	✓ 31%	❖ 3%	❖ 7%	❖ 2%	❖ 0%
Internal Efficiency & Quality:					
Repetition Rate – Primary	✓ 4%	!! 9%	!! 10%	❖ 8%	!! 12%
Repetition Rate – Secondary	❖ 8%	❖ 9%	!! 11%	❖ 8%	❖ 4%
No Books – Primary	✓ 4%	!! 29%	❖ 7%	!! 24%	!! 61%
No Books – Secondary.	✓ 5%	❖ 12%	❖ 9%	❖ 12%	!! 19%

Source: Panama LSMS 1997. See Annex 4 for detailed figures. (a) Percent over aged 9 who can read and write. (b) Average years of education completed for those aged 12 and older. (c) Net enrollment rates. (d) Large gender disparities with lower rates of literacy and educational attainment for indigenous women.
✓ Represents fairly comprehensive coverage, not a key priority.
❖ Represents incomplete coverage.
!! Represents very low coverage and key priority.

Box 2.3 – The Language Poverty Trap: Language Ability, Education and Poverty among the Ethnic Indigenous

Spanish-speaking ability appears to be an important determinant of educational outcomes and even poverty status:

- One fifth of the ethnic indigenous population in Panama does not speak Spanish (monolingual indigenous speakers).
- **Literacy** is lowest among the indigenous who do not speak Spanish: only 20% of monolingual indigenous speakers read and write (as compared with 79% and 98% of bilingual and monolingual Spanish-speakers of indigenous ethnic origin)
- **Educational attainment** is also lower. Monolingual indigenous speakers average less than one year of schooling.
- Among the indigenous, **poverty** is highest among households that are headed by monolingual indigenous speakers. Virtually all households headed by monolingual indigenous speakers live in extreme poverty.
- An inability to speak Spanish is also associated with lower **enrollment** for the current generation: just one-half of monolingual indigenous speaking children aged 6-11 are currently enrolled in primary school.
- Though Spanish is clearly the dominant language for schooling in Panama (even among the indigenous), a few indigenous students (15%) do report speaking indigenous languages in class at the primary level. Bilingual education at the primary level should be promoted where necessary to help monolingual indigenous children make the transition into the Spanish speaking world – and eventually escaping poverty.

Source: Panama LSMS 1997. See Annex 6 for details.

Gaps in Current Coverage

2.7.   **There are a number of gaps in current educational coverage, primarily among the poor and indigenous**, which can be summarized as follows:

- Despite efforts to boost national **pre-school enrollment**, the increase has not been well-targeted and there are serious gaps for the poor and indigenous. Of those who do attend, the poor are highly reliant on public facilities while a third of the non-poor attend private schools.

- Despite widespread **primary school** coverage for both boys and girls, even among the poor, there are serious gaps for indigenous children. The net enrollment rate is highest among the Kuna and the Embera-Wounan and lowest among the Ngobe-Buglé. Almost all poor primary students and the majority of the non-poor enroll in public facilities.

- There are large gaps in **secondary school** enrollment among rural, poor and indigenous children.[13] More girls enroll than boys, and most students enroll in public facilities.

- Access to **higher education** is extremely unequal in Panama, with virtually none of the poor attending. Some 95 percent of students in higher education are not poor and half of those enrolled belong to the highest quintile of the population.[14] These disparities reflect inequities in public education, since over three-quarters of all students of higher education attend public facilities. Enrollment rates in higher education are much higher for women than men.

2.8.   **Demand-side factors, more than the availability of schools, appear to be the key obstacles to increased enrollment by the poor and indigenous.** "Lack of money" was the single most common reason given for not enrolling in primary and secondary school (accounting for roughly half of absentees).[15] This suggests that the direct costs (fees, materials, etc.) of attending school are prohibitively high for the poor and indigenous. Indeed, the costs to households of public schooling (particularly informal fees and the cost of school supplies) are quite high in Panama (Box 2.4). Indirect costs – such as foregone earnings from work or domestic duties – are not frequently cited as barriers to enrollment. "Lack of interest" is the second main impediment to enrollment for the poor, particularly at the secondary level (accounting for one fifth of absentees).[16] Disinterest is particularly high among poor urban boys (accounting for 40 percent of poor male non-enrollees), although none cited work as an obstacle. This suggests a rather large cohort of poor, young urban males opting neither to work nor to attend school, who are at risk for both crime and continued poverty. Only four percent of poor non-enrollees at the secondary level and 18 percent at the primary level cited supply-side factors – such as distance to schools, inadequate class space, and lack of facilities – as key obstacles.[17]

Box 2.4 – Economic Barriers to Education

The direct costs of schooling in Panama are high, and could constitute a barrier to enrollment among the poor. Households allocate 6.2% of their total consumption to education. Even the average total annual cost of attending public school is high: B./109 per student for primary and B./253 for secondary. To put this in context, these direct costs of schooling represent 12% and 28% of the full poverty line respectively. Private school is over nine times more costly at the primary level and four times more costly for secondary school. Formal fees for public schools constitute only a small share of the cost. In fact, informal fees (covering fundraisers, field trips, extra-curricular activities, etc.) are much higher than formal fees. The largest single cost of attending school appears to be supplies (uniforms, materials), followed by transport and books.

Higher spending by the non-poor – particularly for key educational inputs – could signal differences in the quality of education being received by the poor and non-poor. There is substantial variation in costs by poverty group and geographic area, with much higher spending among the non-poor and in urban areas. These differences arise primarily in spending on school supplies and books; as discussed below, an important share of poor and indigenous students do not possess textbooks. Spending on informal fees – which contribute to educational and extra-curricular activities – is also higher among the non-poor and in urban areas.

Source : Panama LSMS, see Annex 4 for details.

Disparities in Internal Efficiency and the Quality of Education

2.9.   **Poor children tend to repeat grades more than non-poor children at the primary level.** Twelve percent and nine percent of extremely poor and poor primary school students respectively report repeating their current grade, as compared with only four percent of non-poor children. Roughly double the share of indigenous primary students report repeating their current grade than those in urban and rural

---

[13] In fact, national secondary school enrollment lags below what would be expected given Panama's level of per capita income. See Hicks and Peeters (September 17, 1998).

[14] With an average total annual per capita consumption of B./4,812, or 5.3 times the full poverty line.

[15] Figures from the LSMS household questionnaire. These results were confirmed in the LSMS community questionnaire, in which economic factors were given as the main reason children did not attend school.

[16] Additional research (perhaps via focus group discussions) would be worthwhile to better pinpoint the factors underlying this disinterest. It could reflect social factors (parents who didn't attend school, lack of family support, peer pressure, etc.) or a lack of relevance of the curriculum. Lack of family support was cited as a key factor (after economic reasons) for children not attending school in the LSMS community questionnaire.

[17] Lack of facilities is a much more serious constraint at the pre-primary level, though demand-side factors (such as poverty status, mother's education, etc.) do play a role in determining pre-primary enrollment. See Annex 13.

areas. Dropout rates are also higher among indigenous primary-school students.[18] These disparities in internal efficiency could arise due to differences in the quality of education or demand-side constraints. They are less apparent at the secondary level, where very few poor students enroll.

2.10.   **The quality of education received by poor and indigenous children lags that received by the non-poor.** There are two ways to assess educational quality: the quality of learning (via standard achievement tests) and the quality of inputs (materials, books, teachers, etc.). The LSMS suggests that the poor and indigenous lack access to key quality-related inputs. **First,** a large share of poor and indigenous children do not have textbooks (Box 2.5). **Second,** lower household spending on school supplies among the poor and indigenous suggests lower use of educational materials in their learning process (see Box 2.4). **Third,** a lack of bilingual materials and instruction at the primary level apparently creates an obstacle to better attainment among indigenous children (see Box 2.3). **Fourth,** poor and indigenous children are much more likely to belong to communities reporting an insufficient number of teachers. **Finally,** poor and indigenous children are much more likely to live in communities with dilapidated school facilities (infrastructure, classrooms, desks, etc.).

Box 2.5 – Poverty and Access to Textbooks in Panama: Inadequacy of a Key Quality Input
♦   **Lack of books among the poor.** Close to 30% of poor primary and 12% of poor secondary students do not have textbooks, as compared with only 5% of the non-poor (at both levels). "Lack of money" is the main reason cited by the poor for not possessing books (over half of those without books). One-third indicated that "they weren't asked" for books at school, suggesting a complete neglect of book use in these schools and a symptom of poverty (teachers may not ask students for books if they know they cannot afford them). ♦   **Lack of books among indigenous children.** Close to 60% of all primary and one fifth of secondary students in indigenous areas do not have books (in any language). "Lack of money" is the main reason (70% of those without books). ♦   **Sources of books.** The majority of poor and indigenous children who *do* have books purchase or borrow them. Very few receive free books from the Government or schools, although existing donations do appear to be well targeted: 9% and 2% of poor primary and secondary students respectively received free books, as compared with only 1% of the non-poor at both levels; 33% and 7% of primary and secondary indigenous students respectively received free books.
Source: Panama LSMS 1997 Household Questionnaire.

HEALTH

2.11.   **Disparities in both health status and access to health care services are prevalent between the poor and non-poor in Panama.** Good health contributes directly to individual well-being. It is also an important complement to labor in terms of its contribution to productivity.

2.12.   **Relatively good health indicators for the nation as a whole mask large differences and poor health status among the poor and indigenous.** Although life expectancy overall is high for Latin America (74 years at birth), it is as low as 63 in the poorest regions in Panama.[19] Likewise, in the poorest 40 districts, infant mortality rates are 40-50 per 1000 live births (on par with low-income countries), despite a national average of 19 per 1000. Intestinal diseases, malnutrition, and respiratory diseases still account for a significant share of deaths in provinces such as Bocas del Toro and the Comarca of San Blas; tuberculosis is also high in Bocas del Toro; and malaria is common in Bocas del Toro, Darien and Veraguas, all of which have a high concentration of poor and indigenous people.[20] Moreover, as discussed in Chapter 1, malnutrition is more prevalent among the poor and indigenous than among the non-poor. Other social concerns frequently reported among the poor include violence, alcoholism, and teenage pregnancy (over half of pregnant teenagers are poor and one quarter of all pregnancies among the poor occur during the teenage years).

2.13.   **Available data suggest that the poor and indigenous have less access to health care.** Access is determined both by the physical availability of services (as measured by the distance or time needed to

---

[18] Of indigenous residents aged 13-17 who enrolled at some point, half did not complete primary school. This compares with only four percent and 13 percent of urban and rural youths respectively.

[19] MINSA (September 1996). Health Statistics. Overall life expectancy in Panama is actually slightly higher than what would be expected given per capita incomes. Hicks and Peeters (September 1988).

[20] MINSA (September 1996). Health Statistics.

reach the nearest facilities) and the ability of households to pay for such services. Though these two constraints call for very different policy responses, their effect is similar for the household: an inability to afford either to travel to distant services or to pay for nearby services (or both). Using the World Health Organization definition of access as living within one hour of a health care facilities (physical availability of services), roughly 20 percent of the population lacks access. LSMS data suggest that this gap is worse among the poor, particularly the indigenous. Among indigenous residents who *did* seek health care when ill, the average time taken to reach health facilities was 52 minutes (Table 2.1). For those who did *not* seek treatment, both cost and distance were key obstacles (over half of those in the poorest quintile and a quarter of those in the second quintile did not seek care when ill due to cost and/or distance).

2.14.   **The poor and indigenous are less likely to seek medical treatment in case of illness than the non-poor.**[21]   Among those reporting illness or an accident, 45 percent of the poor consulted a medical professional, as compared with 64 percent of the non-poor. The share of those seeking treatment is even lower among the indigenous (Table 2.1).

2.15.   **The poor who do seek treatment are more likely to use public services** – such as public clinics, hospitals and health centers – than their non-poor counterparts, though a substantial share of the non-poor do use public services (Table 2.1). The indigenous likewise rely substantially on public facilities (mainly centers and sub-centers), but also self-treat at home. The non-poor are more likely to visit doctors than the poor and indigenous, who also rely on nurses and relatives for treatment.

2.16.   **The low quality of health services also appears to be a problem facing the poor, particularly in rural and indigenous areas.** At present, there are few incentives in the public health system to ensure quality of care. With limited access to services, poor consumers have little choice of provider. Health services are not adequately supervised and there are no appropriate accreditation and quality control systems in place. Though the LSMS did not collect many indicators of quality, the community survey does suggest that medical inputs are less available to the poor, who are more likely to live in communities reporting longer waiting times, unavailability of medicines, and sufficient medical equipment. Lack of medicines appears to be particularly problematic in rural areas, as does medical equipment in indigenous areas. Poor quality of care was the primary reason for not seeking care for three percent of those in the poorest quintile who were ill but did not seek treatment.

---

[21] Data on health consultations should be treated with caution as they are self-reported (cross-country evidence suggests that the non-poor are more likely to report illnesses than the poor) and the poor tend to self-treat more than the non-poor.

Table 2.1 – Health Services by Poverty Group and Geographic Area							
	Extreme Poor	All Poor	Non-Poor	Urban	Rural	Indig.	Total
Health Visits, Sickness During Past Month							
Consultancy Rate[a]	0.7	0.8	1.2	1.2	1.0	0.6	1.1
Coverage Rate[b]	0.4	0.5	0.6	0.6	0.5	0.3	0.6
Concentration Rate[c]	1.9	1.8	1.9	1.9	1.8	2.0	1.9
Place of Treatment							
Public Facility	81%	83%	62%	62%	77%	81%	68%
Private Facility	19%	17%	38%	38%	23%	19%	32%
Public Hospital/Clinic	27%	37%	42%	47%	33%	20%	41%
Health Center/Sub-Center	55%	46%	20%	15%	44%	61%	27%
Private Hospital/Clinic/Physician	7%	9%	32%	32%	17%	2%	26%
Pharmacist/Other	3%	4%	4%	5%	3%	1%	4%
At home	9%	4%	2%	2%	3%	16%	3%
Distance to Treatment (Average minutes to place of treatment, excluding treatment at home)							
Average minutes (for those who sought treatment)	37	32	27	24	35	52	29
Private (Household) Spending on Health Services							
% of sick paying something (B./ > 0)	58%	61%	72%	71%	67%	47%	68%

Source: LSMS 1997. (a) Consultancy rate = number of visits/ number of sick; in other words, the number of visits on average for an individual reporting illness. (b) Coverage rate = number of people with at least one visit/ number of sick; in other words, the percent of people reporting illness who had at least one medical visit. (c) Concentration rate = number of visits/ number of people with at least one visit.

PHYSICAL ASSETS

2.17.   **The distribution of physical assets – such as housing and land – is highly unequal.** Such assets contribute to income-generating potential by providing a base for productive activities. Property also generates rent – through earnings charged to renters or via the savings from imputed rent, which would otherwise be spent by the household. Households can also use property as collateral for leveraging credit. Emergency income can likewise be generated through sales of property or borrowing against it (equity loans). Finally, housing can be used as a tool for extending personal relationships, building trust, and generating social capital. The ability of households to use property as an asset depends largely on their quality, the security of tenure, and the flexibility of land and housing markets.

2.18.   **The poor tend to live in much lower-quality housing than the non-poor.** Although there are significant cultural differences among the poor in Panama, the LSMS suggests many similarities in their housing conditions. A typical poor household lives in an individual house (65 percent) or hut (*choza, rancho;* 28 percent). Their homes tend to be quite crowded (averaging three members per room, as compared with 1.2 among the non-poor), particularly among the indigenous (over four members per room). The materials used to construct these homes are less durable than for the housing of the non-poor; the average estimated value of housing of the non-poor is more than double that of the poor.

2.19. **The majority of the population lacks titling for their homes, but the gap is worse for the poor.** Most households in Panama own their homes, including the poor (76 percent overall, 82 percent of poor households). However, formal proof of ownership – titles or deeds (either registered or unregistered) – is rare, particularly among the poor (Figure 2.3).

2.20. **The distribution of land is highly unequal, particularly untitled land.** The poor, who account for two thirds of the rural population, own less

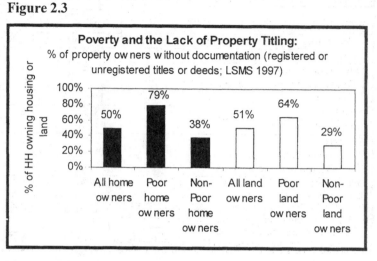

Figure 2.3

than one third of agricultural land and 16 percent of titled land. Of those with land, non-poor households own 3.6 times as much land as poor households (with average holdings of 36 and 10 hectares respectively), and nine times more titled land. The Gini coefficient for total land owned was 77 in 1997.[22]

2.21. **Land – particularly untitled land – may be a constraint for the poor.** Half the poor and 70 percent of the non-poor in rural areas are landless. Among the poor, those with small- and medium-sized plots have the lowest incomes – even lower than the landless. Only those with larger farms (greater than 15 hectares) have incomes that approach those of the landless.[23]

2.22. **The lack of property titles reduces the ability of the poor to obtain credit** (since titles are often required as collateral). In fact, as discussed in para. 2.30, lack of guarantees (property titles or other assets) was the main reason poor households were refused credit. Without formal claim, the poor also cannot sell or borrow against this asset for emergency income. Titling contributes significantly to land values (adding an average of B./456 per hectare taking into account other differences in land value), lending promise to the use of a titling program as part of an anti-poverty strategy.

2.23. **The poor also have fewer durable goods than the non-poor.** On average, the total value of the durable goods owned by the non-poor is 16 times higher than the value of those owned by the poor. In addition to the overall store of wealth that can be used for emergency income, the poor lack the conveniences and productive opportunities that these assets can help generate.

BASIC INFRASTRUCTURE

2.24. **The poor – particularly the rural poor and the indigenous – also lack access to many basic services** (Box 2.6). Households without basic services (water, sanitation, electricity, telephones) are more vulnerable than those who command these services. Potable water and sanitation services contribute directly to overall welfare and health status. Electricity and telephones help households use their homes productively for income generation.

---

[22] Source: Panama LSMS 1997. A previous national estimate put the Gini coefficient for land at 87 in 1990. These compare with 84 in Guatemala (1979), 81 in Costa Rica (1973) and El Salvador (1971), 78 in Honduras (1974), 56 in Indonesia (1973), 53 in the Philippines (1980), and 35 in Korea (1980). Source: Deininger (1997).

[23] This does not take into account differences in land quality. While the LSMS does not include information on many indicators of land quality (climate, soil type, slope, etc.), it does suggest that the poor have very little access to irrigated land (see Annex 5). Other indicators could be included in the next LSMS through the use of GIs data collection techniques.

Box 2.6 – Disparities in Basic Infrastructure Services: Key Gaps Facing the Poor in Panama, by Geographic Area					
	Non-Poor	All Poor	Urban Poor	Rural Poor	Indigenous Poor
Piped Water: (a)					
Access (house, yard, community)	✓ 95%	❖ 72%	✓ 92%	❖ 72%	‼ 42% (d)
o/w % with uninterrupted service	❖ 70%	❖ 46%	❖ 65%	❖ 45%	‼ 23% (d)
Sanitation Services:	❖	❖	❖	❖	‼
Formal connection (sewer/septic)	70%	15%	44%	6%	8%
Latrine/pit	28%	66%	48%	80%	32%
No facility	2%	20%	8%	14%	60%
Garbage Collection:	❖ 73%	❖ 20%	❖ 77%	❖ 6%	❖ 0%
Energy:					
Electric lighting in home (b)	✓ 92%	❖ 45%	✓ 92%	❖ 38%	❖ 7%
Gas/electricity for cooking (c)	✓ 93%	❖ 45%	✓ 91%	‼ 38%	‼ 8% (e)

Source: Panama LSMS 1997. See Annex 4 for detailed figures. (a) Other sources include wells, river, other; uninterrupted service refers to receipt of water 30 days/month, 24 hours/day. (b) Other sources include candles, gas, fuel, nothing. (c) Other sources include firewood, other. (d) 57% of indigenous poor obtain water from rivers/lakes; only 3% treat their unpiped water. (e) 92% of indigenous poor use firewood.
✓ Represents fairly comprehensive coverage, not a key priority.
❖ Represents incomplete coverage.
‼ Represents very low coverage and key priority.

2.25.   **Although the majority of the poor have access to piped water, a large share of indigenous residents lack access, and service quality problems abound.** Three-quarters of the poor receive piped water.[24] Close to 60 percent of indigenous residents, however, lack any form of connection to piped water; the remainder collect water from rivers, lakes, rain or other sources.[25] The lack of access to potable water in indigenous areas is a likely cause of the high levels of diarrhea and hence malnutrition among indigenous children. Although the Government is undertaking a number of projects to extend piped water to rural and indigenous communities, anecdotal evidence suggests problems with overlapping efforts and a lack of coordination in service delivery and approach. Of those who do receive piped water, a large share of the poor in all areas report problems with service quality (irregular flow, inadequate water pressure, contamination and pollution problems, and inadequate maintenance). Higher efficiency and cost recovery in the provision of water services could help finance improvements in quality and coverage of services (Box 2.7).

2.26.   **There are large disparities in access to sanitation services by area and by poverty group.** Overall, 55 percent of the Panamanian population has connections to the sewer system or a septic tank. Access, however, varies greatly by poverty group, with formal connections serving the majority of the non-poor but very few poor households. Instead, most poor households have pit toilets or latrines, while one-fifth have no formal toilet system. Differences are also apparent by geographic area, though the pattern of inequities in service delivery remains. In urban areas, half of poor households rely on pit toilets or latrines, raising public health concerns. Sanitation connections are rare in the countryside, particularly among the poor. While the majority of poor rural (non-indigenous) households have pit toilets or latrines, only a third of indigenous residents do, with the remainder having no formal toilet access. With respect to garbage collection services, differences are largely geographic, with most of the urban population covered (though qualitative data suggest that services are sporadic), and few rural and indigenous residents receiving the services.

---

[24] The majority of the poor receive piped water on their property (*en el patio*), but not in their homes.
[25] The lack of access to piped water is particularly widespread among the Ngobe-Buglé.

19

Box 2.7 – Incomplete Cost Recovery for Water and Electricity
Incomplete cost recovery for basic services leads to waste, and lower quantity and quality of service provision. **Water.** Close to one-fifth of Panamanian households with water connections do not pay anything for their water consumption.[26] This figure is higher for the poor (27%) than the non-poor (15%), and is particularly high among the urban poor (40%). For those who do pay something, the cost is minimal: the poor pay less than B./8.4 per person per year (2% of their average total consumption) while the non-poor pay B./35 per person per year (1% of their average total consumption). **Electricity.** Some 13% of households with connections to the electricity grid do not pay anything for their service. Illegal connections (tapping into public lighting for example) appear to be particularly widespread among poor city dwellers: 40% of poor urban households with connections did not pay for their consumption.
Source: Panama LSMS 1997.

2.27.   **While virtually all urban residents have access to electric lighting and gas for cooking, coverage is extremely limited in rural and indigenous areas, particularly among the poor.** The majority of the poor in rural and indigenous areas rely on kerosene lighting and firewood for cooking. The widespread use of firewood for cooking in these areas raises serious concerns regarding deforestation[27] in already marginal areas and respiratory diseases. Low cost recovery and efficiency reduces the funds available for expanding electric service coverage (Box 2.7).

2.28.   **Virtually no poor households have telephone connections.** Only 14 percent of all households in Panama report owning telephone lines and only two percent of the poor have a line.

Box 2.8 – Transportation Bottlenecks and the Urban Poor
Urban communities cited transportation – inadequate public services, deteriorating roads, and traffic congestion – as a top priority. The urban poor are largely reliant on public transportation. Half of all poor urban residents (71% in Panama City and San Miguelito) rely on public transportation to commute to work. The main form of public transportation is buses, which are run by private operators. Relatively low fixed prices and a complex system of licensing for entry and route assignments have dampened competition in service provision and greatly reduced the quality of services. Commuting times are lengthy: on average, it takes the poor close to one hour to commute to work using public transportation, thereby reducing time available for productive activities. The Government is currently exploring ways to reduce distortions in public transport, improve the quality of service provision, and strengthen the regulatory framework for vehicle standards, inspection, and pollution control.
Source: Panama LSMS 1997. See Annex 7 for details.

FINANCIAL ASSETS

2.29.   **The non-poor are much more likely to save than the poor.** Savings[28] can be an important asset for the poor, for consumption smoothing and investment purposes. Only eleven percent of the poor maintained savings, however, compared with close to half of the non-poor. Geographic differences are also notable, with half of urban households maintaining savings as compared with one fifth and one tenth of rural and indigenous households respectively. The poor tend to put their savings in public institutions, while the non-poor are more likely to use private banks.

2.30.   **The overall volume of lending to the poor is much smaller than their contribution to the economy.** Borrowing and making purchases on credit are another important way for households to smooth their consumption and invest for future earnings potential. Whereas poor households receive three percent of total credit, they account for ten percent of total consumption and income in the economy. Information constraints, physical distance, lack of guarantees, and high costs-per-dollar borrowed could present obstacles to lending to the poor. Thus:

---

[26] This compares with Ecuador, for example, where 74 percent who are connected pay nothing for their water services. Source: World Bank, Ecuador Poverty Report, Volume II, June 30, 1995.

[27] Most deforestation in Panama, however, is not caused by households, but by forestry and livestock enterprises.

[28] The Panama LSMS questionnaire did not include questions on household food stocks, a form of in-kind savings that can be quickly liquidated for cash. Hence a complete picture of savings cannot be assembled. In addition, data collected by the LSMS on amounts saved per month and total savings are not consistent and the figures cannot be reconciled. Use of these figures is not recommended. Future LSMS questionnaires should try to correct for these errors.

- **A smaller share of the poor solicited credit than non-poor households.** Although the approval rate is fairly similar (slightly higher among the non-poor), the expectation of rejection was an important deterrent for soliciting credit among the poor. Other factors that discouraged the poor from soliciting credit include risk and excessive paperwork.

- **Lack of guarantees (titles or other assets) is the main reason that the poor were refused credit in all areas.** The size of land holdings and the possession of land titles are the two main factors influencing access to, and volume of, agricultural lending in rural areas.

- **Physical distance to lenders affects the sources of loans obtained by the poor.** Physical distance affects the ability of the borrower to access lenders and the ability of the lender to assess the borrower's credit risk and supervise repayment. The sources of credit accessed by the rural poor, for example, are on average only three kilometers away, compared with ten kilometers for the non-poor. Formal credit sources (private banks or producers associations) are much further from borrowers than government programs, cooperatives, moneylenders, NGOs and family. Thus the more distant, formal sources seek collateral to substitute for knowledge of the borrowers, and thereby exclude the poor.

- **The poor borrow a greater amount for consumption purposes, and the size of loans they obtain is much smaller than those obtained by the non-poor.** Three quarters of borrowing by the poor is for consumption purposes, as compared with about half for the non-poor. Average annual borrowing by the poor is B./730 as compared with about B./4,600 for the non-poor.

- **Poor borrowers pay a higher average annual interest rate for farm lending.** Effective annual interest rates vary greatly with source, term, collateral, and riskiness of the borrower. In rural areas, poor borrowers pay a median rate of 24 percent versus 12 percent for non-poor borrowers.

- **Repayment varies significantly by lender, with a high delinquency rate for government programs.** Among those who repaid something, median repayments were only 12 and 17 percent for government banks and programs respectively, but 100 percent for all other sources of cash loans.

SOCIAL CAPITAL

2.31. **Social capital is one of the assets of the poor.**[29] Social capital – defined as norms, trust, and reciprocity networks that facilitate mutually beneficial cooperation in a community – is an important asset that can reduce vulnerability and increase opportunities. The poor and the extreme poor account for a disproportionate share of those living in communities with high social capital.[30] Among those in the poorest quintile, it is more than double the share living in communities with low social

Figure 2.4 – Poverty and Social Capital

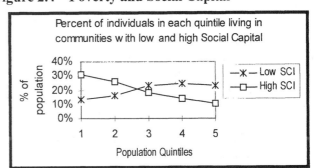

capital (Figure 2.4). The reverse is true for the highest quintile.

2.32. **The poor tend to associate for "public goods" purposes, whereas the non-poor join associations which yield higher private gains.** The poor tend to participate more in community committees and associations than the non-poor, whereas wealthier households tend to participate in cooperatives. The poor are close to two times more likely to join local committees and four times more

---

[29] The LSMS included a number of questions pertaining to social capital in both the household survey and the community focus group interviews. In addition, to gather in-depth information on social capital, focus group discussions were conducted in 16 communities as part of a complementary Social Capital Qualitative Survey (SCQS).

[30] Though this could be explained by cultural differences, with over-representation of the indigenous (who have higher social capital) in the lower quintiles, social capital does appear to be stronger among the poor even within geographic areas (within urban areas for example).

likely to participate in local associations than the non-poor. In contrast, wealthier households were close to three times more likely to join cooperatives than the poor. These patterns suggest that the poor substitute community action for a lack of public services.

2.33.   **Social capital helps communities to leverage assistance.** Communities with high social capital report a higher frequency of assistance from the Government and NGOs. Overall, they are close to four times more likely to receive Government assistance and two times more likely to receive NGO assistance than those with low social capital. This correlation is observed in all three geographic areas, and is particularly strong in rural and indigenous areas.

2.34.   **The SCQS and the LSMS reveal a sharp contrast between urban, rural and indigenous communities in terms of the prevalence of community organizations and social capital.** Some 75 percent and 80 percent of rural and indigenous communities in the LSMS sample affirm having some sort of community organization, as compared with just half of urban communities in the sample. Indigenous households also participate in organizations much more than their urban and rural counterparts (40 percent of indigenous households report participating in some type of organization, as compared with only 28 and 30 percent of urban and rural households respectively). Not surprisingly, indigenous and rural communities also have higher social capital than urban communities,[31] reflecting more numerous and active networks of associations in these communities. The SCQS found that horizontal connections are stronger among communities with higher social capital, and consequently among indigenous communities. These horizontal connections manifest themselves either through different organizations in the same community cooperating with each other, or through the establishment of links with groups in neighboring communities.

Box 2.9 – Community Perceptions of the Quality of Life: Urban Pessimism & Social Problems

◆ **A Paradox of Perceptions?** Community perceptions of changes in overall well-being contradict the profile of poverty as measured by annual consumption. Despite having higher average total consumption and a lower incidence of poverty, urban communities have more pessimistic perceptions of recent changes in their overall living standards than their "poorer" rural and indigenous counterparts. In contrast, urban communities were more optimistic when asked about specific changes in living conditions (basic services and housing). Clearly non-economic factors are causing the apparent paradox between economic conditions and community perceptions.

◆ **Social Problems as Priorities.** Social issues – particularly crime and safety but also drugs, alcohol addiction, gangs, and youth problems – were the most frequently cited priority among urban communities. Over 80% reported problems with theft, drugs and alcohol, and close to half reported problems with gangs and prostitution. Official statistics suggest that crime and violence are rising, and that most crime (particularly violent crime) is concentrated in urban areas, particularly Panama City and Colón.

◆ **Poverty, Crime and Violence.** Although the LSMS does not reveal a strong correlation with poverty, crime and violence can exact a high cost on the poor, who are more vulnerable to shocks, in a number of ways:

   * **Direct costs**: Stolen property, lost productivity, lost life, destruction of public infrastructure, etc.
   * **Prevention costs**: Investments in metal doors, window bars, etc. Common in the low-income *barriadas* surrounding Panama City.
   * **Lost employment opportunities**: Deterred investors in high-crime areas; reduced safety for commuting, etc.
   * **Erosion of social capital**: reduced trust in communities and between households limits the use of this important asset.

See Sollis et. al. (1995) for a discussion of crime and violence in Panama's *barriadas* and Moser (1996) on impact of crime and violence on the poor.

---

[31] As measured by a Social Capital Index (SCI), see Annex 18.

Chapter 3 - The Determinants of Poverty, Malnutrition, and Inequality

3.1.   Chapter 2 examines the disparities in key assets between the poor and non-poor and by geographic area.   This chapter analyzes the relative importance of these and other determinants of poverty, malnutrition, and inequality in a multi-variate setting. It summarizes the key results for each problem, highlighting key priorities for policy interventions.   Two key conclusions emerge from the multi-variate analysis of all three problems (Box 3.1):

- The correlates of poverty, malnutrition, and inequality overlap substantially – and most involve crucial policy levers.
- Disparities in key assets – labor, education, basic services, and physical and financial assets – are indeed strongly correlated with poverty, malnutrition, and inequality.

Box 3.1 – Determinants of Poverty, Malnutrition and Inequality: Summary of Key Factors			
	Poverty	**Nutritional Status**	**Inequality**
Labor	✓ Agriculture & informal sector earnings		✓ Sector of employment, dependency ratio
Education	✓ Household head/companion	✓ Mother's	✓ Household head/companion, all members
Basic Services	✓ Depending on geographic area	✓ Health services, vaccinations	✓ Telephones, electricity, Sanitation (covers water)
Physical Assets	✓ Housing quality & tenancy, titled land holdings	✓ Durable goods, titled land holdings	✓ Housing tenancy, titled land holdings
Financial Assets	✓ Credit		✓ Credit
Location	✓ Geographic area	✓ Geographic area	✓ Geographic area
Fertility, Household Structure	✓ Household size	✓ Fertility, pregnancies, number of children under 5	✓ Household size
Other Factors	✓ Social Capital (some types)	✓ Economic situation (food consumption) ✓ Diarrhea (correlation with water) ✓ Exclusive breastfeeding ✓ Age, gender of child	✓ Prices and incentives ✓ Language

PROBABILITY OF BEING POOR / CORRELATES OF POVERTY

3.2.   This section examines the correlates of poverty in a multi-variate setting. The analysis is useful, first, to verify the relative role of the various factors in determining poverty status, and second, to assess the potential impact that policy-induced changes in these factors are likely to have on the probability of being poor, holding all other factors constant. The probability of a household being poor was examined for the nation as a whole, as well as for urban, rural and indigenous areas.[1]

3.3.   It is important to note the limitations of this analysis at the outset. **First** and foremost, the analysis does not capture the dynamic impact of certain causes of poverty over time. Most notably, the impact of changes in economic growth – most certainly a key determinant of poverty – cannot be assessed using this static, cross-section model. **Second,** the analysis is limited by the variables available at the household level from the 1997 LSMS. Other factors -- such as social conditions like crime and violence, or physical conditions such as variations in climate or access to markets -- could not be included due to a lack of data at this level. **Finally,** though theory holds that many of the variables included in the analysis do indeed contribute to (cause) poverty (or poverty reduction), the statistical relationships should be interpreted as correlates and not as determinants since causality can run both ways for some variables.

---

[1] See Annex 8 for a more detailed description of the methodology and results.   Annexes 5 and 6 include detailed models for rural areas and for the ethnic indigenous (as opposed to geographic areas).

3.4.   **Poverty is clearly associated with lower levels or constrained use of key assets**, including labor, education, physical assets, basic services, credit and social capital. Geographic location and household size are also found to be important correlates of poverty. Key findings are summarized below.

- **Informal-sector and agricultural employment are correlated with poverty.** Households deriving most of their income from agriculture or the informal sector have a higher probability of being poor due to lower earnings (and hence productivity) in these sectors.

- **Education can serve as an important elevator for escaping poverty.**[2] The higher the educational attainment of the household head or his/her companion, the lower the household's probability of being poor. Overall, if a household head or companion has completed primary education, the household is close to ten percent less likely to be poor than if he/she had no education. Even a few years of secondary education further reduce the probability of being poor.

- **Low quality housing and lack of housing titles are strongly correlated with poverty,** though the direction of causality is not clear. Poverty itself is a cause of makeshift housing, but low quality housing can also limit the ability of households to use their homes as a productive asset – as a location of independent businesses for example (particularly when accompanied by a lack of basic infrastructure services as discussed below). Not owning a house is also associated with a higher probability of being poor, as does the lack of a registered housing title in urban and rural areas.

- **Small land holdings are associated with poverty, even if they are titled.** Households with titled land holdings greater than 15 hectares are less likely to be poor. Land holdings of less than 15 hectares does not lower the probability of being poor.

- **Access to basic services significantly reduces the probability of being poor for the nation as a whole** (Box 3.2). The correlation between basic services and poverty depends largely on the existing coverage of these services. In urban areas, water and electricity are not significant determinants of poverty status because most city-dwellers (including the poor) are covered by these services. Likewise, in indigenous areas, lack of sanitation services and formal water supply do not register as significant correlates of poverty because almost no indigenous households have access to these services.

Box 3.2 – The Correlation Between Basic Services and Poverty in Panama				
	Nation	Urban Areas	Rural Areas	Indigenous Areas
Water Supply	✔	✘	✔	✘
Sanitation Services	✔	✔	✔	✘
Electricity	✔	✘	✔	✔
Telephone Services	✔	✔	✔	✔
✔ Indicates significant correlation between the lack of access to the service and a higher probability of being poor. ✘ Indicates no significant correlation between service and probability of being poor.				

- **Limited access to credit is strongly correlated with being poor**, though the direction of causality is unclear. Low incomes and assets could prevent the poor from obtaining credit; likewise, low access to credit could hamper the poor's ability to use their labor and other assets productively.

- **Membership in certain types of organizations reduces households' probability of being poor.** Households that belong to a cooperative – which generates "private gains" to members – are less likely to be poor, particularly in urban areas. In indigenous areas, participation in community organizations (such as committees, associations, *juntas*, and *consejos*) is associated with higher total consumption, which is consistent with the findings discussed above.

- **Even after accounting for disparities in assets, geographic location is a major factor in explaining poverty in Panama**, particularly for indigenous poverty. Households in indigenous and

---

[2] The analysis uses the maximum educational attainment of the household head or his/her companion. Since the educational attainment of these members (adults) precedes their current economic status, it could validly be considered as having a causative influence on poverty status (whereas the educational levels of young dependents in the household may be low because poverty prevents them from affording an education).

24

remote areas are 25 percent more likely to be poor than urban households, even after other differences are taken into account. Finally, living in rural (non-indigenous, non-remote) areas increases the probability of being poor by nine percent.

- **Larger households tend to be poorer.** Overall, each additional child under five increases the probability of being poor by 16 percentage points. The correlation between fertility and poverty is particularly strong in rural areas, underscoring the importance of access to family planning services.

DETERMINANTS OF NUTRITIONAL STATUS

3.5. **Malnutrition is strongly correlated with poverty** in Panama, as discussed in Chapter 1. Not surprisingly, the determinants of nutritional status largely coincide with the correlates of poverty. The key determinants of nutritional status are summarized below.[3]

- **More education is associated with better nutritional status, holding consumption and other factors constant.** Mothers' education significantly affects nutritional status: children whose mothers have some secondary education or more are less likely to be malnourished than those whose mothers have no education.

- **Access to health services improves nutritional status.** Closer proximity to health facilities and timely receipt of vaccines are correlated with improved nutritional status. Children with recent bouts of diarrhea are significantly more likely to be underweight, underscoring the importance of access to water and sanitation services, as well as the availability of oral rehydration therapy and deworming interventions.

- **The possession of physical assets affects nutritional status.** Children living in households with few durable goods – a proxy for wealth – are more likely to be malnourished.

- **Paradoxically, children of farmers are more likely to be malnourished.** Children living in households with agricultural land holdings (even titled) of 1-15 hectares are more likely to be malnourished than those living in households within little or no land.

- **Geographic disparities are a significant determinant of nutritional status.** Children in indigenous areas are significantly more likely to be stunted than those in urban areas.

- **Older children are more likely to be malnourished** – which highlights the vulnerability of children during the weaning period. Boys are also more likely to be malnourished, which is a common result in an absence of discriminatory practices.

- **Competition with other children under five lowers nutritional status.** The more members under five, the worse the nutritional status of each child. Similarly, a higher number of pregnancies reduces the nutritional status of each child. This could relate to health problems associated with short birth spacing (for both mother and child), shorter periods of exclusive breastfeeding for each child, and competition for food and child care among siblings. These findings highlight the need for increased availability of family planning services and outreach.

- **Exclusive breastfeeding strongly improves nutritional status.** The benefits of breastfeeding (stronger immune systems, safe source of nutrients, etc.) are well known.

---

[3] The determinants of nutritional status were ascertained using several multi-variate linear regression models on z-scores expressed in percentage terms (continuous variables) for height-for-age (indicator of chronic malnutrition or stunting) for children under five and for weight-for-age for children under five. Other variables that were tested but were not significant include an index of housing quality, lack of sanitation services, rooms-per-person, lack of electricity, cooking with firewood, lack of piped water (with and without treatment), garbage dump in yard, gender and marital status of household head, childcare providers, health status of mother (smoking, illness), etc. Some of these variables may indeed have an impact on nutritional status but did not prove significant due to correlation with other variables (e.g., water with diarrhea and indigenous areas). See Annex 9 for details.

3.6.   **In Panama, the sources of inequality overlap substantially with the determinants of poverty.** As with poverty, disparities in assets – labor, education, housing, land, basic services, and credit – explain a large share of inequality (Table 3.1). Other sources of inequality include geographic location and household size and composition.[4] Two-thirds of Panama's consumption inequality can be explained by disparities in labor, education, land, certain services, geography and household size.[5] Education constitutes the single most important determinant of inequality, reflecting the large disparities in access to education (particularly secondary and higher education) and the large wage differentials associated with the various levels of educational attainment.

Table 3.1 – Decomposition of Inequality in Panama			
	Group	Sub-Group	% Inequality of Explained by:
1	Labor	# of workers per household member	14%
2		Formal vs. Informal Earnings (largest source in HH)	13%
3		Public/Private/Canal Earnings (largest source in HH)	7%
4	Years of Education	All household members	13%
5		Maximum for HH Head or Companion	41%
6		Household Head	39%
7	Housing Ownership	With registered title vs. no title vs. doesn't own house	15%
8	Hectares of	Owned (6 groups)[a]	11%
9	agricultural land	Worked (6 groups)[a]	14%
10		With title (6 groups)[a]	5%
11	Access to	No telephone line (vs. possesses line)	35%
12	Basic Services	No electricity connection (vs. has connection)	22%
13		No sanitation services (vs. has services)[b]	33%
14	Credit	More than B./100 in annual credit obtained	6%
15	Geography &	Four Areas: Urban, Rural, Indigenous, Remote	29%
16	Language	Indigenous Areas vs. Non-Indigenous	10%
17		Indigenous Language vs. Non-Indigenous Language	8%
18	Gender	Male/Female	0%
19	Household Size	# members from 0-23 years of age	26%
20		# members from 24-59 years of age	2%
21		# members aged 59+	0%
	Total: % of inequality explained by factors 2, 5, 9, 13, 15, 19		61%

Based on a decomposition of Entropy Measures of Inequality. Figures presented for the E-2 measure of inequality. See Annex 10 for detailed methodology and results.a\ Divided by sizes of 0-0.01, 0.01-1, 1-3, 3-10, 10-30 and more than 30 hectares. b\ Sanitation services include connection to sewer system or septic tank. This variable also reflects access to water.

3.7.   **The long-term nature of many of these variables is significant: as international experience has shown, it is very difficult to reduce inequality.** Most of these variables are somewhat structural (geography), difficult for Governments to change (land distribution, sectoral employment opportunities), or affect consumption over various generations (e.g., education and fertility).[6]

3.8.   **One measure that can reduce inequality in the short term is the reduction of trade barriers and price controls.** As discussed in Chapter 4, simulations suggest that reductions in trade and price distortions for agricultural products are likely to reduce inequality: complete trade liberalization would reduce the consumption Gini by 0.6 points. Although small, such reductions are significant, particularly in light of the tendency for Gini coefficients to show little variation over time.

[4] The analysis reveals that gender (the ratio of males to females and the sex of the household) is not an important personal attribute in explaining inequality in Panama (or poverty, as discussed above). The unimportance of gender consistent with international evidence for developing countries (see Ferreira and Litchfield, 1997). It is important to note, however, that inequality within households is not captured by LSMS data.
[5] It is important to note that, with the exception of this "joint" analysis (analyzing the different variables together), the decomposition of inequality using each individual variable is not additive. See Annex 10 for additional explanations.
[6] Even Chile, which has aggressively pursued structural policies to promote growth, and reduce poverty and inequality for some time (trade policies, education reform and targeted public investments, etc.), has only reduced the Gini index of inequality by 1.5 percentage points in seven years. See Ferreira and Litchfield (January 1997) and World Bank (June 10, 1997).

Chapter 4 – Poverty, Duality and Distortions in Panama's Economy

4.1. Chapters 2 and 3 establish the links between disparities in the distribution of assets and poverty, malnutrition, and inequality. These disparities in economic opportunity reflect Panama's uniquely dualistic pattern of development, which has in turn been spawned by a legacy of policy distortions adopted largely in the 1970s. This chapter examines these distortions and their likely impact on poverty and inequality. It also reviews recent reforms that have sought to correct these distortions and highlights actions remaining on the reform agenda that are key for reducing poverty and inequality.

THE LEGACY OF DISTORTIONS AND DUALITY IN PANAMA'S ECONOMY

4.2. With a GDP per capita of US$3,080 (1997) and low inflation, the Panamanian economy is among the more prosperous and stable in the region. Its privileged geographic location and its monetary regime anchored in the use of the U.S. dollar as legal tender have fostered a comparative advantage in services, which contribute over three quarters of GDP and generate two-thirds of employment in Panama. Such services are becoming even more competitive with increased privatization (e.g., in ports services).

4.3. **Panama's Modern Service "Enclaves" as a Source of Duality.** These strategic factors have also spurred the rapid development of internationally-oriented, modern, dynamic service "enclaves," including the Canal Zone, the Colón Free Zone, and the International Banking Center. While these enclaves generate an important share of GDP (eight percent for the Colón Free Zone, seven percent for the Canal Zone) they create little employment (three percent of the labor force) or fiscal revenue that could be used for investment in other regions of the country. Moreover, they inject negative spillovers into the economy: the huge wage differentials between those paid in the enclaves, particularly in the Canal Zone where the U.S. minimum wage is enforced, and the rest of the Panamanian economy sharply raise wage expectations relative to the opportunity cost of labor.

4.4. **Factor Market Segmentation.**   Indeed, factor markets have been segmented by policies that drive up the cost of labor and cheapen the cost of capital. Panama's labor market is characterized by a multiplicity of labor regimes (Box 4.1), which have created large wage differentials between workers in the Panama Canal Commission, public sector employees, and those employed in the rest of the economy.

4.5. These interventions not only hamper growth, but also have a direct link to poverty. Although poverty is measured by consumption rather than income (Chapter 1), income is a key determinant of consumption levels and the poor derive most of their income from labor earnings. By increasing the relative price of labor – and thus reducing demand for the poor's most abundant asset – these distortions swelled the ranks of the unemployed and encouraged informality. Indeed, unemployment rose sharply and remained fairly unresponsive to changes in growth following the introduction of the Labor Code in 1972.[1] Moreover, while they benefit those who are lucky enough to find formal sector jobs, the resulting segmentation of the labor market can put a heavy toll on informal sector workers by reducing their wages, making it difficult for the working poor to grow out of poverty through their own labor. Indeed, the LSMS reveals that the poor in Panama do not benefit from the generous provisions mandated by labor legislation – and they may even be hurt by the distortions they create. A number of aspects support this conclusion: (i) the majority of the working poor receive wages that are below the lowest official minimum wage;[2] (ii) they do not receive the fringe benefits mandated by the Labor Code (such as the "13th month" salary bonuses); (iii) the majority of the working poor are employed in the informal sector, where wages are lower and employment terms less favorable; and (iv) the working poor throughout the country appear to be underemployed and the urban poor are hurt by high rates of open unemployment.

---

[1] Following the introduction of the Labor Code in 1972, unemployment climbed from an average of 6.5% in the 1960s to an average 7.3% in the 1970s and 11.9% in the 1980s. (Source: MIPPE/DPS). Moreover, Gonzalez (1998) shows that unemployment became less responsive (elastic) to changes in economic growth after the Labor Code was instituted.
[2] Close to two thirds of extremely poor paid workers and over half of all paid workers living below the poverty line receive less than the lowest hourly minimum wage (as compared with only 17 percent of the non-poor).

```
┌─────────────────────────────────────────────────────────────────────────────────────────┐
│              Box 4.1 – Panama's Labor Market: Multiple and Stringent Policy Regimes        │
├─────────────────────────────────────────────────────────────────────────────────────────┤
│ A multiplicity of policy regimes govern Panama's Labor Market:                             │
└─────────────────────────────────────────────────────────────────────────────────────────┘
```

Box 4.1 – Panama's Labor Market: Multiple and Stringent Policy Regimes

A multiplicity of policy regimes govern Panama's Labor Market:

- The generous **Labor Code**, which was introduced in 1972 and modified in 1995, is the principle regulatory mechanism for the private sector. The Labor Code and associated legislation still distorts the private labor market in a number of ways:
    - A complex structure of minimum wages (by region and sector) and prohibition on wage reductions under any circumstances.
    - Short probationary period after which strong severance restrictions apply (the 1995 reform maintained the probationary period but removed the automatic conversion of workers to permanent status at its end)
    - Severe limits and penalties for dismissal.
    - Numerous fringe benefits including, *inter alia*, an extra "13th month" salary bonus, length-of-service bonuses, and overtime bonuses.
- Some 100 special labor laws govern **public sector employment**, with even more generous provisions for state workers and higher wage schedules than those of the Labor Code.
- U.S. labor laws cover workers in the **Panama Canal Commission** (PCC) and this regime is being maintained as assets are transferred to Panamanian ownership. Wages paid by the PCC are far higher than those paid in the rest of the economy (even higher than those in the public sector).
- A separate – and less restrictive – legislative regime governs employment in the **Export Processing Zones**.

See Annex 11 for details.

4.6.   **The Traditional Sector: Further Distortions.** The modern services sector is juxtaposed with a domestically-oriented traditional sector (primarily agriculture and industry), that has been constrained by policy-induced rigidities and low productivity for decades. Until recently, a highly distorted **trade regime** (one of the most protective in Latin America), combined with a complex web of **price controls** in the domestically-oriented sectors, had the result of protecting inefficient sectors, distorting resource allocation, generating rents for certain groups, and raising the cost of the basic consumption basket. Simulations using the LSMS suggest that the net redistributive effect of such protection was highly regressive, effectively taxing the poor and increasing poverty and inequality (Box 4.2).

Box 4.2 – Redistributive Effects of Trade Protection on Households

Until recently, Panama maintained one of the most highly protected trade and pricing regimes in Latin America. These interventions had a direct redistributive effect on the economy, and thus a potential direct impact on poverty and inequality.

The redistributive impact of complete trade and price liberalization for basic food items was simulated using household data from the LSMS. Food is important from a poverty perspective because food consumption represents 59% of the total budgets of the poor, and because agriculture generates 29% of the total incomes of the poor and 41% of the incomes of the rural poor. **The net impact of complete trade liberalization on poverty and inequality is expected to be positive.** Simulations suggest that:

- Overall poverty would fall close to two percentage points from the 1997 level (from 37.3% to 35.6%).
- Inequality would fall (with a reduction in the consumption Gini of 0.6 percentage points).
- Poor households would incur a net gain of B./26 per capita or 5% of total consumption (as compared with B./57 per capita or 2% of total consumption for the non-poor).
- Although some producers would lose in net terms (even taking into account their gains as consumers from the fall in the cost of basic staples), net losers represent only 2% of the population and less than one third are poor.
- Despite the fact that very few poor producers (under 15,000 people in total) would lose in net terms from an elimination of trade barriers, a significant share of these poor net losers are concentrated in the Provinces of Darién and Veraguas. Geographically-targeted compensating measures might thus be warranted to protect poor producers in these regions from the localized adverse effects of possible future trade liberalization measures.

See Annex 12 for details on tariff rates and the methodology used in the simulations.

4.7.   **Effects of Distortions and Duality.** The highly protectionist and distortionary policies ultimately stifled growth, and generated a large external debt. They also exacerbated poverty and engendered a highly unequal distribution of income. In the 1980s, these distortions and the confrontation with the U.S. plunged the economy into severe crisis. By end-1989, GDP had fallen by 16 percent, mismanagement and external sanctions had demonetized the economy, and unemployment had climbed to 20 percent (using the national definition).

4.8.   Since 1990, Panama has gone a long way toward achieving political and economic recovery. In the first several years, growth was based mainly on a boom in construction and other non-tradables, as well as arrears accumulation. By 1994, GDP reached pre-crisis levels, but, in the absence of fundamental structural changes, growth fell back to a modest two percent.

4.9.   In an attempt to stimulate more inclusive growth and reduce poverty and inequality, the Government has undertaken a number of fundamental reforms since 1994. It has dismantled a labyrinth of trade barriers and price controls, launched a far-reaching privatization program, issued anti-trust and consumer protection legislation, unified fiscal incentives for manufacturing firms, and adopted modest but important reforms to the Labor Code (Box 4.3).

4.10.   After several years of little growth, the economy began to respond in 1997, despite a series of climatic and economic shocks.[3] Real GDP rose from 2.9 percent in 1994 to 4.7 percent in 1997. Unemployment started to fall for the first time in years, declining from over 14 percent in 1994 to 13.2 percent in 1997 (using the national definition). Even more important for the long-term, employment has apparently become more responsive to changes in growth since the introduction of modest, but important, reforms to the Labor Code in 1995.[4]

Box 4.3 – Key Achievements of the Economic Reform Program
Liberalizing the Trade Regime. Reduced tariffs on many commodities, transformed specific tariffs into ad valorem rates, eliminated non-tariff barriers to imports, removed price controls. Transformed most highly distorted trade regime in LAC to one of the most open.
Promoting Domestic Competition. Passed the Competition Law, which removed remaining price controls and established anti-trust and consumer protection framework.
Reforming the Labor Code. Modest reforms to the Labor Code, including: (i) curbing the intervention of government in employer-employee relations; (ii) giving employers more flexibility to reassign employees within firms; and (iii) easing the automatic conversion of employees to permanent employment status after the three-month probationary period.
Reforming and Privatizing Public Enterprises. (i) Privatizing the state telecommunications institute (INTEL); (ii) reforming pricing principles and passing law to permit private generation of electricity; (iii) privatizing service delivery functions of state port authority (APN); (iv) opening traditionally state-dominated activities in the financing, construction, operation, and maintenance of major highways.
Unifying Fiscal Incentives in Manufacturing Sector. Passing Law 28/1995 "*Ley de Universalización a los Incentivos Tributarios*" to equalize fiscal incentives for all manufacturing firms irrespective of their size.
Sources: Republic of Panama: *Desarrollo Social con Eficiencia Economica 1997-1999*, Cabinet Resolution No. 222 of September 19, 1997; World Bank (1998): Economic Reform Loan (ERL), Implementation Completion Report.

CONSOLIDATING ECONOMIC REFORMS

4.11.   Though progress has been made in reducing some distortions and disparities in economic opportunity, an important economic reform agenda remains for Panama to sustain growth and reduce unemployment.[5] With timely implementation of these reforms, growth in real GDP is expected to climb from four percent in 1998 to five percent by 2001.[6] Assuming a constant distribution of consumption, these expected growth rates could reduce poverty by up to 3.3 percentage points by the year 2001 (from 37.3 percent in 1997 to 34.0 percent in 2001). Extreme poverty, which tends to be more stable, is projected to fall by 2.0 percentage points over that same period (from 18.8 percent to 16.8 percent).

---

[3] Notably, the El Niño climatic phenomenon, a downturn in Canal operations (due to decreased grain imports by China), and declining U.S. Defense Department demand.
[4] Gonzalez (1998).
[5] As discussed in detail in the Country Assistance Strategy for Panama, World Bank (October 29, 1998).
[6] See Country Assistance Strategy for Panama for details on base case reform and growth projections.

4.12.   In addition to fostering growth, which is critical for poverty reduction, four areas also have the potential to weaken disparities in key assets and economic opportunity and are crucial for reducing poverty and inequality:

- Deepening **reforms to the labor code** and related legislation to ease restrictions on dismissal and lower the relative cost of labor.   Such distortions continue to hurt the poor by encouraging unemployment, underemployment, and informality.   Further reforms to reduce these distortions would allow the poor more flexible use of their most abundant asset.

- Expanding the **land tenure regime**, by modernizing land administration services and launching a massive national land titling program focusing on peri-urban and rural areas.   This program should fill the gaps in land titling that currently prevent the poor from leveraging credit and buying and selling property.   It would also have a likely impact on inequality, since disparities in titled property assets explain a significant share of inequality in Panama (see Chapter 3).

- Continuing **trade reforms**.   Though tariffs have come down substantially, further reductions are still needed (particularly for rice and milk).   Simulations using the LSMS suggest that further reductions in tariffs would indeed reduce poverty and inequality (Box 4.2).   Although some producers would lose in net terms from lower prices (even taking into account their gains as consumers), these net losers represent a very small share of the population and the majority are non-poor.

- Reducing distortions in **public and freight transport.**   The Government should actively pursue reforms to reduce distortions in the provision of public transport, which is largely used by the urban poor.   Barriers to competition in freight transport would also reduce the cost of living in general.

Chapter 5 – Poverty and Social Spending

5.1. Disparities in human capital reflect a lack of targeting of social policy and public resources. Despite high public spending on the social sectors, inefficiencies and inequities have prevented improved outcomes for the poor (Figure 5.1).[1] Although the Government has attempted to compensate for some of these biases against the poor by developing a number of social assistance programs, the impact of these programs could be improved through systematic targeting and improvements in program delivery. Given the clear links between disparities in human capital and poverty, inequality and

Figure 5.1

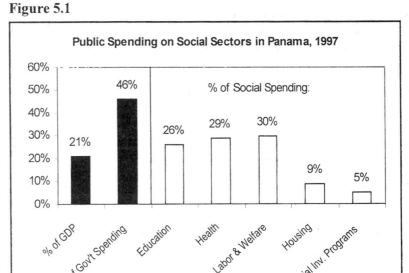

malnutrition established Chapters 2 and 3, this chapter highlights the crucial need for a reallocation of public spending on the social sectors toward areas that benefit the poor.

INEQUITIES AND INEFFICIENCIES IN THE PROVISION OF PUBLIC EDUCATION

5.2. With close to six percent of GDP allocated to public spending on education, Panama ranks among the highest in Latin America.[2] Moreover, education has absorbed an increasing share of resources, rising from 4.7 percent of GDP in 1992 to 5.6 percent in 1997 and from nine percent of total public spending in 1992 to twelve percent in 1997 (Table 5.1). The LSMS reveals that household spending on education accounts for about three percent of GDP, yielding a total of nine percent of GDP (public and private spending) allocated to education in 1997.

5.3. While the overall level of public expenditures on education appears to be adequate, its distribution is inequitable. Indeed, disparities in educational outcomes largely reflect biases in public spending:

- **Overall, public spending on education is regressive, with the non-poor benefiting more in absolute terms.** Whereas the poor represent 43 percent of the school-aged population aged 5-24, they only receive 28 percent of total public spending on education (Figure 5.2). In relative terms, however, subsidies are more important to the poor, representing 35 percent of the poor's average per capita total consumption as compared with eleven percent for the non-poor.

---

[1] A lion's share (93 percent) of spending on labor and social welfare is absorbed by the Social Security Fund's Disability, Old Age, and Life Insurance Fund (*invalidez, vejez, y muerte* under the *Caja de Seguridad Social*, CSS). The remainder goes to employment and training, worker-employer relations, sick and maternity leave benefits, a CSS fund for professional risks, welfare and social assistance, and administration and regulation. The majority (83 percent) of housing spending goes to investments in public housing channeled through the Ministry of Housing (MIVI), the CSS, and the National Mortgage Bank (BHN). Social Investment Programs include spending by the Ministry of the Presidency on the Social Fund (FES) and programs supported by the Office of the First Lady, and on MIPPE/MEF's Local Investment Program (PROINLO).

[2] Other top spenders include Mexico (5.8%), Venezuela (5.1%), and Costa Rica (4.7%). Like Panama, these countries not only allocate a high share of GDP to public spending on education, but such spending is high in on a per capita basis in absolute purchasing-power-parity (PPP) terms. The average share of GDP allocated to public spending on education in developed countries is about 5.3 percent. Sources: World Bank and UNICEF EdStats database; World Bank World Development Reports; MIPPE and MINEDUC.

- **Public spending on pre-primary and secondary education is regressive in absolute terms** (Figure 5.2). In relative terms, however, subsidies at these levels are more important to the poor than the non-poor (as a share of the poor's relatively lower average total consumption per capita).

- **Public subsidies to higher education are extremely regressive, in both absolute and relative terms.** Virtually all public spending (94 percent) on higher education benefits the non-poor. Over forty percent of subsidies on public higher education accrues to the top quintile of the population. Moreover, public spending on higher education is regressive in relative terms, representing over five percent of the average per capita total consumption of the non-poor, compared with only three percent for the poor (despite the poor's having relatively lower levels of total consumption). Hence, with a lower rate of cost recovery at this level,[3] the large government subsidies to higher education truly benefit the upper echelons of Panamanian society.

Table 5.1 – Public Spending on Education						
	1992	1993	1994	1995	1996	1997 (P)
Total Spending on Education (B./000) (a)	313,668	338,143	364,377	373,022	431,859	490,355
% Recurrent	95%	87%	92%	91%	91%	n.a.
% Investment	5%	13%	8%	9%	9%	n.a.
Total Spending on Education as Share of:						
GDP	4.7%	5.4%	4.7%	4.7%	5.2%	5.6%
Total Government Spending (b)	9.2%	12.8%	12.0%	11.0%	11.5%	12.2%
Total Gov't Spending on Social Sectors (c)	25.1%	26.6%	23.9%	21.6%	23.9%	26.5%
Education Spending by Level (% of total) (d)						
Primary and Pre-Primary	40%	30%	33%	34%	29%	29%
Secondary	25%	37%	30%	29%	34%	33%
Higher	29%	27%	29%	30%	29%	30%
Other	6%	7%	7%	7%	7%	8%
Total Subsidies Per Student (B./) (d)						
Primary and Pre-Primary	358	326	342	351	342	374
Secondary	476	831	641	604	805	872
Higher	1,623	1,676	1,722	1,683	1,747	2,142

Sources: MIPPE/MEF: Dirección de Presupuesto de la Nación; MINEDUC; Contraloria de la Republica. 1997 figures are preliminary. a\ Data on education expenditures exclude spending on education investments by FES and PROINLO (demand-driven local investment programs) as well as the School Lunch Program supported by FES. b\ As share of Non-Financial Public Sector Spending. c\ Includes Government spending on Education, Health, Labor and Social Security, and Housing. Excludes spending on FES, programs supported by the First Lady, PROINLO, and the "Proyectos de Desarrollo Social" (Circuitales), some or all of which could be considered as "social" spending. d\ Includes administrative spending.

- **Only at the primary level are subsidies progressive in both absolute and relative terms.** While the poor represent 49 percent of primary-school aged children, they receive 56 percent of total government spending on primary education. In relative terms, primary school subsidies are ten times more important for the poor, representing 18 percent of the poor's per capita consumption as compared with 1.6 percent for the non-poor.

- **Geographic inequities in public spending on education are also apparent, with biases in favor of urban areas and against indigenous and non-indigenous rural areas.** While indigenous residents (virtually all of whom are poor) represent ten percent of the school-aged population (5-24 years), they only receive five percent of total government spending on education (Figure 5.3). Rural residents also receive a disproportionately low amount of education subsidies, despite the fact that the majority of the poor are concentrated in the countryside. In contrast, whereas about half of the population aged 5-24 lives in urban areas, city-dwellers receive two thirds of public spending on education. As with biases against the poor, geographic inequities in public spending arise at the preschool, secondary, and higher education levels.

---

[3] Cost recovery is lowest for higher education: subsidies account for 84 percent of the total cost of public higher education, as compared with 78 percent for primary and secondary school

5.4.   **Despite these patterns, the share of total spending allocated to primary education has fallen substantially in recent years.** The share allocated to basic education[4] now equals that accorded to higher education – which almost exclusively benefits the non-poor (Table 5.1).

Figure 5.2

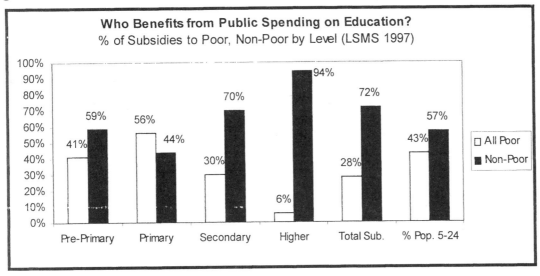

Figure 5.3

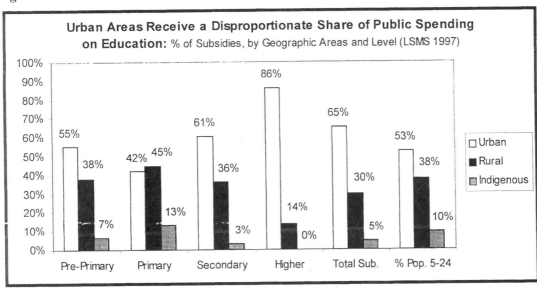

5.5.   **Disparities in household spending on education exacerbate inequities in the distribution of total resources devoted to education.** The non-poor spend substantially more than the poor on education (Figure 5.4). As discussed in Box 2.4 in Chapter 2, these differences arise primarily in

---

[4] The Government does not systematically disaggregate spending allocations to primary and pre-primary (basic) education. Available data for 1993, however, indicate that primary school absorbs 96 percent of the allocation to basic education. Source: World Bank Report No. 13701-PAN "Panama: Issues in Basic Education," March 1995.

spending on school supplies, books, and informal fees. Such disparities probably add to inequities in the quality of education received.

Figure 5.4

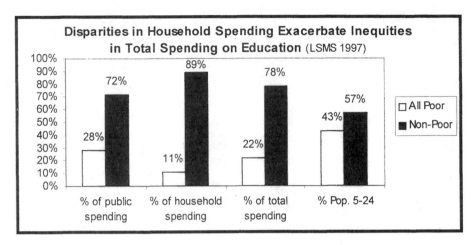

5.6. **Functional inefficiencies in education management have also prevented improved educational outcomes among the poor.** The poor quality of public education also stems from inefficiencies in the delivery of education, including: (i) highly centralized decision-making and lack of parent and community participation; (ii) weak policy-making and planning capacity in the Ministry of Education; (iii) the lack of a management information system and standardized evaluation system as decision-making tools; and (iv) a disconnect between the pay and performance of teachers and administrators. While such inefficiencies are not limited to the poor, the resulting quality of the education received by the poor lags that of the non-poor (as discussed above).

5.7. **Although the Government has recently started to address some of these deficiencies, the major challenge is to remove existing biases in public spending.** The Government's ten-year Education Strategy (1997-2006) outlines four major policy objectives: (i) equity of access; (ii) quality improvements; (iii) institutional efficiency with an emphasis on decentralization of administrative and educational decisions; and (iv) expanded community and family participation. The key challenge for translating these principles into action and for reducing disparities in human capital is to reallocate public spending on education such that a larger share benefits the poor. Cost recovery for higher education, which exclusively benefits the non-poor, should be increased in order to liberate resources that could be allocated toward basic education, which is a priority for helping the poor grow out of poverty.

INEQUITIES AND INEFFICIENCIES IN THE PROVISION OF PUBLIC HEALTH CARE SERVICES

5.8. **With over seven percent of GDP and 15 percent of government expenditures allocated to public spending on health in 1996, Panama ranks among the top spenders in Latin America.**[5] Moreover, health has absorbed an increasing share of resources, with public spending, rising from six percent of GDP and twelve percent of government expenditures in 1992. Despite this large investment, health outcomes and performance indicators are lower than expected, particularly among the poor and indigenous (see Chapter 2). Inequities in public spending and inefficiencies in the sector largely explain this apparent paradox.

---

[5] Other high spenders include Argentina (10.6 percent of GDP), Costa Rica (8.5 percent), and Colombia (7.4 percent). Source: Govindaraj et. al. (March 1995).

Table 5.2 – Public Spending on Health					
	1992	1993	1994	1995	1996
Total Spending on Health (B./000)	406,709	442,724	475,859	547,090	584,510
% Recurrent	91%	89%	88%	81%	79%
% Investment	9%	11%	12%	19%	21%
Total Spending on Health as Share of:					
GDP	6.1%	6.1%	6.2%	6.9%	7.1%
Total Government Spending	11.9%	14.6%	15.7%	16.1%	15.6%
Total Gov't Spending on Social Sectors	32.5%	30.3%	31.2%	31.7%	32.3%
Health Spending by Type (% of total)					
Maternal-Infant Health	28%	28%	28%	26%	25%
Adult Health	34%	34%	32%	30%	29%
Environmental Health	16%	15%	17%	13%	12%
Construction of Health Centers	6%	8%	8%	17%	20%
Administration and Regulation	16%	15%	16%	15%	14%
Health Spending by Agency (% of total)					
Ministry of Health (MINSA)	33%	36%	31%	29%	30%
Social Security Fund (CSS)	51%	50%	53%	59%	59%
Water and Sanitation Institute (IDAAN)	3%	3%	3%	3%	3%
Metropolitan Waste Management (DIMA)	13%	11%	13%	10%	9%
Source: MIPPE/MEF: Dirección de Presupuesto de la Nación.					

5.9.   **While the overall level of public resources allocated to health care appears to be adequate, disparities in health outcomes reflect biases in public spending.** Extensive data from the LSMS on use patterns, poverty status and geographic location support the following conclusions (see Annex 17):[6]

- **The poorest and richest quintiles benefit the least from public spending on health care.** For those in the top quintile, this is due to reliance on private health care. For the poorest, however, this bias reflects low levels of health care use in general, regardless of the type of care.

- **Health care spending on curative care is regressive, while spending on maternity-related care is progressive.** However, a lack of institutional data on the costs of different types of health care prevents an assessment of the overall incidence of public spending.

- **Hospital-based care is used more by the non-poor and those in urban areas and thus spending on hospital care is likely to be regressive.** Poorer groups tend to use health centers, posts and sub-centers more, and hence spending on these services is likely to be progressive.

5.10.   **Inefficiencies in the health sector have also prevented better health outcomes among the poor.** Such inefficiencies arise largely due to the existence of a fragmented health system comprised of three major players: the Ministry of Health (MINSA), the Social Security Fund (CSS) and the private sector. Disintegration in the financing and provision of health services among these three players promotes duplication and under-utilization of services, negates economies of scale, and creates unnecessary increases in the cost of services. In addition, MINSA has weak policy-making, financing, and regulatory capabilities, deteriorated infrastructure, and obsolete management and information systems. There is also an excessive reliance on physicians in instances in which nurses could more cheaply provide services. Decision-making and management are overly-centralized, which combined with high levels of bureaucracy, has promoted a culture of poor management, lack of accountability for results and performance, and an inability to respond to local needs in a timely fashion. There is no link between payment transfers to providers and performance, with little incentive to improve efficiency and effectiveness. Moreover, health service delivery and referral systems are disorganized and lack appropriate regulation and financial incentives to manage demand for health services. While these issues are not limited to the poor, it is the poor who suffer the results in terms of less access to quality services and worse health outcomes.

---

[6] A complete analysis of the incidence of public spending on health was not possible due to a lack of data on the value of health care services and the share of this value that was covered by government subsidies (versus the share covered by household payments). The patterns presented here largely reflect the incidence of the *use* of public services. See Annex 17 for details.

5.11.   **While the Government is undertaking a number of steps to improve efficiency in the health sector, it should also seek to correct biases in public spending.** MINSA and CSS have launched a health sector reform program to be piloted in the San Miguelito region that seeks to improve <u>efficiency</u> by (i) establishing a strategic partnership between the two institutions; (ii) separating the financing and provision of services; (iii) increasing private-sector participation in service provision; (iv) strengthening the policy-making, regulatory and management capabilities of MINSA; (v) decentralizing services to the regional level and increasing the administrative and financial autonomy of service providers; and (vi) increasing community participation in health affairs and health care. Increasing efficiency is only half the story, however. The Government should also seek to improve <u>equity</u> of access to health care services by: (i) improving the targeting of public spending using the new poverty map developed by MIPPE/MEF; and (ii) expanding the coverage of cost-effective primary health interventions in poor rural, indigenous, and urban areas. A thorough review of public spending on health services, combined with data from the LSMS, would facilitate the identification of specific actions needed for such a reallocation.

PROTECTING THE POOR: NUTRITION & SOCIAL ASSISTANCE INTERVENTIONS

5.12.   **To compensate for some of the biases against the poor, the Government has mobilized considerable resources for social assistance programs.** An estimated one percent of GDP is currently allocated to social programs, most of which were initiated since the early 1990s (see Box 5.1).

5.13.   **These programs rightly address key poverty issues and several appear quite effective at reaching the poor.** While Panama does not have a comprehensive social safety net, its existing assistance programs do seek to reduce key disparities, including:

Figure 5.5 (NOTE: all poor includes extreme poor)

- **Removing economic barriers to increased school enrollment by the poor.** Panama's compensatory education programs – several school feeding schemes and a new cash transfer program – seek to remove economic barriers to education by providing assistance needed to generate incentives for increased enrollment, attendance, and performance. While an evaluation of the educational impact of these

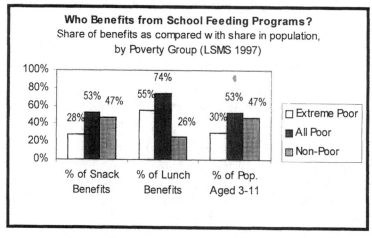

programs is currently underway, there is evidence that some are quite effective at reaching the poor.[7] In particular, the LSMS suggests that the FES School Lunch Program is extremely well targeted, reaching a disproportionate share of poor and extreme poor children (Figure 5.5).

- **Responding to community requests for basic and social infrastructure.** Disparities in access to basic services are closely linked to poverty, inequality and malnutrition. The Government currently operates a number of demand-driven local investment programs – including the FES and PROINLO – designed to respond to community needs to fill gaps in basic service provision.

---

[7] The FES and the World Bank are currently designing an evaluation of the impact of school feeding programs on school attendance and performance.

Box 5.1 – INVENTORY OF MAIN GOVERNMENT SOCIAL ASSISTANCE PROGRAMS		
Program	Explicit Targeting of Poor?	Key Issues for Improved Poverty Effectiveness
COMPENSATORY EDUCATION PROGRAMS		
MINEDUC School Feeding Program Early-morning snack (milk with enriched cookies or an enriched cereal-based *crema*). Average annual cost per student: B./23; for milk: B./35; for the cookies; B./9; for the *crema*: B./12.	✗ None. Explicitly universal by law (all school children).	♦ Targeting ♦ Improve efficiency in delivery to remote areas ♦ Improve cost-effectiveness, particularly for milk
New MINEDUC School Lunch Program To be provided to children in extended-day programs. New program.	✗ None.	♦ Targeting ♦ Reduce overlap with FES program
FES School Feeding Program Lunch (rice, beans, and oil). Implementation with community participation. Average annual cost per student: B./21.	✔ Targeted according to nutrition & poverty map criteria	♦ Targeted expansion ♦ Reduce inefficiencies in delivery to remote areas
Cash School Transfer (Balboa per day) Program New program to transfer B./1 per student for each day of school attendance (being piloted in Barú)	✔ To be targeted according to new poverty map and enrollment / dropout indices	♦ Targeting ♦ Efficient administration & monitoring
OTHER NUTRITION & FEEDING PROGRAMS		
MINSA Supplementary Feeding Program Monthly food rations accompanied by micronutrient supplements via health system to malnourished children under 5 and underweight pregnant and lactating women. Clear eligibility and exit criteria (anthropometric screening).	✔ Targeted using anthropometric indicators of malnutrition and nutritional risk; program also self-targeted due to bland taste of meal	♦ Evaluate impact on poor and efficiency of implementation; expand program
Other Nutrition Interventions (MINSA/PATRONATO DE NUTRICION) Other nutrition interventions include micronutrient supplements in areas with deficiencies, deworming interventions, school gardens, etc.	✔ Most are targeted by need (e.g., micronutrient deficiencies)	♦ Evaluate impact and efficiency of implementation
SPECIAL GROUP ASSISTANCE PROGRAMS		
FES Grupos Vulnerables Programs New programs. NGO-executed programs funded by FES for special vulnerable groups, including: street children, poor elderly, poor women, poor and at-risk youths, Afro-Panamanians, and the indigenous.	✔ Various criteria: geographic targeting, self-targeting of street children; elderly not covered by CSS or other social security programs; etc.	♦ Ensure targeting, especially for women and youth programs ♦ Program impact evaluations needed
LOCAL SOCIAL INVESTMENT PROGRAMS		
FES Infrastructure & Credit Programs Demand-driven social and economic infrastructure investment projects and a new program to support micro-enterprises. It also funds a number of regional development programs (e.g., FIDA-Ngobe Program)	✔ ✗ Many – but not all – FES investments are targeted using geographic poverty criteria	♦ Design new criteria for targeting with new poverty map ♦ Expand share of FES spending subject to targeting criteria
MIPPE/MFF – PROINLO Demand-driven community investments.	✗ None. Explicitly universal with equal amounts to each *corregimiento*	♦ Targeting ♦ Evaluate possible functional overlap with FES

- **Responding to the specific needs of vulnerable groups.** The Government also provides tailored assistance to specific vulnerable groups through a number of smaller programs, including housing assistance to the low-income families, and NGO-executed social programs for street children, poor elderly, poor women and youths, indigenous groups and Afro-Panamanians. MINSA also operates a supplemental feeding and micronutrient program for malnourished children and mothers, which appears to be quite well targeted.[8]

5.14. **Nonetheless, a number of weaknesses reduce the effectiveness of these transfers,** including:

- **A lack of targeting.** Some of Panama's larger assistance programs – notably MINEDUC's school snack program (see Figure 5.5)[9] and MIPPE/MEF's local investment program (PROINLO) – are explicitly universal. Others, such as the FES, are only partially targeted to the poor.[10] The considerable amount of resources devoted to these programs would have a much larger impact on poverty reduction if they were concentrated on the poor.

- **Inefficiencies in program delivery.** Inefficiencies in the delivery of transfers also reduce the cost-effectiveness of these safety-net programs. The MINEDUC school snack program, for example, includes unnecessarily costly inputs, most notably milk (which is backed by the milk processing and packaging lobby).[11] Cost-effectiveness would be improved with the removal of milk from the program (to be replaced by the cheaper cereal-based *crema* or the fortified cookies). Both the MINEDUC snack program and the FES lunch program also suffer from inefficiencies in the physical delivery of food to remote areas (see Box 5.2), which could be remedied through a decentralization of food procurement in these areas.

- **Possible duplication of functions.** A possible duplication of functions of the various social investment programs (between the FES and PROINLO and potentially with the line ministries) could reduce their effectiveness.

Box 5.2 – Decentralizing School Feeding Programs in Remote Areas: the Potential of Block Grants

Both the MINEDUC Snack Program and the FES Lunch Program suffer inefficiencies in the physical delivery of food to remote areas. Before the start of the next school year, both programs need to design more cost-effective mechanisms for transferring resources to these communities (which have high incidences of poverty and malnutrition). Some options:

- **Government delivery is costly.** In some instances, the food has had to be delivered via helicopter (at a cost of B./800 per hour per helicopter!), horses, or boats.
- **Community pick-up is costly and ineffective.** One option that has been tried involves requiring communities to pick up the food themselves at satellite delivery points (the cost remains, but is borne by the communities). This has not been effective, however, and there are numerous reports of the food being left to waste.
- **Block grants are a promising alternative.** An alternative involves the decentralization of food purchases to the communities themselves. The Government could transfer funds as block grants directly to the communities, who would then purchase the food locally (according to pre-advised nutritional criteria consistent with local food supplies). A cost-benefit analysis suggests that, with proper monitoring and mechanisms for accountability, this would be by far the most cost-effective option.

---

[8] Poor children receive over three quarters of MINSA food rations (with the remaining quarter going to the non-poor). Coverage of the program is limited, however, reaching 14% of indigenous children and 8% of all poor children (compared with 3% of the non-poor). See Annex 17.

[9] Panamanian law requires that MINEDUC's snack program be expanded to reach all children. In fact, it is slightly self-targeted to the poor due to the fact that wealthier children voluntarily attend private – rather than public – schools (and the snacks are not provided at private schools).

[10] While targeting criteria are applied to some of the investments supported by the FES (notably those funded by international donors such as the World Bank), the remainder of FES investment spending is not explicitly targeted according to poverty criteria.

[11] In terms of the cost per thousand calories transferred, milk is 1.6 times more costly than enriched cookies and 2.4 times more costly than the enriched *crema*. Moreover, the common prevalence of milk allergies (particularly among the indigenous) makes the use of milk less attractive.

Chapter 6 – Principles, Priorities, and Actions to Reduce Poverty

SOCIAL AGENDA AND A STRATEGY TO REDUCE POVERTY: MAIN PRINCIPLES

6.1.   **Poverty reduction is the top priority of the new Government,** as emphasized in the Social Agenda.[1] This Social Agenda outlines broad strategic principles for reducing poverty, seeking to strengthen the key assets of the poor, taking into account geographic differences in poverty and priorities (see Box 6.1). The main principles for this strategy include:

- Improved efficiency in social spending to improve its investment impact on human capital;

- Targeting of resources to the poor to improve the likelihood of impact on poverty;

- Decentralization and "de-bureaucratization" for improved efficiency and quality of interventions;

- Increased community participation for improved effectiveness; and

- Monitoring of the poverty situation and of the implementation of actions to reduce poverty.

Box 6.1 – Community Priorities by Geographic Area		
Rural Areas	**Indigenous Areas**	**Urban Areas**
Transport, roads	Education	Safety, crime
Electricity, telephones	Potable water	Transportation, roads
Potable water	Alcohol, drugs	Employment, labor
Health care	Transport, roads	Sanitation services
Employment, labor	Health care	Potable water
Education	Housing	Social & community centers
Housing	Safety, crime	Housing, titling
Social & community centers	Employment / labor	Alcohol, drugs
Safety, crime	Sanitation services	Health care
Land, titling	Electricity, telephones	Gangs, youth problems
Sanitation services	Social & community centers	Lighting, telephones
Alcohol, drugs		Garbage collection
		Education

Source: Panama LSMS 1997 Community Questionnaire; community priorities ranked in order of frequency.

PRIORITIES FOR TRANSLATING THESE PRINCIPLES INTO ACTION

6.2.   In addition to sustaining and deepening the economic reform program as a vehicle for promoting growth, several priority actions are needed to translate the above principles into results, including: (i) prioritizing among poverty groups; (ii) reallocating public spending as the top priority action; (iii) decentralizing and promoting participation for effectiveness of service delivery; (iv) implementing specific policy reforms to reduce disparities in assets; (v) explicitly using and developing targeting mechanisms; and (vi) allocating resources for monitoring the poverty situation and actions to reduce poverty.

Prioritizing Among Key Poor and Vulnerable Groups

6.3.   **The Government should prioritize among poverty groups according to the prevalence, depth and severity of poverty** (Box 6.2). First priority should be given to the rural poor, the indigenous, and poor and malnourished children. Second priority should be assigned to combating urban poverty. Finally, third priority should be given to programs that target the elderly poor, child laborers, poor informal-sector workers and the poor unemployed.

---

[1] *Agenda Social*, 5 Volumes, August 1999.

Box 6.2 – Priority Poverty Groups (●●● = high priority; ●● = medium priority; ● = priority according to scope & severity of poverty)	
GEOGRAPHIC GROUPS:	**PRIORITY**
◆ **The poor in rural areas.** A high share of the rural population is poor. The new Poverty Map (see below) would help identify specific districts with high concentrations of rural poor.	●●●
◆ **All residents of indigenous areas.** Geographic targeting to indigenous areas would be administratively simple: virtually all residents of indigenous areas are poor; most live in extreme poverty.	●●●
◆ **The poor in urban areas.** In terms of their absolute number, the urban poor are an important group. A significant share of city dwellers also live just above the poverty line and could be considered vulnerable. Urban poverty is less extreme, severe, or deep, however.	●●
ETHNIC GROUPS:	**PRIORITY**
◆ **The Ngobe-Buglé.** The analysis reveals that Panama's largest ethnic indigenous group has the highest rate of poverty in the country. Most Ngobe-Buglé are concentrated in indigenous areas in Chiriquí and Bocas del Toro, making geographic targeting feasible (see above). They tend to live in dispersed clusters of 6-8 households, however, making, service provision difficult.	●●●
◆ **Other indigenous groups.** Poverty rates are also high among other indigenous groups, but primarily for those who live within the indigenous areas.	●●●
DEMOGRAPHIC & ECONOMIC GROUPS:	**PRIORITY**
◆ **Poor children and youths.** One half of Panamanian children under 18 live in poverty. One quarter of poor children under five years old are malnourished. The developmental status of children renders them extremely vulnerable to the risks of living in an impoverished environment. Youth is the point in the life cycle when physical, cognitive and psycho-social development occurs at its most accelerated pace and is most susceptible to abnormal development from poverty conditions. Poverty is particularly costly to individuals, society, and future generations when it occurs at these stages of life.	●●●
◆ **Undernourished children and pregnant & lactating women.** The Social Agenda also identifies these groups as priority for interventions. With strong correlation between poverty and malnutrition, they are largely captured by other priority group classifications. There are some specific interventions needed for these groups, however (see Part 3).	●●●
◆ **Poor elderly.** Though a smaller share of the elderly are poor (29%), demographic changes indicate that these will become an important group in the future. There are very few programs in Panama at present to assist poor elderly citizens who fall outside the social security system.	●
◆ **Poor child laborers, informal-sector workers, and unemployed (particularly women and youths).** The Social Agenda also identifies these groups as priority for interventions. Indeed, poverty is correlated with child labor, informal work, and unemployment (for urban women and youths). Though they are probably already captured by the above priority group classifications, they may have specific needs.	●

Main Priority Action: Reallocating Public Spending

6.4.   **Reallocating public expenditures is the top priority for effective action to reduce poverty.** Given the high level of social spending in Panama, it is unlikely that a large amount of additional resources will be forthcoming. As such, the Government urgently needs to reallocate existing spending toward areas that benefit the poor, boost cost recovery for services used by the non-poor, and improve efficiency in service delivery. Explicit use of targeting mechanisms (see below) in program and service delivery plans would also help ensure that more resources are channeled to the poor. A thorough review of public spending should be conducted in 1999 to provide additional guidance on such reallocations. This review should emphasize both the functional aspects of the budget (including the distributional incidence of spending in the main sectors) as well as the administration and management of public expenditures. The LSMS analysis already provides insights into some of the main reallocations that are needed to reduce disparities in assets.

6.5.   **Public spending on education must be reallocated for improved effectiveness in combating poverty.** The analysis clearly shows that disparities in education are the key causes of poverty, malnutrition and inequality in Panama. Investing in the education of the poor is also the principal lever for helping the poor lift themselves out of poverty in the long run. Clear candidates for reallocation in the education sector include:

- Higher cost recovery for higher education (benefits the non-poor) would liberate resources that could be allocated toward basic education (priority for the poor and indigenous). The annual cost of completing coverage of primary schooling for all children aged 6-11 who are not currently enrolled is expected to be quite small: about B./12 million in total (0.14 percent of GDP), including B./9 million to the Government and B./3 million to households (in the form of fees, informal fees, transport costs, books, and materials).[2] The annual cost of completing coverage of secondary education for all children aged 12-17 not currently enrolled would be larger: about B./89 million in total (1% of GDP), including B./69 million in public spending and B./20 million in contributions from households. Completing secondary school coverage of only the *poor* would cost about three quarters of this amount. Nonetheless, given the substantially higher rates of return to secondary school education – and the corresponding impact on reducing poverty and inequality – such investments are warranted.

- In many areas demand-side factors (economic constraints) pose larger obstacles to increased enrollment by the poor than supply-side factors (availability of facilities). As such, spending should be focused on compensatory education interventions (e.g., *targeted* school feeding and/or attendance-based cash transfer programs) and the provision of textbooks and school materials (largest cost items for attending school; benefits for quality of education). Investments in instruments such as the TELEBASICA program would also reduce constraints to increased school access in remote rural areas.

6.6. **The Government should complement its efforts to boost efficiency in the health sector with a reallocation of public spending designed to improve equity.** A thorough review of public spending on health services that combines use information from the LSMS with unit cost data on specific services should be undertaken to identify specific actions needed for such a reallocation. Though unit cost data are not currently available, the analysis of the LSMS does highlight some candidates for reallocated public spending:

- In terms of the types of services provided, higher cost recovery should be sought for curative care (disproportionately benefits the non-poor) and resources should be shifted toward the expansion of cost-effective primary health interventions in poor, rural, and indigenous areas (using the poverty map, see below), with an emphasis on maternal-infant health, oral rehydration, potable water in rural and indigenous areas, prevention and early detection of TB, family planning, and health education.

- In terms of facilities, higher cost recovery (and private rather than public provision) should be sought for hospital-based care (disproportionately benefits the non-poor and urban residents), and public spending on inputs (including medicines), investment and rehabilitation should focus on health centers, sub-centers, and posts (used primarily by the poor).

6.7. **Spending on social security and assistance programs should be streamlined to ensure a comprehensive, efficient, and well-targeted social safety net.** Although existing assistance programs rightly address key poverty issues (compensatory education, local investment, nutrition, and tailored-interventions for specific vulnerable groups), a number of actions should be taken to streamline spending on these programs and ensure a more comprehensive and efficient safety net:

- Explicitly target spending on all social assistance programs, including existing school feeding and community investment programs, reducing or eliminating allocations to areas with a low incidence of poverty and shifting these resources to poorer areas (see targeting discussion below);

- Reduce duplication in spending on local investment programs by combining these programs or focusing them on specific areas (sectoral or geographic);

- Develop mechanisms to protect annual budget allocations for programs and interventions (such as the targeted programs supported by the FES, primary education, etc.) with a proven record for reaching the poor. This does not include "all social spending" or "all social investment" and excludes the more political programs such as the "social investment" spending under the "Circuitales" legislators fund.

---

[2] These figures are based on average per student costs of schooling at the primary and secondary levels (Source: MIPPE) and the number of children in each age cohort that are not currently enrolled in school (Source: LSMS 1997). These do not include the incremental investment cost associated with the extension of the school day.

- Use resources generated from better targeting of above programs to expand existing pilot programs that are tailored to specific vulnerable groups if evaluations show them to be successful (e.g., those being supported by the FES and the new Ministry of Youth, Women, Children and Family, MJMNF); allocate resources to develop new social programs using similar model to tackle social problems such as crime, violence, and alcoholism, which were cited by urban and indigenous communities as priorities in the LSMS; and

- Conduct a thorough review of the distributional incidence of public spending on social security programs.

6.8. **Public spending allocations for basic infrastructure should be allocated according to gaps and poverty criteria.** The precise mix of infrastructure needs differs significantly by geographic area. In broad terms, communities in LSMS focus-group discussions voiced the following priorities: potable water in indigenous areas; transportation, electricity, telephones, and water in rural areas; and transportation and sanitation services in urban areas. These priorities are completely consistent with the analysis of disparities in assets using quantitative data from the LSMS (Chapter 2). The upcoming Census 2000 will provide detailed information on existing gaps and coverage in infrastructure services. A mapping of these gaps should then be overlayed with the new poverty map to facilitate the allocation of public spending according to poverty and service gaps (giving priority to *corregimientos* and districts that have a high prevalence of poverty and service gaps).

Improving the Effectiveness and Efficiency of Service Delivery

6.9. **Decentralization of, and community participation in, service delivery should improve the effectiveness of poverty-reduction interventions.** The Government's Social Agenda emphasizes decentralization of the administration and implementation of various functions and services to the local level in order to improve accountability, quality, and efficiency of service delivery. It also highlights the importance of community participation as a way to boost local ownership and client satisfaction, mobilize additional resources, improve accountability among service providers, and build social capital. Some examples include:

- Decentralizing personnel decisions to regional education boards and expanding innovative participatory informal pre-school programs (CEFACEIs, *Madre-a-Madre*);

- Decentralizing food purchases under the school feeding programs by transferring block grants to remote communities for local food procurement;

- Expanding use of NGOs and communities as intermediaries for the design, development and execution of social programs tailored to the specific needs of vulnerable groups (e.g., those being supported by the FES and MJMNF); and

- Greater reliance on community expression of preferences for investments, both for services provided by line ministries and for demand-driven local investment funds (such as the FES).

Box 6.3 - The Challenge of Poverty Reduction Among Remote, Dispersed Populations

A key challenge facing the Government of Panama in its fight against poverty is the development of remote areas with highly dispersed populations. Panama has over 6,000 dispersed villages of less than 50 inhabitants and over 4,300 hamlets of less than 2,000 people. The LSMS indicates that close to two percent of the population lives in non-indigenous "remote areas" (*áreas de difícil acceso*), many of which are only accessible by air, boat, or by horseback. Many indigenous areas are likewise remote, with no road access and dispersed hamlets of 6-8 households each. A lack of Spanish-speaking ability can be a further barrier distancing these groups from the rest of the economy.

There is no "magic bullet" in the fight against poverty in remote areas. The costs of delivering basic physical and social services to dispersed populations is extremely high on a per person basis. In an era of tight fiscal budgets, these costs mean even fewer total poor people who can be reached by government assistance, and hence a smaller impact of public spending on poverty reduction. Productive activities, whether small-scale manufacturing, agro-processing or agriculture, are hampered by high transaction costs and little access to markets. Fragile environmental and ecological conditions further constrain the development of these areas.

Experiences around the world has shown that ultimately, a common solution and natural response is migration to larger local towns, regional centers or major metropolitan areas, either by entire families or individual members who then send remittances back.

Nonetheless, there are some actions that can help improve the living standards of these dispersed populations, including:

- providing basic services in local towns;
- expanding the use of innovative approaches to service delivery that are well-adapted to reach dispersed populations, such as (i) the contracting of NGOs and community groups already active in these areas to provide services (an existing example is the contracting of NGOs in remote areas of Darién (e.g., Pro-Niños del Darién) to deliver food supplements and other nutrition interventions to school-aged children); (ii) the decentralization of service delivery, social investment decisions, and project implementation via municipalities or regional FES offices; and (iii) the use of TELEBASICA and mobile health personnel to provide education and health services to dispersed populations (which would raise their human capital and expand their employment potential even if they do migrate);
- reducing transaction costs in and out of these areas to promote private sector activity and improve market access by improving road access or boat service connections (albeit taking into account environmental and ecological considerations) and expanding telecommunications;
- providing technical assistance that is targeted to the specific needs of these populations with respect to agricultural production, marketing, and financial services via the use of travelling extension agents and the media;
- supporting integrated regional or area development initiatives; and
- continuing the economic reform program to promote overall economic growth – particularly in labor-intensive centers – to help mitigate the employment effects of on-going migration of these populations.

Key Policy Reforms to Reduce Disparities in Assets

6.10. **Implementing key policy reforms to promote broad-based economic growth and reduce duality and disparities in assets.** The agenda for the second-generation of economic reforms designed to promote economic growth is large, encompassing reforms to improve state efficiency, foster competition, improve governance, modernize basic infrastructure, and manage the canal and develop the inter-oceanic region (See Chapter 4). The Government also needs to prevent against backsliding against reforms that have already been implemented since the beginning of the 1990s. Special efforts should be made to ensure that key reforms to reduce disparities in assets, and hence poverty, are undertaken, including:

- **Deepening reforms to the labor code** and related legislation to ease restrictions on dismissal and lower the relative cost of labor, the poor's most abundant asset. A thorough study of labor policies and their impact on the labor market would help identify the specific reforms that should be undertaken.

43

- **Expanding coverage of land titling**, by modernizing land administration services and launching a massive national land titling program focusing on peri-urban and rural areas. Expanding titling would greatly reduce disparities in land and housing, which are closely associated with poverty and inequality. It is also one of the most effective ways of allowing the poor access to credit – which can help in income generation – since a lack of collateral is the primary barrier to obtaining credit.

- **Continuing trade reforms and promoting competition in domestic markets.** Simulations using the LSMS show that reforms to liberalize trade and domestic markets would indeed reduce poverty and inequality in Panama. Though tariffs have come down substantially, further reductions are still needed, particularly for rice and milk. Moreover, the introduction of new distortions – including non-tariff barriers (such as phytosanitary permits) – should be avoided.

- **Reducing distortions in public and freight transport.** Although efficient public transport is a top priority for the urban poor, particularly as a complement to labor assets, subsidies and price distortions and a complex system of licensing have reduced quality and competition in service provision. Competition is also limited by barriers to entry and exit in freight transport, reducing efficiency and increasing the cost of living in Panama. The Government should actively pursue reforms to reduce these distortions.

Explicit Targeting of Programs and Interventions to the Poor is Crucial

6.11.   **Targeting resources to the poor is a crucial tool for improving the impact and cost-effectiveness of public spending and interventions.** Targeting improves cost-effectiveness and impact by concentrating public resources on those who need them the most. **Geographic targeting** (via the poverty map) is the main tool being used for targeting in Panama. It entails a number of advantages, most notably administrative ease: communities can be selected *ex ante* for interventions based on their concentrations of poor people. The current effort to improve the poverty map by combining data from the Census and LSMS will be useful in promoting this approach.[3] In some areas (e.g., large urban cities), however, districts and *corregimientos* are quite diverse in their poverty profiles and sample limitations prevent creating poverty mapping tools at more disaggregated community or neighborhood levels. As such, some programs (e.g., transfer programs such as maternal-infant food supplements or the PARVIS housing subsidy) should attempt to further fine-tune targeting by combining the poverty map with additional targeting mechanisms. **Individual indicators**, such as income (means-testing) or anthropometric assessments can be useful (though administratively burdensome) to further fine-tune targeting in such instances. **Self-targeting** can also be used for the delivery of services clearly used more by the poor than the non-poor (e.g., targeting benefits via health posts, sub-centers and centers which are used disproportionately by the poor).

Sufficient Resources for Monitoring and Evaluation

6.12.   **Monitoring of both the poor and poverty reduction interventions is necessary, and adequate resources should be made available for this task. First,** the Government is developing a **poverty monitoring system** to track living conditions and provide data for the evaluation of the impact of interventions. The system will build on the 1997 LSMS by executing such surveys every three years. Two more are planned: one in 2001 and one in 2004. In addition, the Government is exploring the possibility of incorporating key supplements into the annual household survey system (managed by the Directorate of Statistics and Census, DEC) to generate ongoing data for monitoring poverty. Finally, the upcoming Census 2000 (which is quite extensive in its breadth of topic coverage in Panama) will provide additional information for the monitoring of poverty. **Second,** the Government is also developing **tools to monitor actions to reduce poverty**, including: elaborating an action plan, specifying actions for each year (as was done for 1999), and developing monitoring indicators that will be tracked by each institution.

---

[3] A repeat of this exercise using data from the upcoming Census 2000 and LSMS 2000 will be necessary to update this map.

Program-specific questions should be included in the upcoming LSMSs to facilitate such monitoring. Resources should also be made available for evaluating the poverty impact of specific interventions.

ROAD MAP OF KEY ACTIONS FOR POVERTY REDUCTION

6.13.   Box 6.4 outlines key constraints and actions in the main strategic areas for poverty reduction as well as areas for further research.   The general timing of the implementation of these actions is also indicated. Some key steps for immediate implementation include:

- Conducting a thorough review of public expenditure allocations (see above) and developing proposals for reallocating expenditures such that they better reach the poor for the next fiscal budget;

- Developing a set of indicators to monitor actions to reduce poverty (including key budget categories) and agreeing on an inter-ministerial process for reporting on such indicators and implementation (see above). Funds from the on-going IDF grant could be used to contract consultants to build the capacity of MIPPE/MEF staff for developing and monitoring such indicators;

- Utilizing the new Poverty Map prepared by MIPPE/MEF/FES as a tool for targeting and resource allocation; and

- Continuing dissemination efforts for the Poverty Assessment and the Poverty Map in Government circles and public forums.

Box 6.4 – ROAD MAP OF KEY ACTIONS FOR POVERTY REDUCTION			
CONSTRAINTS		**RECOMMENDATIONS**	
Key Issues	**Priority**	**Key Actions**	**Period**
DEEPENING ECONOMIC REFORMS: Priority for poor in all areas			
Economic growth is essential for poverty reduction. It is also the most effective way to reduce unemployment (more effective than direct labor interventions). Removing key distortions will also reduce disparities in assets, such as labor, property, and credit.	•••	Key reforms: ♦ Deepening reforms to the labor code ♦ Modernizing the land tenure regime (also crucial for improving access to credit) ♦ Continuing trade reforms ♦ Reducing distortions in transport sector	Act: on-going Imp: ST, MT
EDUCATION: Priority for poor in all areas, large gaps for all indigenous			
CONSTRAINTS		**RECOMMENDATIONS**	
Key Issues	**Priority**	**Key Actions**	**Period**
Disparities in access. Main gaps: ♦ Pre-primary: all poor, especially rural and indigenous ♦ Primary: indigenous ♦ Secondary: all poor, esp. rural & indigenous ♦ Higher: all poor (but less of priority) Direct costs, other demand-side factors are key constraints. Availability of schools more of a problem at pre-primary level.	••• ••• ••• ••	Reallocate spending by: ♦ Increasing cost recovery in higher education (raising fees) to free up resources ♦ Increasing the share of spending allocated to basic and secondary education *in poor areas* (via PM) using freed resources from above Ease demand constraints through: ♦ Targeted compensatory education programs ♦ Targeted scholarships for the poor (especially rural and indigenous poor) for primary, secondary education	Act: ST, MT Imp: LT Act: ST Imp: ST, LT
	•••	Ease supply constraints for pre-primary schools through targeted expansion of informal programs (CEFACEIs, Madre-a-Madre); ease supply constraints in rural and remote areas at other levels through expansion and use of TELEBASICA program	Act: ST, MT Imp: LT
••• = top priority; •• = medium priority; • = priority; PM = poverty map; ST = one year period; MT = 1-3 years; LT = more than 3 years; Act = period for implementation of actions; Imp = period for impact on poverty			

Box 6.4 Cont'd – EDUCATION: Priority for poor in all areas, large gaps for all indigenous			
CONSTRAINTS	**RECOMMENDATIONS**		
Key Issues	Priority	Key Actions	Period
Low quality schooling (lack of books, materials, bilingual materials & instruction, insufficient teachers, dilapidated infrastructure)		Improve quality by providing inputs to schools in poorest *corregimientos* (using PM):	Act: ST, MT Imp: LT
	●●●	◆ Providing textbooks at primary, secondary level free of charge on a loan basis	
	●●●	◆ Providing school materials including bilingual materials at primary level	
	●●●	◆ Training bilingual teachers	
	●●	◆ Improving facilities on a demand-driven basis with priority to poor areas (via PM)	
Functional inefficiencies		Improve efficiency of public spending by:	Act: ST, MT Imp: LT
	●●	◆ Decentralizing administration and some spending decisions (e.g., materials); implementing Law 28/1997	
	●●	◆ Building planning capacity in MINEDUC	
	●●	◆ Introducing MIS, evaluation system	
	●●	◆ Improving incentive system for teachers by linking pay to performance	
HEALTH CARE: Priority for poor, especially in indigenous areas			
Low access to health care among poor, esp. indigenous; **Traditional infectious and communicable diseases**: intestinal diseases, malnutrition, respiratory diseases, TB, malaria; **Social public health issues**: teenage pregnancy, high fertility, violence & alcoholism	●●●	◆ Evaluate factors limiting access (cost, availability of facilities, etc.)	Act: ST, MT Imp: MT for all
	●●●	◆ Expand coverage of poor of cost-effective interventions, with emphasis on maternal-infant health, oral rehydration, potable water in rural and indigenous areas, prevention and early detection of TB, family planning, health education, mobile health personnel to reach dispersed populations, etc.	
	●●	◆ Train bilingual, indigenous health personnel	
Low quality health care for poor (limited competition among providers; lack of supervision & incentives; lack of medicines, medical equipment)	●●●	To improve quality and efficiency: ◆ Establish a strategic partnership between MINSA and the CSS ◆ Separate financing and provision of services ◆ Increase private-sector participation in the provision of services ◆ Strengthen policy-making, regulation and management capabilities in MINSA ◆ Decentralize services, increase community participation	Act: MT Imp: MT
Biases in public spending in favor of non-poor (especially middle classes)	●●●	To improve equity in public spending: ◆ Collect data on cost by type and level of service for thorough incidence analysis ◆ Target spending on new investments and rehabilitation according to poor using PM ◆ Reorient spending in favor of primary care via clinics and away from tertiary care	Act: ST Imp: MT Act: ST, MT Imp: MT Act: ST, MT Imp: MT
Weaknesses in the health services network	●●●	◆ Development and strengthening of the health services network by improving infrastructure, sanitary technology and human resource capacity, and management capacity; implementing new models for financing and management of services; developing and implementing supervision, monitoring and evaluation mechanisms	Act: CP, PM Imp: PM

●●● = top priority; ●● = medium priority; ● = priority; PM = poverty map; ST = one year period; MT = 1-3 years; LT = more than 3 years; Act = period for implementation of actions; Imp = period for impact on poverty

Box 6.4 Cont'd – SOCIAL ASSISTANCE & NUTRITION: Priority for poor in all areas, esp. indigenous			
CONSTRAINTS	**RECOMMENDATIONS**		
Key Issues	**Priority**	**Key Actions**	**Period**
Compensatory Education Programs:		(School feeding, cash transfers)	
◆ Targeting to poor is crucial	●●●	Improve/maintain targeting to poor using nutritional and PM criteria as follows: ◆ Modify law to introduce targeting of MINEDUC feeding programs; graduate schools with low levels of malnutrition ◆ Maintain targeting of FES lunch program during expansion ◆ Target new cash transfer (Balboa) program	Act: ST, MT Imp: ST, MT & LT
◆ Inefficiencies in implementation	●●●	Reduce inefficiencies as follows: ◆ Decentralize food procurement in remote areas under school feeding programs ◆ Replace milk with more cost-effective foods under MINEDUC snack program ◆ Review international experiences with school-based cash transfers for design of Balboa cash-transfer program	Act: ST, MT Imp: ST, MT & LT
Various transfer and nutrition programs: MINSA food supplements, various nutrition interventions, PARVIS housing subsidy, new FES *Grupos Vulnerables* programs	●●●	◆ Evaluate impact and targeting of programs (with specific questions in LSMS 2000); introduce explicit targeting mechanisms in all new programs (e.g., FES programs)	Act: ST, MT Imp: LT
Social Investment Programs **FES Infrastructure & Credit Programs** Key issues: targeting to poor	●●●	◆ Design new criteria for targeting with new poverty map;	Act: ST Imp: MT
	●●	◆ Expand share of FES spending subject to targeting criteria	Act: MT Imp: MT
MIPPE/MEF's PROINLO Key issues: targeting to poor	●●●	◆ Introduce targeting to poorer *corregimientos* using new PM	Act: MT Imp: MT
	●	◆ Review possible functional overlap with FES	Act: MT Imp: LT
BASIC INFRASTRUCTURE			
General: Investments should be targeted to the poor by overlapping PM with inventory of existing infrastructure services Priorities should be demand-driven based on community participation			
Key issues for poor in rural areas: Access to transport, roads	●●●	◆ Construction, rehabilitation and maintenance of rural access roads	Act: MT, Imp: MT for all
Access to electricity	●●	◆ Installation of rural electrification	
Access to potable water where deficient	●●●	◆ Coordinated multi-agency effort to improve access to potable water	
Key issues in indigenous areas: Access to potable water	●●●	◆ Coordinated multi-agency effort to improve access to potable water	Act: MT, Imp: MT for all
Access to latrines	●●●	◆ Support community/NGO efforts to promote construction of latrines	
Access to electricity, gas (excessive use of firewood for cooking)	●●	◆ Promote use of gas over firewood for cooking	
Key issues for poor in urban areas: Efficiency of public transport services	●●	◆ Reforms to promote entry and competition in public bussing; rehabilitation and maintenance of urban streets; improvement of traffic management	Act: MT, Imp: MT for all
Access to sanitation & garbage services	●●	◆ Expand access using PM	
Quality of water services	●	◆ Improve quality of service delivery	
Access to & maintenance of public lighting	●	◆ Improve access & maintenance of public lighting with community participation	
●●● = top priority; ●● = medium priority; ● = priority; PM = poverty map; ST = one year period; MT = 1-3 years; LT = more than 3 years; Act = period for implementation of actions; Imp = period for impact on poverty			

Box 6.4 Cont'd – LAND AND PROPERTY TITLING			
CONSTRAINTS		**RECOMMENDATIONS**	
Key Issues	Priority	Key Actions	Period
In urban areas, poor lack titles to their homes. Lack of titles also hampers ability to leverage credit for income generation.	•••	Identify and rectify inefficiencies in titling and registry system; adopt outreach campaign to inform poor of procedures and opportunities; expand titling and registry giving priority to *corregimientos* with high concentrations of poor (via PM)	Act: ST, MT, LT Imp: LT
In rural areas, poor lack titles to their land. Lack of titles also hampers ability to leverage credit for income generation.	•••	Improve efficiency of land cadastre, titling, and registry system; complete and evaluate land-titling pilot project in Veraguas; expand and refine pilot approach to nationwide land titling campaign, giving priority to *corregimientos* with high concentrations of poor (via PM)	Act: ST, MT, LT Imp: LT
INCOME GENERATION & FINANCIAL SERVICES			
Poor lack access to savings and credit services, which are crucial for consumption smoothing and income generation	•••	♦ Adopt actions to extend titling of land and property to poor (above), which can be used as guarantees for credit to improve credit-worthiness of poor	Act: MT, LT Imp: LT
	•••	♦ Evaluate in detail constraints on demand and supply side for providing better access to financial services among poor; tailor solutions to key constraints	Act: ST Imp: MT
	•••	♦ Adopt innovative, market-friendly approaches to providing financial services (e.g., solidarity groups)	Act: MT Imp: MT
	•••	♦ Remove any existing interest-rate subsidies	Act: ST, MT Imp: MT
The poor rural communities do not have access to appropriate technology to enable them to diversify production and improve productivity.	•••	♦ Provide TA for the agricultural production and marketing of traditional and non-traditional products, using cost-effective methodologies.	Act: MT, LT Imp: MT, LT
BUILDING SOCIAL CAPITAL			
Social capital helps communities reduce vulnerability, increase opportunities and leverage assistance. While the poor tend to live in communities with higher social capital, these ties are stronger in indigenous areas and weaker in urban areas.	••• •	♦ Work with community groups in determining local investment needs ♦ Provide funds to communities for direct investment in social capital in response to their requests (e.g., via community centers, sports areas, etc.)	Act: ST, ,LT Imp: MT, LT

••• = top priority; •• = medium priority; • = priority; PM = poverty map; ST = one year period; MT = 1-3 years; LT = more than 3 years; Act = period for implementation of actions; Imp = period for impact on poverty.

Box 6.4 Cont'd – AREAS FOR FURTHER RESEARCH

- Public expenditure analysis, including the distributional incidence and efficiency of public expenditures in key sectors and the management of public expenditures
- More thorough analysis of the impact of existing labor legislation on the labor market in terms of overall segmentation, unemployment, and the informal sector; leading to specific reform proposals
- Research to explore the links between poverty and the environment
- Analysis of the distributional incidence of the social security system and its impact on the poor
- Evaluation of the impact of social assistance programs, including: (i) School feeding programs (educational impact); (ii) MINSA supplementary feeding program; (iii) MIVI's PARVIS housing subsidy program; (iv) FES investments, social programs, and credit scheme; (v) MIPPE/MEF's PROINLO program.
- Participatory research via focus groups and other qualitative tools to further examine obstacles to increased school enrollment and attendance by indigenous children
- Participatory research via focus groups and other instruments on crime and violence, possible solutions, and links to poverty

References for Main Report[1]

Deininger, Klaus and Lyn Squire. November 1997. "New Ways of Looking at Old Issues: Inequality and Growth." The World Bank. Draft.

Ferreira, F.H.G. y Litchfield, J.A. 1997. "Poverty and Income Distribution in a High-Growth Economy Chile: 1987-1995" Capítulo 2 "Income Distribution and Poverty: A Statistical Overview".

Fundación Istmeña de Estudios Económicos y Sociales. November 1994. *Empleo, Pobreza y Economia Informal.* FIEES Series No. 3.

Gonzalez, José Antonio. 1998. *Labor Market Flexibility in 13 Latin American Countries and the United States: Stylized Facts about Structural Relationships Between Output and Employment-Unemployment-Wages.* The World Bank.

Government of Panama. September 19, 1997. *Desarrollo Social Con Eficiencia Económica 1997-1999.* Cabinet Resolution No. 222.

Government of Panama. September 17, 1998. *Nuevo Enfoque Estratégico Frente a la Pobreza.* Cabinet Resolution No. 134.

Hicks, Norman and Pia Peeters. September 17, 1998. "Poverty in Latin America and the Caribbean: A Survey." The World Bank. Draft.

Maloney, William F. February 1998. "Are LDC Labor Markets Dualistic?" The World Bank. Draft.

Maloney, William F. October 26, 1998. "Self-Employment and Labor Turnover in LDCs: Cross-Country Evidence." The World Bank. Draft.

Maloney, William F. and Tom Krebs. April 1998. "Informality, Distribution, Rigidity, and Labor Market Institutions in Latin America: An Applied Efficiency Wage Model." The World Bank. Draft.

McLure, Charles E. 1974. The distribution of income and tax incidence in Panama. Public Finance Quarterly Vol. 2 No. 2.

Ministerio de Planificación y Política Económica and RUTA Social. April 1997. *El Gasto Público Social en Panama: Tendencias y Prioridades.*

Ministerio de Planificación y Política Económica. December 1993. *Panamá: Niveles de Satisfacción de las necesidades básicas. Mapa de Pobreza. Documento de Trabajo No. 44.*

Ministerio de Planificación y Política Económica. 1996. *Perfil e Indicadores de Pobreza en Panamá.* Data calculated by SIAL/OIT.

Ministerio de Planificación y Política Económica, Dirección de Políticas Sociales. March 1998. *Panamá: Informe Social 1997.*

---

[1] Additional references included in Annexes.

Ministerio de Planificación y Política Económica, Dirección de Políticas Sociales. December 1997. Programa de Desarrollo Social: Periodo 1994-1999.

Ministerio de Planificación y Política Económica, Dirección de Políticas Sociales and *Fondo de Población de las Naciones Unidas.* 1997. *Panamá: Pasos Hacia Un Futuro Mejor: Políticas con Enfoque de Género, Población y Pobreza.*

Ministerio de Salud. September 1996. *Estadisticas de Salud.*

Molina, S., Sergio. December 1982. *La Pobreza: Descripción y análisis de políticas para superarla. Revista de la CEPAL 18.*

Moser, Caroline O.N. 1996. Confronting Crisis: A Summary of Household Responses to Poverty and Vulnerability in Four Poor Urban Communities. The World Bank. ESSD Series No. 7.

Ravallion, Martin and Shaohua Chen. May 1997. "What Can New Survey Data Tell Us about Recent Changes in Distribution and Poverty?" The World Bank Economic Review, Vol. 11 No. 2.

Sahota, Gian S. 1990. Poverty Theory and Policy: A Study of Panama. Johns Hopkins University Press.

UNICEF and *Ministerio de Planificación y Política Económica.* July 1997. *Panamá: La Niñez y la Mujer en la Encrucijada del Año 2000.* Second Edition.

UNICEF and *Ministerio de Trabajo y Bienestar Social.* July 1997. *Desarrollo Humano en Panamá: Trabajo Infantil y Educación.*

Wodon, Quentin. 1999. Poverty and Policy in Latin America. The World Bank. Draft.

World Bank. October 29, 1998. Country Assistance Strategy of the World Bank Group for the Republic of Panama. Report No. 18421-PAN.

World Bank. June 1, 1995. Republic of Nicaragua: Poverty Assessment. Report No. 14038-NI.

World Bank. June 30, 1995. Ecuador Poverty Report. Volume 2.

World Bank. July 20, 1995. Panama: A Dual Economy in Transition. Report No. 13977-PAN.

World Bank. March 17, 1995. Panama: Issues in Basic Education. Report No. 13701-PAN.

World Bank. June 10, 1997. Poverty and Income Distribution in a High-Growth Economy: Chile: 1987-1995. Report No. 16377-CH.

World Health Organization. 1997. Global Database on Child Growth and Malnutrition.

Yrarrazaval, Rafael E. October 1997. "Panama: Política Comercial y de Precios de Productos Agropecuarios 1992-1997." The World Bank. Draft.

ANNEXES

ANNEX 1 – THE CONSUMPTION AGGREGATE

MEASURING WELFARE: TOTAL CONSUMPTION

1.   Assessing poverty relies on some measure of welfare. Since well-being, or utility, cannot be measured directly, consumption is used as an indirect measure of welfare. Consumption is used instead of income for several reasons. **First,** consumption is considered a better indicator of standards of living since it fluctuates less than income during a month or year. When incomes change (e.g., in different seasons), individuals tend to use their savings (in cash and kind) to smooth consumption throughout the year. **Second,** consumption data tend to be more accurate than information on individuals' incomes. International experience has shown that respondents tend to provide more accurate information on consumption than income. The latter is often underestimated or difficult to measure due to informal or in-kind income. **Finally,** using consumption as a measure of welfare has the advantage that poverty lines can be derived from the same data and not from other information sources.

2.   Consumption also has several advantages over other welfare measures, such as indicators of basic needs (as access to water, electricity, and schooling; malnutrition; etc.). While consumption is an *objective* measure of welfare, indicators of basic needs are based on various *subjective* definitions, including the level at which such needs would be "satisfied" and the respective weights assigned to their components. Moreover, indicators of basic needs are not responsive to short-term changes, since they mainly reflect public investments. As such, they are less useful for monitoring changes in economic conditions. Although the Poverty Assessment uses consumption as the basis to measure welfare and poverty, the vast array of data available from the LSMS allow for the use of basic social indicators (as malnutrition access and use of basic services) to complement this quantitative measure of poverty.

COMPONENTS OF TOTAL CONSUMPTION

Overview

3.   The LSMS includes the data necessary to construct a measure of total consumption. This measure includes the annual consumption of food (both purchased and non-purchased, including own-production), housing (using an imputed value for owned housing), durable goods, spending on consumer goods and services, basic services (water, gas, electricity), and outlays on health and education. These components are described in detail below. The prices used to value the consumption of these components come mainly from the household and community surveys. A price index was established to adjust for geographical cost differentials (see below). Finally, information on household members was used to convert household consumption (collected in the survey) into a measure of the individual (per capita) welfare, taking into account both household size and composition.

Box 1 – Components of Total Consumption
Consumption of purchased food
Consumption of non-purchased food (own-production, gifts, donations)
Spending on consumer goods and services
Household services
Annual use value of durable goods
Annual use value of housing
Basic services (water, electricity, gas)
Education
Health

Food Consumption

4.   **Purchased Food.** The main data source for purchased foods is Section 8.A.I of the LSMS household questionnaire ("Spending and Consumption of Food, Drinks, and Tobacco"). Question 3 (variable GA103) indicates if household members purchased each item during the last 12 months. Using this section, the number of months (question 4, variable GA104) in which each food item was consumed was multiplied by the average monthly value (question 5, variable GA105) to obtain the annual value of consumption.

5.   To calculate annual spending on foods purchased in supermarkets, Section 8.A.III of the LSMS ("Frequency and Value of Purchases in Supermarkets") was used, multiplying the total value of purchases (question 2, variable GA302) by the annual frequency of purchases (question 1, variable GA301[1]). In addition, the annual value of food consumed *outside* the household was calculated by multiplying question 5 (variable GB105) in Section 8.B.I (spending the last 7 days) by 52 (weeks per year).

6.   Adding the annual expenses of all purchased foods, food purchased in supermarkets, and food consumed outside the home yields the total annual spending on purchased foods.

7.   **Non-Purchased Food.** Even though the consumption of these items does not involve a monetary outlay, household welfare increases in the same way as with purchased food. The main data source for the consumption of non-purchased foods is Section 8.A.I in the LSMS household questionnaire ("Spending and Consumption of Food, Drinks, and Tobacco"). Question 7 (variable GA107) indicates whether the item was obtained by own production or through other means (donations, partial reimbursement, or from a business) during the last 12 months. To obtain the annual *quantity*, the number of months in which each food was consumed (question 8, variable GA108) was multiplied by the average monthly amount (question 9, variable GA109A[2]).

8.   To obtain the annual *value* of non-purchased food consumption, the annual amount was multiplied by a *price*. In the case of non-purchased food, however, prices and values were not reported (since such quantities were never purchased or sold). Therefore, prices were imputed as follows. **First,** if the household also purchased the item (in addition to being consumed from non-purchase acquisitions), the price paid for the purchased quantities was used. To impute this paid price, the total value of purchases during the last 15 days (question 6c, variable GA106C) was divided by the amount purchased during the last 15 days (question 6a, variable GA106A). **Second,** if this price was unknown (because the good was never purchased), its value was estimated using the prices paid by nearby households (geographically), since they would presumably have access to similar markets.[3]

9.   The consumption of free food was also included (from Section 4, Education). To obtain the annual value of free food in schools, the value of the rations was estimated by the respondent in questions 3 and 23 (variables P403c y P423c) and was multiplied by 34 (weeks in the school year).

10.   The total annual value of non-purchased food consumption is obtained by adding the imputed annual expenses of all non-purchased foods (internal consumption, gifts, donations) and free food in health centers and schools.

---

[1] For daily purchases, the frequency was 365, for weekly purchases it was 52, for monthly purchases it was 12 and for annual purchases the frequency was one.
[2] After taking into consideration the product unit from question GA109B.
[3] Out of the total food consumption, non-purchased food represents 16%; and out of these, 8% had prices from the same good in the household, while the price paid by nearby households was used for 92%.

Spending on Consumer Goods and Services

11.   The main data source for outlays on goods and services that are generally consumed in one year or less (such as matches, soap, detergent, newspaper, deodorants, books, school or non-work related transportation expenses, shoes, clothing, etc.) are Sections 8.B.I, 8.B.II, and 8.B.III of the LSMS.   For expenses during the last 7 days (Section 8.B.I), the value reported in question 4 was multiplied by 52 weeks to obtain the annual value.[4]   For expenses during the last month (Section 8.B.II), the value reported in question 2 was multiplied by 12 months for the annual value.[5] All annual expenses of Section 8.B.III were included directly, except for variables GB305, GB317, GB318 (durable goods purchases and repairs), the variable GB319, which was included in health expenses, and variables GB321 (direct taxes), GB323, GB324, and GB325 (transfers and donations made), which were not included in the component for annual spending on consumer goods and services. Total annual spending on consumer goods and services is the sum of the annual value of spending on all consumer good and services (each item).

Household Services: Energy, Water, Telephone

12.   Data on household services expenses come from Section I of the LSMS. To obtain the annual value of household water consumption, monthly consumption (question 20, variable V120) was multiplied by 12 months.   Annual spending on household electricity consumption was derived by multiplying monthly consumption (question 26, variable V126A) by 12 months.   To obtain annual expenses on lighting (kerosene, gas, candles, and other power sources), monthly consumption (question 27, variable V127) was multiplied by 12 months.   The annual value of household cooking fuel consumption was derived by multiplying monthly consumption (question 30, variable V130) by 12 months. To obtain annual spending on telephone services, monthly consumption (question 28, variable V128) was multiplied by 12 months. Total annual spending on household services equals the sum of annual spending for each of the household services.

Annual Use Value of Housing

13.   The annual use value of the housing must be included in total consumption for each household. Data on housing come from Section 1 of the LSMS household questionnaire ("Information on Housing and Households").

14.   **Rented housing.** Rent is considered to be a good estimate of the use value of housing for those households that pay for the use of their house, apartment, or other type of home. As such, for rented housing, the annual rent value was calculated by multiplying monthly rent (question 37, variable V137) by 12 months and included in the consumption aggregate.

15.   **Owned Housing (not rented).** The annual use value of owned housing was imputed as follows: (i) in most cases, the value estimated by the owners was used; or (ii) for households that did not provide an estimated value, the use value of housing was estimated by a regression (as discussed below).

16.   *(i) Value estimated by owners.* The use value estimated by owners was used for most cases of owned housing. Fortunately, the LSMS asked households that did not rent: "If you had to pay rent for this housing, how much would you pay on a monthly basis?" (question 36, variable V136). The answer

---

[4] From Section 8.B.I, variables GB101, GB102, GB103, GB104, GB106, GB107, GB108 were included in the consumption of consumer goods and services, but variable GB105 (food consumption outside the household) was included in food consumption.

[5] From Section 8.B.II, variables GB201-GB224 were included in the consumption of consumer goods and services. However, variables GB225-GB229, insurance, retirement, and Social Security Fund (*Caja de Seguro Social*) contributions and payments, were not included in the consumption of consumer goods and services, since they were included in health expenses and "other" expenses (see below for more details). Non-food expenses in supermarkets (questions 30, 31, variables GB230-231) were included (multiplying the value indicated in question 31, by the annual purchase frequency indicated in question 30).

to this question was used as an estimate of the rental value of the housing and therefore as an estimate of its use value (the estimated value was multiplied by 12 months to obtain the annual value).

17.   Three steps were involved in verifying the validity of answers to question 36 (variable V136) as an estimate of the rental value of owned housing. **First,** households that reported having paid rent were selected and a linear regression was estimated by regressing the paid value on the various descriptive and geographic characteristics of the housing.. **Second,** households that did not report having paid rent were selected and the rental value was estimated using the selected household characteristics and the parameters estimated in the first equation. **Third,** a second linear regression was estimated for the households that did not pay rent. The variables used were the value from the estimated parameters and the value reported in question 36. Table 1 shows the regression results of the first step, using the value of rent paid as the dependent variable.

Table 1 – Linear Regression of Rented Housing Value of paid rent = dependent variable		
Variable	Estimated Parameter	t Value
Constant	10.9	0.2427
Cement concrete or tile roof (1 or 0)	36.8	0.0000
Mosaic/brick/granite, or vinyl floor (1 or 0)	20.02	0.0205
Number of rooms	16.57	0.0000
Private shower (1 or 0)	29.99	0.0013
Monthly electricity bill (Balboas)	0.5116	0.0002
Monthly telephone bill (Balboas)	0.4416	0.0003
Number of additional sanitary services (in excess of 1)	145.58	0.0000
Urban area (1 or 0)	-27.51	0.0248
Rural area (1 or 0)	-38.48	0.0003
Indigenous area (1 or 0)	-59.55	0.0000
With a multiple R of 0.78, an adjusted R^2 of 0.61, and a F value of 79.3, with an error probability below 0.000099 (p < 0,000099). Data source: LSMS Panama, 1997.		

18.   Comparing the rental value obtained from the estimated parameters (for households that paid no rent) with the rental value estimated by household members (question 36, variable V136) yielded a correlation coefficient of 0.732 (p<0.000099). The average value estimated with these parameters was 89.61, as compared with 99.57 with question 36 (a 1:1.1 ratio). The average difference between both values was 9.9 (between 6.6 and 13.2, with a confidence interval of 95%). Given the high similarity of the values achieved with the estimated parameters and the answers to question 36 (variable V136), as well as the high correlation between the two, the use of variable V136 as an estimate of the rental value is deemed appropriate.

19.   *(ii) Value not estimated by owners.* In 2% of the 4,938 households, the respondents did not provide an estimate of the rental value for owned housing; consequently, the estimated parameters in regression of Table 1 were used to impute the use value of housing.

Value of the Annual Use of Durable Goods

20.   Many goods are only partially consumed during the study period, such as cars, refrigerators, stoves, etc. Even if a television set has been purchased during the time period of the survey, it is expected to be used (and hence consumed) during many years to come. To reflect the current welfare that these goods provide to the household, the "value of one year of use" (annual use value) must be estimated and incorporated (rather than the actual purchase cost of these goods), whether the item was purchased in the current year or in previous years.

21.   Data on the consumption value of household durables come from Section 8.F of the LSMS. Since these goods are generally not entirely consumed during one year, the value of their use during the past year had to be estimated. For example, if someone bought a television set this year for B/.300.00, the annual consumption value of this television set is not B/.300.00, since the individual can also use the television during the following year, i.e., the B/.300.00 will be consumed during a time period of more than one year. Food and other consumer goods do not have this characteristic, because if someone buys one liter of milk, this milk will be consumed in less than one year.

22.   Three data points are needed to estimate the consumption value of the household durables (i) the age of the durable good (variables F301 to F325); (ii) the remaining use life of the durable good; and (iii) the current value of the durable good (variables F401 to F425).

23.   To obtain the remaining use life of durable goods, we need to know the average lifetime of each good or, as commonly referred to, its use life or expected lifetime. If the use life of the durable good is known, we will only need to subtract its age to obtain the remaining lifetime. Fortunately, LSMS data allow for an estimate of the expected lifetime of each durable good. Assuming that in one year a similar percentage of the population buys a durable good (say a television), it is likely that some individuals will have a new television, some will have televisions that are one-year old, others two-years old, etc. As such, calculating the average age of all televisions sets (average of F307) yields the mean life or average age of all televisions. By multiplying the mean life by two, the result would be the expected lifetime of a television set in years. If the reported age (variable F307) is subtracted from the expected lifetime of a television set, the remaining use life of each television set is obtained. Finally, dividing the current value of a television set (variable F401) by the remaining use life yields the annual use value of the television set.

24.   Applying this procedure for all durable good and adding the values of each item yields the annual value of the consumption of household durable goods.

Education

25.   Data on household expenses on education (such as registration and enrollment fees, uniforms, books or material, travel) come from Section 4 of the LSMS. The LSMS asked households for *annual* pre-primary school expenses for children under 6 years (questions 4-6, variables P404-P406 in Section 4) and for students aged 6 and over (questions 24, 25, 26, 29, 30; variables P424, P425, P426, P429, P430). Households were also asked for the *monthly* expenses for children under 6 (questions 7-10, variables P407-P410) and students aged 6 and over (questions 31-34, variables P431-P434). To obtain the annual value of the monthly expenses, they were multiplied by 12 months.

26.   Total annual education consumption is obtained by adding the educational expenses and scholarships for all household members.

Health

27.   The data source for health expenses is Section 8. Health spending in question 19 of Section 8.B.III (variable GB319) included: annual expenses on drugs, medical fees, medical tests, hospital admissions, and other expenses associated with the health care of household members.

28.   Annual expenses on health insurance reported in questions 27, 28, 29 of Section 8.B.II (variables GB227, GB228, GB229) were also included.

29.   Likewise, contributions to social security for illness and mother-child benefits were also included, since these expenses represent the consumption of health services. Not included were social

security contributions for disability, senior citizen benefits, and death, since they represent various forms of savings.[6] However, Section 8.B.II of the LSMS questionnaire asked about the *total* contribution to the Social Security Fund (question 25, variable GB225), making no distinction between contributions for illness and mother-child benefits (representing consumption) versus disability, senior citizen benefits, and death contributions (representing savings). To distinguish between these two types of expenditures, the annual value reported in question 25 was adjusted by a factor of 7.4%, which represents the share of the total social security contributions paid by workers for illness and mother-child health care benefits.[7]

30.   Total annual health spending is obtained by adding all expenditures reported in these questions.

Other

31.   Total consumption also includes donations-in-kind received from institutions, family members, friends, and neighbors (questions 8 and 9 of Section 8.E.II, variables GE208 and GE209).[8] Likewise, alimony payments (question 26 in Section 8.B.II, variable GB226) were included.

Total Consumption

32.   Finally, by adding all consumption values for each component (by household), we obtain the **total consumption** variable. Seven households were excluded from the original figure of 4,945 households (yielding a total of 4,938) because a large share of the consumption aggregate had to be estimated or imputed due to missing values.[9]

WEIGHTING TOTAL CONSUMPTION BY THE REGIONAL PRICE INDEX

33.   The cost of living is not uniform throughout the country; as such, the value of total consumption was adjusted to account for regional variation in prices. Price indices were constructed for each Primary Sampling Unit (PSU) using the information collected in the price questionnaire and the household questionnaire (Section 8.A) in the following manner.

34.   Using consumption data from Section 8.A.I, **"national average consumption in pounds"** was calculated for each food article. This was achieved dividing the value of annual consumption (variables GA104 * GA105) by the national average price per item (estimated dividing variables GA106C by GA106A).[10] At least 45 observations per item, with units expressed in pounds, were required to obtain nationwide prices

35.   Next, prices for each article were estimated both at regional (PSU) and national level using the price questionnaires as the main source of information. If such information was not available in the price questionnaire, prices reported in the LSMS household questionnaire in Section 8.A.I, variables GA106C and GA106A, were used, selecting cases where units were expressed in pounds. With these prices, the purchase cost of **"national average consumption in pounds"** in each PSU was estimated (using prices at PSU level), as well as the purchase cost at national level (using national price averages).

---

[6] They would be included in an income variable.

[7] From contributions paid by workers to the Social Security Fund (C.S.S.,*Caja de Seguro Social*), 92.6% is allocated to disability, senior citizen benefit, and death (I.V.M., *Invalidez, Vejez y Muerte*) program and 7.4% to the illness and mother-child benefit (EyM, *Enfermedad y Maternidad*) program. Source: C.S.S.

[8] However, cash grants were not included, in order to avoid double-counting such transfers, since consumption associated to these cash grants was already included in other consumption forms. (Grants in kinds and cash would be included in an income variable).

[9] Also, only households with complete interviews were selected.

[10] This national average price per item was used only for the estimation of the average national consumption quantities. Later, another "national average price" is estimated using a methodology based in the price questionnaire information.

36.   Finally, to obtain a variable that allows for standardization of any expense at the national level (to be used as a multiplier), the purchase cost at national level of the **"average national consumption level in pounds"** was divided by the purchase cost in each PSU of the **"national average consumption level in pounds"**, obtaining a value for each PSU (PESO variable).

37.   Using the national average as a basis (national average = 1), the PESO variable was found to vary between 0.67 and 1.22.

VALUE OF TOTAL CONSUMPTION PER CAPITA

38.   For the final step to rank the population by welfare level (consumption) from the lowest to the highest, a share of the total consumption must be allocated to each household member. Per capita consumption is used in the Poverty Assessment, i.e., the total value of consumption of the household divided by the number of household members. There are several other ways of allocating household consumption to the different members, taking into account different requirements, economies of scale, and the presence of public services in the household. Per capita consumption was used due to its transparency, but other methods were used for sensitivity tests of the consumption aggregate.

LEVELS OF TOTAL CONSUMPTION PER CAPITA: PANAMA 1997

39.   The population from the lowest to the highest according to total annual consumption per capita (welfare). Per capita consumption varies considerably in Panama (see graph). On average, annual per-capita consumption is B/.1,821. The richest ten percent of the population has an average consumption level of B/.6,451 while the poorest ten percent has an annual average per-capita consumption of B/.207.

Total Consumption Levels: Republic of Panama, 1997

% of population	Level of total annual per-capita consumption (B$)
100	6,451
90	3,165
80	2,256
70	1,713
60	1,372
50	1,097
40	853
30	646
20	432
10	207

Lowest level of total consumption

Source: LSMS, 1997

ANNEX 2 – MEASURING POVERTY

1.   This study uses the following method to classify individuals as extreme poor, poor, or non-poor: (i) individuals are ranked according to their level of welfare, as measured by total consumption (Annex 1); (ii) the value of the full poverty line and extreme poverty line is calculated; and (iii) individuals whose consumption levels fall below these lines are classified accordingly.

(I)   RANKING INDIVIDUALS

FIG. 1: POPULATION RANKING BASED ON PER CAPITA CONSUMPTION

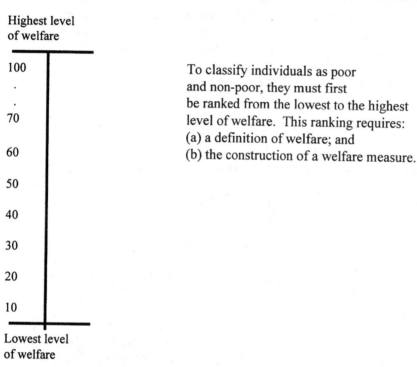

Highest level
of welfare

100
·
·
70

60

50

40

30

20

10

Lowest level
of welfare

To classify individuals as poor
and non-poor, they must first
be ranked from the lowest to the highest
level of welfare. This ranking requires:
(a) a definition of welfare; and
(b) the construction of a welfare measure.

2.   **Defining Welfare.**   Since welfare, or well-being, cannot be measured directly consumption was used as an indirect measure of welfare. Consumption is used because it is not subject to the underestimation and biases of an income measure, and because it avoids the subjectivity associated with measures of basic needs and indicators of human development. Annex 1 provides details on the construction of total consumption as a measure of welfare.

3.   Individuals were ranked from the lowest to the highest level of annual per-capita consumption (welfare).   The graph shows major differences in the current per-capita consumption in Panama. On average, annual per-capital consumption is B$1,821. Consumption ranges from an average of B/.6,451 for the richest ten percent of the population to an average of B/.207 for the poorest ten percent.

FIG. 2: LEVELS OF CONSUMPTION: REPUBLIC OF PANAMA, 1997

% of population	Level of average annual per-capita consumption (B/.)
100	6,451
90	3,165
80	2,256
70	1,713
60	1,372
50	1,097
40	853
30	646
20	432
10	207

Lowest level of consumption
Source: LSMS 1997

(II) CONSTRUCTING POVERTY LINES

4.   Two poverty lines were constructed for this study: an extreme poverty line and a full poverty line.

5.   **The Extreme Poverty Line.** The extreme poverty line represents the cost of the minimum caloric requirement recommended for Panama (2,280 on average, see Table A2.1), using the observed consumption basket of the "low income" population. When the consumption level of any individual is below such value, he/she is unable to consume the minimum recommended calorie level. That is, even if the individual spends all his/her resources on food, he/she would still not be able to acquire the minimum level of recommended calories.

6.   The extreme poverty line was calculated as follows:

a) Using the ranking based on total annual per-capita consumption, households with the lowest consumption levels were selected (those in the lowest 10% - 40% of the population).

b) On the basis of the food consumption *patterns* of the households in the lowest 10% - 40%, the amount of calories supplied by each type of food[1] and the percentage of

---

[1] Using food caloric composition data from 'Valor Nutritivo de los alimentos de Centroamérica." Instituto de Nutrición de Centro América y Panamá (INCAP) y la Organización Panamericana de la Salud (OPS). Ciudad de Guatemala, Guatemala, 1998.

these calories in the total consumption of this population group (on average) was calculated. For example, for this group of households, rice provides more calories than any other type of food (27.2 percent of the calories consumed). Next in importance are vegetable oils and sugar, which supply 9.1 and 8.5 percent respectively of the calories consumed by this group (see Table A2.2 for consumption patterns of all products).

c) The minimum average calorie requirements of a Panamanian were calculated using data from INCAP: 2,280 kcal/day (see Table A2.1).

d) The amount of food required to satisfy the minimum calorie requirements were calculated, using the shares (consumption patterns) for each type of food for households within the lowest 10% - 40% of consumption. The absolute amounts consumed by this group are adjusted to meet the amounts required to achieve the recommended calorie level (2280) using their consumption shares.

e) On the basis of these amounts, the cost of food required to satisfy the minimum calorie requirements was determined. This is the cost of the minimum calorie requirements, in other words, the value of the extreme poverty line. For Panama in 1997, the extreme poverty line was calculated as B/.519 per-capita per year.

7.   Figure 3 below shows the method used for calculating the extreme poverty line.

8.   **The Full Poverty Line.** Total consumption, even among the poorest, almost always includes the consumption of non-food goods and services. As such, the general poverty line includes an additional amount for the percentage of the **non-food** consumption. The share of non-food consumption is based on the observed consumption patterns of individuals whose total consumption is close to the extreme poverty line.

9.   The full poverty line equals the extreme poverty line plus an allowance for non-food consumption, as follows:

a) Individuals with *total consumption* (C_T) levels close to (+/-10%) the extreme poverty line ($C_T = Z_{pe} = 519$) were selected. These individuals are those who, even if they spent all their resources on food consumption, would barely meet their minimum calorie requirements.

b) *Consumption coefficients* were calculated for this group: that is, the share of total consumption allocated to food (in this case, 57.3%) and non-food products (42.7%).

c) To obtain the full poverty line, the value of the extreme poverty line was divided by this share of food consumption (57.3%).

10.   Figure 4 below shows the method used to calculate the general poverty line.

Table A2.1 - Panama: Minimum Calorie Requirements: Average by Age and Gender					
Age in Years	Population			Calories/Per-Capita	
	Total	Men	Women	Men	Women
0-1	60,406	30,867	29,539	738	738
1-2	60,737	31,064	29,673	1,100	1,100
2-3	60,906	31,167	29,739	1,300	1,300
3-4	121,739	62,311	59,428	1,500	1,500
5-6	120,797	61,800	58,997	1,750	1,600
7-9	177,660	90,751	86,909	2,000	1,700
10-11	115,271	58,749	56,522	2,200	1,900
12-13	112,285	57,134	55,151	2,350	2,000
14-15	108,994	55,437	53,557	2,650	2,100
16-17	105,704	53,737	51,967	3,000	2,150
18-64	1,528,139	769,357	758,782	3,100	2,100
65 and more	146,048	70,975	75,073	2,300	1,850
Minimum Calorie Requirements: Weighted Average					**2,280**

Source: *Instituto de Nutrición de Centro América y Panamá* (INCAP) of the Pan American Health Organization (PAHO). Moderate activity is assumed. *Contraloría General de la República*. DEC.
a\ Projections of the population by province, gender, and specific age, by July l, 1990-2000.
b\Special Bulletin. Projection of total country population by gender and age cohorts. Years 1990-2000.

Item	Calories per Pound	Individuals lowest 10-40%			Calorie % Pattern/ day/capita	Calories to obtain 2,280 cal./ day/person	Average cost per calorie	Annual Cost of 2280 calories
		Average Amount						
		Lb./year/ HH	Calories/day/ household	person				
Rice (all)	1634	568.8	2545	530.1	27.2%	619.2	0.000192	43.36
Vegetable Oil	4013	77.5	852	177.4	9.1%	207.3	0.000216	16.32
Sugar	1725	167.6	791	164.9	8.5%	192.6	0.000185	12.99
Corn (Grain)	1725	143.9	680	141.6	7.3%	165.4	0.000148	8.92
Bread	1279	109.3	383	79.8	4.1%	93.2	0.000602	20.48
Flour	1819	67.1	334	69.6	3.6%	81.3	0.000181	5.36
Beans (*frijoles*)	1559	54.0	230	48.0	2.5%	56.0	0.000329	6.72
Pasta (Spaghetti, etc.)	1684	48.9	225	47.0	2.4%	54.8	0.000330	6.61
Chicken or Hens	625	131.4	225	46.8	2.4%	54.7	0.001761	35.18
Cereals & Creams	1643	48.0	216	45.0	2.3%	52.6	0.000542	10.40
Powdered Milk	1618	48.4	214	44.6	2.3%	52.1	0.001622	30.88
Beef Meat	673	115.6	213	44.4	2.3%	51.8	0.002229	42.20
Beans (*Porotos*)	1562	45.7	195	40.7	2.1%	47.5	0.000557	9.67
Lentils	1544	46.0	194	40.5	2.1%	47.3	0.000422	7.29
Plantains (all)	389	177.4	189	39.4	2.0%	46.0	0.000452	7.60
Liquid Milk	261	225.8	161	33.6	1.7%	39.3	0.001205	17.29
Pork Meat	970	48.3	128	26.7	1.4%	31.2	0.001485	16.94
Processed Corn	699	63.8	122	25.4	1.3%	29.7	0.000614	6.66
Peas, legumes	1557	27.6	118	24.5	1.3%	28.7	0.000359	3.76
Butter/Margarine	2916	14.0	112	23.3	1.2%	27.2	0.000437	4.33
Eggs	1020	39.6	111	23.1	1.2%	26.9	0.000939	9.24
Yuca	374	105.9	108	22.6	1.2%	26.4	0.000400	3.86
Cookies/candies/etc.	2111	18.2	105	21.9	1.1%	25.6	0.000739	6.90
Evaporated Milk	608	60.0	100	20.8	1.1%	24.3	0.001713	15.20
Cheese	1209	25.1	83	17.3	0.9%	20.2	0.001695	12.51
Sausages (ham, etc.)	1004	28.0	77	16.0	0.8%	18.7	0.001892	12.92
ñame	409	60.9	68	14.2	0.7%	16.6	0.000996	6.04
Sardines & Tuna Fish	591	39.6	64	13.4	0.7%	15.6	0.001457	8.30
Guineos/bananas	299	74.9	61	12.8	0.7%	14.9	0.000910	4.96
Potatoes	307	71.5	60	12.5	0.6%	14.6	0.001237	6.61
Fish	296	67.6	55	11.4	0.6%	13.3	0.002877	14.01
Otoe	414	35.0	40	8.3	0.4%	9.7	0.000972	3.43
All Soups	1518	9.4	39	8.2	0.4%	9.5	0.001686	5.88
Tomato Paste & Sauce	427	25.8	30	6.3	0.3%	7.4	0.003255	8.74
Sodas, Drinks, Juices	194	46.6	25	5.2	0.3%	6.0	0.005951	13.10
Avocados	378	23.5	24	5.1	0.3%	5.9	0.001721	3.72
Mangos	121	70.5	23	4.9	0.3%	5.7	0.001725	3.58
Pineapple	139	46.2	18	3.7	0.2%	4.3	0.001710	2.67
Garlic	608	10.9	18	3.8	0.2%	4.4	0.002017	3.26
Carrots	168	36.3	17	3.5	0.2%	4.1	0.002394	3.55
All peppers	162	35.1	16	3.2	0.2%	3.8	0.002665	3.68
Seafood	165	26.2	12	2.5	0.1%	2.9	0.009858	10.39
Orange	131	32.4	12	2.4	0.1%	2.8	0.003140	3.25
Tomatoes	93	39.0	10	2.1	0.1%	2.4	0.005405	4.77
Apple	209	17.8	10	2.1	0.1%	2.5	0.003615	3.27
Cabbage	127	27.7	10	2.0	0.1%	2.3	0.003743	3.21
Pumpkin/Challote	90	35.0	9	1.8	0.1%	2.1	0.003437	2.63
Lemons	67	43.0	8	1.6	0.1%	1.9	0.003285	2.30
Sugar Beet	126	18.8	6	1.4	0.1%	1.6	0.004061	2.34
Lettuce	64	26.1	5	1.0	0.1%	1.1	0.009073	3.69
Papaya	107	17.1	5	1.0	0.1%	1.2	0.010894	4.84
Cucumber	52	29.5	4	0.9	0.0%	1.0	0.007267	2.72
Celery	73	16.6	3	0.7	0.0%	0.8	0.008556	2.53
Whole Onions	100	14.0	4	0.8	0.0%	0.9	0.016747	5.70
Melon	76	12.5	3	0.5	0.0%	0.6	0.007833	1.80
Total: Calories			2025			2280		
EXTREME POVERTY LINE								519
Source: LSMS 1997								

Table A2.2 - Calculation of Food Consumption Patterns for Extreme Poverty Line

FIG. 3: CALCULATING THE EXTREME POVERTY LINE

A. Ranking Individuals

Highest level of total annual per-capita consumption

B. Calculating the Value of Minimum Caloric Requirements

Actual level of average calories for households in the lowest 10-40%. Total level in this group = 2,025/person. *For example:*

27.2% of calories comes from rice

9.1% of calories comes from vegetable oil

8.5% of calories comes from sugar

7.3% of calories comes from corn

See patterns for all products in Table A2.2

The number of calories corresponds to a physical amount of food (in pounds)

Average recommended calorie level = 2280

The quantity of each food item is adjusted to obtain a basket that provides the 2,280 calories maintaining the *consumption patterns* of households in the 10-40% per-capita consumption range.

C. Value of the Extreme Poverty Line

The value is calculated by adding the quantity of items estimated in the last step using the prices actually faced by households in the 10-40% group. Using LSMS data, the annual value of the extreme poverty line is B/.519 per capita.

$$Z_{pe} = B\ 519$$

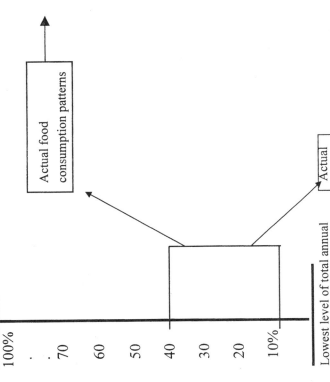

Actual food consumption patterns

Actual prices

100%

70

60

50

40

30

20

10%

Lowest level of total annual per-capita consumption

FIG. 4: CALCULATING THE FULL POVERTY LINE

Ranking Individuals
Highest level of total
per-capita consumption (Balboas)

The full poverty line includes the cost of the extreme poverty line, Z_{pe}, plus an additional amount for non-food consumption.

$C_T = C_A + C_{NA}$
C_T = Total consumption
C_A = Food consumption
C_{NA} = Non-food consumption

What share of total consumption is allocated to non-food?
To calculate the poverty line, actual *consumption coefficients* of the group of individuals with a *total consumption* near (+/-10%) the extreme poverty line (Z_{pe}) were used.
In this case, this group allocates 42.7% to non-food consumption and 57.3% to food consumption.

These consumption shares were used to calculate the full poverty line:
$C_A = (1 - .427)Z_{pg}$
$Z_{pg} = 519/.573$

Zpe = Extreme Poverty Line = 519
Zpg = General Poverty Line = 905

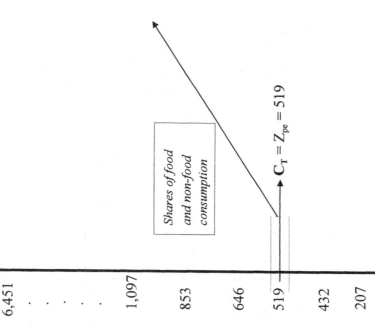

Shares of food
and non-food
consumption

$C_T = Z_{pe} = 519$

6,451
. . . . .
1,097
853
646
519
432
207

Lowest level of
total consumption

(III) POVERTY MEASURES

11.   The poverty indices used in this study are three special cases of additively separable measures developed by Foster, Greer and Thorbecke (FGT, 1984). The general poverty measure is:

$$P_\alpha = \frac{1}{n} \sum_{n=1}^{q} \left(\frac{Z - y_i}{Z} \right)^\alpha$$ [Eq. 1]

where:

y_i = estimated consumption of the ith person in a population of size n

Z = the poverty line

q = number of persons whose y_i is below poverty line Z and;

α = is a non-negative parameter that reflects the measure's aversion to poverty

12.   **Head Count Index.** The first case is that where $\alpha = 0$. This is the Head Count measure (H) and, as can be seen from Eq. 1, it is simply q/n or the proportion of the population below the poverty line. In short, the Head Count Index provides information on the incidence of poverty. It says nothing about the depth or severity of poverty and treats as equal any two populations where the proportion of the population living in poverty is the same.

13.   **Poverty Gap.** To determine the depth of poverty, a second version of the FGT poverty measure, called the Poverty Gap index (PG), is used. This index is the case where $\alpha = 1$ (in Eq. 1). The index is the aggregate poverty deficit of the poor relative to the poverty line.

14.   **FGT P$_2$ (Severity).** The third case of the poverty measure is that where $\alpha = 2$. This measure, often called the Foster-Greer-Thorbecke P$_2$ measure (FGT P$_2$), identifies the severity of poverty and demonstrates the relative inequalities among the poor. It is distributionally sensitive and, essentially, weights the average poverty gaps by the population at each level.

15.   Ravallion (1992[2]) presents a good example to illustrate the differences between the FGT P$_2$ index and the previous two. For example, it is possible for two populations to have the same head count and poverty gap indices but have very different distributions of levels of poverty. Ravallion (1992) presents the example of two populations A and B where A is made up of four individuals with consumption levels 1, 2, 3, 4 and B is made up of four individuals with consumption levels 2, 2, 2, 4. If the poverty line equals three, the head count for both populations is 75 percent, the poverty gap measure is 25 percent. But the FGT P$_2$ measure is 14 in population A and 8 in population B, thus demonstrating that the poorest person in Population A has half the expenditures of the poorest person in Population B.

---

[2] Ravallion, Martin, "Poverty Comparisons: A Guide to Concepts and Methods," World Bank LSMS Working Paper No. 88, 1992.

ANNEX 3 – THE INCOME AGGREGATE

1.   The income aggregate is a measure of all incomes obtained by each household in a year. It can be divided into two large groups: (i) direct earnings obtained from labor activities; and (ii) incomes not related to labor activities during the year.   Labor earnings are divided into agricultural and non-agricultural; both groups consist of wages (either in the formal or informal sector) and self-employment or businesses.   Non-labor earnings include interest from savings or investments (stocks, dividends), equipment or property leases (including own house), retirement or allowance benefits, donations from institutions, friends or family, and other non-classified income.

```
Box 1 – Components of Total Income
Formal and informal agricultural earnings
Net benefit of independent agricultural activities
Formal and informal non-agricultural earnings
Net benefit of formal and informal non-agricultural activities
Interests received
Equipment and property leases
Retirement and allowance benefits
Donations from institutions and private persons
Other incomes
```

2.   All data were previously "cleaned" and reviewed to identify "outliers," estimate or re-codify missing data, and generally, to organize the data files into a more user-friendly format.

LABOR EARNINGS

3.   Although data are reported as agricultural and non-agricultural, variables are developed from three sections of the LSMS and will be explained on the basis of these sections. There is an obvious allocation of the different variables in the report, and it requires no special explanation. The following sections were used: Section 6-Economic Activity (labor), Section 9-Non-Agricultural Business of the Household, and Section 10-Agricultural Activities.

Economic Activity, Labor (Section 6)

4.   Since up to three different jobs were reported in one year, the common variables of the three jobs were first unified. Table A3.1 has the original name of the variable, its source, and the given common name. Part B is the first job, part C the second one, and part D the third.

5.   The total wage is the sum of "Salario 1" and 'Salario 2". The net benefit of independent business is the value of the "Neto" variable (both variables are in their annual value). The first classification is wages or self-employment.

6.   The second classification was agricultural or non-agricultural incomes. The variable "Rama" was used for this purpose: values of 1, 2 or 5 in this variable correspond to agricultural jobs, and the remaining ones to non-agricultural jobs. The third classification was either formal or informal sector. The variables used for the formal or informal classification included: job category (p618), company size (p617), and the type code given by the national job codes (p611).

7.   Government and Canal employees (p618=1 or p618=3) were classified as FORMAL. Private sector employees and daily workers (p618=2 o p618=4) were classified as INFORMAL if the firm or farm has less than 6 workers: (p617<3), or as FORMAL if the firm or farm has more than 5 workers: (p617>2). Firm or farm owners or active partners (p618=5), were classified as INFORMAL if the firm or

farm has less than 6 workers: (p617<3) and they are not professionals (p611>16), and as FORMAL for the rest. Independent workers or workers in their own farm (p618=6), were classified as FORMAL if the firm or farm has more than 5 workers: (p617>2) and they are professionals (p611<17), and as INFORMAL for the rest. Helpers or family workers without pay (p618=7 o p618=8), were classified as INFORMAL if the firm or farm has less than 6 workers: (p617<3), or as FORMAL if the firm or farm has more than 5 workers: (p617>2). Domestic employees (p618=9) were classified as INFORMAL[1].

Table A3.1- Re-Coding Some Variables of Section 6	
QUESTION (S) #	**NEW NAME**
B-11, C-37, D-50	Occupacion
B-12, C-38, D-51	Rama (sector)
B-14, C-39, D-52	**Meses** (months worked)
B-18, C-42, D-53	Tipo (type of job)
(B-26, C-45, D-56) * **Meses**	Salario 1
Part B: 24b + **Meses** *(25b+27b+28b+29b+30b)	
Part C: 44b + (**Meses** *46b) + 47b	Salario 2
Part D: 55b + (**Meses** *57b) + 58b	
B-26b, C-44b, D-55b	Aguinaldo
B-19c, C43c, D-54c	**Veces (frequency)**
(B-19c, C43c, D-54c) * **Veces**	Neto
A-17	Size
A-22	Sindicato (union)

Non-Agricultural Self-Employment and Family Businesses (Section 9)

8.   Even though this section was completely reviewed, the resulting net incomes were extremely exaggerated, both in terms of high earnings and high losses. In addition, there were many inconsistencies among the data reported on various variables, and due to the section's nature, it was often impossible to differentiate between real data and potential errors. This problem commonly occurs in the business section, since it is very difficult to place a ceiling or identify the "exaggerated" cases when there is no biological or agricultural parameter to compare with. For example, if someone declares that corn production was 300 quintals in one hectare of land, it is evident that such data must be incorrect, since the past reported production never exceeded 100 quintals[2]. Also, if a household that consists of only one person reports a 4,000 pound consumption of potatoes, we know that one person cannot have consumed more than ten pounds of potatoes each day during an entire year. For self-employment, however, one merchant may well trade merchandise for B/. 1,000.00 in one month and another B/.100,000.00. There are no applicable parameters to differentiate between likely and unlikely cases.

9.   Due to these problems, the results of Section 9 were not used. Instead, data reported in Section 6, the variable "Neto," were used when the classification was "non-agricultural."[3] We deem that the problems introduced by using this variable are much less than the alternative option to use the results of Section 9.

Agricultural Business (Section 10)

10.   Agricultural activities are divided into two areas: **First,** farming and its applicable by-products, and forestry, and **Second,** animal production and its by-products. Several expenses were also reported jointly and were allocated on a pro-rata basis to farming and ranching activities.

---

[1] Using this definition with the LSMS 97, 12 cases were left without classification, and were assigned as follows: 8 persons working in the private sector and one owner were classified as FORMAL, one daily worker and two independent workers were classified as INFORMAL.
[2] Outputs of 70 quintals are considered to be outstanding.
[3] Since values of B/. 0.00 were recorded even when respondents reported losses, it must be taken into account that data from this variable will tend to overestimate the average income for any group.

11.   Incomes of the farming activities are composed of crop output (10-B.I-3a), less amounts left as seeds (10-B.I-8), less amounts lost or wasted (10-B.I-12), less amounts received for lands under share cropping (10-B.I-14), multiplied by the unit price. In a first instance, the sales price reported by the farmer itself was used as the unit price. When no such sales price was reported, the mean price obtained for such output/unit was used. The output value of by-products was also added, estimating their prices in a similar way as for the farming output; finally, the total value of cut down trees was added.

12.   The first group of farming disbursements is the sum of all values reported in the Input Section 10-B.II, question one to five, and Expenses 10-B.III, question one to nine.

13.   Incomes from ranching include: the sum of all animals sold, animals consumed in the household, animals exchanged, as well as any changes in the value of the herd. These were multiplied by the sale prices when such prices were reported, and multiplied by the mean sale price of each type of animal when such sale prices were not reported. To calculate the change in the value of the herd, the current value of the herd is subtracted from the value of the herd twelve months ago (10-D.I, question three). To calculate the value of the herd twelve months ago, the price of each animal was multiplied by the number of animals owned twelve months ago. The number of animals owned twelve months ago was calculated on the basis of the current animal stock (10-D.I, question two), less animals purchased or born (10-D.I, question four and five, respectively), plus dead animals, animals sold alive, animals sold slaughtered, animals consumed in the household, animals used for barter trade, and those used for the preparation of by-products (10-D.I, questions six, seven "a" (7a), ten "a" (10a), and section 10-D.III, questions eleven, twelve, thirteen, and fourteen, respectively). The output value of animal by-products was added to this value, using the new reported sales price, when reported, and the mean value when no sale was reported, multiplying it by the produced quantity (10-D.V, question two "a" (2a)).

14.   The first group of animal production disbursements is the sum of all values of purchased animals (10-D, question four), multiplied by the price per animal, plus the animals' maintenance and breeding costs (10-D.VI, question one to five), and the value of crops used to feed the animals (10-B.I, question nine).

15.   The remaining disbursements in agricultural outputs are composed by the net expenses to **rent land** which is to be cultivated: 10-A.I, question eleven, less 10-A.II, question twenty two ; the value of **wages paid** to workers: $10\text{-B.IV.2a} * 10\text{-B.IV.2b} + 10\text{-B.IV.3a} * (1.5^{4} + 10\text{-B.IV.3b}) + 10\text{-B.IV.5} + 10\text{-B.IV.6d}$; disbursements for **technical assistance**: 10-B.V, question one "d" (1d); and the annual usage value of **equipment and facilities** described in sections 10-B.VI and 10-B.VII (all categories). The usage value of these durable consumer goods was estimated in the same way as described in the consumption aggregate for durable household goods. Basically, the average age per good reported in questions number two of both sections is calculated, then this number is multiplied by two to obtain the expected lifetime of the good. Next, the reported age of each good is subtracted from its expected lifetime (again question number two), achieving the remaining lifetime of that good. Finally, the current value of the good (10-B.VI.7 and 10-B.VII.6) is divided by its remaining lifetime and this value is the annual usage value of such good.

16.   Except for the use value of milking machines and dipping stations (Sections 10-B.VI and 10-B.VII), it was impossible to differentiate if the remaining expenses were used for animal production or crop outputs; therefore, they had to be allocated on a pro-rata basis to each activity. The share used was given by the net benefit of each activity on the basis of the previously calculated incomes and disbursements. Obviously, this process is applied only when both outputs (crops or trees, and animals) were produced in the same household.

---

[4] "1.5" is to take into account the value or cost to feed workers, since the question refers to daily wages of workers who also received food.

NON LABOR INCOME

Interest Received

17.   This includes interest from savings accounts and other similar sources, and dividends of shares and interests in stock companies and cooperatives. In the Living Standards Measurement Survey (LSMS), these incomes are reported in Section 8.E.II, question one and two. Both questions are on an annual basis and did not require any transformation.

Leasing Equipment, Properties, and Own House

18.   This includes the rent received from properties, construction, equipment, and goods, and the estimated use value of owned housing. Values of received rentals are in Section 8.E.I, question one of the LSMS. Since the question asked was on monthly basis, the reported amount was multiplied by twelve to obtain its annual equivalent.

19.   The use value of owned housing was also included. It is common to include such a value as income, since it is also included as an expense (it was in the consumption aggregate, see Annex 1). The rationale is similar to the one used to include the production value of foods consumed in the household, since it is an owned good which the household decides to sell, rent, or consume, and whatever is done with the good must not affect the income aggregate. Another way to look at this "income" is to think that the household is self-renting the house.

20.   Most homeowners reported the estimated rental value of their property. In those cases in which no estimated value was reported, the rental value was estimated using the same equation as described in for consumption aggregate in Annex 1 and is shown in Table A3.2.

Table A3.2- Linear Regression of Rented Housing		
Variable	Estimated Parameter	t Value
Constant	10.9	0.2427
Cement concrete or tile roof (1 or 0)	36.58	0.0000
Mosaic/brick/granite, or vinyl floor (1 or 0)	20.02	0.0205
Number of rooms	16.57	0.0000
Private shower (1 or 0)	29.99	0.0013
Monthly electricity bill (Balboas)	0.5116	0.0002
Monthly telephone bill (Balboas)	0.4416	0.0003
Number of additional sanitary services (in excess of 1)	145.58	0.0000
Urban area (1 or 0)	-27.51	0.0248
Rural area (1 or 0)	-38.48	0.0003
Indigenous area (1 or 0)	-59.55	0.0000
With a multiple R of 0.78, an adjusted R^2 of 0.61, and a F value of 79.3, with an error probability below 0.000099 (p < 0,000099). Data source: LSMS Panama, 1997.		

21.   Owners' estimates are in Section 1, question thirty-six. This amount, as well as the amount estimated with the equation for missing cases is equal to the monthly value, and is thus multiplied by twelve to obtain the annual value.

Pensions, Compensations

22.   This includes child care allowances, orphan and widow pensions, retirement benefits, unemployment allowance, compensations for work or contract termination, life insurance, fire, or losses caused to property or due to labor accidents. In the LSMS questionnaire, these sources of income can be found in Section 6.E, questions fifty nine, sixty, and seventy one, and in Section 8.E.II, questions three,

four, five, and eleven. For annual income, the reported figures of both sections were taken and multiplied by twelve.

Donations and Support of Institutions

23.   This includes free food received for children under 5, and students both under and over six, cash or in-kind received from institutions and the value of scholarships.

24.   The value of donated food received for children under five was reported in the LSMS Section 3.A, questions twelve and thirteen. Question twelve, which refers to the coded frequency of the received food, was newly codified to represent the annual frequency of the received values (for example, 4-monthly was codified into "12", since it was received twelve times in a year). This figure was multiplied by the value of question thirteen to obtain the annual value of such food.

25.   Food received in educational institutions was reported in Section 4.A, question three C (3c), and in Section 4.B, question twenty-three C (23c). In both cases, the reported value is on a weekly basis. To obtain the annual value, the reported figure was multiplied by thirty-two, deeming that a school year has 32 weeks.

26.   Cash values from institutions are from Section 6.D, question sixty-four, and Section 8.E.II, question seven. The value of in-kind grants from institutions can be found in Section 8.E.II, question eight. All of these variables were given on an annual basis and therefore needed no transformation.

27.   The value of scholarships (multiplied by twelve) is reported in Section 8.E.I, question two. This item was included since scholarships were deemed to refer more to donations from institutions than to any other category.

Donations and Support from Private Individuals

28.   This includes cash or in-kind gifts from family, friends, or neighbors. The cash portion was reported as "Remittances" in Section 6.D, question sixty-five, and the in-kind portion in Section 8.E.II, question nine of the LSMS. Both cases were reported as annual values and therefore need no transformation.

Other Income

29.   Inheritance, lottery, games of chance, and others (not classified). In the LSMS, these amounts were reported on an annual basis in Section 8.E.II, questions six, ten, and twelve, and there was no need to transform the reported data.

ANNEX 4 – STATISTICAL APPENDIX
List of Tables

Table A4.1 - TOTAL CONSUMPTION: Absolute Value (per capita) by Area and Poverty Group

ABSOLUTE VALUE, B./	URBAN AREAS				RURAL AREAS			
	XP	AP	NP	TOT	XP	AP	NP	TOT
Yearly Consumption PC	406	674	2881	2544	334	517	1773	1036
Food	213	338	917	829	205	297	751	485
Bought	190	308	876	788	133	214	638	389
Produced	4	6	8	8	49	56	70	62
Received	18	23	25	25	23	26	34	29
Other	2	1	4	3	1	2	9	5
Education	25	45	169	150	17	33	103	62
Health	4	6	116	99	3	6	37	18
Personal goods/serv.	52	101	498	438	35	63	285	155
Durable goods	7	12	125	108	4	7	83	39
Transport, trips	17	32	220	192	12	25	161	81
Rent	63	100	637	555	46	66	251	142
Electricity, gas, etc	13	23	106	93	8	15	61	34
Water & phone	10	16	88	77	2	4	37	18
In-kind transfers (non-food)	1	2	5	4	1	2	4	3
	INDIGENOUS AREAS				ALL PANAMA			
	XP	AP	NP*	TOT	XP	AP	NP	TOT
Yearly Consumption PC	236	277	1434	330	307	506	2604	1821
Food	162	183	787	211	191	284	876	655
Bought	66	83	660	110	115	210	816	589
Produced	52	55	42	55	46	45	24	31
Received	41	42	77	43	29	29	28	28
Other	3	3	8	3	2	2	5	4
Education	11	15	173	22	16	32	153	108
Health	1	4	31	5	3	5	96	62
Personal goods/serv.	21	27	171	33	32	65	445	303
Durable goods	4	5	63	8	4	8	115	75
Transport, trips	5	7	83	11	10	23	205	137
Rent	26	30	95	33	41	67	540	363
Electricity, gas, etc	4	5	29	6	7	15	95	65
Water & phone	0	0	3	1	2	6	75	49
In-kind transfers (non-food)	0	0	0	0	1	2	5	3

Panama LSMS 1997; XP = Extreme Poor; AP = All Poor (includes extreme poor); NP = Non-Poor; TOT = Total

* Very small sample; results should be treated with caution

Table A4.2 - CONSUMPTION PATTERNS: Percent of Total Consumption, by Area and Poverty Group

	URBAN AREAS				RURAL AREAS			
	XP	AP	NP	TOT	XP	AP	NP	TOT
Food(%)	52.3	50.3	37.0	39.0	62.0	58.9	45.8	53.5
Bought (%)	46.8	45.8	35.3	36.9	38.2	40.2	38.1	39.4
Produced (%)	0.8	0.9	0.4	0.5	15.8	12.4	4.8	9.3
Received (%)	4.3	3.5	1.3	1.7	7.9	6.1	2.3	4.5
Others (%)	0.4	0.1	0.2	0.2	0.3	0.3	0.6	0.4
Education (%)	6.4	6.6	6.4	6.4	4.8	5.9	6.2	6.0
Health (%)	1.1	0.9	2.8	2.6	1.0	1.0	1.6	1.3
Personal goods/serv.(%)	12.7	14.8	17.4	17.0	10.1	11.5	15.8	13.3
Durable goods (%)	1.6	1.8	3.6	3.3	1.0	1.3	3.6	2.2
Transport, trips (%)	4.2	4.6	7.2	6.8	3.5	4.4	8.1	5.9
Rent (%)	15.6	14.9	18.9	18.2	14.3	13.1	13.6	13.3
Electricity, gas, etc.%	3.3	3.4	3.7	3.6	2.4	2.7	3.4	3.0
Water & phone (%)	2.5	2.4	2.9	2.9	0.6	0.8	1.6	1.2
In-kind Transfers (non-food)(%)	0.3	0.2	0.2	0.2	0.3	0.4	0.3	0.3
Total(%)	100.0	100.0	100.0	100.0	100.0	100.0	100.0	100.0
	INDIGENOUS AREAS				ALL PANAMA			
	XP	AP	NP*	TOT	XP	AP	NP	TOT
Food(%)	68.7	67.7	55.3	67.1	63.4	58.6	39.2	46.5
Bought (%)	25.7	26.8	44.8	27.7	34.6	38.9	36.0	37.1
Produced (%)	24.4	23.3	3.5	22.4	17.4	11.9	1.5	5.4
Received (%)	17.8	16.8	6.3	16.3	11.0	7.6	1.6	3.8
Others (%)	0.8	0.8	0.7	0.8	0.5	0.3	0.3	0.3
Education (%)	4.2	4.5	12.5	4.9	4.7	5.8	6.4	6.2
Health (%)	0.5	0.9	1.6	0.9	0.8	1.0	2.5	2.0
Personal goods/serv.(%)	8.9	9.2	11.8	9.3	10.0	11.8	17.0	15.0
Durable goods (%)	1.7	1.8	4.6	1.9	1.3	1.5	3.6	2.8
Transport, trips (%)	1.7	2.0	5.4	2.1	2.9	4.0	7.4	6.1
Rent (%)	12.2	12.0	6.5	11.7	13.7	13.3	17.5	15.9
Electricity, gas, etc.%	1.9	1.9	2.1	1.9	2.3	2.7	3.6	3.3
Water & phone (%)	0.2	0.2	0.2	0.2	0.6	1.0	2.6	2.0
In-kind Transfers (non-food)(%)	0.1	0.1	0.0	0.1	0.2	0.3	0.2	0.2
Total(%)	100.0	100.0	100.0	100.0	100.0	100.0	100.0	100.0

Panama LSMS 1997; XP = Extreme Poor; AP = All Poor (includes extreme poor); NP = Non-Poor; TOT = Total
* Very small sample; results should be treated with caution

Table A4.3 - Average Total Consumption Per Capita, by Quintile

	CONSUMPTION QUINTILES				
	Q1	Q2	Q3	Q4	Q5
Total Consumption, B./	320	750	1235	1984	4812

Table A4.4 - Average annual food consumption per capita, by Area and Poverty Group

Balboas Per Capita/Year

	URBAN AREAS				RURAL AREAS			
	XP	AP	NP	TOT	XP	AP	NP	TOT
FOOD INSIDE THE HOME	189.1	301.3	694.5	634.4	183.5	271.4	653.5	429.3
MILK PRODUCTS	22.3	39.7	80.3	74.1	11.6	21.6	66.8	40.3
Powdered milk	7.9	13.5	17.8	17.2	6.4	9.2	18.1	12.9
Liquid milk	3.0	8.3	26.1	23.3	1.9	4.2	20.4	10.9
Evaporated milk	5.9	9.7	17.9	16.7	2.5	5.7	16.6	10.2
Cheese	5.5	8.2	18.4	16.9	0.8	2.6	11.6	6.3
MEAT/CHICKEN EGGS	50.3	86.6	234.8	212.2	42.6	72.5	216.0	131.8
Beef	12.8	25.3	69.3	62.6	10.1	21.4	68.1	40.7
Pork	3.2	6.5	20.0	17.9	3.3	5.8	19.9	11.6
Chicken or hens	17.7	28.9	64.7	59.3	14.0	22.1	63.9	39.4
Fish	4.9	6.7	19.8	17.8	5.2	7.8	18.1	12.1
Shellfish (shrimps)	0.6	0.9	8.4	7.3	0.8	1.3	5.6	3.1
Sardine and tuna-fish	2.3	3.8	8.5	7.8	2.9	4.0	7.7	5.5
Sausages	3.0	6.8	29.1	25.7	1.1	2.6	15.3	7.9
Cattle innards	1.2	1.8	4.0	3.7	0.4	0.9	3.6	2.0
Chicken/hen innards	1.3	1.0	2.1	2.0	0.4	0.6	1.5	1.0
Chicken eggs	3.4	4.9	8.8	8.2	4.3	6.1	12.3	8.7
BASIC GRAINS	34.2	44.3	61.0	58.5	47.8	60.0	92.5	73.4
Rice (all)	25.7	31.0	37.0	36.1	33.5	40.2	53.2	45.6
Dry beans	2.6	5.0	8.8	8.2	3.3	5.0	11.4	7.6
Lentils	2.9	4.2	6.8	6.4	2.9	4.1	8.5	6.0
Beans (Frijoles)	1.5	1.8	3.4	3.1	3.9	5.0	6.9	5.8
Green and yellow peas	0.7	0.7	1.9	1.7	0.2	0.6	1.9	1.1
Grain corn	0.7	0.9	1.4	1.3	2.9	3.9	8.1	5.6
Ear corn	0.1	0.6	1.8	1.6	1.1	1.3	2.4	1.8
GREENS AND VEGETABLES	16.7	30.5	77.5	70.3	22.9	31.6	76.2	50.0
Greens	9.9	18.3	48.6	44.0	10.7	16.5	46.6	28.9
Tomatoes	1.4	2.5	8.3	7.4	0.9	1.7	6.3	3.6
Cabbage	0.4	1.1	3.4	3.1	0.2	0.6	3.0	1.6
Carrot	0.5	1.2	4.5	4.0	0.2	0.7	3.6	1.9
Pumpkin/Shallot	0.2	0.5	1.8	1.6	0.3	0.4	1.5	0.8
Lettuce	0.5	0.9	4.6	4.1	0.1	0.3	2.7	1.3
Cucumber	0.6	0.8	2.6	2.3	0.1	0.4	1.9	1.0
Beet	0.2	0.3	1.3	1.2	0.1	0.2	1.3	0.6
Whole Onion	2.3	4.5	7.0	6.6	2.5	3.6	8.0	5.4
Chili Pepper/Pepper/hot	1.0	1.9	3.8	3.5	1.1	1.7	4.1	2.7
Celery	0.3	1.0	3.1	2.8	0.3	0.6	2.2	1.2
Garlic	1.5	1.9	4.0	3.7	1.2	1.8	4.4	2.9
Coriander/parsley/chives	1.0	1.8	4.1	3.7	3.6	4.6	7.7	5.9
Vegetables	6.7	12.2	29.0	26.4	12.2	15.1	29.6	21.1
Potatoes	1.6	3.6	9.8	8.9	1.0	2.2	8.4	4.7
Unripe/ripe bananas	3.2	4.7	9.9	9.1	3.9	4.5	8.9	6.3
Ñame	0.8	1.9	5.0	4.5	3.4	4.1	6.8	5.2
Yucca	0.7	1.3	2.3	2.2	2.9	3.2	3.8	3.5
Otoe	0.4	0.7	2.0	1.8	1.0	1.1	1.7	1.4
FRUITS	5.8	12.2	31.9	28.8	11.0	15.1	32.2	22.1
Guineo banana/banana	1.7	2.2	4.4	4.1	3.1	3.5	5.1	4.2
Orange	0.3	1.1	2.9	2.6	1.3	1.8	3.7	2.5
Apple	0.5	1.3	5.1	4.5	0.2	0.6	3.7	1.9
Coconut (pip)	0.8	1.7	3.1	2.9	1.8	2.6	3.9	3.1
Avocado	0.6	1.2	2.7	2.5	0.7	1.3	2.9	2.0
Mango	0.6	1.8	2.8	2.6	2.0	2.2	3.2	2.6
Lemmon	0.4	1.5	2.8	2.6	0.7	0.9	2.0	1.3
Papaya	0.7	0.6	2.9	2.5	0.5	1.1	3.0	1.9

Table A4.4 - CONT'D - Average annual food consumption per capita, by Area and Poverty Group

Balboas Per Capita/Year

	URBAN AREAS				RURAL AREAS			
	XP	AP	NP	TOT	XP	AP	NP	TOT
Pineapple	0.1	0.4	2.5	2.2	0.6	0.6	2.3	1.3
Melon	0.0	0.1	0.8	0.7	0.0	0.1	0.5	0.2
Watermelon	0.1	0.5	1.9	1.7	0.2	0.5	1.9	1.1
BREAD/FLOUR/CREAM/PASTAS	24.0	34.7	78.7	72.0	14.7	23.8	58.8	38.3
Bread, Cookies, Candies	15.4	19.6	39.2	36.2	7.2	11.2	29.9	18.9
Salty and sweet bread	14.3	16.7	28.5	26.7	6.2	9.4	22.9	15.0
Cookies/pastry/candies	1.1	2.9	10.6	9.5	1.0	1.8	6.9	3.9
Other	8.6	15.1	39.5	35.8	7.5	12.6	29.0	19.4
Cereals and creams	3.2	5.4	17.7	15.8	1.7	3.4	10.6	6.4
Macaroni products	1.9	3.4	8.7	7.9	2.4	3.6	6.7	4.8
Infant food	1.3	2.7	4.7	4.4	0.6	1.1	3.1	1.9
Ready-cooked corn	1.0	1.8	5.4	4.8	1.5	1.8	4.3	2.8
Wheat flour/puff pastry	1.2	1.8	3.1	2.9	1.4	2.8	4.3	3.4
SUGAR/HONEY	8.5	9.5	13.9	13.3	8.8	11.0	18.8	14.2
Sugar (castor/brown)	8.0	8.7	11.8	11.4	7.8	9.6	14.9	11.8
Sugar loaf, brown sugar, honey	0.4	0.8	2.1	1.9	1.0	1.5	3.9	2.5
FATS	11.1	15.6	32.0	29.5	7.2	11.8	28.6	18.7
Vegetable oil	8.1	11.2	20.4	19.0	6.5	10.0	21.3	14.7
Butter/margarine	1.8	2.3	5.0	4.6	0.5	1.0	2.8	1.7
Mayonnaise	1.2	2.1	6.6	5.9	0.3	0.8	4.5	2.3
SOFT DRINKS/ICE CREAM/COFFEE/TEA	10.0	16.0	48.4	43.5	9.6	13.2	36.8	23.0
Soda water/soft drinks/juices	4.4	7.6	30.2	26.8	2.3	3.9	17.1	9.4
Ice creams and brown sugar	0.9	3.0	8.2	7.4	0.4	1.2	6.7	3.5
Coffee and tea	4.8	5.4	10.0	9.3	7.0	8.1	13.0	10.2
OTHER FOODS INSIDE THE HOME	6.3	12.4	36.0	32.4	7.3	10.8	26.9	17.4
Pastas/Tomato sauce	2.9	5.1	12.5	11.4	2.0	3.6	10.6	6.5
Canned/package soup	1.1	2.7	5.7	5.2	1.6	2.4	6.0	3.8
Seasoning	0.8	1.9	5.1	4.6	1.1	1.5	3.5	2.3
Salt	1.2	1.7	2.9	2.7	2.3	2.5	4.0	3.1
Canned food	0.2	0.8	6.4	5.6	0.0	0.2	2.0	0.9
Other food	-	0.2	3.4	2.9	0.3	0.6	0.9	0.7
FOOD CONSUMED OUTSIDE THE HOME								
HOME OR PURCHASED, GROUP	24.0	36.6	222.7	194.3	21.8	25.7	97.9	55.5
SUPERMARKETS AND RESTAURANTS	8.6	14.3	189.0	162.3	2.5	6.0	61.7	29.0
FOOD AT SCHOOL	11.9	16.3	10.7	11.6	16.9	15.6	12.6	14.4
ALCOHOL AND TOBACCO	3.6	6.0	23.0	20.4	2.4	4.0	23.6	12.1
GRAND TOTAL OF ALL CONSUMED								
FOOD (+alcohol and tobacco)	213.1	337.9	917.2	828.7	205.3	297.1	751.4	484.8

Panama LSMS 1997; XP = Extreme Poor; AP = All Poor (includes extreme poor); NP = Non-Poor; TOT = Total

* Very small sample; results should be treated with caution

Table A4.4 CONT'D - Average annual food consumption per capita, by Area and Poverty Group

Balboas per capita/year

	INDIGENOUS AREAS				ALL PANAMA			
	XP	AP	NP*	TOT	XP	AP	NP	TOT
FOOD INSIDE THE HOME	121.2	139.3	639.8	162.3	162.5	252.7	684.2	523.1
MILK PRODUCTS	2.8	3.9	45.2	5.8	9.6	22.3	76.8	56.5
Powdered milk	1.5	2.1	15.9	2.7	4.8	8.8	17.9	14.5
Liquid milk	0.2	0.4	5.8	0.6	1.4	4.4	24.6	17.0
Evaporated milk	0.7	0.9	15.8	1.6	2.2	5.7	17.6	13.2
Cheese	0.5	0.5	7.7	0.9	1.1	3.5	16.7	11.8
MEAT/CHICKEN EGGS	22.2	27.9	190.1	35.4	36.2	67.1	230.0	169.2
Beef	2.2	3.6	36.1	5.1	7.6	18.8	68.8	50.1
Pork	1.0	1.4	9.5	1.8	2.5	5.1	19.9	14.4
Chicken or Hen	6.8	8.2	56.1	10.4	11.8	21.0	64.5	48.2
Fish	5.4	6.2	30.0	7.3	5.2	7.3	19.4	14.9
Shell-fish (shrimps)	1.5	1.5	3.2	1.5	1.0	1.2	7.7	5.3
Sardine and tuna-fish	2.9	3.6	20.9	4.4	2.8	3.9	8.4	6.7
Sausages	0.1	0.4	10.1	0.8	0.9	3.1	25.7	17.3
Cattle innards	0.1	0.1	2.7	0.2	0.4	1.0	3.9	2.8
Chicken/hen innards	0.4	0.4	3.2	0.5	0.5	0.6	2.0	1.5
Chicken eggs	1.9	2.6	18.4	3.3	3.4	5.2	9.7	8.0
BASIC GRAINS	27.3	30.7	109.0	34.3	39.5	50.8	68.9	62.2
Rice (all)	19.4	22.0	79.7	24.7	27.9	34.6	41.2	38.7
Dry beans	0.8	0.9	7.5	1.2	2.4	4.2	9.4	7.4
Lentils	0.6	0.8	9.0	1.2	2.1	3.5	7.2	5.8
Beans	2.9	3.3	7.2	3.5	3.3	3.9	4.2	4.1
Green and yellow peas	0.0	0.0	0.1	0.0	0.2	0.5	1.9	1.4
Grain corn	2.6	2.7	4.9	2.8	2.6	3.0	3.1	3.0
Ear corn	1.0	1.0	0.7	1.0	1.0	1.1	2.0	1.7
VEGETABLES AND GREENS	17.4	18.7	54.7	20.3	20.4	28.9	77.1	59.1
Greens	5.2	5.9	32.2	7.1	8.7	14.9	48.0	35.6
Tomatoes	0.1	0.2	1.8	0.3	0.7	1.6	7.8	5.5
Cabbage	0.2	0.2	1.1	0.3	0.2	0.7	3.3	2.3
Carrot	0.0	0.1	0.8	0.1	0.2	0.7	4.3	2.9
Pumpkin/Shallot	0.3	0.3	0.3	0.3	0.3	0.4	1.7	1.2
Lettuce	0.2	0.2	-	0.2	0.2	0.4	4.1	2.7
Cucumber	0.1	0.1	0.2	0.1	0.2	0.5	2.4	1.7
Beet	0.0	0.0	0.5	0.0	0.1	0.2	1.3	0.9
Whole Onion	1.2	1.4	11.5	1.9	2.1	3.4	7.3	5.8
Chili Pepper/Pepper/Hot	0.7	0.9	4.0	1.1	1.0	1.6	3.9	3.0
Celery	0.4	0.4	2.9	0.5	0.4	0.6	2.9	2.0
Garlic	0.3	0.3	4.3	0.5	0.9	1.5	4.1	3.2
Coriander/parsley/chives	1.8	1.8	4.9	1.9	2.7	3.4	5.0	4.4
Vegetables	12.2	12.8	22.5	13.2	11.7	14.0	29.1	23.4
Potatoes	0.2	0.3	5.3	0.5	0.8	2.1	9.5	6.7
Unripe/ripe bananas	4.0	4.2	11.3	4.5	3.8	4.5	9.7	7.7
Ñame	2.4	2.6	4.7	2.7	2.9	3.3	5.4	4.6
Yucca	2.9	3.1	1.0	3.0	2.7	2.8	2.7	2.7
Otoe	2.7	2.6	0.3	2.5	1.5	1.3	1.9	1.7
FRUITS	19.2	19.6	33.5	20.3	13.4	15.3	31.9	25.7
Guineo banana/banana	8.1	8.1	12.9	8.3	4.7	4.1	4.6	4.4
Orange	0.9	0.9	3.9	1.0	1.1	1.4	3.1	2.5
Apple	0.0	0.0	1.6	0.1	0.2	0.7	4.7	3.2
Coconut (pip)	2.6	2.6	3.3	2.6	2.0	2.4	3.3	3.0
Avocado	1.8	1.9	2.3	1.9	1.1	1.4	2.8	2.3
Mango	4.5	4.8	5.2	4.8	2.7	2.6	2.9	2.8
Lemmon	0.8	0.8	1.6	0.9	0.7	1.0	2.6	2.0
Papaya	0.1	0.1	1.5	0.2	0.4	0.8	2.9	2.1

Table A4.4 CONT'D - Average annual food consumption per capita, by Area and Poverty Group

Balboas per capita/year	INDIGENOUS AREAS				ALL PANAMA			
	XP	AP	NP*	TOT	XP	AP	NP	TOT
Pineapple	0.3	0.3	0.8	0.3	0.4	0.5	2.5	1.7
Melon	-	-	-	-	0.0	0.1	0.7	0.5
Watermelon	0.2	0.2	0.4	0.2	0.2	0.4	1.9	1.3
BREAD/FLOUR/CREAMS/PASTA	6.2	7.4	65.7	10.1	12.6	23.1	73.8	54.9
Bread, Cookies, Candies	3.2	3.6	22.8	4.4	6.6	11.6	36.8	27.4
Salty and sweet bread	2.5	2.8	15.8	3.4	5.7	9.8	27.1	20.6
Cookies/pastry/Candy	0.7	0.8	7.0	1.1	0.9	1.9	9.7	6.8
Other	3.0	3.9	42.9	5.7	6.1	11.5	37.0	27.5
Cereals and creams	0.6	0.8	10.4	1.2	1.5	3.4	15.9	11.3
Macaroni products	1.0	1.3	9.8	1.7	1.9	3.1	8.2	6.3
Infant food	0.4	0.4	8.0	0.8	0.6	1.3	4.3	3.2
Ready-cooked corn	0.2	0.4	0.5	0.4	1.0	1.5	5.1	3.7
Wheat flour/puff pastrys	0.8	1.0	14.2	1.6	1.2	2.2	3.5	3.0
SUGAR/HONEY	9.2	11.6	34.7	12.7	8.9	10.8	15.2	13.6
Sugar (castor/brown)	9.1	10.4	34.4	11.5	8.3	9.5	12.7	11.5
Sugar loaf, brown sugar, honey	0.1	1.3	0.3	1.2	0.6	1.3	2.5	2.1
FATS	3.3	3.7	22.4	4.6	6.2	11.1	31.1	23.6
Vegetable oil	3.1	3.5	19.2	4.2	5.5	9.0	20.6	16.3
Butter/margarine	0.2	0.2	1.4	0.3	0.5	1.1	4.4	3.2
Mayonnaise	0.0	0.0	1.8	0.1	0.3	1.0	6.1	4.2
SOFT DRINK/ICE CREAM/COFFEE/TE	7.2	8.2	51.4	10.2	8.8	12.9	45.6	33.4
Soda water/soft drinks/juices	1.3	1.8	21.5	2.7	2.1	4.3	27.0	18.5
Ice creams and brown sugar	0.1	0.3	5.3	0.5	0.3	1.4	7.8	5.4
Coffee and tea	5.8	6.1	24.6	7.0	6.4	7.1	10.8	9.4
OTHER FOOD INSIDE THE HOME	6.6	7.5	33.3	8.7	6.9	10.5	33.7	25.1
Pastas/Tomato sauce	1.0	1.3	11.3	1.7	1.7	3.5	12.0	8.8
Canned/package soup	1.4	1.9	11.0	2.3	1.5	2.3	5.8	4.5
Seasoning	0.2	0.2	2.9	0.3	0.8	1.4	4.7	3.4
Salt	3.1	3.3	4.6	3.3	2.5	2.5	3.2	2.9
Canned foods	0.1	0.1	1.1	0.1	0.1	0.3	5.3	3.5
Other foods	0.9	0.8	2.4	0.9	0.5	0.6	2.8	1.9
FOOD CONSUMED OUTSIDE THE HOME								
HOME OR PURCHASED, GROUP	40.9	43.6	146.9	48.4	28.6	31.6	192.0	132.1
SUPERMARKETS AND RESTAURANTS	1.7	2.5	64.6	5.4	2.8	7.2	157.4	101.3
FOOD AT SCHOOL	37.2	37.8	46.7	38.2	23.5	20.1	11.4	14.6
ALCOHOL AND TOBACCO	2.0	3.3	35.6	4.8	2.4	4.3	23.2	16.2
GRAND TOTAL OF ALL CONSUMED								
FOOD (+alcohol and tobacco)	162.1	182.9	786.7	210.6	191.1	284.3	876.2	655.2

Panama LSMS 1997; XP = Extreme Poor; AP = All Poor (includes extreme poor); NP = Non-Poor; TOT = Total

* Very small sample; results should be treated with caution

Table A4.5 - Consumption of Durable Goods, by Area and Poverty Group (% of households consuming each item)

	URBAN AREAS				RURAL AREAS				INDIGENOUS AREAS				ALL PANAMA			
	XP	AP	NP	TOT	XP	AP	NP	TOT	XP	AP	NP*	TOT	XP	AP	NP	TOT
Stove	85%	91%	97%	96%	29%	51%	85%	69%	11%	13%	73%	19%	29%	54%	94%	83%
Iron	64%	78%	92%	90%	18%	35%	67%	52%	7%	10%	45%	13%	19%	40%	85%	73%
Grinder	15%	24%	24%	24%	56%	58%	53%	55%	46%	46%	12%	43%	50%	48%	32%	36%
Radio	49%	54%	65%	64%	64%	66%	69%	67%	50%	50%	63%	51%	58%	61%	66%	64%
Refrigerator	31%	47%	86%	82%	4%	15%	50%	34%	2%	4%	26%	6%	6%	20%	76%	60%
Washer	9%	21%	62%	58%	3%	7%	31%	20%	1%	1%	5%	2%	3%	9%	53%	41%
TV	69%	86%	95%	94%	21%	37%	72%	56%	6%	8%	32%	10%	21%	43%	88%	76%
Phone line	2%	4%	21%	20%	0%	1%	10%	6%	0%	0%	0%	0%	1%	2%	18%	14%
Sewing machine	13%	17%	28%	27%	10%	15%	22%	18%	29%	30%	16%	29%	16%	18%	27%	24%
Fan	43%	64%	85%	83%	5%	17%	47%	33%	2%	3%	13%	4%	8%	25%	74%	61%
Blender	17%	25%	65%	61%	1%	7%	34%	22%	0%	0%	0%	0%	2%	10%	56%	43%
Bicycle	22%	32%	33%	33%	13%	21%	34%	28%	1%	1%	3%	2%	10%	21%	33%	30%
Toaster	4%	6%	31%	28%	0%	1%	10%	6%	0%	0%	0%	0%	0%	2%	25%	19%
Stereo	23%	27%	52%	50%	1%	5%	19%	13%	0%	1%	10%	2%	3%	9%	43%	34%
VCR	2%	6%	34%	31%	0%	1%	10%	5%	0%	0%	0%	0%	0%	2%	27%	20%
Typewriter	4%	7%	27%	25%	0%	2%	14%	8%	0%	0%	9%	1%	0%	3%	23%	17%
Computer	0%	0%	8%	7%	0%	0%	1%	0%	0%	0%	0%	0%	0%	0%	6%	4%
Air conditioner	0%	0%	12%	11%	0%	0%	1%	1%	0%	0%	0%	0%	0%	0%	9%	7%
Car	0%	2%	36%	33%	0%	2%	19%	11%	0%	0%	0%	0%	0%	1%	31%	23%
Boat/motor	3%	1%	1%	1%	3%	2%	2%	2%	14%	14%	16%	14%	6%	4%	1%	2%
Motorcycle	0%	0%	1%	1%	0%	0%	1%	1%	0%	0%	0%	0%	0%	0%	1%	1%
Other	2%	1%	3%	3%	0%	0%	3%	2%	1%	1%	5%	1%	0%	0%	3%	2%

Panama LSMS 1997; XP = Extreme Poor; AP = All Poor (includes extreme poor); NP = Non-Poor; TOT = Total
* Very small sample; results should be treated with caution

Table A4.6 - Total Value of Household Durables, by Area and Poverty Group

	URBAN AREAS				RURAL AREAS				INDIGENOUS AREAS				ALL PANAMA			
	XP	AP	NP	TOT	XP	AP	NP	TOT	XP	AP	NP*	TOT	XP	AP	NP	TOT
Present value of Household durables	$251	$411	4764	4323	$112	$220	2241	1296	$119	$150	$877	$217	$126	$250	4051	3005

Panama LSMS 1997; XP = Extreme Poor; AP = All Poor (includes extreme poor); NP = Non-Poor; TOT = Total
* Very small sample; results should be treated with caution

Table A4.7 - Income Aggregate, by consumption quintile

| | CONSUMPTION QUINTILES | | | | | |
	1	2	3	4	5	TOTAL
Total Income per capita	$ 440	$ 812	$ 1,379	$ 2,354	$ 6,469	$ 2,292
LABOR INCOME	78%	77%	73%	73%	67%	70%
1.AGRICULTURAL	45%	18%	9%	5%	1%	6%
Salaries	13%	9%	4%	2%	0%	2%
Formal Sector	5%	5%	2%	2%	0%	1%
Informal Sector	8%	4%	1%	0%	0%	1%
Net Inc. from Production	32%	9%	5%	3%	1%	4%
2.NON-AGRICULTURAL	34%	58%	64%	68%	65%	64%
Salaries	30%	50%	54%	56%	55%	54%
Formal Sector	22%	38%	46%	52%	51%	48%
Informal Sector	8%	11%	8%	4%	4%	5%
Own Business	4%	9%	10%	12%	11%	11%
Formal Sector	0%	1%	1%	2%	6%	4%
Informal Sector	4%	7%	9%	10%	4%	6%
NON LABOR INCOME	22%	23%	27%	27%	33%	30%
1.RETURNS TO CAPITAL	9%	10%	11%	13%	17%	15%
Interest Received	0%	0%	0%	0%	1%	1%
Rent on equip., property	9%	10%	11%	12%	17%	14%
2.DONATIONS, GIFTS	9%	6%	5%	4%	2%	4%
From institutions	7%	3%	2%	2%	1%	2%
From friends, family	3%	3%	3%	2%	1%	2%
3.PENSIONS, INDEMN.	3%	6%	9%	9%	13%	11%
4.OTHER INCOME	0%	1%	1%	1%	1%	1%

Table A4.8 - Income Aggregate, by income quintile

| | INCOME QUINTILE | | | | | |
	1	2	3	4	5	TOTAL
Total Income per capita	$ 174	$ 606	$ 1,191	$ 2,304	$ 7,178	$ 2,292
LABOR INCOME	46%	68%	71%	71%	70%	70%
1.AGRICULTURAL	14%	19%	11%	4%	4%	6%
Salaries	16%	11%	6%	2%	1%	2%
Formal Sector	5%	5%	4%	1%	0%	1%
Informal Sector	11%	6%	3%	0%	0%	1%
Net Inc. from Production	-2%	8%	5%	2%	4%	4%
2.NON-AGRICULTURAL	33%	48%	60%	67%	66%	64%
Salaries	25%	39%	51%	56%	55%	54%
Formal Sector	17%	27%	42%	50%	51%	48%
Informal Sector	8%	11%	9%	6%	4%	5%
Own Business	8%	10%	9%	11%	11%	11%
Formal Sector	1%	0%	1%	2%	6%	4%
Informal Sector	7%	9%	8%	9%	5%	6%
NON LABOR INCOME	54%	32%	29%	29%	30%	30%
1.RETURNS TO CAPITAL	25%	15%	14%	13%	15%	15%
Interest Received	0%	0%	0%	0%	1%	1%
Rent on equip., property	25%	15%	14%	13%	14%	14%
2.DONATIONS, GIFTS	23%	10%	6%	4%	2%	4%
From institutions	16%	5%	3%	2%	1%	2%
From friends, family	7%	4%	4%	2%	1%	2%
3.PENSIONS, INDEMN.	4%	6%	8%	11%	12%	11%
4.OTHER INCOME	2%	1%	1%	1%	1%	1%

Cuadro A4.9 - Income Aggregate, by Poverty Group and Area

	EXTREME POVERTY				ALL POOR (INCL. EXT. POOR)			
	Urban	Rural	Indigenous	Total	Urban	Rural	Indigenous	Total
Total Income per capita	$ 627	$ 469	$ 303	$ 426	$ 849	$ 593	$ 328	$ 600
LABOR INCOME	82%	80%	73%	79%	78%	77%	74%	77%
1.AGRICULTURAL	2%	57%	44%	46%	3%	41%	39%	29%
Salaries	2%	17%	7%	12%	3%	17%	6%	11%
Formal Sector	2%	6%	3%	5%	2%	7%	3%	5%
Informal Sector	0%	11%	4%	8%	1%	9%	3%	6%
Net Inc. from Production	0%	40%	38%	34%	0%	25%	33%	18%
2.NON-AGRICULTURAL	79%	24%	29%	33%	75%	36%	35%	48%
Salaries	73%	20%	24%	28%	66%	30%	31%	41%
Formal Sector	56%	13%	21%	21%	51%	22%	27%	32%
Informal Sector	17%	7%	3%	7%	15%	8%	4%	10%
Own Business	6%	4%	5%	4%	9%	6%	4%	7%
Formal Sector	0%	0%	0%	0%	2%	1%	0%	1%
Informal Sector	6%	4%	4%	4%	7%	5%	4%	6%
NON LABOR INCOME	18%	20%	27%	21%	22%	23%	26%	23%
1.RETURNS TO CAPITAL	7%	9%	8%	9%	9%	10%	8%	9%
Interest Received	0%	0%	0%	0%	0%	0%	0%	0%
Rent on equip., property	7%	9%	8%	9%	9%	10%	8%	9%
2.DONATIONS, GIFTS	7%	8%	16%	10%	5%	8%	16%	8%
From institutions	2%	5%	14%	7%	2%	5%	14%	5%
From friends, family	5%	3%	2%	3%	3%	3%	2%	3%
3.PENSIONS, INDEMN.	4%	2%	3%	3%	8%	4%	3%	5%
4.OTHER INCOME	0%	1%	0%	0%	1%	1%	0%	1%

Cuadro A4.9 CONT'D - Income Aggregate, by Poverty Group and Area

	NON POOR				ALL PANAMA, BY AREA			
	Urban	Rural	Indigenous	Total	Urban	Rural	Indigenous	Total
Total Income per capita	$ 3,796	$ 1,807	$ 1,349	$ 3,299	$ 3,346	$ 1,095	$ 375	$ 2,292
LABOR INCOME	69%	70%	83%	69%	69%	72%	75%	70%
1.AGRICULTURAL	1%	20%	8%	3%	1%	27%	34%	6%
Salaries	0%	6%	2%	1%	1%	10%	5%	2%
Formal Sector	0%	4%	2%	1%	0%	5%	2%	1%
Informal Sector	0%	2%	0%	0%	0%	5%	3%	1%
Net Inc. from Production	0%	14%	6%	2%	0%	17%	29%	4%
2.NON-AGRICULTURAL	68%	50%	75%	66%	68%	46%	41%	64%
Salaries	57%	37%	72%	55%	58%	35%	37%	54%
Formal Sector	53%	31%	67%	50%	53%	28%	33%	48%
Informal Sector	4%	6%	5%	5%	5%	7%	4%	5%
Own Business	11%	13%	3%	11%	11%	11%	4%	11%
Formal Sector	5%	2%	0%	5%	5%	1%	0%	4%
Informal Sector	5%	11%	3%	6%	6%	9%	4%	6%
NON LABOR INCOME	31%	30%	17%	31%	31%	28%	25%	30%
1.RETURNS TO CAPITAL	16%	14%	3%	15%	15%	12%	7%	15%
Interest Received	1%	1%	0%	1%	1%	0%	0%	1%
Rent on equip., property	15%	13%	3%	15%	15%	12%	7%	14%
2.DONATIONS, GIFTS	3%	5%	14%	3%	3%	6%	15%	4%
From institutions	1%	3%	14%	1%	1%	4%	14%	2%
From friends, family	2%	2%	0%	2%	2%	3%	2%	2%
3.PENSIONS, INDEMN.	11%	10%	0%	11%	11%	8%	2%	11%
4.OTHER INCOME	1%	1%	0%	1%	1%	1%	0%	1%

Table A4.10 - Poverty by Age Group
(% of individuals in each group who are poor)

	Age: 0-5	Age: 6-11	Age: 12-17	Age: 18-24	Age: 25-59	Age: >=60	Table Total
Extreme Poor							
% below XPL	30%	27%	23%	17%	14%	12%	19%
# of persons	102,244	98,332	81,915	55,394	145,420	31,326	514,839
All Poor (a)							
% below FPL	53%	49%	44%	35%	30%	27%	37%
# of persons	183,440	175,340	153,260	117,028	318,526	72,355	1,020,158
Non-poor							
% above FPL	47%	51%	56%	65%	71%	73%	63%
# of persons	163,425	183,945	197,324	213,409	761,603	191,819	1,712,158
Table Total							
Total %	100%	100%	100%	100%	100%	100%	100%
# of persons	346,866	359,285	350,584	330,437	1,080,129	264,174	2,732,316

XPL = extreme poverty line; FPL = full poverty line.
a\ "All poor" includes extreme poor.

Table A4.11 - Malnutrition Among Children Under 5, by Poverty Group and Geographic Area

	URBAN AREAS				RURAL AREAS			
	XP	AP	NP	TOT	XP	AP	NP	TOT
Chronic (HFA) (a)	24%	11%	4%	6%	25%	18%	6%	15%
Underweight (WFA) (b)	17%	6%	2%	3%	13%	9%	2%	7%
Acute (WFH) (c)	6%	2%	1%	1%	1%	1%	1%	1%
Any Form (d)	33%	14%	5%	7%	28%	20%	6%	17%
	INDIGENOUS AREAS				ALL PANAMA			
	XP	AP	NP*	TOT	XP	AP	NP	TOT
Chronic (HFA) (a)	51%	50%	7%	49%	34%	23%	4%	14%
Underweight (WFA) (b)	23%	22%	0%	21%	17%	11%	2%	7%
Acute (WFH) (c)	2%	2%	0%	2%	2%	2%	1%	1%
Any Form (d)	53%	52%	7%	51%	37%	26%	5%	16%

Panama LSMS 1997; XP = Extreme Poor; AP = All Poor (includes extreme poor); NP = Non-Poor; TOT = Total
* Very small sample; results should be treated with caution
a\ HFA = height for age. Defined as children whose height is two or more standard deviations below reference value.
b\ WFA = weight for age. Defined as children whose weight is two or more standard deviations below reference value.
a\ WFH = weight for height. Defined as children whose WFH is two or more standard deviations below reference value.
d\ Children who are counted as malnourished under any of the above definitions.

Table A4.12 - Undernourished Children by Poverty Group
(% of malnourished kids who are poor, extreme poor, non-poor)

	Chronic (HFA)	Underweight (WFA)	Acute (WFH)	Any Form
Extreme Poor (below XPL)	70%	73%	48%	68%
All Poor (below FPL, incl. XP)	86%	87%	73%	85%
Non Poor (Above FPL)	14%	13%	27%	15%
Total	100%	100%	100%	100%

Table A4.13 - Household Structure, by Poverty Group and Geographic Area

	URBAN AREAS				RURAL AREAS			
	XP	AP	NP	TOT	XP	AP	NP	TOT
HOUSEHOLD SIZE AND COMPOSITION								
Persons per HH	6.74	6.05	3.79	4.02	5.92	5.22	3.23	4.16
Age: 0-5	1.34	1.05	0.37	0.44	1.14	0.91	0.29	0.58
Age: 6-11	1.25	0.99	0.40	0.46	1.10	0.87	0.35	0.59
Age: 12-17	1.07	0.85	0.43	0.47	0.89	0.77	0.39	0.57
Age: 18-24	0.87	0.78	0.50	0.52	0.61	0.57	0.34	0.45
Age: 25-59	1.88	1.98	1.70	1.73	1.73	1.67	1.40	1.52
Age: >=60	0.33	0.40	0.39	0.39	0.45	0.43	0.46	0.45
DEPENDENCY ON WORKING MEMBERS								
Workers in the Household	1.75	1.85	1.67	1.68	2.00	1.81	1.40	1.59
Dependency ratio \a	5.24	3.89	2.78	2.89	3.22	3.16	2.78	2.96
CHARACTERISTICS OF HOUSEHOLD HEAD (HH)								
Household head: age	48.20	45.90	48.50	48.20	49.30	48.80	51.00	50.00
Household head: female	38%	29%	29%	29%	12%	14%	20%	17%
HH Head: With partner	58%	71%	65%	65%	78%	77%	64%	70%
HH Head: Separated/divorced	19%	11%	13%	12%	4%	7%	11%	9%
HH Head: Widowed	6%	5%	8%	8%	8%	8%	10%	9%
HH Head: Single	17%	12%	14%	14%	9%	9%	14%	12%

	INDIGENOUS AREAS				ALL PANAMA			
	XP	AP	NP*	TOT	XP	AP	NP	TOT
HOUSEHOLD SIZE AND COMPOSITION								
Persons per HH	7.44	7.15	3.39	6.80	6.45	5.70	3.63	4.20
Age: 0-5	1.55	1.48	0.50	1.39	1.28	1.02	0.35	0.53
Age: 6-11	1.50	1.41	0.60	1.33	1.23	0.98	0.39	0.55
Age: 12-17	1.29	1.20	0.49	1.14	1.03	0.86	0.42	0.54
Age: 18-24	0.81	0.82	0.35	0.77	0.69	0.65	0.45	0.51
Age: 25-59	2.00	1.95	1.36	1.90	1.82	1.78	1.61	1.66
Age: >=60	0.29	0.29	0.07	0.27	0.39	0.40	0.41	0.41
DEPENDENCY ON WORKING MEMBERS								
Workers in the Household	2.31	2.26	1.47	2.18	2.07	1.89	1.59	1.67
Dependency ratio \a	3.47	3.35	1.74	3.20	3.47	3.35	2.77	2.93
CHARACTERISTICS OF HOUSEHOLD HEAD (HH)								
Household head: age	45.20	45.00	35.30	44.10	48.00	47.60	49.10	48.70
Household head: female	16%	15%	15%	15%	15%	17%	26%	24%
HH Head: With partner	85%	85%	81%	84%	79%	77%	65%	68%
HH Head: Separated/divorced	6%	6%	6%	6%	6%	8%	12%	11%
HH Head: Widowed	4%	4%	2%	4%	7%	7%	9%	8%
HH Head: Single	4%	5%	11%	5%	8%	9%	14%	13%

Panama LSMS 1997; XP = Extreme Poor; AP = All Poor (includes extreme poor); NP = Non-Poor; TOT = Total

* Very small sample; results should be treated with caution. All the figures in the table are the average of each household's value

\a Dependency ratio = # of non-working members/# of working members (excluding persons w/o info.)

Households without workers were given a value of 13 since this is the highest value in the sample

Table A4.14 - Fertility, by Poverty Group and Geographic Area

	URBAN AREAS				RURAL AREAS			
	XP	AP	NP	TOT	XP	AP	NP	TOT
Live births (avg. number)	4.6	3.4	2.3	2.5	4.5	4.0	2.6	3.4
Children alive today (avg. #)	4.5	3.4	2.4	2.5	4.4	3.9	2.6	3.4

	INDIGENOUS AREAS				ALL PANAMA			
	XP	AP	NP*	TOT	XP	AP	NP	TOT
Live births (avg. number)	4.7	4.6	3.3	4.5	4.6	4.0	2.4	3.0
Children alive today (avg. #)	4.3	4.2	3.3	4.5	4.3	3.9	2.4	3.0

Panama LSMS 1997; XP = Extreme Poor; AP = All Poor (includes extreme poor); NP = Non-Poor; TOT = Total

* Very small sample; results should be treated with caution

Table A4.15 - LITERACY (% of those over age 9 who can read and write)

	URBAN AREAS				RURAL AREAS			
	XP	AP	NP	TOT	XP	AP	NP	TOT
Male >9 years	88%	94%	99%	98%	83%	86%	93%	89%
Female > 9 years	90%	94%	98%	97%	79%	84%	92%	88%
Total > 9 years	89%	94%	98%	98%	81%	85%	92%	88%
	INDIGENOUS AREAS				ALL PANAMA			
	XP	AP	NP*	TOT	XP	AP	NP	TOT
Male >9 years	72%	73%	88%	74%	80%	85%	97%	93%
Female > 9 years	51%	51%	84%	53%	69%	80%	97%	92%
Total > 9 years	61%	62%	86%	63%	75%	83%	97%	92%
	BY QUINTILE							
	Q1	Q2	Q3	Q4	Q5			
Male >9 years	81%	91%	95%	97%	99%			
Female > 9 years	71%	90%	94%	97%	99%			
Total > 9 years	76%	90%	95%	97%	99%			

Panama LSMS 1997; XP = Extreme Poor; AP = All Poor (includes extreme poor); NP = Non-Poor; TOT = Total
* Very small sample; results should be treated with caution

Table A4.16 - EDUCATIONAL ATTAINMENT (average number of years of schooling for those age 12+)

	URBAN AREAS				RURAL AREAS			
	XP	AP	NP	TOT	XP	AP	NP	TOT
Male by Age Group								
12-17 years	5.5	6.4	7.8	7.5	5.2	5.7	7.3	6.3
18-24 years	8.0	7.8	10.8	10.3	5.6	6.3	9.1	7.3
25-39 years	6.5	8.6	11.3	10.9	5.9	6.6	8.4	7.4
>40 years	4.2	4.9	9.9	9.4	2.9	3.2	5.4	4.4
Female by Age Group								
12-17 years	5.7	6.8	7.9	7.7	5.7	6.4	7.7	6.9
18-24 years	6.7	8.7	11.6	11.2	5.5	6.7	10.2	8.3
25-39 years	6.1	8.0	12.0	11.5	5.6	6.9	9.2	7.8
>40 years	4.6	5.0	9.4	9.0	2.2	2.8	5.5	4.3
Total by Age Group								
12-17 years	5.6	6.6	7.8	7.6	5.4	6.0	7.5	6.5
18-24 years	7.4	8.3	11.2	10.8	5.6	6.4	9.7	7.8
25-39 years	6.4	8.3	11.7	11.2	5.8	6.7	8.8	7.6
>40 years	4.4	4.9	9.6	9.2	2.6	3.1	5.5	4.3
Total, All Age Groups								
Male	6.1	6.9	10.1	9.7	4.5	5.0	7.0	5.9
Female	6.0	7.1	10.3	9.9	4.3	5.2	7.5	6.3
GRAND TOTAL	6.0	7.0	10.2	9.8	4.4	5.1	7.3	6.1
	INDIGENOUS AREAS				ALL PANAMA			
	XP	AP	NP*	TOT	XP	AP	NP	TOT
Male by Age Group								
12-17 years	4.2	4.2	6.4	4.3	4.9	5.5	7.6	6.7
18-24 years	5.0	5.1	5.7	5.1	5.7	6.4	10.4	8.9
25-39 years	5.0	5.1	8.0	5.2	5.7	6.9	10.6	9.4
>40 years	1.9	2.0	5.3	2.1	2.7	3.3	8.5	7.0
Female by Age Group								
12-17 years	3.7	3.9	7.2	4.0	4.9	5.9	7.8	7.0
18-24 years	3.3	3.7	6.1	3.8	4.8	6.6	11.3	9.8
25-39 years	2.8	2.9	8.3	3.4	4.7	6.5	11.5	9.9
>40 years	0.6	0.8	5.0	0.8	1.9	3.0	8.5	7.1
Total by Age Group								
12-17 years	4.0	4.1	6.8	4.2	4.9	5.7	7.7	6.8
18-24 years	4.2	4.4	5.9	4.5	5.3	6.5	10.9	9.3
25-39 years	3.8	3.9	8.3	4.2	5.2	6.7	11.1	9.7
>40 years	1.3	1.4	5.2	1.5	2.3	3.2	8.5	7.1
Total, All Age Groups								
Male	3.8	3.9	6.6	4.0	4.4	5.2	9.3	7.9
Female	2.5	2.6	7.6	2.9	3.8	5.2	9.7	8.3
GRAND TOTAL	3.2	3.3	7.1	3.5	4.1	5.2	9.5	8.1

Table A4.16 CONT'D - EDUCATIONAL ATTAINMENT (average number of years of schooling for those age 12+)

	Q1	Q2	Q3	Q4	Q5
			BY QUINTILE		
Male by Age Group					
12-17 years	4.9	6.4	7.1	7.8	8.1
18-24 years	5.7	7.5	9.1	10.5	12.0
25-39 years	5.8	7.7	8.8	10.7	13.0
>40 years	2.8	4.1	5.9	7.9	11.1
Female by Age Group					
12-17 years	5.0	7.0	7.5	8.0	8.1
18-24 years	4.9	8.3	10.3	11.5	12.1
25-39 years	4.7	8.2	9.8	11.7	13.2
>40 years	2.0	3.9	5.8	7.8	10.8
Total by Age Group					
12-17 years	5.0	6.7	7.3	7.9	8.1
18-24 years	5.4	7.9	9.7	11.1	12.1
25-39 years	5.3	7.9	9.3	11.2	13.1
>40 years	2.4	4.0	5.9	7.8	10.9
Total, All Age Groups					
Male	4.5	6.2	7.6	9.0	11.4
Female	3.9	6.5	8.0	9.6	11.3
GRAND TOTAL	4.2	6.3	7.8	9.3	11.3

Panama LSMS 1997; XP = Extreme Poor; AP = All Poor (includes extreme poor); NP = Non-Poor; TOT = Total
* Very small sample; results should be treated with caution

Table A4.17 - NET ENROLLMENT RATES, by Education Level

	URBAN AREAS				RURAL AREAS			
	XP	AP	NP	TOT	XP	AP	NP	TOT
Pre-Kinder (age cohort = 3-4)								
Male	0%	5%	13%	11%	3%	4%	12%	6%
Female	0%	6%	11%	10%	3%	3%	4%	3%
Total	0%	5%	12%	11%	3%	3%	8%	5%
Pre-Primary (kinder age cohort = 5)								
Male	22%	44%	77%	66%	10%	25%	54%	35%
Female	21%	49%	71%	67%	11%	21%	52%	30%
Total	21%	46%	73%	67%	11%	23%	53%	32%
Primary (age cohort = 6-11)								
Male	83%	92%	94%	93%	92%	92%	96%	93%
Female	84%	93%	95%	95%	91%	91%	94%	92%
Total	83%	92%	94%	94%	91%	91%	95%	93%
Secondary (age cohort = 12-17)								
Male	35%	59%	86%	81%	15%	29%	69%	43%
Female	34%	61%	84%	80%	27%	46%	77%	58%
Total	34%	60%	85%	80%	20%	37%	73%	50%
Higher Education (age cohort = 18-24)								
Male	4%	6%	31%	27%	1%	1%	11%	5%
Female	5%	8%	38%	34%	1%	2%	25%	12%
Total	4%	7%	35%	31%	1%	2%	18%	8%

Table A4.17 CONT'D - NET ENROLLMENT RATES, by Education Level

	INDIGENOUS AREAS				ALL PANAMA			
	XP	AP	NP*	TOT	XP	AP	NP	TOT
Pre-Kinder (age cohort = 3-4)								
Male	0%	0%	0%	0%	1%	3%	13%	7%
Female	0%	1%	0%	1%	2%	3%	10%	7%
Total	0%	1%	0%	1%	2%	3%	11%	7%
Pre-Primary (kinder age cohort = 5)								
Male	7%	13%	32%	14%	10%	27%	69%	45%
Female	12%	16%	100%	18%	12%	25%	67%	47%
Total	9%	14%	49%	16%	11%	26%	68%	46%
Primary (age cohort = 6-11)								
Male	82%	83%	100%	83%	87%	90%	94%	92%
Female	81%	83%	82%	83%	87%	90%	95%	92%
Total	82%	83%	89%	83%	87%	90%	95%	92%
Secondary (age cohort = 12-17)								
Male	16%	16%	78%	18%	17%	32%	81%	59%
Female	13%	16%	61%	17%	22%	43%	82%	66%
Total	15%	16%	70%	18%	19%	37%	82%	62%
Higher Education (age cohort = 18-24)								
Male	0%	0%	0%	0%	1%	2%	27%	17%
Female	0%	1%	18%	1%	1%	3%	35%	25%
Total	0%	0%	7%	1%	1%	3%	31%	21%

Table A4.17 CONT'D - NET ENROLLMENT RATES, by Education Level

	BY QUINTILE				
	Q1	Q2	Q3	Q4	Q5
Pre-Kinder (age cohort = 3-4)					
Male	2%	5%	6%	11%	31%
Female	2%	7%	7%	9%	14%
Total	2%	6%	6%	10%	21%
Pre-Primary (kinder age cohort = 5)					
Male	13%	46%	61%	73%	88%
Female	15%	43%	57%	74%	74%
Total	14%	45%	59%	74%	79%
Primary (age cohort = 6-11)					
Male	87%	93%	96%	95%	90%
Female	87%	93%	95%	94%	95%
Total	87%	93%	96%	95%	92%
Secondary (age cohort = 12-17)					
Male	17%	54%	70%	87%	92%
Female	22%	68%	79%	85%	84%
Total	19%	61%	75%	86%	88%
Higher Education (age cohort = 18-24)					
Male	1%	4%	10%	25%	53%
Female	1%	6%	18%	36%	53%
Total	1%	5%	14%	31%	53%

Panama LSMS 1997; XP = Extreme Poor; AP = All Poor (includes extreme poor); NP = Non-Poor; TOT = Total
* Very small sample; results should be treated with caution
Net enrollment rates are calculated as: number of individuals of expected age cohort who are enrolled
   in school level / number of individuals of expected age cohort

Table A4.18 - REASONS FOR NOT ATTENDING SCHOOL - PRIMARY AGE GROUP

	URBAN AREAS				RURAL AREAS			
	XP	AP	NP	TOT	XP	AP	NP	TOT
TOTAL SAMPLE SIZE: # not attending	6	12	3	15	25	35	1	36
PRIMARY AGE - All kids aged 6-11								
Age								
Lack of Money	31%	25%		19%	40%	41%		40%
Work					5%	4%		4%
Domestic duties					4%	3%		3%
Not interested								
Sickness		23%		17%	12%	17%	100%	19%
Distance/transport					3%	5%		5%
Lack of class space	53%	27%		20%				
Lack of special facilities					23%	22%		21%
Other	16%	26%	100%	44%	14%	9%		9%
Group Total	100%	100%	100%	100%	100%	100%	100%	100%
PRIMARY AGE - Girls aged 6-11								
Age								
Lack of Money		26%		26%	41%	38%		36%
Work					8%	7%		6%
Domestic duties					6%	5%		5%
Not interested								
Sickness					18%	25%	100%	29%
Distance/transport						5%		5%
Lack of class space	100%	24%		24%				
Lack of special facilities					11%	9%		8%
Other		49%		49%	15%	12%		11%
Group Total	100%	100%		100%	100%	100%	100%	100%
PRIMARY AGE - Boys aged 6-11								
Lack of Money	38%	25%		16%	38%	45%		45%
Not interested								
Sickness		35%		23%		6%		6%
Distance/transport					8%	5%		5%
Lack of class space	43%	28%		19%				
Lack of special facilities					43%	38%		38%
Other	19%	13%	100%	42%	11%	6%		6%
Group Total	100%	100%	100%	100%	100%	100%		100%

Panama LSMS 1997; XP = Extreme Poor; AP = All Poor (includes extreme poor); NP = Non-Poor; TOT = Total
Small sample in many categories; results should be interpreted with caution.

Table A4.18 CONT'D - REASONS FOR NOT ATTENDING SCHOOL - PRIMARY AGE GROUP

	INDIGENOUS AREAS				ALL PANAMA			
	XP	AP	NP*	TOT	XP	AP	NP	TOT
TOTAL SAMPLE SIZE: # not attending	69	71	2	73	100	118	6	124
PRIMARY AGE - All kids aged 6-11								
Age	3%	3%		3%	2%	1%		1%
Lack of Money	49%	49%	62%	50%	44%	43%	15%	41%
Work					2%	1%		1%
Domestic duties					1%	1%		1%
Not interested	12%	13%		12%	7%	6%		6%
Sickness	2%	2%	38%	3%	5%	10%	22%	11%
Distance/transport	7%	7%		7%	5%	5%		5%
Lack of class space					5%	4%		4%
Lack of special facilities	1%	1%		1%	8%	9%		8%
Other	27%	26%		25%	22%	20%	63%	23%
Group Total	100%	100%	100%	100%	100%	100%	100%	100%
PRIMARY AGE - Girls aged 6-11								
Age	6%	6%		6%	4%	3%		3%
Lack of Money	31%	31%	62%	34%	35%	34%	40%	34%
Work					3%	3%		3%
Domestic duties					3%	2%		2%
Not interested	16%	16%		15%	9%	8%		7%
Sickness			38%	3%	8%	11%	60%	14%
Distance/transport	10%	10%		9%	5%	6%		6%
Lack of class space					3%	3%		2%
Lack of special facilities					5%	4%		4%
Other	37%	37%		34%	27%	27%		26%
Group Total	100%	100%	100%	100%	100%	100%	100%	100%
PRIMARY AGE - Boys aged 6-11								
Lack of money	63%	63%		63%	54%	51%		47%
Not interested	8%	10%		10%	5%	5%		5%
Sickness	3%	3%		3%	2%	9%		8%
Distance/transport	5%	5%		5%	5%	4%		4%
Lack of class space					6%	5%		5%
Lack of special facilities	3%	2%		2%	11%	13%		12%
Other	19%	18%		18%	17%	13%	100%	20%
Group Total	100%	100%		100%	100%	100%	100%	100%

Panama LSMS 1997; XP = Extreme Poor; AP = All Poor (includes extreme poor); NP = Non-Poor; TOT = Total
Small sample in many categories; results should be interpreted with caution.

Table A4.18 CONT'D - REASONS FOR NOT ATTENDING SCHOOL - PRIMARY AGE GROUP

	BY QUINTILE				
	Q1	Q2	Q3	Q4	Q5
TOTAL SAMPLE SIZE: # not attending	100	19	4		1
PRIMARY AGE - All kids aged 6-11					
Age	2%				
Lack of Money	44%	34%	28%		
Work	2%				
Domestic duties	1%				
Not interested	7%	4%			
Sickness	5%	30%	42%		
Distance/transport	5%	4%			
Lack of class space	5%				
Lack of special facilities	8%	11%			
Other	22%	18%	30%		100%
Group Total	100%	100%	100%		100%
PRIMARY AGE - Girls aged 6-11					
Age	4%				
Lack of Money	35%	30%	40%		
Work	3%				
Domestic duties	3%				
Not interested	9%				
Sickness	8%	28%	60%		
Distance/transport	5%	12%			
Lack of class space	3%				
Lack of special facilities	5%				
Other	27%	31%			
Group Total	100%	100%	100%		
PRIMARY AGE - Boys aged 6-11					
Lack of money	54%	37%			
Not interested	5%	6%			
Sickness	2%	31%			
Distance/transport	5%				
Lack of class space	6%				
Lack of special facilities	11%	17%			
Other	17%	10%	100%		100%
Group Total	100%	100%	100%		100%

Panama LSMS 1997; XP = Extreme Poor; AP = All Poor (includes extreme poor); NP = Non-Poor; TOT = Total
Small sample in many categories; results should be interpreted with caution.

Table A4.19 - REASONS FOR NOT ATTENDING SCHOOL - SECONDARY AGE GROUP

	URBAN AREAS				RURAL AREAS			
	XP	AP	NP	TOT	XP	AP	NP	TOT
TOTAL SAMPLE SIZE: # not attending	26	48	65	113	202	316	70	386
SECONDARY AGE - All kids aged 12-17								
Age			1%	1%	3%	2%		1%
Lack of money	66%	49%	23%	33%	64%	57%	44%	55%
Work			20%	12%	8%	7%	7%	7%
Domestic duties			1%	1%	1%	2%		2%
Finished studies		2%		1%	1%	1%	4%	1%
Not interested	17%	24%	25%	25%	13%	18%	27%	20%
Sickness	4%	2%	3%	2%	2%	2%		1%
Distance/transport					3%	4%	3%	4%
Pregnancy		4%	9%	7%	3%	2%	3%	2%
Lack of class space						1%	4%	1%
Lack of special facilities		4%	1%	2%	1%	1%	1%	1%
Had to repeat	4%	2%	4%	3%	1%	1%	4%	2%
Other	8%	13%	13%	13%	2%	2%	4%	3%
Group Total	100%	100%	100%	100%	100%	100%	100%	100%
SECONDARY AGE - Girls aged 12-17								
Age			1%	1%	6%	4%		3%
Lack of Money	92%	67%	26%	40%	59%	57%	46%	55%
Work			26%	17%	5%	4%		3%
Domestic duties			2%	2%	3%	5%		4%
Finished studies					1%	1%	6%	2%
Not interested		8%	14%	12%	10%	10%	20%	12%
Sickness					2%	2%		2%
Distance/transport					3%	5%	3%	5%
Pregnancy		8%	14%	12%	8%	6%	7%	6%
Lack of class space						1%	4%	1%
Lack of special facilities		8%	2%	4%	1%	2%	3%	2%
Had to repeat	8%	4%	2%	3%		1%	7%	2%
Other		4%	12%	9%	3%	3%	4%	3%
Group Total	100%	100%	100%	100%	100%	100%	100%	100%
SECONDARY AGE - Boys aged 12-17								
Age					1%	1%		0%
Lack of money	39%	29%	20%	24%	66%	58%	43%	55%
Work			11%	6%	10%	8%	11%	9%
Finished studies		4%		2%	0%	1%	2%	1%
Not interested	36%	40%	42%	41%	14%	23%	31%	25%
Sickness	9%	5%	7%	6%	2%	1%		1%
Distance/transport					3%	3%	2%	3%
Lack of class space						1%	4%	1%
Lack of special facilities					2%	1%		1%
Had to repeat			7%	4%	2%	2%	2%	2%
Other	16%	22%	14%	17%	1%	2%	4%	3%
Group Total	100%	100%	100%	100%	100%	100%	100%	100%

Panama LSMS 1997; XP = Extreme Poor; AP = All Poor (includes extreme poor); NP = Non-Poor; TOT = Total
Small sample in many categories; results should be interpreted with caution.

Table A4.19 CONT'D - REASONS FOR NOT ATTENDING SCHOOL - SECONDARY AGE GROUP

	INDIGENOUS AREAS				ALL PANAMA			
	XP	AP	NP*	TOT	XP	AP	NP	TOT
TOTAL SAMPLE SIZE: # not attending	188	196	4	200	416	560	139	699
SECONDARY AGE - All kids aged 12-17								
Age	9%	10%		9%	5%	4%	1%	3%
Lack of money	49%	46%	44%	46%	59%	53%	33%	48%
Work	3%	2%		2%	5%	5%	14%	7%
Domestic duties	5%	5%		4%	2%	2%	1%	2%
Finished studies	2%	2%		2%	1%	1%	2%	1%
Not interested	18%	19%	56%	20%	15%	19%	27%	21%
Sickness	2%	2%		2%	2%	2%	1%	2%
Distance/transport		1%		1%	2%	3%	1%	2%
Pregnancy	1%	2%		2%	2%	3%	6%	3%
Lack of class space						0%	2%	1%
Lack of special facilities					1%	1%	1%	1%
Had to repeat	1%	1%		1%	1%	1%	4%	2%
Other	11%	11%		11%	5%	6%	9%	7%
Group Total	100%	100%	100%	100%	100%	100%	100%	100%
SECONDARY AGE - Girls aged 12-17								
Age	6%	6%		6%	5%	4%	1%	3%
Lack of money	46%	43%	28%	43%	56%	54%	32%	48%
Work	2%	2%		2%	3%	3%	17%	7%
Domestic duties	9%	9%		9%	5%	6%	1%	4%
Finished studies	1%	1%		1%	1%	1%	2%	1%
Not interested	22%	21%	72%	22%	14%	13%	17%	15%
Sickness	2%	2%		2%	2%	2%		1%
Distance/transport		1%		1%	2%	3%	1%	3%
Pregnancy	2%	5%		4%	4%	6%	12%	8%
Lack of class space						1%	1%	1%
Lack of special facilities					1%	2%	2%	2%
Had to repeat					1%	1%	4%	2%
Other	10%	11%		11%	6%	6%	9%	7%
Group Total	100%	100%	100%	100%	100%	100%	100%	100%
SECONDARY AGE - Boys aged 12-17								
Age	13%	13%		13%	4%	3%		3%
Lack of money	52%	49%	100%	50%	60%	53%	33%	49%
Work	3%	3%		3%	7%	6%	11%	7%
Finished studies	3%	3%		3%	1%	2%	1%	2%
Not interested	14%	17%		17%	16%	23%	36%	26%
Sickness	1%	1%		1%	2%	1%	3%	2%
Distance/transport					2%	2%	1%	2%
Lack of class space						0%	2%	1%
Lack of special facilities					1%	1%		1%
Had to repeat	2%	2%		2%	2%	2%	4%	2%
Other	12%	12%		11%	5%	6%	9%	7%
Group Total	100%	100%	100%	100%	100%	100%	100%	100%

Panama LSMS 1997; XP = Extreme Poor; AP = All Poor (includes extreme poor); NP = Non-Poor; TOT = Total
Small sample in many categories; results should be interpreted with caution.

Table A4.19 CONT'D - REASONS FOR NOT ATTENDING SCHOOL - SECONDARY AGE GROUP

	BY QUINTILE				
	Q1	Q2	Q3	Q4	Q5
TOTAL SAMPLE SIZE: # not attending	436	137	72	35	19
SECONDARY AGE - All kids aged 12-17					
Age	5%	1%		2%	
Lack of money	60%	35%	39%	31%	23%
Work	5%	3%	10%	7%	43%
Domestic duties	2%	2%	2%		
Finished studies	1%	3%	1%		
Not interested	14%	33%	27%	31%	14%
Sickness	2%	1%		3%	4%
Distance/transport	2%	4%	2%		
Pregnancy	2%	5%	3%	10%	7%
Lack of class space		1%	3%		
Lack of special facilities	1%	2%	1%	3%	
Had to repeat	1%	2%	4%	5%	
Other	5%	8%	9%	9%	8%
Group Total	100%	100%	100%	100%	100%
SECONDARY AGE - Girls aged 12-17					
Age	5%			4%	
Lack of money	58%	40%	41%	28%	28%
Work	3%	2%		14%	46%
Domestic duties	6%	5%	4%		
Finished studies	1%	3%			
Not interested	13%	14%	23%	16%	12%
Sickness	2%	2%			
Distance/transport	2%	6%	3%		
Pregnancy	4%	13%	6%	20%	9%
Lack of class space		2%	3%		
Lack of special facilities	1%	6%	3%	5%	
Had to repeat	1%	4%	3%	6%	
Other	5%	5%	15%	7%	6%
Group Total	100%	100%	100%	100%	100%
SECONDARY AGE - Boys aged 12-17					
Age	4%	1%			
Lack of money	61%	32%	37%	34%	
Work	7%	4%	17%		27%
Finished studies	1%	3%	2%		
Not interested	15%	46%	29%	46%	25%
Sickness	2%			5%	25%
Distance/transport	2%	3%	2%		
Lack of class space		1%	4%		
Lack of special facilities	1%				
Had to repeat	2%	1%	5%	4%	
Other	5%	10%	5%	11%	22%
Group Total	100%	100%	100%	100%	100%

Panama LSMS 1997; XP = Extreme Poor; AP = All Poor (includes extreme poor); NP = Non-Poor; TOT = Total
Small sample in many categories; results should be interpreted with caution.

Table A4.20 - NUMBER OF STUDENTS IN SCHOOL, BY LEVEL AND TYPE OF FACILITY (PUBLIC OR PRIVATE)

	URBAN AREAS				RURAL AREAS			
	XP	AP	NP	TOT	XP	AP	NP	TOT
PUBLIC SCHOOLS								
Pre-Kinder	.	633	3,167	3,800	884	1,334	957	2,291
Pre-Primary (Kinder)	845	3,860	11,079	14,939	1,522	5,634	4,591	10,225
Primary	8,756	41,035	102,912	143,947	61,166	109,014	44,542	153,555
Secondary	3,233	21,736	105,186	126,921	9,595	35,751	39,888	75,639
Higher Education	387	3,475	72,427	75,902	204	1,385	10,589	11,974
PRIVATE SCHOOLS								
Pre-Kinder	.	291	3,312	3,603	.	247	581	827
Pre-Primary (Kinder)	.	339	9,156	9,496	105	238	584	822
Primary	.	.	36,145	36,145	559	1,146	3,258	4,404
Secondary	.	932	44,378	45,309	328	1,093	3,498	4,591
Higher Education	.	.	23,516	23,516	.	417	1,516	1,933
ALL SCHOOLS								
Pre-Kinder	.	924	6,479	7,403	884	1,580	1,538	3,118
Pre-Primary (Kinder)	845	4,199	20,235	24,434	1,626	5,872	5,175	11,047
Primary	8,756	41,035	139,057	180,093	61,725	110,160	47,800	157,960
Secondary	3,233	22,667	149,563	172,231	9,923	36,844	43,387	80,230
Higher Education	387	3,475	95,943	99,418	204	1,802	12,104	13,906

	INDIGENOUS AREAS				ALL PANAMA			
	XP	AP	NP*	TOT	XP	AP	NP	TOT
PUBLIC SCHOOLS								
Pre-Kinder	222	291	.	291	1,106	2,258	4,124	6,382
Pre-Primary (Kinder)	1,270	1,647	139	1,786	3,637	11,141	15,809	26,950
Primary	39,898	43,458	1,575	45,033	109,820	193,507	149,029	342,535
Secondary	4,966	5,811	1,046	6,857	17,794	63,298	146,120	209,417
Higher Education	.	75	69	145	591	4,935	83,085	88,020
PRIVATE SCHOOLS								
Pre-Kinder	.	.	.	.	.	537	3,893	4,430
Pre-Primary (Kinder)	.	.	.	.	105	577	9,740	10,318
Primary	1,021	1,021	.	1,021	1,580	2,167	39,404	41,571
Secondary	109	109	.	109	437	2,134	47,876	50,010
Higher Education	.	.	.	.	.	417	25,031	25,448
ALL SCHOOLS								
Pre-Kinder	222	291	.	291	1,106	2,795	8,017	10,812
Pre-Primary (Kinder)	1,270	1,647	139	1,786	3,741	11,718	25,550	37,267
Primary	40,919	44,479	1,575	46,054	111,400	195,674	188,432	384,106
Secondary	5,076	5,920	1,046	6,966	18,231	65,431	193,996	259,427
Higher Education	.	75	69	145	591	5,352	108,116	113,468

	BY QUINTILE				
	Q1	Q2	Q3	Q4	Q5
PUBLIC SCHOOLS					
Pre-Kinder	1,224	1,517	1,970	1,249	421
Pre-Primary (Kinder)	4,330	7,608	6,686	6,621	1,706
Primary	115,436	89,462	75,767	47,182	14,688
Secondary	18,964	50,057	58,549	58,202	23,644
Higher Education	903	4,847	13,394	31,015	37,860
PRIVATE SCHOOLS					
Pre-Kinder	.	537	102	900	2,891
Pre-Primary (Kinder)	105	600	1,326	2,454	5,833
Primary	1,580	587	3,572	10,932	24,899
Secondary	437	2,188	5,418	10,931	31,036
Higher Education	.	521	1,606	4,207	19,114
ALL SCHOOLS					
Pre-Kinder	1,224	2,054	2,073	2,149	3,313
Pre-Primary (Kinder)	4,434	8,208	8,012	9,075	7,539
Primary	117,016	90,049	79,339	58,115	39,587
Secondary	19,401	52,245	63,967	69,133	54,681
Higher Education	903	5,368	15,001	35,223	56,974

Panama LSMS 1997; XP = Extreme Poor; AP = All Poor (includes extreme poor); NP = Non-Poor; TOT = Total
* Very small sample; results should be treated with caution

Table A4.21 - NUMBER OF PERSONS BY SCHOOL AGE LEVEL (whether in school or not)

	URBAN AREAS				RURAL AREAS			
	XP	AP	NP	TOT	XP	AP	NP	TOT
Age: 3-4 years (pre-kinder age cohort)	2,808	11,005	39,181	50,186	19,525	35,351	12,137	47,488
Age: 5 (kinder age cohort)	1,316	6,374	20,225	26,599	8,591	16,093	7,103	23,196
Age: 6-11 (primary age cohort)	8,793	37,979	137,248	175,227	53,603	98,566	45,014	143,579
Age: 12-17 (secondary age cohort)	7,509	32,619	145,621	178,239	43,587	87,504	50,326	137,831
Age: 18-24 (higher ed. age cohort)	6,096	30,047	168,432	198,479	29,938	64,471	43,982	108,453

	INDIGENOUS AREAS				ALL PANAMA			
	XP	AP	NP*	TOT	XP	AP	NP	TOT
Age: 3-4 years (pre-kinder age cohort)	11,726	12,794	341	13,135	34,059	59,149	51,659	110,809
Age: 5 (kinder age cohort)	6,088	6,679	283	6,963	15,994	29,146	27,612	56,757
Age: 6-11 (primary age cohort)	35,936	38,795	1,684	40,479	98,332	175,340	183,945	359,285
Age: 12-17 (secondary age cohort)	30,819	33,137	1,377	34,514	81,915	153,260	197,324	350,584
Age: 18-24 (higher ed. age cohort)	19,360	22,510	994	23,504	55,394	117,028	213,409	330,437

	BY QUINTILE				
	Q1	Q2	Q3	Q4	Q5
Age: 3-4 years (pre-kinder age cohort)	35,727	27,006	18,607	17,721	11,748
Age: 5 (kinder age cohort)	17,391	13,248	10,462	9,724	5,933
Age: 6-11 (primary age cohort)	103,251	82,855	74,926	57,878	40,376
Age: 12-17 (secondary age cohort)	86,040	75,046	69,525	67,399	52,574
Age: 18-24 (higher ed. age cohort)	59,210	66,961	68,161	72,615	63,490

Panama LSMS 1997; XP = Extreme Poor; AP = All Poor (includes extreme poor); NP = Non-Poor; TOT = Total
* Very small sample; results should be treated with caution
Table includes total number of people by age group (whether in school or not)

Table A4.22 - Incidence of Spending on Education, by Poverty Group and Quintile

	ALL PANAMA				BY QUINTILE				
	XP	AP	NP	TOT	Q1	Q2	Q3	Q4	Q5
Incidence of Public Spending									
Pre-Primary (Kinder) (unit cost = B./374 per student)									
Public Spending ('000)	1,360	4,167	5,913	10,079	1,619	2,845	2,500	2,476	638
Percent of total public spending	13%	41%	59%	100%	16%	28%	25%	25%	6%
Primary (unit cost = B./374 per student)									
Public Spending ('000)	41,073	72,372	55,737	128,108	43,173	33,459	28,337	17,646	5,493
Percent of total public spending	32%	56%	44%	100%	34%	26%	22%	14%	4%
Secondary (unit cost = B./872 per student)									
Public Spending ('000)	15,516	55,196	127,417	182,612	16,537	43,650	51,055	50,752	20,618
Percent of total public spending	8%	30%	70%	100%	9%	24%	28%	28%	11%
Higher Education (unit cost = B./2142 per student)									
Public Spending ('000)	1,267	10,571	177,968	188,539	1,935	10,383	28,690	66,434	81,096
Percent of total public spending	1%	6%	94%	100%	1%	6%	15%	35%	43%
Total Public Spending (excludes spending on other types of education)									
Public Spending ('000)	59,216	142,306	367,034	509.338	63,264	90,337	110,582	137,309	107,845
Percent of total public spending	12%	28%	72%	100%	12%	18%	22%	27%	21%
Incidence of Household Spending									
Per capita (from cons. patterns)	16	32	153	108	16	50	84	132	255
Number of people	514,839	1,020,158	1,712,158	2,732,316	546,463	546,463	546,463	546,463	546463
Total (B./ '000)	8,237	32,645	261,960	295,090	8,907	27,159	46,121	72,133	139,348
Percent of total household spending	3%	11%	89%	100%	3%	9%	16%	24%	47%
Incidence of Total Spending on Education (Public + Household)									
Total (B./ '000)	67,453	174,951	628,994	804,428	72,171	117,496	156,703	209,442	247,193
Percent of total spending	8%	22%	78%	100%	9%	15%	19%	26%	31%
Reference: % Pop. Aged 5-24	23%	43%	57%	100%	24%	22%	20%	19%	15%

Panama LSMS 1997; XP = Extreme Poor; AP = All Poor (includes extreme poor); NP = Non-Poor; TOT = Total
Unit costs from MIPPE: Dirección de Presupuesto de la Nación; MINEDUC.
Public incidence figures calculated from Table A4.20. Household spending on education from Table A4.1

Table A4.23 - INTERNAL EFFICIENCY - REPETITION RATES: % of kids in school who report repeating current grade

	URBAN AREAS				RURAL AREAS			
	XP	AP	NP	TOT	XP	AP	NP	TOT
Repeating Primary - TOTAL	20%	10%	4%	6%	10%	8%	4%	7%
Male	17%	10%	4%	5%	14%	11%	4%	9%
Female	23%	11%	4%	6%	6%	4%	4%	4%
Repeating Secundary - TOTAL	12%	11%	10%	10%	10%	8%	5%	6%
Male	14%	11%	11%	11%	10%	8%	6%	7%
Female	9%	12%	8%	9%	9%	7%	4%	6%

	INDIGENOUS AREAS				ALL PANAMA			
	XP	AP	NP*	TOT	XP	AP	NP	TOT
Repeating Primary - TOTAL	12%	12%	0%	12%	12%	9%	4%	7%
Male	12%	12%	0%	12%	13%	11%	4%	8%
Female	12%	12%	0%	11%	10%	8%	4%	6%
Repeating Secundary - TOTAL	5%	4%	0%	3%	9%	9%	8%	8%
Male	0%	0%	0%	0%	8%	9%	10%	9%
Female	12%	9%	0%	8%	10%	9%	7%	8%

	BY QUINTILE				
	Q1	Q2	Q3	Q4	Q5
Repeating Primary - TOTAL	12%	7%	4%	2%	4%
Male	13%	9%	5%	2%	3%
Female	10%	5%	3%	2%	5%
Repeating Secundary - TOTAL	8%	9%	10%	9%	6%
Male	7%	9%	11%	10%	6%
Female	9%	9%	8%	8%	6%

Panama LSMS 1997; XP = Extreme Poor; AP = All Poor (includes extreme poor); NP = Non-Poor; TOT = Total

* Very small sample; results should be treated with caution

Table A4.24 - AVAILABILITY OF BOOKS: % of kids with books, by level of education

	URBAN AREAS				RURAL AREAS			
	XP	AP	NP	TOT	XP	AP	NP	TOT
Primary	90%	93%	98%	97%	70%	76%	92%	81%
Secondary	83%	91%	96%	95%	83%	88%	94%	91%
	INDIGENOUS AREAS				ALL PANAMA			
	XP	AP	NP*	TOT	XP	AP	NP	TOT
Primary	38%	39%	86%	41%	60%	71%	96%	84%
Secondary	79%	81%	93%	83%	82%	88%	95%	93%
	BY QUINTILE							
	Q1	Q2	Q3	Q4	Q5			
Primary	61%	87%	96%	97%	99%			
Secondary	82%	90%	96%	94%	96%			

Table A4.25 - SOURCES OF BOOKS, For those students with books

	URBAN AREAS				RURAL AREAS			
	XP	AP	NP	TOT	XP	AP	NP	TOT
PRIMARY								
Own, loan, friends	24%	20%	8%	11%	43%	36%	17%	29%
Free: School or Gov. prog.	.	.	1%	1%	11%	7%	2%	5%
Subsidy: School/Gov. prog.	.	.	1%	1%	1%	1%	.	0%
Bought or rented	76%	80%	90%	88%	45%	57%	81%	65%
Group Total	100%	100%	100%	100%	100%	100%	100%	100%
SECONDARY								
Own, loan, friends	41%	30%	21%	22%	53%	44%	26%	34%
Free: School or Gov. prog.	.	2%	1%	1%	2%	0%	1%	1%
Subsidy: School/Gov. prog.	.	.	0%	0%	.	0%	0%	0%
Bought or rented	59%	69%	78%	77%	45%	55%	72%	65%
Group Total	100%	100%	100%	100%	100%	100%	100%	100%
	INDIGENOUS AREAS				ALL PANAMA			
	XP	AP	NP*	TOT	XP	AP	NP	TOT
PRIMARY								
Own, loan, friends	19%	19%	14%	18%	35%	29%	11%	19%
Free: School or Gov. prog.	37%	35%	5%	33%	16%	9%	1%	4%
Subsidy: School/Gov. prog.	1%	1%	.	1%	1%	0%	1%	1%
Bought or rented	44%	46%	81%	48%	48%	62%	88%	77%
Group Total	100%	100%	100%	100%	100%	100%	100%	100%
SECONDARY								
Own, loan, friends	24%	24%	25%	25%	43%	37%	22%	26%
Free: School or Gov. prog.	8%	9%	.	7%	3%	2%	1%	1%
Subsidy: School/Gov. prog.	.	.	. .		.	0%	0%	0%
Bought or rented	69%	67%	75%	68%	54%	61%	77%	73%
Group Total	100%	100%	100%	100%	100%	100%	100%	100%
	BY QUINTILE							
	Q1	Q2	Q3	Q4	Q5			
PRIMARY								
Own, loan, friends	36%	22%	17%	6%	4%			
Free: School or Gov. prog.	15%	2%	1%	0%	2%			
Subsidy: School/Gov. prog.	1%			0%	2%			
Bought or rented	49%	76%	82%	94%	92%			
Group Total	100%	100%	100%	100%	100%			
SECONDARY								
Own, loan, friends	44%	35%	27%	24%	14%			
Free: School or Gov. prog.	3%	1%	1%	1%	2%			
Subsidy: School/Gov. prog.		0%	0%	0%	1%			
Bought or rented	54%	64%	73%	75%	84%			
Group Total	100%	100%	100%	100%	100%			

Panama LSMS 1997; XP = Extreme Poor; AP = All Poor (includes extreme poor); NP = Non-Poor; TOT = Total
* Very small sample; results should be treated with caution

Table A4.26 - REASONS FOR NOT HAVING BOOKS, for those students who do not have books

| | URBAN AREAS | | | | RURAL AREAS | | | |
	XP	AP	NP	TOT	XP	AP	NP	TOT
PRIMARY								
Not asked for	15%	48%	55%	51%	47%	49%	71%	52%
Lack of money	85%	52%	33%	44%	41%	38%	20%	36%
Use library	.	.	6%	3%	12%	12%	9%	11%
Not available	.	.	6%	3%	.	1%	.	1%
Group Total	100%	100%	100%	100%	100%	100%	100%	100%
SECONDARY								
Not asked for	28%	55%	72%	68%	26%	39%	36%	38%
Lack of money	48%	19%	12%	14%	33%	29%	8%	21%
Use library	24%	27%	16%	19%	41%	32%	57%	41%
Group Total	100%	100%	100%	100%	100%	100%	100%	100%

| | INDIGENOUS AREAS | | | | ALL PANAMA | | | |
	XP	AP	NP*	TOT	XP	AP	NP	TOT
PRIMARY								
Not asked for	25%	25%	100%	26%	34%	38%	66%	41%
Lack of money	70%	70%	.	69%	59%	54%	24%	51%
Use library	5%	5%	.	5%	8%	8%	7%	8%
Not available	.	.	.	.	.	0%	2%	1%
Group Total	100%	100%	100%	100%	100%	100%	100%	100%
SECONDARY								
Not asked for	19%	18%	.	17%	24%	40%	61%	52%
Lack of money	81%	76%	100%	77%	51%	33%	12%	21%
Use library	.	6%	.	6%	25%	27%	28%	27%
Group Total	100%	100%	100%	100%	100%	100%	100%	100%

| | BY QUINTILE | | | | |
	Q1	Q2	Q3	Q4	Q5
PRIMARY					
Not asked for	34%	51%	70%	80%	100%
Lack of money	58%	39%	19%	11%	.
Use library	8%	7%	11%	9%	.
Not available	.	3%	.	.	.
Group Total	100%	100%	100%	100%	100%
SECONDARY					
Not asked for	23%	51%	32%	76%	80%
Lack of money	49%	22%	25%	4%	.
Use library	27%	27%	43%	20%	20%
Group Total	100%	100%	100%	100%	100%

Panama LSMS 1997; XP = Extreme Poor; AP = All Poor (includes extreme poor); NP = Non-Poor; TOT = Total

* Very small sample; results should be treated with caution

Table A4.27 - MEANS OF TRANSPORTATION TO SCHOOL

	URBAN AREAS				RURAL AREAS			
	XP	AP	NP	TOT	XP	AP	NP	TOT
TOTAL (primary & secondary)								
Walk	75%	63%	27%	33%	82%	68%	32%	53%
Bus, Taxi	25%	35%	56%	53%	11%	25%	57%	38%
Car	.	0%	15%	13%	1%	1%	8%	4%
Other	.	3%	1%	1%	6%	6%	3%	5%
Group Total	100%	100%	100%	100%	100%	100%	100%	100%
PRIMARY								
Walk	89%	80%	47%	54%	89%	85%	57%	76%
Bus, Taxi	12%	17%	41%	35%	4%	9%	31%	16%
Car	.	0%	11%	9%	0%	1%	8%	3%
Other	.	3%	2%	2%	6%	6%	5%	6%
Group Total	100%	100%	100%	100%	100%	100%	100%	100%
SECONDARY								
Walk	47%	38%	23%	25%	40%	22%	12%	17%
Bus, Taxi	53%	61%	66%	65%	52%	70%	81%	76%
Car	.	.	10%	9%	1%	2%	6%	4%
Other	.	1%	1%	1%	7%	6%	2%	4%
Group Total	100%	100%	100%	100%	100%	100%	100%	100%

	INDIGENOUS AREAS				ALL PANAMA			
	XP	AP	NP*	TOT	XP	AP	NP	TOT
TOTAL (primary & secondary)								
Walk	96%	95%	65%	94%	87%	72%	28%	44%
Bus, Taxi	2%	3%	32%	5%	9%	23%	56%	45%
Car	0%	0%	3%	0%	0%	1%	14%	9%
Other	2%	2%	.	2%	4%	4%	2%	3%
Group Total	100%	100%	100%	100%	100%	100%	100%	100%
PRIMARY								
Walk	98%	98%	100%	98%	93%	87%	50%	69%
Bus, Taxi	.	.	.		3%	9%	38%	23%
Car	0%	0%	.	0%	0%	0%	10%	5%
Other	2%	2%	.	2%	4%	4%	3%	3%
Group Total	100%	100%	100%	100%	100%	100%	100%	100%
SECONDARY								
Walk	82%	74%	10%	64%	53%	33%	21%	24%
Bus, Taxi	18%	26%	81%	34%	43%	63%	69%	68%
Car	.	.	8%	1%	1%	1%	9%	7%
Other	.	.	.	.	4%	4%	1%	2%
Group Total	100%	100%	100%	100%	100%	100%	100%	100%

Table A4.27 CONT'D - MEANS OF TRANSPORTATION TO SCHOOL

| | BY QUINTILE | | | | |
	Q1	Q2	Q3	Q4	Q5
TOTAL (primary & secondary)					
Walk	86%	57%	43%	28%	10%
Bus, Taxi	10%	37%	52%	61%	59%
Car	0%	1%	3%	10%	31%
Other	4%	5%	2%	1%	1%
Group Total	100%	100%	100%	100%	100%
PRIMARY					
Walk	92%	78%	66%	46%	16%
Bus, Taxi	4%	16%	27%	43%	58%
Car	0%	1%	5%	9%	26%
Other	4%	5%	3%	2%	1%
Group Total	100%	100%	100%	100%	100%
SECONDARY					
Walk	51%	27%	23%	23%	13%
Bus, Taxi	45%	68%	74%	68%	66%
Car	1%	1%	1%	9%	21%
Other	4%	4%	2%	0%	0%
Group Total	100%	100%	100%	100%	100%

Panama LSMS 1997; XP = Extreme Poor; AP = All Poor (includes extreme poor); NP = Non-Poor; TOT = Total
* Very small sample; results should be treated with caution

Table A4.28 - MINUTES TO SCHOOL, Average minutes to school, by level

| | URBAN AREAS | | | | RURAL AREAS | | | |
	XP	AP	NP	TOT	XP	AP	NP	TOT
TOTAL (primary & secondary)	15	20	26	25	24	24	27	25
Primary	12	15	17	16	20	18	15	17
Secondary	21	27	28	28	50	42	34	37

| | INDIGENOUS AREAS | | | | ALL PANAMA | | | |
	XP	AP	NP*	TOT	XP	AP	NP	TOT
TOTAL (primary & secondary)	20	21	28	21	22	22	26	25
Primary	18	18	14	18	19	17	16	17
Secondary	38	44	49	45	42	37	29	31

| | BY QUINTILE | | | | |
	Q1	Q2	Q3	Q4	Q5
TOTAL (primary & secondary)	22	23	23	27	29
Primary	19	16	13	15	23
Secondary	41	34	30	29	28

Panama LSMS 1997; XP = Extreme Poor; AP = All Poor (includes extreme poor); NP = Non-Poor; TOT = Total
* Very small sample; results should be treated with caution

Table A4.29 - Household Spending on Education, Primary Level, by Poverty Group and Area
Students who pay something (B,/>0) as share of all students

	XP	AP	NP	Urban	Rural	Indigenous	TOT
Public							
Fees	42	57	79	83	64	27	67
School Supplies	89	94	100	100	97	81	96
Informal Fees	40	47	63	58	56	36	54
Transport	2	7	28	25	13	0	16
Other	6	10	26	26	12	5	17
Total	91	95	100	100	98	84	97
Private							
Fees	28	37	97	98	83	n.a	94
School Supplies	92	94	99	98	97	n.a	98
Informal Fees	20	36	45	43	63	n.a	44
Transport	0	0	67	69	36	n.a	64
Other	20	15	35	36	20	n.a	34
Total	100	100	100	1	99	n.a	99
All							
Fees	42	57	83	86	64	27	70
School Supplies	89	94	100	100	97	81	97
Informal Fees	40	47	63	55	56	36	53
Transport	2	7	28	34	13	0	21
Other	6	10	26	28	12	5	19
Total	91	95	100	100	98	84	97

Mean Expenditures for All Students (including those who don't pay)

	XP	AP	NP	Urban	Rural	Indigenous	TOT
Public							
Fees	1	2	4	5	2	1	3
School Supplies	26	42	101	116	60	22	78
Informal Fees	3	3	7	6	5	1	5
Transport	1	3	27	23	8	0	13
Other	2	3	11	10	5	1	7
Total	34	58	169	159	80	25	106
Private							
Fees	1	1	571	593	246	n.a	540
School Supplies	14	21	188	271	173	n.a	255
Informal Fees	1	1	13	13	10	n.a	13
Transport	0	0	139	144	54	n.a	131
Other	3	2	37	38	19	n.a	35
Total	19	28	1027	1060	503	n.a	973
All							
Fees	1	2	120	120	9	1	59
School Supplies	26	41	118	146	62	21	99
Informal Fees	2	3	8	7	5	2	6
Transport	1	3	50	47	10	0	26
Other	2	3	16	15	5	1	10
Total	34	57	344	335	92	25	198

Table A4.29 CONT'D - Household Spending on Education, Primary Level, by Poverty Group and Area
Mean Expenditures for Students Who Pay Something (B./>0)

	XP	AP	NP	Urban	Rural	Indigenous	TOT
Public							
Fees	2	4	5	6	3	2	2
School Supplies	29	44	101	116	61	27	81
Informal Fees	4	5	7	9	9	4	11
Transport	27	37	96	90	65	102	121
Other	29	32	44	40	42	23	39
Total	38	61	169	159	82	30	109
Private							
Fees	3	3	586	604	293	n.a	574
School Supplies	15	22	191	276	179	n.a	12
Informal Fees	2	3	14	31	16	n.a	29
Transport	0	0	206	210	149	n.a	206
Other	14	14	104	104	94	n.a	102
Total	19	28	1038	1072	503	n.a	983
All							
Fees	2	4	145	140	13	2	87
School Supplies	29	44	119	146	64	26	100
Informal Fees	4	5	8	13	9	4	11
Transport	27	37	138	138	71	102	121
Other	29	32	59	56	44	22	52
Total	37	61	345	336	94	30	203
Sample Size	XP	AP	NP	Urban	Rural	Indigenous	TOT
Public	1158	1842	1112	1019	1337	598	2954
Private	18	23	231	204	37	13	254
All	1176	1865	1343	1223	1374	611	3208

Panama LSMS 1997; XP = Extreme Poor; AP = All Poor (includes extreme poor); NP = Non-Poor; TOT = Total

Table A4.30 - Household Spending on Education, Secondary Level, by Poverty Group and Area
Students who pay something (B,/>0) as share of all students

	XP	AP	NP	Urban	Rural	Indigenous	TOT
Public							
Fees	92	93	93	92	95	97	93
School Supplies	99	100	100	100	99	100	99
Informal Fees	58	58	55	52	63	50	56
Transport	43	61	65	57	77	36	64
Other	11	16	25	26	15	18	22
Total	100	100	100	100	100	100	100
Private							
Fees	50	90	100	100	95	n.a	96
School Supplies	75	95	98	97	97	n.a	97
Informal Fees	25	48	42	41	57	n.a	43
Transport	75	67	61	60	75	n.a	62
Other	0	17	27	27	21	n.a	27
Total	100	100	100	100	100	n.a	100
All							
Fees	91	93	94	94	95	97	94
School Supplies	98	99	99	99	99	100	99
Informal Fees	58	58	52	49	62	50	53
Transport	44	61	64	58	77	35	63
Other	11	16	25	26	16	18	23
Total	100	100	100	100	100	100	100

Mean Expenditures for All Students (including those who don't pay)

	XP	AP	NP	Urban	Rural	Indigenous	TOT
Public							
Fees	9	13	16	16	14	8	15
School Supplies	64	86	134	157	126	88	144
Informal Fees	6	7	10	9	10	6	9
Transport	39	62	71	54	95	43	68
Other	3	8	20	20	11	17	16
Total	129	192	280	256	256	161	253
Private							
Fees	6	259	606	616	389	n.a	594
School Supplies	45	89	167	244	203	n.a	240
Informal Fees	7	27	14	14	21	n.a	15
Transport	62	99	103	105	117	n.a	106
Other	0	4	33	34	23	n.a	33
Total	127	489	1001	1013	753	n.a	987
All							
Fees	9	21	161	174	36	8	127
School Supplies	63	86	142	181	131	88	163
Informal Fees	6	8	11	10	11	6	10
Transport	40	64	79	67	96	42	76
Other	3	8	23	24	11	16	20
Total	129	201	457	456	284	160	395

Table A4.30 CONT'D - Household Spending on Education, Secondary Level, by Poverty Group and Area
Mean Expenditures for Students Who Pay Something (B./>0)

	XP	AP	NP	Urban	Rural	Indigenous	TOT
Public							
Fees	9	14	17	18	15	8	16
School Supplies	64	86	134	158	127	88	164
Informal Fees	10	13	18	17	13	12	16
Transport	90	102	109	94	123	119	107
Other	28	55	81	76	70	90	75
Total	129	192	280	256	256	161	253
Private							
Fees	12	289	608	618	408	n.a	598
School Supplies	59	93	171	250	208	n.a	246
Informal Fees	29	57	32	34	36	n.a	34
Transport	83	146	169	174	154	n.a	172
Other	0	25	125	124	111	n.a	123
Total	127	489	1001	1013	753	n.a	987
All							
Fees	9	22	171	186	38	8	135
School Supplies	65	86	144	182	131	88	164
Informal Fees	10	14	21	20	20	12	19
Transport	90	104	123	115	125	119	119
Other	28	54	92	90	73	90	86
Total	129	201	458	456	284	160	395
Sample Size							
	XP	AP	NP	Urban	Rural	Indigenous	TOT
Public	171	532	1071	880	638	85	1603
Private	4	17	291	270	39	1	310
All	175	549	1362	1150	677	86	1913

Panama LSMS 1997; XP = Extreme Poor; AP = All Poor (includes extreme poor); NP = Non-Poor; TOT = Total

Table A4.31 - Health Services by Poverty Group, Geographic Area

	URBAN AREAS				RURAL AREAS			
	XP	AP	NP	TOT	XP	AP	NP	TOT
HEALTH VISITS, SICKNESS DURING PAST MONTH								
Consultancy Rate	0.8	1.0	1.2	1.2	0.7	0.8	1.2	1.0
Coverage Rate	0.5	0.5	0.7	0.6	0.4	0.5	0.6	0.5
Concentration rate	1.6	1.8	1.9	1.9	1.9	1.8	1.9	1.8
PLACE OF TREATMENT: PUBLIC VS. PRIVATE FACILITIES								
Public facility	91%	86%	58%	62%	81%	82%	73%	77%
Private facility	9%	14%	42%	38%	19%	18%	27%	23%
PLACE OF TREATMENT: BY TYPE OF FACILITY								
Public Hospital/Clinic	62%	60%	45%	47%	24%	30%	35%	33%
Health Center/Sub-center	28%	26%	14%	15%	56%	52%	37%	44%
Private Hosp./Clinic/Doc	8%	10%	35%	32%	9%	10%	24%	17%
Pharmacist/Other	2%	3%	5%	5%	4%	4%	2%	3%
At home	0%	1%	2%	2%	6%	3%	2%	3%
DISTANCE TO TREATMENT (Average minutes to place of treatment, excluding treatment at home)								
Minutes health facility	29.1	24.8	23.8	24.1	37.9	32.4	39.9	35.4
PRIVATE SPENDING ON HEALTH CARE								
% of sick paying something (B./>0)	63%	61%	73%	71%	62%	64%	71%	67%

	INDIGENOUS AREAS				ALL PANAMA			
	XP	AP	NP*	TOT	XP	AP	NP	TOT
HEALTH VISITS, SICKNESS DURING PAST MONTH								
Consultancy Rate	0.6	0.6	1.0	0.6	0.7	0.8	1.2	1.1
Coverage Rate	0.3	0.3	0.6	0.3	0.4	0.5	0.6	0.6
Concentration rate	2.0	2.0	1.6	2.0	1.9	1.8	1.9	1.9
PLACE OF TREATMENT: PUBLIC VS. PRIVATE FACILITIES								
Public facility	79%	80%	97%	81%	81%	83%	62%	68%
Private facility	21%	20%	3%	19%	19%	17%	38%	32%
PLACE OF TREATMENT: BY TYPE OF FACILITY								
Public Hospital/Clinic	17%	18%	42%	20%	27%	37%	42%	41%
Health Center/Sub-center	62%	62%	55%	61%	55%	46%	20%	27%
Private Hosp./Clinic/Doc	2%	2%	3%	2%	7%	9%	32%	26%
Pharmacist/Other	1%	1%	0%	1%	3%	4%	4%	4%
At home	18%	17%	0%	16%	9%	4%	2%	3%
DISTANCE TO TREATMENT (Average minutes to place of treatment, excluding treatment at home)								
Minutes health facility	39	55	15	52	37	32	27	29
PRIVATE SPENDING ON HEALTH CARE								
% of sick paying something (B./>0)	48%	47%	43%	47%	58%	61%	72%	68%

Panama LSMS 1997; XP = Extreme Poor; AP = All Poor (includes extreme poor); NP = Non-Poor; TOT = Total

* Very small sample; results should be treated with caution

Consultancy Rate = number of visits/number of sick; in other words, the number of visits on average
    for an individual reporting illness

Coverage Rate = number of people with at least one visit/number of sick; in other words the percentage of people
    reporting illness who had at least one medical visit

Concentration rate = number of visits/number of people with at least one visit.

Table A4.32 - HOUSING OWNERSHIP & CONDITIONS

	URBAN AREAS				RURAL AREAS			
	XP	AP	NP	TOT	XP	AP	NP	TOT
HOUSING OWNERSHIP								
TYPE OF DWELLING								
Dwelling: House	74%	71%	70%	70%	60%	73%	90%	82%
Dwelling: Hut	4%	4%	0%	1%	37%	25%	7%	15%
Dwelling: Apartment	4%	8%	21%	19%	1%	1%	2%	1%
Dwelling: Other	18%	17%	9%	10%	2%	2%	1%	1%
TYPE OF OWNERSHIP								
Rent House	6%	8%	21%	19%	2%	2%	4%	3%
Own House	60%	62%	70%	69%	89%	87%	86%	87%
- with registered title	20%	15%	35%	33%	6%	9%	21%	15%
- with title in process	11%	17%	17%	17%	4%	6%	11%	9%
- no title or deed	29%	30%	18%	20%	79%	72%	54%	63%
Other House \a	34%	29%	10%	12%	10%	10%	10%	10%
HOUSING CONDITIONS								
CONDITION OF ROOF								
Roof: Quality 1 \b	92%	95%	96%	96%	77%	83%	95%	89%
Roof: Quality 2 \c	8%	5%	4%	4%	23%	17%	5%	11%
CONDITION OF WALLS								
Walls: Quality 1 \d	58%	69%	92%	90%	20%	36%	70%	54%
Walls: Quality 2 \e	35%	25%	6%	8%	29%	25%	15%	20%
Walls: Quality 3 \f	7%	6%	1%	2%	50%	39%	15%	26%
CONDITION OF FLOOR								
Floor: Quality 1 \g	2%	5%	38%	35%	0%	0%	8%	4%
Floor: Quality 2 \h	68%	73%	56%	57%	35%	50%	75%	63%
Floor: Quality 3 \i	12%	12%	5%	6%	10%	7%	5%	6%
Floor: Quality 4 \j	14%	9%	1%	1%	53%	41%	12%	26%
Floor: Quality 5 \k	4%	1%	1%	1%	2%	1%	1%	1%
NUMBER OF ROOMS (CROWDING)								
Rooms: Total No. \k	2.1	2.6	3.6	3.5	2.4	2.6	3.3	3.0
Rooms: Persons per room \l	4.0	2.9	1.3	1.5	3.1	2.5	1.1	1.8

	INDIGENOUS AREAS				ALL PANAMA			
	XP	AP	NP*	TOT	XP	AP	NP	TOT
HOUSING OWNERSHIP								
TYPE OF DWELLING								
Dwelling: House	19%	23%	66%	27%	49%	65%	75%	72%
Dwelling: Hut	80%	76%	29%	72%	47%	28%	2%	9%
Dwelling: Apartment	1%	1%	0%	1%	1%	3%	15%	12%
Dwelling: Other	0%	0%	5%	0%	3%	5%	7%	6%
TYPE OF OWNERSHIP								
Rent House	0%	1%	18%	2%	2%	3%	16%	13%
Own House	91%	89%	46%	85%	87%	82%	74%	76%
- with registered title	4%	4%	0%	4%	7%	10%	31%	25%
- with title in process	1%	1%	0%	1%	4%	8%	15%	13%
- no title or deed	86%	83%	46%	80%	77%	65%	28%	38%
Other House \a	8%	10%	35%	13%	11%	14%	10%	11%
HOUSING CONDITIONS								
CONDITION OF ROOF								
Roof: Quality 1 \b	33%	37%	67%	39%	65%	78%	95%	91%
Roof: Quality 2 \c	67%	63%	33%	61%	35%	22%	5%	9%
CONDITION OF WALLS								
Walls: Quality 1 \d	5%	7%	39%	10%	19%	39%	86%	73%
Walls: Quality 2 \e	15%	18%	23%	18%	25%	24%	9%	13%
Walls: Quality 3 \f	80%	75%	39%	72%	56%	37%	5%	14%
CONDITION OF FLOOR								
Floor: Quality 1 \g	0%	0%	0%	0%	0%	1%	30%	22%
Floor: Quality 2 \h	7%	10%	47%	13%	29%	49%	61%	58%
Floor: Quality 3 \i	17%	18%	20%	18%	12%	10%	5%	6%
Floor: Quality 4 \j	65%	61%	18%	57%	53%	37%	4%	13%
Floor: Quality 5 \k	11%	11%	14%	12%	5%	3%	1%	1%
NUMBER OF ROOMS (CROWDING)								
Rooms: Total No. \k	1.9	1.9	2.6	2.0	2.2	2.5	3.5	3.2
Rooms: Persons per room \l	4.9	4.6	1.4	4.3	3.7	2.9	1.2	1.7

Panama LSMS 1997; XP = Extreme Poor; AP = All Poor (includes extreme poor); NP = Non-Poor; TOT = Total

* Very small sample; results should be treated with caution

\a House was borrowed, given, used as payment for services, occupied, other. \b Concrete, cement, teja, zinc. \c Concrete-fiber wood, straw, other.

\d Concrete blocks, bricks, stone, concrete, cement. \e Concrete-fiber, wood. \f Sticks, mud, straw, pieces, no walls, others

\g Concrete tile, bricks, granite. \h Concrete, cement. \i Wood. \j Dirt, sand. \k Vinyl, sticks, other \l Excluding kitchen and bathrooms

Table A4.33 - BASIC INFRASTRUCTURE SERVICES (% of households)

	URBAN AREAS				RURAL AREAS			
	XP	AP	NP	TOT	XP	AP	NP	TOT
WATER								
Water: Piped	87%	92%	99%	98%	62%	72%	87%	80%
- Inside house	25%	39%	79%	75%	9%	18%	49%	36%
- In the yard	64%	53%	19%	22%	87%	79%	49%	61%
- Outside property	11%	9%	2%	3%	4%	3%	2%	3%
Water: from well	2%	2%	0%	0%	13%	11%	8%	10%
Water: from river, other	11%	6%	1%	1%	25%	17%	4%	10%
Treat unpiped water \a	14%	9%	12%	11%	13%	18%	30%	22%
Uninterrupted water service \b	63%	65%	75%	74%	35%	45%	59%	52%
SANITATION & GARBAGE COLLECTION								
Toilet: Sewer system/septic tank	41%	44%	84%	80%	3%	6%	33%	21%
Toilet: Latrine or pit	50%	48%	15%	18%	76%	80%	62%	70%
Toilet: None	10%	8%	1%	1%	22%	14%	5%	9%
With trash collection	67%	77%	93%	91%	3%	6%	23%	15%
ENERGY SOURCES								
Lighting: Electricity	81%	92%	99%	98%	22%	38%	75%	58%
Lighting: Candles/gas/fuel	17%	7%	1%	1%	77%	61%	24%	41%
Lighting: Other/nothing	2%	1%	0%	0%	1%	1%	1%	1%
Cooking: Gas, electricity	84%	91%	99%	98%	20%	38%	76%	58%
Cooking: Wood, others	16%	9%	1%	2%	80%	62%	24%	42%

	INDIGENOUS AREAS				ALL PANAMA			
	XP	AP	NP*	TOT	XP	AP	NP	TOT
WATER								
Water: Piped	42%	42%	41%	42%	58%	72%	95%	89%
- Inside house	17%	16%	20%	17%	13%	23%	71%	61%
- In the yard	74%	74%	61%	72%	81%	71%	26%	36%
- Outside property	9%	10%	19%	11%	6%	5%	2%	3%
Water: from well	1%	1%	0%	1%	8%	8%	2%	4%
Water: from river, other	57%	57%	59%	57%	33%	21%	2%	7%
Treat unpiped water \a	3%	3%	22%	5%	9%	13%	26%	17%
Uninterrupted water service \b	24%	23%	13%	22%	34%	46%	70%	64%
SANITATION & GARBAGE COLLECTION								
Toilet: Sewer system/septic tank	6%	8%	31%	10%	7%	15%	70%	55%
Toilet: Latrine or pit	31%	32%	49%	34%	60%	66%	28%	38%
Toilet: None	62%	60%	19%	56%	33%	20%	2%	7%
With trash collection	0%	0%	0%	0%	8%	20%	73%	59%
ENERGY SOURCES								
Lighting: Electricity	7%	7%	18%	8%	23%	45%	92%	79%
Lighting: Candles/gas/fuel	88%	85%	60%	83%	75%	53%	7%	20%
Lighting: Other/nothing	6%	8%	22%	10%	2%	2%	1%	1%
Cooking: Gas, electricity	6%	8%	72%	14%	21%	45%	93%	79%
Cooking: Wood, others	94%	92%	28%	86%	79%	55%	7%	21%

Panama LSMS 1997; XP = Extreme Poor; AP = All Poor (includes extreme poor); NP = Non-Poor; TOT = Total
* Very small sample; results should be treated with caution
\a Boiled or clorinated; % of households who treat water that is obtained from sources other than piped connections
\b % of households with connections to piped water who receive water 30 days/month, 24 hours/day

Table A4.34 - COST RECOVERY FOR WATER

	URBAN AREAS				RURAL AREAS			
	XP	AP	NP	TOT	XP	AP	NP	TOT
Per Household (with HH weights)								
% paying nothing, with connection	58%	44%	16%	18%	25%	19%	12%	15%
Monthly water payments, B./								
All households (HH)	4.0	4.5	11.3	10.6	1.0	1.6	3.4	2.6
All HH paying something (B./ > 0)	11.3	9.1	14.0	13.7	2.2	2.7	4.4	3.7
HH without connections (B./ > 0)	.	5.0	13.1	12.0	2.5	3.4	3.2	3.3
HH with connections (B./ > 0)	11.3	9.1	14.0	13.7	2.2	2.7	4.4	3.7
Per Capita (with individual weights)								
% paying nothing, with connection	56%	41%	14%	18%	23%	18%	11%	15%
Monthly water payments, B./								
All individuals	0.6	0.8	2.9	2.5	0.2	0.3	1.1	0.6
All indiv. paying something (B./ > 0)	1.5	1.4	3.5	3.2	0.4	0.5	1.3	0.9
Without connections (B./>0)	.	1.7	5.3	4.7	0.7	0.9	1.1	1.0
With connections (B./ > 0)	1.5	1.4	3.5	3.2	0.4	0.5	1.3	0.9

	INDIGENOUS AREAS				ALL PANAMA			
	XP	AP	NP*	TOT	XP	AP	NP	TOT
Per Household (with HH weights)								
% paying nothing, with connection	29%	29%	0%	26%	30%	27%	15%	17%
Monthly water payments, B./								
All households (HH)	0.2	0.3	0.3	0.3	1.1	2.0	8.8	6.8
All HH paying something (B./ > 0)	0.8	0.8	0.7	0.8	2.4	3.6	10.9	9.5
HH without connections (B./ > 0)	0.5	0.5	.	0.5	2.2	3.4	6.8	5.4
HH with connections (B./ > 0)	0.8	0.8	0.7	0.8	2.6	3.8	11.1	9.5
Per Capita (with individual weights)								
% paying nothing, with connection	27%	26%	0%	25%	29%	26%	13%	17%
Monthly water payments, B./								
All individuals	0.0	0.0	0.1	0.0	0.2	0.4	2.4	1.6
All indiv. paying something (B./ > 0)	0.1	0.1	0.2	0.1	0.4	0.7	2.9	2.2
Without connections (B./>0)	0.1	0.1	.	0.1	0.5	0.9	2.5	1.7
With connections (B./ > 0)	0.1	0.1	0.2	0.1	0.4	0.7	2.9	2.2

Table A4.35 - COST RECOVERY FOR ELECTRICITY

	URBAN AREAS				RURAL AREAS			
	XP	AP	NP	TOT	XP	AP	NP	TOT
Per Household (with HH weights)								
% paying nothing, with connection	60%	40%	12%	14%	13%	12%	9%	10%
Monthly payments, B./								
All households (HH)	3.3	7.5	27.7	25.7	5.7	7.3	14.5	12.3
All HH paying something (B./ > 0)	8.55	12.7	31.5	30.3	6.57	8.26	16.1	13.7
Per Capita (with individual weights)								
% paying nothing, with connection	57%	37%	10%	14%	12%	12%	9%	10%
Monthly payments								
All individuals	0.5	1.2	7.2	6.3	1.0	1.4	4.1	3.0
All indiv. paying something (B./ > 0)	1.1	1.9	8.1	7.4	1.1	1.6	4.5	3.4

	INDIGENOUS AREAS				ALL PANAMA			
	XP	AP	NP*	TOT	XP	AP	NP	TOT
Per Household (with HH weights)								
% paying nothing, with connection	28%	24%	0%	19%	29%	25%	11%	13%
Monthly payments, B./								
All households (HH)	4.4	4.5	4.6	4.5	4.8	7.3	24.6	21.9
All HH paying something (B./ > 0)	6.0	6.0	4.6	5.6	6.9	9.7	27.9	25.4
Per Capita (with individual weights)								
% paying nothing, with connection	30%	27%	0%	25%	30%	24%	10%	13%
Monthly payments								
All individuals	0.4	0.5	1.4	0.6	0.7	1.3	6.5	5.4
All indiv. paying something (B./ > 0)	0.6	0.7	1.4	0.7	1.0	1.7	7.3	6.2

Panama LSMS 1997; XP = Extreme Poor; AP = All Poor (includes extreme poor); NP = Non-Poor; TOT = Total

* Very small sample; results should be treated with caution

Table A4.36 - Savings by Institution, by Poverty Group and Area

	URBAN AREAS				RURAL AREAS			
	XP	AP	NP	TOT	XP	AP	NP	TOT
SAVES	13%	19%	52%	48%	3%	9%	31%	21%
...In Private Banks	0%	8%	43%	41%	0%	3%	14%	12%
...In the National Bank of Panama	31%	13%	22%	21%	8%	18%	34%	31%
...In 'Caja de ahorros'	64%	58%	39%	40%	63%	48%	41%	42%
...Neighborhood & workers coop.	22%	11%	10%	10%	15%	10%	7%	8%
...Saving & Credit Unions	0%	15%	19%	19%	8%	17%	22%	21%
...Clubs, comercial stores	0%	4%	10%	9%	0%	1%	4%	3%
	INDIGENOUS AREAS				ALL PANAMA			
	XP	AP	NP*	TOT	XP	AP	NP	TOT
SAVES	5%	6%	48%	10%	5%	11%	46%	36%
...In Private Banks	14%	10%	0%	5%	4%	6%	37%	34%
...In the National Bank of Panama	52%	46%	16%	32%	27%	19%	24%	23%
...In 'Caja de ahorros'	21%	34%	39%	36%	50%	51%	40%	40%
...Neighborhood & workers coop.	27%	19%	6%	13%	20%	11%	10%	10%
...Saving & Credit Unions	0%	9%	59%	32%	3%	16%	20%	20%
...Clubs, comercial stores	0%	0%	0%	0%	0%	2%	8%	8%

Panama LSMS 1997; XP = Extreme Poor; AP = All Poor (includes extreme poor); NP = Non-Poor; TOT = Total

* Very small sample; results should be treated with caution

Table A4.37 - Consumer Credit and Uses, by Poverty Group and Area

	URBAN AREAS				RURAL AREAS			
	XP	AP	NP	TOT	XP	AP	NP	TOT
RECEIVED CONSUMPTION CREDIT LAST YEAR	12%	19%	20%	20%	11%	15%	18%	17%
...Bought clothes, shoes	80%	69%	78%	77%	14%	28%	52%	42%
...Bought food	20%	29%	22%	23%	85%	76%	44%	58%
...Bought HH appliances	0%	14%	27%	26%	4%	5%	15%	10%
...Bought other consumption goods	0%	8%	13%	13%	0%	1%	4%	3%
	INDIGENOUS AREAS				ALL PANAMA			
	XP	AP	NP*	TOT	XP	AP	NP	TOT
RECEIVED CONSUMPTION CREDIT LAST YEAR	7%	8%	23%	9%	10%	15%	20%	18%
...Bought cloths, shoes	4%	7%	18%	10%	19%	37%	71%	64%
...Bought food	91%	89%	89%	89%	79%	64%	28%	36%
...Bought HH appliances	5%	4%	0%	3%	4%	7%	24%	20%
...Bought other consumption goods	0%	0%	11%	2%	0%	3%	11%	9%

Panama LSMS 1997; XP = Extreme Poor; AP = All Poor (includes extreme poor); NP = Non-Poor; TOT = Total

* Very small sample; results should be treated with caution

Table A4.38 - Applications for Cash Credit, by Poverty Group, Area

	URBAN AREAS				RURAL AREAS			
	XP	AP	NP	TOT	XP	AP	NP	TOT
APPLIED FOR CASH CREDIT LAST YEAR								
...NO	96%	88%	82%	82%	97%	94%	87%	90%
...YES	4%	12%	18%	18%	3%	6%	13%	10%
TOTAL	100%	100%	100%	100%	100%	100%	100%	100%
WHY DID NOT APPLY FOR CASH CREDIT?								
..Does not need it	3%	11%	43%	40%	4%	8%	24%	16%
..Too risky	28%	30%	28%	28%	57%	54%	46%	50%
..To much paper work	7%	16%	12%	13%	14%	15%	14%	14%
..Fear of rejection	33%	24%	8%	10%	21%	19%	13%	16%
Other	28%	18%	9%	10%	4%	5%	4%	4%
TOTAL	100%	100%	100%	100%	100%	100%	100%	100%
WAS THE CREDIT APPROVED?								
...NO		7%	4%	5%	9%	6%	6%	6%
...YES	100%	93%	96%	95%	91%	94%	94%	94%
TOTAL	100%	100%	100%	100%	100%	100%	100%	100%
IF YES, WAS THE QUANTITY ENOUGH?	45%	49%	71%	70%	32%	58%	62%	61%
IF NO, WHY WAS CASH CREDIT REFUSED?								
..No collateral		52%	5%	9%	100%	32%	38%	36%
..No land title		48%		5%		39%	12%	20%
..Low income			40%	36%			12%	8%
..Other			55%	50%		29%	39%	36%
TOTAL		100%	100%	100%	100%	100%	100%	100%

	INDIGENOUS AREAS				ALL PANAMA			
	XP	AP	NP*	TOT	XP	AP	NP	TOT
APPLIED FOR CASH CREDIT LAST YEAR								
...NO	96%	95%	83%	94%	97%	93%	83%	86%
...YES	4%	5%	17%	6%	3%	7%	17%	14%
TOTAL	100%	100%	100%	100%	100%	100%	100%	100%
WHY DID NOT APPLY FOR CASH CREDIT?								
..Does not need it	4%	7%	38%	9%	4%	8%	38%	29%
..Too risky	46%	44%	38%	44%	51%	48%	33%	37%
..To much paper work	13%	12%	10%	12%	13%	15%	13%	13%
..Fear of rejection	27%	27%	6%	25%	24%	21%	9%	13%
Other	10%	11%	8%	10%	8%	8%	7%	8%
TOTAL	100%	100%	100%	100%	100%	100%	100%	100%
WAS THE CREDIT APPROVED?								
...NO	22%	15%		11%	13%	7%	5%	5%
...YES	78%	85%	100%	89%	87%	93%	95%	95%
TOTAL	100%	100%	100%	100%	100%	100%	100%	100%
IF YES, WAS THE QUANTITY ENOUGH?	26%	49%	100%	63%	32%	54%	69%	67%
IF NO, WHY WAS CASH CREDIT REFUSED?								
..No collateral					40%	31%	13%	17%
..No land title						33%	3%	9%
..Low income	67%	67%		67%	40%	15%	33%	29%
..Other	33%	33%		33%	20%	21%	51%	45%
TOTAL	100%	100%		100%	100%	100%	100%	100%

Panama LSMS 1997: XP = Extreme Poor; AP = All Poor (includes extreme poor); NP = Non-Poor; TOT = Total

* Very small sample; results should be treated with caution

Table A4.39 - Total Credit and Loans (expanded to all households), by Poverty Group, Area

Units = '000 Balboas	URBAN AREAS				RURAL AREAS			
	XP	AP	NP	TOT	XP	AP	NP	TOT
Personal loan								
Total Loans to all households	215	4,330	304,111	308,441	670	8,051	52,910	60,961
Average lending per household	0.216	0.393	2.189	2.057	0.114	0.406	1.255	0.984
Personal credit								
Total Loans to all households	69	1,490	34,112	35,603	157	3,164	5,962	9,126
Average lending per household	0.069	0.135	0.246	0.237	0.027	0.16	0.141	0.147
Business Loan								
Total Loans to all households	0	93	111,745	111,838	1,371	4,916	49,427	54,342
Average lending per household	0	0.008	0.804	0.746	0.233	0.248	1.173	0.877
Business Credit								
Total Loans to all households	0	0	151,593	151,593	476	594	126,709	127,304
Average lending per household	0	0	1.091	1.011	0.081	0.03	3.006	2.054
All Personal (loans and credit)								
Total Loans to all households	284	5,821	338,224	344,044	827	11,215	58,872	70,087
Average lending per household	0.285	0.528	2.435	2.295	0.141	0.566	1.397	1.131
All Business (loans and credit)								
Total Loans to all households	0	93	263,338	263,431	1,847	5,510	176,136	181,646
Average lending per household	0	0.008	1.896	1.757	0.314	0.278	4.179	2.931
All Loans (business and personal)								
Total Loans to all households	215	4,423	415,856	420,279	2,041	12,967	102,337	115,304
Average lending per household	0.216	0.401	2.994	2.803	0.347	0.654	2.428	1.861
All Credit (business and personal)								
Total Loans to all households	69	1,490	185,705	187,196	633	3,758	132,671	136,430
Average lending per household	0.069	0.135	1.337	1.249	0.108	0.19	3.147	2.202
ALL LOANS AND CREDIT -- GRAND TOTAL								
Total Loans to all households	284	5,913	601,561	607,475	2,674	16,725	235,008	251,733
Average lending per household	0.285	0.537	4.331	4.052	0.455	0.844	5.575	4.062
Number of Households Borrowing	996	11,019	138,912	149,931	5,880	19,819	42,152	61,971
Number of Individuals Borrowing	8,083	73,073	560,652	633,725	38,295	117,229	159,079	276,308

	INDIGENOUS AREAS				ALL PANAMA			
	XP	AP	NP*	TOT	XP	AP	NP	TOT
Personal loan								
Total Loans to all households	577	1,389	360	1,748	1,461	13,770	357,381	371,151
Average lending per household	0.308	0.449	0.601	0.474	0.167	0.406	1.967	1.722
Personal credit								
Total Loans to all households	58	598	180	778	285	5,252	40,255	45,506
Average lending per household	0.031	0.193	0.301	0.211	0.033	0.155	0.222	0.211
Business Loan								
Total Loans to all households	0	0	78	78	1,371	5,008	161,250	166,258
Average lending per household	0	0	0.13	0.021	0.157	0.148	0.888	0.771
Business Credit								
Total Loans to all households	87	129	0	129	563	723	278,302	279,026
Average lending per household	0.046	0.042	0	0.035	0.064	0.021	1.532	1.294
All Personal (loans and credit)								
Total Loans to all households	635	1,986	540	2,526	1,746	19,022	397,635	416,657
Average lending per household	0.339	0.643	0.902	0.685	0.2	0.561	2.189	1.933
All Business (loans and credit)								
Total Loans to all households	87	129	78	207	1,934	5,732	439,552	445,284
Average lending per household	0.046	0.042	0.13	0.056	0.221	0.169	2.42	2.065
All Loans (business and personal)								
Total Loans to all households	577	1,389	437	1,826	2,832	18,778	518,630	537,409
Average lending per household	0.308	0.449	0.731	0.495	0.324	0.553	2.855	2.493
All Credit (business and personal)								
Total Loans to all households	145	727	180	907	847	5,975	318,557	324,532
Average lending per household	0.077	0.235	0.301	0.246	0.097	0.176	1.754	1.505
ALL LOANS AND CREDIT -- GRAND TOTAL								
Total Loans to all households	721	2,115	618	2,733	3,680	24,754	837,187	861,941
Average lending per household	0.385	0.685	1.032	0.741	0.421	0.73	4.608	3.998
Number of Households Borrowing	1,872	3,090	598	3,688	8,748	33,928	181,663	215,591
Number of Individuals Borrowing	15,422	23,460	2,425	25,886	61,801	213,762	722,156	935,918

Panama LSMS 1997, XP = Extreme Poor; AP = All Poor (includes extreme poor); NP = Non-Poor; TOT = Total

* Very small sample; results should be treated with caution

Annex 5 - Agriculture and Rural Poverty

Tom Wiens, Carlos Sobrado, Kathy Lindert
April 7, 1999

Poverty in the Rural Economy

1.   Poverty in Panama is concentrated in rural areas, making the reduction of rural poverty a key priority. The LSMS reveals the following patterns of poverty in the rural economy:

- Close to two thirds of residents of the rural economy (including urban farmers)[1] live below the poverty line (Table A5.3);
- Rural poverty is highest in indigenous areas (95 percent) and lowest among urban farmers (8 percent, Table A5.3);
- Interestingly, rural poverty is lowest among the landless and highest among those with less than 15 hectares of land (Table A5.4); it is also higher among farmers than non-farmers (Table A5.3).

Rural Employment and Incomes: Agriculture's Surprisingly Small Role

2.   **Agriculture plays a remarkably small role in rural Panama.** Overall, agriculture accounts for seven percent of Panama's GDP and 22 percent of total employment.[2] In rural areas, agriculture generates just over one quarter of total incomes (Table A5.5) and half of total employment. The non-farm sector contributes to close to half of total incomes in rural areas.[3] Even among farmers, agriculture contributes just half of their total incomes. As discussed below, this relatively small role reflects the high percentage of landless people (regardless of poverty status), as well as a comparative absence of plantation or estate agriculture which traditionally employs substantial amounts of hired labor.

3.   **Agriculture is more important among the rural poor, but still limited in its role.** The farm and non-farm sectors generate similar shares of average per capita incomes of the rural poor (41 percent and 35 percent respectively, Table A5.5).[4] The non-farm sector employs over one third of poor rural workers. Poor rural women in particular are engaged in non-farm employment, primarily community services, commerce and manufacturing. The extreme poor in rural areas are more dependent on agriculture, deriving 53 percent of their average total incomes from the farm sector.

4.   **Among the rural poor, most agricultural income is used for subsistence purposes.** Own-production accounts for two thirds of the total agricultural incomes of the rural poor, and is particularly important for residents of indigenous areas, who have fewer opportunities to supplement farm incomes with agricultural wage earnings (Table A5.7).

5.   **The non-poor derive a much larger share of their agricultural incomes from livestock.** While most rural households raise a few animals, ranching (specialization in livestock) is found among the largest farmers. Livestock and dairy products contribute over half of the total agricultural incomes of the non-poor, as compared with less than one fifth of the incomes of the poor (Table A5.9). Moreover, more than 80 percent of the total value of production of livestock and dairy products is produced by the non-poor (Table A5.10). This has implications for trade protection patterns: milk tariffs – which remain

---

[1] The rural economy in this Annex includes: rural non-indigenous areas (including remote), indigenous areas, and urban farmers. Urban farmers represent less than two percent of this "total rural" population (Table A5.1). Farmers are defined as those who derive at least ten percent of their total incomes from agriculture and who possess at least 0.25 hectares of land available for work.
[2] This compares with 25 percent of GDP and one third of employment in Nicaragua (1993), 14 percent of GDP (1995) and 36 percent of employment (1990) for El Salvador, and 25 percent of GDP (1995) and 52 percent of employment (1990) in Guatemala.
[3] The remainder comes from non-labor earnings. It is important to note that agriculture impacts the non-farm sector by generating demand for such services in rural areas.
[4] With the remainder coming from non-labor earnings, such as the imputed value of housing (returns to capital), transfers, and pensions.

63.   **Language Spoken at School.** Spanish is clearly the dominant language for schooling in Panama (Table A6.21), even among the indigenous. Some indigenous students (15 percent) do report indigenous languages as the main language spoken at school, particularly at the primary level (Tables A6.21 and A6.22). Poor indigenous students are almost three times more likely than their non-poor indigenous counterparts to attend schools in which indigenous language is the dominant language spoken, which reflects the larger share of monolingual indigenous speakers among the poor. Among indigenous groups, the Kuna are the most likely to attend school in indigenous language.

Health and Health Care Services

64.   Good health is another important aspect of maintaining human capital and labor assets (as well as a general source of wellbeing). Although health indicators are relatively strong in Panama, these indicators mask poor health status among the poor, particularly the indigenous. Infant mortality rates are 40-50 per 1000 live births in indigenous areas (on par with low-income countries), despite a national average of 19 per 1000. As discussed above, malnutrition among indigenous children is high. Intestinal diseases, malnutrition, and respiratory diseases still account for a significant share of deaths in predominantly indigenous areas such as Bocas del Toro and San Blas; tuberculosis is also high in Bocas del Toro; and malaria is common in Bocas del Toro, Darien, and Veraguas, all of which have high concentrations of indigenous people. Indigenous communities in the LSMS also report problems with alcoholism.

65.   The indigenous are less likely to seek medical treatment in case of illness or accidents than the non-indigenous. Among those reporting illness or an accident, some forty percent of the indigenous consulted a medical professional, as compared with about sixty percent of the non-indigenous (Table A6.23). This gap persists even among those below the poverty line (with the poor non-indigenous seeking treatment more commonly than the poor indigenous). The indigenous generally use public health facilities, as do the poor non-indigenous in Panama (Table A6.23). The indigenous are four times more likely to self-treat illness at home than the non-indigenous, suggesting lower access to health facilities among the indigenous population. The Ngobe-Buglé in particular have a higher frequency of self-treatment for illness at home. This might be due to the fact that the Ngobe-Buglé traditionally live in very small, dispersed household clusters, which hinders the provision of basic services. Indeed, the average distance to medical facilities for the indigenous who *sought* treatment is 41 minutes and 55 minutes for the Ngobe-Buglé, as compared with 32 minutes for the non-indigenous (it is presumably even further for those who did not seek treatment).

66.   When the indigenous do seek treatment, they are much more likely to use health centers and sub-centers – and less likely to use hospitals -- than the non-indigenous, irrespective of poverty status. They are also less likely to pay for medical services. Close to half of all non-indigenous people who sought treatment paid something for medical services, as compared with just over one-quarter of the indigenous (Table A6.23).

Physical Assets & Basic Services

67.   **Housing Conditions.** Although there are significant cultural differences between the indigenous groups in Panama, the LSMS suggests many similarities in the housing conditions among these groups (Table A6.24). A "typical" indigenous household lives in a hut (*choza o rancho*) or individual house. Indigenous houses tend to be quite crowded -- averaging two rooms and 5-6 members per room. In addition, the materials used to construct these houses are less durable than the ones for non-indigenous houses. Specifically, only half of the indigenous houses have ceilings made out of more durable materials such as concrete or metal compared with 94 percent for non-indigenous houses. Similarly, walls and floors in most indigenous houses are made using wood, earth or thatch.

68.   **Housing Tenancy.** Although the majority of indigenous households report "owning" their homes, the majority lack proof of ownership (62 percent of all households or 79 percent of those who own their homes), such as titles or deeds (Table A6.24). The lack of titling is higher among the poor indigenous versus the poor non-indigenous. While differences in titling could reflect cultural traditions with respect to property allocations, the lack of titles can serve to block indigenous people from obtaining credit -- an important lever for escaping poverty and smoothing consumption -- as these groups lack formal forms of guarantees for borrowing.

69.   **Basic Services.** In terms of access to basic services, indigenous groups are under-served for all services, even in comparison with the *poor* non-indigenous population (Table A6.24). The Ngobe-Buglé have the least access to all types of basic services. This probably reflects the fact that a larger share of the Ngobe-Buglé live in indigenous areas compared with the Kuna and Embera-Wounan (Table A6.3 above) and the fact that the Ngobe-Buglé traditionally live in small, dispersed clusters of households, which greatly hinders the provision of services.

70.   Roughly half of all indigenous households have access to formal **water supply** (public or private piped connections), compared with more than ninety percent for non-indigenous households (Table A6.24). About forty percent of the indigenous get their water from rivers and streams while three percent get water from wells. Among the indigenous groups, while four-fifths of the Kuna and Embera-Wounan possess access to piped water (a similar share as that of poor non-indigenous households), only one-third of the Ngobe-Buglé have access. Of those households that do not receive water from piped service, very few treat the water (via boiling, filtration, or chlorine), giving rise to health concerns. In particular, while only 23 percent of non-indigenous households treat water, even fewer indigenous households do so (seven percent). Interestingly, the Kuna treat water more than any other group (including non-indigenous).

71.   Likewise, about half of all indigenous households lack any form of **sanitation service** (sewer connections or latrines), raising concerns about potential contamination, environmental and public health problems (Table A6.24). The situation is particularly severe among the Ngobe-Buglé: almost two thirds lack sanitation services. Formal trash collection services are virtually non-existent among indigenous households. The lack of proper waste removal services in the Comarca Kuna Yala in San Blas has already caused significant environmental damage and pollution in the fragile sea life surrounding the archipelago.

72.   In terms of **energy sources** for lighting and cooking, most indigenous households do not have connections to electricity or gas, relying on informal sources such as kerosene, candles, and firewood Table A6.24). Again, indigenous households have even less access to formal energy sources than *poor* non-indigenous households and the Ngobe-Buglé have the least access.

73.   **Access to Land.** Half of all indigenous households own *some* land (Table A6.25). This is in contrast to the non-indigenous, the majority of whom are landless. However, of those who do own land, the non-indigenous own more land (19 hectares of land compared with only seven for indigenous households). The Kuna, who are the least poor of the indigenous groups, own the least amount of land (six hectares). Land might actually be a constraint to indigenous

Figure A6.2

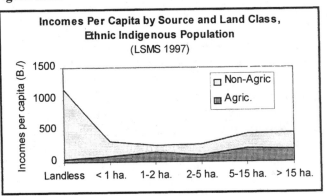

incomes: the landless have by far the highest per capita incomes (Figure A6.2). Those with some, but little land have the lowest; even those with a lot of land have lower incomes than the landless.

74.   **Land Tenancy and Titling.** Due to legal restrictions on private ownership of land in indigenous *Comarcas*[39], LSMS shows that over three fourths of indigenous people who own land have no ownership title; in the case of non-indigenous people, this proportion is slightly less than half (Table A6.26).

Financial Assets

75.   **Savings.**   Savings are an important asset for consumption smoothing and investment. The LSMS reveals that 19 percent of the indigenous have savings, compared with more than 37 percent for the non-indigenous (Table A6.27).   As expected, the poor have low savings (nine percent for the indigenous).   Among the indigenous, the Kuna have the highest savings rates.   This is consistent with the findings above that the Kuna are the wealthier among the indigenous groups. Of those who do save, the majority of indigenous use public institutions to put their savings, such as the National Bank of Panama and the Caja de Ahorros.

76.   **Credit.** The ability to purchase goods and services on credit is also an important tool for consumption smoothing and investment.   While most of the households requesting credit were approved, only eight percent of the indigenous solicited any credit, compared with fourteen percent for non-indigenous (Table A6.28). The most common reasons for not soliciting credit include the risks associated with indebtedness and a belief that they would not be approved.   Of the indigenous who did solicit credit, low income was the main reason for being refused.   Average borrowing amounts for the indigenous and non-indigenous do not differ substantially overall (B./3,742 and B./ 4,007 respectively). They are much lower among the poor (particularly the indigenous poor).   They are also lowest among those living within indigenous areas (B./741 on average), suggesting limited geographical proximity to credit institutions in these areas (as well as limited assets for collateral).   Most credit obtained by the indigenous was for personal use (consumption smoothing).

Social Capital

77.   Social capital – defined as norms, trust, and reciprocity networks that facilitate mutually beneficial cooperation in a community – is an important asset that can reduce vulnerability and increase opportunities.   The LSMS and the associated Social Capital Qualitative Survey (SCQS) indicate the following trends in social capital among the indigenous (See Annex 18 of the Poverty Assessment for details):

- **Indigenous communities have higher social capital than non-indigenous communities.** Four fifths of indigenous communities in the LSMS community sample report having some sort of community organization, as compared with just half of urban communities and three quarters of non-indigenous rural communities.   Horizontal connections, which manifest themselves through different organizations within the same community or via the establishment of links with groups in neighboring communities – were also found to be the strongest in indigenous communities in the SCQS.

---

[39] The laws creating the *Comarcas Emberá* (Law 22 of 1983) and the *Comarca Ngobe-Buglé* (Law 10 of 1997) state that lands delimited by such laws constitute collective property of the respective *Comarcas* and that the right to use collective lands is administered by traditional indigenous authorities, in accordance with procedures in the corresponding Organic Acts.   The laws only acknowledge private properties and rights of possession registered at the time such laws were enacted and establish restrictions on the sale of these properties to persons other than those of the *Comarca*.

- **Among the ethnic indigenous, social capital appears to be stronger for those living *within* indigenous areas as compared with those living *outside* indigenous areas.**[40] A larger share of indigenous households living within indigenous areas report participation in public-good type "community-oriented" organizations (local, community *juntas*, congresses, committees, and associations) than their counterparts living in urban and non-indigenous rural areas (36 percent versus 26 percent respectively). Close to twice as many ethnic indigenous households living within indigenous areas report participation in community committees and associations as those living outside indigenous areas. In contrast, ethnic indigenous households living outside indigenous areas are close to two times more likely to join associations which yield higher private gains, such as cooperatives, a pattern also found in urban areas and among the non-poor in general. Migrating or settling in non-indigenous areas does seem to have an effect on social capital and community ties.

- **Social capital appears to contribute to more positive perceptions of overall well-being.** Despite the abysmal rate of poverty among indigenous communities, they report more positive perceptions of changes in overall well-being than their non-indigenous rural and urban counterparts. This optimism contrasts with their perceptions of specific living conditions (such as the delivery of basic services), which were more negative than their non-indigenous counterparts. Stronger community ties – social capital – could account for the relatively positive perceptions of overall well-being among the indigenous, which otherwise contrast with generally abysmal economic conditions.

- **Social capital also appears to be important as a tool to leverage external assistance.** A higher share of indigenous communities with high or medium levels of social capital report receiving external assistance (from the Government or NGOs) than those with low social capital.

PART IV: THE DETERMINANTS OF INDIGENOUS POVERTY

78. While the univariate analysis presented above is crucial in understanding the relationship between the indigenous and poverty, it is important to understand the interaction of all these factors as well. This section examines the correlates of poverty for the ethnic indigenous and non-indigenous in a multi-variate setting so as to shed light on their relative importance. The analysis is useful, first, to verify the relative role of the various factors in determining poverty status (and any differences for the indigenous and non-indigenous), and second, to assess the potential impact that policy-induced changes in these factors are likely to have on the probability of being poor, holding all other factors constant.

79. It is important to note the limitations of this analysis at the outset. First and foremost, the analysis does not capture the dynamic impact of certain causes of poverty over time. Most notably, the impact of changes in economic growth -- most certainly a key determinant of poverty -- cannot be assessed using this static, cross-section model. Other dynamic factors that are likely correlates of poverty include variables such as past nutritional status of household members (which could affect their current productivity for example). Second, the analysis is limited by the variables available at the household level from the 1997 LSMS household survey. Other factors -- such as social conditions, like social exclusion, discrimination, alcoholism or crime, or physical conditions, such as variations in climate or access to markets -- could not be included due to a lack of data at this level. Finally, though theory holds that many of the variables included in the analysis do indeed contribute to ("cause") poverty (or poverty reduction), the statistical relationships should be interpreted as correlates and not as determinants since causality can run both ways.

---

[40] The results in this paragraph were tabulated using language indicators of ethnicity (Definition 3) and are not included in Annex 18.

Key Correlates of Indigenous Poverty

80.   Estimation results for the probability of ethnic indigenous households being poor[41] are presented in Table A6.29. The findings are discussed below.

81.   The key assets described above – labor, education, basic services, and physical assets – are clearly correlated with poverty status among the indigenous.   Other correlates of poverty include geographic location and household size and composition.

82.   **Labor: Sources of Income and Employment**. Informal-sector employment is clearly correlated with poverty among indigenous households.   Those whose main income is derived from informal employment have a significantly higher probability of being poor than those with incomes coming from the private formal sector, the public sector, or non-labor earnings.

83.   **Education**. Education is clearly correlated with poverty status and plays an important role in reducing poverty.[42] The higher the education of the household head or his/her companion, the lower the household's probability of being poor. *Completing* schooling (primary or secondary) significantly reduces a household's chances of being poor.

84.   **Housing Conditions and Tenancy**. Low quality housing is strongly correlated with poverty, though the direction of causality is not clear. Poverty itself is a cause of makeshift housing, but low quality housing can also limit the ability of households to use their homes as a productive asset – as a location of independent businesses for example. Larger houses (more rooms per capita) are correlated with lower levels of poverty. Home ownership and tenancy status does not appear to have a significant impact on the probability of being poor for the indigenous.

85.   **Basic Services.** Access to basic infrastructure services improves the well-being and productivity of the poor and enhances their ability to use their homes for independent businesses. Lack of access to sanitation services (with only latrines) is strongly correlated with poverty. Further distances from the water source (as a proxy for access to water) are associated with a higher probability of being poor.

86.   **Other Physical Assets**. Ownership of equipment is associated with a lower probability of being poor. Equipment can be viewed as a proxy of wealth or physical assets, which would clearly be related to poverty status.

87.   **Credit**. Access to credit is significantly correlated with a lower probability of being poor. Credit allows households to smooth consumption in the face of income fluctuations and to invest in productive activities for future income generation.

88.   **Fertility, Household Size and Composition**. Larger indigenous households tend to be poor. Households with more young children (reflecting higher fertility) have a higher probability of being poor, presumably due to the dependency status of these members.

89.   **Geographic Location.** Even after controlling for key household characteristics, geography plays an important role in determining poverty status.   Ethnically indigenous households *within* indigenous areas are more likely to be poor than those located *outside* indigenous areas, even after other differences

---

[41] The "marginal effects" column shows the percentage change in poverty status associated with a unit change in the explanatory variable. A negative sign on a coefficient generally means that an increased value of the variable reduces the probability of being poor. Maddala (1983) offers a comprehensive exposition of the econometric methodology implemented in this section.

[42] The analysis uses the maximum educational attainment of the household head or his/her companion to gauge the relationship between education and poverty. Since educational attainment of these members (adults) precedes their current economic status, it could validly be considered as having a causative influence on poverty status.

are taken into account. Interestingly, indicators of ethnicity were not significant, again supporting the notion that geography is a more powerful determinant of poverty (as discussed above).

Comparison with the Determinants of Poverty for the Non-Indigenous

90.   The factors associated with indigenous poverty are largely the same as those correlated with poverty among the non-indigenous (Table A6.30).[43]   This suggests that, while the determinants of poverty are fairly constant regardless of ethnicity – and include endowments and use of key assets, such as labor, education, basic services and physical assets, as well as geographic location and household structure – the ethnic indigenous have a higher incidence of poverty because of poorer endowments of these assets. In fact, in a joint regression for all Panama, ethnicity did not turn out to be significant as a correlate of poverty, whereas key assets and geographic location (inside vs. outside indigenous areas) did, suggesting that it is these factors and not ethnicity *per se* that are associated with poverty.

PART IV: SUMMARY AND RECOMMENDATIONS

91.   A number of key patterns emerge with respect to the profile of poverty among the indigenous in Panama:

- **Poverty** among the indigenous is abysmal (83 percent of ethnic indigenous live below the poverty line and 70 percent live in extreme poverty). Poverty is highest among the Ngobe-Buglé (the largest indigenous group: 92 percent are poor), followed by the Embera-Wounan (80 percent), and the Kuna (65 percent). Indicators of child malnutrition mirror these patterns.

- **Geography** is an important determinant of poverty: indigenous people living within indigenous areas have a significantly higher incidence of poverty than those living outside these areas. This result is particularly pertinent for the Kuna and the Embera-Wounan, about half of whom live outside indigenous areas. Indeed, economic factors appear to be the prime motivation for migration among the Kuna. A loss of indigenous language speaking ability, however, seems to be one of the costs of such decisions, as a larger share of ethnic indigenous people living outside indigenous areas speak only Spanish.

- An inability to **speak Spanish** is also associated with destitution. Poverty among the ethnic indigenous is highest among those households that are headed by monolingual indigenous speakers: virtually all live in *extreme* poverty.

- Large households and high **fertility** are strongly associated with indigenous poverty, as lower incomes must be spread across more members.

92.   A review of the assets of the indigenous suggest that indigenous poverty reflects insufficient endowments of key assets – or obstacles to their efficient use in the market:

- While **labor** is one of the most abundant assets among the indigenous, returns to this asset are low due to: underemployment and low productivity, limited employment opportunities outside the informal sector (where earnings are significantly lower, see Annex 11), and probable wage discrimination in labor markets.

- Although **education** is a clear vehicle for escaping poverty (and serves as an input into other needed areas such as family planning), educational attainment among indigenous people is very low, particularly among the Ngobe-Buglé. Despite almost complete coverage of primary schooling in Panama (even among the non-indigenous poor), a substantial share of indigenous children do not enroll in, or complete, primary school. Very few attend secondary school. An inability to speak

---

[43] Significance levels are stronger overall because the non-indigenous sample is larger.

Spanish appears to be a significant deterrent of school enrollment and there are few opportunities for indigenous children to attend bilingual schools.

- **Health** indicators are also worse among the indigenous, and access to health services is much more restricted.

- **Housing** quality is low among the indigenous, and most do not possess titles or proof of ownership for their homes.

- The indigenous are largely under-served with respect to **basic services**, such as water, sanitation services, and energy sources, particularly the Ngobe-Buglé.

- The indigenous have few **financial assets** either in the form of savings or access to credit.

- In contrast with the above assets, **social capital** is quite high among the indigenous. These community bonds seem to be effective in generating positive perceptions of overall well-being and in leveraging external assistance.

93. The above analysis sheds light on a number of policy recommendations:

- **Additional public resources** need to be allocated to poverty reduction efforts among the indigenous. Geographic targeting to indigenous areas can be a useful tool in making (and monitoring) such allocations since: (a) poverty is highest and most widespread in these areas (even among the ethnic indigenous); and (b) geographic targeting is more administratively simple than targeting based on ethnicity or language.

- The Government should seek to make effective use of the high degree of **social capital** in indigenous communities, working with indigenous organizations to prioritize, design, and implement solutions and interventions for poverty reduction.

- Two key priority areas for **public investment** that are crucial for longer-term poverty reduction were identified by the indigenous communities themselves (see Table A6.31) include **education** and **potable water**:

  - With respect to **education**, the Government should provide additional resources for bilingual materials, textbooks, and teacher-training at the primary level. Additional research using qualitative methods (focus groups, etc.) would also be beneficial to further explore the barriers to higher educational attainment among indigenous children.

  - With respect to **potable water**, the Ngobe-Buglé have by far the highest gaps in access to this vital input into well-being (and consequently the highest rates of malnutrition). Additional resources should be provided in a coordinated manner (to avoid overlaps and conflicts between programs) so as to improve the access of indigenous groups (particularly the Ngobe-Buglé) to potable water.

- Given the high degree of poverty and extreme poverty among the indigenous (particularly those living within indigenous areas), **social assistance** in the form of transfers is urgently needed for alleviating poverty in the short run. For larger impact, such transfers should include those with long-term investment benefits, such as those linked to educational attendance (e.g., targeted school feeding programs or cash transfers tied to attendance).

REFERENCES

Alvarado, Eligío. February 28, 1998. *Panamá: Perfil de los Pueblos Indígenas.* Draft.

Davis V. Enriqueta. December 1997. *Informe Sobre la Pobreza en Panamá: Componente de Capital Social.*

Deaton, A. 1997. *The Analysis of Household Surveys.* The World Bank.

Maddala, G. 1983. *Limited Dependent and Qualitative Variables in Econometrics.* Cambridge University Press.

Oaxaca, R.L. 1973. *Male-Female Wage Differentials in Urban Labor Market*s. International Economic Review, Vol. 14, No. 1, p.p. 693-709.

Psacharapoulos, G. and H. Patrinos. 1994. *Indigenous People and Poverty in Latin America.* The World Bank.

Ravallion, M. 1992. *Poverty Comparisons.* LSMS Working Paper No. 88. The World Bank.

The World Bank. May 1998. Panama: Atlantic Mesoamerican Biological Corridor Project. Global Environment Facility Project Document.

APPENDIX A6.1: AGRICULTURAL PRODUCTION BY ETHNIC GROUP

Table A6.1.1. - Absolute Value of Agricultural Production						
B./'000	TOT	NI	I	NB	K	EW
Vaca, toros, ternero	117,582	115,641	1,940	1,005	935	0
Arroz	57,255	55,553	1,701	677	108	915
Ñame	34,123	23,926	10,197	7,156	11	3,029
Cerdos o puercos	34,578	34,073	504	376	15	112
Mazorca/grano seco	22,656	19,317	3,338	939	1,472	927
Café	24,061	23,534	527	527	0	0
Leche	16,491	16,491	0	0	0	0
Gallinas o pollos	11,412	10,400	1,011	636	249	126
Plátano	5,789	4,077	1,711	30	231	1,450
Frijol de bejuco	4,720	3,322	1,398	1,268	22	108
Zapallo	5,616	5,153	462	0	461	1
Yuca	4,239	3,975	264	158	49	57
Aguacate	4,982	4,579	403	8	27	368
Pimento	5,676	5,676	0	0	0	0
Maracuya	4,923	4,923	0	0	0	0
Mazorca/maiz nuevo	4,058	3,933	125	90	1	35
Banano-Guineo	2,983	770	2,211	1,409	680	122
Tomate perita	3,598	3,594	4	0	4	0
Papaya	3,169	3,169	0	0	0	0
Caña de azucar	3,340	3,340	0	0	0	0
Poroto	2,945	2,945	0	0	0	0
Perejil	2,332	2,332	0	0	0	0
Madera	2,148	1,776	373	42	54	277
Bollos/tortillas	1,950	1,789	161	51	48	61
Sorgo	2,329	2,329	0	0	0	0
All other crops	28,390	25,798	2,592	1,001	728	863
Total	411,345	382,415	28,922	15,373	5,095	8,451

Source: Panama LSMS 1997

NI = non-indigenous; I = indigenous; NB = Ngobe-Buglé; K = Kuna

EW = Embera-Wounan

Table A6.1.2 - Percent of Agricultural Production per Group						
	All	**NI**	**I**	**NB**	**K**	**EW**
Vaca, toros, ternero	29%	30%	7%	7%	18%	0%
Arroz	14%	15%	6%	4%	2%	11%
Ñame	8%	6%	35%	47%	0%	36%
Cerdos o puercos	8%	9%	2%	2%	0%	1%
Mazorca/grano seco	6%	5%	12%	6%	29%	11%
Café	6%	6%	2%	3%	0%	0%
Leche	4%	4%	0%	0%	0%	0%
Gallinas o pollos	3%	3%	3%	4%	5%	1%
Platáno	1%	1%	6%	0%	5%	17%
Frijol de bejuco	1%	1%	5%	8%	0%	1%
Zapallo	1%	1%	2%	0%	9%	0%
Yuca	1%	1%	1%	1%	1%	1%
Aguacate	1%	1%	1%	0%	1%	4%
Pimento	1%	1%	0%	0%	0%	0%
Maracuya	1%	1%	0%	0%	0%	0%
Mazorca/maiz nuevo	1%	1%	0%	1%	0%	0%
Banano-Guineo	1%	0%	8%	9%	13%	1%
Tomate perita	1%	1%	0%	0%	0%	0%
Papaya	1%	1%	0%	0%	0%	0%
Caña de azucar	1%	1%	0%	0%	0%	0%
Poroto	1%	1%	0%	0%	0%	0%
Perejil	1%	1%	0%	0%	0%	0%
Madera	1%	0%	1%	0%	1%	3%
Bollos/tortillas	0%	0%	1%	0%	1%	1%
Sorgo	1%	1%	0%	0%	0%	0%
All other crops	7%	7%	9%	7%	14%	10%
Total	100%	100%	100%	100%	100%	100%

Source: Panama LSMS 1997

NI = non-indigenous; I = indigenous; NB = Ngobe-Buglé; K = Kuna

EW = Embera-Wounan

APPENDIX A6.2: SAMPLING AND ETHNICITY IN THE LSMS

Sample design

In the Panama LSMS 1997, indigenous households were over-sampled so as to ensure adequate sample size. In addition, a two-stage sampling design was implemented in which primary sampling units (PSU) were first randomly chosen from regions and households were then randomly chosen from each PSU. As such, statistical analysis must take into account the sample design. Furthermore, even with over-sampling of indigenous populations, there are cases in which the sample size is small and careful statistical treatment is essential.

With this in mind and, given the data collection design, the statistical analysis in this paper is performed using stratification tools that takes into account both the sample design as well as the sample sizes of each sub-population.[44] As a basic check, Tables A6.2.1 through A6.2.4 summarize the sample sizes of some of the main categories used in this analysis.

Statistical Significance

All results discussed in the paper were tested for statistical significance. Since the LSMS does not use a standard random sample and the sample size for the indigenous is not large, standard tests of significance based on large sample properties and random sampling are not valid. As such, statistical testing for significance for all means comparisons discussed in the paper takes into account the non-random design of the data by using the appropriate weights and stratification tools to correct for any biases. All results presented in the paper were statistically significant (most at the 99% level of confidence), with the exception of the means comparisons for dependency ratios, as noted in the text.

Table A6.2.1 - LSMS Sample Distribution for the Indigenous Population			
	Definition 1	Definition 2	Definition 3
Ngobe-Buglé	1442	1457	1957
Kuna	361	373	583
Embera-Wounan	335	349	493
Other Indigenous	13	17	52
Total	2151	2196	3085
Source: LSMS Panama 1997. Definition 3 includes children < age 6.			

---

[44] See Deaton (1997) for further readings on stratification.

Table A6.2.2 - Sample Size by Geographic Area and Ethnicity Definition				
	Geographic Area			
	Urban	Rural	Indigenous	TOTAL
Ethnic Definition 1: Maternal Language				
Total Population	8782	7485	2160	18437
Non-Indigenous	8660	7424	202	16286
Ngobe-Buglé	37	49	1356	1442
Kuna	39	15	307	361
Embera-Wounan	46	7	295	348
Ethnic Definition 2: Maternal or Second Language				
Total Population	8782	7485	2160	18437
Non-Indigenous	8634	7411	196	16241
Ngobe-Buglé	43	57	1357	1457
Kuna	48	17	308	373
Embera-Wounan	57	10	299	366
Ethnic Definition 3: Any Indigenous Language in Household (INCLUDES children < 6)				
Total Population	9965	8743	2729	21437
Non-Indigenous	9622	8549	181	18352
Ngobe-Buglé	83	110	1764	1957
Kuna	124	60	399	583
Embera-Wounan	136	24	385	545

Table A6.2.3 - Sample Size by Language Abilities and Ethnic Group Using Definition 3				
Ethnic Group:	Monolingual Spanish	Monolingual Indigenous	Bilingual	TOTAL
Total Population	16473	579	4327	21437
Non-Indigenous Population	16371	0	1981	18352
Ethnic Indigenous Population	190	549	2346	3085
Living in indigenous area	27	514	2007	2548
Living outside indigenous area	163	35	339	537
Male	96	282	1225	1603
Female	94	267	1121	1482
Age 6-11	32	108	449	589
12-17	26	99	378	503
18-24	23	66	268	357
25-39	42	90	385	517
40-59	20	69	274	363
> 60	10	29	74	113
Ngobe-Buglé				
Living in indigenous area	27	373	1364	1764
Living outside indigenous area	58	9	126	193
Male	44	206	797	1047
Female	41	176	693	910
Age 6-11	16	78	294	388
12-17	11	70	250	331
18-24	8	46	161	215
25-39	17	60	237	314
40-59	10	52	162	224
> 60	7	12	33	52
Kuna				
Living in indigenous area	0	135	264	399
Living outside indigenous area	82	21	81	184
Male	42	72	162	276
Female	40	84	183	307
Age 6-11	14	27	46	87
12-17	12	28	58	98
18-24	8	20	44	72
25-39	22	29	59	110
40-59	9	15	57	81
> 60	3	16	24	43
Embera-Wounan				
Living in indigenous area	0	6	379	385
Living outside indigenous area	23	5	132	160
Male	10	4	266	280
Female	13	7	245	265
Age 6-11	2	3	109	114
12-17	3	1	70	74
18-24	7	0	63	70
25-39	3	1	89	93
40-59	1	2	55	58
> 60	0	1	17	18

Table A6.2.4 - Household Sample Sizes by Ethnicity and Poverty Group									
	Tot.	NI	I	N-B	K	E-W	MS	MI	B
Extreme Poor	6003	3526	2477	1695	414	368	3544	520	1939
All Poor	9413	6665	2748	1834	442	472	6549	523	2341
Non Poor	12024	11687	337	123	141	73	10012	26	1986
Source: LSMS 1997. NI = Non-indigenous; I = Indigenous; N-B = Ngobe-Buglé; K = Kuna; E-W = Embera-Wounan.									

APPENDIX A6.3 – WAGE DISCRIMINATION AGAINST ETHNIC INDIGENOUS WORKERS

Methodology for Measuring Wage Discrimination. Using Oaxaca 's (1973) technique it is possible to decompose the earnings gap between two groups (in this case between non-indigenous and indigenous workers) into a component which is largely attributable in human capital endowments, and a component that reflects largely wage discrimination. The technique involves estimating separate wage regressions for the two groups of interest (A and B) as:

$$(1) \qquad \ln w_A = X_A (b_A) + \varepsilon_A \text{ for group A and}$$

$$(2) \qquad \ln w_B = X_B (b_B) + \varepsilon_B \text{ for group B}$$

where the subscripts 'A' and 'B' refers to group A and B respectively; ln (w)'s are the log of wages, X's are a vector of characteristics, b's are the coefficients and ε's are the error terms.

The analysis in this paper is based on *wage* regressions, excluding earnings from self-employment (since a self-employed individual would not discriminate against him/herself). The difference in the average log of wages is equivalent to the percentage difference between non-indigenous and indigenous pay. Given that the error term in the non- indigenous and indigenous wage functions has a mean of zero, we can show that:

$$(3) \ln w_A - \ln w_B = [\ \overline{X}_A (b_A) -\ \overline{X}_B (b_B)]$$

where $\overline{X}_A$ and $\overline{X}_B$ are the average values of non- indigenous and indigenous characteristics in the sample. Re-arranging, equation (3) yields:

$$(4) \ln w_A - \ln w_B = [\ \overline{X}_B (b_A - b_B)] + [b_A (\ \overline{X}_A -\ \overline{X}_B)]$$

Therefore, the difference in pay comes from two different sources. The first term represents wage gaps attributed to differences in the returns (b_A - b_B) that groups A and B receive for the same endowment of income generating characteristics. The second term represents wage gaps attributed to differences in the endowments of income generating characteristics ($\overline{X}_A$ - $\overline{X}_B$) evaluated with group A's worker pay structure. The former part is said to reflect wage discrimination while the latter captures wage differentials from differences in endowments.

The use of earning functions to estimate discrimination means that there will be omitted variables not "explaining" wage differentials. Therefore, the discrimination part of the decomposition does not only explain wage differences due to discrimination but in addition, due to omitted variables. In this sense it is often said that the discrimination part serves as the upper bound of "unjustified" or "unexplained" wage discrimination.

Table A6.3.1 - Log of Hourly Earnings Regressions by Ethnic Group		
	Non-Indigenous	Indigenous
Individual Characteristics		
Education		
# years of education	0.065***	0.026*
Experience[a]	0.032***	0.061**
Experience squared	-0.005***	-0.001
Had training	0.172***	0.404***
# of household members		
Ages 0-5	-0.021	-0.045
Ages 6-11	-0.054***	0.033
Ages 12-17	-0.026***	0.090*
Geographic Area		
Rural	-0.358***	0.045
Indigenous	-0.371***	-0.527***
Other		
Female	0.016	-0.145
Single[b]	-0.140***	0.193
Job Characteristics		
Public[c]	0.280***	0.503***
Belong to union	0.110***	0.300***
Constant	-0.543***	-1.087***
Selectivity	0.205***	0.412***
Sample Size	4554	274
R-squared	0.36	0.32

Dependent Variable: Log of Hourly Earnings. (a) Experience = How long have you worked in your current profession (e.g., as a mechanic in any firm)? (b) Single = unmarried + widowed + divorced. (omitted variable: married = married + *unida*). (c) The omitted variable for the sectors is private and for the geographic area is urban. Significance levels: * = 90%, ** = 95%, *** = 99%

Table A6.1 - Distribution of Indigenous Population by Ethnic Group and Province, 1990	Guaymí		Kuna	Embera-Wounan		Naso-Teribe	Other	TOTAL
	Ngobe	Buglé		Embera	Waunana			
TOTAL ('000)	**123.6**	**3.8**	**47.3**	**14.7**	**2.6**	**2.2**	**0.1**	**194.2**
Bocas del Toro	41%	47%	1%	0%	1%	84%	0%	29%
Coclé	0%	0%	0%	0%	0%	0%	2%	0%
Colón	0%	1%	5%	1%	1%	1%	2%	1%
Chiriquí	51%	2%	0%	0%	0%	10%	3%	33%
Darien	0%	1%	3%	78%	75%	0%	0%	8%
Herrera	0%	0%	0%	0%	0%	0%	1%	0%
Los Santos	0%	0%	0%	0%	0%	0%	1%	0%
Panama	2%	7%	24%	19%	22%	4%	89%	9%
Veraguas	6%	39%	0%	0%	0%	0%	5%	4%
Comarca San Blas	0%	0%	67%	0%	0%	0%	0%	16%

Source: E. Davis (1997): 1990 Census. Numbers may not add due to rounding.

Table A6.2 – Comparing Definitions of Ethnicity Percent of population per group (using expanded population)			
	Definition 1	Definition 2	Definition 3[a]
Percent of National Population			
Indigenous	7	8	10
Non-Indigenous	93	92	90
Total	100	100	100
Percent of Indigenous Population			
Ngobe-Buglé	65	64	59
Kuna	19	50	23
Embera-Wounan[b]	16	17	18
Total	100	100	100

Source: LSMS Panama 1997. Percentages may not add up to 100 due to rounding. (a) Definition 3 includes children under 6. (b) Includes the "other" indigenous groups.

Table A6.3 - Language Classification by Geographic Area and Ethnic Definition Percentages by ethnic group (using expanded sample)				
	Geographic Area			TOTAL
	Urban	Rural	Indigenous	
Ethnic Definition 1: Maternal Language				
% of Area Pop.	100	100	100	100
Non-Indigenous	99	99	10	93
Ngobe-Buglé	0	1	62	5
Kuna	1	0	15	1
Embera-Wounan	0	0 (a)	13	1
% of Ethnic Group				
Non-Indigenous	60	39	1	100
Ngobe-Buglé	4	7	90	100
Kuna	24	5	71	100
Embera-Wounan	22	3 (a)	75	100
Ethnic Definition 2: Maternal or Second Language				
% of Area Pop.	100	100	100	100
Non-Indigenous	98	99	9	92
Ngobe-Buglé	0	1	62	5
Kuna	1	0	15	2
Embera-Wounan	1	0 (a)	13	1
% of Ethnic Group				
Non-Indigenous	60	39	1	100
Ngobe-Buglé	4	7	88	100
Kuna	27	5	68	100
Embera-Wounan	25	4 (a)	71	100
Ethnic Definition 3: Any Indigenous Language in Household				
% of Area Pop.	100	100	100	100
Non-Indigenous	97	97	7	90
Ngobe-Buglé	1	2	65	6
Kuna	2	1	15	2
Embera-Wounan	1	0 (a)	13	2
% of Ethnic Group				
Non-Indigenous	60	40	1	100
Ngobe-Buglé	6	10	84	100
Kuna	38	11	50	100
Embera-Wounan	38	6 (a)	56	100
Source: LSMS Panama 1997. Percentages may not add up to 100 due to rounding. (a) Small sample				

Table A6.4 – Language Abilities by Ethnic Group[a,b] (% of people in each group)		Monolingual Spanish	Monolingual Indigenous	Bilingual	TOTAL
Total Population		83	2	15	100
Non-Indigenous Population		90	0	10	100
Ethnic Indigenous Population		15	21	64	100
Living in indigenous area		3	27	70	100
Living outside indigenous area		44	7	49	100
	Male	17	15	69	100
	Female	13	28	59	100
	6-11	18	24	58	100
	12-17	18	14	68	100
Age	18-24	14	17	69	100
	25-39	13	20	68	100
	40-59	10	29	61	100
	> 60	14	29	57	100
Ngobe-Buglé		8	25	67	100
Living in indigenous area		2	28	69	100
Living outside indigenous area		34	8	58	100
	Male	8	18	75	100
	Female	7	33	59	100
	6-11	8	28	63	100
	12-17	9	16	75	100
Age	18-24	5	20	75	100
	25-39	6	24	70	100
	40-59	7	37	56	100
	> 60	17	29	54	100
Kuna		29	25	46	100
Living in indigenous area		4	43	54	100
Living outside indigenous area		53	9	38	100
	Male	33	19	49	100
	Female	25	32	43	100
	6-11	41	32	27	100
	12-17	35	17	49	100
Age	18-24	29	25	46	100
	25-39	27	25	49	100
	40-59	21	24	55	100
	> 60	17	33	50	100
Embera-Wounan		19	2	79	100
Living in indigenous area		2	3	96	100
Living outside indigenous area		41	2	57	100
	Male	23	2	75	100
	Female	13	4	83	100
	6-11	28	1	71	100
	12-17	29	0	71	100
Age	18-24	21	0	79	100
	25-39	13	1	87	100
	40-59	3	9	89	100
	> 60	na	16	84	100

Source: LSMS Panama 1997. Percentages may not add up to 100 due to rounding. (a) Ethnic groups are selected using the language classification criterion (Definition 3). (b) Excludes children under age 6 for whom the language questions in the LSMS were not asked.

Table A6.5 – Poverty Indicators by Ethnicity						
	% of population under the poverty line	# of individuals below the poverty line ('000)	Average consumption[a] (B/.)	Absolute Gap (mn.B/.)	Depth Index (P1)	Severity Index (P2)
Poverty Line = B./905						
Total (all Panama)	37.3	1020	506	407	16.4	9.7
Non-indigenous[b]	32.2	793	559	274	12.3	6.5
Ethnic indigenous[b]	83.8	227	319	133	54.2	39.2
Ngobe-Buglé	92.3	147	277	92	64.1	48.3
Kuna	65.5	41	377	21	38.2	25.2
Embera-Wounan	79.5	39	419	19	42.7	27.9
Indigenous Areas[c]	95.4	197	277	124	66.2	49.2
Extreme Poverty Line = B./519						
Total (all Panama)	18.8	515	307	109	7.7	4.2
Non-indigenous[b]	13.3	326	343	57	4.5	2.1
Ethnic indigenous[b]	69.6	189	245	52	36.8	23.0
Ngobe-Buglé	81.5	130	223	38	46.5	30.2
Kuna	50.0	31	291	7	21.9	11.7
Embera-Wounan	56.3	28	294	6	24.3	14.1
Indigenous Areas[c]	86.4	178	236	50	47.0	29.7

Source: LSMS Panama 1997. (a) For the whole sample. (b) Using the language definition of ethnicity (Definition 3 above). (c) Using the geographic area definition (regardless of ethnicity).

Table A6.6 – Poverty Indicators by Ethnicity and Area						
	% of population under the poverty line	# of individuals below the poverty line	Average consumption (B/.)	Absolute Gap (mn.B/.)	Depth Index (P1)	Severity Index (P2)
Poverty Line= B./905						
Ethnic Indigenous						
Within indigenous areas	96.4	185	275	117	67.0	49.9
Outside indigenous areas	52.8	41	516	16	22.7	13.2
Within Indigenous Areas						
Ngobe-Buglé	96.4	128	259	83	68.8	52.4
Kuna	96.5	30	297	18	64.8	45.4
Embera-Wounan	95.9	27	327	16	61.1	42.7
Outside Indigenous Areas						
Ngobe-Buglé	70.9	18	398	9	39.6	27.1
Kuna	33.9	10	609	3	11.1	4.5
Embera-Wounan	58.6	13	608	4	19.2	9.1
Extreme Poverty Line = B./519						
Ethnic Indigenous						
Within indigenous areas	87.5	168	236	48	47.6	30.1
Outside indigenous areas	25.8	20	315	4	10.2	5.6
Within Indigenous Areas						
Ngobe-Buglé	87.6	117	218	35	50.8	33.2
Kuna	92.1	29	281	7	42.2	23.1
Embera-Wounan	81.5	22	272	5	38.7	23.2
Outside Indigenous Areas						
Ngobe-Buglé	49.8	13	265	3	24.4	14.8
Kuna	7.1	2	429	0.2	0.1	0.002
Embera-Wounan	24.1	5	392	1	5.9	2.5

Source: LSMS Panama 1997.

Table A6.7 - Migration by Ethnic Classification and Language Ability (in %)									
	National Total	NI	I	N-B	K	E-W	MS	MI	B
Migration incidence[a]	11	10	12	8	15	18	11	9	12
Reason for migrating:									
More money/work	21	22	10	10	12	9	21	13	24
Agricultural work	2	2	2	3	0	4	2	3	3
Non-agric. Work	3	3	6	0	8	10	3	5	5
Studies/education	11	10	17	8	40	4	11	0	13
Marriage	14	14	16	31	7	6	14	19	13
Sickness	2	2	3	3	4	2	2	6	2
Retirement	1	1	0	0	0	0	1	0	0
Family reasons	38	38	41	37	30	57	39	52	28
Other	9	9	6	9	0	10	8	3	13
Total	100	100	100	100	100	100	100	100	100

Source: LSMS Panama 1997. Percentages may not add up to 100 due to rounding. Tot.=Total Panama, NI= Non-Indigenous, I= Indigenous, N-B=Ngobe-Buglé , K=Kuna,E-W=Embera- Wounan, MS=Monolingual Spanish, MI=Monolingual indigenous, B=Bilingual. (a) % of people who report migrating since 1992. Excludes children under 10 (who were not asked question in LSMS).

Table A6.8 - Poverty Indicators for the Indigenous Population by Household Head' s Language Ability						
	% of population under the poverty line	# of individuals below the poverty line ('000s)	Average consumption (B/.)	Absolute Gap (mn.B/.)	Depth Index (P1)	Severity Index (P2)
Poverty Line = B./905						
Monolingual Spanish	36.4	776	558	269	13.9	7.3
Monolingual Indigenous	93.9	40	228	27	70.2	54.3
Bilingual	36.8	201	360	110	22.2	15.6
Extreme Poverty Line = B./519						
Monolingual Spanish	15.1	322	343	57	5.1	2.4
Monolingual Indigenous	92.5	39	220	11	53.1	34.7
Bilingual	27.9	152	250	41	14.4	8.9

Source: LSMS Panama 1997.

Table A6.9 – Malnutrition by Ethnic Group: % of Children Under Age 5				
	Chronic (HFA)	Weight (WFA)	Acute (WFH)	Total (Any kind)
All Panama				
Total	14	7	1.1	16
Ethnic Non-indigenous	9	5	1.0	11
Ethnic Indigenous	44	17	1.4	44
Ngobe-Buglé	48	17	1.2	49
Kuna	32	20	2.6	35
Embera-Wounan	33	14	0.8	36
All Poor				
Total	23	11	1.6	26
Ethnic Non-indigenous	16	9	1.6	18
Ethnic Indigenous	46	19	1.5	48
Ngobe-Buglé	50	18	1.3	51
Kuna	42	26	3.4	45
Embera-Wounan	36	16	0.9	40
Extreme poor				
Total	32	15	1.8	34
Ethnic Non-indigenous	22	12	2.0	25
Ethnic Indigenous	48	19	1.4	51
Ngobe-Buglé	52	20	0.9	54
Kuna	43	27	3.5	47
Embera-Wounan	35	10	1.3	39
Ethnic Indigenous by Area				
Within Indigenous Areas	50	20	1.9	51
Outside Indigenous Areas	22	8	n.a	24
Ethnic Ind. by Language Ability				
Household Head Monolingual Spanish	8	3	n.a	8
Household Head Bilingual	45	18	1.8	46
Household Head Monolingual Indigenous	46	16	n.a	47
Ethnic Indigenous by Gender				
Girls	40	19	1.5	43
Boys	46	17	1.5	48

Source: LSMS Panama 1997. Chronic malnutrition (HFA) defined as height for age being less than two standard deviations below the reference value. Underweight (WFA) defined as weight for age being less than two standard deviations below the reference value. Acute malnutrition (WFH) defined as weight for height being less than two standard deviations below reference value. N.A. reported due to small sample size.

Table A6.10 - Household Structure by Ethnicity and Poverty Group											
	All Poor						Total					
	Tot.	NI	I	N-B	K	E-W	Tot.	NI	I	N-B	K	E-W
Avg. household (HH) size	5.7	5.4	7.3	7.3	7.6	7.2	4.2	4.0	6.6	6.8	6.3	6.3
Avg. # children aged 0-5	1.1	0.9	1.5	1.5	1.2	1.4	0.5	0.4	1.3	1.5	0.8	1.3
Avg. # children aged 6-11	1.0	0.7	1.4	1.6	1.3	1.6	0.6	0.5	1.2	1.3	0.9	1.3
Avg. # children aged 12-17	0.7	0.8	1.3	1.3	1.4	1.0	0.6	0.5	1.1	1.2	1.1	0.9
Avg. # adults aged 18-59	2.4	2.4	2.9	2.7	3.1	3.0	2.1	2.1	2.7	2.6	2.9	2.6
Avg. # adults over 60	0.5	0.5	0.2	0.2	0.5	0.2	0.4	0.4	0.3	0.2	0.6	0.2
Avg. HH head age	47	49	43	42	48	39	49	49	45	44	52	40
Avg. # workers per HH	1.9	1.8	2.2	2.1	2.4	2.9	1.7	1.6	2.2	2.0	2.3	2.5
Dependency ratio[a]	3.3	3.3	3.5	3.8	2.9	2.4	2.9	2.9	3.2	3.8	2.6	2.3
% HH with female head	15	16	14	16	15	13	24	24	16	14	20	16
% of HH heads who are:												
Married	80	74	86	87	79	89	68	67	85	87	76	88
Separated/divorced	7	9	5	5	5	3	11	11	6	5	9	5
Widowed	5	7	3	3	5	1	8	8	3	3	6	1
Single	8	9	6	5	11	6	12	13	6	5	10	6

Source: LSMS Panama 1997. Percentages may not add up to 100 due to rounding. Tot.= Total Panama, NI = Non-Indigenous, I=Indigenous, N-B=Ngobe-Buglé, K=Kuna, E-W=Embera-Wounan. (a) Dependency ratio = number of non-working members/number of working members.

Table A6.11 - Determinants of Fertility [a]		
	All Panama	Indigenous
# years of education	-0.175***	-0.071**
Age	0.327***	0.505***
Age squared	-0.003***	-0.005***
Indigenous	0.689***	
Kuna[b]		-1.266***
Embera-Wounan[b]		0.343
Household Consumption	-.00001***	-.0001**
Constant	-2.529***	-5.937***
Sample Size	3544	480
R-squared	0.39	0.52
Mean Fertility	3.0	3.5

(a) The dependent variable is number of live births ever born by a woman (for women between the ages 15-49). (b) The omitted variable for the indigenous group binary variables is the Ngobe-Buglé. Significant levels: * = 90%, ** = 95%, *** = 99%.

Table A6.12 – Labor Force Participation for the Indigenous [a]				
% of Population Aged 15+	All Indigenous	Ngobe Buglé	Kuna	Embera-Wounan
Area				
All	54	47	58	73
Within indigenous	53	47	56	78
Outside indigenous	56	44	58	68
Age Groups (yrs)				
15-17	34	32	37	39
18-24	55	41	64	81
25-39	61	52	66	77
40-59	62	56	61	85
60+	46	41	46	56
Education				
No Education	45	40	42	69
Primary	57	51	59	73
Secondary	62	51	63	80
Vocational/other[b]	76	100	71	100
Higher [b,c]	72	100	34	100

Source: Panama LSMS 1997. (a) Using the international definition (See Annex 11 of Volume 2 of Poverty Assessment). (b)Very small sample. (c) Includes graduate and post graduate schooling.

Table A6.13 - Intensity of Work, by Ethnic Group		
	Indigenous	Non-Indigenous
No. of months worked:		
First Job	8.4	9.3
First two jobs	9.4	10.3
Days worked per week	5.1	5.2
Hours worked:		
Per week (first job)	31	39
Per year (two jobs)	1186	1670
% with more than one job	12	13

Source: LSMS 1997.

Table A6.14 - Distribution of Indigenous Workers by Sector						
% of employed individuals	All Indigenous	Ngobe Buglé	Kuna	Embera-Wounan	Within Indigenous Areas	Outside Indigenous Areas
Agriculture	50	65	28	45	67	16
Mining	1	1	0	0	1	1
Manufacturing	7	3	10	12	8	6
Basic services[a]	1	1	1	0	1	1
Construction	2	1	3	4	1	5
Commerce	20	19	21	22	16	29
Transport	3	2	4	2	1	6
Financial services	2	1	3	2	1	5
Community services[b]	16	7	31	14	6	33
All	100	100	100	100	100	100
Total # employed ('000)	75	36	22	19	50	25

Source: Panama LSMS 1997. (a) Basic services such as electricity, water, sanitation, garbage collection etc. (b) Public and community services such as public administration, defense, sports associations, NGOs, domestic services. Numbers may not add up due to rounding.

Table A6.15 - Distribution of Indigenous Workers by Type of Employment						
% of all employed individuals	All Indigenous	Ngobe Buglé	Kuna	Embera-Wounan	Within Indigenous Areas	Outside Indigenous Areas
Public sector	9	4	17	9	5	15
Canal	0	0	0	1	0	1
Private sector:	91	96	83	90	95	84
White Collar	21	22	22	18	12	39
Blue Collar	8	7	11	6	9	5
Domestic laborer	3	2	6	2	1	7
Self-employed	33	35	29	34	39	22
Unpaid laborer	27	30	16	30	34	11
All	100	100	100	100	100	100
Total # employed ('000)	75	36	22	19	50	25

Source: Panama LSMS 1997.

Table A6.16 – Share of Indigenous Workers in the Informal Sector						
Informal sector workers as % of all workers in category	All Indigenous	Ngobe Buglé	Kuna	Embera-Wounan	Within Indigenous Areas	Outside Indigenous Areas
All	63	68	56	63	74	47
Type of Employment						
Public sector	0	0	0	0	0	0
Canal	0	0	0	0	0	0
Private sector:	70	71	64	70	79	58
Enterprise	12	12	16	7	15	21
Day laborer	39	40	34	48	38	73
Domestic Employee	100	100	100	100	100	100
Self-employed	96	97	95	98	99	89
Unpaid laborer	87	90	98	76	87	86
Geographic Area						
Outside indigenous	43	36	50	38	-	-
Within indigenous	73	75	63	79	-	-

Source: Panama LSMS 1997.

Table A6.17 - Sources of Income, by Ethnic Group		
	Ethnic Groups	
	Indigenous	Non-Indigenous
Labor Earnings	59	66
Wages and Salaries	36	50
Self-Employment	23	16
Non-Labor Income	41	34
Returns to Capital[a]	16	17
Donations/Transfers	21	8
From institutions	19	4
From family, friends	2	4
Pensions, Indemnities	4	8
Other Income	0	1
Total Income Per Capita (B./)	693	2407

Source: LSMS 1997. (a) Returns to capital include: interest received (negligible) plus the imputed value of physical assets and property.

Table A6.18– Agriculture's Contribution to Incomes, by Ethnic Group						
	All	Non-indigenous	Indigenous	Ngobe-Buglé	Kuna	Embera-Wounan
Per capita Income	2237	2407	693	395	1393	762
% from Agriculture	27	26	33	30	23	52
% of Agriculture Income: [a]						
From wages	14	13	23	23	17	35
From own production	86	87	77	77	83	65
% of Own Production:[a]						
For sales	43	51	11	8	13	21
For own consumption	57	49	89	92	87	79
Source: Panama LSMS 1997. a\ Includes farming households only.						

Table A6.19 - Education Characteristics by Ethnicity and Poverty Group												
	All Poor						Total					
	Tot.	NI	I	N-B	K	E-W	Tot.	NI	I	N-B	K	E-W
Literacy												
Read and write (age >9, in %):												
All	83	88	65	62	69	72	92	94	70	64	80	75
Men	85	88	74	73	77	79	93	94	79	75	85	82
Women	80	87	55	50	64	64	92	94	61	53	74	67
Net Enrollment Rate												
Net Enrollment Rate (%): [a]												
Primary	89	92	83	81	85	91	92	94	83	82	89	88
Secondary	37	43	16	16	31	16	62	67	18	19	51	24
Educational Attainment: Years of schooling												
Years of Schooling (age >12):												
All	5.1	5.4	3.5	3.1	4.7	3.8	8.1	8.4	4.5	2.8	6.8	4.6
Men	5.1	5.4	4.1	3.6	5.3	4.4	7.9	8.1	5.1	3.2	7.3	5.3
Women	5.0	5.5	2.9	2.5	4.1	3.1	8.3	8.7	3.9	2.8	6.3	3.7
Between 12-17	5.6	6.0	4.2	4.1	4.9	4.0	6.8	7.1	4.8	4.3	6.2	4.4
Between 18-24	6.4	7.0	4.6	3.8	5.0	5.8	9.3	9.8	5.1	4.2	6.4	6.1
Between 25-39	6.0	6.6	3.8	3.0	5.7	4.4	9.5	8.2	5.0	3.6	7.9	5.4
Between >40	3.1	3.4	1.6	0.9	3.5	0.9	7.0	7.3	3.3	1.5	6.4	2.1
Max. educ. for HH head/comp. [b]												
No Education (%)	46	39	69	76	45	67	23	19	60	71	34	58
Primary (%)	48	54	28	22	46	30	44	45	32	26	46	34
Secondary (%)	6	7	4	2	9	3	22	24	6	3	16	6
Higher (%)	0	0	0	0	0	0	11	12	1	0	4	1
Educational Services												
Students in:												
Public schools	98	98	98	99	90	100	84	83	97	99	90	98
Private schools	2	2	2	1	10	0	16	17	3	1	10	2
Household Spending on Education												
(% of students in public or private school who pay anything for school)												
Students who pay something B.>0	65	72	42	43	44	37	80	83	50	47	61	45

Source: LSMS Panama 1997. Percentages may not add up to 100 due to rounding. Tot.=Total Panama, NI= Non-Indigenous, I= Indigenous, N-B=Ngobe-Buglé , K=Kuna,E-W=Embera-Wounan. (a) Net Enrollment Rate = all students enrolled in primary who are also of primary school age / all primary school enrollment (same for secondary). (b) Maximum level of education for household head or his/her companion.

Table A6.20 – Education by Poverty group and Language Ability for the Ethnic Indigenous Population						
	All Poor			**Total**		
	MS	**MI**	**B**	**MS**	**MI**	**B**
Literacy						
Read and write (age >12 in %):						
All	88	17	79	94	20	92
Men	88	27	83	94	32	93
Women	87	12	75	94	15	91
Net Enrollment Rate						
Net Enrollment Rate (%): [a]						
Primary	92	54	94	94	55	94
Secondary	43	1	21	66	8	52
Educational Attainment: Years of Schooling						
Years of Schooling (age > 12):						
All	4.9	0.6	3.9	7.1	0.9	8.8
Men	4.8	0.9	4.1	6.8	1.2	8.6
Women	5.0	0.5	3.6	7.3	0.8	9.0
Between 12-17	5.7	1.4 *	4.4	6.8	1.7 *	6.1
Between 18-24	7.3	1.0 *	5.4	9.7	1.6 *	10.1
Between 25-39	6.6	0.4 *	4.8	9.5	0.6 *	10.7
Between >40	3.4	0.4 *	2.9	6.6	0.7 *	10.3
Max. educ. for HH head/companion[b]						
No Education (%)	39	87 *	63	22	84 *	26
Primary (%)	53	12 *	33	47	14 *	29
Secondary (%)	7	1 *	4	22	1 *	26
Higher (%)	0	0 *	0	10	0 *	19
Educational Services						
Students in: (%)						
Public schools	99	97	97	87	97	70
Private schools	1	3	3	13	3	30
Household Spending on Education (% of students in public or private school who pay anything for school)						
Students who pay something > B./0	73	19	41	83	25	64

Source: LSMS Panama 1997. Percentages may not add up to 100 due to rounding. MS = monolingual Spanish speaking, MI = monolingual indigenous speaking, B = bilingual speakers. (a) Net Enrollment Rate = all students enrolled in primary who are also of primary school age / all primary school enrollment (same for secondary). (b) Maximum level of education for household head or his/her companion. * indicates very small sample.

Table A6.21 – Language Spoken at School for Currently Enrolled Students				
	Spanish	Indigenous Lang.	Other Lang.[a]	Total
Panama: All	96.9	1.4	1.6	100
Panama: Bilingual Speakers	87.0	1.6	11.4	100
Ethnic Indigenous: All	84.9	14.8	0.2	100
Ethnic Indigenous: Bilingual	96.3	3.3	0.3	100

Source: LSMS Panama 1997. Percentages may not add up to 100 due to rounding. (a) This includes mainly English.

Table A6.22 – Language Spoken at School: For Currently Enrolled Ethnic Indigenous Students				
	Spanish	Indigenous Lang.	Other Lang.[a]	Total
Aged 6-11	80.4	19.2	0.4	100
Aged 12-17	93.0	7.0	na	100
Aged 18-24	85.4	14.6	na	100
All Poor	83.3	16.7	0.0	100
Non-poor	92.1	6.7	1.2	100
Ngobe-Buglé	85.8	14.2	0.0	100
Kuna	83.0	17.0	0.0	100
Embera-Wounan	85.0	13.9	1.2	100

Source: LSMS Panama 1997. Percentages may not add up to 100 due to rounding. (a) This includes mainly English.

Table A6.23 - Use of Health Services, by Ethnicity and Poverty Group											
	All Poor						Total				
	Tot.	NI	I	N-B	K	E-W	Tot.	NI	I	N-B	K	E-W
Health Visits, Sickness During Past Month											
Consultancy rate [a]	0.8	0.9	0.6	0.6	0.7	0.6	1.1	1.1	0.7	0.7	0.8	0.6
Coverage rate[b]	0.4	0.5	0.3	0.3	0.4	0.3	0.6	0.6	0.4	0.3	0.5	0.4
Concentration rate[c]	1.8	1.8	2.0	2.2	1.8	1.7	1.9	1.9	1.9	2.1	1.6	1.7
Place of Treatment											
Place of treatment:											
Public	83	83	83	79	88	86	68	67	79	81	72	86
Private	17	17	17	21	12	14	32	33	21	19	28	14
Total	100	100	100	100	100	100	100	100	100	100	100	100
Public hospital	37	39	26	33	18	16	41	41	33	36	32	26
Health center	46	44	57	46	70	70	27	26	46	45	40	60
Clinic/private office	9	10	3	2	4	7	26	27	9	2	18	7
Pharmacy	4	4	1	1	1	2	4	4	3	2	5	3
Own home	4	3	12	18	7	6	3	2	9	15	5	4
Total	100	100	100	100	100	100	100	100	100	100	100	100
Avg. time to treatment (minutes)	40	39	44	60	23	37	32	32	41	55	25	44
Maternal Care											
Prenatal visits (avg. #)	6	6	5	5	6	6	7	7	6	6	7	6
Births in hospital or clinic (%)	97	97	97	94	99	100	97	97	98	97	97	100
Tetanus shots (%)	74	77	56	47	85	65	77	78	68	60	90	70
Household Expenditures on Health Care											
% paying for medical services	36	38	23	20	32	22	44	45	27	23	38	22

Source: LSMS Panama 1997. Percentages may not add up to 100 due to rounding. Tot.=Total Panama, NI= Non-Indigenous, I= Indigenous, N-B=Ngobe-Buglé, K=Kuna,E-W=Embera- Wounan. (a) Consultancy rate = number of visits/ number of sick, in other words, the number of visits on average for an individual reporting illness. (b) Coverage rate = number of people with at least one visit/ number of sick; in other words, the percent of people reporting illness who had at least one medical visit. (c) Concentration rate = number of visits/ number of people with at least one visit.

Table A6.24- Housing and Access to Basic Services by Ethnicity and Poverty Group												
% of households unless		All Poor					Total					
otherwise indicated		Tot.	NI	I	N-B	K	E-W	Tot.	NI	I	N-B	K	E-W
Housing Ownership and Tenancy													
Rent		4	4	2	0	10	2	13	13	6	0	17	7
Own		83	83	83	83	84	83	76	76	78	78	78	80
Other		13	13	15	17	6	15	11	11	16	22	5	13
With registered title/deed		11	12	6	6	5	7	25	26	10	6	15	13
With title in process		8	9	3	2	5	3	13	13	7	4	11	10
No title or deed		64	62	74	75	74	73	38	37	62	68	51	57
Housing Conditions													
Type of dwelling	House	65	73	28	22	50	28	72	74	40	31	59	39
	Hut	27	19	67	74	42	66	9	7	54	65	29	52
	Apartment	3	3	2	1	6	0	12	12	4	1	9	5
	Other	5	5	4	2	3	5	6	7	3	3	3	4
Ceiling	Quality 1[a]	79	86	46	49	29	48	91	94	50	42	59	61
	Quality 2[b]	25	18	63	66	68	51	9	6	50	48	41	39
Walls	Quality 1[a]	6	6	4	3	9	0	15	15	6	4	15	2
	Quality 2[b]	95	95	96	96	89	100	85	85	94	96	85	98
Floor	Quality 1[a]	53	60	19	16	27	19	80	83	33	24	46	30
	Quality 2[b]	48	40	83	84	75	82	20	17	67	76	54	70
# of rooms		2.5	2.6	2.0	2.0	2.1	1.9	3.2	3.3	2.3	2.2	2.7	2.2
# of people per room		2.8	2.5	4.6	4.3	4.9	5.0	1.7	1.6	3.8	3.9	3.4	4.0
Water Access													
Water Source													
Piped water supply		73	78	48	31	78	80	89	91	56	33	86	85
From well		9	13	3	4	4	0	5	5	3	4	3	0
From river, other		18	9	49	65	18	20	6	4	41	63	12	15
Treat water if water source is not piped water		14	21	6	3	42	7	17	23	7	4	35	7
% with water service		47	51	27	22	47	31	64	66	33	22	57	38
Sanitary Services													
% sewer service		17	18	12	13	11	10	55	57	25	20	37	23
% latrine		64	70	31	22	42	55	38	39	31	24	34	49
% with none		19	12	57	65	47	35	7	4	44	56	29	28
Trash collection		24	27	7	2	8	24	59	61	20	5	36	41
Energy Sources													
Lighting Source:													
Electricity		47	53	17	11	21	36	79	82	32	16	55	49
Kerosene, candles		51	45	75	79	77	60	20	17	60	71	45	48
Other or none		2	2	8	10	2	4	1	1	8	12	1	3
Cooking With:													
Gas, electricity		46	51	19	13	23	35	78	80	36	23	55	50
Firewood		52	47	79	84	77	63	20	17	62	75	44	48

Source: LSMS Panama 1997. Percentages may not add up to 100 due to rounding. Tot.=Total Panama, NI=Non-Indigenous, I=Indigenous, N-B=Ngobe-Buglé, K=Kuna, E-W=Embera-Wounan. (a) Quality 1: cement, concrete, tile, brick, metal. (b) Quality 2: wood, thatch, earth.

Table A6.25 - Land Ownership						
	All	NI	I	N-B	K	E-W
% HH owning some land	18	15	52	61	34	48
Avg. land owned (in ha) [a]	17	19	7	7	6	10
Avg. rented land (in ha) [a]	2.7	3.1	0.7	0.5	0.5	1.5
Land for farming (in ha) [a],[b]	19.7	22.1	7.7	7.5	6.5	11.5
Percent of HH with:						
No land (in %)	82	85	48	39	66	52
0-1 Ha (in %)	4	4	8	9	9	6
1-2 Ha (in %)	3	2	11	13	5	10
2-5 Ha (in %)	5	3	19	24	15	10
5-15 Ha (in %)	3	3	8	9	3	12
More than 15 Ha (in %)	4	4	6	7	3	10
Total (in %)	100	100	100	100	100	100

Source: LSMS Panama 1997. Percentages may not add up to 100 due to rounding. NI= Non-Indigenous, I= Indigenous, N-B= Ngobe-Buglé , K= Kuna, E-W= Embera-Wounan. (a) Calculated for households with more than 0.25 hectares of land (minimum land size to engage in farming activities). (b) Total land in hectares available to the household for farming.

Table A6.26 - Land Tenancy by Ethnicity						
% of households owning some land	Total	NI	I	N-B	K	E-W
With registered title or deed	25	28	10	12	6	6
With unregistered title	22	25	13	16	7	0
Cooperative land	2	2	1	0	0	4
No title/ owner without title	51	45	76	72	87	90
Total	100	100	100	100	100	100

Source: LSMS Panama 1997. Percentages may not add up to 100 due to rounding. Total =Total Panama, NI= Non-Indigenous, I= Indigenous, N-B=Ngobe-Buglé , K=Kuna, E-W= Embera-Wounan.

Table A6.27 – Savings, by Ethnicity and Poverty Group											
	All Poor						Total				
	Tot.	NI	I	N-B	K	E-W	Tot.	NI	I	N-B	K	E-W
% with savings[a]	11	11	9	7	13	11	36	37	19	12	36	16
% by place of savings[b]												
Private Banks	6	6	11	11	n.a	n.a	35	35	21	11	32	13
National Bank of Panama	19	16	34	31	58	12	23	23	31	19	38	38
Caja de ahorros	51	54	31	21	41	44	40	40	38	31	51	20
Local Cooperatives[c]	11	10	28	28	n.a	n.a	10	10	7	15	0	10
Credit/Savings Unions	16	14	25	29	n.a	44	20	19	28	39	23	20
Savings/storage clubs	2	2	n.a	n.a	n.a	n.a	8	8	7	n.a	7	n.a

Source: LSMS Panama 1997. Tot.=Total Panama, NI= Non-Indigenous, I= Indigenous, N-B=Ngobe-Buglé , K=Kuna,E-W=Embera-Wounan. (a) % of households. Reference period is last 12 months. (b) % of those with savings. People can have savings in more than one place; hence figures do not add up to 100%. (c) Neighborhood and worker cooperatives.

TableA6.28 – Credit, by Ethnicity and Poverty Group						
	All Poor			**Total**		
Credit in Cash (Loans)						
	Tot.	NI	I	Tot.	NI	I
% soliciting credit[a]	7	7	5	14	14	8
% received credit[b]	93	94	86	95	95	94
Was credit amount sufficient[c]	54	55	42	67	68	54
Reason for not soliciting credit[d]						
Did not need it	8	9	7	29	30	15
Too risky	48	49	43	37	37	41
Too much paperwork	15	15	14	13	13	13
They wouldn't give it to me	21	21	25	13	12	21
Other	8	8	11	8	7	11
Reason for being refused credit[e]						
No assets for guarantee	31	40	0	17	18	0
Lack of property title	33	43	0	9	9	0
Low income	15	0	67	29	28	67
Other	21	17	33	45	45	33
Credit in Kind (Purchases on Credit)						
% making purchases on credit[g]	15	16	10	18	19	14
% using credit for :						
Clothing	6	6	2	12	12	5
Food	10	10	8	7	6	9
Household durables	1	1	1	4	4	2
Other consumption goods	0	0	0	2	2	1
Total Credit (in Cash and Kind)						
Average amount received (B./)[h]						
Consumer loans and credit	561	569	503	1933	1918	2350
Loans or credit for businesses	169	188	29	2065	2089	1392
Total loans and credit	730	757	532	3998	4007	3742

Source: LSMS Panama 1997. Tot.=Total Panama, NI= Non-Indigenous, I= Indigenous. (a) Households soliciting credit as % of all households. Reference period is past 12 months. (b) Those who solicited and received credit as % of all households soliciting credit. (c) Those who believed amount received to be sufficient as % of all households receiving credit. (d) Households who did not solicit credit as % of all households. (e) % of households who solicited but did not receive credit (f) Average value of those households receiving credit. (g) Those who believed amount received to be sufficient as % of all households receiving credit. (h) Average value of those households receiving credit.

Table A6.29 – Determinants of Poverty for Among the Ethnic Indigenous Population (Probit Estimates)	Marginal Effects
Geographic area:	
Within indigenous areas (vs. outside)	0.025**
Number of household members:	
Age 0-5	0.017***
Age 6-11	0.011***
Age 12-17	0.010**
Age 18-24	0.016***
Age 25-59	0.005
Age over 60	0.007
Female head	0.003
Max. education of head or companion:	
1-5 years (vs. none)	-0.076**
Primary completed (vs. none)	-0.082***
7-11 years (vs. none)	-0.018
Secondary completed (vs. none)	-0.160**
Higher (vs. none)	-0.260**
Ethnic Group	
Ngobe-Buglé (vs. Kuna)	0.001
Embera-Wounan (vs. Kuna)	0.012
Housing conditions	
Rooms per capita	-0.018**
With latrine (vs. none)	-0.053***
Minutes to water source	0.002***
Access to electricity	-0.005
Biggest source of household income	
Private formal (vs. public formal)	0.003
Private informal (vs. public formal)	0.025*
Non labor (vs. public formal)	0.001
Wealth	
Land owned (in hectares)	-0.017*
House ownership with registered title (vs. no ownership)	0.005
House ownership without registered title (vs. no ownership)	0.010
Value of equipment owned	-0.084***
Cooperative (membership)	0.003
Sample Size	459
Fit (% of correct predictions)	0.94
Dependent Variable: Poor (Yes/No). Significant levels: * = 90%, ** = 95%, *** = 99%	

Table A6.30 – Determinants of Poverty for Among the Ethnic Non-Indigenous Population (Probit Estimates)	
	Marginal Effects
Geographic area:	
Within indigenous areas (vs. outside)	0.199**
Number of household members:	
Age 0-5	0.077***
Age 6-11	0.052***
Age 12-17	0.045***
Age 18-24	0.037***
Age 25-59	0.021***
Age over 60	0.052***
Female head	-0.009
Max. education of head or companion:	
1-5 years (vs. none)	-0.015
Primary completed (vs. none)	-0.040*
7-11 years (vs. none)	-0.070***
Secondary completed (vs. none)	-0.074***
Higher (vs. none)	-0.142***
Housing conditions	
Rooms per capita	-0.082***
With latrine (vs. none)	-0.136***
Minutes to water source	0.002
Access to electricity	-0.098***
Biggest source of household income	
Private formal (vs. public formal)	0.048***
Private informal (vs. public formal)	0.044***
Non labor (vs. public formal)	0.063***
Wealth	
Land owned (in hectares)	-0.030**
House ownership with registered title (vs. no ownership)	-0.050***
House ownership without registered title (vs. no ownership)	-0.086***
Value of equipment owned	-0.190***
Cooperative (membership)	-0.040***
Sample Size	4478
Fit (% of correct predictions)	0.86
Dependent Variable: Poor (Yes/No). Significant levels: * = 90%, ** = 95%, *** = 99%	

Table A6.31 - Ranking of Community Priorities, Indigenous Communities in LSMS Sample		
	Ranking	**% of Communities in Sample**
Education	1	37%
Potable water	1	37%
Drugs, alcohol	2	29%
Transport, roads	3	25%
Health	4	22%
Housing	4	22%
Safety / crime	4	22%
Employment / labor	5	17%
Sanitation services	5	17%
Electricity, telephones	6	12%
Social / community centers	7	5%
Source: LSMS 1997; Community Survey. Communities were asked to list their two most important priority issues / problems. Results presented in this table aggregate the two responses. Note that the sample is not statistically representative of communities in Panama. Percents refer to the share of 24 indigenous communities in the sample with completed questionnaires.		

Annex 7 - Urban Poverty in Panama

Kathy Lindert,[1] April 21, 1999

OVERVIEW OF PANAMA'S URBAN AREAS

1.   As a consequence of general migration to the cities, the size of Panama's urban population has grown faster than that of rural areas. The most recent census shows that the growth rate for urban areas averaged 3.7 percent p.a. as compared with 2.0 percent in rural areas and 2.9 percent for the nation as a whole from 1980 to 1990. Census data indicate that close to 54 percent of Panama's population of 2.7 million lives in urban areas.[2] This compares with South American countries,[3] which are generally more urbanized, and Central American countries,[4] which are typically more rural.

2.   Panama's urban areas can be divided into two distinct categories: (i) the two "major urban" metropolitan areas of Panama City and Colón at both ends of the canal; and (ii) smaller provincial centers, many of which have important ties to the rural economy. Table A7.1 below ranks various "urban" districts in Panama by their degrees of urbanization.[5]

3.   With a total of over one million people in 1990, the Panama province accounts for 46 percent of the national population. Some eighty percent of the provincial population live in urban areas. The average population density for Panama City is 3,883 per square kilometer. Population density within the District of Panama ranges greatly across the various *corregimientos* from just over one thousand in Pedregal to 51,220 per square kilometer in El Chorrillo.

4.   Colon is the Panama's second largest city and the capital of a large province of the same name. The City of Colon is squeezed into a small island-like peninsula spanning less than three square kilometers. Population density is extremely high (18,846 persons per square kilometer). With 140,908 inhabitants in 1990, the District of Colón accounts for 84 percent of the population in Colón Province. Outside the District of Colón, much of the region is rural and largely undeveloped.

5.   David is Panama's third largest city, the capital of the Chiriqui province, a productive agricultural region that is home to the majority of Panama's indigenous Guaymí (Ngobe-Buglé) population.[6] With its location along the Pan-American Highway near the Costa Rican border, David is an important transportation hub. Approximately 103 thousand inhabitants live in the district of David.[7] Population density is not nearly as high as Panama City: 118 persons per square kilometer on average and 925 in the city center (see Table A7.1 above).[8]

6.   Other urban centers primarily include provincial capitals, such as Santiago, Panama's fourth largest city and the capital of the province of Veraguas, Penonomé the capital of the province of Coclé, and Chitré, the capital of the province of Herrera and the largest town of the peninsula of Azuero (see

---

[1] The author would like to thank Carlos Sobrado for assistance with the LSMS analysis of urban poverty and Renos Vakis for assistance with the labor analysis for urban areas.

[2] The Census and the LSMS define urban areas as any area with more 1,500 residents with the following characteristics: electricity, public water supply, a sewer system, and paved streets. To classify as urban, these areas should also have secondary schools, commercial establishments, social and recreation centers, and sidewalks.

[3] Over three quarters of the population in Argentina, Brazil, Chile, Colombia, and Peru is urban, the urban population in Bolivia (57%), Ecuador (57%) and Paraguay (52%) is on par with Panama's.

[4] Urban residents account for less than half of the total population in all Central American countries except Nicaragua.

[5] Herrera, Ligia J. "Regiones de Desarrollo Socioeconomico de Panama: 1980-1990: Transformaciones ocurridas en la decada." CELA, 1994.

[6] The 1990 census indicates that 51% of the Guaymí (also called Ngobe-Buglé) population lives in Chiriquí; another 41% live in Bocas del Toro, with the remainder living in other provinces.

[7] 1990 Census.

[8] 1990 Census.

Table A7.1). Many of these centers maintain important links to the rural economy (both direct and indirect).

District	Province	Urbanization Index[a]	Population[b]	Pop. Density[c]
Table A7.1 - The Urban Population in Panama **For Districts with High and Medium Degrees of Urbanization**				
Entire Country (1990)	--	n.a.	2,329,329	31
High Urbanization				
Panama	Panama	83.1	584,803	228
o/w: Panama City	Panama	n.a.	389,172	3,883
Medium-High Urbanization				
San Miguelito	Panama	77.2	243,025	4,861
Chitré	Herrera	70.0	34,747	381
David	Chiriquí	65.1	102,678	118
Aguadulce	Coclé	61.7	32,434	70
Colón	Colón	62.9	140,908	94
o/w City of Colón	Colón	n.a.	54,654	18,846
Arraiján	Panama	64.0	61,849	364
La Chorrera	Panama	61.7	89,780	131
Medium Urbanization				
Las Tablas	Los Santos	55.4	21,110	30
o/w city center	Los Santos	n.a.	6,706	798
Santiago	Veraguas	53.7	60,959	63
o/w city center	Veraguas	n.a.	43,874	144
Changuinola	Bocas del Toro	52.7	56,430	14
Bugaba	Chiriquí	49.7	57,890	66
Antón	Coclé	40.9	37,137	50
Taboga	Panama	40.2	1,810	151

Sources: 1990 Census (population and population density); Ligia Herrera J. (1994), based on 1990 census data.
a\The urbanization index is based on a composite set of indicators of urbanization including the share of the population of the district living in "urban" areas (as defined by the census), demographic growth rates, population density, the share of the population *not* engaged in agricultural activities, and telecommunications service access.
b\Population from 1990 Census.
c\Population density (individuals per square kilometer) from 1990 Census.

A PROFILE OF URBAN POVERTY[9]

Incidence of Urban Poverty

7.   Although poverty is less widespread in urban areas than in the countryside, there are a considerable number of pockets of urban poverty in Panama, and a significant share of city-dwellers live just above the poverty line and could be considered vulnerable. Moreover, given demographic trends and urban migration, it is likely that a higher share of the poor will be concentrated in urban areas in the future.

8.   Approximately 15 percent of the urban population (over 230 thousand people) fall below the full poverty line, accounting for 23 percent of Panama's poor (Table A7.2). Urban poverty is not very deep in Panama, and only three percent of city dwellers live below the extreme poverty line.

9.   Nonetheless, the presence of a significant group of urban residents who could be considered "vulnerable" or "at risk" of poverty is apparent from the flatter slope of the cumulative distribution of the population living just above the full poverty line. In fact, raising the poverty line (or alternatively, reducing total consumption) by ten percent (from B./905 to B./995) would increase the incidence of urban

---

[9] This report defines the extreme poor as those whose total annual per capita consumption falls below B./519 and the poor as those whose total annual per capita consumption falls below B./905 (including the extreme poor). See Annex 2 of the Poverty Assessment for details.

poverty by about 22 percent, from 15 to 19 percent of the urban population (from 232 to 284 thousand people), raising the contribution of the urban poor to national poverty from 23 to 25 percent (Table A7.2 and Figure A7.1).

Table A7.2 – Incidence of Urban Poverty and Vulnerability					
	Poverty Line (B./)	Head Count Index (Incidence)	Contribution to National Poverty	Poverty Gap Index (P1, Depth)	Severity Index (P2)
Extreme Poverty Line	519	3.1%	9.2%	0.7	0.2
Full Poverty Line (FPL)	905	15.3%	22.7%	3.9	1.5
FPL + 10%	995	18.7%	25.4%	5.1	2.0
FPL + 20%	1085	22.0%	27.4%	6.4	2.6
FPL + 30%	1176	25.9%	29.9%	7.7	3.3
Source: LSMS 1997.					

Urban Children and Youths in Poverty

Figure A7.1

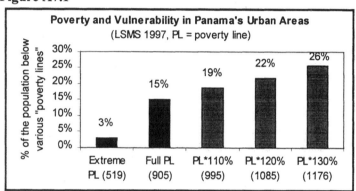

10.   Moreover, one quarter of all urban children under five live in poverty, with six percent in extreme poverty. A similar figure (22 percent) of children aged 6-11 and youths aged 12-17 (18 percent) are growing up in poverty in urban areas. In fact, children and youths under aged 18 account for close to one half (46 percent) of all city dwellers living under the poverty line. The concentration of poverty among children and youths in urban areas has important generational implications and possible poverty trap effects.

Geographic Distribution of the Urban Poor

11.   The LSMS sample was selected to be statistically representative for the Panama City - San Miguelito metropolitan area (PCSM) and at the *regional* level for both urban and rural areas within each region.[10] This allows for a more detailed analysis of the geographic distribution of urban poverty. As shown in Table A7.3 below, a significant share (29 percent) of the urban population of the Occidental region is poor. This region accounts for 23 percent of urban poverty and includes Panama's third largest city, David, as well as a number of other smaller towns such as Bugaba, Barú, and Boquete in the Chiriquí province and Changuinola in Bocas del Toro. While 19 percent of the urban population of the Central region (which includes smaller cities like Chitré, Aguadulce, las Tablas, Santiago, and Anton) lives in poverty, this region only accounts for 15 percent of Panama's urban poor due to its relatively smaller population. In contrast, although a relatively small share of the population of the Panama City - San Miguelito (PCSM) greater metropolitan area falls below the poverty line, PCSM accounts for close to forty percent of the country's urban poor. Many neighborhoods in PCSM are mixed, with pockets of poverty juxtaposed with wealthier areas. Likewise, although 12 percent of the urban areas in the rest of

---

[10] The regions ("dominio" variable) include: (i) Metropolitana, which includes the provinces of Panama and Colón (without PCSM which is its own separate "region") and which can be split into urban and rural; (ii) Central, which includes the provinces of Cocle, Herrera, los Santos and Veraguas (excluding indigenous areas) and which can be split into urban and rural; (iii) Occidental, which includes the western provinces of Chiriquí and Bocas del Toro (excluding indigenous areas) and which can be split into urban and rural; (iv) the indigenous "region" (areas), which include the indigenous areas of the above provinces plus those in San Blas and Darien; and (v) the "remote access" region (areas), which include the non-indigenous areas of San Blas, Darien, and other provinces.

the Metropolitana region (which covers the provinces of Colón and Panama excluding PCSM) is poor, this region accounts for one quarter of the urban poor.

	Percent of Urban Population	Distribution of Poverty (Using Full Poverty Line = B./905)				
		# Below PL	Head Count Index (%)	Contribution to Urban Poverty	Poverty Gap Index[a]	Severity Index[b]
All Urban						
All Urban	100%	232,006	15%	100%	3.9	1.5
By Region (Urban Areas Only) – SAMPLE NOT STTATISTICALLY REPRESENTATIVE[c]						
PCSM	51%	90,064	12%	39%	3.0	1.2
Other Metropolitana	25%	54,169	14%	23%	2.9	0.1
Central	12%	34,288	19%	15%	5.2	2.0
Occidental	12%	53,484	29%	23%	8.6	3.7

Source: LSMS 1997. a\The poverty gap index (P$_1$) represents the depth of poverty, measuring the amount needed to bring the poor to the poverty line, expressed as a percentage of the poverty line taking into account the share of the poor in the total population. b\The poverty severity index (P$_2$) is a derivation of the poverty gap index that takes into account the distribution of consumption between the poor. In other words, this measure indicates the degree of inequality among the population below the poverty line. c\Regional sample *is* statistically representative. Urban areas within the regions of: (i) Panama City - San Miguelito (PCSM), (ii) other Metropolitana (includes the urban areas in the provinces of Panama and Colón excluding PCSM), (iii) the Central Region (includes the urban areas in the provinces of Veraguas, Coclé, Herrera and los Santos), and (iv) the Occidental Region (includes the urban areas in the provinces of Chiriquí and Bocas del Toro). There were no urban areas in the sample of the Province of Darien.

Household Characteristics of the Urban Poor

12.   Poor and extreme poor households in urban areas tend to have larger households and more children than their non-poor counterparts (Table A7.4). Consequently, with a similar number of workers, they tend to have higher dependency ratios.

13.   A more thorough analysis of headship reveals that some types of female headed households do have a higher incidence of poverty than male headed households (though this result does not hold for female headed households overall).[11] Specifically, a larger share of extreme poor households are reportedly headed by females than moderately poor and non poor households. In addition, a higher share of urban households headed by females who are *unida* (unmarried partners) is poor (moderately or extremely) than their male counterparts,[12] and this difference is significant.[13]

[11] See Annex 19 of the Poverty Assessment for a more thorough analysis of headship by gender.
[12] Close to 30 percent of households headed by females who are *unidas* are poor, compared with eleven percent of households headed by males who are *unidos*.
[13] Significant with a t-statistic of 3.105.

Table A7.4 - Characteristics of Poor Urban Households in Panama				
	Extreme Poor	All Poor	Non Poor	Total Urban
# Household members	6.7	6.1	3.8	4.0
# Kids 0-5 years old/household	1.3	1.1	0.4	0.4
# Kids 6-11 years old/household	1.3	1.0	0.4	0.5
# Adults > 60 years old/household	0.3	0.4	0.4	0.4
Age of household head	48.2	45.9	48.5	48.2
# Workers/household	1.8	1.9	1.7	1.7
Dependency Ratio	5.2	3.9	2.8	2.9
Reported Female Head (%)	38%	29%	29%	29%
% of Household Heads who are:				
With partner	58%	71%	65%	65%
Separated/Divorced	19%	11%	13%	12%
Widowed	6%	5%	8%	8%
Single	17%	12%	14%	14%
Source: LSMS 1997.				

Child Malnutrition in Urban Areas

14.   Like poverty, malnutrition is not as widespread in urban areas as in the countryside, though the incidence of malnutrition is higher among poor urban children than their non-poor counterparts. Overall, six percent of urban children under age five are stunted (using the height-for-age indicator of malnutrition).[14] Malnutrition is close to three times more prevalent among poor children than among the non-poor in urban areas. Eleven percent and 24 percent of poor and extreme poor children in urban areas are stunted, as compared with only four percent of non-poor urban children. In urban areas, malnutrition peaks among children aged 12-17 months, with twelve percent of children in this age group being stunted. This is a common result in which malnutrition rises during the transition from breast-feeding to a diet based completely on solids. There is no significant difference the prevalence of undernutrition among boys and girls in urban areas.

ASSETS OF THE URBAN POOR

15.   Poverty is not a static situation. Rather, people tend to move in an out of poverty,[15] as economic, household, and personal conditions change in the face of various risks. Multi-country analyses of the various coping strategies of vulnerable populations reveal that the poor possess a number of assets, or means of resisting worsening living conditions.[16] These assets can be grouped as follows: (i) labor; (ii) human capital (education and health); (iii) physical and financial assets, notably housing, credit and infrastructure; and (iv) social capital at the community level.[17] This section examines these key assets of the urban poor.

Labor

16.   Labor is the poor's most valuable asset. In a context of increasing economic insecurity, due to changes in prices, wages, and public expenditures, the poor's response is to diversify income resources

---

[14] The figures are three percent for weight-for-age and one percent for weight-for-height for urban children.

[15] There is some evidence, and much debate, over the degree to which those in extreme poverty are able to move out of their destitute living conditions. Data from several countries suggest that while the "moderately poor" are a fairly dynamic group, it is much more difficult for individuals to move out of extreme poverty.

[16] Moser (1996) plus specific country studies.

[17] Household relations (extended families, etc.) can also be viewed as an asset. Moser (1996).

by mobilizing their labor. This can involve either intensifying existing income-generating strategies or creating new ways of earning income.[18]

17.   Indeed, most income for the urban poor comes from labor earnings. As shown in Table A7.5 below, labor earnings accounted for over three-quarters of the total incomes of the poor, compared with roughly two-thirds for the non-poor. Of this, urban workers obtain roughly ninety percent of their labor earnings from wages and salaries, with the remaining tenth coming from self-employment.

18.   Panama's urban poor are primarily employed in commerce and community/public services (particularly women), followed by manufacturing and construction (Table A7.6 below). A smaller share of the poor are employed in the financial services and the transport sector than the non-poor in urban areas. Likewise, the non-poor are more likely to work in the public sector than the poor (Table A7.7). Among the poor working in the private sector (89 percent), a larger share of poor urban men work in private enterprises and as day laborers, as compared with poor urban women who tend to work as domestic laborers or for themselves as self-employed workers. The relatively strong share of poor urban women who are self-employed has important implications for the targeting of micro-credit schemes (discussed more below).

Table A7.5 - Sources of Annual Income, by Type of Earnings, Urban Areas			
	Urban Areas		
Types of Earnings	Extreme Poor	All Poor	Non-Poor
Labor Earnings	**82%**	**78%**	**69%**
Wages and Salaries	75%	69%	57%
Self-Employment	6%	9%	11%
Non-Labor Earnings	**18%**	**22%**	**31%**
Returns to Capital[a]	7%	9%	16%
Donations/Transfers	7%	5%	3%
From institutions[b]	2%	2%	1%
From family, friends	5%	3%	2%
Pensions, Indemnities	4%	8%	11%
Other Income	**0%**	**1%**	**1%**
Total Income Per Capita (B./)	**627**	**849**	**3,796**

Source: LSMS 1997. a\ Returns to capital include: interest received (negligible) plus the imputed value of physical assets and property. b\ It is not possible to distinguish between public and private institutions.

19.   Poor urban workers – particularly poor urban women – tend to be concentrated in the informal sector (Table A7.6). Close to three quarters of all poor urban workers hold jobs in the informal sector, as compared with 40 percent of non-poor city dwellers. Eighty percent of poor working women in urban areas work in the informal sector. Indeed, controlling for other variables such as education and experience, lower levels of total household consumption are associated with informal-sector employment (see Appendix Table A7.A1). Moreover, the LSMS reveals that jobs held by poor workers appear to be less secure, with just over one third of poor urban workers holding a contract for their positions compared with close to sixty percent of non-poor employees.

---

[18] Moser (1996).

Table A7.6 - Distribution of Urban Workers by Sector, Gender and Poverty Group (%)									
	All Poor			Non-poor			All		
% of All Urban Workers	M	F	Both	M	F	Both	M	F	Both
Agriculture	8	1	6	3	1	2	3	1	2
Mining	0	0	0	1	0	1	0	0	0
Manufacturing	16	9	14	13	7	10	13	7	11
Basic services[a]	2	2	2	3	1	2	3	1	2
Construction	13	0	9	9	1	6	10	1	6
Commerce	36	31	35	25	26	26	27	26	26
Transport	5	0	3	13	5	9	12	4	9
Financial services	1	2	2	8	9	8	7	9	8
Community services[b]	18	55	30	26	52	38	25	52	37
All	100	100	100	100	100	100	100	100	100
% in Informal Sector[c]	68	80	71	39	41	40	31	41	35
Total # employed ('000)	38	17	55	311	247	558	351	265	616

a\ Basic services such as electricity, water, sanitation, garbage collection etc. b\ Public and community services such as public administration, defense, sports associations, NGOs, domestic services. c\ See Annex 11 of the Poverty Assessment for definition of informal sector. Source: Panama LSMS 1997

Table A7.7 - Distribution of Urban Workers by Type of Employment, Gender and Poverty Group (%)									
	All Poor			Non-poor			All		
% of All Urban Workers	M	F	Both	M	F	Both	M	F	Both
Public sector	10	13	11	21	28	24	19	27	22
Canal	1	0	1	3	1	2	3	1	2
Private sector:	89	87	89	76	71	74	78	73	76
Enterprise (white collar)	56	21	45	51	37	45	52	36	45
Day labor (blue collar)	14	1	10	3	1	2	4	1	3
Domestic laborer	1	30	10	1	13	6	1	15	7
Self-employed	17	28	21	22	18	20	22	19	20
Unpaid laborer	2	7	4	2	3	3	2	4	3
All	100	100	100	100	100	100	100	100	100
Total # employed ('000)	38	17	55	311	247	558	351	265	616

Source: Panama LSMS 1997.

20.	An important coping strategy for the urban poor and vulnerable in Panama has been to mobilize more workers -- mainly women -- among household members.[19] As shown in Table A7.4 above, the urban poor average 1.9 workers per household in Panama. Due to higher family size, the *extreme* poor in urban areas have higher dependency ratios (5.2 non-working members per working member compared with 3.9 for all urban poor). Urban women are much more likely to join the labor force than in those living in rural areas.[20] Over half of women participate in the labor force in urban areas, compared with about one third in rural and indigenous areas.[21] A smaller share of poor women enter the labor force, however: 40 percent in urban areas. Indeed, controlling for other variables (such as education, household size and age), higher levels of total household consumption were slightly but significantly correlated with higher probability of labor force participation for urban women (See Appendix Table A7.A2). Multi-variate regressions also suggest that the presence of children, particularly adolescents aged 12-17, in the household reduces the probability for urban women to enter the labor force. This suggests that after-school programs could be an important strategy for reducing constraints to women's income generation.

---

[19] Available data suggest that the urban poor have *not* relied on child labor in a significant manner in Panama. The LSMS found that only 23 thousand children ages 10-14 were employed in Panama in 1997. Of these, 27 percent lived in urban areas.

[20] See Annex 11 of the Poverty Assessment for details. Controlling for other variables, the difference between women's labor force participation in urban and rural areas is significant.

[21] Just over three quarters of men participate in the labor force in urban areas.

21. Increasing the number of jobs held or the intensity of work per worker does *not* seem to be used as a coping strategy by the average poor urban worker in Panama (Table A7.8). Indeed, the share of workers with more than one job is virtually the same for poor and non-poor city dwellers (about ten percent). Moreover, the poor seem to work fewer hours per week and months per year than the non-poor. To the extent that "underemployment" is measured by

Table A7.8 – Intensity of Work, by Poverty Group		
	Poor	Non-Poor
No. of months worked:		
All jobs	7.8	9.6
First two jobs	8.5	10.4
Days worked per week	5.0	5.4
Hours worked:		
Per week (first job)	35	41
Per year (two jobs)	1277	1790
% with more than one job	11%	10%
Source: LSMS 1997		

intensity of work, these figures seem to suggest that the urban poor tend to be underemployed (compared to their non-poor counterparts). Unemployment is also higher among the urban poor, suggesting that important structural factors (such as market segmentation or human capital mis-matches) could be limiting the poor's use of their most important asset (as discussed in more detail below).

Human Capital: Education and Health

(a) Education

22. Education *is* indeed an asset of Panama's urban poor. Virtually all are literate (Table A7.9). Average educational attainment is relatively high: on average the urban poor have completed primary school (seven years of schooling), with two and four more years of schooling than their poor rural and indigenous counterparts respectively. An analysis of the LSMS finds significant returns to primary education: controlling for other factors, there is a ten percent rate of return on primary school (as compared with no or incomplete education).[22]

23. Some important gaps and deficiencies remain, however, for the urban poor. **First,** less than half of poor urban children enroll in pre-primary school,[23] which has been shown to have an important impact on cognitive development and later success in school. This compares with three-quarters of non-poor city dwellers. **Second,** non-poor urban children also tend to stay in school longer (on average three years longer) than poor urbanites. Only sixty percent of poor urban kids aged 12-17 enroll in secondary school, compared with 85 percent of their non-poor counterparts. **Finally,** repetition and drop out rates are higher among the poor than the non-poor in Panama's cities (particularly for boys). Close to half of poor boys who did not enroll in secondary school cited a "lack of interest" as the main reason for their absenteeism, though none cited work as an obstacle. This suggests a rather large cohort of poor, young urban males opting neither to work nor to attend school, who are at risk both for crime and continued poverty.

---

[22] See Annex 14 of the Poverty Assessment for details on the returns to education calculations.
[23] See Annex 13 of the Poverty Assessment for more details on pre-primary school in Panama.

Table A7.9 - Educational Indicators by Poverty Group, Urban Areas				
	Extreme Poor*	All Poor	Non-Poor	All Urban
Literacy	89%	94%	98%	98%
Educational Attainment[a]				
All individuals 12+ years old	6.0	7.0	10.2	9.8
Males	6.0	6.9	10.1	9.7
Females	6.1	7.1	10.3	9.9
Aged 12-17	5.6	6.6	7.8	7.6
Aged 18-24	7.4	8.3	11.2	10.8
Aged 25-39	6.4	8.3	11.7	11.2
Aged 40+	4.4	4.9	9.6	9.2
Net Enrollment Rates[b]				
Pre-Primary (kinder)	21%	46%	73%	67%
Primary	83%	92%	94%	94%
Secondary	34%	60%	85%	80%
Superior	4%	7%	35%	31%
Repetition Rates[c]				
Kids aged 6-11 (Primary)	20%	10%	4%	6%
Males aged 6-11	17%	10%	4%	5%
Females aged 6-11	23%	11%	4%	6%
Kids aged 12-17 (Secondary)	12%*	11%	10%	10%
Males aged 12-17	14%*	11%	11%	11%
Females aged 12-17	9%*	12%	8%	9%
Drop Out Rates, Primary School[d]				
All kids aged 6-11	5%	2%	1%	1%
Males aged 6-11	5%	2%	1%	2%
Females aged 6-11	4%	1%	0%	0%

Source: LSMS 1997. a\Years of schooling completed for those aged 12+. b\ Net enrollment rate = (all individuals of primary age who are in primary school) / (all individuals of primary age), where primary age = 6-11. Same for pre-primary (age 5), secondary (age 12-17), superior (age 18-24). c\Percent of kids in age cohort who report repeating their *current* grade. d\ Percent of kids in age cohort who enrolled at some point but are not currently enrolled. * Denotes a very small sample. Results should be interpreted with caution.

(b) Health

24. Access to health services is another asset of the urban poor. In general, the poor are just as likely to seek medical treatment as the non-poor in urban areas (Table A7.10). Poor city-dwellers are much more likely to use public facilities – such as clinics, hospitals, and health centers – than their non-poor counterparts (a large share of whom use private services). The urban poor generally live within close proximity to health facilities, with an average distance of 25 minutes to medical services (as compared with 35 minutes and 52 minutes for residents of rural and indigenous areas). Compared with the non-poor, slightly lower share of the poor make any payment for health services, however, in urban areas, suggesting a certain degree of targeting of health service subsidies.

Physical and Financial Assets: Housing, Credit, and Infrastructure

(a) Housing

25. Housing can serve as an important asset for the poor. The poor commonly use housing as a base for productive activities and enterprises. Housing also generates rent -- through earnings charged to renters or via the savings from "imputed rent" which would otherwise be spent by the household. Emergency income can likewise be generated from the sale of housing as a last resort. Finally, households can use housing as a tool for extending personal relationships, building trust and generating social capital.[24] The ability of households to use housing as an asset depends largely on their security of tenure and the flexibility of housing markets. Access to assets that complement home ownership, such as

---

[24] Moser (1996).

electricity, water and credit also contributes to households' ability to use their homes for income-generating activities (as discussed below).

26.   The LSMS reveals that 70 percent of Panama's urban population lives in individual houses (*casas individuales*), the remainder live in apartments (19 percent) and other types of dwellings.[25] Renting is rare in Panama: only 19 percent of city dwellers rent[26] and the majority of renters are non-poor. A small share of all "homeowners" possess registered titles for their homes, and most of those without title are poor.

Table A7.10 – Health Services: Urban Areas by Poverty Group, Nation by Geographic Area							
	Urban Areas by Poverty Group			Panama by Geographic Area			
	Extreme Poor	All Poor	Non-Poor	Urban	Rural	Indig.	Total
Health Visits, Sickness During Past Month							
Consultancy Rate[a]	0.8	1.0	1.2	1.2	1.0	0.6	1.1
Coverage Rate[b]	0.5	0.5	0.7	0.6	0.5	0.3	0.6
Concentration Rate[c]	1.6	1.8	1.9	1.9	1.8	2.0	1.9
Place of Treatment							
Public Facility	91%	86%	58%	62%	77%	81%	68%
Private Facility	9%	14%	42%	38%	23%	19%	32%
Public Hospital/Clinic	62%	60%	45%	47%	33%	20%	41%
Health Center/Sub-Center	28%	26%	14%	15%	44%	62%	27%
Private Hospital/Clinic/Physician	8%	10%	35%	32%	17%	2%	26%
Pharmacist/Other	2%	3%	5%	5%	3%	1%	4%
At home	0%	1%	2%	2%	3%	16%	3%
Distance to Treatment (Average minutes to place of treatment, excluding treatment at home)							
Average minutes	29	25	24	24	35	52	29
Private (Household) Spending on Health Services							
% of those who were sick who paid anything (B./>0) for medical services	63%	61%	73%	71%	67%	43%	68%
Source: LSMS 1997. Numbers may not add to 100 due to rounding. a\ Consultancy rate = number of visits/ number of sick; in other words, the number of visits on average for an individual reporting illness. b\ Coverage rate = number of people with at least one visit/ number of sick; in other words, the percent of people reporting illness who had at least one medical visit. c\ Concentration rate = number of visits/ number of people with at least one visit.							

27.   **Property Acquisition.**   Close to half of poor urban households first acquired vacant lots and then built their homes themselves, compared with only one-third of the non-poor.[27] Invasion (squatting) is a fairly common way in which poor urban Panamanians obtain their land.[28] Invasion is often quite organized: professional squatters locate a piece of land (usually state-owned), draw up a rudimentary "development plan" for these *barriadas* and then enlist families to purchase the land for a fee. The organizers sometimes give the families a document without legal value "certifying" their rights to ownership.[29]

28.   **Housing Construction and Improvements.** Construction work usually begins immediately, as building allows the "owners" to stake a "claim" on the land and avoid losing the property to other

---

[25] These results from the LSMS are very similar to those found in the 1990 census.

[26] Even fewer residents of rural areas rent their homes.

[27] Source: LSMS 1997.

[28] Sources: Heber et. al. (September 1995, based on 1990 census) and Sollis et. al. (September 1995, based on household interviews in seven communities in metropolitan area of Panama City). In the sample used in Sollis et. al., 43% of households obtained their property through invasion and another 43% purchased their plots from original (often professional) squatters. The LSMS did not ask questions about how the plots were acquired.

[29] Heber et. al. (September 1995).

squatters.[30] The process is usually gradual (depending largely on available funds as discussed below), beginning with the construction of a one-room wooden house with a zinc metal roof and either a dirt or cement floor; the walls are then converted to cement block (usually 2-6 years after acquisition), followed by expansions and improvements (generally 1-5 years after cement construction).[31] Windows are typically made of breached concrete "decorative blocks" (*bloques ornamentales*), which are preferred to glazed windows not only for economic but also for safety reasons.[32]

29.   The LSMS shows that twenty percent of the urban poor had acquired their houses in the past three years; another quarter had moved in during the past 4-10 years. One third of poor urban residents live in houses with walls made of wood or other "temporary" materials, compared with just seven percent of the non-poor. The majority of poor urban residents live in houses with metal or cement roofs, while another 22 percent lived in dwellings with dirt or wood floors. The poor live in dwellings with less than three rooms (compared with close to four for the non-poor), with an average of three members per room (compared to 1.3 members per room in non-poor households).

30.   One quarter of poor urban households report having made improvements to their homes in the past twelve months (as compared with one third of the non-poor). The primary improvements include changing the walls or floor (one-third), adding rooms (one-third) and changing the door or windows (one fifth).[33]

31.   In general, housing construction and improvements are carried out by the owners themselves, assisted by relatives, friends and neighbors. The LSMS reveals that, among the urban poor, two thirds of those who constructed their houses report building it themselves (most with help from family members) and 87 percent report receiving help from "friends." Paid labor is also used, though primarily for longer-term construction and improvement projects. Most paid labor consists of bricklayers and their assistants, who sometimes also perform basic plumbing and electrician tasks and who generally reside in the local community.[34]

32.   **Sources of Financing for Construction/Improvements.** The urban poor report spending an average of B./369 per household (B./69 per person or 10 percent of average total annual per capita consumption) on housing improvements in the past year (compared with B./1431 per household or B./460 per person for non-poor urban residents).[35] Household savings are an extremely important source of financing for housing construction and improvements among the poor (Table A7.11): two thirds of poor urban households report using savings as a source of financing for home improvements. Help from family and/or friends was the second most frequently cited source, followed by loans from private and public institutions. Loans from private institutions are a much more common source of financing for the non-poor. These patterns underscore the need for financial services (with savings accounts) -- not just credit -- for the poor. These findings are consistent with those found in other studies.[36]

---

[30] Focus group discussions and a household survey in the greater metropolitan area of Panama City conducted by Sollis et. al. (September 1995) found evidence of an informal "squatters code" in which squatters only take plots that do not have completed or semi-completed houses -- unless the owners have been absent for a significant period of time.

[31] Sollis et. al. (September 1995).

[32] Heber et. al. (September 1995).

[33] Source: LSMS 1997.

[34] Sollis et. al. (September 1995).

[35] Source: LSMS 1997.

[36] Sollis (September 1995) found that savings represented two thirds of the *value* of financing for home improvements. Although loans were used less frequently than savings, they made up 18% of the total value of financing. The evidence in that study suggests that the larger, more expensive jobs are typically completed with loan financing: the median value of loans from any source used in a housing improvement was $1000, while the median value of savings allocated to home improvements was $390.

33.   **Housing Subsidies.** The Ministry of Housing (MIVI) has recently developed a new program, called PARVIS,[37] to support the housing needs of the poor. The program provides eligible households with a **grant** of up to B./1,500, of which B./1,000 goes to housing materials. The other B./500 is a matching grant whereby the Government contributes B./1 for every B./0.50 provided by the applicant up to a total of B./500 to be used for housing improvements. PARVIS also finances a series of sub-programs to provide basic **infrastructure** to eligible beneficiaries (water, sanitation, drainage, latrines, etc.). Communities are involved at all stages, including the prioritization of proposals, implementation, operation and maintenance. Finally, PARVIS provides **land tenure** and legalization services for the plots acquired by the families.

Table A7.11 - Housing Improvements in Urban Areas, by Poverty Group			
	All Poor	**Non-Poor**	**All Urban**
% Reporting Improvements[a]	26%	32%	31%
Spending on Improvements:[b]			
Per Household	369	1431	1331
Per Person	69	460	423
Sources of Financing for Housing Improvements:[c]			
% using own savings	67%	75%	75%
% with loan from public inst.	12%	11%	11%
% with loan from private inst.	13%	19%	18%
% with help from family/friends	21%	11%	12%
% with donations	3%	1%	1%
% with lottery winnings	4%	4%	4%
Source: LSMS 1997. Percent of households. a\% of those with "own" home. b\% of those reporting improvements. c\% of those reporting improvements. Can have more than one source.			

34.   The program is targeted to the families with incomes less than B./300 per month (means-testing). Beneficiaries cannot benefit from other housing assistance programs or have owned a land plot for longer than three years. They must also prove possession of a legal right to the land (e.g., an *asignación de lote*, as discussed below). Communities of ten or more eligible families can apply jointly for community improvement funding. The program was launched in 1997 and an evaluation has not yet been conducted.

35.   **Titling.** The lack of titling of homes is widespread in urban areas, though a larger share of the poor lack titles to their homes than the non-poor (Table A7.12). Less than half of *all* urban "homeowners" have a registered title. The situation is worse for the poor: only 24 percent of those with their "own" home (only 15 percent of all poor urban residents) have a registered title. While

Table A7.12 - House Titling in Urban Areas, by Poverty Group			
	All Poor	**Non-Poor**	**All Urban**
% with "own" home[a]	62%	70%	69%
% with registered title[b]	24%	50%	48%
% with unregistered title[b]	27%	24%	25%
% with no title or contract[b]	48%	26%	29%
Source: LSMS 1997. a\% of all urban residents. b\% of all homeowners.			

another 27 percent of poor urban homeowners claims to have an "unregistered" title or a "title" in process, 48 percent have no formal claim to their home or lot.

36.   The lack of housing titles seriously limits the poor's ability to use their homes as an asset. Without housing titles, the ability of the poor to obtain credit is compromised (since titles are often required as collateral for borrowing). In fact, as discussed below, lack of guarantees (housing title or other assets) was the sole reason poor urban households were refused credit. Without formal claim, they also lack the possibility of borrowing against (equity loans) or selling this asset for emergency income. The lack of title also lowers their incentives for investing in their homes (e.g., for housing improvements) by reducing their security of tenure.

37.   MIVI has attempted to expand titling and legalize property "ownership." The process, however, is complex and lengthy, partly reflecting the desire on behalf of the Government to avoid promoting

---

[37] PARVIS is the *Programa de Apoyo Rápido para Vivienda de Interés Social*. It was launched in February 1997 with support from the Inter-American Development Bank. The overall budget for 1997 was B./3.1 million (0.04% of GDP).

incentives for organized invasion and to guard against professional squatters benefiting from owning multiple lots. Once MIVI has taken the decision to get involved, the process of titling and legalization occurs in several stages. **First,** if privately owned land has been occupied, the ministry tries to purchase the lot from the legal owner. **Second,** MIVI conducts a topographical study, explains the process to potential beneficiaries, and drafts an official plan for ownership and service delivery.[38] **Third,** the "owners" can apply for the right to acquire legal title to the property (*asignación de lote*) and to purchase their individual lot.[39] **Fourth,** MIVI and the applicant agree on the conditions of the sale.[40] In general, the Government sells the land to occupants on credit with a maturity of five years and at an interest rate of eight percent, which means that they can gradually pay off their debt in monthly installments that rarely exceed B./10.[41] Only when the purchase price has been paid in full is the *asignación de lote* exchanged for full legal title to the property. The process averages between a year and a half to five years to complete, though some communities report incomplete titling some twenty years after its initiation.[42]

(b) Basic Infrastructure

38. The urban poor possess relatively more physical assets in terms of their access to basic infrastructure services than their rural and indigenous counterparts. Most urban households -- poor and non-poor -- have access to water, gas and electricity. The results of the LSMS suggest problems with quality of service delivery, however, as well as inefficiencies in cost recovery for these services. Sanitation services are less widespread, however, and garbage collection is intermittent, causing concern for public health problems in poor neighborhoods.

39. **Water.** Most urban households report access to piped water (Table A7.13).[43] Half of the poor have outdoor connections, compared with 79 percent of the non-poor who have connections within their homes.

40. Over a quarter of urban residents report irregularity in service delivery; a similar figure was found in the LSMS community questionnaire.[44] Close to three-quarters of urban communities in the LSMS sample reported problems with the quality of service delivery and the water itself. Inadequate water pressure was a common complaint (one-fifth of communities). Another fifth complained of contamination and pollution problems (*agua chocolate*, dirty water, sedimentation, contamination, etc.), suggesting that the water being delivered is less than potable. Maintenance is commonly viewed as inadequate.

---

[38] In many cases this inevitably involves officially adopting the illegal plan and partitioning of lots, since the sites have already been built on. This can create problems, especially as far as the size of the plots is concerned, because the official regulations stipulate that, for health reasons, plots of land without drainage must have an area of at least 600 squared meters -- a standard with which the illegal plans rarely comply, yet which can hardly be imposed retroactively after the houses have gone up. Heber et. al (September 1995).

[39] This phase requires that the "owner" present a number of documents with his/her application, including: a certificate of *Ho propiedad*," proof of employment (*carta de trabajo*) from either an employer or the municipality, copies of birth certificates of everyone intending to live on the property, the *cedula* of the person aspiring to be the owner, and social security documents. Sollis et. al. (September 1995).

[40] A 1995 study found that the price of the lots ranged from as low as $0.25 per square meter to as high as $2. The higher end prices were usually charged in cases where the Government had had to purchase the land from a private owner. Heber et. al. (September 1995).

[41] These loans appear in the balance sheet of the Banco Hipotecario Nacional (BHN), the financial arm of MIVI. Heber et. al. (September 1995).

[42] For more information and specific examples, see Sollis et. al. (September 1995) and Heber et. a. (September 1995).

[43] Private trucking of water in Panama is rare: although MIVI does pay some private trucks to deliver water to underserved areas, the service is generally irregular and residents have low confidence in the quality and sanitation of trucked water. Some report that the trucks had previously been used for other purposes (e.g., fuel transportation!). Sollis et. al. (September 1995).

[44] One quarter of urban communities in the LSMS sample report problems with irregularity of service delivery. Residents complained that water would only arrive at night or in the day. At one LSMS community focus group, for example, community members recounted that "we only get water at 3 a.m.!" (Personal notes from LSMS interviews).

41.   Cost recovery for piped water is incomplete.[45] Overall, close to one-fifth of households with connections to the water system do not pay anything for their water consumption.[46] This figure is higher for the urban poor (58 percent). For those who do pay something, the cost is minimal (Table A7.13). In absolute terms, the poor pay less per capita than the non-poor, though this could reflect lower quantities consumed. Spending on water consumption did, however, represent a slightly higher share of the total per capita annual consumption of the poor than the non-poor.

42.   **Sanitation Services.** The LSMS reveals that over 80 percent of all urban residents are hooked up to the sewage system or septic tanks (Table A7.13). Only 41 percent of poor city-dwellers, however, have such connections; the remainder use latrines, pits, or no formal facility, raising public health concerns. A recent study of urban slums found that only a few residents of *barriadas* are connected to main sewage lines or septic tanks. Sewage seeping from neighbors' latrines was also cited as a common problem.[47]

Table A7.13 - Infrastructure Assets in Urban Areas, by Poverty Group				
	Extreme Poor	**All Poor**	**Non-Poor**	**Total Urban**
WATER				
Access to public/community system (acueducto)	87%	92%	99%	98%
o/w connection in house	25%	39%	79%	75%
o/w connection outside house on property	64%	53%	19%	22%
o/w community source (no conn. on property)	11%	9%	2%	3%
Permanent water supply[a]	63%	65%	75%	74%
% of households not paying anything for water:				
% of those with connections (acueducto)	58%	44%	16%	18%
Average payments (per capita): (B./)				
for all (including those who pay nothing)	4.0	4.5	11.3	10.6
for those who pay something	11.3	9.1	14.0	13.7
SANITATION AND GARBAGE COLLECTION				
Access to sanitation services				
% with sewage services/septic tank	41%	44%	84%	80%
% with latrine or pit	50%	48%	15%	18%
% with no service	10%	8%	1%	1%
% with access to garbage collection services	67%	77%	93%	91%
ENERGY				
Lighting with:				
Electricity	81%	92%	99%	98%
Other (gas, kerosene, etc.)	19%	8%	1%	2%
Cooking with:				
Gas	84%	91%	99%	98%
Other (mainly firewood)	16%	9%	1%	2%
% of households not paying for electricity	60%	40%	12%	14%
Average electricity payments (per capita): (B./)				
for all (including those who pay nothing)	15.0	20.3	103.6	94.6
for those who pay something	26.2	31.3	118.4	111.2

Source: LSMS 1997. a\Permanent water supply refers to those who have a connection to the water system and receive water 30 days/month and 24 hours/day.

43.   **Energy: Gas, Electricity, Street Lighting.** As for water, though most urban households have access to gas and electricity, communities report problems with quality and irregularity, and cost recovery is incomplete. Virtually all urban households cook with gas and light their homes with electricity (Table A7.13). Close to half of the urban communities in the LSMS sample complained of poor quality and

---

[45] See Oxford Economic Research Associates Ltd. (July 9, 1998), "La demanda de servicios de agua y saneamiento entre las comunidades pobres: experiencia internacional y evidencia en Panama" for more information on cost recovery for water services in Panama.
[46] Panama LSMS 1997.
[47] Sollis et. al. (September 1995). In one case in Samaria (San Miguelito), a woman respondent recalled how she was forced from her bedroom due to foul odors emanating from her neighbor's overflowing latrine during the rainy season.

irregular service delivery. Common complaints include: frequent blackouts (announced, unannounced), voltage problems, poor installations, and inadequate maintenance.

44.   Illegal connections (tapping into public lighting for example) appear to be common among the poor: sixty percent of poor city dwellers report not paying anything or their electricity. This is similar to the result found in a recent study of urban *barriadas*, which found that half of all *barriada* residents had illegal connections.[48] Those with legal connections do tend to pay -- either via collective contracts (flat quotas) or individual (metered) contracts. In absolute terms, the poor pay less per capita than the non-poor (Table A7.13), though this could reflect lower quantities consumed.

45.   As for street lighting, virtually all urban communities in the LSMS report the existence of some public lighting. However, over half of the urban poor live in communities that report incomplete coverage in their areas. Quality, maintenance and vandalism of public lighting also seem to be problems (irregular replacement of lightbulbs, etc.). Inadequate street lighting has been linked to crime and violence (which are discussed below).

46.   **Garbage Collection.** Although the majority of urban residents ostensibly receive garbage collection services, close to half of urban communities in the LSMS sample report irregular or occasional collection. In many areas, households are supposed to bring garbage to regular collection points; collection at these points is frequently interrupted, resulting in a build up of piles of trash (on street corners, in open lots, etc.). MINSA does send environmental health teams to the *barriadas* for periodic checks, and community organizations are also involved in lobbying local municipalities for collection.[49]

(c) Savings and Credit

47.   **Savings.** Savings can be an important asset for the poor. In addition to smoothing consumption, savings are commonly used by the poor for investment purposes (such as housing improvements, as discussed above). The LSMS reveals that one fifth of poor urban households hold savings, as compared with half of the non-poor (Table A7.14).[50] An even smaller share of the extreme urban poor maintain savings,

Table A7.14 - Savings in Urban Areas, by Poverty Group				
	Ext. Poor	All Poor	Non-Poor	Total Urban
% with savings[a]	13%	19%	52%	48%
% by place of savings[b]				
Private banks	0%	8%	43%	41%
Bank of Panama	31%	13%	22%	21%
Caja de ahorros	64%	58%	39%	40%
Local Cooperatives[c]	22%	11%	10%	10%
Savings Unions/Coops	0%	15%	19%	19%
Savings/storage clubs	0%	4%	10%	10%
Source: LSMS 1997 (Section 8.E.III). a\% of households. Reference period is past 12 months. b\% of those with savings. People can have savings in more than one place; hence figures do not add up to 100%. c\Neighborhood and worker cooperatives.				

which makes sense given this group's inability to meet minimum caloric requirements.[51] The poor tend to put their savings in public institutions, such as the National Bank of Panama and the *Caja de Ahorros*. Unlike the non-poor, the urban poor do no commonly use private banks for their savings. Private institutions probably find it less profitable to offer services geared towards the poor, who generally maintain smaller accounts.

---

[48] Sollis et. al. (September 1995).
[49] Sollis et. al. (September 1995).
[50] Data collected by the LSMS on amounts saved per month and total savings are not consistent and the figures cannot be reconciled. Use of these figures is not recommended. Future LSMS questionnaires should try to correct for these errors.
[51] See Annex 2 of the Poverty Assessment for a discussion of the definition of poverty lines.

Table A7.15 - Credit in Urban Areas, By Poverty Group			
	All Poor	**Non-Poor**	**Total Urban**
Credit in Cash (Loans)			
% soliciting credit[a]	12%	18%	18%
o/w % who received credit[b]	93%	96%	95%
Was credit amount sufficient?[c]	49%	71%	70%
Reason for not soliciting credit[d]			
Did not need it	11%	44%	40%
Too risky	30%	28%	28%
Too much paperwork	16%	12%	13%
They wouldn't give it to me	24%	8%	10%
Other	18%	9%	10%
Reason for being refused credit[e]			
No assets for guarantee	52%	5%	9%
Lack of property title	48%	0%	5%
Low income	0%	40%	36%
Other	0%	55%	50%
Credit in Kind (Purchases on Credit)			
% making purchases on credit[f]	19%	20%	20%
o/w % making purchases on credit for:			
Clothing	70%	78%	77%
Food	29%	22%	23%
Household durables	14%	27%	27%
Other consumption goods	8%	13%	13%
Total Credit (in Cash and Kind)			
Average Value Received Per Household (B./)[g]			
Consumer loans and credit	528	2,435	2,295
Loans and credit for enterprises/businesses	11	1,896	1,757
Total value of loans and credit	537	4,331	4,052
Total Value Received by Group as Percent of:			
National loans and credit	0.7%	70.0%	70.5%
Loans and credit in urban areas	1.0%	99.0%	100%

Source: LSMS 1997; Sections 8.D, 8.E.I, 8.E.III, 9.A.IX, 10.E. a\Households soliciting credit as % of all households. Reference period is past 12 months. b\Those who solicited and received credit as % of all households soliciting credit. c\Those who believed amount received to be sufficient as % of all households receiving credit. d\ Households who did not solicit credit as % of all households. e\% of households who solicited but did not receive credit. f\ Households making purchases on credit as % of all households in group. g\ Average value for those receiving credit.

48.   **Credit.** Borrowing and making purchases on credit are another important way that households can smooth their consumption and invest for future earnings potential. The LSMS reveals a number of important trends with respect to borrowing and credit in urban areas (Table A7.15).[52] **First,** a smaller share of poor households solicited loans and made purchases on credit than non-poor households. Although a similar share of those soliciting credit were approved, among the reasons reported by poor households for not soliciting loans were the belief that they would not be approved. Risk and excessive paperwork also appear to be significant deterring factors for poor city dwellers. **Second,** a lack of guarantees (property titles or other assets) fully explains the reasons poor households were refused for credit. **Third,** there is very little borrowing (either in cash or kind) by the urban poor for independent businesses, which corroborates the small share of incomes that the urban poor derive from such activities (see above). It appears that most urban poor borrow for consumption purposes (such as clothing) or for home improvements. **Fourth,** the size of loans and purchases on credit obtained by poor urban households is much smaller than those obtained by the non-poor, averaging under B./401 for lending and

---

[52] The LSMS does not have a single comprehensive section on credit and loans. Rather, this analysis draws from questions in sections 8.D (household loans and credit); 8.E.I (student loans); 8.E.III. (household loans and credit -- qualitative questions); 9.A.IX (loans for independent enterprises); and 10.E (agricultural credit and purchases on credit).

about B./135 for purchases on credit.[53] The design of credit programs intended to reach the poor should take into account the small size of loans apparently needed by the poor. Moreover, the targeting of micro-credit schemes should take into account the large share of poor urban women who are self-employed (see above). **Finally,** urban areas account for the majority of the total volume of lending in Panama (71 percent). Virtually all (99 percent) of this volume accrues to non-poor city dwellers, however, with the urban poor only accounting for one percent of lending and purchases on credit.

Social Capital

49.   Unlike their rural and indigenous counterparts, social capital[54] does not appear to be a strong asset of the urban poor. Evidence of weaker social capital in urban areas in general is a pervasive result of both the LSMS and an associate Social Capital Qualitative Survey (SCQS).[55] Urban communities scored much lower on a Social Capital Index (SCI) than rural and indigenous communities, revealing much lower participation in community activities (Table A7.16 below).[56] In terms of networks of associations,[57] urban communities have fewer community organizations, and participation by urban households is less common (Table A7.16). When urban households do participate, it is primarily in the more "private good" types of organizations such as cooperatives, rather than those which stand to serve the public good, such as committees or community groups (Table A7.16). The SCQS also revealed fewer horizontal connections and less trust among urban communities in the sample.[58] Perhaps as an indication of their desire for improved social capital, urban communities in the LSMS sample ranked community and social centers ranked as the fifth most frequently identified priority. Examples given in the survey included: safe community centers, parks, sports centers, youth centers, community institutions, and market places.

Table A7.16 – Quantitative Indicators of Social Capital by Geographic Area	Urban	Rural	Indigenous
% of Communities:[a]			
Reporting No Community Organizations Present	49%	25%	19%
With Low Social Capital Index (SCI)	45%	11%	16%
With Medium Social Capital Index (SCI)	40%	54%	51%
With High Social Capital Index (SCI)	15%	35%	32%
% of Households Participating in:[b]			
Junta comunal or *consejo municipal*	7%	12%	9%
Committees	5%	14%	14%
Local Associations	1%	0%	24%
Cooperatives	22%	13%	14%
Any of Above	28%	30%	41%
Mean number of groups	0.34	0.39	0.61
a\From LSMS community questionnaire (sample not representative). b\From LSMS household questionnaire (representative sample).			

---

[53] This may explain the importance of "excessive paperwork" as a deterrent for applications for loans by the poor: the amount of bureaucracy required is prohibitively expensive for such small sums.

[54] Social capital is defined as "features of social organization such as trust, norms, and networks, that can improve the efficiency of society by facilitating coordinated actions." Some of the key ingredients of social capital are trust, norms of reciprocity, and networks of civic engagement. See Annex 18 of the Poverty Assessment for more details and description.

[55] See Annex 18 of the Poverty Assessment for more details.

[56] The SCI is a composite index of indicators of social capital based on data from the LSMS community questionnaire. See Annex 18 of the Poverty Assessment for details.

[57] The SCQS revealed that even when formal networks are present, these organizations do not guarantee the presence of social capital. Several examples of problems with community organizations in urban communities emerged from the SCQS discussions: several communities cited political motivations as lying behind individuals' efforts to organize; others pointed to disputes and alcohol problems arising in group-sponsored events; still others cited low community interest in participating in group meetings and activities. See Annex 18 of the Poverty Assessment for details.

[58] For example, one urban resident described the lack of trust in his community in the SCQS focus group interviews: "We lack self-esteem, there are no values...there is no unity...envy prevails... Here each one lives in his/her own world...there is no friendship." Lindo-Fuentes (1997; SCQS mission report).

50.   Although social capital appears to be weaker among urban communities as a whole (as compared with rural/indigenous communities), the LSMS does suggest that *within* urban areas, the poor account for a slightly higher share of those living in communities with higher social capital. Although the poor represent about 19 percent of the urban population for which community data are available,[59] they account for 30 percent of the population living in communities with a high Social Capital Index.

51.   Moreover, there is evidence that social capital is important for leveraging external assistance. The results of the LSMS community questionnaire suggest a fairly strong correlation between social capital and external assistance in all areas, including urban communities.[60] Indeed, some Government programs, such as the FES and PROINLO, rely on the existence of community organizations to function. In a survey of low income squatter communities around Panama City (*barriadas*), Sollis et. al. also describe the important role of community groups (particularly issue-specific *comites*, and *directivas*) in raising funds for community-based development solutions and in leveraging government agencies for service delivery and property titling. The focus groups conducted under the SCQS and by Sollis et. al. both revealed that the stronger presence of electoral waves in urban communities tends to undermine incentives for community-based initiatives, with electoral handouts breaking the momentum of community groups.[61]

CORRELATES OF URBAN POVERTY

52.   The above descriptive analysis hints at some of the individual factors that determine urban poverty and potential levers for reducing poverty in Panama's cities. This section examines the correlates of urban poverty in a multi-variate setting so as to shed light on their relative importance. The analysis is useful, first, to verify the relative role of the various factors in determining poverty status, and second, to assess the potential impact that policy-induced changes in these factors are likely to have on the probability of being poor, holding all other factors constant.

53.   It is important to note the limitations of this analysis at the outset. **First** and foremost, the analysis does not capture the dynamic impact of certain causes of urban poverty over time. Most notably, the impact of changes in economic growth -- most certainly a key determinant of urban poverty -- cannot be assessed using this static, cross-section model. Other dynamic factors that are likely correlates of urban poverty include variables such as past nutritional status of household members (which could affect their current productivity for example). **Second,** the analysis is limited by the variables available at the *household* level from the 1997 LSMS household survey. Other factors -- such as social conditions like crime and violence -- could not be included due to a lack of data at this level. **Finally,** though theory holds that many of the variables included in the analysis do indeed contribute to ("cause") poverty (or poverty reduction), the statistical relationships should be interpreted as correlates and not as determinants since causality can run both ways for some variables.

54.   The probability of a household being poor was examined for urban areas (See Appendix Table A7.A3 for results).[62] The key correlates of poverty include household size (fertility), education, sources of income, housing quality and tenancy, some (but not all) basic services, credit, transportation (cars), and membership in certain types of organizations.[63]

---

[59] Some urban communities were not surveyed for the LSMS community questionnaire due to difficulties in defining community boundaries.

[60] See Annex 18 of the Poverty Assessment for details.

[61] For example, one focus group participant in the SCQS survey explained "When election time comes, they 'roar' and always say that they will give and then do not return." Lindo-Fuentes (1997; SCQS mission report).

[62] See Annex 8 of the Poverty Assessment for a more detailed description of the methodology.

[63] Contrary to conventional wisdom, female-headed households do *not* have a higher probability of being poor than those headed by males (which confirms the analysis of descriptive statistics in Annex 19 of the Poverty Assessment). Likewise, different types of marital status are not correlated with being poor, nor is the number of workers per household member.

55.   **Larger urban households tend to be poor.** In particular, households with more young children (reflecting higher fertility) and more elderly members have a higher probability of being poor, presumably due to the dependency status of these members.

56.   **Education is correlated with poverty status and plays a role in reducing poverty.**[64] The higher the educational attainment of the household head or his/her companion, the lower the household's probability of being poor. Even a few years of secondary education reduce the probability of being poor by about four percent.[65]

57.   **Urban households deriving most of their income from the informal sector have a higher probability of being poor.** Higher poverty associated with informal work is consistent with the finding (discussed in Annex 11 of the Poverty Assessment) that earnings in the informal sector are significantly lower than those in the formal sector even when other variables, such as education and experience, are taken into account.

58.   **Low quality housing and lack of housing titles are strongly correlated with urban poverty,** though the direction of causality is not clear. Poverty itself is a cause of makeshift housing, but low quality housing can also limit the ability of households to use their homes as a productive asset – as a location of independent businesses for example (particularly when accompanied by a lack of basic infrastructure services as discussed below). Not owning a house also increases the probability of being poor, as does the lack of a registered housing title in urban and rural areas.

59.   **A lack of some – but not all – basic services is correlated with urban poverty.** Lack of sanitation services, electricity, and telephones is correlated with higher urban poverty. However, water is not a significant determinant of poverty status in Panama's cities, which makes sense given that most city-dwellers (including the poor) are covered by water services.

60.   **Access to credit significantly reduces a household's probability of being poor.** Credit allows households to smooth consumption in the face of income fluctuations and to invest in productive activities for future income generation.

61.   **Ownership of assets significantly reduces a household's probability of being poor as proxied by car ownership as a measurement of wealth.** Cars can also be interpreted as a useful complement to labor inputs: they allow an efficient means of commuting to better, more lucrative jobs, and they reduce time lost commuting (see below).

62.   **Membership in certain types of organizations reduces urban households' probability of being poor.** Households that belong to a cooperative – which generates "private gains" to members – are less likely to be poor. Affiliation with a sports or cultural club likewise is correlated with higher economic status in urban areas.

---

[64] The analysis uses the maximum educational attainment of the household head or his/her companion. Since the educational attainment of these members (adults) precedes their current economic status, it could validly be considered as having a causative influence on poverty status (whereas the educational levels of young dependents in the household may be low because poverty prevents them from affording an education).

[65] It is interesting to note, however, that the *extra* effect of *completing* secondary is not as strong a factor in reducing the probability of being poor as the impact of attending some secondary education (as shown by the small difference in the coefficients on incomplete secondary and complete secondary education).

KEY ISSUES FACING THE URBAN POOR

Community Perceptions of Quality of Life, Priorities

63.   **Pessimistic Perceptions Among City Dwellers.** Despite having higher average per capita incomes and a lower incidence of poverty, urban communities have more pessimistic perceptions of recent changes in their overall well-being than their rural and indigenous counterparts.   Of all communities interviewed in the LSMS Community Survey,[66] 41 percent of urban communities perceive that conditions have worsened in the past five years, compared with 31 percent of rural communities and only 14 percent of indigenous communities. Interestingly, in contrast, when asked about specific changes in living conditions (such as housing, garbage collection, water and sanitation, and public lighting), urban communities were more optimistic in their perceptions than residents of rural and indigenous communities.[67] Clearly, a variety of other, non-economic factors -- such as social problems, inconveniences and hassles due to traffic congestion, a lack of community unity, etc. -- are causing the apparent paradox between higher economic conditions and more pessimistic views of the overall quality of life in Panama's cities.

64.   **Overall Ranking of Community Priorities.** Table A7.17 sheds some light on the factors that may be driving these somewhat negative perceptions of general well-being. **Social issues** -- particularly crime and safety but also including the highly related issues as drugs and alcohol, gangs, and youth problems -- which are not directly captured by economic measures of living standards (poverty, incomes), were most frequently ranked as top priority by urban communities in the LSMS sample. **Transportation** -- including inadequate public services, deteriorating roads, and traffic congestion -- was also a top priority. Reflecting higher unemployment rates in urban areas, **unemployment** ("*falta de empleo*") was a common concern among urban communities.   In terms of **infrastructure**, sanitation services and potable water were frequently cited as priorities, followed by public lighting and telephones and garbage collection. Communities also complained about **housing conditions and titling**, as well as **health** and **education**. The first three are discussed in more detail below; the rest were discussed above.

Table A7.17 - Ranking of Community Priorities, Urban Communities in LSMS Sample		
	Ranking	% of Communities in Sample
Safety / Crime	1	25%
Transportation, Roads	1	25%
Employment, Labor	2	22%
Sanitation Services	3	16%
Potable Water	4	13%
Social, Community Centers	5	10%
Housing / Titling	5	10%
Drugs, Alcohol	6	9%
Health	6	9%
Gangs, Youth Problems	7	5%
Lighting, Telephones	7	5%
Garbage Collection	8	4%
Education	9	3%
Social problems (safety/crime, drugs, alcohol, gangs / youth problems)	1	39%

Source: LSMS 1997; Community Survey. Communities were asked to list their two most important priority issues / problems. Results presented in this table aggregate the two responses. Note that the sample is not statistically representative of urban communities in Panama. Percents refer to the share of 206 urban communities in the sample with completed questionnaires. A number of urban communities covered by the LSMS Household Survey were not covered by the Community Survey due to difficulties in defining community boundaries (these were primarily in Panama City / San Miguelito).

Social Problems: Crime, Safety, Social Decline

65.   **Community Perceptions.** Crime, personal security and related social problems are clearly priority issues for urban communities in Panama. In fact, public safety tied with transportation as *the*

---

[66] The community survey consisted of focus-group type discussions.
[67] See Annex 18 of the Poverty Assessment for details.

most frequently cited priority among urban communities in the LSMS.[68] Closely related, drugs, alcohol, gangs and "youth problems," and public lighting and telephones were also commonly ranked as key priorities among urban communities in the sample.

66.   Over eighty percent of urban communities in the LSMS survey reported having problems with theft, drugs and alcohol, and close to half reported problems with gangs (*pandillas*) and prostitution (Table A7.18). A higher frequency of urban communities reported problems with these social ills than rural or indigenous communities.

67.   Less than half of urban communities in the LSMS sample reported coverage by police services. Of those with coverage, many reported inadequate coverage (insufficient police units, police transportation and presence) and over half reported irregular coverage (completely irregular or only at night). A few also reported inadequate "professionalism" on behalf of police (*amiguismo*, corruption).

68.   **Official Crime Statistics.**   In fact, although crime statistics are notoriously inadequate,[69] available data do suggest that (i) crime and violence[70] are rising in Panama; and (ii) most crime, particularly violent crime, is concentrated in urban areas, particularly Panama City and Colón. The total number of detained criminals has increased in the past few years (Table A7.19).   Colon has the highest incidence of incarceration (56 per thousand inhabitants), followed by

Table A7.18 - Crime and Social Problems: % of Communities in LSMS Reporting Various Problems			
% of Communities	Urban	Rural	Indigenous
Theft	82%	47%	42%
Gangs	52%	14%	16%
Drugs	82%	30%	18%
Alcohol	86%	68%	42%
Prostitution	45%	14%	3%
Other	18%	13%	0%
Source: LSMS Community Survey. Figures refer to % of communities in the sample.			

Panama City (35 per thousand residents).   Males appear to be responsible for a majority of crimes in Panama, accounting for 91 percent of guilty criminals in 1995.

69.   The **homicide** rate[71] in Panama increased *five* times between the late 1970s/early 1980s and the late 1980s/early 1990s (Table A7.20). With the exception of Trinidad and Tobago, this increase was higher than other Latin American countries. Available statistics indicate that 16 percent of all deaths in Panama are caused by acts of violence and accidents. Criminals detained

Table A7.19 – Detained Criminals in Panama					
	1991	1992	1993	1994	1995
Total Number	32,463	40,833	42,753	44,673	48,600
Panama City	10,498	12,736	13,957	15,198	15,842
Colon	3,356	3,889	2,448	3,025	3,261
Per 1,000 persons	13.3	16.4	16.9	17.3	18.5
Panama City	16.4	29.4	31.8	34.1	35.0
Colon	58.7	67.5	42.2	51.8	55.8
Sources: MIPPE, collected from: Zonas de Policía y Alcaldias de la República; Tribunales y juzgados en la República.					

---

[68] There could be some bias in favor of higher reporting of crime/safety issues as "priorities" due to the placement of the "key priorities" question in the LSMS questionnaire immediately after questions pertaining to specific crime/safety issues. Two factors could reduce this bias however: (i) the "key priorities" question follows questions pertaining to all sorts of types of issues (education, health, water, lighting, electricity, etc.), not just crime and safety; and (ii) a much smaller share of rural and indigenous communities cited crime/safety problems as "priority issues" in the "key priority" question (the questionnaire was the same for all areas).

[69] Due to severe underreporting by victims and a lack of systematic and consistent data collection.

[70] While violence and crime are frequently categorized as synonymous, there are important distinctions between the two: violence is the unlawful exercise of physical force, crime is an act punishable by law. Different types of violent crimes include homicide, assault (including domestic violence, which is widely underreported), burglary, etc. Moser (Briefing Note, 1996).

[71] Homicide rates are the most commonly used proxy for crime and violence in general. Ayres (1998). Fajnzylber, Lederman and Loayza (1998). The high rate for the late-1980s and early-1990s could present an upward bias in the trend due to exceptional events associated with the U.S. invasion and ensuing crisis at that time.

for homicide represent one percent of all detainees and five percent of all criminals detained for personal-security crimes for the country as a whole. Homicide accounts for a higher share of crimes in Colon, accounting for two percent of all detainees and six percent of criminals detained for personal security crimes.[72]

70. **Theft** is also a key problem in Panama's cities. Theft-related crimes are the most frequent type of crime in Panama, accounting for 28 percent of all detained criminals for the nation as a whole, and 40 percent for Panama City. A survey of low income *barriadas* in communities around Panama City, found that 32 percent of households in the sample had been burglarized. In some *barriadas* (e.g. Sinai, Las Malvinas) 80-100 percent of households in the sample had experienced theft.[73]

71. Direct **drug-related crimes** (possession, use, trafficking) accounted for six percent of all detained criminals in Panama's urban areas, and as high as nine percent in Colon in 1995. Cocaine and marijuana appear to be the primary illegal drugs in Panama,[74] though alcohol abuse is also a significant problem.[75] The total quantity of drugs seized by police has increased substantially in recent years, particularly in 1995-96. Possession and internal drug trafficking account for the majority of drug-related convictions (34 and 57 percent respectively), though international trafficking accounts for the largest share of the volume of drugs seized by police and other officials (75 percent), reflecting Panama's convenient geographic position for international drug shipments.[76] Most drugs were seized in the Panama province (92 percent), followed by Colon (seven percent). Of adults convicted for direct drug-related crimes in Panama, one half were young adults aged 18-29 years old and most were of Panamanian nationality (88 percent, followed by Colombians who accounted for ten percent).[77] Close to 57 percent of youths convicted for drug-related crimes were age 16-17, with another 29 percent between the ages of 14-15 and the remainder aged 13 and under.

72. Another related and important problem in Panama is **youth crime**, particularly in urban areas. Youths (under age 20) account for five percent of all detained criminals in Panama, with young adults (aged 20-29) representing another nine percent. Half of these are in Panama City and Colon. Most criminal youths appear to be boys.[78] Data for Panama City reveals that theft is the main form of youth crimes (accounting for 26 percent in 1995), followed

Table A7.20 - Homicide Rates Per 100,000 Persons			
	Late 70s/ Early 80s (A)	Late 80s/ Early 90s (B)	Ratio B/A
Colombia	20.5	89.5	4.37
Brazil	11.5	19.7	1.71
Mexico	18.2	17.8	0.98
Venezuela	11.7	15.2	1.30
Trinidad & Tobago	2.1	12.6	6.00
Peru	2.4	11.5	4.79
Panama	**2.1**	**10.9**	**5.19**
Ecuador	6.4	10.3	1.61
United States	10.7	10.1	0.94
Argentina	3.9	4.8	1.23
Costa Rica	5.7	4.1	0.72
Uruguay	2.6	4.4	1.69
Paraguay	5.1	4.0	0.78
Chile	2.6	3.0	1.15
Source: Ayres (1998).			

---

[72] Source: MIPPE, collected from Zonas de Policía y Alcaldias de la República.

[73] Sollis et. al. (1995).

[74] Cocaine typically accounts for about 95% of the total weight of drugs seized by officials, followed by marijuana (2-4%), though marijuana represented about two-thirds of the total weight seized in 1996 due to exceptionally large quantities of that drug seized that year. Source: Ministerio Publico: Fiscalia Especializada en Delitos Relacionados con Drogas, Seccion de Computo y Estadistica.

[75] Source: Comision Nacional para el Estudio y la Prevencion de los Delitos Relacionados con la Droga (CONAPRED), August 1992.

[76] Figures for the first half of 1997. Source: Ministerio Publico: Fiscalia Especializada en Delitos Relacionados con Drogas, Seccion de Computo y Estadistica.

[77] Source: Ministerio Publico: Fiscalia Especializada en Delitos Relacionados con Drogas, Seccion de Computo y Estadistica.

[78] According to a survey of children and adolescents detained in Tocumen, 95% are boys. Source: Coordinacion de la Magistrada Esmeralda A. de Troitino, Departamento de Estadistica. Figures for 1997.

by physically violent crimes (assault, fighting, homicide). Direct drug-related crimes and possession of illegal arms each account for five percent of youth crimes. Sexual crimes – including sex abuse, rape, and illegal prostitution – account for less than two percent of youth crimes.

73.   Quantitative data on **domestic violence** are generally deficient in Panama, as in most countries. Available crime statistics indicate that domestic violence (abuse, domestic disputes, incest, etc.) represented just over one percent of total detained criminals in Panama. These figures are likely under-estimated, however, due to problems of under-reporting, lack of awareness on behalf of victims (regarding their rights) and police, and definitional problems. A number of qualitative studies have been conducted on domestic violence for various parts of Panama.[79] The Government has included domestic violence in its recent anti-poverty strategy[80] and is looking for opportunities to collaborate with communities and NGOs to help combat this domestic violence. For example, the Social Emergency Fund (FES) is currently exploring the possibility of funding programs to help abused women via NGOs as part of its *"grupos vulnerables"* initiative.

74.   **Poverty and Crime.** The LSMS community survey does not reveal a strong correlation between poverty and the share of urban communities reporting problems with crime. The share of city dwellers living in communities reporting various crimes and social ills was very similar for both the poor and the non-poor. Only a slightly larger share of the urban poor live in communities which report problems with theft, alcohol and prostitution. For other types of problems, the frequencies were the same.[81]

Box 1 - Low Social Capital, Crime and Social Decline in Urban Panama

Crime and violence can erode social capital by reducing trust and cooperation within the community. Indeed, urban communities with low social capital (SCI) frequently talked of the problems of crime, personal security, and social decline in the SCQS focus group interviews. Some examples of the discussions by urban dwellers in low social capital communities:

"There are young people who are unemployed and there are robberies, and with the drug issue, they are on the look out to see what to rob....people are afraid to denounce because they fear retaliation."

"Girls who are twelve or thirteen years old are already women. Drug dealers give them money, they see that they have developed breasts...they offer them money, invite them to lunch and buy them new shoes....fifteen and sixteen year old girls lure the younger ones who sometimes [spontaneously] offer themselves to older men." Participants in the focus group meeting explained how the result of this process was that young girls end up as mistresses of drug dealers or as prostitutes. Boys run drugs.

"Listen, even in children's parties there is a horrendous aggressive attitude." "I don't let my children go out of the apartment." "[When teachers try to discipline children,] they feel that they have the right to respond to the teacher and even tell him what he will die of." "In school there are forty pregnant girls." "Older kids beat younger kids."

"The situation went out of control after the [1989] invasion. There were weapons everywhere and the police was disbanded." "[Now] there are revolvers day and night... at every hour...last week they killed a 20 year old kid."

Source: Panama SCQS 1997

---

75.   Nonetheless, crime and violence can exact a high cost on the poor, who are more vulnerable to shocks, in a number of ways. First, crime and violence can impose direct costs on the poor. These direct costs can take the form of stolen property, lost productivity (and hence earnings), and, in the extreme case of homicide, lost life (and earnings or potential earnings of the victim). It can also lead to the outright

---

[79] See for example, "Márquez de Pérez et. al. (1991),"Approximación diagnóstica a las violaciones de mujeres en los distritos de Panamá y San Miguelito;" Atencio et. al. (1994), "La Familia en Panamá: Situación Actual y Perspectivas;" and Santamaria R. et. al. (December 1996), "Proyecto Acción de Prevencion de la Violencia Intrafamiliar."

[80] "Nuevo Enfoque Estrategico para Reducir la Pobreza." August 20, 1998.

[81] This does not mean that the intensity or frequency of crime is the same between poor and non-poor communities. The questions in the LSMS simply asked if the community had experienced problems with theft, gangs, drugs, alcohol, prostitution, other crimes (not how often or what share of the community was affected).

destruction of public infrastructure (via acts of vandalism), which is a crucial asset to the poor.[82] When households invest in measures to protect themselves from crime/violence, such as installing locks, metal doors, window bars, or perimeter walls on their homes, they also incur direct prevention costs. A study of home improvements in low income *barriadas* surrounding Panama city found these types of improvements to be quite costly and common (half of all households in the sample).[83]

76.   Crime and violence can also reduce employment opportunities. High levels of crime and violence can deter investors (e.g., in image-sensitive tourist areas or in low wage cost factory areas), thereby reducing potential jobs. Crime and violence also hamper the ability of workers to travel safely to work.[84] This is particularly constraining for the urban poor (especially women) living in marginalized *barriadas* on the outskirts of the city, those who must walk along unlit interior pathways (as is common among poorer communities in the Panama City area), and for those who work odd hours of the day when safe transportation is not guaranteed.[85] In the same manner, violence can erode human capital when it reduces or limits access to education and health facilities by both users and providers.[86]

77.   Furthermore, crime and violence can erode social capital, when it reduces trust and cooperation between community members and organizations (see Box 1). It can also impair household relations (particularly when the problems involve alcohol or domestic violence), by reducing the capacity of households to function effectively as a unit.[87]

Transportation

78.   Safe and reliable transportation is an important complement to labor as an asset, particularly in Panama's urban areas where residential areas are often located in peripheral areas, quite far from centers of business and employment. A lack of *safe* transportation can hinder people from obtaining gainful employment -- particularly women and those who work odd hours. As discussed above, transport was one of the most frequently ranked priorities among urban communities in the LSMS sample.

79.   Few poor city dwellers in Panama have direct access to roads. Rather, access roads generally encircle dense, poor urban communities that are characterized by intricate mazes of cement pathways (only a few feet wide, with stairs or ramps in hilly areas) that criss-cross between lots. As such, safe parking of vehicles is limited in poor urban neighborhoods. Indeed, very few (one percent) poor urban households own cars, compared with one third of the non-poor. Virtually none have motorcycles, and while one third report owning bicycles, these are not reported as common methods of transportation to school or work.

80.   Consequently, the poor are largely reliant on public transportation. In fact, half of all poor urban residents, and 71 percent of those living in the PCSM greater metropolitan area rely on public transportation to commute to work (Table A7.21). The main form of public transportation is busses. Bus passenger transport in Panama is provided mostly by private operators. The Ministry of Government and Justice (MJG) allocates licenses (*cupos*) for entry and route assignments. Although measures have recently been taken to improve competition, anecdotal evidence suggests that the majority of these *cupos* are owned by a few individuals, who then rent them out to bus operators for a profit. Passenger tariffs are

---

[82] Ayres (1998).
[83] Sollis et. al. (1995). The average cost of installing metal doors was $90-120; locks cost another $35. The average cost of window bars was $40-$50 per window; the cost of a perimeter walls ranged from $50 for a barbed wire fence to $800 for a block wall.
[84] Moser (Briefing Note, 1996).
[85] In Cerro Cocobolo, a low income *barriada*, for example, a community with prevalent street crime where gunshots are heard at night, an aunt of one women in focus group discussions was killed while resisting robbery, with a bus terminal ten minutes walk away along an ill-lit street that is prone to late-night robberies. Sollis et. al. (1995).
[86] Moser (Briefing Note, 1996).
[87] Moser (Briefing Note, 1996); Ayres (1998).

fixed at 15 *centavos*, based on negotiations between the Government and transport unions.[88]   The Government recently commissioned a study[89] to explore ways to improve the efficiency of bus passenger transport, reduce distortions, improve the quality of service provision, and improve the regulatory framework for vehicle standards, inspection, and pollution control.   Two options include organizing cooperatives among bus drivers and permitting the creation of organized bus companies.

81.   On average, the urban poor spend roughly B./28 per person per year (over four percent of total consumption) on bus transport, as compared with B./74 (three percent of total consumption) for the non-poor in urban areas.   Adding to this monetary cost is the time taken for the poor to get to work.   As discussed above, the physical layout and spatial development of Panama's urban areas (particularly the greater metropolitan areas of Panama City and Colón) have led to long travel distances as people commute from peripheral residential areas along busy, narrow corridors (such as the Transisthmian Highway) to central areas for work.   Deterioration of roads, streets and bridges due to years of inadequate maintenance, unacceptably high levels of traffic congestion, and inadequate traffic management (including poor use of traffic lights) have increased the time needed for such commutes, thus raising the true cost of commuting.   In fact, the LSMS reveals that, on average, it takes close to one hour for the poor to commute to work using public transportation (Table A7.21).   Lengthy, congested commutes undoubtedly contribute to the frustration and pessimism expressed by urban community members in the LSMS survey.

Table A7.21 – Transportation to Work, Urban Areas & PCSM					
	All Urban Areas			Panama City and San Miguelito (PCSM)		
	All Poor	Non-Poor	Total	All Poor	Non-Poor	Total
% of Workers Using Various Modes of Transport to Commute to Work						
Public Service	49%	49%	49%	70%	52%	54%
Own Car	2%	25%	22%	2%	28%	26%
Bicycle	9%	2%	3%	0%	0%	0%
Business/Institution	7%	4%	5%	5%	4%	4%
Walking	30%	13%	15%	22%	10%	11%
Other	3%	6%	6%	1%	6%	5%
Average Time Taken To Commute to Work, by Mode of Transportation						
Public Service[a]	52	46	47	49	47	47
Own Car	34	28	28	37	30	30
Bicycle	19	15	16	0	10	10
Business/Institution	57	40	43	106	46	52
Walking	18	13	14	10	12	12
Other	29	29	29	52	30	30
Average Total	38	35	36	43	38	38
Source: LSMS 1997. Numbers may not add to 100 due to rounding. a\ Includes waiting time.						

Unemployment Among the Poor

82.   **Urban Unemployment and Market Segmentation.**   Unemployment was one of the top three priority concerns of urban communities sampled in the LSMS community survey.   Indeed, unemployment is high in urban areas, averaging 7.4 percent using the international definition, and over ten percent when seasonal and "discouraged" workers are counted (national definition).   Unemployment is twice as high in urban areas as rural and indigenous areas.   Indeed, controlling for other variables, unemployment is significantly higher in urban areas.[90]   This may arise from a higher degree of distortion-induced segmentation in urban labor markets, arising from the multiplicity of legislative regimes (including separate legislation governing the public sector, the Panama Canal Commission,

---

[88] Though the price is not subsidized directly on an operational basis, owners do receive tax breaks on spare parts and the import of buses.
[89] With the support of the World Bank-funded Roads project.
[90] See Annex 11 of the Poverty Assessment for details.

export processing zones, and the private sector). Arguably a larger share of the urban labor market is subject to this multiplicity of labor regimes than labor markets in rural and indigenous areas.

83.   **Urban Unemployment and Poverty.** Although unemployment is not correlated with poverty for the nation as a whole, unemployment *is* higher among the urban poor than the urban non-poor (Table A7.22). In fact, controlling for other variables such as education and age, lower levels of total household consumption are indeed associated with a higher probability of being unemployed (Table A7.23). Hence, unemployment is a poverty issue in Panama's cities.

84.   **Unemployment Among Poor Urban Youths, Women.** Unemployment is particularly high among urban women, especially the poor. In fact, controlling for other variables, urban women have a higher likelihood of being unemployed than men (Table A7.23). One fifth of poor urban women in the labor force cannot find jobs; this compares with eight percent for their non-poor counterparts. Unemployment is also high among urban youths in general, and poor young women in particular. One fifth of urban teenagers aged 15-19 cannot find jobs (Table A7.22). A lack of experience – or unrealistically high expectations about "deserved" earnings (perhaps fueled by the demonstration effect of high incomes in urban areas) – could be hampering young adults' transition from school to work in Panama. Interestingly, while unemployment is quite high for adolescent males aged 15-19, it drops significantly for those aged 20-24. In contrast, for urban women, particularly the poor, unemployment starts high for teenagers aged 15-19 and jumps even higher for those aged 20-29. This pattern holds for both the poor and the non-poor in urban areas, but is particularly notable for the poor. One third of poor urban women aged 20-24 and over one quarter of those aged 25-29 cannot find jobs. A number of factors may make firms hesitant to hire women during their most fertile years: even stronger restrictions on the dismissal of pregnant women,[91] mandatory maternity leave, and perceptions by employers that children and pregnancy might distract women from their professional responsibilities.

Table A7.22 - Urban Unemployment Rates for 1997 Using International Definition and LSMS Data											
	Extreme Poor			All Poor			Non-poor			All		
	M	F	All	M	F	All	M	F	All	M	F	All
Age-groups												
15-19 yrs	Obs	10.2	10.2	17.9	21.6	19.2	23.8	16.3	20.3	22.2	16.9	19.9
20-24 yrs	8.2	52.1	23.0	3.6	34.2	14.4	12.0	17.6	14.4	10.8	19.3	14.4
25-29 yrs	10.7	Obs	10.7	8.8	27.9	15.6	4.9	14.2	9.1	5.9	15.7	10.2
30-39 yrs	Obs	4.1	4.1	6.9	19.9	11.5	4.3	5.6	4.9	4.7	7.0	5.7
40-49 yrs	Obs	Obs	Obs	2.5	7.5	4.6	2.8	4.6	3.6	2.8	4.8	3.7
50-59 yrs	Obs	Obs	Obs	Obs	4.9	4.9	1.7	1.6	1.7	1.6	2.3	1.9
Above 60	Obs	Obs	Obs	Obs	Obs	Obs	4.1	Obs	4.1	3.7	4.2	3.8
Education												
None	Obs	Obs	Obs	Obs	Obs	Obs	Obs	Obs	Obs	Obs	Obs	Obs
Primary	3.1	15.2	6.4	5.1	11.0	6.9	4.3	5.6	4.9	4.5	6.6	5.4
Secondary	3.9	52.7	19.6	7.1	27.1	14.6	7.1	11.2	8.9	7.3	13.0	9.6
Vocational/other	Obs	Obs	Obs	21.7	30.1	24.3	5.9	9.2	7.2	4.7	6.5	5.7
Higher	Obs	Obs	Obs	6.6	23.2	14.2	4.5	6.3	5.4	7.6	10.8	8.8
Total	**3.1**	**29.8**	**11.0**	**6.7**	**20.9**	**11.7**	**5.9**	**8.2**	**6.9**	**6.0**	**9.3**	**7.4**
obs. = small or no sample. Source: Panama LSMS 1997. See Annex 11 of the Poverty Assessment for definitions.												

---

[91] As stipulated by the Labor Code. See Annex 11 of the Poverty Assessment for details.

Table A7.23 – Determinants of Unemployment[a] in Urban Areas Probit Estimates of Unemployment			
	Marginal Effects		
	Male	Female	All
Education			
# years in primary	-0.0037	-0.0018	-0.0042
# years in secondary	0.0028	0.0019	0.0033**
# years in higher	0.0010	-0.0057*	-0.0025
Diploma received	-0.0047	0.0069	0.0024
Age	-0.0052***	-0.0003	-0.0056***
Age squared	.00005***	-.00005	.00004**
Head of the household	-0.0541***	0.0090	-0.0267***
Female			0.0238***
Single[b]	0.0176*	0.0092	0.0235***
# of household members	-0.0003	0.0073***	0.0029**
Poverty/economic status			
Total household consumption	$-1.79e-6$*	$-6.50e-6$***	$-4.11e-6$***
Sample Size	2479	1878	4357
Fit (% of correct predictions)	0.93	0.89	0.92
Dependent variable = 1 if individual is unemployed, 0 if he/she is employed. a\ Uses the international definition (see Box 1 of Annex 11 of the Poverty Assessment). b\ Single = unmarried + widowed + divorced. (Necessary omitted variable: married = married + *unida*). Significant levels: * = 90%, ** = 95%, *** = 99%			

RECOMMENDATIONS FOR REDUCING URBAN POVERTY

85.   Reducing poverty in urban areas in Panama requires (a) continued reforms to promote broad-based economic growth in order to increase the incomes and employment opportunities of the poor; and (b) a number of key direct actions to improve the equity and efficiency of public spending in order to help build the assets of the poor. This paper focuses primarily on the direct interventions to reduce urban poverty.

Strategic Principles

86.   A number of strategic principles should guide the direct actions for urban poverty reduction in Panama. These include:

- **Targeting interventions and public spending to the poor.** Targeting seeks to concentrate public resources on those who need them most so as to increase their impact on poverty reduction. **Geographic targeting** (via a poverty map) is the main tool being used for targeting in Panama. Geographic targeting has a number of advantages, most notably administrative ease: communities can be selected ex ante for interventions or increased public spending based on their concentration of poor people. By selecting entire communities for eligibility (e.g., for the development of a pre-primary school program) rather than distinguishing among individuals (e.g., kids within the school), geographic targeting can particularly useful in areas such as education. The current effort to improve the poverty map by combining data from the Census and LSMS will be useful in promoting this approach.[92] In urban areas, however, *corregimientos* can be quite diverse with respect to their poverty profile and sample limitations prevent creating poverty mapping tools at more disaggregated community or neighborhood levels. As such, some programs – particularly transfer programs such as maternal-infant food supplements or the PARVIS housing subsidy scheme – should attempt to further fine tune targeting via **individual indicators**, such as means-testing or anthropometric assessments. **Self-targeting** can also be used for the delivery of services clearly used more by the poor than the non-poor (e.g., targeting resources to public primary school rather than higher education).

---

[92] A repeat of this exercise using data from the 2000 Census and 2000 LSMS will be even more useful for geographic targeting.

- **Emphasis should be placed on interventions that target poor children and youths.** As discussed above, 46 percent of the urban poor in Panama are under age 17. Close to one quarter of all urban children under 17 live in poverty. The developmental status of children renders them extremely vulnerable to the risks of living in an impoverished environment. Youth is the point in the life cycle when physical, cognitive and psycho-social development occurs at its most accelerated pace and is most susceptible to abnormal development from poverty conditions. Poverty is particularly costly to individuals and to society when it occurs at these stages of life. An urban poverty strategy should help focus on helping young people develop their human capital to maximize their chances to thrive and contribute to future improvements in living conditions.

- **Community participation should be promoted to build social capital in Panama's urban neighborhoods and to increase the effectiveness of poverty reduction efforts and service delivery.** As discussed above, social ties in urban areas tend to be weaker than in rural areas. Low social capital, combined with a wide range of social problems, appear to have contributed to pessimism among Panama's city dwellers (as discussed above). Social capital can be a key asset for communities to be able to weather economic crises. Community participation in efforts to reduce poverty can also improve the effectiveness of interventions by (a) addressing the specific needs of communities as they perceive them; and (b) building ownership of the solutions and programs. The Government should seek to build social capital, local ownership and impact by designing mechanisms to work in direct partnerships with communities (as is being done under the FES and in the CEFACEI and mother-to-mother pre-school programs, see main Poverty Assessment report).

Key Areas for Direct Action

87.   The analysis of urban poverty sheds light on a number of key priorities for poverty reduction in urban areas, including: (a) continuing the reform process to generate labor-intensive growth and improving the access of the urban poor to credit, which would both serve to generate income and employment; (b) undertaking a number of reforms and investments in the transport sector (particularly in the area of passenger bus transport); (c) improving the equity and quality of public schooling; (d) evaluating the PARVIS housing support program and expanding the titling of housing and property in urban areas; (e) supporting infrastructure investments, in particular sanitation, garbage collection services, and public lighting, in poor areas; and (f) embarking on a participatory-research program to explore key crime, violence, and social problems and solutions in poor communities.

Labor, Credit and Income Generation

88.   **Employment Generation via Growth.** Unemployment is clearly an important issue for Panama's urban areas – both because urban areas have the highest rates of unemployment in the country and because unemployment was ranked one of the top three priority problems by urban communities. Unemployment is also an urban poverty issue in light of the fact that the poor have a higher probability of being unemployed in Panama's cities.

89.   In many countries, governments feel compelled to take "direct" action to reduce unemployment, embarking on ambitious training and vocational education programs. Such interventions should be treated with caution, however, as they tend to be quite costly and have limited proven returns in terms of reducing unemployment. Rather, the *key* instrument for reducing unemployment is the deepening of economic reforms for the promotion of labor-intensive growth. Indeed, unemployment has started to fall in recent years as growth has picked up and the Labor Code has become more flexible.[93] Key actions on the Government's reform agenda that would help promote growth include: transport sector liberalization

---

[93] See Annex 11 of the Poverty Assessment for more information on Labor Code reforms and the resulting increasing responsiveness of labor markets and unemployment to growth.

(see below), continued tariff and pricing reforms (particularly for rice and milk), petroleum sector reform (liberalizing entry and exit), liberalizing the investment regime to promote foreign investment, and strengthening the financial system (modernizing banking and securities market legislation). In addition, the Government should undertake an analysis of the current Labor Code (since the 1995 reforms) to identify areas that require reform for additional flexibility (such as wage setting and restrictions on dismissal).

90.   **Micro-Credit and Income Generation**. A number of actions could be undertaken to improve the access of the urban poor to credit, which could serve as a mechanism for helping generate income and employment for poor city-dwellers:

(a) To improve the individual credit-worthiness of the urban poor, an expansion of property titling and an improvement in the efficiency of the titling and registry process should be rigorously pursued (as discussed below);

(b) To reduce the costs of information about the credit-worthiness of the urban poor, small-scale loan cooperatives ("solidarity groups" in which members-borrowers use peer pressure to encourage other members to repay) could be targeted; likewise, the creation of loan pools or independent lending agencies that specialize in loans to the poor could be explored;

(c) To better meet the needs of the urban poor, credit schemes (such as the new initiative by the FES) should take into account the small size of borrowing generally required by the poor (under B./500 for loans and B./140 for purchases on credit);

(d) To improve the productivity in the use of credit by the urban poor, credit schemes should also include technical assistance;

(e) Finally, to actually reach the poor in urban areas, the schemes should adopt some form of targeting. This could include a combination of geographic targeting (locating specialized lending agencies in poor areas according to the poverty map) and indicators targeting (means-testing, proxy means-testing). The schemes should also take into consideration key vulnerable groups, such as poor women, who tend to be self-employed and hence could have a particular need for micro-credit.

Transportation

91.   A related issue is transportation, which was also ranked highly as a priority issue facing Panama's urban communities. Existing distortions and bottlenecks in the transport system increase the cost to workers of commuting (reducing their number of productive hours per day) as well as the overall cost of living. As discussed above, these bottlenecks have been particularly taxing to the poor, who are largely reliant on an inefficient public transport system. With the support of the World Bank's Second Roads Rehabilitation project, the Government should seek to reduce urban commuting costs by:

(a) implementing the recommended reforms of the recent bus passenger transport study[94] in order to reorganize the urban bus system, improve the transparency of license allocation (through regular competitive bidding), and reduce distortions and deficiencies in the public transport system;

(b) continuing to improve the Ministry of Public Works' administrative capacity and maintenance of urban roads; and

---

[94] The study was supported by the first World Bank-supported Roads Project.

(c) continuing to increase investment in the rehabilitation of urban roads and streets, as well as the investment in intersection management (traffic lights to reduce congestion).

In addition to these measures, though politically difficult due to the strong presence of trucking unions, the Government should attempt to enforce the liberalization of road shipments (trucking)[95] in Panama (particularly in the Colón area) to reduce the cost of living in general.

Education

92.   As discussed above, educational achievement is clearly correlated with a reduction in urban poverty. Differences in education are also key determinants of inequality, accounting for *half* of existing inequality in Panama.[96] As such, efforts should be made to reduce inequities in public spending on education in urban areas and to improve the educational attainment of poor urban children.

93.   In terms of **access** in urban areas, the Government should increase allocations to community-based informal *initial education* and *pre-primary education* programs for the urban poor.[97] Early childhood education has been shown to improve children's readiness for reading and writing and to reduce repetition and dropout rates in primary schools. Non-formal approaches are less costly and make it possible to provide early educational services to children in poor urban families and to encourage parental involvement in and understanding of better child-rearing practices. Emphasis should also be on improving the access of poor urban children to *secondary* schools. To ensure that these programs reach the poor, an expansion of initial, pre-primary, and secondary education in urban areas should be carefully geographically targeted to *corregimientos* with high concentrations of the poor using the new poverty map prepared by MIPPE. This poverty map should be combined with information on educational attainment for the proper selection of poor and needy communities in Panama's urban areas.

94.   In terms of improving the **quality** of basic education in urban areas, the Government should allocate more resources towards investments in school infrastructure, quality materials and library packages, and textbooks. Again, these investments should be targeted in priority order to those urban *corregimientos* with a high concentration of the poor according to the new poverty map. In addition, further work should be done to explore the factors causing higher dropout rates among poor urban children at the secondary level, particularly boys.

Housing

95.   As discussed above, housing is a key asset of the poor, for general living standards, use as a base for productive activities, as an emergency asset for sale, and as a tool for extending personal relationships and building social capital. Poor quality housing (roofing, floors, walls, shacks) is significantly correlated with poverty (see above). While housing investments are generally considered a private activity (rather than a "public good"), the Government has recently initiated an IDB-supported program, "PARVIS," to support the housing improvement needs of the poor (as discussed above). The program is largely focused on urban areas. The Government should undertake an independent evaluation of the effectiveness of the program as a whole and of its means-tested targeting mechanism in order to assess its impact on the urban poor.

96.   Expanding the coverage of housing/property titles is also a clear priority in urban Panama, both in general and for the poor. The Government should seek to identify and rectify bottlenecks in the titling process, covering all phases (awareness and outreach, cadastre, application and approval, and registry).

---

[95] There are a number of restrictions to entry into the trucking business in Panama, particularly in the Colón Free Zone.

[96] See Annex 10 of the Poverty Assessment for a decomposition of inequality in Panama.

[97] The proposed World Bank-supported Second Basic Education Project intends to support the expansion of pre-primary education to children living in poor urban areas.

This would greatly boost the use of housing as a key asset of the urban poor and improve their access to credit.

Basic Infrastructure

97.   For the most part, communities have better knowledge of their priorities for infrastructure investments than central planners. These community-based choices usually take into account existing coverage and gaps, as well as local preferences (which can be driven by a number of factors including primary occupation, natural resources, and location). As such, infrastructure priorities should be determined by the communities themselves. Demand-driven schemes, such as the Social Fund (FES) can play an important role in responding to these priorities. Working with communities can also strengthen social capital and ownership and future maintenance of the investments.

98.   Nonetheless, the above analysis sheds light on a number of gaps in infrastructure provision facing the urban poor in Panama. These include **sanitation** services (sewerage**), garbage collection**, and the provision of **public lighting**, which also happen to rely on some degree of central strategy for efficient delivery. The Government should seek to target funds for these services to the urban poor using the new poverty map (to select *corregimientos* with high concentrations of the poor) combined with institutional and census data on coverage (or lack of it) of these services (to identify poor communities with inadequate coverage).

Crime, Violence and Social Problems

99.   Crime, violence and social problems are clearly a priority for the urban poor. Additional work should be done, however, to better assess the types of problems that plague poor urban neighborhoods as well as possible solutions. Such research should be done in a participatory manner, involving the communities themselves, as well as local organizations and the numerous NGOs which appear to have emerged to help combat the problems (e.g., youth associations such as those in San Miguelito, anti-drug groups, organizations focusing on domestic violence, etc.). The Social Emergency Fund (FES) could also be used to pilot Government funding for anti-violence initiatives through NGOs (building on the mechanism being developed for funding NGO-initiatives to reach *grupos vulnerables*). Some such initiatives could include community-based youth-oriented recreational facilities and after-school programs.

APPENDIX A7.1

Table A7.A1 – Determinants of Employment Choice, Urban Areas Probit Estimates			
	Marginal Effects		
	Male	**Female**	**Female**
Individual Characteristics			
Education			
# years in primary	-0.0178	-0.0232	-0.0214**
# years in secondary	0.0131***	0.0646***	0.0334***
# years in higher	0.0271***	0.0383***	0.0354***
Diploma received	-0.0607	0.2563***	0.0343
Experience[a]	0.0014	0.0264***	0.0097***
Experience Squared	-0.00005	-0.0006***	-0.0002**
Training	0.2302***	0.2489***	0.2434***
Other			
Female			-0.1182***
Single[b]	-0.0373	0.0128	-0.0097
Household characteristics			
# of household members			
Ages 0-5	-0.0111	-0.0425**	-0.0178*
Poverty/economic status			
Total household consumption	5.58e-6**	-7.78e-6***	-7.64e-7
Selectivity	0.0899***	0.0937***	0.0957***
Sample Size	2306	1675	3981
Fit (% of correct predictions)	0.69	0.74	0.70
Dependent variable = 1 if individual works in the formal sector; 0 if he/she works in the informal sector. See Annex 11 of the Poverty Assessment for definitions.a\ Experience variable comes from a question in the LSMS that asks "how long have you worked as [...current profession....]?" b\ Single = unmarried + widowed + divorced. (The necessary omitted variable is: married = married + *unida*) Significant levels: * = 90%, ** = 95%, *** = 99%			

Table A7.A2 – Determinants of Urban Labor Force Participation Probit Estimates Using the International Definition of LFP[a]			
	Marginal Effects		
	Male	**Female**	**All**
Individual Characteristics			
Education			
# years in primary	0.0088	0.0022	0.0089
# years in secondary	-0.0046	0.0025	-0.0008
# years in higher	0.0167***	0.0468***	0.0388***
Diploma received	0.2004***	0.1304***	0.1739***
Currently in school	-0.1988***	-0.1940***	-02458***
Age[a]			
Between 20-24	0.1518***	0.2070***	0.2184***
Between 25-29	0.1883***	0.2870***	0.2772***
Between 30-39	0.1986***	0.3567***	0.3037***
Between 40-39	0.1543***	0.3727***	0.2875***
Between 50-59	0.0844***	0.1702***	0.1440***
Over 60	-0.2897***	-0.2888***	-0.3247***
Other			
Female			-0.2503***
Single[b]	-0.0763***	0.1912.***	0.0677***
Head of the household	0.1407***	0.1004***	0.2213***
Household characteristics			
# of household members			
Ages 0-5	0.0092	- 0.0103	-0.0026
Ages 6-11	0.0155	-0.0173	-0.0039
Ages 12-17	0.0023	-0.0034***	-0.0152*
Ages 18-59	0.0110**	-0.0363	0.0126**
Ages over 60	-0.0190	-0.0046	-0.0028
Poverty/economic status			
Total household consumption	6.03e-7	6.90e-6***	4.97e-6***
Sample Size	3303	3719	7022
Fit (% of correct predictions)	0.85	0.70	0.91

Dependent variable = 1 if individual participates in the labor force (employed or unemployed); 0 if not.

a\ See Annex 11 of the Poverty Assessment for definitions.

a\ The omitted variable for the age dummies is age between 15-19.

b\ Single = unmarried + widowed + divorced. (Necessary omitted variable: married = married + *unida*)

Significant levels: * = 90%, ** = 95%, *** = 99%

Table A7.A3 – Correlates of Poverty: Multi-Variate Analysis: Urban Areas	
Probability of being poor; marginal values	Urban Areas
Area	
Panama City & San Miguelito	NS
Household Size & Composition	
Number of members 0-5 years old	8.4%**
Number of members 6-11 years old	6.2%**
Number of members 12-17 years old	6.7%**
Number of members 18-24 years old	5.4%**
Number of members 25-59 years old	4.1%**
Number of members >=60 years old	8.1%**
Number of females/ Number of males	-0.8%*
Sex of household head	NS
Education: Maximum for HHH/companion	
Primary completed (vs. Primary incomplete or none)	NS
Secondary incomplete (vs. Primary incomplete or none)	-6.1%*
Secondary completed (vs. Primary incomplete or none)	NS
Advanced education (vs. Primary incomplete or none)	-1.4%**
Labor and Income Sources	
Workers per persons in HH	NS
Biggest Source of Income:	
Formal-Private (vs. Formal-Public)	4.5%*
Informal-Private (vs. Formal-Public)	6.4%**
Non-labor (vs. Formal-Public)	6.3%*
Agriculture represents more than half of total income	NS
Housing & Basic Services	
Hut + Bad roof + Bad walls + Bad floor (from 0 to 4)	8.0%**
Latrine, pit or none	11.2%**
No telephone	12.7%**
No electricity	16.3%**
Hours w/water during last month (Max 30 * 24 =720)	NS
Water in the yard (not inside house)	NS
Rooms per Person	NS
Housing tenancy	
No registered title (vs. registered)	7.5%**
Does not own house (vs. registered)	17.6%**
Credit & Assets	
Less than $100 in all credits & loans	5.9%**
Has a car	-17.5%**
Social Capital	
Belongs to community organization	NS
Belongs to a cooperative	-9.1%**
Belongs to a sports or cultural group	-6.9%**
Constant	**
Source: Panama LSMS 1997. See Annex 8 of Poverty Assessment for details on methodology.	
a\ Determinants of Consumption Regressions. Marginal change in consumption. Original function:	
Probability < 5% (**), 10% (*), NS = Non-Significant	

REFERENCES

Atencio M. Nira et. al. (1994). "La Familia en Panamá: Situación Actual y Perspectivas."

Ayres, Robert L. (1998). Crime and Violence as Development Issues in Latin America and the Caribbean. The World Bank.

Comisión Nacional Para el Estudio y la Prevención de los Délitos Relacionadas con la Droga (CEDEM) (August 1992). "Supérate, no permitas que las drogas te detengan."

Dames & Moore, Inc. et. al. (December 1997). "Plan de Desarrollo Urbano de las Areas Metropolitanas del Pacífico y del Atlántico."

Ministerio de Planificación y Política Económica, Departamento de Planificación Social (September 1994) - de De la Cruz, Rosa Elena et. al: "Breve Informe Sobre la Situación de los Sectores Sociales en Panamá: 1992-1993."

Fajnzylber Pablo, Daniel Lederman and Norman Loayza (March 1998). "What Causes Violent Crime?" The World Bank.

Heber, Gabriele et. al. (September 1995). "Small Scale Finance for Housing Improvement in Panama.

Herrera, Ligia J (1994). "Regiones de Desarrollo Socioeconomico de Panama: 1980-1990: Transformaciones ocurridas en la decada." CELA.

Katsura, Harold M. and Clare Romanik (January 1996). "Housing Demand Among Panama's Middle- and Low-Income Population." The Urban Institute.

Lindo-Fuentes, Hector (December 1997). "Qualitative Study of Social Capital in Selected Communities in Panama."

Márquez de Pérez, Amelia et. al. (1991). Aproximación Diagnóstica a las Violaciones de Mujeres en los Distritos de Panamá y San Miguelito." CEDEM.

Ministerio de Vivienda (1997). "Programa Parvis y Otros Programas Dirigidos a los Pobres."

Ministerio de Salud (1996). "Ventanas Epidemiologicas Sobre Uso Indebido de Drogas, Panamá."

Moser, Caroline O.N. (1996). Confronting Crisis: A Summary of Household Responses to Poverty and Vulnerability in Four Poor Urban Communities. The World Bank. ESSD Series No. 7.

Moser, Caroline. (1996). Urban Violence: Briefing Note. The World Bank. Memo.

Oxford Economic Research Associates Ltd. (July 9, 1998). "La demanda de servicios de agua y saneamiento entre las comunidades pobres: experiencia internacional y evidencia en Panamá."

Santamaría Nilda et. al. (December 1996). "Ruta Crítica de las Mujeres Afectadas por la Violencia Intrafamiliar." Organización Panamericana de la Salud: Programa Mujer, Salud y Desarrollo.

Sollis, Peter ct. al. (September 1995). "Building a Future: The Housing Improvement Process in the *Barriadas* of Panama City."

Annex 8 – The Determinants of Poverty in Panama

Carlos E. Sobrado
April 12, 1999

1.   This paper examines the correlates of poverty with multi-variate models that predict the probability of being poor using data from the Panama LSMS (1997). The analysis is useful, first, to verify the relative role of the various factors in determining poverty status, and second, to assess the potential impact that policy-induced changes in these factors are likely to have on the probability of being poor, holding all other factors constant. The probability of a household being poor was examined for the nation as a whole, as well as for urban, rural (non-indigenous) and indigenous areas.

2.   It is important to note the limitations of this analysis at the outset. **First** and foremost, the analysis does not capture the dynamic impact of certain causes of poverty over time. Most notably, the impact of changes in economic growth – most certainly a key determinant of poverty – cannot be assessed using this static, cross-section model. **Second,** the analysis is limited by the variables available at the household level from the 1997 LSMS. Other factors -- such as social conditions like crime and violence, or physical conditions such as variations in climate or access to markets -- could not be included due to a lack of data at this level. **Finally,** though theory holds that many of the variables included in the analysis do indeed contribute to (cause) poverty (or poverty reduction), the statistical relationships should be interpreted as correlates and not as determinants since causality can run both ways for some variables.

3.   The analysis was conducted using probabilistic regressions with poverty classifications for each household[1] (0=non-poor, and 1=poor) and household characteristics (Table A8.A1.1 in Appendix A8.1). All the regressions were calculated using the households as the base unit, and taking into consideration the sampling design.

4.   The paper is organized as follows: **first**, a regression for the entire country was estimated, **second**, geographic area regressions were estimated (urban, rural non-indigenous and indigenous), **third**, the cumulative impact on the probability of being poor is presented for a hypothetical household due to changes in several variables is calculated, and **finally**, several conclusions are suggested.

THE PROBABILITY OF BEING POOR IN PANAMA

5.   This section presents regression results for the probability of being poor for Panama as a whole. A probit model[2] was estimated to determine which variables are relevant to the poverty classification and which variables are not (Table A8.1).

Marginal effects

6.   The marginal effect of each significant variable on the probability of being poor was calculated. The marginal effects are the changes in the percentage of the probability of being poor (dependent variable), due to a change of one (1) on any independent variable. A change of one (1) in a categorical variable (including the dummies) implies a movement from one category to the other. The marginal effects of the independent variables on the probability of being poor were calculated for the entire sample, and the results are presented in Table A8.1.

---

[1] Based on actual per capita consumption.
[2] See Appendix A8.A2 for a more technical explanation of the probit model.

Geographical Location

7.   **Even after controlling for other characteristics, geographical location is a key variable associated with poverty.** Holding all other variables constant, a household in the indigenous or remote area is 25 percentage points more likely to be poor than an urban household. Households in rural (non-indigenous, non-remote) areas are 10 percentage points more likely to be poor than an otherwise similar urban household.

Household Size

8.   **Larger households are more likely to be poor.**   Overall, each additional child under five increases a household's probability of being poor by 16 percentage points; each member over 60 years old increases the household's likelihood of being poor by about 13 percentage points. As expected, economically active members (25-59 years old) are associated with the lowest increase in the probability of being poor (less than 7 percentage points). Given the high number of family members in extreme poor households,[3] family size and composition is clearly an important correlate of poverty status, suggesting a potentially strong role for family planning interventions.

Gender and Marital Status

9.   **Neither gender nor marital status are significantly correlated with poverty status.** Neither of the two gender variables (female/male ratio and gender of the household head) nor the marital status of the household head were significantly related to the probability of being poor (not even at the $p \leq 0.15$ significance level).

Education

10.   **The education of the household head or companion is strongly significant in reducing the probability of being poor**. Finishing primary education, starting secondary and finishing secondary education each decrease the probability of being poor by around ten percentage points. Higher education reduces the probability of being poor by about 30 percentage points compared to no education by either household head or companion.

Labor

11.   **Informal-sector and agricultural employment are correlated with poverty.** Households deriving most of their income from agriculture or the informal sector have a higher probability of being poor due to lower earnings (and hence productivity) in these sectors. Deriving most income from the public sector reduces a household's probability of being poor by about ten percentage points. Dependence on agriculture for the main source of earnings increases a household's probability of being poor by about six percent (as compared to non-farm earnings).

Land Titling

12.   **Small holdings of land are associated with poverty, even if they are titled.** Only land titles over 15 hectares were associated with a lower probability of being poor.

---

[3] An average of 6.5 members: 1.4 average members ages 0 to 5, 1.23 ages 6 to 11, 1.03 ages 12 to 17, 0.7 ages 18 to 24, 1.8 ages 25 to 59 and 0.4 average members 60 years and older.

Table A8.1 – Statistical Significance and Marginal values for the Probability of Being Poor	
Variables b	Panama d/x a
Observed household poverty rate	**27.5%**
Area group	
Rural non-indigenous, non-remote (vs. Urban)	0.102**
Indigenous area (vs. Urban)	0.252**
Remote (vs. Urban)	0.282**
Panama City & San Miguelito	
Minutes to public health facility	-0.0004*
Number of Members in Household by age group	
Number of members 0-5 years old	0.158**
Number of members 6-11 years old	0.106**
Number of members 12-17 years old	0.094**
Number of members 18-24 years old	0.097**
Number of members 25-59 years old	0.067**
Number of members >=60 years old	0.131**
Number of females/number of males	ns
Gender of household head	ns
HHH/companion education (Max) group	
Primary incomplete (vs. None)	ns
Primary completed (vs. None)	-0.090**
Secondary incomplete (vs. None)	-0.122**
Secondary completed (vs. None)	-0.126**
Advanced education (vs. None)	-0.293**
Workers per persons in HH	ns
Biggest Source of Income group	
Formal-Private (vs. Formal-Public)	0.086**
Informal-Private (vs. Formal-Public)	0.098**
Non-labor (vs. Formal-Public)	0.117**
Agriculture represents > 50% of total income	0.058**
Land titled group	
1 to 15 ha (vs. less than one hectare)	ns
>15 ha (vs. less than one hectare)	-0.129**
Hut + low quality roof + low quality walls + low quality floor (from 0 to 4)	0.084**
Latrine, pit or none	0.183**
No telephone	0.226**
No electricity	0.181**
Source of water: river	0.103*
Hours with water last month (Max 30 * 24 =720)	ns
Water in the yard (not inside house)	ns
Rooms per Person	-0.092**
House tenancy group	
No registered title (vs. registered)	0.072**
Does not own house (vs. registered)	0.170**
Less than $100 in all credits & loans	0.143**
Has a car	-0.280**
Belongs to community organization	ns
Belongs to a cooperative	-0.100**
Belongs to a sports or cultural group	-0.073**
Constant	.**

Source: Panama LSMS 1997
a All the marginal values were calculated at the observed poverty rate using only significant variables or variables in a group
 with at least one significant variable (the groups can be identified by a title line before each group)
probability < : 5% (**), 15% (*), non-significant (ns), and not used because perfect multicolliniarity (nu)
b Household head marital status was included but none of the categories was significant.

Basic Services and Housing

13.   **A lack of access to basic services is correlated with poverty.** Households that lack telephone services are significantly more likely to be poor than those with connections (23 percentage points more likely).   Similarly, those lacking electricity connections or toilets connected to the sewer system electricity are more likely to be poor than those with connections (18 percentage points more likely for

each). Households that rely on river water are ten percent more likely to be poor than those who receive water from the IDAAN/MINSA water system.

14. **Housing quality and titling are also related to poverty status.** The probability of being poor increases by more than eight percentage points for each on an index of poor housing quality (which ranges from 0 to 4). Owning a house with title is associated with a lower probability of being poor by seven percentage points as compared with owners with no title and 17 percentage points when compared with households that do not own their homes.

Credit and Other Physical Assets

15. **Limited access to credit is correlated with poverty status,** though the direction of causality is not clear. Households may be poor because they lack credit to make investments that would boost productivity or smooth consumption. Alternatively, households may lack access to credit because they do not have the collateral or incomes needed to qualify for loans. Households with less than B./100.00 in credit per year are 14 percentage points more likely to be poor than those with more than that amount of borrowing over the past year.

16. **Owning a car reduces a households probability of being poor by 28 percentage points.** Car ownership could indicate a store of wealth or an important complement to labor (efficient means of transportation).

Social Capital

17. **Membership in certain types of organizations is correlated with poverty status.** Participation in cooperatives or sport/cultural groups lowers the probability of being poor by ten and seven percentage points respectively. Membership in community organizations is not significantly related to poverty status.

THE DETERMINANTS OF POVERTY FOR SPECIFIC GEOGRAPHIC AREAS

18. The determinants (or correlates) of poverty can vary from one segment of the population to the other. For instance, additional years of education can have a different impact for an urban household compared to a rural household. The LSMS sample representative for urban, rural and indigenous areas and, as such, separate logistic regressions can be estimated for each area. It is important not to confuse the results for each separate area regression with the results of a national regression applied to a specific area. In the former, the estimated parameters are based only on households in that specific area, and in the latter the parameters reflect the conditions of the entire country.[4]

Marginal Effects and Statistical Significance

19. The logistic regressions for urban, rural, and indigenous areas (separately) included the same independent variables as the national regression (excluding the geography variables). The marginal values and the significance level are presented in Table A8.2. The marginal effects were evaluated at the following probabilities of being poor: 10.1% probability of being poor for urban households, 46.7% for rural, and at 90.8% for the indigenous households.

---

[4] Also, the national regression only allows to adjust the intercept to take into consideration specific areas, but not the slope of the individual variables (i.e. the effect of household size is assumed to be the same regardless of the area the household is located at).

20.   With the exception of housing tenancy for indigenous households,[5] **all the significant parameters in the individual areas show exactly the same tendency[6] as each other and as the results at the national level.** Since all the tendencies are essentially the same, only notable characteristics of the marginal values are discussed here.

Non-significant parameters

21.   The lack of significance for some variable parameters can be a result of too little variation in the dependent variable for the individual areas. For instance, the number of *poor* households in the urban areas is only 10.1%, and the number of *non-poor* households in the indigenous area is only 9.2%. Non-significant values can also be a product of little variation in the independent variables. For example, in urban areas, less than 2% of household heads or their companions had no education. It is important to take into consideration these specific characteristics before concluding the importance (or not) of any variable in the poverty status of a household because **as correlation does not mean causality, lack of correlation does not suggest an absence of causality.**

Urban Households: Notable Characteristics

22.   Households size is strongly related to higher levels of poverty and the very young and very old have more effect over the probability of being poor. Housing characteristics, tenancy type as well as credit and durable goods are also strongly related to poverty (only water access was not). Participation in cooperatives and sports or cultural groups is inversely related to poverty. Poverty is not significantly higher or lower in Panama City and San Miguelito than in other urban areas.

Rural Non-Indigenous Households: Notable Characteristics

23.   The marginal effect of household size is stronger in rural households than any other area or for the entire country. Again, a larger number of younger and older members is related with higher levels of poverty. The reduction in the probability of being poor related to the education level of the household head or companion is very similar than the national results. Labor characteristics, such as the source of earnings (formal, public, private or other), also yield the same tendencies in rural areas as the country as a whole with respect to their correlation with poverty status. Similar results are also found for land titling (only more than 15 ha. of land are significantly related to lower levels of poverty), and the basic housing characteristics and services. Participation in cooperatives and cultural groups is not significantly correlated with poverty status, nor is housing tenancy.

Indigenous Households: Notable Characteristics

24.   In terms of household size and composition, only the members older than 17 years were significant related to higher levels of indigenous poverty. Education is strongly related to the probability of being poor. Households whose household head or companion has completed secondary or higher education are 50 percentage points less likely to be poor than those with no education; the figure is 40 percentage points for those who have completed primary education. Two other variables show strong relation to the probability of being poor: not having a telephone (34 percentage points), and lack of access to credit (29 percentage points).

---

[5] Traditional interpretation does not apply because only 4% of all indigenous households in the sample (16 out of 402) had registered title, and all of them are poor households making the parameter a comparison between non registered house title and not owning the house.

[6] Tendency as the direction of the relationship between the dependent variable and any of the independent variables observed in the sign of the significant parameters estimated.

Variables [b]	Urban d/x [a]	Rural non-Indig. d/x [a]	Indigenous d/x [a]
Table A8.2 Marginal values for the probability of being poof for individual areas			
Observed household poverty rate	**10.1%**	**46.7%**	**90.8%**
Remote	nu	0.153**	nu
Panama City & San Miguelito	ns	nu	nu
Minutes to public health facility	-0.001**	ns	ns
Number of Members in Household by age group			
Number of members 0-5 years old	0.084**	0.228**	0.037*
Number of members 6-11 years old	0.062**	0.135**	ns
Number of members 12-17 years old	0.067**	0.104**	ns
Number of members 18-24 years old	0.054**	0.116**	0.170**
Number of members 25-59 years old	0.041**	0.082**	0.117**
Number of members >=60 years old	0.081**	0.150**	0.103**
Number of females/ Number of males	-0.008*	ns	ns
Female household head	ns	ns	0.100*
HHH/companion education (Max) group			
Primary incomplete (vs. None)	ns	ns	ns
Primary completed (vs. None)	ns	-0.108**	-0.394**
Secondary incomplete (vs. None)	-0.061*	-0.105*	-0.150*
Secondary completed (vs. None)	ns	-0.132*	-0.501**
Advanced education (vs. None)	-0.014**	-0.391**	-0.477**
Workers per persons in HH	ns	ns	ns
Biggest Source of Income group			
Formal-Private (vs. Formal-Public)	0.045*	0.135**	ns
Informal-Private (vs. Formal-Public)	0.064**	0.110*	ns
Non-labor (vs. Formal-Public)	0.063*	0.143**	ns
Agriculture represents > 50% of total income	ns	0.066*	0.177**
Land titled group			
1 to 15 ha (vs. less than one hectare)	nu	ns	ns
>15 ha (vs. less than one hectare)	nu	-0.153**	nu
Hut + Bad roof + Bad walls + Bad floor (from 0 to 4)	0.080**	0.091**	0.053**
Latrine, pit or none	0.112**	0.232**	ns
No telephone	0.127**	0.305**	0.338*
No electricity	0.163**	0.211**	ns
Source of water: River	nu	0.152*	0.100*
Hours with water last month (Max 30 * 24 =720)	ns	ns	0.0002*
Water in the yard (not inside house)	ns	0.052*	ns
Rooms per Person	ns	-0.108**	ns
House tenancy group			
No registered title (vs. registered)	0.075**	ns	ns.
Does not own house (vs. registered)	0.176**	ns	-0.985**
Less than $100 in all credits & loans	0.059**	0.232**	0.293**
Has a car	-0.175**	-0.347**	nu
Belongs to community organization	ns	ns	0.072*
Belongs to a cooperative	-0.091**	ns	ns
Belongs to a sports or cultural group	-0.069**	ns	ns
Constant	**	**	*

Source: Panama LSMS 1997
[a] All the marginal values were calculated at the observed poverty rate using only significant variables or variables in a group with at least one significant variable (the groups can be identified by a title line before each group) probability < : 5% (**), 15% (*), non-significant (ns), and not used because perfect multicoliniarity (nu)
[b] Household head marital status was included but it was not significant in any of the regressions.

TWO HYPOTHETICAL HOUSEHOLDS

25.   To illustrate the cumulative effects of different household characteristics on poverty status, two hypothetical households are analyzed by changing one characteristic at a time and estimating the new probability of being poor for the new values. This exercise is not the same as adding up the reported marginal values in Tables A8.1 and A8.2 because such values are only valid at the level of the probability of being poor that they were evaluated at.

26.   The characteristics for both households are described in Appendix A8.3. For these exercises the entire sample was used to estimate the probabilistic regression using the significant variables (at $p \leq 5\%$) reported in Table A8.1.

27.   Table A8.3 shows the change in the probability of being poor as the households' characteristics are changed, starting at 4.3% for Household 1 and ending at 95.3% for Household 2. The seven changes (for five variables) increase the probability of being poor by 91%.[7]

28.   Even a small difference between household characteristics can make a big difference in the expected probability of being poor. For example, by improving the education level of the household head (or companion) from no education to completed primary education, and reducing the housing quality index by two points, the expected probability of being poor would be reduced from 65.6% to 35.0% (that is, the difference between rows five and three in Table A8.3).

Table A8.3 Estimated probability of being poor with different household characteristics	
Changes in household characteristics (variables value)	Estimated probability of being poor
Original characteristics Household 1 [a]	4.3%
One additional member aged 0 to 5 years old	10.6%
Only completed primary as the highest level attained [b]	35.0%
No education attained by the household head or companion	45.6%
Housing quality index increased by 2 points [c]	65.6%
One additional member aged 0 to 5 years old	81.0%
Move to rural area	88.0%
Household does not have electricity (final characteristics are equal to Household 2)	95.3%
[a] All the household characteristics are described in Appendix 3. [b] By the household head or companion. [c] The lower the index the better the house construction materials.	

CONCLUSIONS

29.   The general relationship between household characteristics and their probability of being poor is similar across geographical areas and for the entire country.

30.   Even after taking into consideration all the household characteristics, the geographic location has a strong effect in poverty. This result is commonly due to structural differences between areas that are not accounted for in the models.[8] Targeted efforts to improve these specific opportunities and infrastructure in these areas (mainly in indigenous and remote areas) should be considered.

31.   Regardless of the level of analysis, household size is one of the most critical factors in determining poverty status. Government programs to improve the access to information and family planning services should be a priority.

32.   Education is another important factor for determining poverty status – and a crucial vehicle for escaping poverty. This is not only due to the relevance of education but also because the important and unique role the public sector plays in providing education. The Government of Panama should build on its existing base of widespread coverage of primary education to complete coverage of primary and secondary education among the poor.

---

[7] The magnitude of each change is related to the variable changed but also is related to the probability of being poor before the change. The marginal value of any variable will be the greatest at a 50% probability of being poor, and will be the smallest a probabilities closer to 0% and 100%.

[8] For instance, a rural region with good roads can take better advantage of the land than an area without roads (remote).

33.	Credit is important as an input to several of the variables related to poverty status, such as durable goods, housing and land ownership, housing quality, etc. Local credit or micro-credit programs can make a big difference in households' ability to smooth consumption and invest for productive earnings potential.

34.	Access to general services (electricity, water, sanitation, etc.) is strongly related to the probability of being poor, though the direction of causality is not readily discerned from the regressions.

35.	Finally, the cumulative effect of few relevant household characteristics makes a tremendous difference in the probability of being poor. For example, a large household with many children and little education has an extremely high probability of being poor in any area of Panama.

APPENDIX A8.A1

Table A8.A1.1 - Mean and percentage household values for different household characteristics				
	GEOGRAPHICAL AREA			
HOUSEHOLD CHARACTERISTICS	Urban	Rural non-Ind.	Rural Indigenous	Panama
Area: Urban area	100%	0.0%	0.0%	58.1%
Rural non-indigenous, non-remote area	0.0%	96.8%	0.0%	36.0%
Indigenous area	0.0%	0.0%	0.0%	4.7%
Remote	0.0%	3.2%	100%	1.2%
Panama City & San Miguelito	52.3%	0%	0%	30.4%
Minutes to public health facility	23.3	42.4	74.8	32.7
Number of members 0-5 years old	0.44	0.58	1.39	0.53
Number of members 6-11 years old	0.46	0.59	1.33	0.55
Number of members 12-17 years old	0.47	0.57	1.14	0.54
Number of members 18-24 years old	0.52	0.45	0.77	0.51
Number of members 25-59 years old	1.73	1.52	1.9	1.66
Number of members >=60 years old	0.39	0.45	0.27	0.41
Number of females/ Number of males	1.89	1.41	1.28	1.68
Sex of household head: female	28.7%	17.1%	15.0	23.7%
Marital status: together/married	65.3%	70.0%	84.3%	68.0%
Separated/Divorced/Widowed	20.3%	18.0%	9.9%	18.9%
Single	13.7%	11.8%	5.2%	12.6%
Do not know	0.7%	0.2%	0.6%	0.5%
HH Head or companion education (Max.): None	1.8%	12.7%	46.8%	7.9%
Primary incomplete	7.4%	24.6%	20.7%	14.5%
Primary completed	13.2%	32.9%	14.6%	20.6%
Secondary incomplete	26.0%	15.4%	11.9%	21.4%
Secondary completed	20.1%	9.3%	4.5%	15.3%
Advanced education	31.5%	5.1%	1.5%	20.3%
Workers per persons in HH	0.61	0.65	0.49	0.62
Biggest Source of Income: Formal-Public	25.7%	10.7%	8.7%	19.3%
Formal-Private	38.1%	22.5%	20.9%	31.5%
Informal-Private	18.8%	47.9%	48.5%	31.0%
Non-labor	17.4%	18.9%	21.9%	18.2%
Agriculture represents more than half of total income	10.0%	67.7%	79.7%	34.7%
Land titled: less than one hectare	98.8%	83.4%	84.8%	95.5%
1 to 15 ha	0.5%	11.0%	13.4%	2.0%
>15 ha	0.7%	5.6%	1.8%	2.5%
Hut + Bad roof + Bad walls + Bad floor (from 0 to 4)	0.82	1.44	2.87	1.15
Latrine, pit or none	19.8%	79.5%	89.6%	45.2%
No telephone	40.6%	89.3%	98.3%	61.5%
No electricity	1.4%	41.0%	82.7%	20.0%
Source of water: River	0.0%	5.8%	44.3%	4.2%
Hours w/water during last month (Max. 30 * 24 =720)	618	466	228	544
Water in the yard (not inside house)	21.7%	49.4%	30.6%	32.4%
Rooms per Person	1.11	1.01	0.43	1.04
House tenancy: registered	32.7%	15.3%	3.9%	24.9%
No registered title	36.2%	71.5%	80.9%	51.4%
Does not own house	31.1%	13.2%	15.2%	23.7%
Less than $100 in all credits & loans	67.4%	81.8%	94.0%	74.0%
Has a car	32.9%	10.7%	0.0%	2301%
Belongs to community organization	11.0%	21.2%	37.6%	16.1%
Belongs to a cooperative	21.8%	13.0%	13.2%	18.1%
Belongs to a sports or cultural group	20.1%	13.7%	17.5%	17.6%
Source: LSMS 1997				

APPENDIX A8.A2

TECHNICAL NOTE ON THE PROBABILITY OF BEING POOR

Significance level

The significance level for all variables was calculated taking into consideration the sample design of the LSMS (strata and primary sampling units) using the statistical package STATA, and the procedure "svyprobt" (the probit procedure estimates a maximum-likelihood model)

Marginal value definition

For the marginal values, the STATA procedure "dpropit" was used. The probability of being poor for any household (p) is given by the equation:

$$\Pr\left(y_i \neq 0 \mid x_j\right) = \Phi\left(x_j \, \beta\right)$$

where Φ is the standard cumulative normal. The marginal value for a unit change in variable x_i is:

$$\frac{\partial \Phi}{\partial x_i} = f(xb) b_i$$

Where "x" is a matrix with a value for each variable "i." Since the marginal effects can be calculated at any probability of being poor, first we have to determine which are the relevant or desirable probability to use. Traditionally it is evaluated at the probability of being poor related with the mean values for each variable (at x-bar[9]). For this study it was deem more relevant to evaluate the marginal values at the observed poverty level.[10]

---

[9] This probability of being poor is calculate by using the mean variable values and the estimated parameters from the "probit" equation:
$$\Pr obability = \Phi\left(b_0 + b_1 \, \bar{x}_1 + b_2 \, \bar{x}_2 + \ldots + b_n \, \bar{x}_n\right)$$

[10] That is at any x_i values such that: $\Phi\left(b_0 + b_1 \, x_1 + b_2 \, x_2 + \ldots + b_n \, x_n\right) = Observed \ poverty \ level$

APPENDIX A8.A3

A8.A3.1 – Characteristics of Two Hypothetical Household [a]		
Variables	Household 1	Household 2
Area	**Urban**	**Rural**
Number of members 0-5 years old	**1**	**3**
Number of members 6-11 years old	1	1
Number of members 12-17 years old	0	0
Number of members 18-24 years old	0	0
Number of members 25-59 years old	2	2
Number of members >=60 years old	0	0
Education of household head or companion (highest)	**Advanced studies**	**None**
Biggest Source of Income	Non Labor Income	Non Labor Income
Agriculture represents more than half of total income	No	No
Land titled: hectares	Less than 1	Less than 1
Hut + Bad roof + Bad walls + Bad floor (from 0 to 4)	**2**	**4**
Indoor pluming toilet	Yes	Yes
Telephone	No	No
Electricity	**Yes**	**No**
Rooms per Person	0.5	0.5
House tenancy: registered title	Yes	Yes
Less than $100 in all credits & loans	Yes	Yes
Has a car	No	No
Belongs to a cooperative	No	No
Belongs to a sports or cultural group	No	No

[a] Variables in bold are the only differences between each household

Annex 9 – Malnutrition in Panama: an Analysis of LSMS Anthropometric Data

Carlos Sobrado, Kathy Lindert, and Gloria Rivera[1]
April 14, 1999

1.   Poverty and malnutrition are closely linked. The link can be as direct as a family not having enough money to purchase a basic and balanced basket of food. It can also be indirect, through illness, such as diarrheal diseases (often due to a lack of potable water), which can weaken the body and interfere with the absorption of nutrients, particularly if families cannot afford treatment.

2.   Malnutrition in infants and young children has serious long-term implications. As a consequence of chronically inadequate food consumption or repeated episodes of illness (such as diarrhea), many children die in infancy. Those who survive often fail to thrive and grow, suffer more frequent and more severe illness, cannot learn, and end up being less productive as adults. Micronutrient deficiencies, such as iron, iodine and vitamin A, also carry irreversible consequences, such as irreversible mental retardation, blindness, etc.

3.   This study, which was prepared as input into the Poverty Assessment, uses anthropometric measures for children collected in the Living Standards Measurement Survey (LSMS 1997) to review the patterns and determinants of malnutrition in Panama. The paper is divided in four parts: the **first** section provides a general description of the data; **second**, basic patterns of under-nutrition are examined using means comparisons; **third**, a multi-variate regression is estimated; and **finally**, the obesity problem in Panama is explored.

THE DATA: ANTHROPOMETRIC MEASURES IN THE LSMS

4.   Anthropometry, the measurement of human growth and size, is widely considered to be a non-invasive, inexpensive way to assess the nutritional status of large samples of individuals. It can provide information on one dimension of an individual's health status, which reflects his or her intake of nutrients and morbidity history. These are important dimensions of welfare and can influence the consumption and investment choices of the household.[2] Unlike the consumption and specially the income aggregate, nutritional status has a "long term memory" reflecting not only the present day (or present year) conditions of the households, but it can reflect the conditions of several years. Also, the nutritional status is a direct measure of well being, lacking shortcomings like intra-household distribution of goods and services assumptions[3], or household ability to maximize the utility derived from goods and services.

5.   The LSMS collected anthropometric measures (weight and height) for 2,255 children aged 0-59 months (Table A9.1). Using these data, three nutritional measures were calculated: (i) height for age (HFA), an indicator of chronic malnutrition or "stunting;" (ii) weight for age (WFA), which indicates if a child is underweight; and (iii) weight for height (WFH), an indicator of acute malnutrition or "wasting." By comparing the measures to worldwide standards the Z scores are calculated.[4] Z-scores values lower

---

[1] With the guidance of Judy McGuire and Harold Alderman.
[2] Alderman (1997).
[3] Consumption and income aggregates are commonly reported in per capita or "per adult equivalent" units, assuming a predetermined intra-household distribution of the goods and services.
[4] By subtracting the worldwide mean and dividing by the worldwide standard deviation (gender and age specific).

than minus two are considered indicators of undernourishment, and Z-score values above two are considered indicators of obesity.[5]

Table A9.1 – Anthropometric Data for Children 0-59 Months, LSMS 1997		
	LSMS Sample	Expanded to National Population
Number of children 0-59 months	2,255	273,360
Number of households	1,569	195,255
Number of kids per household	1.44	1.40

BASIC PATTERNS OF UNDER-NUTRITION

Geographic Patterns of Malnutrition

6.   Over 16 percent of all children under five in Panama suffer from any form of malnutrition, with 14 percent who are chronically malnourished, seven percent who are underweight, and one percent who suffer from acute malnutrition (Table A9.2). Using the HFA indicator of chronic malnutrition, children living in urban areas are statistically significantly less likely to be malnourished than those in non-urban areas (regardless of poverty level). Children in indigenous or remote areas are always worse off than children in any other area.[6] With respect to the provincial distribution of malnutrition, the Provinces of Veraguas, Cocle and Bocas del Toro have the highest rates of malnutrition, followed by Chiriqui and Colón. The Provinces of Los Santos, Herrera, and Panama have the lowest rates of malnutrition. This ranking of provinces by malnutrition rates is statistically significant based on a provincial means comparison analysis.[7]

Poverty and Malnutrition

7.   There is a strong correlation between poverty and malnutrition in Panama (Table A9.2). As such, anthropometric measures appear to be good objective indicators of living standards and well-being. Close to one quarter of poor children and one third of extreme poor under five are malnourished, compared to four percent among non-poor children. These differences are significant. About 86 percent of malnourished children in Panama are poor (Table A9.3).

8.   The incidence of malnutrition mirrors the geographic patterns of poverty (Table A9.2). Geographically, malnutrition is highest in children living in indigenous areas – where poverty is highest – and lowest in urban areas – where poverty is lowest. These differences are statistically significant.

---

[5] Each Z-score is associated with a specific probability in the normal distribution expressed in percentage terms.

[6] The mean percentage "Chronic" values between the non urban, non poor kids and the urban poor or extreme poor kids can not be statistically differentiated at $p < 5\%$

[7] With the exception of Chiriquí and Bocas del Toro since their malnutrition rates are not statistically different.

	Chronic (HFA)	Underweight (WFA)	Acute (WFH)	Any Form	Means Comparisons for HFA*							
Table A9.2 – Malnutrition and Poverty: Anthropometric Measures and Means Comparisons for Children Aged 0-59 months, by Poverty Group and Geographic Area					1	2	3	4	5	6	7	8
Total Population												
Total Population	14.4%	6.8%	1.1%	**16.1%**								
Urban	5.6%	2.9%	0.9%	**7.1%**	a	a						
Non-Urban (Rural)	22.5%	10.3%	1.3%	**24.4%**	b							
Non-Indigenous	13.7%	6.8%	1.2%	**15.7%**		b						
Indigenous**	48.7%	21.0%	1.7%	**50.5%**		c						
Remote	33.5%	14.2%	1.1%	**34.6%**		c						
Non-Poor												
Total Population	4.3%	1.8%	0.6%	**5.1%**			a	a				
Urban	4.0%	1.7%	0.6%	**4.9%**					a	a	a	a
Non-Urban (Rural)	5.4%	2.2%	0.7%	**5.7%**					b	b		
Non-Indigenous	5.0%	2.1%	0.7%	**5.3%**							b	b
Indigenous**	n.s.	n.s.	n.s.	**n.s.**							n.s.	n.s.
Remote	n.s.	n.s.	n.s.	**n.s.**							n.s.	n.s.
All Poor*												
Total Population	24.4%	11.7%	1.6%	**27.0%**		b						
Urban	11.5%	7.2%	2.0%	**14.9%**					b		b	
Non-Urban (Rural)	27.7%	12.8%	1.5%	**30.2%**					c			
Non-Indigenous	17.5%	8.9%	1.4%	**20.3%**							c	
Indigenous**	50.1%	21.6%	1.8%	**52.0%**							d	
Remote	33.1%	13.9%	1.1%	**34.2%**							d	
Extreme Poor*												
Total Population	34.5%	17.0%	1.9%	**37.7%**			b					
Urban	26.1%	18.8%	6.9%	**38.0%**						c		bc
Non-Urban (Rural)	35.2%	16.8%	1.5%	**37.6%**						c		
Non-Indigenous	23.5%	12.6%	1.4%	**26.5%**								c
Indigenous**	50.6%	22.6%	1.6%	**52.2%**								d
Remote	39.5%	17.1%	1.4%	**40.9%**								d

Source: Panama LSMS 1997

*Means comparisons are used to gauge whether or not differences between nutrition rates of various groups are statistically significant. They use the HFA indicator of malnutrition. Each column compares the rows indicated by the letters in the column to determine whether or not there are statistically significant differences in their nutrition rates. A higher letter (with "a" being the highest) indicates better nutritional status. For example, in Column 1, urban children (with an "a") have a statistically lower frequency of malnutrition than their non-urban counterparts (with a "b"). Groups with the same letter have rates of malnutrition that can not be differentiated (statistically at p<5%). "n.s." indicates non significant groups due to the small number of observations.

** Indigenous in this table is the geographic classification (not ethnic).

*** All poor includes extreme poor.

Table A9.3 – The Poverty Status of Malnourished Children				
	Chronic (HFA)	Underweight (WFH)	Acute (WFH)	Any Form of Malnutrition
All Poor	86.1%	86.9%	72.7%	85.2%
Non-Poor	13.9%	13.1%	27.3%	14.8%
Total	100%	100%	100%	100%

Malnutrition, Age and Gender

9.   Malnutrition is slightly – but significantly higher among boys than girls (Table A9.4). This is quite common in an absence of discriminatory practices (boys generally require higher daily caloric intakes than girls and tend to suffer higher rates of disease and infant mortality).[8]

---

[8] World Health Organization (1997) "Global Database on Child Growth and Malnutrition."

Table A9.4 – Malnutrition and Gender		
	Boys	Girls
Chronic (HFA)	16%	13%
Underweight (WFA)	7%	7%
Acute (WFH)	1%	1%
Any form of malnutrition	18%	14%
Source: Panama LSMS 1997.		

10.   Malnutrition rates are fairly low among children aged 0-5 months (Table A9.5), when they are commonly exclusively breastfed. This suggests a small share of children who are born with low birthweights. Malnutrition rates jump significantly among children aged 12-17 months, when they are fed solid foods. Stunting rates (chronic malnutrition as indicated by HFA) remain high among older children, reflecting cumulative deviations from normal skeletal or linear growth. Indicators of acute undernutrition (low WFH) and underweight (low WFA) decline somewhat after the 12-17 month age span, suggesting that this is the period during which they are most nutritionally vulnerable (due to high risks of poor diet on solid foods and infection).

Table A9.5 – Percent of Malnourished Children by Age Group (in months)				
Age in months:	Chronic (HFA)	Underweight (WFH)	Acute (WFH)	Any Form of Malnutrition
0-5	4	2	0	4
6-11	6	5	1	9
12-17	17	11	3	22
18-23	13	10	2	16
24-35	14	6	1	15
36-47	21	8	2	22
48-59	19	6	0	19
Total	100%	100%	100%	100%

DETERMINANTS OF UNDER-NUTRITION: MULTI-VARIATE REGRESSIONS

11.   Multivariate regressions using the HFA and WFA indicators were constructed to assess the relative importance of key determinants of malnutrition. It is important to recognize the limitations of this analysis at the outset. First, the analysis excludes a number of possible determinants of malnutrition, such as birth weight, the nutritional status of the children's parents, etc. Second, it assumes that the independent variables (household, individual and maternal characteristics) are exogenous or unrelated, which may not always be the case. The results of these regressions are presented in Table A9.6.

12.   **Geography.** Geographic disparities are a significant determinant of malnutrition. Even after taking in consideration all the other variables, children living in the indigenous areas (compared to urban areas) and in the province of Veraguas (compared to the province of Panama) are more likely to be stunted.

Table A9.6 - Determinants of Malnutrition: Multivariate Linear Regression Analysis		
	Height by age	Weight by age [a]
Variable		
Other rural area (Urban area omitted)	-3.53	n.s.
Indigenous area (Urban area omitted)	-12.09***	n.s.
Remote access (Urban area omitted)	-6.59*	n.s.
Province of Bocas del Toro (Panama province omitted)	5.561*	9.93***
Province of Chiriqui (Panama province omitted)	n.s.	3.24
Province of Veraguas (Panama province omitted)	-6.90***	n.s.
Province of Los Santos (Panama province omitted)	n.s.	7.61
Province of Colon (Panama province omitted)	n.s.	n.s.
Province of Cocle (Panama province omitted)	n.s.	n.s.
Province of Herrera (Panama province omitted)	n.s.	n.s.
Province of Darien (Panama province omitted)	n.s.	n.s.
Age of the Child in months	-0.2852***	-0.2565***
Female Child	2.984**	n.s.
Number of household members 0 to 5 years old	-2.15**	-2.88***
Number of household members 6 to 11 years old	-1.23	-1.60**
Number of household members 12 to 17 years old	n.s.	n.s.
Number of household members 18 to 24 years old	n.s.	n.s.
Number of household members 25 to 59 years old	n.s.	n.s.
Number of household members 60 years and older	n.s.	n.s.
Minutes to public health facility	-0.0303**	-0.0240
Child more than 10 months old and without the measles vaccine	-6.529**	-5.050
Child without diphtheria-tosferina-tetanus vaccine (& > 3 months old)	n.s.	12.23**
Child with diarrhea last month	n.s.	-3.647**
Child currently is exclusively breastfeed	10.59***	14.23***
Mothers age in years	0.2660	n.s.
Mother with incomplete primary education (no education omitted)	n.s.	-4.89**
Mother with complete primary education (no education omitted)	n.s.	n.s.
Mother with incomplete secondary education (no education omitted)	8.996***	7.701***
Mother with completed secondary education (no education omitted)	7.158**	9.771***
Mother with some advanced education (no education omitted)	8.345**	12.294***
Mother not present in the household	9.053	n.s.
Mother sick last month	n.s.	2.2315
Mother number of pregnancies	-1.246**	n.s.
Per capita yearly food consumption	n.s.	0.005898**
Per capita yearly food consumption squared	n.s.	n.s.
Household with less than $250 value in durable goods	-6.543***	-4.975**
Household with less than $100 in credit (any type) last year	-2.692	n.s.
1 to 15 hectares of tittle land (0 to 1 hectares of tittle land omitted)	-4.846**	n.s.
More than 15 hectares of title land (0 to 1 hectares of tittle land omitted)	n.s.	n.s.
Workers per capita	n.s.	n.s.
Formal or Informal is the biggest share of household income	n.s.	n.s.
Agriculture is the biggest share of household income	n.s.	n.s.
Intercept	45.49***	57.31***
R square	0.260	0.236

Source: Panama LSMS 1997
[a] Probability ≤ : 0.5% (***), 5%(**), 10% (*), 15%( ) n.s.: not significant at probability ≤ 15%
Independent variables: Height by Age and Weight by Age anthropometric figure expressed in percentage terms.
Other variables included in the model but not significant at p≤15% were: Sibling birth order (from the siblings present in the household), mother number of prenatal visits during last pregnancy, child attending an educational or care institution, house construction materials index, rooms per person in the house, lack of sanitation services, lack of electricity, cooking with firewood in bedroom or living room with walls, water source is a river (with and without water treatment), garbage is dump in the yard, household head sex by with or without companion, father or mother takes care of the Child at home, TB vaccine, polio vaccine, respiratory problems last month, other disease last month, exclusive breastfeeding after six months of age, mother smoke, mother drink, and mother sick last month and mother works

13.   **Child Characteristics**. As is common in other countries,[9] malnutrition increases with age. This increase arises due to the cumulative "memory" of the HFA indicator: once children are stunted (e.g., between 12-17 months of age), they do not catch up in terms of their height. As indicated by the descriptive patterns of malnutrition discussed above, girls are significantly less likely to be malnourished than boys. Breastfeeding is strongly associated with better nutritional status (not only because the "quantity" effect but also due to the "quality" effect of breast milk and the lower likelihood of contracting diarrheal infections when children are exclusively breastfed). Two proxies serve to indicate the effect of child health on nutritional status: close proximity to health facilities and receipt of at least one measles vaccine are associated with better nutritional status.

14.   **Maternal Characteristics**. Mothers' education significantly affects nutritional status: children whose mothers have some education higher than primary school are less likely to be malnourished than those with no education. A negative relationship between the number of pregnancies (of the mother), and the child's nutritional condition was found, showing the negative impact of pregnancies too close to each other.

15.   **Household characteristics**. Competition with other children under five lowers nutritional status. The more members under five, the worse the nutritional status of each child. This could relate to health problems associated with short birth spacing (for both mother and child), shorter periods of exclusive breastfeeding for each child, and competition for food and child care among siblings. These findings highlight the need for increased availability of family planning services. As a proxy for wealth and ability to cope with economic fluctuations, children living households with less than $250 in durable goods or with less than $100 in credit and loans (yearly) were were more likely to be malnourished (using the HFA indicator). Kids in households with 1-15 hectares of titled land have worse nutritional status than those living in households with little or no land.[10]

OBESITY

16.   Over-nutrition is also a problem in Panama. Over-nutrition can have high costs, including, *inter alia*, the burden of diseases associated with obesity, such as cardio-vascular disease, stroke, certain types of cancer, and non-insulin dependent diabetes. Some 4-5 percent of all Panamanian children are obese (recording scores greater than two standard deviations higher than the reference standard for WFA and WFH). Obesity in Panama tends to be higher urban areas, and also higher for the children in non-poor households (Table A9.7).

Table A9.7 - Obesity in Panama, by Consumption Quintile and Geographic Area									
	CONSUMPTION QUINTILE					GEOGRAPHIC AREA			All Panama
	1	2	3	4	5	Urban	Rural[a]	Indigenous	
Weight for Age[b]	1.9%	3.7%	3.0%	6.4%	9.4%	5.6%	2.9%	1.5%	4.0%
Weight for Height[b]	3.5%	4.6%	5.2%	9.2%	8.9%	7.3%	3.1%	6.4%	5.5%

[a] Includes all non-indigenous rural households
[b] Overweight according to the specific indicator imply the value for the child was two or more standard deviations above the average

---

[9] Keller and Fillmore (1983).
[10] Studies of the same data sample have shown a higher probability of being poor for the households with 1 to 15 ha.

REFERENCES

Alderman, Harold. Anthropometry. Chapter in "Designing Household Survey Questionnaires for Developing Countries: Lessons from Ten Years of LSMS Experience," Edited by Margaret Grosh and Paul Glewwe. World Bank. Draft May 6, 1997.

Bouis H., and Haddad L. Effects of Agricultural Commercialization on Land Ternure, Household Resource Allocation, and Nutrition in the Philippines. International Food Policy Research Institute, Research Report 79, January 1990.

Kennedy E., and Cogill B. Income and Nutritional Effects of the Commercialization of Agriculture in southwestern Kenya. International Food Policy Research Institute, Research Report 63, November 1987.

Von Braun J., Hotchkiss D., and Immink M. Nontraditional Export Crops in Guatemala: Effects on Production, Income, and Nutrition. International Food Policy Research Institute, Research Report 73, May 1989.

Annex 10 - Inequality in Panama

Carlos Sobrado, April 20, 1999

1.   International evidence indicates that inequality is a handicap to longer-term poverty reduction for two reasons.[1] First, greater income inequality leads to lower investment in physical and human capital, and hence slower economic growth – which translates into higher poverty. Second, cross-country evidence suggests that, at any given growth rate, higher inequality results in a lower rate of poverty reduction.

2.   This paper examines the degree and sources of inequality in Panama using data from the 1997 Living Standards Measurement Survey (LSMS). Two welfare measures are used: total consumption and total income.[2] Although consumption is generally considered to be a better measure of welfare, income is also useful to verify the trends exhibited by the consumption aggregate, to illustrate difference between the two measures, and to compare current trends in inequality to past trends in Panama and to patterns in other countries.

THE DEGREE OF INEQUALITY IN PANAMA

3.   This section examines the degree of inequality in Panama using a number of different measures, including quintiles (for income and consumption), Lorenz curves and Gini Indices. It also compares the degree of inequality in Panama to measures in other countries.

Inequality Across Quintiles

4.   Average per capita consumption in Panama was B/.1,821 in 1997, ranging from B/.320 for the first quintile (Q1) to B./4,812 for the fifth quintile (Q5). Average per capita income was B/.2,292, ranging from B/.174 for the bottom quintile to B/.7178 for the top quintile (Table A10.1).

5.   To illustrate inequality, ratios of average consumption and income were calculated for quintiles 1-4 with respect to quintile 5 (Table A10.1). For each Balboa of consumption reported by households of fifth quintile, those in the first quintile had 7 cents. The ratio for income was 2 cents. Comparing consumption and income of the top quintile with the national average yields values of 38% for consumption and 32% for income; in other words, those in the top quintile reported levels of consumption and income three times higher than the national average.

Table A10.1 – Distribution of Consumption and Income by Quintile						
	Quintile[a]					Total
	Q1	Q2	Q3	Q4	Q5	
Consumption aggregate[b]	B/ 320	B/ 750	B/ 1,235	B/ 1,984	B/ 4,812	B/ 1,821
Percentage above Q5 consumption	7%	16%	26%	41%	100%	38%
Income aggregate[b]	B/ 174	B/ 606	B/ 1,191	B/ 2,304	B/ 7,178	B/ 2,292
Percentage above Q5 income	2%	8%	17%	32%	100%	32%
a\ Consumption quintiles for consumption aggregate and income quintiles for income aggregate						
b\ In per capita Balboas per household, taking account of price differences in Panama extrapolated to the total number of Panamanians.						

---

[1] See Deininger and Squire (1997), Ravallion and Chen (1997), and Ravallion (mimeo, February 12, 1998) for a survey of cross-country evidence.

[2] See Annexes 1 and 3 of the Poverty Assessment for details on the construction of the consumption and income aggregates.

6.   Table A10.2 presents the shares of each quintile in total consumption and income and ratios of these percentages in the indicated quintiles. The largest jumps in consumption and income occur at the two extremes of the spectrum: at the bottom, between the first and second quintiles, and at the top between the fourth and fifth quintiles. While the bottom quintile consumes 3.5 percent of total consumption, the top quintile consumes 53 percent. The disparities are even more striking for income. These patterns are consistent across geographic areas (Table A10.2).

Table 10.2 – Inequality in Panama						
	National	Urban	Total Rural [a]	Rural Non-Indi-genous	Indi-genous [b]	Remote Access
Total Consumption Inequality						
GINI Index of Consumption	49	41	45	41	40	34
% of Total Cons.: [c]	100%	100%	100%	100%	100%	
Quintile 1 (Q1) %	3.5	5.8	4.3	5.5	6.2	6.7
Quintile 2 (Q2) %	8.2	10.0	9.1	10.2	10.6	12.3
Quintile 3 (Q3) %	13.6	14.3	14.4	15.1	14.5	16.2
Quintile 4 (Q4) %	21.8	21.9	22.6	22.3	20.9	23.4
Quintile 5 (Q5) %	52.9	47.9	49.7	46.9	47.6	41.3
Ratios: [c]						
Q2/Q1	2.3	1.7	2.1	1.9	1.7	1.9
Q3/Q2	1.6	1.4	1.6	1.5	1.4	1.3
Q4/Q3	1.6	1.5	1.6	1.5	1.4	1.4
Q5/Q4	2.4	2.2	2.2	2.1	2.3	1.8
Q5/Q1	15.1	8.2	11.6	8.5	7.6	6.2
Income Inequality						
GINI Index of Income	60	53	58	55	56	59
% of Total Income: [d]	100%	100%	100%	100%	100%	
Quintile 1 (Q1) %	1.5	3.0	1.5	1.9	2.6	2.9
Quintile 2 (Q2) %	5.3	7.2	6.0	6.9	6.6	6.6
Quintile 3 (Q3) %	10.4	12.3	11.6	12.5	11.3	9.3
Quintile 4 (Q4) %	20.1	21.1	20.5	20.8	19.8	16.5
Quintile 5 (Q5) %	62.7	56.4	60.4	58.0	59.7	64.8
Ratios: [d]						
Q2/Q1	3.5	2.4	3.9	3.7	2.5	2.2
Q3/Q2	2.0	1.7	2.0	1.8	1.7	1.4
Q4/Q3	1.9	1.7	1.8	1.7	1.8	1.8
Q5/Q4	3.1	2.7	3.0	2.8	3.0	3.9
Q5/Q1	41.5	18.9	39.9	31.3	22.8	22.0

[a] "Rural - Total" population includes: "other rural," indigenous, and difficult access.
[b] In this Table, indigenous refers to a geographical classification based on the concentration of indigenous people in several areas. It is not based on the language or on the ethnic origin of individuals.
[c] Quintiles of national population ordered per total annual per capita consumption.
[d] Quintiles of national population ordered per total annual per capita income.

Lorenz Curves and GINI Coefficients

7.   The Lorenz curve is a graphical representation of welfare distribution for the entire population. It ranks the population's consumption (income) from bottom to top and calculates each person's share of national consumption (income), as well as the percentage that each person represents in the overall population. Finally, the accumulated value of both variables is calculated.

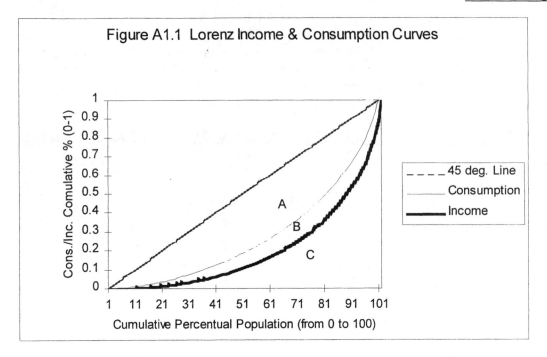

Figure A1.1 Lorenz Income & Consumption Curves

8.   Lorenz curves were calculated for both consumption and income aggregates and are shown in Figure A1.1. The Lorenz curve for consumption is always above the Lorenz curve for income (stochastic dominance[3]), indicating that consumption is more equitably distributed than income. It is worth noting that inequality differences result from the behavior of individuals and not from the method used in the calculations, that is, results are not contradictory, but complementary.

9.   The GINI coefficient is used as a summary measure of inequality for the entire population. This coefficient can be defined from the Lorenz curves: the **consumption GINI** corresponds to the division of area A by the sum of areas A, B and C, and the **income GINI** is the division of area A + B by the sum of areas A, B and C. Table A10.2 shows results at national and regional level.

10.   GINI index based on *consumption* is 49 for the entire country, while GINI index based on *income* is 60 for the entire country (see Table A10.2). As expected, the value of income GINI is higher, since household earnings tend to fluctuate more throughout the years due to changes in employment, variations in agricultural outputs, etc. Consumption is usually more stable, since households generally keep or save profits from more favorable years so as to use them in more difficult years (generally in savings accounts, real estate, durable goods, and animals).[4]

11.   Regardless of the GINI used (consumption or income), inequality is lower in urban areas than in "Total Rural" area (Table 10.2).[5] The GINI consumption index for urban areas is 41, as compared with 45 for all rural areas. The income GINI for urban areas is 53, as compared with 58 for all rural areas.

12.   The remote access area is a particular case, since it accounts for the lowest consumption Gini of all groups and in turn, the highest income GINI of all groups, with a 25 point difference between the two (34 to 59). If we consider that the difference between both GINIs is a result of the adjustment made by

---

[3] By definition, the last point of both curves should be on the coordinate (100,100), which makes impossible a stochastic dominance in strict terms. Stochastic dominance occurs on all other points of the curves.

[4] While total consumption measures annual welfare, earnings could have been used in articles not completely consumed in that year, as is the case of acquisition or maintenance of durable goods, direct and indirect taxes (in formal wages), increases in animal herds, and savings.

[5] It is entirely consistent for total inequality in a given country to be higher than inequality in geographic areas (urban, rural) because total inequality captures inequality between the areas as well as within them.

households to achieve a stable welfare level throughout the years, this large difference can be partly explained by the fact that these households lack external sources to smooth their consumption, such as pensions and reliable and constant wages. In fact, 70% of incomes in difficult access areas are a result of net profits from agricultural output[6], often heavily fluctuating from one year to another according to seasons, weather conditions, and plagues, among others.

Comparisons with Other National and International Surveys

13.   Appendix A10.1 compares Gini coefficients for Panama and other countries. Only one country out of the 26 reported has a higher income GINI than Panama (South Africa, with 62 in 1993). When comparing with Latin American countries only, none of them shows higher income inequality than Panama (using the most recent years in Appendix A10.1). If we compare the GINI index based on consumption, there are three countries in Latin America with higher consumption GINIs and five with lower consumption GINIs than Panama.

14.   Comparisons of inequality across time are difficult for Panama due to a lack of comparability of samples and the methodologies used to measure welfare. GINI coefficients were calculated using data from the Socio-Economic Household Survey in 1983. However, this survey did not include a representative sample for indigenous or remote areas. As such, an additional GINI coefficient was calculated using the 1997 LSMS data to exclude these areas for the purposes of closer comparability. This index yields a GINI of 58, which is slightly higher than the GINI of 56 calculated for 1983.

SOURCES OF INEQUALITY IN PANAMA

15.   This section examines possible sources of inequality in Panama, including geographic location, access to basic services, household composition and size, labor and employment, land holdings, education, and gender of household head.

16.   This analysis is based on "entropy measures" of inequality, which allow for the decomposition of inequality for various household characteristics. Total inequality calculated using entropy measures may be partly related with different household characteristics; for example, we expect that different geographic areas explain part of total inequality in Panama. The share of inequality explained by the different characteristics and its percentage with respect to national inequality were calculated.

17.   Three entropy measures of inequality and its decomposition were calculated (See Appendix A10.2): **E1** or the logarithm of mean deviation, which is the most sensitive to consumption at the lower end of the spectrum, **E2** or the Theil index, with a similar sensitivity at all consumption levels, and **E3** or a transformation of the variance ratio, which more sensitive to consumption at the top end of the spectrum.[7] Each decomposition was made regardless of the others, that is, results from different decompositions are non-additive. Each decomposition illustrates how much of total inequality can be explained by the characteristic in question (in absolute terms).

18.   The population was divided according to seven characteristics: geographic location[8], basic household services, household size and composition, employment, agricultural land, education, and others. Three variables were selected for each characteristic, for which the decomposition value (I_B) and corresponding percentages on total inequality in Panama were calculated (See Table A10.3). The most representative variable for each of the seven characteristics was selected to create a composite division.

---

[6] As compared with 4% at national level and 17% in all rural areas, including difficult access areas and 29% in indigenous area.

[7] Ferreira and Litchfield (1997).

[8] The definition of indigenous based on language was included here, due to its similitude with the same definition based on geographic area.

The final selection of the most appropriate variables is based on the total R_B values and on the interpretation and clarity of the groups.

Geographic Location

19.   The initial division of population in urban, indigenous, difficult access, and other rural explains between one third (35%) and one fifth (17%) of total inequality in Panama. The main difference between indigenous area and households with indigenous language is that the second classification includes indigenous people living outside the indigenous areas. Both classifications explain a smaller share of inequality (as compared with the four-area division) and the language classification explains even less than the geographic classification (with indigenous areas), due to the higher per capita consumption of indigenous people living outside indigenous areas.   When households with a higher per capita consumption are included in the indigenous group, inequality explained by such classification decreases.

Access to Basic Household Services

20.   Access to sanitation services[9] explains between one third and one fifth of total inequality. Other services such as electricity and telephone are also highly related with inequality in Panama (explaining between 12% and 35% of total inequality).

Household Size and Composition

21.   The number of persons per household under age 24 accounts for between 16-30% of total inequality. The number of persons over 23 years explains only 2% of nationwide inequality. Most persons under 24 do not contribute to family earnings (because they are too young or studying), resulting in a lower per capita consumption for the household. Persons over 23 years affect household consumption in two ways: first, since total household consumption must be divided by more members, they reduce household's per capita consumption; and second, since they contribute to earnings, per capita consumption increases. In the explanation of nationwide inequality, these two effects seem to cancel each other.

Sector of Employment

22.   Some 9-13% of inequality is explained by the sector of employment that generates the most earnings (formal or informal) or the fact that a household's main income comes from non-wage income. Even though the subdivision "number of workers per member" explains a slightly higher share of national inequality (10%-14%), this results from the combined effect of household size and the number of working members in the household; as such, it was not selected as the best measure.

Land Holdings

23.   The number of hectares of land available for work accounts for 8-18% of inequality in Panama. Hectares of owned and titled land explain a lower share of inequality (6-14% and 3-5%, respectively).

Education

24.   Education is the single largest determinant of inequality in Panama. The number of years of schooling of the household head or companion[10] is the subdivision which best explains national inequality (32-41%).   An alternative variable, the total number of years of schooling of the entire

---

[9] Which is closely related to water services in the household.
[10] The one with more years of schooling was selected.

household, is correlated with the number of persons per household and explains a smaller share of inequality. Education of the household head explains inequality slightly less, since it does not account for the education attainment of the partner.

Other Sources of Inequality

25.   **Gender**, measured by the ratio of males to females in the household,[11] explains less than one percent (1%) of inequality in Panama. It is not possible to examine the degree of inequality existing within households due to the fact that the consumption aggregate is constructed from household-level data (and hence assumed to be equally distributed among household members on a per capita basis).[12] The annual use of **credit** of more than B\100 explains 5-6% of inequality, while **home ownership** explains between 11-15%.

#	GROUP	SUBGROUP	E-1	E-2	E-3	E-1	E-2	E-3
colspan table title								

<table>
<tr><th colspan="9">Table A10.3 – Sources of Inequality in Panama</th></tr>
<tr><th></th><th></th><th></th><th colspan="3">Entropy Measures and R_B's [1]</th><th colspan="3">% of total inequality explained by variables</th></tr>
<tr><th>#</th><th>GROUP</th><th>SUBGROUP</th><th>E-1</th><th>E-2</th><th>E-3</th><th>E-1</th><th>E-2</th><th>E-3</th></tr>
<tr><td></td><td>All Panama</td><td></td><td>.44</td><td>.42</td><td>.61</td><td>100%</td><td>100%</td><td>100%</td></tr>
<tr><td>1</td><td rowspan="3">Geographic</td><td>Indigenous Language</td><td>.05</td><td>.03</td><td>.03</td><td>11%</td><td>8%</td><td>4%</td></tr>
<tr><td>2</td><td>Indigenous area</td><td>.07</td><td>.04</td><td>.03</td><td>16%</td><td>10%</td><td>4%</td></tr>
<tr><td>3</td><td>Geographic area (4)</td><td>.16</td><td>.12</td><td>.10</td><td>35%</td><td>29%</td><td>17%</td></tr>
<tr><td>4</td><td rowspan="3">Basic Household Services</td><td>No telephone</td><td>.15</td><td>.15</td><td>.15</td><td>33%</td><td>35%</td><td>25%</td></tr>
<tr><td>5</td><td>No electricity</td><td>.13</td><td>.09</td><td>.07</td><td>30%</td><td>22%</td><td>12%</td></tr>
<tr><td>6</td><td>No sanitation services</td><td>.16</td><td>.14</td><td>.13</td><td>35%</td><td>33%</td><td>21%</td></tr>
<tr><td>7</td><td rowspan="3"># of Persons per Household</td><td>Aged 24 to 59</td><td>.01</td><td>.01</td><td>.01</td><td>2%</td><td>2%</td><td>1%</td></tr>
<tr><td>8</td><td>Aged over 59</td><td>.00</td><td>.00</td><td>.00</td><td>0%</td><td>0%</td><td>0%</td></tr>
<tr><td>9</td><td>Aged 0 to 23 [2]</td><td>.13</td><td>.11</td><td>.10</td><td>30%</td><td>26%</td><td>16%</td></tr>
<tr><td>10</td><td rowspan="3">Employment</td><td># of workers per member [3]</td><td>.06</td><td>.06</td><td>.06</td><td>13%</td><td>14%</td><td>10%</td></tr>
<tr><td>11</td><td>Public/Private/Canal/$=0 [3]</td><td>.03</td><td>.03</td><td>.04</td><td>6%</td><td>7%</td><td>6%</td></tr>
<tr><td>12</td><td>Formal/Informal/$=0 [3]</td><td>.06</td><td>.06</td><td>.05</td><td>13%</td><td>13%</td><td>9%</td></tr>
<tr><td>13</td><td rowspan="3">Hectares of agricultural Land</td><td>Own [4]</td><td>.06</td><td>.05</td><td>.04</td><td>14%</td><td>11%</td><td>6%</td></tr>
<tr><td>14</td><td>With land title [4]</td><td>.02</td><td>.02</td><td>.02</td><td>5%</td><td>5%</td><td>3%</td></tr>
<tr><td>15</td><td>Worked [4]</td><td>.08</td><td>.06</td><td>.05</td><td>18%</td><td>14%</td><td>8%</td></tr>
<tr><td>16</td><td rowspan="3">Years of education</td><td>Of all members</td><td>.05</td><td>.05</td><td>.05</td><td>11%</td><td>12%</td><td>9%</td></tr>
<tr><td>17</td><td>Of household head</td><td>.16</td><td>.16</td><td>.19</td><td>36%</td><td>39%</td><td>31%</td></tr>
<tr><td>18</td><td>Highest of household head or partner [5]</td><td>.17</td><td>.17</td><td>.19</td><td>38%</td><td>41%</td><td>32%</td></tr>
<tr><td>19</td><td rowspan="3">Others</td><td>Man/Woman</td><td>.00</td><td>.00</td><td>.00</td><td>0%</td><td>0%</td><td>0%</td></tr>
<tr><td>20</td><td>More than B\100 in annual credit</td><td>.03</td><td>.03</td><td>.03</td><td>6%</td><td>6%</td><td>5%</td></tr>
<tr><td>21</td><td>House ownership [6]</td><td>.06</td><td>.06</td><td>.07</td><td>14%</td><td>15%</td><td>11%</td></tr>
<tr><td colspan="2">TOTAL (composite):</td><td>3,6,9,12,15 & 18= 616 Groups</td><td>.32</td><td>.28</td><td>.33</td><td>73%</td><td>68%</td><td>54%</td></tr>
</table>

[1] Entropy measures for all Panama and R_B decomposition value for the remainder.
[2] Divided into 4 groups: 0, 1-3, 4-6, and more than 6. Initially, this group was also divided in number of persons aged 0 to 5 (E1%=19, E2%=16% & E3%=9%) and number of persons aged 6 to 23 (E1%=23, E2%=20% & E3%=12%).
[3] Selected for the worker with the highest annual hourly wage.
[4] Divided by sizes of 0-0.01, 0.01-1, 1-3, 3-10, 10-30, and more than 30 hectares.
[5] Divided into 7 groups: 0, 1-3, 4-6, 7-9, 10-12, 13-15, and more than 15 years of education.
[6] Divided into house owner with registered title, house owner with no registered title, and house's owner.
  Was also calculated for households with aqueduct, well, and river as water source (E1%=12, E2%=7% & E3%=3%), number of literate individuals over nine years old (6%, 5% & 3%), number of literate individuals over 23 years old (5%, 4%, & 2%), sum of years of schooling of persons over 24 and less than 60 (20%,21% & 16%), sum of years of schooling of household head and partner (31%, 33% & 26%).

Note: **E-1** or the logarithm of mean deviation.
      E-2 or the Theil index.
      E-3 or a transformation of the variance ratio.

---

[11] But for biological reasons, such ratio is often 1:1, that is, the same number of men and women is expected, and we do not expect that proportion to vary in average according to household's consumption level.
[12] To determine such differences, other type of studies are required, which collect consumption data about each household's member.

Total Inequality: Composite Analysis

26.   Using the combination of the selected variables, it is possible to examine the share of inequality explained by the above sources. Some 54-73% of total inequality in Panama is explained by a combination of the following variables (shaded in Table A10.3): geographic area (4 groups), sanitation services (2 groups), members under 24 years (4 groups), sector of employment (3 groups), hectares of land available for work (6 groups), and the maximum number of years of education of the household head or companion (7 groups).[13] As expected, the combination of subdivisions explains less than the sum of individual values, since these characteristics are not totally independent from the others.

27.   In sum, education, the number of children in the household, geographic area, and access to basic services are the main determinants of inequality in Panama, and individually explain about three quarters of the inequality captured in measure E1, which is the most sensitive to poor households.

---

[13] This composite variable splits the sample into 616 groups (of the 4,032 possible).

Appendix A10.1 – INTERNATIONAL GINI INDEX COMPARISON

APPENDIX A10.1 –International Comparison of Inequality with the GINI Index		
Region/Country	GINI for Consumption (year)	GINI for Income (year)
Latin America: median	**45**	**57**
Panama	**49* (1997)**	**60ᵃ (1997), 58ᵇ (1997), 56ᵇ (1983)**
Bolivia	42 (1990)	n.a.
Brazil	55 (1974)	60 (1976), 62 (1985), 60 (1989)
Chile	n.a.	58 (1989)
Colombia	43 (1972)	53 (1972), 51 (1991)
Costa Rica	n.a.	46 (1977)
El Salvador	n.a.	48 (1977)
Guatemala	n.a.	59 (1989)
Ecuador	43 (1994)	n.a.
Honduras	n.a.	62 (1968), 54 (1993)
Jamaica	38 (1993)	n.a.
Mexico	50 (1992)	55 (1989)
Nicaragua	50 (1993)	n.a.
Peru	45 (1994)	49 (1981)
Asia: median	**32**	**39**
Bangladesh	28 (1992)	37 (1986)
India	32 (1992)	n.a.
Indonesia	32 (1993)	n.a.
Sri Lanka	30 (1990)	47 (1987)
Taiwan	26 (1991)	30 (1991), 31 (1993)
Thailand	46 (1992)	52 (1992)
Vietnam	36 (1992)	n.a.
Western Europe: median	**32**	**33**
Denmark	33 (1987)	33 (1987 & 1992)
Germany	27 (1983)	31 (1983)
Greece	35 (1988)	n.a.
Portugal	32 (1990)	37 (1990)
Spain	26 (1989)	37 (1973)
United Kingdom	34 (1986)	29 (1986), 32 (1991)
East Europe: median	**36**	**33**
Estonia	37 (1995)	40 (1995)
Hungary	27 (1993)	30 (1993)
Kazakhstan	35 (1996)	33 (1993)
Kyrgyzstan Republic	46 (1993)	35 (1993)
Poland	31 (1993)	33 (1993)
Russia	46 (1993)	n.a.
Middle East/North Africa: med.	**39**	**--**
Algeria	39 (1988)	n.a.
Egypt	32 (1991)	n.a.
Jordan	41 (1991)	n.a.
Morocco	39 (1991)	n.a.
Tunisia	40 (1990)	n.a.
Africa: median	**48**	**--**
Ghana	34 (1992)	n.a.
Kenya	54 (1992)	n.a.
Madagascar	43 (1993)	n.a.
Malawi	54 (1993)	n.a.
South Africa	n.a.	62 (1993)
Tanzania	38 (1993)	59 (1991)
Uganda	41 (1992)	n.a.
Zambia	52 (1996)	51 (1976)
Zimbabwe	57 (1990)	n.a.

Source: Panama: LSMS 1997; Russia, Kyrgyzstan Republic, Kazakhstan: World Bank Poverty Assessments; the remaining: Deininger & Squire (1996). a\ Total Population. b Population excluding indigenous and difficult access areas.

APPENDIX A10.2 - INEQUALITY MEASURES AND THEIR DECOMPOSITION

ENTROPY MEASURES (E) OF INEQUALITY

General formula

$$G(\alpha) = \frac{1}{\alpha^2 - \alpha}\left[\frac{1}{n}\sum_{i=1}^{n}\left[\frac{y_i}{\mu(y)}\right]^{\alpha} - 1\right] \qquad \alpha \in R$$

Logarithm of the mean deviation $\qquad\qquad\qquad E(0) \rightarrow \quad \alpha = 0$
Theil index $\qquad\qquad\qquad\qquad\qquad E(1) \rightarrow \quad \alpha = 1$
Using the l'Hospital rule, we obtain

$$E(0) = \frac{1}{n}\sum_{i=1}^{n}\log\left(\frac{\mu(y)}{y_i}\right) \qquad \text{and,} \qquad E(1) = \frac{1}{n}\sum_{i=1}^{n}\frac{y_i}{\mu(y)}\log\left(\frac{y_i}{\mu(y)}\right)$$

Half of variance ratio square $\qquad E(2) \rightarrow \quad \alpha = 2$

$$E(2) = \frac{1}{2n\mu(y)^2}\sum_{i=1}^{n}(y_i - \mu(y))^2$$

DECOMPOSITION OF ENTROPY MEASURES

Any entropy measure of inequality can be decomposed into inequality between groups (I_B) and inequality throughout groups (I_W).[14] If we divide the population into k_j subgroups, where j is the number of subgroups and $\mu(y)_j$ is the mean of subgroup j, $E(\alpha)_j$ is the measure for the inequality of subgroup j, $f_j = n_j/n$ is the share of population in subgroup j, and $v_j = \frac{n_j\,\mu(y)_j}{n\,\mu(y)}$ is the share of total consumption of subgroup j, we obtain:

$$I_B = \frac{1}{\alpha^2 - \alpha}\left[\sum_{j=1}^{k}f_j\left(\frac{\mu(y)_j}{\mu(y)}\right)^{\alpha} - 1\right] \qquad y \qquad I_W = \sum_{j=1}^{k}w_j\,E(\alpha)_j \qquad y \quad w_j = v_j^{\alpha}\,f_j^{1-\alpha}$$

With these definitions, entropy measures can be divided into $E(\alpha) = I_B + I_W$, where I_B reflects the inequality given by the subdivision "k" and I_W is the remaining inequality.

---

[14] Cowell and Jemkins (1995), who used previous researches by Bourguignon (1979), Cowell (1980) and Shorrocks (1980 y 1984).

REFERENCES

Cowell, F.A. (1980): "On the Structure of additive Inequality Measures", Review of Economic Studies, 47, págs. 521-31.

Cowell, F.A. y S.P. Jenkins (1995): "How Much Inequality Can We Explain? A methodology and an application to the USA." Economic Journal, 105, págs. 421-430.

Deininger, Klaus and Lyn Squire (November 1997). "New Ways of Looking at Old Issues: Inequality and Growth." World Bank. Draft.

Ferreira, F.H.G. y Litchfield, J.A. (1997): "Poverty and Income Distribution in a High-Growth Economy Chile: 1987-1995" Chapter 2 "Income Distribution and Poverty: A Statistical Overview"

Ravallion, Martin and Shaohua Chen. (May 1997). "What Can New Survey Data Tell Us about Recent Changes in Distribution and Poverty?" The World Bank Economic Review, Vol. 11 No. 2.

Shorrocks, A.F. (1980): "The Class of Additively Decomposable Inequality Measures", Econometrica, 48, págs 613-625.

Shorrocks, A.F. (1984): "Inequality Decomposition by Population Subgroup", Econometrica, 52, oo.1369-1385.

Annex 11 - Poverty, Vulnerability and Labor Markets in Panama: A Study Using LSMS Data

Renos Vakis, Ana-Maria Arriagada and Kathy Lindert[1]
January 27, 1999

1.   This paper reviews the labor-market conditions facing a number of traditionally vulnerable (or "socially excluded") groups in Panama: the poor, women, the indigenous population, youths, and child laborers. The analysis suggests that the **poor** generally do not benefit from – and could be hurt by – Panama's generous but complex labor legislation due to open unemployment, likely underemployment and employment under less favorable terms in the informal sector. Although **women** do not appear to suffer discrimination in terms of wages and benefits in Panama, they do seem to face fewer opportunities for work than men. **Indigenous workers** fare poorly in Panama's labor markets, with linguistic obstacles to labor force participation, few opportunities for formal sector work (which generates higher earnings), few fringe benefits, and apparent wage discrimination.[2] Unemployment is quite high among **youths** in Panama, particularly urban youths and young women, suggesting difficulties in the transition from school to work. Finally, although **child labor** does not appear to be a widespread problem in Panama, child laborers tend to be poor and complete fewer years of schooling than their non-working counterparts.

2.   The paper is organized as follows. Part 1 explores the determinants of labor force participation, unemployment and employment choices. Part 2 examines the determinants of hourly earnings. Part 3 reviews existing labor market policies and whether or not the poor benefit from these generous provisions. Finally, Part 4 brings the various elements together to summarize the labor market conditions facing key vulnerable groups in Panama.

PART 1: LABOR FORCE PARTICIPATION, UNEMPLOYMENT, EMPLOYMENT

LABOR FORCE PARTICIPATION

Patterns and Determinants of Labor Force Participation

3.   Table A11.1 examines labor force participation (LFP) rates for males, females, and the entire population over age 15 (see Box 1 for definitions)[3] in Panama by geographic area, poverty group,[4] age, and education level. The overall participation rate was 60 percent in 1997, which is similar to rates found in other surveys for recent years. Labor force participation is significantly higher for men (78 percent)

---

[1] The authors would like to thank Amit Dar for his advice and help on the econometric analysis. They are also grateful to Carlos Becerra, Carlos Sobrado, and Cecilio Gadpaille for working to reconcile national and international labor force definitions and to define informality using the LSMS. They are also extremely thankful for comments received from Rosa Elena de De la Cruz, Edith Kowalzyk, Eudemia Perez, and Roberto Gonzalez, all of the Ministry of Planning and Economic Policy (MIPPE), during a collaborative mission in Washington in April, and from representatives of MIPPE and the Ministry of Labor who participated in a "Reunion de Alto Nivel" on poverty issues held in Panama in May 1998. Finally, they would also like to thank Ian Bannon, Wendy Cunningham, Nobu Fuwa, Jose Gonzalez, Richard L. Ground, William Maloney, Andrew Mason, and Martin Rama for their very useful comments on an earlier phase of the analysis. Saji Thomas and Amit Dar also contributed to an earlier phase of the analysis.
[2] These issues are also explored in more detail in Annex 6.
[3] Table A-1 in Appendix A presents labor force participation rates using Panama's standard national definitions (see Box 1 for definitions).
[4] Poverty groups are defined as: (i) the extreme poor, whose total per capita consumption falls below B./519 per year; (ii) the poor (including the extreme poor), whose total per capita consumption falls below B./905 per year; and (iii) the non-poor, whose total per capita consumption is higher or equal to B./905 per year. The methodology for defining these poverty lines is described in Annex 2 of the Poverty Assessment.

than for women (43 percent), although a relatively high share of females enter the labor force in Panama, as compared with other Latin American countries.[5]

4.   Multi-variate regressions allow for an analysis of the relative importance of different variables in determining labor force participation.   Table A11.2 presents results of estimates of labor force participation regressions using probit models for men and women. The results are discussed below.

5.   **Education and LFP.**[6] Education seems to have a fairly small impact on men's participation in the labor force. Indeed, there is little variance in male LFP (as shown in Table A11.1). As such, neither primary nor secondary education affect men's decision to participate (as compared with having no education), once other determinants have been taken into account (Table A11.2). For women, however, education does have an impact on labor force participation. In fact, the share of women in the labor force increases with education levels (Table A11.1). Women with higher education are over two times more likely to enter the labor force than those with no formal education. Controlling for other variables, women in secondary and higher education are indeed significantly more likely to participate than those with no education (Table A11.2). Interestingly, women with a primary education are no more likely to join the labor force than those with no formal training (Table A11.2). This suggests that the relatively low potential earnings from working are outweighed by the "opportunity cost" of other responsibilities (such as child care) for a significant share of women with little or no education. Having some diploma does increase the probability of entering the labor force for both men and women (even after controlling for years of education), suggesting a certain degree of "credentialism" in Panama. As expected, students are less likely to participate in the labor force than individuals not currently enrolled in school.

Box 1 - Labor Force Definitions Using LSMS Data: International and National Definitions[a]			
	Employed	Unemployed	In Labor Force
International Definition	A person is employed if he/she: a) Worked in reference period (last week) (601=1 or 602=1) b) didn't work last week but has a job (603=1) c) has a sporadic job (609=3)	A person is unemployed if he/she: a) didn't work in the past week and was actively looking for a job (604=1) b) didn't work last week but was waiting for a response about a new job (609=1)	A person is in the labor force if he/she: a) is employed (see definition); or b) is unemployed (see international definition)
National Definition	Same.	A person is unemployed if he/she: a) didn't work in the past week and was actively looking for a job (604=1) b) didn't work last week but was waiting for a response about a new job (609=1) c) didn't work last week but was waiting for the harvest or a seasonal job (609=2) d) is a discouraged worker: i.e., he/she didn't work last week and didn't look for a job because he/she was tired of looking for a job (609=8), thinks that there are no jobs (609=10), thinks that there are jobs but he/she won't get one (609=11)	A person is in the labor force if he/she: a) is employed (see definition); or b) is unemployed (see national definition)
Source of data: Panama LSMS 1997 (mainly Section 6 of household questionnaire). Numbers in parentheses refer to question codes from LSMS. a\This analysis uses only the population aged 15 and older. The LSMS did collect labor information for children aged 10-14, but these are analyzed separately as "child labor."			

---

[5] Data from the late 1980s reveal that fewer than thirty percent of women participate in the labor force in Chile (28), Colombia (25), Costa Rica (27), and Guatemala (28). Those at the other end of the spectrum, which are more similar to Panama in this respect, include Bolivia (44), Ecuador (46), Uruguay (52), and Venezuela (44). Source: Psacharapoulos and Tzannatos (1992).

[6] Alternative specifications of the education regressions yielded similar results. These included: the number of years in school and the level of education completed.

6.   **Age and LFP.** As observed in other countries, the age-participation profile for both genders is concave, as younger and older individuals have lower participation rates than their prime-aged counterparts (Table A11.1). The rates are considerably higher in the 25-60 year age group (prime-age group) for males. As expected, the probability of participating in the labor force decreases after age 60. Controlling for other variables, the probability of joining the labor force increases with age for both men and women, but the marginal effects are stronger for those in the middle of the age spectrum (Table A11.2).

7.   **Language Ability and LFP.** Language abilities – notably the ability to speak Spanish – can affect individuals' decisions regarding labor force participation if, for example, opportunities are fewer or earnings lower for those who do not speak Spanish. Not surprisingly, an inability to speak Spanish (speaking only an indigenous language) does create barriers to entry in the labor force in Panama, even controlling for other variables (Table A11.2).[7] While bilingual speakers are not less likely to participate than monolingual Spanish speakers, those who speak only an indigenous language do indeed have a lower probability of joining the labor force.

8.   **Geographic Area.** Overall participation rates in urban areas are slightly higher than in rural[8] and indigenous areas (Table A11.1). Controlling for other variables, rural men are more likely to participate than their urban counterparts (Table A11.2). Rural women, on the other hand, are less likely to join the labor force. The reverse is true in indigenous areas (Table A11.2).

9.   **Household Size and Composition.** The presence of children in the household affects men and women in different ways. While for men, more children (especially between ages 6-11) increases their probability of joining the labor force, whereas for women the opposite occurs. The greater the number of young children, the greater the demand for income as well as for child care. While on one hand this pushes the men to seek work and generate income, women may increase time devoted to childcare, thus reducing their likelihood of joining the labor force. These results suggest that childcare is perceived as the primary responsibility of women in Panamanian households.

10.   **Poverty.** Labor force participation is somewhat lower among the poor than the non-poor (Table A11.1). Although male labor-force participation does not vary much by poverty group, poor women are less likely to enter the labor force than their non-poor counterparts. This result is somewhat surprising, given that the mobilization of female labor force participation is a common response to poverty and vulnerability. It could result from the higher fertility rates among the poor and hence larger domestic responsibilities for poor women. These results are validated in the multi-variate analysis:[9] controlling for other variables, poor women participate less, whereas labor force participation does not seem to be influenced by household consumption levels.

---

[7] Only two percent of the total Panamanian population does not speak Spanish. However, 21 percent of ethnic indigenous people do not speak Spanish. Because a fair amount of ethnically indigenous people live outside indigenous areas, the correlation between these language variables and the geographic variables was found to be small. See Annex 6 for details.

[8] In this paper "rural" refers to "non-indigenous rural" since residents of official "indigenous" areas (largely rural) are included as a separate group.

[9] This study generally uses individual consumption as a measure of welfare. However, due to potential simultaneity between per capita consumption and labor force participation (and likewise for unemployment, as discussed below), household rather than individual consumption is used.

Box 2 – Child Labor in Panama

Child labor is thought to be a problem in many developing countries. Children work for a variety of reasons, the most important being poverty.[a] The concept of child labor is problematic, since it can apply to a range of activities, from domestic work to wage work. The 1997 LSMS collected information on labor activities for children aged 10-14 (but not younger). The results of the LSMS are consistent with the findings of a previous study[b] conducted using data from the 1994 Household Survey. The LSMS has the advantage of covering a nationally representative sample (indigenous and remote areas had been excluded from the 1994 survey) and allowing for an analysis of child labor by poverty group. A summary of the findings:

- **Child labor is not a widespread problem in Panama.** Only eight percent of children ages 10-14 work in Panama. The majority of these child laborers are older: close to two thirds are 13-14 years old; only eight percent are aged 10.
- **A disproportionate share of child laborers live in rural and indigenous areas.** Close to three quarters of child laborers live in the countryside, whereas roughly half of all children aged 10-14 live in urban areas.
- **The majority are boys.** Overall, three quarters of child workers are male. This is also reflected in the fact that girls tend to stay in school longer in Panama than boys. The shares are more equal in indigenous areas, where forty percent of child laborers are female (and where the gender gap in education is reversed).
- **Most child laborers are poor.** A disproportionate share of child laborers are poor. While poor children account for 46 percent of the age cohort, two thirds of child workers are poor. Similarly, extreme poor children represent 27 percent of their age cohort but 46 percent of child laborers. Eleven percent of poor children work, as compared with only five percent of non-poor children.
- **Most work in agriculture and commerce.** Close to half of all child laborers work in agriculture; a quarter work in commerce. A slightly higher share of girls work in services (as domestic servants) and manufacturing. Most work as unpaid family laborers (particularly girls), followed by blue collar workers. About 12 percent are self employed. Some 15 percent of female child laborers work as domestic servants.
- **Hours worked and wages vary substantially.** On average, child laborers work 27 hours per week. Average hours worked are slightly higher for boys in agriculture (31) and much higher for girls in services (47; mostly domestic servants). Most child laborers are not paid (over half). On average, those who are paid earn less than their adult counterparts but more than the minimum wage in most sectors. Girls are paid significantly less than boys, adults and the minimum wage, however, in manufacturing and commerce.
- **Lower education is the price of child labor.** On average, educational achievement is lower for children who work than for those who don't. Among 13-year olds, for example, school children who don't work average one more year of schooling than those who work and go to school and two years more than those who only work.

Source: Panama LSMS 1997 (using the nationally representative sample). See Appendix A for detailed tables. a\ Kanbur and Grooetart (1995). b\ UNICEF and Ministry of Labor and Social Welfare (July 1997).

UNEMPLOYMENT IN PANAMA

The General Level of Unemployment

11.   Using the international definition of unemployment (see Box 1), the LSMS indicates that the overall unemployment rate was 5.9 percent in 1997, which is quite low, probably reflecting the recent upturn in economic growth in Panama. Including seasonally unemployed and discouraged workers (the national definition, see Box 1) brings the rate to 9.2 percent which is still fairly low. Indeed, Table A11.3 also suggests that unemployment dropped in 1997, though the comparisons should be interpreted with caution due to definitional and sampling differences between the LSMS and the annual Household Surveys.[10]

Patterns and Determinants of Unemployment in Panama

12.   Tables A11.4 and A11.5 present unemployment rates for various groups using the international and national definitions of unemployment. The results of multivariate probit regressions, which allow for

---

[10] In addition to the different treatment of seasonal and discouraged workers (see Box 1), unemployment figures from the Household Surveys rely on different **definitions** of "actively looking for work" than the figures used in the LSMS (looking for work in the past three months versus in the past week). Moreover, the **samples** for the two types of surveys differed substantially: the LSMS sample is nationally representative, whereas the sample used in the Household Surveys excluded indigenous and remote areas (which have lower unemployment rates).

an analysis of the relative importance of different factors in determining unemployment, are included in Table A11.6. The analysis also corrects for selectivity bias.[11]

13.   **Gender and Unemployment.** Tables A11.4 and A11.5 suggest that unemployment is higher for women than for men regardless of definition.[12] In fact, female unemployment is close to *twice as high* as unemployment among males.

14.   **Youth Unemployment.** As in other countries, youth unemployment is a serious problem in Panama, with those individuals below 25 at least twice as likely to be unemployed as those above that age (Tables A11.4 and A11.5). Unemployment is notably high among young women (aged 15-24).[13] The regression analysis in Table A11.6 confirms the positive relationship between youth and unemployment, particularly for women, after controlling for other factors. A lack of experience – or unrealistically high expectations about "deserved" earnings – could be hampering young adults' transition from school to work in Panama.

15.   **Urban Unemployment and Market Segmentation.** Unemployment is largely an urban phenomenon in Panama, with the urban unemployment rate almost twice the rates in rural and indigenous areas (Tables A11.4 and A11.5).[14] Indeed, controlling for other variables, unemployment is significantly higher in urban areas Table A11.6).[15] This may arise from a higher degree of distortion-induced segmentation in urban labor markets. Arguably, a larger share of the urban labor market is subject to the multiplicity of legislative regimes than labor markets in rural and indigenous areas (as discussed in more detail below).

16.   **Unemployment and Poverty.** The relationship between poverty and unemployment is complex. In general, the poor cannot afford to be unemployed and their low reservation wages mean that they take up even less attractive jobs. At first glance, the overall unemployment rate does not appear to be correlated with poverty in Panama (using the international definition, Table A11.4).[16] The unemployment rate is lowest among the extreme poor (3.5 percent) and highest among the non-poor (6.2 percent). In fact, of the 66,000 unemployed individuals in Panama in 1997 (see definition in Box 1 above), close to three-quarters are *not* poor (though this essentially replicates the distribution of workers across poverty groups).[17]

17.   However, while the above is true for men, poor women have higher rates of unemployment than their non-poor counterparts (Table A11.4). Multivariate regressions confirm these observations: although there is no correlation between poverty (using household consumption as a proxy)[18] and unemployment for men, poor women are indeed significantly more likely to be unemployed (Table A11.5).

18.   Urban unemployment *is* substantially higher among the poor: unemployment among poor city-dwellers is almost twice as high as the rate for non-poor urban residents (see Table A11.4). The difference is even higher when taking into account seasonal and discouraged workers (using the national

---

[11] Human capital endowments, regional attributes or idiosyncratic household characteristics may affect an individual's decision to participate in the labor force. Thus, individuals will self select into or out of the labor force, which may bias the estimates from the unemployment regressions. Using the selectivity correction term, derived by Heckman (78) the regression yields consistent estimates of the parameters.

[12] Indeed, a statistical test comparing the unemployment rates between men and women shows that the distributions of the two populations are significantly different from each other. As such, separate regressions were constructed for each sub-population.

[13] Given that dismissal policies are more restrictive for pregnant women (as discussed below), firms may be hesitant to hire women in their more fertile years.

[14] *Underemployment* may be a more relevant problem in rural and indigenous areas, though this is quite difficult to measure.

[15] "Urban" was the necessary omitted binary variable in the regressions.

[16] Counting seasonal and discouraged workers as unemployed (the national definition), however, suggests higher unemployment rates for the poor than the non-poor.

[17] Approximately three-quarters of all workers are non-poor.

[18] Per capita consumption cannot be included in these regressions because of potential problems of simultaneity. As such, household consumption is used as a proxy.

definition, see Table A11.5), indicating an important contingent of poor unemployed and discouraged urban workers. Controlling for other variables, lower levels of household consumption were significantly correlated with higher levels of unemployment for both men and women in separate regressions for urban unemployment.[19] Again, the likely higher degree of distortion-induced segmentation in urban labor markets could result in depriving a higher share of the poor urban labor force of employment. The duality of Panama's urban economy -- which is ever present in metropolitan areas like Colón -- bears testament to the effects of this segmentation.

19.   **Education.** The pattern of unemployment rates with respect to education appears to suggest a certain duality in the Panamanian economy, with lower unemployment rates at the two ends of the spectrum and higher unemployment in the middle (Tables A11.4 and A11.5). Unemployment is fairly low among those with little or no education. It seems that, in the absence of a broad formal safety net in Panama, those with no education have low reservation wages and are willing to accept less "attractive" forms of employment. Unemployment is also relatively low at the other end of the spectrum, among individuals with university or post-graduate education. While those with higher education have high reservation wages, there may be greater demand for their relatively scarce skills.

20.   In contrast, unemployment in Panama is considerably higher among those with secondary and vocational education (Tables A11.4 and A11.5). Indeed, after controlling for other factors, men with secondary and vocational education are more likely to be unemployed (Table A11.6). Individuals with secondary and vocational education have higher reservation wages, but may not have the specific skills required in the labor market and appear to be at a disadvantage.

21.   This pattern suggests a mis-match between education and job expectations versus the characteristics of the jobs available in the economy. It seems that Panama's economy has more capacity to absorb those at the extremes of the education spectrum: unskilled workers (with no or primary education) and highly skilled workers (with higher education), but lesser demand for those in the middle (with secondary and vocational education). This excess supply of labor at the secondary and vocational levels could result from problems with the educational system (i.e., problems with quality of education and/or inappropriate skills training vis-à-vis the demands of the labor market). Alternatively, it could be caused by distortions induced by the complex structure of minimum wages described in Part 3 below. Indeed, the setting occupation-specific minimum wages above the basic minimum wage could distort training and education decisions by encouraging individuals to over-invest in certain types of skills that cannot be absorbed in the labor market.

22.   **Household Characteristics.** A higher number of household members appears to be correlated with higher unemployment, particularly for women (Table A11.6). Employers might be hesitant to hire women with substantial domestic duties, such as childcare or transporting children to-and-from school, which could interfere with work responsibilities.

UNDEREMPLOYMENT

23.   Available figures suggest that the working poor are probably underemployed. As shown in Table A11.7, the poor work fewer total hours than the non poor in all geographic areas. Though these data do not reveal if the poor work fewer hours due to personal preferences, given the lower living conditions facing those below the poverty line, they do suggest likely underemployment and low productivity among the poor.

---

[19] See Annex 7 for additional details on the determinants of urban unemployment.

EMPLOYMENT

24.   Close to sixty percent of the population aged 15 and older and over ninety percent of the labor force was employed in Panama in 1997. Close to twice as many males are employed as females. A slightly higher share of the non-poor is employed as compared with the poor. While two-fifths of the non-poor workforce are women, females comprise only one quarter of poor workers.

Employment by Sector

25.   Table A11.8 examines the distribution of workers by sector of employment. Over one third of workers are employed in services (community, basic or financial) while another twenty percent each are employed in commerce and agriculture. About ten percent of Panama's labor force is employed in manufacturing.

26.   There are significant differences in the sector of employment by gender. While 83 percent of all women work in commerce and services, male workers are spread more evenly across more sectors, including agriculture, services, trade occupations, and manufacturing (as shown in Table A11.8). While a larger absolute number of women work in service-related positions, the agriculture sector employs over nine times more men than women (in absolute terms). The lack of women working in certain sectors could be policy induced. In fact, legislation bars women from working in physically demanding jobs in certain sectors (such as mining and construction).[20]

27.   The sectoral profile of employment also varies substantially by poverty group. Among the non-poor, a larger share of both men and women are employed in commerce and services, with very few in agriculture, whereas agriculture employs a much more significant share of poor workers, particularly poor males (see Table A11.8). This is not surprising since three quarters of the poor live in rural areas where agriculture generates an important source of income.[21]

Public Versus Private Sector Employment

28.   Table A11.9 examines the distribution of the workforce by public versus private sector of employment. Overall, close to one fifth of the workforce is employed in the public sector and in the canal area, with the remainder working in the private sector. White-collar employees working in private enterprises constitute the main form of private sector employment, followed by self-employment and blue-collar day laborers (*jornaleros*).

29.   Not surprisingly, there are significant differences in employment patterns by gender and poverty group. The non-poor are much more likely to be employed in the relatively higher paying types of jobs – in the public sector, by the Canal Commission, or as white collar workers in private enterprises. In contrast, the poor are more likely to work as blue-collar day laborers (*jornaleros*) or as unpaid workers. Women are more likely to be employed in the public sector than men, who are more likely to be employed as white-collar workers in private enterprises.

---

[20] The Labor Code specifies in Article 104 that 'Está prohibido el trabajo de la mujer en: (1) los subterráneos, minas, subsuelo, canteras y actividades manuales de construcción civil; y (2) las actividades peligrosas o insalubres determinadas por el Ministerio de Trabajo y Bienestar Social."

[21] Agriculture represents 27 percent and 34 percent of total incomes in rural and indigenous areas respectively. Among the rural poor, it accounts for over one half of the incomes of the extreme poor and forty percent for the poor. See Annex 4.

Patterns and Determinants of Informal Sector Employment in Panama

30.   LSMS data on type of employment and firm size are used to classify the *firm* where the individual works as informal or formal (see Box 3 for details). Table A11.10 reveals the incidence of formal and informal employment in Panama. The results of a probability model for the likelihood of employment in the formal sector (correcting for selectivity)[22] are presented in Table A11.11.

31.   *One half* of the workforce in Panama is employed in the informal sector (Table A11.10). This compares with 70 percent in Nicaragua (1993), 52 percent in El Salvador (1992)[23] and 41 percent in Ecuador (1994). There are no significant gender differentials in informality for the population as a whole – both men and women are equally likely to be employed in the formal sector. Most informal workers are either blue-collar day laborers (*jornaleros*), domestic employees, self-employed, or unpaid workers.

32.   Informality and poverty are strongly correlated for both genders, but even more so for women (Table A11.10). The results of the probit regressions also support this conclusion: controlling for other variables (such as education), lower levels of household consumption increase the probability of being employed in the informal sector (Table A11.11). While the majority of non-poor workers (equally for men and women) have formal-sector employment, 79 percent of the extreme poor and 70 percent of all poor workers are employed in the informal sector (Table A11.10). Almost all poor and extreme poor women work in the informal sector, indicating that informality is not completely explained by employment in agriculture since the majority of poor women are employed in the trade and service sectors (see Table A11.8 above). Indeed, while four fifths of workers in agriculture are employed informally, the informal sector also accounts for a significant share of employees in commerce, manufacturing, and services (see Table A11.10).

33.   Not surprisingly, informality is also associated with lower levels of education. Both Table A11.10 and the probit results in Table A11.11 suggest that education increases the likelihood of being employed in the formal sector at all levels. One exception is primary school for women: women with primary education are less likely to be employed formally than those with no education (Table A11.11). Experience[24] and receiving a diploma appear to increase women's chances of working in the formal sector. Finally, professional training increases the likelihood of being employed in the formal sector for both men and women.

34.   Opportunities for formal sector employment in indigenous areas appear to be scarce. Three fourths of workers living in indigenous areas are employed in the informal sector (Table A11.10). Table A11.11 also confirms that, controlling for other variables, workers in indigenous and rural areas are more likely to be employed informally than those in urban areas. As discussed below, these workers are generally paid dismally low wages and do not receive "mandated" benefits, such as the thirteenth month salary bonus. Moreover, while working conditions are generally worse in the informal sector, they are notoriously abysmal for indigenous workers in Panama.

---

[22] An individual will first decide to participate in the labor force and then which sector to work. Some men and women will be more likely to participate in the labor force than others. The reasons may be due to their human capital endowments, regional attributes or household characteristics. Thus, individuals will self select to be in the labor force. Without taking this into account, the sector employment choice regressions will be biased. The selectivity variable corrects for this selection-bias problem.

[23] Urban areas only.

[24] The Panama LSMS includes a question "how long have you worked as [current profession]," which is a better proxy for experience than age or age minus years of schooling (which are commonly used in employment regressions).

Box 3 – Defining Informal versus Formal Sector Employment using the LSMS
The following classifications using LSMS data aim to classify the *firm* where the individual works as informal or formal.

Formal Sector. A person is classified as working in the formal sector if he/she is employed in any of the following situations:
a) Employees of the Government or the Canal Commission (618=1 or 3)
b) Employees in private enterprises that have 6 or more workers (618=2 and 617>2)
c) Unpaid workers in private enterprises that have 6 or more workers (618=7 or 8 and 617>2)
d) Day laborers in private enterprises of 6 or more workers (618=4 and 617>2)
e) Owners of private enterprises of 6 or more workers (618=5 and 617>2)
f) Owners of private enterprises with 1-5 employees in a professional field (618=5 and 617=1 or 2 and 611=0-16)
g) Self-employed, independent workers who work in a professional field (618=6 and 611=0-16)

Informal Sector. A person is classified as working in the informal sector if he/she is employed in any of the following situations:
a) Employees of private enterprises of 1-5 workers (618=2 and 617=1 or 2)
b) Unpaid workers in private enterprises of 1-5 workers (618=7 or 8 and 617=1 or 2)
c) Domestic employees (618=9)
d) Day laborers in private enterprises of 1-5 workers (618=4 and 617=1 or 2)
e) Owners of private enterprises with 1-5 employees in non-professional fields (618=5 and 617= 1 or 2 and 611>16)
f) Self-employed, independent workers who work in non-professional fields (618=6 and 611>16).

Figures in parentheses refer to variable codes in Section 6 of LSMS household questionnaire. Population aged 15+ and the first job worked.

PART 2: WAGES AND EARNINGS

Patterns of Hourly Labor Earnings

35.   Calculating hourly earnings functions can be challenging due to the wide variety of types of earnings needed to be taken into account, including base salaries, tips, in-kind payments, and 13th month salary bonuses. Box 4 provides an explanation of the types of labor earnings used in this analysis. Table A11.12 presents mean hourly labor earnings for various groups by gender.

36.   On average, women earn slightly more than men on a per hour basis. Statistical tests, however, indicate that this difference is not significant (as discussed below). In contrast, men earn significantly more than women on a monthly basis, owing to a higher number of hours worked per month.[25] On average, men earn B./456 per month, as compared with B./436 per month for women (see Table A-3 in the Appendix A).

37.   Thanks to more generous labor legislation governing the public sector,[26] state workers earn significantly more than those in the private sector.[27] Public sector employees earn 1.8 times more than those in the private sector on an hourly basis. Within the private sector, white-collar employees of private enterprises earn the most, while blue-collar workers (*jornaleros*) earn the least. Hourly earnings for employees in the formal sector are 1.6 times higher on average than those of informal sector workers.

38.   As expected, non-poor workers earn significantly more than poor workers. Similarly, workers in urban areas earn far more than those residing in indigenous and rural areas. Not surprisingly, mean hourly earnings increase considerably with levels of education. The hourly wages of a worker with primary education is 1.3 times the wages of someone with no education. Likewise, someone with a secondary education earns almost twice as much than someone with only a primary education. A worker with higher education earns more than four times from someone with no education.

---

[25] These results refer to the *first* (primary) job held by each individual.
[26] It should be noted, however, that only two thirds of public sector employees are covered by this legislation, as discussed in more detail below.
[27] Employees of the Panama Canal Commission earn even more (averaging B./10 per hour), thanks to their coverage by the U.S. Labor Code. These employees have been excluded from this analysis, however, due to an extremely small sample in the LSMS.

Methodology for Analyzing the Determinants of Hourly Labor Earnings

39.   The level of hourly earnings can be explained as a function of individual and job characteristics. Individual characteristics are intended to capture differences in human capital and labor productivity, and include educational variables (two different specifications) and lifetime experience in current occupation.[28] A quadratic specification of this variable is also included so as to allow for non-linearities in the returns to experience. Other individual characteristics include gender, geographic location,[29] and information on the number of children in the household.[30] Job characteristics include sector of employment[31] and a variable for union membership.

40.   Correction for selection bias is also necessary. Some men and women are more likely to participate in the labor force than others. The reasons may be due to their human capital endowments, regional attributes or household characteristics. Thus, individuals will self select into or out of the labor force. Without taking this into account, the wage regressions will be biased. Using the methodology introduced by Heckman, the wage regressions below are corrected for selectivity. In fact, in all the regressions the selectivity term is positive and significant (see Table A11.13), suggesting that the determinants of labor force participation are positively correlated with wages.

Box 4 – Defining Hourly Labor Earnings Using the LSMS
Total Labor Earnings. This analysis includes all types of labor earnings, whether cash or in-kind. It includes: wages/salaries; the value of the "13th month" bonus; the value of any tips received; the value of any in-kind benefits (food, housing, clothing, transport) received from employment; and independent earnings.
Hourly Labor Earnings as Unit of Analysis. It is preferable to analyze these data on an hourly basis to take into account differences in the time worked (days per month, hours per day, etc.). Most labor earnings data were collected on a monthly basis. These can be converted using data collected on "hours worked per week" (616), and assuming that the person worked four weeks per month (since the LSMS did not ask how many weeks were worked per month). For those types of labor earnings that were collected on a yearly basis, the earnings can be converted using data collected on "hours worked per week" (616) assuming that the person worked four weeks per month) and months worked per year (614).
Figures in parentheses refer to variable codes in Section 6 of LSMS household questionnaire. Population aged 15+ and the first job worked. a\Independent earnings are not included in the analysis of discrimination (Oaxaca decomposition), since one would not discriminate against himself/herself, or in the comparison of actual labor earnings to minimum wages (inappropriate comparison).

Results: the Determinants of Hourly Labor Earnings

41.   Two different specifications are constructed for males, females and all workers using different education variables. The results are presented in Table A11.13.

42.   **Gender and Earnings Differentials.** As discussed above, women earn slightly more than men on an hourly basis in Panama. This small wage differential can be explained by differences in human capital:[32] women in Panama have higher levels of educational attainment than men.[33] The differential is not significant however: as shown in Table A11.13, being a woman does not affect hourly earnings (the coefficients are not significant). Statistical t-tests also found the difference between men's and women's hourly earnings to be insignificant. It is important to note, however, that men earn significantly more than women on a *monthly* basis (as discussed above and as shown in Table A-3 of Appendix A).

---

[28] The Panama LSMS includes a question "how long have you worked as [current profession]," which is a better proxy for experience than age or age minus years of schooling (which are commonly used in earnings/wage regressions).

[29] Rural and indigenous "dummy" (binary) variables are included with urban being the necessary omitted variable for comparison.

[30] Individuals might receive lower pay if domestic duties (childcare, transporting children to/from school, leaving work to go home when a child is ill, etc.) interfere with professional functions.

[31] Public and private formal sector "dummy" (binary) variables are included; private informal sector employment is the necessary omitted variable for comparison.

[32] In fact, a Oaxaca decomposition of male-female earnings differentials was conducted. The decomposition found that women's earnings are indeed brought up by higher human capital (education), but that these gains are partially offset by "unexplained" factors that could be considered an upper bound on discrimination.

[33] See Annex 4.

43.   **Education and Training.** As discussed above, mean hourly earnings increase considerably with levels of education (Table A11.12). The earnings regressions confirm the positive returns to education. Each year of schooling yields about five percent increase in hourly earnings.[34] An alternative specification, which splits years of schooling by level of education (splines), also shows that returns to education increase by levels of education in a linear fashion. For example, an additional year of secondary education raises wages by five percent, while an additional year in higher education increases wages by seven percent. Interestingly, additional years of primary education do not seem to increase wages significantly. Although the results are similar for both men and women, the returns to education appear to be slightly higher for women, providing support for the importance of girls' education.

44.   Obtaining a diploma does appear to increase hourly earnings, but this variable was not robust to alternative specifications. Finally, professional training[35] does seem to boost earnings (and hence marginal productivity), particularly for men.

45.   **Experience.**[36] The earnings-experience profile is concave with respect to earnings, increasing with experience, and then peaking after about 20 years of experience, as is common in other countries.

46.   **Public Sector Premiums.** The regression analysis highlights the generosity of the separate legislative regime for state workers (discussed below). As shown in Table A11.12 above, public sector workers earn significantly more than those in the private sector. Different regression specifications confirm that public sector workers enjoy a large wage premium that is not explained by differences in human capital (which are already controlled for by the other variables in the regressions, see Table A11.13). The high premiums for employment in the public sector may also partly explain the high unemployment rates in urban areas, particularly among urban youth: with high expectations, secondary and university graduates are willing to queue up until a high paying job in the public sector opens up.

47.   **Informal Sector Earnings.** Controlling for other variables such as education and experience, informal sector[37] workers are paid significantly less than those in the formal sector (public or private, see Table A11.13). These results hint at the fact that informal sector work might not be preferable (over formal sector jobs) to those with, say, lower levels of education, but rather serves as an alternative to unemployment in a segmented labor market.[38]

48.   **Union Membership.** Union members receive a significant earnings premium that is not explained by other variables (such as human capital, see Table A11.13). Union membership appears to be particularly beneficial to women. Controlling for other variables, female union members earn 26-27 percent more than non-members, while male union members earn about 18 percent more. (See Box 6 below for a discussion of union membership in Panama).

49.   **Geographic Area.** As discussed above, workers in urban areas earn much more than their rural and indigenous counterparts: two times more than non-indigenous rural workers and three times more than workers in indigenous areas (Table A11.12). Even after controlling for the difference in the sector of employment and human capital characteristics, workers in rural areas earn significantly less than their

---

[34] The coefficient on the education variables can be interpreted as the gross private rate of return to schooling (not taking into account the cost of schooling), based on Mincer's earnings function.

[35] Training refers to the question 441 in the LSMS questionnaire, which asks "have you attended any courses in the last twelve months to facilitate you job performance?"

[36] The lifetime experience variable comes from question 613b in the LSMS questionnaire (variable P613), which asks "How long have you worked as [...profession...]?" As individuals do not frequently change occupations, this variable is a much better proxy for work experience than age or the Mincerian experience variable (which calculates an experience proxy as experience = age minus years of schooling).

[37] The informal sector was the necessary omitted comparison variable in the regressions in Table A11.13.

[38] In an analysis of the informal sector in Mexico, Maloney (February 1998) finds that in certain circumstances, there are reasons for workers to prefer informal employment due to both lower levels of human capital and inefficiencies in labor codes.

urban counterparts. This gap is strongly exacerbated for the indigenous workers, suggesting a certain degree of discrimination, as discussed in Box 5 below.

Box 5 – Ethnicity and Wage Discrimination?[a]

Hourly wages for ethnic[b] indigenous people in Panama are around 38 percent less than those for non-indigenous workers. Wage functions were estimated to decompose the wage gap between ethnic indigenous and non-indigenous workers using the Oaxaca technique described in Appendix B. While 43 percent of the wage differential can be explained by differences in observable characteristics (education, experience, sector of employment, area of residence, etc.), 57 percent of the gap is unexplained and can be thought of as an upper bound on discrimination against indigenous workers.[c]

a\ Independent earnings were not included in this analysis, since one would not discriminate against himself/herself. bEthnicity is defined using language variables from the LSMS. See Annex 6 for details. c\ These results are consistent with the results of a study of indigenous employment on banana plantations by Bourgois (1985), which found significant economic discrimination against indigenous workers (particularly the Ngobe-Buglé), through lower wages paid, harsher types of work conducted, and the abysmal occupational conditions facing indigenous workers.

PART 3: LABOR MARKET POLICIES AND POVERTY: DO THE POOR BENEFIT?

Overview of Panama's Labor Regimes[39]

50.   Panama's labor market is characterized by a multiplicity of labor regimes. First, the Labor Code is the principal regulatory mechanism for the private sector, which accounts for over eighty percent of the workforce. Second, some 100 special labor laws govern public sector employment,[40] with even more generous provisions for state workers (and higher wage schedules) than the formal labor code. Third, workers in the Panama Canal Commission and related services are covered by the U.S. Labor Code, and this regime is essentially being replicated as assets are transferred to Panamanian ownership. Finally, a separate -- and less restrictive -- legislative regime governs employment in the Export Processing Zones.[41] As discussed above, the existence of a vast informal sector in Panama could be a symptom of the segmentation that has arisen as a result of the multiplicity of Panama's labor regimes.

51.   The cornerstone of labor legislation in Panama is the Labor Code, which was introduced in 1972 and recently modified in 1995.[42] Studies conducted before the 1995 reforms concluded that Panama's Labor Code was more restrictive and onerous than labor legislation in a number of other Latin American Countries.[43] Indeed, following its introduction in 1972, unemployment climbed from an average of 6.5 percent in the preceding decade to an average of 7.3 percent in the 1970s and 11.9 in the 1980s (using the national definition of unemployment).[44] A recent study[45] found that the elasticity of unemployment with respect to changes in growth dropped substantially (and even became pro-cyclical) soon after the

---

[39] Other labor-related interventions, such as payroll taxes and social security have not been addressed in this study due to limited availability of data in the LSMS. They will be addressed in the planned CEM/PER.

[40] It is important to note, however, that these laws only cover about two-thirds of all state employees. The remainder is not covered by any legislation.

[41] Law No. 3 of January 1997, which is an addition to Law No. 25 of November 30, 1992, establishes labor practices for workers in the Export Processing Zones (EPZ). While the minimum wage structure established by the Labor Code (see below) still applies to workers in EPZ enterprises, these firms are allowed to determine rest day policies (días de descanso) and vacation terms (with some limitations). EPZ employers are also allowed to dismiss workers more freely, provided that they inform authorities of the cause.

[42] Labor Code: Decreto de Gabinete 252 of 1971 (it was put into effect in 1972); Modifications to the Labor Code: Law No. 44, August 12, 1995 "Por la cual se dictan normas para regularizar y modernizar las relaciones laborales."

[43] Gregory (July 1991) and Gregory and Davila (April 1993). Labor legislation was compared for five countries in addition to Panama, including: Mexico, Honduras, Costa Rica, the Dominican Republic, and Chile. The studies found that Panama's Labor Code imposes burdens on employers that appear to be greater than the codes of these other countries, particularly with respect to (i) restrictions on dismissal of employees (which remain largely in effect even after the 1995 reform); (ii) regulations of piece-rate payment systems (which have been moderated by the recent reforms); and (iii) the relatively high level of minimum wages in Panama combined with a high ratio of days paid to days worked.

[44] Source: MIPPE, Dirección de Políticas Sociales: "Tasa de Desocupación, Años 1963-1997."

[45] Gonzalez (1998).

introduction of the Labor Code, suggesting that it did indeed introduce important rigidities in Panama's labor markets.

52.   Interestingly, there are signs that Panama's labor markets have become more flexible since the 1995 Modernization Law. Though many believed the 1995 law to be too modest in terms of reducing rigidities, even these reforms (discussed below) have had an important impact. Indeed, composite indices of labor-market distortions suggest that Panama's labor markets have become more flexible since the introduction of the 1995 reforms.[46] A recent study found that unemployment has become more responsive to changes in growth since the 1995 reforms.[47] In fact, as discussed above, unemployment has fallen in recent years (particularly 1997). The following section discusses the key elements of the Labor Code and associated legislation, with reference to the main changes introduced by the 1995 reform.

53.   **Wage Distortions.** The Labor Code and associated legislation interfere with wage setting in a two ways.[48] **First,** in addition to the basic legal minimum wage,[49] the Government defines a complex structure of additional occupation-specific minimum wages that vary by region.[50] This wage schedule essentially imposes wage differentials according to administratively-determined premiums for differences in associated risks, responsibilities, and skill-requirements.[51] The minimum wage also applies to lump-sum (piece rate) payment schemes.[52] The wage structure could serve to discourage the production of goods requiring lower skill levels within any occupational class.[53] Moreover, it could distort training and education decisions by encouraging individuals to over-invest in certain types of skills that cannot be absorbed in the labor market (as suggested by the pattern of unemployment discussed above). **Second,** the Labor Code prohibits wage reductions under *any* circumstances (even with employee consent).[54] This restriction also applies to lump sum (piece rate) payment schemes. Thus an enterprise in financial difficulty is not allowed to reduce wages even if the lower wages remain above the minimum wage.

54.   **Short Probationary Periods.** The Panamanian Labor Code mandates a very short probationary period after which severance restrictions apply (see below). The original 1972 Labor Code established a two-week trial period, which is hardly long enough for firms to evaluate the quality of service for many professions.[55] If an employee continued to be employed after this period, he/she would automatically be converted to "permanent" status, with the associated job security benefits.

---

[46] Source: Burki and Perry (1997). *The Long March: A Reform Agenda for Latin America and the Caribbean in the Next Decade.* The World Bank. Composite indices include a number of indicators of labor-market interventions, including: severance restrictions and penalties, flexibility for temporary contracts, contribution-benefit links, and social security tax rates. Panama's composite index improved from −1.0 in 1990 to −0.3 in 1995.

[47] Gonzalez (1998).

[48] These restrictions continue even after the 1995 Modernization Law. The main changes in this area involved the treatment of lump-sum tasks. The paragraph above describes the regulations as applied since the 1995 law.

[49] The first setting of minimum wages was implemented in 1959 (Law No. 51). The minimum wage schedule has been modified periodically since then through a number of decrees and laws: (i) in 1971 via Decree No. 53; (ii) in 1974 via Law No. 33; (iii) in 1979 via Decree No. 49; (iv) in 1982 via Decree No. 21; (v) in 1991 via Decree No. 70; (vi) most recently in 1995 via Executive Decree No. 91 of November 14, 1995.

[50] There are three minimum wage regions specified in the Presidential Decrees on minimum wages: Region 1, which includes districts of Panamá, Colón, and San Miguelito; Region 2, which includes districts in David, Chitré, Chorrera, Aguadulce, Santiago Barú, Changuinola, las Tablas, Penonomé, Bugaba, Arraiján, Capira, Chepo and Taboga; and Region 3, which includes all other districts. Minimum wages were higher for most sectors in Region 1 in the Executive Decree No. 91 of November 14, 1995.

[51] A recent law, however, does permit the payment of sub-minimum wages for approved apprenticeship programs.

[52] As per Article 19 of Law No. 44, August 12, 1995.

[53] For example, construction firms will have an incentive to restrict their building activities to commercial and upscale real estate, rather than building more modest homes, which require employment of a lower level of woodworking skills at the same minimum wage for the construction sector.

[54] This restriction was originally stipulated in the Constitution. It was then legislated in Article 159 of the 1971 Labor Code (Decreto de Gabinete 252). It was reaffirmed in Article 22 of the 1995 Labor Code Modernization Law No. 44 of August 12, 1995. While the 1995 revision still prohibits any downward adjustment to wages (even with the consent of the employee), it does allow for a *temporary* reduction in the paid work day or work week in cases of official "severe national economic crises."

[55] Article 78 of the 1971 Cabinet Decree No. 252.

55.   The terms surrounding the probationary period appear to be one of the more major changes introduced by the 1995 Labor Code Modernization Law. Although the 1995 reforms[56] re-affirmed the three-month probation period, the requirement for *automatic* conversion to "permanent" status for employment beyond this period was abolished. Instead, the new article simply includes a clause that the probationary status does not apply if the worker is being re-hired to a position he/she previously held in the same company (to discourage incentives for continuous firing and re-hiring within the three month period). However, anecdotal evidence suggests that firms have found it easy to get around this clause by hiring workers for three months, and then re-hiring them after a short "severance" period (without paying penalties) for a "different" position.

56.   **Excessive Restrictions and Employer Penalties for Job Suspension.** One of the most restrictive aspects of the Labor Code is the provisions governing job dismissal.[57] The basic provision for job suspension in Panama is that once an employee has served longer than the probationary period (three months), he/she cannot be dismissed without "just cause" without the payment of a severance allowance and penalties. The key components of this restriction are as follows:

a)   Any dismissal requires a 30-day notice during which time the employer must pay equivalent wages.

b)   "Just causes" include:[58] (i) unacceptable conduct by an employee (which requires certified documentation and official approval); (ii) prolonged incapacitation of a worker for non-employment related reasons (e.g., mental or physical incapacity, non-employment related accidents) after the period of one year; and (iii) "economic causes,"[59] which must be officially approved by the Ministry of Labor.[60]

c)   Severance allowances depend on the date at which the worker was initially hired in relation to the 1995 Labor Code Modernization law.[61] As an example, for those hired since Law No. 44 of 1995 law, severance payments are equivalent to 3.4 weeks of salary for each year worked in the first ten years and one week for every additional year worked after that. Severance allowances must be paid for "unjust dismissals" *and* in cases of dismissals for "economic just causes" described above.

d)   An employee who feels unjustly discharged can appeal through an administrative and judicial process that can be very protracted. Available data indicate that, on average, 90 percent of workers claim wrongful dismissal. Hearings average one year, but can take up to three. Workers do not pay the costs of judicial disputes -- even if they lose. An analysis of 100 cases in 1983 found that only two percent of cases were decided in the employers' favor, indicating that the expected cost of dismissal is well approximated by the average cost of the severance payments.[62]

e)   When workers are dismissed for an "unjust cause," employers must pay an additional penalty (in addition to the severance allowance) *or* reinstate the worker to his/her position. In addition, the employer must pay retroactive wage payments (*salarios caidos*), for 3-5 months depending on when the worker entered employment in relation to Law No. 44 of 1995. [63]

---

[56] Article 13 of Law No. 44 of 1995.

[57] Severance restrictions are included in Articles 32, 33, 34, 35, and 36 of the 1995 Modernization Law (replacing Articles 213, 218, 219, 224, and 225 of the 1971 Labor Code.

[58] New "justified causes" are considered in detail in Article 32 of Law No. 44 of August 12, 1995 (which are added to Article 213 of Cabinet Decree No. 252 of 1971).

[59] Economic causes are described in part C of Article 32 of Law No. 44 of August 12, 1995.

[60] In the case of "economic causes," Article 32 of Law No. 44 of August 12, 1995 clearly states the order of priority for downsizing: (a) lay-offs should begin with those who have the least seniority; (b) followed by those who are not Panamanian, those who are not union members, and those who are the "least efficient," (c) followed by pregnant women (who should be the last to be dismissed). In cases where the above circumstances are equal, union membership takes preference over workers who do not belong to unions.

[61] Severance allowances are detailed in Article 36 of Law No. 44 of August 12, 1995, which replaces Article 225 of Cabinet Decree 252 of 1971.

[62] Spinanger (1983), Gregory and Davila (April 1993) and World Bank (July 1995).

[63] The additional penalty is equivalent to 50 percent of the severance allowance for those who began working before the 1995 Labor Code Modernization law and 25 percent for those who began working after the law went into effect. Articles 33 and 34 of Law 44 of August 12, 1995 (which replace Articles 218 and 219 of Cabinet Decree No. 252 of 1971).

57.   **Numerous Mandated Fringe Benefits.** On top of the base minimum wage, the Labor Code also mandates a broad array of benefits. **First,** several benefits give rise to a high ratio of days paid to days worked. The Labor Code requires firms to pay thirty days vacation, plus an extra "13th month salary." Workers in Panama are thus essentially paid six days a week for five days work and thirteen months a year for eleven months work.[64] **Second,** the Labor Code mandates that workers receive a length-of-service bonus (*prima de antiguedad*) equivalent to one week of salary for every year worked is paid to all workers at the end of their employment regardless of the cause of the end of the contract.[65] **Third,** the Code includes a complex set of calculations governing payments for overtime work.

Labor Policies and the Poor

58.   An analysis of the LSMS reveals that, for the most part, the poor do *not* benefit from the generous provisions mandated by the Labor Code.[66] Rather, it is possible that the poor are *hurt* by the segmentation that can arise from the multiplicity of stringent labor regimes that characterizes Panama's labor markets. A number of factors support these conclusions. **First,** although unemployment is not correlated with poverty for the nation as a whole,[67] unemployment *is* higher for the poor in urban areas (as compared with the non-poor), which tend to be more segmented by the more dominant presence of multiple labor regimes. **Second,** for the poor who do work, they tend to be employed in the informal sector with lower wages and less favorable terms. A **third** and related point is the fact that the majority of the poor do not benefit from the mandated "thirteenth month" bonuses, which suggests that they are not covered by labor legislation. And **finally**, the majority of poor and extreme poor workers[68] receive wages that are below the official minimum wage. These results are discussed in more detail below.

59.   **Unemployment and the Poor.** Those who are unemployed clearly do not benefit from generous provisions mandated by labor regulations. In fact, labor policies could worsen unemployment, due to the segmentation that can arise from a multiplicity of labor regimes and due to the extra costs associated with the hiring of workers due to the generous terms mandated by labor laws (which may cause firms to substitute capital for labor).

60.   Although the LSMS suggests that overall unemployment was not particularly high in Panama in 1997, unemployment in urban areas -- which are arguably more affected by the multiplicity of labor regimes -- has been a chronic problem, particularly for the poor (see Tables A11.4 and A11.5). As discussed above, urban labor markets are segmented by the more dominant presence of the public sector, the Panama Canal Commission, and the Export Processing Zones, in addition to the private sector, all of which are governed by separate legislative regimes. In contrast, agriculture, which tends to have a higher share of self-employment (which is exempt from labor legislation) tends to be the more dominant form of employment in rural and indigenous areas.

61.   While unemployment is not correlated with poverty for the nation as a whole, the poor are more likely to be unemployed than the non-poor in urban areas (see Tables A11.4 and A11.5). Indeed,

---

[64] Taking into account national holidays, this yields a ratio of days paid to days worked of 1.66, compared with 1.26 for workers in Mexico, 1.27 in Honduras, 1.34 in Costa Rica, and 1.41 in the Dominican Republic. Gregory and Davila (April 1993) report that the number of days paid in Panama is 290 (260 = 5 days/week multiplied by 52 weeks/year plus 30 bonus days for the 13th month salary). The total number of days off is 85 (52 weekly *días de descanso*, 30 vacation days, plus national holidays taking into account overlaps between holidays and *días de descanso*), yielding a total number of days worked of 175 (260-85), and a ratio of days paid to days worked of 1.66. Comparable figures for Mexico are 380 days paid, 302 days worked; Honduras: 312 days paid, 245 days worked; Dominican Republic: 342 days paid, 241 days worked; and Costa Rica: 303 days paid, 226 days worked.

[65] As per Article 35 of Law 44 of August 12, 1995 (and Article 35 of the 1971 Labor Code). If a worker has been employed less than one year, he/she receives the pro-rated share of one week's salary.

[66] As discussed above, the majority of Panama's poor (94 percent) work in the private sector (formal and informal private sector). Less than six percent work in the public sector and the Panama Canal Commission employs virtually no poor workers. The Labor Code (and associated legislation including the minimum wage laws governing the private sector) is thus the most relevant regime for the poor.

[67] It is correlated for women (see Table A11.6 above).

[68] This includes paid workers, not unpaid laborers or the self-employed.

unemployment *is* higher among poor city dwellers, particularly women. Using the standard international definition (see Box 1), the unemployment rate was twelve percent for the urban poor, compared with under seven percent for their non-poor counterparts. The inclusion of seasonal and discouraged workers brings the figure to 18 percent for poor city dwellers, compared with just nine percent for the urban non-poor (using the national definition). Unemployment is even higher for poor urban women and youths (see Tables A11.4 and A11.5). Indeed, controlling for other variables, lower levels of household consumption are associated with higher unemployment in separate regressions on the determinants of urban unemployment.[69] Thus a substantial share of poor labor force participants in urban areas do not benefit from the generous provisions of labor legislation, but rather could be hurt by these interventions if they are prevented from obtaining jobs.

62. **Poverty and Informal Employment.** Even those who do find work do not necessarily benefit from the generous provisions "mandated" by labor legislation. This is particularly true for those employed in the informal sector, where wages tend to be lower and employment terms less favorable (Tables A11.11 and A11.12 above).[70] Indeed, a high degree of informality is commonly interpreted as a sign of market segmentation caused by stringent and multiple labor codes. In this respect, Panama's labor market is no exception. As discussed above, close to *half* of the workforce in Panama is employed in the informal sector. The figure is even higher for the poor: 79 percent of the extreme poor and 70 percent of the poor are employed in the informal sector, compared with only forty percent for the non-poor (Table A11.10 above).

63. **Compliance with Labor Regulations: the 13th Month Benefit.** The share of private-sector workers receiving the "thirteenth month" salary bonus, as mandated by the Labor Code, serves as another indicator of the degree of compliance with labor regulations. Overall, 50 percent of workers do not receive the benefit (Table A11.14). While roughly one third of *white collar* private sector workers do not receive the benefit; 79 percent of *blue collar* (excluding unpaid laborers and the self-employed) do not receive it, indicating fairly incomplete compliance with the Labor Code.[71]

64. It is clear from Table A11.14 that, for the most part, the poor and extreme poor do not benefit from these bonuses. One-third of all paid private-sector workers living below the poverty line received the benefit, compared with 69 percent for the non-poor (Table A11.14). Very few indigenous workers (virtually all of whom are poor[72]) receive the 13th month benefit: only 33 percent of paid private sector indigenous workers received the bonus, and only 13 percent of all indigenous workers received it.

65. **Minimum Wages and the Poor.** Table A11.15 suggests that, in most sectors, the minimum wage is not binding. For the most part, average wages are not clustered right at the minimum wage. For manufacturing, for example, the average wage exceeds the minimum wage by more than two times; those who earn more than the minimum wage earn close to four times more than the average minimum wage for that sector. For community/public services, the gap between the average and the minimum wage is even higher. The exception is agriculture: on average, paid workers (excluding the self-employed) in the agricultural sector received close to 13 percent *less* than the minimum wage, suggesting that the minimum wage is set *above* the market wage (and is not consistently enforced).[73]

---

[69] See Annex 7.

[70] As discussed above, controlling for other variables (such as education and experience), earnings in the informal sector are significantly lower than in the formal (public or private) sector. In his study of duality in Mexico's labor markets, Maloney (February 1998), however, finds that in some circumstances, there are reasons for workers to prefer informal employment due to both lower levels of human capital and inefficiencies in labor codes.

[71] Labor legislation governing the public sector also mandates the payment of the 13th month benefit. Only eight percent of public sector workers did not receive the benefit. Interestingly, a higher share of the poor (17 percent) did not receive the benefit than the non-poor (7 percent).

[72] See Annex 6.

[73] These results hold true even the comparison is done using only the basic wages as a reference.

66.   Indeed, Table A11.16 suggests that the minimum wage is not fully enforced. Close to one quarter of all paid workers[74] receive less than the average minimum hourly wage. Enforcement appears to be weakest for agricultural, trade, and manufacturing workers. In the case of agriculture, the physical dispersion of workers, the seasonality of agricultural employment and the frequent use of task specific (piece rate) payment schemes hampers enforcement, despite moderately high levels of union membership among farm workers (see Box 6). For commerce, common informality and the dispersion of workers, combined with weaker union membership (see Box 6) likewise hamper enforcement. In contrast, minimum wages seem to be enforced more in mining and most services which are characterized by more widespread union membership. As discussed in above, union membership generally carries a premium on earnings, controlling for other variables (Table A11.13).

67.   Finally, it is clear from Table A11.16 below that the poor do not generally benefit from the minimum wage provisions in Panama's labor legislation. Close to two thirds of paid workers living in extreme poverty and over a half of all paid poor workers receive less than the minimum hourly wage. This compares with only 17 percent for the non-poor. A larger share of the poor earn less than the minimum wage than the non-poor for all significant categories (very few poor workers are employed in mining and utilities).

Box 6 - Union Membership in Panama

Unions sometimes serve as informal enforcers of labor legislation, informing officials when minimum wages are not paid or benefits not granted. As shown in Table A11.13, union members do indeed tend to earn more than non-members (even when other differences are taken into account).

Panama's Labor Code includes strong language regarding the role of the state in defending labor in employment negotiations and in actively promoting union organization. Indeed, the very first Article of the 1995 Labor Code Modernization Law states that "the present Code regulates relations between capital and labor [...ensuring...] state protection to the benefit of workers."

The LSMS reveals that roughly eleven percent of all workers (excluding the self-employed) belong to unions in Panama. This pattern is found irrespective of gender and poverty group. In terms of widespread membership, unions appear to be stronger in the basic and public/community services sectors (28 and 16 percent respectively of workers belong). Not coincidentally, workers in these sectors have a much higher likelihood of receiving at least the minimum wage and the thirteenth month salary benefit than workers in other sectors. Membership is fairly common in manufacturing and transportation (both around 14 percent), followed by construction (nine percent) and financial services (eight percent). Agricultural workers are the least likely to join unions (three percent belong).

PART 4: SUMMARY AND CONCLUSIONS

68.   This paper reviews the labor-market conditions facing a number of traditionally vulnerable (or "socially excluded") groups in Panama: the poor, women, indigenous workers, youths and child laborers.

Labor Markets and the Poor: Unemployment and Informal Jobs

69.   **The poor generally do not benefit from – and may even be hurt by – Panama's generous but complex labor legislation.** Through its multiplicity of labor regimes, the Panamanian Government intervenes in the labor market in a number of ways: (i) it sets a complex structure of minimum wages; (ii) it establishes a very short period of probation for new hires (though recent reforms have created a number of loopholes for getting around these requirements); (iii) it severely restricts job suspension; and (iv) it mandates numerous fringe benefits. The LSMS analysis suggests that, for the most part, the poor do not benefit from these interventions. Rather, they could be hurt by the market segmentation that arises

---

[74] Excluding unpaid laborers and the self-employed.

from the multiplicity of labor regimes both in terms of higher open unemployment and from less favorable terms for those who do find work.

70.　**First,** although unemployment is not correlated with poverty for the nation as a whole, the poor are more likely to be unemployed than the non-poor in urban areas. Arguably, urban labor markets may be more segmented by the more dominant presence of the public sector, the Panama Canal Commission, and the export processing zones, in addition to the private sector, all of which are governed by separate legislative regimes. Unemployment is higher in urban areas – and even higher among the urban poor (twelve percent), even when other variables (such as education) have been taken into account. It seems that the poor tend to bear the cost of labor market distortions in Panama in the form of open unemployment. Recent reforms, however, do seem to have eased the restrictiveness of the Labor Code, resulting in lower unemployment in recent years. Further work is needed to identify the key aspects of existing labor legislation that merit additional reform to make Panama's labor markets even more flexible so as to better absorb the excess supply of labor (particularly among the poor).

71.　**Second,** the analysis suggests that market segmentation squeezes a large share of those among the poor who are lucky enough to find work into informal sector jobs with far less favorable terms. Indeed, the large informal sector in Panama (covering half of all workers) is a symptom of such segmentation. Moreover, a larger share of the poor (close to three quarters) work in the informal sector than the non-poor. The employment of such a large share of the poor in the informal sector suggests that the majority of the poor are not covered by Panama's generous labor legislation. Indeed, over one half of the poor are paid less than the minimum wage, and over two thirds do not receive the "mandates" thirteenth month salary bonus. In fact, the analysis shows that the returns to informal sector employment are significantly lower than formal sector earnings – even after differences in education and experience have been taken into account. These results suggest that informal sector work might not be preferable (over formal sector jobs) to the poor, but rather serves as an alternative to unemployment in a segmented labor market.

Women in the Labor Market: Equal Pay, but Fewer Opportunities

72.　**While women do not appear to suffer discrimination in terms of wages and benefits in Panama, they do seem to face fewer opportunities for work than men.** Wage discrimination against women does not seem to be a systematic problem in Panama. In fact, the LSMS shows that women earn slightly more than men on an hourly basis, though the advantage is insignificant (and easily explained by higher levels of education among women in Panama).

73.　A number of factors, however, suggest that Panamanian women seem to have fewer opportunities for work than their male counterparts. **First,** as is typical throughout the world, a much smaller share of women participate in the labor force, probably reflecting higher opportunity costs for women (such as providing dependent care). **Second,** women (particularly young women) have higher rates of unemployment than men. It could be that, despite relatively higher education levels among Panamanian women, employers perceive additional costs of hiring women. Possible costs include generous maternity leave and additional restrictions on the dismissal of pregnant women (which might deter firms from hiring women in their fertile years) or perceived interruptions in daily duties due to domestic responsibilities (such as child care). **Third,** among those who do work, women are much more concentrated in certain sectors (such as commerce and public/community services) than men. This concentration could arise from policy (as discussed above, women are barred from working physically-demanding jobs in certain sectors) or tradition. **Fourth,** women work fewer hours[75] – and hence generate lower average *monthly* earnings – than men. It is not clear whether these shorter work days are

---

[75] On average women work about 171 hours a month as opposed to 191 hours for men (for first two jobs).

by choice (for better balance with domestic responsibilities, for example) or because of a lack of demand for full-time employment of women. Nonetheless, policy makers should explore options for reducing the constraints on poor women's opportunities in the labor force. Some of these options could include (i) providing support for community-based care for children under five in poor areas (initial education programs); (ii) extending the school day for primary and secondary school students (as is currently being initiated in some schools in Panama); and (iii) providing support for community-based after school programs.

Indigenous Workers: Informal Jobs, Wage Discrimination, and Few Benefits

74.   Despite relatively high union membership, a number of factors suggest that indigenous workers do not appear to fare well in Panama's labor markets.[76] **First,** labor force participation is significantly lower for monolingual indigenous speakers, whose inability to speak Spanish could create obstacles to employment. **Second,** for those who do find work, a vast majority (74 percent) work in the informal sector, which yields earnings that are significantly lower than those in the formal sector (as discussed above). **Third,** indigenous workers earn significantly less than their non-indigenous counterparts. Over half of this wage gap cannot be explained by differences in education (which tends to be lower among the indigenous) and experience, and could be viewed as representing an upper bound on discrimination. **Finally** (and related), only a small share of indigenous workers (one third) receive the mandated "thirteenth month" salary bonus, indicating that these workers are not covered by the provisions and protection of the Labor Code.

Youths in the Labor Market: High Unemployment

75.   Unemployment is high among Panama's youths, particularly among young women and urban youths living below the poverty line. This suggests a mis-match between the education and job expectations of young job seekers and the characteristics of the jobs available in the economy.

76.   In many countries, governments feel compelled to take "direct" action and place unemployed youths in publicly subsidized retraining programs in order to equip them with new skills. Such interventions should be approached with caution. International experience shows that retraining programs are extremely costly and do not lead to significant reductions in unemployment. Rather, the Government should focus on deepening economic reforms (including liberalizing the labor market) to promote broad-based growth as the primary tool for reducing unemployment. In addition, further work should be done to explore the causes of relatively higher unemployment among those with secondary and vocational education. Finally, the Government could help reduce unemployment in a cost-effective manner to address the problem of frictional unemployment by providing and disseminating better labor market information to job seekers and employers through employment exchanges.

Child Labor in Panama: Not Widespread, but Concentrated Among the Poor

77.   Finally, although child labor is not a widespread problem in Panama, it is concentrated more among the poor. Moreover, the cost of child participation in the labor market is lower education: child laborers have lower educational attainment than their non-working counterparts. Lower education among poor child laborers has serious implications for perpetuating poverty in the future.

---

[76] See Annex 6 for a more detailed analysis of indigenous living conditions, including labor market conditions, in Panama.

REFERENCES

Arends, M. 1992. *Female Labor Force Participation and Wages: A Case Study of Panama,* In Case Studies on Women's Employment and Pay in Latin America. (Ed.) George Psacharopoulos and Zafiris Tzannatos. The World Bank.

Bourgois, Philippe. 1985. *Ethnic Diversity on a Corporate Plantation: Guaymí Labor on a United Fruit Brands Subsidiary in Costa Rica and Panama.* Cultural Survival, Inc.

Burki, Shahid Javed and Guillermo E. Perry. 1997. *The Long March: A Reform Agenda for Latin America and the Caribbean in the Next Decade.* The World Bank.

Dar, A. 1994. *The Labor Market in Trinidad and Tobago: An Analysis of the SLC.*

Gonzalez, José Antonio. 1998. *Labor Market Flexibility in 13 Latin American Countries and the United States: Stylized Facts about Structural Relationships Between Output and Employment-Unemployment-Wages.* The World Bank.

Gregory, Peter. July 1991. *Estudio del Empleo en Panamá.*

Gregory, Peter and Alberto Davila. April 1993. *An Evaluation of the Panamanian Labor Code.* Development Technologies. Report prepared for the Ministry of Planning and Economic Policy.

Hammer, Jeffrey S. January 22, 1996. *The Public Economics of Education.* World Bank, Mimeo.

Kanbur, R and C. Grootaert. 1995. *Child Labor: A Review.* Working Paper No. 1454, The World Bank.

Maloney, William F. February 1998. "Are LDC Labor Markets Dualistic?" World Bank. Draft.

Maloney, William F. October 26, 1998. "Self-Employment and Labor Turnover in LDCs: Cross-Country Evidence." World Bank. Draft.

Maloney, William F. and Tom Krebs. April 1998. "Informality, Distribution, Rigidity, and Labor Market Institutions in Latin America: An Applied Efficiency Wage Model." Wold Bank. Draft.

Oaxaca, R.L. 1973. Male-Female Wage Differentials in Urban Labor Markets. *International Economic Review,* Vol. 14, No. 1, p.p. 693-709.

Psacharapoulos, George. 1995. *The Profitability of Investment in Education: Concepts and Methods.* HCO Working Paper No. 63. World Bank.

Psacharapoulos, G. and Z. Tzannatos. 1992. *Women's Employment and Pay in Latin America.* The World Bank.

Spinanger, D. 1983. *El mercado laboral en Panamá: Un análisis del impacto en el empleo del Código del Trabajo.* Mimeo, Kiel Institute for the World Economy, USAID/Panama.

UNICEF and the Ministry of Labor and Social Welfare. July 1997. *Desarrollo Humano en Panamá: Trabajo Infantil y Educación.*

World Bank. July 20, 1995. *Panama: A Dual Economy in Transition.* Country Operations Division, Country Department II, Latin America and the Caribbean Regional Office. Report No. 13977-PAN.

Table A11.1 – Labor Force Participation, by Poverty Group[a] % of Population 15+											
	Extreme Poor			All Poor			Non-poor			All		
	M	F	All	M	F	All	M	F	All	M	F	All
Area												
All Panama	80	28	56	80	30	57	77	48	62	78	43	60
Urban	69	33	52	75	39	57	75	53	63	75	51	62
Rural	85	25	59	83	25	57	82	35	59	83	30	58
Indigenous	73	32	52	74	32	53	89[b]	47[b]	67[b]	75	33	54
Age Groups (yrs)												
15-17	56	25	43	50	18	36	25	15	20	36	16	26
18-24	85	29	60	82	34	60	75	49	61	77	44	60
25-39	88	32	59	92	37	65	95	63	78	94	55	74
40-59	90	29	61	91	33	64	92	60	75	92	54	72
60+	65	11	43	61	10	38	43	13	27	48	12	30
Education												
No Education	72	25	45	72	22	44	64	43	39	69	21	43
Primary	85	28	61	84	29	60	77	44	56	81	33	58
Secondary	78	34	60	79	38	59	74	48	59	75	44	59
Vocational/other[b]	100	n.a	100	91	47	73	86	56	72	86	55	72
Higher[c]	71	39	57	87	59	70	88	46	79	88	71	78

a\ International definition. See Box 1. b\ Very small sample. c\ Includes university and post graduate schooling. Panama LSMS 1997.

Table A11.2 – Determinants of Labor Force Participation		
Probit estimates using international definition of LFP	Marginal Effects	
	Male	Female
Individual Characteristics		
Education:		
# years in primary	0.0026	0.0013
# years in secondary	-0.0001	0.0160***
# years in higher	0.0200***	0.0490***
Diploma received	0.0652***	0.0853***
Currently in school	-02458***	-0.2078***
Age:[a]		
Between 20-24	0.1273***	0.1656***
Between 25-29	0.1466***	0.2261***
Between 30-39	0.1549***	0.2931***
Between 40-39	0.1167***	0.3183***
Between 50-59	0.0452***	0.1375***
Over 60	-0.2582***	-0.2657***
Language ability:[a]		
Monolingual indigenous	-0.1975***	-0.1752***
Bilingual	-0.0174	-0.0211
Other:		
Single[b]	-0.0583***	0.1556***
Head of the household	0.1411***	0.1388***
Household characteristics		
Geographic area:[a]		
Rural	0.0911***	-0.1087***
Indigenous	0.0215	0.0975***
# of household members;		
Ages 0-5	0.0032	-0.0071
Ages 6-11	0.0099*	-0.0134*
Ages 12-17	0.0012	-0.0081
Ages 18-59	0.0029	0.0020
Ages over 60	-0.0177**	0.0101
Poverty/economic status:		
Total household consumption	6.05e-7	5.93e-6***
Sample Size	6992	6960
Fit (% of correct predictions)	0.71	0.71

Dependent Variable: Labor Force Participant (Yes/No). a\ The omitted variable for the age categories is the category for those between 15-19, for language ability is monolingual Spanish, and for geographic areas is urban. b\ Single = unmarried + widowed + divorced. (The necessary omitted variable is married = married + *unida*). Significant levels: * = 90%, ** = 95%, *** = 99%

Table A11.3 – Unemployment Rates in Panama: Comparison of International and National Definitions, LSMS and Labor Force Survey							
	Data from Household Survey Data					LSMS Data	
	National Definition of Unemployment					National Definition[a]	International Definition[a]
Unemployment Rates:	1993	1994	1995	1996	1997	1997	1997
All Panama	13.3%	14.0%	14.0%	14.3%	13.2	9.2%	5.9%
Urban areas	13.0%	15.8%	16.4%	17.0%	n.a	10.3%	7.5%

a\ See Box 1 for definitions.
Sources: 1993-97: Encuesta de hogares (cuadros 441-02, 441-03); Panama LSMS 1997.
Notes on data sources: (i) while the 1997 LSMS sample is nationally representative, the sample used in the Encuestas de hogares excludes indigenous and remote areas; (ii) the data from the Encuestas de hogares were calculated on the basis of a weekly average for the month of August (but classified respondents as unemployed if they did not work but had looked for work some time in the last three months, rather than the last week); the data for the 1997 LSMS were collected over a period from June-September and are based on the week prior to the interview of each household.

Table A11.4 - Unemployment Rates for 1997, Using International Definition and LSMS Data											
	Extreme Poor			All Poor			Non-poor			All		
	M	F	All	M	F	All	M	F	All	M	F	All
Area												
Urban	3.1	29.8	10.3	6.7	21.0	11.7	5.9	8.5	7.0	6.0	9.3	7.4
Rural	2.3	8.8	3.1	2.7	9.7	4.1	3.1	5.7	3.8	2.8	7.2	3.9
Indigenous	2.0	0.6	1.6	1.9	0.5	1.5	0.0	0.0	0.0	1.7	0.4	1.3
Age-groups												
15-19 yrs	2.9	15.1	5.9	5.9	15.7	8.5	16.3	16.5	16.9	11.1	16.3	12.8
20-24 yrs	4.8	17.0	7.0	5.0	22.1	9.1	10.9	17.2	13.9	9.0	17.9	12.2
25-29 yrs	5.6	10.9	7.1	5.8	14.4	8.3	5.1	14.1	8.7	5.5	14.1	8.7
30-39 yrs	0.8	1.6	1.0	2.9	9.2	4.7	3.6	5.0	4.5	3.4	5.5	4.2
40-49 yrs	1.1	4.6	1.9	1.9	7.2	3.4	2.3	4.4	3.3	2.3	4.8	3.3
50-59 yrs	0.9	3.3	1.4	0.1	5.4	1.8	1.2	1.3	1.4	1.1	1.9	1.4
Above 60	0.0	0.0	0.0	0.0	0.0	0.0	2.0	0.0	1.8	1.3	0.0	1.2
Education												
None	0.8	0.8	0.8	1.3	1.6	1.3	1.7	2.4	1.9	1.1	1.8	1.5
Primary	2.0	5.0	2.6	2.5	7.0	3.5	2.5	4.9	3.3	2.5	5.6	3.3
Secondary	5.5	34.2	12.3	6.0	21.6	10.8	7.1	10.9	8.6	6.8	12.2	8.8
Vocational/other	0.0	0.0	0.0	18.6	42.3	25.1	5.7	8.4	6.7	6.9	11.4	8.5
Higher	0.0	0.0	0.0	5.3	17.8	11.8	4.3	6.3	5.4	4.6	6.6	5.6
Total	**2.2**	**7.9**	**3.5**	**3.4**	**11.8**	**5.5**	**5.0**	**8.0**	**6.2**	**4.5**	**8.5**	**5.9**

Source: Panama LSMS 1997. See Box 1 for definitions.

Table A11.5 - Unemployment Rates for 1997, Using National Definition and LSMS Data											
	Extreme Poor			All Poor			Non-poor			All		
	M	F	All	M	F	All	M	F	All	M	F	All
Area												
Urban	9.5	44.0	20.8	11.7	29.7	18.3	7.6	11.5	9.4	8.1	12.9	10.2
Rural	4.6	23.1	8.3	5.1	21.5	8.6	4.5	11.6	6.6	4.8	15.8	7.6
Indigenous	6.2	8.9	7.0	5.6	8.9	6.6	0.0	0.0	0.0	5.2	8.2	6.1
Age-groups												
15-19 yrs	11.9	28.9	16.3	16.2	28.8	19.6	23.4	20.8	22.4	19.7	23.9	21.1
20-24 yrs	7.8	27.2	11.6	10.5	31.5	15.8	15.1	21.8	17.9	13.4	23.6	17.2
25-29 yrs	10.2	14.7	11.5	7.9	21.5	11.9	5.8	18.4	11.1	6.7	18.8	11.4
30-39 yrs	1.9	15.2	5.8	3.7	19.0	8.2	4.4	7.8	5.9	4.0	9.4	6.1
40-49 yrs	1.9	18.3	6.2	2.4	17.1	6.8	3.2	7.1	4.8	2.9	8.6	5.3
50-59 yrs	2.1	14.7	4.9	1.8	14.3	4.6	2.2	6.8	3.6	2.1	6.6	3.7
Above 60	0.7	29.2	4.5	0.3	18.4	2.7	4.0	5.8	4.4	2.8	8.3	3.9
Education												
None	2.9	15.1	7.0	3.3	16.0	7.1	4.1	7.8	5.0	3.3	14.1	6.6
Primary	5.5	18.3	8.2	5.9	18.1	8.6	4.3	9.3	5.9	5.1	12.7	7.2
Secondary	8.8	39.0	16.2	8.9	29.1	15.5	9.1	15.9	11.8	9.1	18.0	12.3
Vocational/other	0.0	0.0	0.0	24.0	52.1	32.1	7.9	10.3	8.8	9.7	14.5	11.4
Higher	1.6	33.6	22.5	9.1	24.1	17.1	4.7	7.7	6.3	5.0	8.2	6.7
Total	**5.5**	**20.4**	**9.1**	**6.6**	**21.9**	**10.7**	**6.7**	**11.5**	**8.7**	**6.6**	**13.4**	**9.2**

Source: Panama LSMS 1997. See Box 1 for definitions.

Table A11.6 – Determinants of Unemployment[a] Probit estimates using the International Definition		
	Marginal Effects	
	Male	**Female**
Individual Characteristics		
Education		
# years in primary	-0.0007	-0.0047
# years in secondary	0.0062***	0.0022
# years in higher	0.0021	-0.0052*
Diploma received	0.0002	0.0037
Age	0.0026	-0.0053**
Age squared	-.00002**	.00001
Household characteristics		
Geographic area[b]		
Rural	-0.0213***	-0.0340***
Indigenous	-0.0283***	-0.0621***
# of household members	0.0004	0.0042**
Poverty/economic status		
Total household consumption	-6.18e-7	-5.21e-7***
Selectivity	-0.0585***	0.0336*
Sample Size	5478	2881
Fit (% of correct predictions)	0.95	0.91
a\ Dependent variable = 1 if unemployed; 0 if employed. b\ The omitted variable for the geographic area is urban. Significant levels: * = 90%, ** = 95%, *** = 99%		

Table A11.7 – Possible Underemployment Among the Poor? Labor Intensity by Area and Poverty Group												
	Urban			Rural			Indigenous			All		
	Poor	Non Poor	All	Poor	Non Poor	All	Poor	Non Poor	All	Poor	Non Poor	All
No. of months worked:												
First Job	8.0	9.6	9.4	8.6	9.3	8.9	8.1	9.7	8.2	8.4	9.5	9.2
First two jobs	8.7	10.4	10.2	10.0	10.7	10.3	9.2	10.9	9.3	9.6	10.4	10.2
Days worked per week	5.0	5.3	5.3	5.0	5.3	5.1	5.0	5.4	5.1	5.0	5.3	5.2
Hours worked:												
Per week (first job)	36	41	40	35	39	37	28	38	28	34	40	38
Per year (two jobs)	1347	1792	1744	1474	1756	1609	1057	1713	1103	1377	1783	1663
% with >1 job	11	10	10	20	18	19	14	13	14	17	12	13
Source: LSMS 1997												

Table A11.8 - Distribution of Workers by Sector, Gender and Poverty Group (%)											
	Extreme Poor			All Poor			Non-poor			All		
	M	F	Both	M	F	Both	M	F	Both	M	F	Both
Agriculture	74	39	67	60	21	51	15	2	10	30	6	22
Mining	0.2	0.0	0.1	0.2	0.0	0.1	0.4	0.1	0.3	0.3	0.1	0.2
Manufacturing	5	16	8	8	13	9	12	7	10	11	9	10
Basic servicesa	0.1	1	0.3	1	1	1	2	1	2	2	1	1
Construction	3	0.0	3	7	0.0	5	9	1	6	8	1	5
Commerce	11	13	11	14	24	16	22	26	24	20	26	22
Transport	2	0.0	1	3	0.2	2	11	4	9	8	4	7
Financial services	0.2	1	0.3	1	1	1	6	8	7	4	7	5
Community servicesb	4	30	10	7	40	15	22	51	34	17	49	29
All	100	100	100	100	100	100	100	100	100	100	100	100
Total # employed ('000)	112	30	142	234	71	305	449	301	750	667	365	1032

a\ Basic services such as electricity, water, sanitation, garbage collection etc.
b\ Public and community services such as public administration, defense, sports associations, NGOs, domestic services.
Source: Panama LSMS 1997

Table A11.9 - Distribution of Workers by Type of Employment, Gender and Poverty Group (%)											
	Extreme Poor			All Poor			Non-poor			All		
	M	F	Both	M	F	Both	M	F	Both	M	F	Both
Public sector	3	3	3	5	7	6	18	28	22	14	24	17
Canal	0.1	0.0	0.1	0.1	0.0	0.1	2	1	2	2	1	1
Private sector:	97	97	97	95	93	94	80	71	76	85	75	82
White Collar	14	7	13	25	13	22	44	34	40	37	29	34
Blue Collar	23	6	20	24	4	19	7	1	4	13	1	9
Domestic laborer	1	20	4	1	24	6	1	14	6	1	15	6
Self-employed	37	26	35	31	26	30	27	20	24	28	21	26
Unpaid laborer	22	39	25	15	26	17	4	4	4	9	10	9
All	100	100	100	100	100	100	100	100	100	100	100	100
Total # employed ('000)	112	30	142	234	71	305	449	301	750	667	365	1032

Source: Panama LSMS 1997.
White collar workers are employees of private enterprises. Blue collar workers are day laborers (*jornaleros*).

Table A11.10 – Share of Workers in the Informal Sector, by Gender and Poverty Group (%)											
	Extreme Poor			All Poor			Non-poor			All		
	M	F	Both	M	F	Both	M	F	Both	M	F	Both
All	77	86	79	68	80	70	39	41	40	50	49	49
Type of Employment												
Public sector	0	0	0	0	0	0	0	0	0	0	0	0
Canal	0	0	0	0	0	0	0	0	0	0	0	0
Private sector:	79	88	81	71	84	74	49	58	52	57	64	59
White Collar	30	51	32	26	39	28	19	20	19	21	21	21
Blue Collar	66	58	66	70	53	70	75	75	75	72	62	71
Domestic Employee	100	100	100	100	100	100	100	100	100	100	100	100
Self-employed	100	98	100	99	97	98	86	87	86	91	89	90
Unpaid laborer	90	87	89	88	84	87	87	84	85	88	84	86
Sector												
Agriculture	86	87	86	83	85	83	78	62	76	81	79	81
Mining[a]	0	0	0	17	0	17	16	0	15	17	0	15
Manufacturing	43	83	61	37	70	48	33	45	37	35	52	40
Basic services[b]	50	0	18	60	0	44	5	0	5	13	0	11
Construction[a]	65	0	65	59	0	59	42	0	41	47	0	45
Commerce	54	83	61	46	78	57	41	51	46	43	56	48
Transport[a]	64	0	64	66	0	64	50	18	43	51	18	45
Financial services[a]	0	100	50	25	73	38	14	26	20	16	27	21
Community services[c]	33	90	71	32	80	62	17	40	31	19	46	35
Geographic Area												
Urban	60	76	63	43	73	52	29	38	33	31	41	35
Rural	79	89	81	73	79	74	63	56	61	68	65	68
Indigenous	76	84	78	74	82	77	23	47	32	71	79	74
Education Level												
No Education	78	83	80	78	84	79	70	79	72	75	83	77
Primary	80	88	81	72	86	75	58	78	64	66	81	70
Secondary	60	81	64	52	67	56	38	41	39	40	46	42
Higher	29	0	35	25	26	26	17	19	18	18	19	18
Vocational/other	58	49	58	35	61	41	30	51	38	5	6	5

a\ Small sample
b\ Basic services such as electricity, water, sanitation, garbage collection etc.
c\ Public and community services such as public administration, defense, sports associations, NGOs, domestic services.
Source: Panama LSMS 1997. White collar workers are employees of private enterprises. Blue collar workers are day laborers (*jornaleros*).

Table A11.11 – Determinants of Employment Choice: Formal vs. Informal Sector Jobs Probit Estimates		
	Marginal Effects	
	Male	Female
Individual Characteristics		
Education		
# years in primary	-0.0080	-0.0334***
# years in secondary	0.0156***	0.7085***
# years in higher	0.0264***	0.0399***
Diploma received	0.0280	0.2410***
Experience[a]	-0.0023	0.0289***
Experience Squared	-0.0001*	-0.0008***
Training	0.2715***	0.2674***
Other		
Single[b]	-0.0795***	-0.0307
Household characteristics[c]		
Geographic area		
Rural	-0.2217***	-0.1232***
Indigenous	-0.2396***	-0.1062**
# of household members		
Ages 0-5	-0.0024	-0.0062
Poverty/economic status		
Total household consumption	7.96e-6***	-8.47e-6***
Selectivity	0.1175***	0.0995***
Sample Size	5202	2615
Fit (% of correct predictions)	0.70	0.75

Dependent variable = 1 if individual works in formal sector; 0 if he/she works in the informal sector. See Box 3 for definitions.

a\ Experience = How long have you been at your current job?

b\ Single = unmarried + widowed + divorced. (Omitted variable: married = married + *unida*).

c\ The omitted variable for the geographic area is urban.

Significant levels: * = 90%, ** = 95%, *** = 99%

Table A11.12 - Mean Hourly Earnings (Including Self-Employment), by Gender			
Balboas	Male	Female	All
Total	2.5	2.8	2.6
By Poverty Group			
Extreme Poor	1.1	1.0	1.1
All Poor	1.3	1.3	1.3
Non-Poor	3.0	3.0	3.0
By Geographic Area			
Urban	3.3	3.1	3.2
Rural	1.4	1.8	1.5
Indigenous	1.2	0.9	1.1
By Public vs. Private Sector			
Public	4.2	3.9	4.0
Private	2.2	2.3	2.2
- Enterprise (white collar)	2.7	2.7	2.7
- Day Laborer (blue collar)	1.0	0.5	0.9
- Domestic Laborer	2.4	1.3	1.4
- Self-Employed	1.9	2.7	2.1
By Formal vs. Informal Sector			
Informal	1.7	1.8	1.7
Private Formal	2.8	3.1	2.8
Public Formal	4.2	3.9	4.0
By Sector			
Agriculture	1.1	1.8	1.1
Mining	3.3	n.a	3.3
Manufacturing	2.4	1.8	2.2
Basic services[a]	3.5	2.7	3.4
Construction	2.5	2.7	2.5
Commerce	2.1	2.4	2.2
Transport	3.2	3.0	3.2
Financial services	4.7	5.1	4.9
Community services[b]	3.9	2.8	3.2
By Education Level			
No Education	1.0	1.2	1.1
Primary	1.4	1.5	1.4
Secondary	2.5	2.4	2.5
Vocational/other	3.2	2.0	2.8
Higher	5.3	4.4	4.8
By Age Level			
15-19	1.1	1.7	1.3
20-24	1.9	2.0	1.9
25-29	2.2	2.5	2.3
30-39	2.5	2.9	2.7
40-49	3.2	3.3	3.2
50-59	2.8	3.2	2.9
>60	2.4	1.7	2.3

a\ Basic services such as electricity, water, sanitation, garbage collection etc.
b\ Public and community services such as public administration, defense, sports associations, NGOs, domestic services.
Source: Panama LSMS 1997. Data exclude earnings of those employed by the Panama Canal Commission because of the very small sample of these workers in the LSMS. Canal employees earn an average of B./10 per hour.

Table A11.13 – Earnings Regressions by Gender

	Model 1			Model 2		
	Male	Female	All	Male	Female	All
Individual Characteristics						
Education						
# years in primary	0.038	0.018	-0.034			
# years in secondary	0.044***	0.050***	0.046***			
# years in higher	0.095***	0.122***	0.071***			
# years of education				0.058***	0.067***	0.048***
Diploma received	0.227***	0.206**	0.252**	0.034	0.165	-0.002
Experience[a]	0.013***	0.015***	0.008	0.013***	0.016***	0.007
Experience squared	-.0003***	-.0004***	-.0001	-.0003***	-0.004***	-.0001
Professional training	0.164***	0.109**	0.237***	0.180***	0.133***	0.246***
Geographic area[b]						
Rural	-0.448***	-0.459***	-0.362***	-0.448***	-0.457***	-0.367***
Indigenous	-0.948***	-0.844***	-1.279***	-0.918***	-0.819***	-1.216***
# of household members						
Ages 0-5	-0.215	-0.009	-0.050*	-0.023	-0.009	-0.521*
Ages 6-11	-0.026	-0.026	-0.025	-0.029*	-0.029	-0.030
Ages 12-17				0.012	0.004	0.021
Other						
Female			0.627			0.077
Job Characteristics						
Public (vs. informal)	0.794***	0.808***	0.779***	0.803***	0.821***	0.793***
Private Formal (vs. inf.)	0.534***	0.587***	0.428***	0.539***	0.591***	0.441***
Belong to union	0.175***	0.263***	0.016	0.182***	0.270***	0.026
Constant	-0.778***	-0.820***	-0.491***	-0.95***	-0.971***	-0.752***
Selectivity	0.206***	0.160***	0.253***	0.215***	0.165***	0.280***
Sample Size	4573	2267	6840	4573	2267	6840
R-squared	0.32	0.33	0.31	0.32	0.33	0.31

Dependent Variable: Log of Hourly Earnings

a\ Experience = How long have you been working as [....current profession...] (e.g., as a mechanic irrespective of specific position0?

b\ The omitted variable for geographic area is urban, and for public and private formal sectors is informal.

Significant levels: * = 90%, ** = 95%, *** = 99%

Table A11. 14 - Applicability of the Labor Code: % of Private Sector Employees[a] Receiving the 13th Month Salary Benefit				
	% Receiving	% Not Receiving	% of Total Recipients	% of Workers
Total Population	50	50	100	100
By Gender				
Male	47	53	61	66
Female	58	42	39	34
By Poverty Group				
Extreme Poor	23	77	17	8
All Poor	34	66	40	24
Non-Poor	69	31	63	78
By Geographic Area				
Urban	61	39	78	66
Rural	32	68	20	32
Indigenous	33	67	2	2
Type of Employment				
White collar[b]	63	37	88	71
Blue collar [c]	21	79	12	29
By Formal vs. Informal Sector				
Informal	28	72	21	39
Formal	65	35	79	61
By Industry				
Agriculture	19	81	6	15
Mining	83	17	1	1
Manufacturing	65	35	17	13
Basic services	44	66	1	1
Construction	39	61	6	8
Commerce	63	37	33	27
Transport	43	57	5	6
Financial services	72	28	10	7
Community/public services	50	50	21	22

a\ Private sector workers including day laborers and those in private enterprises (excluding canal employees, self-employed and unpaid labor).
b\ Private enterprise employees.
c\ Day and domestic laborers.
Source: Panama LSMS 1997.

Table A11.15 - How Binding is the Minimum Wage? Average and Minimum Hourly Wages by Sector					
		Total labor earnings[b]		Basic wages [c]	
	Official Minimum [a]	Actual Average [b]	Average for those earning more than minimum wage	Actual Average [c]	Average for those earning more than minimum wage
Agriculture	0.69	0.60	1.40	0.53	1.27
Mining	0.74	3.35	3.43	2.29	2.85
Manufacturing	0.69	1.64	2.10	1.40	1.82
Basic services	0.74	3.24	3.48	2.99	3.25
Construction	1.00	2.09	2.51	1.95	2.40
Commerce	0.69	1.48	1.89	1.28	1.69
Transport	0.74	2.07	2.41	1.86	2.19
Financial services	1.00	3.63	3.76	3.16	3.35
Community/public services	0.74	2.96	3.42	2.61	3.07
Domestic services	0.43[d]	1.35	1.96	0.84	1.21

Sources:

A\ Official Minimum Wages: the *Decreto Ejecutivo No. 91*, November 14, 1995, which specifies a schedule of different minimum wages for a number of sectors and regions. The analysis uses the lowest of these minimum wages for each sector (across regions and subsectors).

b\ Panama LSMS 1997. Includes all forms of payment (cash, kind, etc.) for *paid* workers (excluding unpaid laborers and the self-employed).

c\ Panama LSMS 1997. Includes only basic wages/salaries for *paid* workers (excluding unpaid laborers and the self-employed).

d\ The minimum wage is based on B/.75 per month and 40 hour weeks.

Table A11.16 - Enforcement of the Minimum Wage: Share of Employees who Receive Less than the Minimum Wage, by Poverty Group				
	% of workers in each group who receive less than the minimum wage			
	Extreme Poor	All Poor	Non-Poor	All
Total % < min. wage	68	54	17	26
Agriculture	82	75	52	67
Mining	0[a]	0[a]	7 [a]	7
Manufacturing	63	42	17	24
Basic services	0[a]	35	1	6
Construction	40	27	15	18
Commerce	48	36	20	24
Transport	28	22	14	15
Financial services	0[a]	12	4	4
Community/public services	43	31	11	14

a\ There are very few paid workers (excluding self-employed and unpaid workers) in this sector and poverty group.

Source: Panama LSMS 1997. Excludes unpaid laborers and the self-employed.

Statistical Appendix A

Table A-1 – Labor Force Participation, by Poverty Group [a]											
% of Population 15+											
	Extreme Poor			All Poor			Non-poor			All		
	M	F	All	M	F	All	M	F	All	M	F	All
Area												
All Panama	83	32	60	83	34	60	78	50	64	80	46	63
Urban	74	39	57	78	44	61	77	55	65	77	53	64
Rural	87	29	62	85	29	60	83	37	61	84	33	61
Indigenous	76	34	55	77	35	56	89 [b]	47 [b]	67 [b]	77	36	57
Age Groups (yrs)												
15-17	64	32	51	58	22	42	28	16	22	40	18	30
18-24	88	32	64	87	39	65	78	51	64	82	47	64
25-39	90	36	63	93	41	68	95	65	79	95	58	76
40-59	91	34	64	92	37	66	93	62	77	92	56	64
60+	65	14	45	61	12	39	44	14	28	40	13	31
Education												
No Education	73	29	48	73	26	47	65	19	41	71	24	45
Primary	88	33	65	87	32	64	79	38	58	83	35	60
Secondary	81	37	63	82	43	63	76	48	62	77	47	61
Vocational[b]	100	n.a	100	96	56	74	88	56	73	89	57	74
Higher[c]	85	59	73	90	64	80	88	73	79	88	72	79

a\ National definition. See Box 1.
b\ Very small sample.
c\ Includes university and post graduate schooling.
Source: Panama LSMS 1997.

Table A-2 - Mean Hourly Earnings (excluding self employment) by Gender			
Balboas	Male	Female	All
Total	1.9	2.2	2.0
By Poverty Group			
Extreme Poor	0.8	0.7	0.8
All Poor	1.0	0.8	1.0
Non-Poor	2.3	2.4	2.4
By Geographic Area			
Urban	2.7	2.5	2.6
Rural	0.9	1.4	1.0
Indigenous	0.9	0.5	0.8
By Public vs. Private Sector			
Public	4.2	3.9	4.1
Private	1.5	1.6	1.5
- Enterprise (white collar)	2.7	2.7	2.7
- Day Laborer (blue collar)	1.0	0.5	0.9
- Domestic Laborer	2.4	1.3	1.3
By Formal vs. Informal Sector			
Informal	0.7	0.9	0.7
Private Formal	2.5	2.6	2.5
Public Formal	4.2	3.9	4.1
By Sector			
Agriculture	0.6	1.1	0.6
Mining	3.3	n.a	3.3
Manufacturing	2.0	0.8	1.6
Basic services[a]	3.5	2.0	3.2
Construction	2.1	2.7	2.1
Commerce	1.5	1.4	1.5
Transport	2.0	2.5	2.1
Financial services	3.4	3.9	3.6
Community services[b]	3.6	2.6	3.0
By Education Level			
No Education	0.6	0.4	0.6
Primary	0.9	0.9	0.9
Secondary	2.0	2.0	2.0
Vocational/other	2.9	1.3	2.3
Higher	4.4	3.7	4.0
By Age Group			
15-19	0.9	1.5	1.1
20-24	1.5	1.8	1.6
25-29	1.6	2.1	1.8
30-39	2.0	2.2	2.1
40-49	2.6	2.7	2.6
50-59	2.0	2.5	2.1
>60	1.6	0.7	1.5

a\ Basic services such as electricity, water, sanitation, garbage collection etc.
b\ Public and community services such as public administration, defense, sports associations, NGOs, domestic services.
Source: Panama LSMS 1997

Table A-3 - Mean Monthly Earnings (excluding self employed) by Gender			
Balboas	Male	Female	All
Total	456	436	449
By Poverty Group			
Extreme Poor	155	96	144
All Poor	200	160	192
Non-Poor	569	477	530
By Geographic Area			
Urban	592	482	545
Rural	241	271	248
Indigenous	243	151	221
By Public vs. Private Sector			
Public	701	620	661
Private	391	338	374
- Enterprise (white collar)	494	444	479
- Day Laborer (blue collar)	100	44	97
- Domestic Laborer	243	162	167
By Formal vs. Informal Sector			
Informal	701	620	661
Private Formal	496	464	487
Public Formal	195	206	199
By Sector			
Agriculture	153	259	158
Mining	446	n.a	691
Manufacturing	499	298	456
Basic services[a]	641	339	598
Construction	451	657	458
Commerce	405	382	397
Transport	555	568	558
Financial services	698	722	709
Community services[b]	624	423	503
By Education Level			
No Education	113	66	101
Primary	186	132	173
Secondary	390	323	345
Vocational/other	486	308	457
Higher	1094	686	887

a\ Basic services such as electricity, water, sanitation, garbage collection etc.
b\ Public and community services such as public administration, defense, sports associations, NGOs, domestic services.
Source: Panama LSMS 1997

Table A-4 – Child Labor by Gender			
	Boys	Girls	Total
Employed:			
Total Number Employed	17539	5764	23303
% of Those Employed	75	25	100
% of Age Cohort (10-14)	12	4	8
% of Child Laborers, by Area:			
Urban	28	22	27
Rural	62	58	61
Indigenous	10	20	12
Total	100	100	100
% of All Children by Area (comparison):			
Urban	48	50	49
Rural	40	39	40
Indigenous	11	11	11
Total	100	100	100
% of Child Laborers in Each Area:			
Urban	80	20	100
Rural	76	24	100
Indigenous	61	39	100

Source: Panama LSMS 1997. The Panama LSMS collected employment information for children aged 10-14 (but not for younger children). These are not included in the standard definitions of labor force.

Table A-5 – Child Labor by Poverty Group, Gender and Age				
	Extreme Poor	All Poor	Non Poor	Total
Child Workers as % of Age Cohort (10-14):				
Boys	18	17	7	12
Girls	6	6	3	4
Total	12	11	5	8
% of Child Laborers by Poverty Group:				
Boys	46	63	34	100
Girls	58	58	42	100
Total	47	65	35	100
% of All Children by Poverty Group (comparison):				
Boys	27	46	54	100
Girls	25	46	54	100
Total	26	46	54	100

Source: Panama LSMS 1997. The Panama LSMS collected employment information for children aged 10-14 (but not for younger children). These are not included in the standard definitions of labor force.

Table A-6 – Distribution of Child Labor & Hours Worked by Sector of Employment						
	Share of Total (%)			Average weekly hours of work		
	Boys	Girls	All	Boys	Girls	All
Agriculture	52	41	46	31	23	29
Mining	n.a	n.a	n.a	n.a	n.a	n.a
Manufacturing	9	12	10	25	23	24
Basic Services	n.a	n.a	n.a	n.a	n.a	n.a
Construction	2	n.a	2	9	n.a	9
Commerce	21	31	24	29	20	26
Transport	6	n.a	6	11	n.a	11
Financial Services	n.a	n.a	n.a	n.a	n.a	n.a
Public/Community Services	10	16	12	26	47	33
Total	100	100	100	28	26	27

Source: Panama LSMS 1997. The Panama LSMS collected employment information for children aged 10-14 (but not for younger children). These are not included in the standard definitions of labor force.

Table A-7 – Distribution of Child Labor & Hours Worked by Type of Employment						
	Share of Total (%)			Average weekly hours of work		
	Boys	Girls	All	Boys	Girls	All
Public Sector	1[a]	0	1[a]	65[a]	0	65[a]
Canal	0	0	0	0	0	0
Private Sector:	99	100	99	30	28	30
White Collar	14	0	10	35	0	35
Blue Collar	20	5	17	32	13	31
Domestic Laborer	2	15	5	10	58	46
Self-Employed	12	10	12	24	32	25
Unpaid Laborer	52	70	56	30	22	28
Total	100	100	100	28	26	27

a\ Small sample. Source: Panama LSMS 1997. The Panama LSMS collected employment information for children aged 10-14 (but not for younger children). These are not included in the standard definitions of labor force.

Table A-8 – Hourly Labor Earnings for Child Labor by Industry (Balboas)			
	Boys	Girls	All
Agriculture	0.84	1.11	0.86
Mining	n.a	n.a	n.a
Manufacturing	0.81	0.46	0.75
Basic Services	n.a	n.a	n.a
Construction	0.92	n.a	0.92
Commerce	3.08	0.15	2.55
Transport	1.08	n.a	1.08
Financial Services	n.a	n.a	n.a
Public/Community Services	0.81	2.50	1.56
All	1.44	1.62	1.47

Source: Panama LSMS 1997. The Panama LSMS collected employment information for children aged 10-14 (but not for younger children). These are not included in the standard definitions of labor force.

Table A-9 – Child Labor and Education			
	Children Aged 10-14 Who Go To:		
	Work Only	Work and School	School Only
Mean years of schooling			
Children aged 10	0.5 [a]	2.9	3.5
Children aged 11	1.6 [a]	4.9	4.3
Children aged 12	4.3 [a]	4.8	5.1
Children aged 13	4.5	5.2	6.4
Children aged 14	5.2	7.3	7.0
All	4.7	5.4	5.2
Percent of:			
Child laborers	36	64	n.a.
All Children	3	5	92

Source: Panama LSMS 1997. The Panama LSMS collected employment information for children aged 10-14 (but not for younger children). These are not included in the standard definitions of labor force. a\ Very small sample.

Appendix B – Methodology for Measuring Wage Discrimination

Using Oaxaca 's (1973) technique it is possible to decompose the earnings gap between two groups (for example, between men and women) into a component which is largely attributable in human capital endowments, and a component that reflects largely wage discrimination. The technique involves estimating separate wage regressions for the two groups of interest (A and B) as:

(1) $\ln w_A = c_A + X_A (b_A) + \varepsilon_A$ for group A and

(2) $\ln w_B = c_B + X_B (b_B) + \varepsilon_B$ for group B

where the subscripts 'A' and 'B' refers to group A and B respectively; ln (w)'s are the log of wages, c's are the constants terms, X's are a vector of characteristics, b's are the coefficients and ε's are the error terms.

The analysis in this paper is based on *wage* regressions, excluding earnings from self-employment (since a self-employed individual would not discriminate against him/herself).[1] The difference in the average log of wages is equivalent to the percentage difference between male and female pay. Given that the error term in the male and female wage functions has a mean of zero, we can show that:

$$(3)\ \ln w_A - \ln w_B = (c_A - c_B) + [\ \overline{X}_A (b_A) - \overline{X}_B (b_B)]$$

where $\overline{X}_A$ and $\overline{X}_B$ are the average values of male and female characteristics in the sample. Re-arranging, equation (3) yields:

$$(4)\ \ln w_A - \ln w_B = [(c_A - c_B) + \overline{X}_B (b_A - b_B)] + [b_A (\ \overline{X}_A - \overline{X}_B)]$$

Therefore, the difference in pay comes from two different sources. The first term represents wage gaps attributed to differences in the returns ($b_A - b_B$) that groups A and B receive for the same endowment of income generating characteristics. The second term represents wage gaps attributed to differences in the endowments of income generating characteristics ($\overline{X}_A - \overline{X}_B$) evaluated with group A's worker pay structure. The former part is said to reflect wage discrimination while the latter captures wage differentials from differences in endowments.

The use of earning functions to estimate discrimination means that there will be omitted variables not "explaining" wage differentials. Therefore, the discrimination part of the decomposition does not only explain wage differences due to discrimination but in addition, due to omitted variables. In this sense it is often said that the discrimination part serves as the upper bound of "unjustified" or "unexplained" wage discrimination.

---

[1] These are slightly different from the earnings regressions in Table 11, which include self-employment earnings.

Annex 12 – The Redistributive Impact of Agricultural Trade and Pricing Reforms

Rafael Yrarrazaval, Kathy Lindert, Tom Wiens, Carlos Sobrado
March 31, 1999

EXECUTIVE SUMMARY

i.   The Panamanian Government, which inherited the most highly distorted trade regime in Latin America, has made radical trade and pricing reforms one of the cornerstones of its economic reform program.   Tariff equivalents on most products have been lowered to a maximum of 15 percent and consolidated to five different rates, coming down from extremely high levels (even as high as 800 percent for basic grains).   On this basis, Panama will have instituted one of the most open economies in Latin America within the short span of twelve months, and will have the lowest average effective protection for agricultural products of any country in the LAC region.

ii.   While the dismantling of trade barriers inevitably generates net gains for the overall economy due to the efficiency gains associated with the reduction of distortions in production and consumption incentives, these reforms can have a negative effect on specific groups in the economy.   In particular, although consumers stand to gain from a reduction in trade protection, producers generally lose due to the fall in prices associated with these reforms.   The objective of this analysis is to quantify these redistributional effects at the household level, so as to identify the characteristics of the net losers and net winners with respect to their poverty status given a free trade scenario.   If the net losers are poor, targeted compensation may be needed to mitigate the poverty impact of these adjustment measures.   The paper also examines the net effect of the free trade scenario on the degree of inequality in the economy (as measured by the Gini index for consumption).

iii.   This paper focuses on the redistributive impact of reforms on basic food items, which have traditionally been highly protected. Food is important from a poverty perspective because (a) spending on food represents a large share of the total budgets of the poor (59 percent of total consumption); and (b) agriculture constitutes an important source of income for the poor (29 percent of total income). Reforms for basic staples have generally involved an elimination of non-tariff barriers and reductions in equivalent tariff rates in recent years. Data from the LSMS are used to simulate the redistributive effects of a hypothetical elimination of all tariffs from their 1997 levels (using 1997 international prices for reference).

iv.   **Overall Effects.** As expected, the reduction in the price of key staples in the consumption basket had a significant and positive net effect on households overall.   The minimum total net benefit of an elimination of all trade tariffs to Panamanian households is estimated at B./124 million per year.   This represents a net average per capita gain of B./45 or over 2.5 percent of total annual consumption. Although non-poor households gained more in absolute terms, the price reduction was more important to the poor as a share of total consumption.

v.   **Characteristics of Net Losers.** Also as expected, some producers did lose in net terms (even taking into account the gains they receive as consumers).   However, these "net losers" represented less than two percent of the population and less than eight percent of producers (or conversely, 97 percent[1] of

---

[1] One percent of the population is not affected by the elimination of trade barriers.

the population and 92 percent of producers were net gainers). A majority of the net losers are non-poor, and on average, non-poor net losers lost almost four times more than net losers below the poverty line. Net losses for the net losers represented a slightly higher share of total consumption for the poor than the non-poor.

vi.   Net losers tend to be concentrated in the provinces of Chiriqui, Los Santos and Darien, followed by Herrera, Veraguas and Cocle. Bocas del Toro and the more urban-dominated provinces of Colon and Panama had the least. The impact of these reforms on Darien and Veraguas, is of particular concern, since more than one half of the "net losers" in these provinces are poor. Likewise, around one third of all "net losers" in Herrera and Chiriqui are poor. Geographically-targeted compensating measures might thus be warranted to protect poor producers in these regions from the localized adverse affects of these reforms. Overall for all the net losers, one third were already poor and two thirds were classified as non poor.

vii.   **Net Losers vs. Net Gainers: Magnitude of the Effects.** The maximum total value of net losses for the net losers is estimated at B./8 million, compared with a minimum net benefit for all net gainers (including the ninety-two percent of producers for whom the net effect is positive) of B./132 million. The higher per capita net loss of B./177 per net loser (compared with the average net gain for net winners of B./50) sheds light on the political forces behind agricultural tariff protection: while the larger *overall* benefits of tariff reductions are dispersed over a large population of net consumers (with smaller per capita benefits), the larger *per capita* losses are concentrated on a small group of producers (who tend to be more politically organized).

viii.   **Impact on Poverty and Inequality.** Simulations suggest an overall decrease in the incidence of poverty and inequality with the hypothetical elimination of trade tariffs. It is estimated that a complete removal of trade barriers would cut the poverty rate 37.3 percent to 35.6 percent and the extreme poverty rate from 18.8 percent to 17.7 percent. The simulations also suggest that the Gini index for consumption inequality would be reduced by 0.58 percentage points, or 1.2 percent for the free trade scenario (bringing the consumption Gini to 47.97, as compared with 48.55 in 1997).

ix.   **Employment Effects.** While some reduction in *employment* (and possibly agricultural wages) would likely occur from cuts in tariff protection, the lower labor intensity of the main crops that were previously makes it improbable that this effect would be large or would spur mass migration to the cities. Moreover, the longer run effect of reducing protective tariffs on activities in which Panama does not have a comparative advantage and of consolidating tariff rates across sectors will create jobs through the promotion of economic growth.

OVERVIEW OF TRADE POLICIES AND RECENT REFORMS

1.   **History of Trade Distortions.** In recent years, the Panamanians Government, which inherited the most highly distorted trade regime in Latin America, has made radical trade and pricing reform one of the cornerstones of its economic program. Prior to implementation of the Bank-supported Economic Reform Loan (ERL, 1992-97), nominal ad valorem equivalent rates of protection ranged from nil for capital and most intermediate goods to 90 percent for final manufactured goods and as high as 800 percent for basic grains. As late as 1996, quotas and other non-tariff barriers were still used extensively, especially to protect domestic producers of foodstuffs. As a result, domestic prices of foodstuffs and other consumer non-durable goods were generally much higher than international prices, whereas the prices of consumer durable goods were close to international prices.

2.   **Trade and Price Reforms.** A first round of tariff and price reforms was launched by the Cabinet in December 1996 and March 1997. These reforms reduced tariffs on many commodities, transformed specific tariffs into ad valorem rates, and eliminated remaining non-tariff barriers to imports.[2] The Government initiated its second round of tariff reductions in July 1997, by lowering the maximum import tariff on vegetable oils, wheat and wheat products, and construction materials from 20-50 percent to 10 percent.[3] Tariffs on all other imports were reduced to a maximum of 15 percent beginning on January 1, 1998, and the number of tariff rates in the economy was consolidated from 108 to five different rates (15, 10, 5, 3, and 0 percent), with the exception of milk products (lowered from 50 to 40 percent), rice (lowered from 60 to 50 percent), and automobiles (whose tariff will remain in the range of 15-20 percent). The tariff on rice will be further lowered to 30 percent by the year 2000.[4] On this basis, Panama will have instituted one of the most open economies in Latin America within the short span of twelve months, and will have the lowest average effective protection for agricultural products of any country in the region.

PRICE AND TARIFF POLICIES FOR BASIC STAPLES[5]

3.   This paper focuses on the redistributive impact of eliminating the trade barriers for basic food items, which have traditionally been highly protected. Food is important from a poverty perspective because (a) spending on food represents a large share of the total budgets of the poor (59 percent of total consumption); and (b) agriculture constitutes an important source of income for the poor (29 percent of total income). Reforms for basic staples have generally involved an elimination of non-tariff barriers and reductions in equivalent tariff rates in recent years. The following section provides an overview of the specific policies and reforms for each of the key products.[6]

Rice

4.   The Government has historically intervened substantially in the rice sub-sector, as rice has been considered a "sensitive" product of national importance. Import quantities have been tightly controlled, subject to strict quotas established by the *Instituto de Mercadeo Agropecuario* (IMA) and licensing requirements overseen by the *Registro Oficial de la Industria Nacional*. In addition to quantitative restrictions, high tariff rates have also been applied to rice imports (consisting of base tariffs and extra-marginal tariffs). Finally, since 1992, producers have been guaranteed a "minimum reference price" for rice sales. An adjustment was made to bring the price of imports up to this minimum price (on top of which the official import tariffs were applied). Wholesale and retail prices for consumers were also fixed by the *Oficina de Regulación de Precios* (ORP). The total effect of these interventions was estimated to constitute a tariff equivalent of 168 percent in 1995.

5.   A series of reforms supported by the ERP and the WTA have succeeded in eliminating most non-tariff barriers on rice, freeing consumer prices, and reducing tariff rates.[7] While import licenses are still required, eligibility for obtaining licenses has been broadened so that other agents (in addition to millers)

---

[2] Specifically, the December 1996 and March 1997 Cabinet decrees: (i) reduced tariffs on all industrial and agro-industrial products from 60% and 90% to 40% and 50% respectively; (ii) reduced tariffs on the main agricultural commodities from a range of 50-180% to 20-60%; (iii) transformed remaining specific tariffs into ad valorem rates; and (iv) eliminated remaining non-tariff barriers. In July 1997, the Legislative Assembly approved the WTO Protocol and associated laws.

[3] This reform was issued as Cabinet Decree No. 37 and went into effect on September 1, 1997.

[4] These reforms were instituted via Cabinet Decree No. 68 issued on November 13, 1997.

[5] For more details on the specifics of trade policies and reforms in Panama, please see Rafael Yrarrazaval (October 1997), "Panamá: Politica Comercial y de Precios de Productos Agropecuarios 1992-1997."

[6] Additional details are described in Yrarrazaval (October 1997).

[7] Three tariffs rates apply: 3% for the 99,336 MT to be imported until April 30, 1998 (due to the consequences of El Niño), 15% for the 1,666.7 MT for the agreed quantity of imports of 5,500 MT for 1998; and 60% for all other imports.

may import with a license. Producer prices are no longer fixed, but are determined based on "negotiations" between agricultural producers, millers and the Government. The tariff equivalents associated with these reforms are estimated at 64 percent in 1997, with further reductions to about 40 percent in 1998. The tariff equivalent on rice is expected to be further reduced to 30 percent by the year 2000.

Corn and Sorghum

6.   A combination of tariff and non-tariff barriers was also applied to corn and sorghum, though the tariff equivalents of these interventions was lower for these products than for rice. As in the case of rice, IMA controlled corn and sorghum imports through a system of quotas and licenses. Minimum reference prices and tariffs also served to maintain high producer prices.[8]   The equivalent tariff rates arising from these interventions were estimated at 109 percent and 82 percent for corn and sorghum respectively.

7.   The ERP supported reforms to eliminate import quotas, restrictions and licensing and reduce the effective tariff rates on corn and sorghum. Indeed, tariff rates have been reduced substantially for these products, and averaged three percent for sorghum and 48-56 percent for corn in 1997. Tariff equivalents for corn have since been brought down to three percent in 1998. Producer prices are now determined based on negotiations between producers, livestock producers (who purchase corn and sorghum for feed), and the Government.

Beans and Lentils

8.   Until the recent waves of reforms, imports of beans (*frijoles*) were subject to quotas overseen by IMA. A system of permits dependent on domestic production of beans was applied to lentils, which are not produced in Panama. Import tariffs were also applied to both beans and lentils. Tariff equivalents were estimated at 36 percent for beans and 18 percent for lentils in 1997. Reforms eliminated quantitative restrictions and brought tariffs down to about 15 percent for both products by 1998. Consumer prices were fixed the ORP the end of 1995.

Sugar

9.   Panama is a net exporter of sugar and has not registered sugar imports since 1991/92. Exports have been destined for the United States, according to Panama's export quota to the U.S. of 2.9 percent at preferential prices (allowing Panama to export roughly 55 thousand metric tons per year in recent years). Producer prices are fixed by the ORP. Consumer prices are fixed by Executive Decree every six months. Reforms supported by the ERP led to the elimination of specific tariffs and import quotas for sugar, as well as the reduction in import tariffs. The equivalent tariff rate on sugar is estimated to have come down from about 43 percent in 1997 to 15 percent in 1998 under the recent wave of reforms.

Milk and Dairy Products

10.   Milk and dairy products remain highly protected in Panama, as ERP conditions did not apply to these products. Although import quotas have recently been eliminated, the total amount to be imported remains negotiated. Tariff rates for the negotiated import quantity (*el contingente negociado*) range from four to fifty percent. Tariff rates for additional imports (*extra-contingente*) for "sensitive" products are much higher than this, ranging from 90 to 173 percent. Both consumer and producer prices remain fixed.

---

[8] Unlike rice, however, consumer prices for these products were not fixed directly.

In 1997, the *average* tariff rate for grade C milk for the producer was 38 percent; tariff equivalents at the consumer level averaged 20 percent. These rates did not change in 1998.

Beef and Pork

11.   Reforms supported by the ERP have substantially reduced interventions in beef, which Panama exports. Export and import quotas have been eliminated and producer and consumer prices have been freed. The actual equivalent tariff rate on imports is zero (though an official nominal rate of twenty percent is in effect).

12.   Likewise, the ERP supported reforms to eliminate the IMA quota on pork imports and consolidate tariffs from fixed amounts to ad valorem rates. Equivalent tariff rates have come down from 60-90 percent in 1993 to 15 percent in 1998 for the first 520 metric tons of imports (which will increase to 880 over the next ten years), with a maximum *"extra-contingente"* rate of 70-90 percent for additional imports (which will come down to 60-70 percent in the next ten years). Consumer prices, which were previously fixed for certain pork products (*patitas, costillas, rabito,* and *hocicos de puerco en salmuera*), have been liberalized since 1996 as one of the ERP conditions.

Poultry

13.   Effective protection has also been substantially reduced for poultry and poultry products. As for most other products, the ERP supported the elimination of quantitative restrictions on poultry imports and the consolidation and reduction of tariff rates. Equivalent tariff rates have been reduced from 60-90 percent in 1993 to 15 percent for the first 324 metric tons of imports in 1997.[9]

Potatoes and Onions

14.   Reforms (which have been supported both by the ERP and under the WTO) have gone a long way in reducing interventions for potatoes and onions in Panama. Quantitative restrictions have been eliminated, and consumer prices freed. Tariffs have been converted to ad valorem rates. Average tariff equivalents, which had been as high as 271 percent for potatoes and 50 for onions, have come down to 13 percent in 1998.

SIMULATED IMPACT OF FREE TRADE REFORMS

15.   **Methodology.** The reduction of trade barriers generally entails two types of impacts: an overall efficiency gain due to the removal of distortions in production and consumption decisions and redistributional effects. In the context of the Panama Poverty Assessment, this paper is primarily concerned with the latter. Producers generally lose from the decrease in prices associated with the removal or reduction of trade barriers. For the economy as a whole, these losses are generally more than offset by the gains to consumers associated with the reduction in the cost of basic staples (as well as by the efficiency gains discussed above). Even some producers stand to gain in net terms if the value of their marketed output is lower than the total value of quantities purchased (e.g., small farmers). But some producers will still lose in net terms, even taking into account the gains that they would accrue as consumers. This paper thus seeks to identify the characteristics of the net losers and net winners, in particular with respect to their poverty status. If the analysis reveals that certain groups of poor producers are net losers, targeted compensation may be needed to mitigate the poverty impact of these adjustment measures.

---

[9] As per the agreement with the WTO. This amount will increase to 756 metric tons in the tenth year of the agreement.

16.   The distributional impact on households of hypothetically removing trade barriers was simulated using consumption and production data from the LSMS. Ideally, elasticities of supply and demand would be used to take into account the behavioral responses of producers and consumers. The cross-sectional nature of the LSMS complicates the estimation of price elasticities, however.[10] Instead, this analysis adopts "zero elasticity of substitution" assumptions for producers and consumers, which has the advantage of providing an upper bound estimate of the losses to producers and a lower bound estimate of the gains to consumers. In other words, by calculating the minimum gain to consumers and the maximum loss to producers, we obtain the smallest net gains due to a free trade scenario. The actual impacts of free trade reforms will be better than these results, because producers have the option of switching to more profitable products and consumers to cheaper substitutes. Using these conservative assumptions, the net losses for producers could indicate the maximum amount that might be needed to compensate them for the reforms. Indeed, if the "net loss" producers are poor, the Government may wish to target some amount of compensation to these producers. Annex 12.1 provides additional details on the methodology used in the analysis, as well as its limitations.

17.   **Reform Scenario.** The continuous and different phasing of reforms for various products and the timing of data collection under the LSMS (conducted in June-September 1997) complicates the analysis of the impact of specific reforms that were undertaken over the 1990s. As such, this analysis simulates the distributional impact of a "free trade scenario," which involves the hypothetical elimination of all tariffs compared to their 1997 levels (using 1997 international prices for reference). Percentage reductions in prices were applied to the actual prices observed in the LSMS data. While the free trade scenario is clearly hypothetical, it does paint a picture of the potential distributional effects of recent and future tariff reductions at the household level. Annex Table A1 at the end of the paper details the magnitude of the price reforms that were simulated under this "free trade" scenario.

Impact on "Net Gainers"

18.   Table A12.1 below presents the results of the simulation for the "net gainers" under the hypothetical free trade scenario. As expected, the reduction in the prices of key staples in the consumption basket would have a significant and positive net effect on a large share of consumers. The minimum net benefit for the "net gainers" of the tariffs elimination is estimated at B./131.7 million per year.[11] This represents an average per capita net gain of B./50 or 2.8 percent of total per capita annual consumption for the "net gainers".

19.   Non-poor "net gainers" would gain more than the poor in absolute per capita terms, probably due to the fact that higher total consumption (or income) allows for larger absolute food consumption. In relative terms, however, the poor and extreme poor would benefit more, which makes sense since, by Engel's Law, food represents a larger share of total consumption of the poor than the rich.

20.   "Net gainers" in urban areas would gain more than their rural and indigenous counterparts in absolute terms, owing to the fact that urban consumers tend to be better off (and can thus purchase larger absolute food quantities) and obtain their food primarily through purchases. Rural consumers, on the other hand, derive more consumption from on-farm production, which is not directly affected by the tariff reforms. However, as a share of total consumption, the net gains from free trade would be more important to rural and indigenous, again conforming to Engel's Law (since a larger share of rural and indigenous consumers are poor).

[10] Elasticities could be estimated using spatial variation in prices with a method developed by Deaton (June 1988).
[11] See Annex 12.1 below for details on the methodology for calculating these minimum gains.

Table A12.1 - Impact of Free Trade Reforms on "Net Gainers"				
	Total Gains (millions B./)	Per Capita Gains (B./)	Gains as % of Per Capita Cons.	Population affected	
				# of persons	%
Total	131.7	49.5	2.8%	2,659,315	97.3%
By Poverty Group:					
Extreme Poor	9.3	18.6	6.1%	504,063	18.4%
All Poor	27.3	27.3	5.4%	1,01,556	36.7%
Non-Poor	104.3	62.9	2.4%	1,657,760	60.7%
By Geographic Area:					
Urban	87.5	58.5	2.3%	1,496,633	54.8%
Rural	40.5	42.3	4.2%	958,495	35.1%
Indigenous	3.6	17.7	5.4%	204,188	7.5%

Source: Panama LSMS 1997 and Yrarrazaval October and November 1997. Simulations assume zero elasticities and thus yield "lower bound" minimum estimates for the gains to consumers. See Annex 12.1 for details on methodology.

Impact on "Net Losers"

21.   Overall, less than two percent of the population would lose in net terms from the hypothetical free trade scenario. Net losers represent about 1.8 percent of the non-poor, 1.4 percent of the poor, and 1.5 percent of the extreme poor population. In non-indigenous rural areas, 4.1 percent of the population would be negatively affected. The figure falls to 1.1 percent in the more subsistence-oriented indigenous areas.

22.   Table A12.2 below presents the net losses for "net losers" arising from the hypothetical elimination of trade tariffs (taking into account the gains arising from lower consumption prices). The maximum total net loss for this group is estimated at B./8.2 million per year. This represents an average per capita net loss of B./177 or 9.7% of total annual consumption per capita for the "net losers."

23.   Non-poor producers[12] would clearly bear the brunt of tariff elimination (or, conversely, are the prime beneficiaries of tariff protection). More than 88 percent of total losses from tariff elimination would come from non-poor households. In per capita terms, non-poor households would lose almost 4-5 times from the free trade scenario than their poor/extreme poor counterparts in the "net loser" group.

24.   In geographic terms, as expected, rural non-indigenous producers accounted for almost 92 percent of all total losses in the "net loser" group. Losses were smaller in indigenous areas in both absolute and relative. This can be explained by the fact that most indigenous producers are subsistence farmers whose output is consumed on-farm and, since it is not marketed, are not directly affected by tariff reductions. Also, many indigenous workers are involved in the production of other crops, such as bananas and coffee, which were not affected by the tariff reforms.

25.   Net losers tend to be concentrated in the provinces of Chiriqui, Los Santos and Darien, followed by Herrera, Veraguas and Cocle. Bocas del Toro and the more urban-dominated provinces of Colon and Panama would have the fewest net losers. The impact of these reforms on Darien and Veraguas, is of particular concern, since more than one half of the "net losers" in these provinces are poor. Likewise, around one third of all "net losers" in Herrera and Chiriqui are poor. Geographically-targeted compensating measures might thus be warranted to protect poor producers in these regions from the localized adverse affects of tariff reforms.

---

[12] By definition only producers of agricultural products can be part of the "Net losers" group.

Table A12.2 - Impact of Free Trade Reforms on "Net Losers"				
	Total Losses (millions B./)	Per Capita Losses (B./)	Losses as % of Per Capita Cons.	Population affected	
				# of persons	%
Total	8.2	177.3	9.7%	46,192	1.7%
By Poverty Group:					
Extreme Poor	0.4	46.9	11.5%	7,883	0.3%
All Poor	0.9	62.8	11.4%	14,692	0.5%
Non-Poor	7.3	230.7	10.4%	31,500	1.2%
By Geographic Area:					
Urban	0.6	212.0	8.8%	2,768	0.1%
Rural	7.5	182.6	10.7%	41,188	1.5%
Indigenous	0.1	36.3	7.4%	2,236	0.1%

Source: Panama LSMS 1997 and Yrarrazaval October and November 1997. Simulations assume zero elasticities and thus yield "upper bound" maximum estimates for the losses to producers. See Annex 12.1 for details on methodology and scenarios.

Net Distributional Impact

26. The net impact of the free trade hypothetical reform scenario on the economy depends on (a) the net gains to households (the balance of consumer gains against producer losses); (b) the balance of net gains to households against the loss of tariff revenue to the government from tariff reductions;[13] and (c) the efficiency gains arising from reductions in distortions. Because this paper is primarily concerned with the direct redistributional effects of trade and pricing reforms, the focus here is on the net effects on households.

27. Despite the losses to "net losers," the gains to "net gainers" would outweigh these losses (even using conservative assumptions), and the free trade scenarios yield an overall net gain, which is shared by more than 97 percent of the Panamanian population. The minimum[14] annual net gain to Panamanian households from the free trade scenario is B./124 million, as shown in Table A12.3 below. The average net gain is B./45 per capita, or 2.5 percent of average annual total per capita consumption.

28. Although the non-poor would receive larger absolute and per capita net gains from these hypothetical tariff reductions, the net gains are more important to the poor in relative terms. The simulations show that the free trade scenario would yield a net gain above five percent of total annual per capita consumption for the poor and extreme poor, compared with 2.2 percent for the non-poor.

29. The geographic distribution of net gains from a hypothetical elimination of trade tariffs would of course favor urban areas, since losses would accrue only to some agricultural producers. More remarkably, rural and indigenous areas would also gain in net terms. Households in the provinces of Colon and Panama appear to be the largest net beneficiaries of tariff reforms in per capita terms (which makes sense due to the small shares of agricultural producers in the populations of these provinces).

---

[13] Or the losses in quota rents to licensed importers in the case of quantitative restrictions.
[14] Minimum because the methodology used did not allow for consumers nor producers to adjust their consumption or production patterns to the new prices.

Table A12.3 - Impact of Free Trade (Hypothetical Elimination of 1997 Protection Levels)			
(+ gain, - loss)	Total Net Impact (millions B./)	Per Capita Net Impact (B./)	Net Impact as % of Per Capita Consumption (%)
Total	123.5	45.2	2.5
By Poverty Group:			
Extreme Poor	9.0	17.4	5.7%
All Poor	26.4	25.9	5.1%
Non-Poor	97.1	56.7	2.2%
By Geographic Area:			
Urban	86.9	57.2	2.2%
Rural	33.0	32.8	3.2%
Indigenous	3.5	17.1	5.2%
By Province:[a]			
Bocas del Toro	3.8	32.3	4.1%
Cocle	7.1	36.1	3.1%
Colon	12.7	56.6	4.3%
Chiriqui	14.0	32.3	2.4%
Darien	1.4	22.0	2.9%
Herrera	4.0	38.8	2.5%
Los Santos	1.8	23.2	1.3%
Panama	70.9	55.0	2.2%
Veraguas	7.8	34.6	3.7%

Source: Panama LSMS 1997 and Yrarrazaval October and November 1997. Simulations assume zero elasticities and thus yield "lower bound" minimum estimates for the gains to consumers and "upper bound" maximum estimates for the losses to producers. The net gains presented in this table thus represent the "lower bound" minimum net gains of tariff reforms. See Annex 1 for details on methodology and scenarios. a\Note that LSMS sample was not statistically representative at the province level.

Overall Redistributional Effects: Impact on Poverty and Inequality

30.   The overall impact of a hypothetical move to free trade for agricultural products was simulated using data from the LSMS. Poverty rates and Gini coefficients were calculated for 1997 as well as for the "free trade scenario" using the predicted *net* change (positive or negative) in per capita consumption, taking into account the gains for consumption and the losses in production incomes associated with the price reductions under the free trade scenario.

31.   Simulations suggest an overall decrease in the incidence of poverty and inequality with the hypothetical elimination of trade tariffs. It is estimated that a complete removal of trade barriers would cut the poverty rate 37.3 percent to 35.6 percent and the extreme poverty rate from 18.8 percent to 17.7 percent. The simulations also suggest that the Gini index for consumption inequality would be reduced by 0.58 percentage points, or 1.2 percent for the free trade scenario (bringing the consumption Gini to 47.97, as compared with 48.55 in 1997).

Impact on Employment and Growth

32.   The above discussion takes into account the effects of trade tariff reforms on consumers and producers. It ignores, however, the effects that these reforms might have on the employment of day laborers. In fact, one common fear of politicians is that a reduction of agricultural tariffs could cause a mass exodus of rural residents to the cities. Such an effect would not be likely for producers themselves (due to the loss of income from sales of agricultural products), because so few of the most marginal farmers or the landless poor are net losers (Table A12.4).

33.   If, however, employment of day laborers and/or wages decreased significantly because of the reforms, and to the extent that income from this source were important to some rural households, it might indeed induce migration.   Decisions by farm producers on the number of "man days" (*jornales*) to employ are influenced by many different factors, and statistically modeling these decisions is difficult. Moreover, the variations in employment observed in a one-time cross-sectional survey (the LSMS), which are the only basis available for statistical estimation, may not be an adequate foundation for predicting changes which occur over time.

Table A12.4 - Net Losers Under the 1998 Tariffs			
Owned Land	All Poor	Non-Poor	Total
Landless	0.2%	0.2%	0.4%
Under 1 ha	0.1%	0.0%	0.1%
1 - 2 ha	0.0%	0.0%	0.1%
2 - 5 ha	0.0%	0.1%	0.2%
5 - 15 ha	0.1%	0.2%	0.4%
Over 15 ha	0.1%	0.5%	0.6%
Table Total	0.5%	1.2%	1.7%
Source: Panama LSMS 1997. Estimates based on Scenario 1.			

34.   Despite these limitations, available information does, however, shed some light on the possible employment effects of tariff reductions. **First,** step-wise regressions using data from the LSMS reveal the sensitivity (or lack of it) of employment and wages to changes in the sales of various agricultural products. These regressions indicate that employment (*jornales*) is somewhat sensitive to changes in the sales of beans, corn, rice, onions and sugar, all of which have traditionally been protected by high agricultural tariffs.[15] It was <u>not</u> sensitive to changes in sales of other protected products, such as milk and milk products, pork or potatoes. Likewise, wages are somewhat sensitive to changes in the sales of beans, corn, rice, onions, sugar, and milk, but not to changes in the sales of other protected products, such as cheese, pork or potatoes. Thus employment and wages could be lowered *if* the reduction in tariff protection were to lower the sales of the above-mentioned products.

35.   **Second**, data on the labor intensity and importance of protected crops yields some indication of the relative importance of possible employment effects of these changes. Labor intensity is rather low for the production of corn and rice, the two highly protected crops that have occupied a large share of the total cultivated area in Panama: available data indicate that rice generally requires five (for rainfed) to thirteen (for irrigated) *jornales* per hectare; for corn, the figure ranges from eleven to 29 *jornales*, depending on the yield and type of technology used. This is quite low when compared with labor input requirements for traditional non-export crops, which do not enjoy such high levels of tariff protection (123 for *ñame*, 126 for *otoe lila*, 81 for okra, and 117 for plantains). The cultivated area of protected crops with higher labor intensity, such as onions, potatoes, tomatoes and peas, has been smaller, with little impact on the total demand for unskilled labor.[16]

36.   Moreover, Panama has traditionally maintained low or zero tariff rates on agricultural inputs -- including machinery. This, combined with tax exemptions for investments in agricultural machinery,

---

[15] The sales of live pigs also had a significant effect on wages and employment, but tariff protection for live pigs was not high in recent years.

[16] Yrarrazaval (October 1997), with data from: Magdaleno Prado (June 1993), "Situación Actual, Oportunidades y Desafíos de la Actividad Arrocera en Panamá" IICA; Rodrigo R. Marciaq (1994), "La cadena agroalimentaria Maíz/Sorgo-Alimentos Balanceados - Aves/Cerdos" IICA; and Technoserve Inc. (March 1995), "Planes de Negocios para la Producción y Exportación de Ñame, Otoe Lila, Ocra, y Plátano."

subsidized interest rates for agricultural credit via the FECI, and minimum wage requirements for agricultural workers,[17] have historically biased production decisions against the hiring of labor.[18]

37.   Thus, while some reduction in employment (and possibly agricultural wages) would likely occur from cuts in tariff protection, given the lower labor intensity of traded crops, it seems improbable that this effect would be large or would spur mass migration to the cities. Moreover, the longer run effect of reducing protective tariffs on activities in which Panama does not have a comparative advantage and of setting lower uniform tariffs across sectors will be to create jobs through the promotion of economic growth.[19]

ANNEX 12.1: SIMPLE METHODOLOGY
FOR ESTIMATING THE REDISTRIBUTIONAL IMPACT OF TRADE REFORMS

Overview of Methodology

1.   The reduction of trade barriers generally entails two types of impacts: an overall efficiency gain due to the removal of distortions in production and consumption decisions and redistributional effects. In the context of the Panama Poverty Assessment, this paper is primarily concerned with the later. Producers generally lose from the decrease in prices associated with the removal of trade barriers. For the economy as a whole, these losses are generally more than offset by the gains to consumers associated with the reduction in the cost of basic staples (as well as by the efficiency gains discussed above). Even some producers stand to gain in net terms if the value of their marketed output is lower than the total value of quantities purchased (e.g., small farmers). But some producers will still lose in net terms, even taking into account the gains that they would accrue as consumers. This paper thus seeks to identify the characteristics of the net losers and net winners, in particular with respect to their poverty status. If the analysis reveals that certain groups of poor producers are net losers, targeted compensation may be needed to mitigate the poverty impact of these adjustment measures.

2.   The distributional impact of trade reforms on households was simulated using the LSMS. Ideally, elasticities of supply and demand would be used to take into account the behavioral responses of producers and consumers. The cross-sectional nature of the LSMS complicates the estimation of price elasticities, however.[20] Instead, this analysis adopts "zero elasticity of substitution" assumptions for producers and consumers, which has the advantage of providing an upper bound estimate of the losses to producers and a lower bound estimate of the gains to consumers. In other words, by calculating the minimum gain to consumers and the maximum loss to producers, we obtain the "worst case" estimate of the potential net losses to producers. The actual impacts of trade reforms will probably be better than these results, because producers have the option of switching to more profitable products and consumers to cheaper substitutes. Using these conservative assumptions, the net losses for producers could indicate the maximum amount that might be needed to compensate them for the reforms. Indeed, if the "net loss" producers are poor, the Government may wish to target some amount of compensation to these producers.

---

[17] The artificially high prices of basic staples due to high tariff protection has also created pressure to maintain high real wages. The incorporation of these higher costs into the calculation of higher minimum wages has thus also contributed to lower employment in the country.

[18] Yrarrazaval (October 1997).

[19] It should also be noted that unemployment appears to have fallen in 1997.

[20] Elasticities could be estimated using spatial variation in prices with a method developed by Deaton (June 1988).

Limitations of Methodology for Analysis

3.   Although this simple methodology has the advantages that (a) it is computationally simple; and (b) it provides the "worst case" estimate of the potential net losses to producers, it has a number of limitations. **First,** by assuming zero elasticities, it is not possible to measure the net gains to the overall economy from improved efficiency that are associated with the removal of distortions in production and consumption incentives.

4.   **Second,** by focusing on the direct redistributive effects of trade reform at the household level, the analysis ignores the impact on licensed importers (in the case of quotas) and government revenue (in the case of tariffs). With quantitative restrictions (quotas, licenses, licensed importers collected rents from buying cheaper imports and selling them in the domestic economy at the minimum guaranteed prices.[21] Given the household focus, this analysis does not take into account the losses that these importers would accrue as quantitative restrictions on imports are phased out and as protection is reduced. It is unlikely that these importers were poor, however, so the redistribution of these rents from importers to consumers would likely have a positive effect on the poor. In the case of tariffs, the analysis does not take into account the lost tariffs revenues that the Government had previously collected on imports. Because of the historical reliance on quantitative restrictions, however, these revenues have been quite small.[22] The poor could be hurt if these lost revenues translate into cuts in government expenditures on programs that are important to the poor. However, if the Government were to maintain its revenues through some other means of tax collection (e.g., via income taxes) in the face of tariff reductions, the effect of switching from tariffs on basic staples (which are quite important to the poor) to other forms of tax collection (e.g., income taxes, which are generally based on a progressive scale), the overall redistributive effect would be progressive.

5.   **Third,** by focusing on the direct redistributive effects of trade reform at the household level, the methodology does not take into account the potential effects on other actors along the marketing chain (e.g., processors who use the products in question as inputs). **Finally,** with its strong "ceteris paribus" assumptions, the methodology does not take into account other reforms (e.g., non-food trade reforms), which could change the relative prices of food products with respect to other products. Instead, the analysis focuses on the direct effects of the trade and pricing reforms involving basic staples. Despite these limitations, the methodology is a computationally simple way to estimate the redistributive effects of trade reforms at the household level.[23]

Reform Scenario: A Hypothetical Elimination of Trade Tariffs

6.   The continuous and different phasing of reforms for various products and the timing of data collection under the LSMS (conducted in June-September 1997) complicates the analysis of the impact of specific reforms. As such, this analysis simulates the distributional impact of a "free trade scenario," which involves they hypothetical elimination of all tariffs compared to their 1997 levels (using 1997 international prices for reference). Percentage reductions in prices were applied to the actual prices

---

[21] Licensed importers only paid a small fee (usually three percent) on importers. This fee was much lower than the difference between the lower CIF prices they paid for imports and the higher domestic prices they received on their sales.

[22] In 1995, total revenues collected represented only ten to eleven percent of the CIF value of all agricultural imports.

[23] An interesting aspect for further research concerns the potential impact of trade reforms at the *intra-household* level on relative gender bargaining situations if there is a clear division of labor between men and women in agriculture (e.g., if men specialize in tradable cash crops while women specialize in non-tradable subsistence crops, as has been found in other countries). Unfortunately, the LSMS did not gather disaggregated information on agricultural production by crop and by gender. The labor section of the questionnaire does show that the number of women working in agriculture as a whole in Panama is very small. Overall, only six percent of employed women work in agriculture. Among the poor, the figure is a bit higher (21 percent). As shown above, very few "net losers" from trade reforms were poor. Thus it is unlikely that a the reforms generated a large number of "net losing" women.

observed in the LSMS data. While this scenario is hypothetical, it does paint a picture of the potential distributional effects of recent and future reductions in equivalent tariffs at the household level. See Annex Table A1 for details of the scenario by product.

Impact on Consumers

7.   **Assumptions.**   A simple, but useful, analysis holds the quantities consumed *constant* and calculates the impact of the above price changes on consumers. This assumption of zero elasticities allows us to gauge the *minimum* benefit to consumers of the price reductions associated with tariff cuts (since, in reality, consumers would adjust their consumption in favor higher consumption of the newly relatively cheaper products, thus obtaining higher benefits). The overall impact thus yields a *lower-bound* minimum gain to consumers from these reforms. This lower-bound is useful for policy analysis because it presents a conservative estimate of the potential benefits from these reforms -- the actual gains to consumers are likely to be higher.

8.   **Quantity Data from LSMS.** The quantity data used for the analysis comes from the "gastos" section of the LSMS. The analysis uses data on *quantities purchased*, since changes in tariffs don't affect un-marketed quantities for own-consumption (particularly since the analysis holds quantities constant). The level of analysis is *per capita* (household consumption divided by number of members) and *per year*. Finally, the analysis is conducted using the "expanded" sample (using the *factores de expansion).*

9.   **Products.** The products analyzed and their prices used in the various scenarios are described in Annex Table A1. An attempt was made to match the product categories from the LSMS as closely as possible with the products specified for tariffs.

10.   **Price Data.** The analysis uses the prices actually faced by consumers at the time of the survey for the base (pre-reform) prices. These come from data collected in the LSMS. The "new" prices are then calculated under the various scenarios using the percentage changes in prices described for each scenario in Annex Table A1.

11.   **Impact on Consumers.** The overall savings to consumers from the price reductions is simulated by adding up the absolute value of savings for each product. The relative importance of these savings is then calculated as a share of the total per capita consumption. Annex Table A2 provides an hypothetical example of this methodology for a hypothetical consumer.

Impact on Producers

12.   **Assumptions.** A simple, but useful, analysis holds the quantities produced *constant* and calculates the impact of the above price changes on producers. This assumption of zero elasticities allows us to gauge the *maximum* loss to producers of the price reductions associated with tariff cuts (since, in reality, producers would eventually adjust their production in favor of lower production of the newly relatively cheaper products, thus reducing their losses). The overall impact thus yields an *upper-bound* maximum loss to producers from these reforms. This upper-bound is useful for policy analysis because it presents a conservative estimate of the potential losses from these reforms -- the actual losses to producers are likely to be lower.

13.   **Quantity Data from LSMS.** The quantity data used for the analysis comes from the "agro-pecuario" section of the LSMS. The analysis uses data on *quantities sold for cash and barter* (4&11)[24], since changes in tariffs don't affect un-marketed quantities for own-consumption, seed, feed, losses, etc. (particularly since we are holding quantities constant). The level of analysis is *per capita* (household production divided by number of members) and *per year*. Finally, the analysis uses the "expanded" sample (using the *factores de expansion).*

14.   **Products.** The products are described in Annex Table A1 below.

15.   **Price Data.** The analysis uses the prices actually received by producers at the time of the survey for the base (pre-reform) prices. These come from data collected in the LSMS. The "new" prices under various scenarios are then calculated using the percentage changes in prices described for each scenario in Annex Table A1 below.

16.   **Impact on Producers.** The overall losses to producers from the price reductions are calculated by adding up the absolute value of losses for each product. The relative importance of these losses is then calculated as a share of total per capita consumption[25]. The method is analogous to the hypothetical example used for consumers in Annex Table A2.

Net Impact on Producers and Consumers

17.   The net impact of reductions in trade barriers on the economy depends on (a) the net gains to the private economy (the balance of consumer gains against producer losses); (b) the balance of net gains to the private economy against the loss of tariff revenue to the government from tariff reductions;[26] and (c) the efficiency gains arising from reductions in distortions. Because this paper is primarily concerned with the direct redistributional effects of trade and pricing reforms, the focus here is on the net effects on households. By measuring producer losses against consumer gains, the analysis highlights the extent of net losses to producers and the characteristics of the net gainers and losers.

18.   The "zero-elasticity" methodology described above is useful because it yields an estimate of the *maximum* adverse effect (maximum net loss or minimum net gain as the case may be) of the trade reforms at the household level. In other words, by calculating the minimum gain to consumers and the maximum loss to producers, we obtain the "worst case" estimate for each scenario. The actual impacts will probably be better than these results. Generally the gains to consumers more than offset the losses to producer, though certain groups of producers tend to lose in net terms. The net losses for these producers could indicate the maximum amount that might be needed to compensate them for the reforms.

19.   Using the outputs obtained for consumers and producers above, the net impact per capita for producers and consumers is calculated as follows:

NET IMPACT = CHANGE IN CONSUMPTION = CONSUMPTION * (%gains from consumption - % losses from production)

20.   The *relative* net impact is the part of the previous equation in parenthesis. This gives an indication of the relative importance of these changes to different groups.

---

[24] Quantities sold for cash and barter represent gross income to the producer. We assume that the producers' input quantities and costs are held constant.

[25] When income in the household is higher than consumption, the relative importance is calculated as a percentage or Income.

[26] Or the losses in quota rents to licensed importers in the case of quantitative restrictions.

Annex Table A1 - PANAMA: TRADE REFORM SCENARIOS

Product	P=producer C=cons. (LSMS code)	Unit	Prices Under Different Scenarios		Tariff Rates	
			1997 Pre-Reform	Free Trade (FT)	Versus Free Trade 1997 Pre-Reform	Free Trade (FT) vs. 1997
RICE						
To the producer, paddy at the farm	P	B/qq	9.27	5.64	64%	-39%
To the consumer	C (20)	B/qq	30.00	20.77	44%	-31%
CORN						
To the producer, at the farm	P	B/qq	10.96	7.02	56%	-36%
At wholesale, MAC, Panama City	C (22, 23, 24)	B/qq	12.37	8.33	48%	-33%
SORGHUM						
To the producer (no consumption)	P (no C)	B/qq	8.75	8.52	3%	-3%
BEANS (frijoles)						
Domestic at wholesale, MAC	P	B/qq	65.04	48.00	36%	-26%
To the consumer	C (17, 18, 19)	B/qq	100.00	73.00	37%	-27%
LENTILS						
At wholesale, MAC	P	B/qq	35.31	29.82	18%	-16%
To the consumer	C (16)	B/qq	60.00	51.00	18%	-15%
POTATOES						
To the producer, at the "plaza"	P	B/qq	24.04	19.01	26%	-21%
To the consumer	C (45)	B/qq	34.75	29.47	18%	-15%
ONIONS						
To the producer, at the "plaza"	P	B/qq	30.00	16.90	78%	-44%
To the consumer	C (36)	B/qq	37.00	26.36	40%	-29%
SUGAR, white, refined						
To the consumer, 100 lb sack	C (28)	B/qq	30.00	21.00	43%	-30%
To the producer, *sugar cane*	P	B/short ton	16.00	11.00	45%	-31%
BEEF, meat						
To the consumer	C (7, 8)	B/lb	1.35	1.35	0%	0%
PORK, meat						
To the consumer: puerco liso (meat)	C (9)	B/lb	1.75	1.75	0%	0%
To the consumer: pernil	C (12 embutidos)	B/lb	1.58	1.01	56%	-36%
CHICKEN, meat						
To the consumer: whole	P, C (10/11)	B/lb	1.05	0.91	15%	-13%
MILK						
To the producer, grade C	P	B/lb	0.225	0.163	38%	-28%
To the consumer:						
Powdered milk, 400 gr. can	C (2)	B/unit	2.24	1.865	20%	-17%
Evaporated milk, 170 gr. can	C (4)	B/unit	0.33	0.27	22%	-18%
Fresh milk, 1 liter	C (3)	B/liter	0.70	0.58	21%	-17%
White cheese, national, 1 pound	C (5)	B/lb	1.98	1.64	21%	-17%

Source: Price scenarios from Yrarrazaval, October and November 1997.

Annex Table A2 - Hypothetical Example of Methodology for Analyzing the Impact of Trade Reforms on Consumers

	LSMS Code	Purchased Quantity per capita 100 g	Actual Price per 100 g	Expenditures per capita B./	Free Trade Scenario		Hold Quantity Fixed	
					% Price Change	New Price	New Outlays	Difference in Outlays
Rice	20	117.8	0.31	37	-0.31	0.21	25	11
Corn (en grano/mazorca)	22&23	34.2	0.21	7	-0.33	0.14	5	2
Corn products (preparados)	24	17.0	0.34	6	-0.33	0.23	4	2
Beans (frijoles)	17	8.4	0.9	8	-0.27	0.66	6	2
Lentils	16	8.4	0.69	6	-0.15	0.59	5	1
Potatos	45	12.8	0.38	5	-0.15	0.32	4	1
Onions	36	9.1	0.47	4	-0.29	0.33	3	1
Sugar	28	35.9	0.31	11	-0.3	0.22	8	3
Pork meat	9	9.1	1.31	12	-0.08	1.21	11	1
Embutidos (pernil)	12	5.8	1.54	9	-0.36	0.99	6	3
Chicken	10	23.6	1.11	26	-0.25	0.83	20	7
Powdered Milk	2	8.5	2.62	22	-0.17	2.17	19	4
Evaporated Milk	4	10.6	1.02	11	-0.18	0.84	9	2
Fresh Milk (liquida)	3	43.7	0.29	13	-0.17	0.24	11	2
Cheese	5	4.7	1.93	9	-0.17	1.60	8	2
TOTAL				185			141	44
As share of total consumption per capita (470)				39%			30%	9%

Annex 13 - Improving the Impact of Pre-Schools in Panama

Kinnon Scott
December 1998

INTRODUCTION

1.   Evidence that attendance in preschool programs can have a positive impact on a child's education and health has spurred countries like Panama to increase the number of such programs and national enrollment levels.   Preschool education is seen as a cost effective intervention that increases a child's school readiness and lowers repetition rates, thus reducing both public and private costs associated with primary level schooling.   In addition, preschool attendance has been shown to increase a child's overall educational attainment, thus improving the earnings profile of the individual in the future.

2.   Panama has begun to focus significant attention on increasing the coverage of preschool programs in the country, either through traditional, school-based, pre-school programs or through new, less expensive community programs.   Although the overall enrollment rate is low compared to that of other countries in the region, in recent years, enrollment rates have increased substantially in Panama. The impact of such increases has not been assessed to date.   On the one hand, the recent nature of much preschool education in Panama precludes the existence of longitudinal studies measuring the impact of preschool attendance on repetition and dropout rates, and educational attainment and earnings.   But even short-term evaluations of the impact of preschool education in Panama have not been done.

3.   The purpose of the present paper is to shed some light on the impact of preschool education in Panama.   While an in-depth study of this topic is not possible at present due to the lack of longitudinal data, the present study does provide a preliminary evaluation of the impact of public spending on preschool in Panama by combining information from studies of other countries with data from several sources in Panama on the present distribution of preschool opportunities.   This assessment provides information on whether the impact of present public spending on preschool education can be increased. Given that attendance in preschool depends not just on government spending but also on each household's decision to enroll preschool age children, an analysis of the determinants of preschool attendance is also included.   While limited by data to only urban areas, the analysis sheds light on other variables amenable to policy intervention.

4.   The paper is organized into five sections. The first section presents a brief overview of the effect preschool education has been shown to have in other countries.   In section two, information on preschool programs in Panama is presented.   Section 3 provides data on the distribution of preschool programs by area and poverty using previous poverty maps and new data from the Living Standards Survey (*Encuesta de niveles de vida*) carried out by the Ministry of Planning.   In the fourth section the determinants of attendance in pre-schools are identified and the final section presents tentative recommendations on increasing the impact of public investment in preschool education.

I.   THE IMPORTANCE OF PRE-SCHOOL

5.   Preschool programs have been shown to provide a variety of benefits both to the children who attend them and to their families. The three main types of benefits that are discussed here are in the areas of education, health and labor markets.   Although improvements in educational results are the most commonly cited effect of preschool, the other two are also important.

(i)   Education

6.   Educational attainment is a key predictor of future income and, hence welfare. A variety of studies have shown the strong impact of years of schooling on income.[1] Equally important, higher levels of educational attainment affect children's welfare directly: parental education (especially the mother's) is related to improved nutrition of children, and to higher probabilities of attending formal education as well as educational attainment of the children.[2]

7.   Given the correlation of education and earnings, increasing educational attainment is a key focus of government education policy. One element of this overall effort to increase attainment is to increase attendance in preschool. Studies have shown that preschool education increases children's cognitive ability[3] both directly after preschool and in the longer term.[4] Repetition rates in primary school are lower for children who have attended preschool[5] and long term studies have shown that overall educational attainment is increased by pre-school attendance.[6]

8.   There is evidence of a 'pro-poor' bias in preschool's impact on children. In some studies, pre-school education has been shown to have a stronger impact on poor and disadvantaged children than on non-poor children. In Chile, it was found that pre-school programs increased reading readiness of poor, rural children but had no noticeable impact on non-poor children.[7] In the United States, pre-school programs have been shown to affect poorer and some minority children more strongly.[8] There is also an equity argument made for preschool: given that fact that poor children start formal schooling with various disadvantages that limit their success in schooling, increasing preschool access to poor children serves to decrease educational inequities in a country.[9] While not all studies show a clear distinction between the impact of preschool on poor and non-poor children,[10] it has been argued that this is a function of the low quality of the preschool programs faced by poor or disadvantaged children.[11]

(ii)   Health

9.   A second benefit from preschool attendance is the health benefit. It is argued that preschool attendance allows for nutritional and other problems to be identified, and addressed, at an earlier age.[12] One outcome of specific pre-school programs in the United States has been increased height-per-age among attendees and increased incidence of vaccination,[13] benefits which accrue even to groups not evidencing educational benefits. Given the greater probability of malnutrition and other health ailments among poor children, non-educational preschool benefits may be greater for this group than for the preschool age population as a whole.

---

[1] See Psacharopoulos, 1993 for a summary of the literature on the topic; and Psacharopoulos and Ng, 1992 for information specific to Latin America.

[2] Scott, 1995; Psacharopoulos and Arriagada, 1989; Cochrane and Jamison, 1981.

[3] Currie and Thomas, 1993; Raudenbush et al, 1991; Filp et al 1983.

[4] Early assessments of the Head Start Program (a preschool program in the United States) appeared to indicate a fading of this initial improvement (see Zigler and Muenchow, 1992 for a history of this program and its evaluations) but later work has shown the effects to be more lasting (Currie and Thomas, 1993).

[5] Meyers and Hertenberg, 1987; MS/INAN, 1983.

[6] Currie and Thomas, 1993; Berrueta-Clement et al, 1983.

[7] Filp et al, 1983.

[8] Currie and Thomas, 1996; Currie and Thomas, 1993.

[9] Filp et al, 1983.

[10] Raudenbush et al, 1991; Pozner, 1983.

[11] Currie and Thomas, 1993; Raudenbush et al, 1991.

[12] Prakasha, 1983.

[13] Currie and Thomas, 1993.

(iii) Labor Force Participation

10.   A third benefit espoused for preschool programs is the labor effect on women. Labor force participation of women is limited by the presence of small children in the household.[14] Preschool programs free mothers' time by taking over childcare functions. This allows mothers' to increase their participation in the labor force. This, in turn, improves household welfare by increasing incomes.

11.   In summary, several studies have shown preschool education to be an important part of the larger educational system. It increases children's abilities to learn and to perform in formal schooling and further serves to increase welfare through the associated benefits to health and labor force participation. Evidence that poorer and disadvantaged children benefit more from preschool indicates that increasing access to such programs for these children will enhance the impact of national investments in preschool. Clearly, along with increased access will need to come increased quality to ensure that the investment provides the benefits expected.

II.   PRE-SCHOOL PROGRAMS IN PANAMA

12.   Panama has worked to increase coverage of preschool programs in recent years. The education reform law of 1995 provides for a basic education package of eleven years of obligatory free schooling: two years of pre-school or pre-primary, six years of primary, and three years of middle school. Although two years of pre-primary schooling are included, attendance will become progressively obligatory in accordance with the capacity of the government. And, in the three years since the law was passed, it has not been possible to expand preschool coverage to a universal level: programs are not available in many areas of the country. It may well be that universal coverage by the public sector is not a desirable goal anyway, but, as is shown below, there is certainly room for increasing and targeting coverage.

13.   There are two main types of preschool program in Panama. The first type can be called 'initial education' and consists of three programs designed to promote socialization among young children as well as provide some measure of nutritional intervention and childcare. The principal programs at this level are the nursery schools provided by the Ministry of Education (for four year olds), Community and Family Centers for Initial Education (CEFACEIs for two to six year olds), known as Centers for Infant and Family Orientation (COIFs for three and four year olds), under the direction of the Ministry of Youth, Women, Children and Family.[15] The second type of program is formal kindergarten for five year olds. The Ministry of Education provides the program for approximately two-thirds of enrolled five year olds and the private sector furnishes the remainder. Overall, approximately 33,000 children were enrolled in this type of program in 1992.[16]

14.   In practice the differences among the programs are not as clear as would be expected. Both types of programs include a mixture of children of different ages; even the formal kindergarten allows four year olds to enroll. In addition, the content of the programs are not distinct: there is overlap in both the content and the teaching methodologies of these programs. Given this overlap it is more useful to talk of all preschool enrollments and not focus on one or another type.

15.   In all programs, enrollment rates have increased substantially in recent decades. In 1970 only 8 percent of children of pre-school age (four and five year olds) attended pre-school programs. In 1996, this net enrollment rate had increased to 30.5 percent.[17] Just in the period between 1990 and 1996, the gross enrollment rate increased approximately 25 percent: for four year olds the rate went from 8.1 percent to 10.5 and for five year olds, from 40.7 percent to 50.6 percent. While having increased

---

[14] See Psacharopoulos and Tzannatos, 1992 for evidence from Latin America.
[15] World Bank 1995.
[16] World Bank, 1996.
[17] World Bank, 1995, and tables provided by the Ministries of Education (MOE) and Planning and Economic Policy (MIPPE) of Panama..

substantially, relative to other countries in the region, the enrollment rates for five year olds are low: in Chile the rate is over 75 percent and in Costa Rica over 90 percent.[18]

16.   Overall education spending in Panama, as a share of GDP, has stayed reasonably constant at 4.7 percent in the 1990s. Its importance in government expenditures, however, has dropped.   As a share of social spending, public spending on education reached a peak in 1993 and has since declined. Present levels are somewhat lower than at the start of the decade. The relatively low number of children attending pre-school programs is reflected in the low share of education spending devoted to pre-school. Unfortunately, no data are available on the trends in pre-school spending but, given the increase in coverage in recent years, it is expected that spending has increased also.[19]

Table 1: Public Expenditures on Education

	1990	1991	1992	1993	1994	1995	1996
Education spending as share of:							
GDP	4.6	4.7	4.7	5.4	4.7	4.7	5.3
Gov. Expend.	11.0	9.3	8.3	11.4	10.8	9.9	9.7
Social Spending	27.7	26.2	27.8	30.1	28.0	25.5	25.9
Education Spending by Level:							
Pre-School & Primary	42.7	43.0	37.3	28.5	32.1	32.2	28.2
Pre-Primary			1.7				
Primary			35.6				
Secondary	26.4	27.0	26.1	37.2	31.6	30.2	35.6
Higher education	29.6	28.4	35.0	32.2	34.0	35.4	33.8

Source: Table created by Ministry of Planning, based on figures of the National Budget Office, figure for pre-primary and primary split for 1992 from World Bank, 1996.
Note: Education spending includes spending by Ministry of Education and INAFORP. Social spending consists of spending on education, health, housing and labor and Social security.

17.   Data from the recent living standards measurement survey (*Encuesta de Niveles de Vida*, ENV)[20], show that 60 percent of all pre-school education (both pre-kinder and kindergarten) is provided by the Ministry of Education, with slightly less than one-third from the private sector. (See Graph 1). The remaining pre-school is provided by other government agencies, municipal governments and community based programs.

---

[18] Unesco, 1993b.

[19] It is important to note that there are also significant expenditures by households on pre-school. As shown by the ENV (see Annex 1), children in public pre-schools incur annual costs of US$158 (in private, US$751). Compared to per capita consumption levels, the amount paid by poor children for pre-school may represent a barrier to enrollment: poor children in preschool, on average spend US$ 88 a year (non-poor children in pre-school, public or private, pay an average of US$460.

[20] The ENV is a multi-topic household survey carried out by the Ministry of Planning of Panama in 1997. The survey used a national sample, the only survey in the country to include rural areas of difficult access and indigenous areas in its sample. Data was collected from approximately 5000 households on consumption, access to and use of social services and infrastruture, as well as wage labor, self-employment and agricultural activities of the households. For further details of the survey see: *Encuesta de Niveles de Vida: Documentacion Basica*," MIPPE, January 1998.

Graph 1: Source of Pre-School

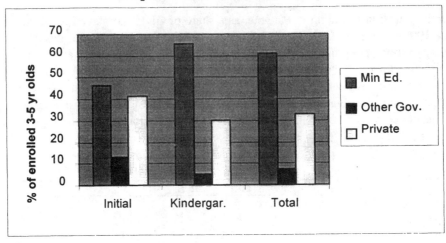

Source: ENV 1997, author's calculations

18.   In summary, while the trend in preschool attendance is positive, with large gains being made nationally, there are still a significant number of children who do not attend pre-school. If the gains to pre-school attendance found in other countries hold true in Panama, and there is no reason to think otherwise, the lack of coverage has the effect of lowering the overall educational attainment in the country relative to what could be achieved if a greater number of children were enrolled in pre-school programs.

19.   While, increasing the overall number of preschools and children attending them clearly will have a significant impact on attainment nationally, it is also important to look at the actual distribution of preschool education in the country.   Are there ways in which the existing resources might be distributed to have more impact overall and/or on breaking the vicious cycle of poverty? The following section addresses these issues.

III.   THE IMPACT OF THE PRESENT DISTRIBUTION OF PRE-SCHOOL

20.   To determine the optimal level of public financing and distribution of public preschool programs in the country, longitudinal data that allow for tracing differences in educational and occupational outcomes of children who did and did not attend preschool would be needed. Such data do not exist, so the present assessment of the impact of preschool spending is based on previous studies in other countries that have identified the key effects of preschool education as well as data from Panama indicating who attends preschool education. The Panama specific information is from one of two sources, administrative records of the Ministry of Education or the household level data collected under the ENV 1997.

21.   If the findings from other countries that preschool attendance lowers repetition rates and may have a greater impact on poorer and disadvantaged children hold true in Panama, it could be argued that the impact of preschool spending would be highest if the existing resources were targeted to either children at high risk of repetition and/or poor or disadvantaged children. The focus of the present section is to determine the extent to which actual preschool programs are, or are not, targeted to such groups in the country.

(i)   Repetition Rates

22.   In the long run, and with universal preschool coverage (either public or private) in a given area, one would hope to see a positive correlation between low repetition rates and high preschool enrollment rates, all else being equal. In Panama, where the increase in preschool attendance is recent and where coverage, even in a specific geographic area, is low, a pattern of low repetition rates in primary and high enrollment in preschool would not yet be expected. Instead, as an effort to decrease high repetition rates, investment in preschool should be highest in those areas of the country with the highest repetition rates. This does not, however, appear to be the case.

23.   In fact, public spending on preschool does not favor areas with high primary school repetition rates. In 1995, the Ministry of Education estimates that repetition rates at the primary level were slightly higher than 10 percent nationally.   As

Table 2: Urban-Rural Primary School Repetition Rates, 1995

Level	Urban	Rural	National
All primary	5.4	13.0	10.2
First grade	9.5	21.6	--

Source: Ministry of Education.

shown in Table 2, the rates varied substantially between rural and urban areas with rural rates being 13 percent and urban ones of 5.4 percent. For first grade only, rural repetition rates were 21.6; more than twice the urban rate of 9.5 percent.   Yet, the household level data, from the ENV, show that rural children are much less likely than urban ones to participate in preschool. In urban areas, over 70 percent of all children attend preschool while only 37 percent of children in rural, non-indigenous areas were enrolled and, in indigenous areas[21] only 19 percent of children attended preschool. (See Graph 2).

Graph 2: Population in Poverty by Geographic Area and Pre-school Attendance

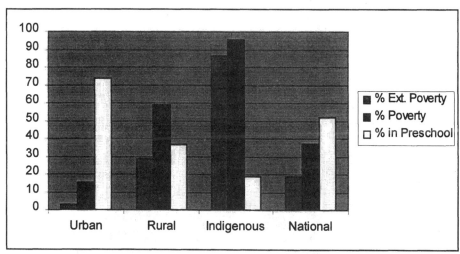

Source: ENV 1997.
Note: Extreme poverty and general poverty refer to percentage of all individuals. Percent in pre-school refers to all children aged five. Pre-school includes both kindergarten and pre-kindergarten.

---

[21] The country is divided, geographically, into four areas: urban and then three rural areas: general rural, difficult access and indigenous. For the administrative records of the Ministry of Education no distinction is made among the types of rural areas. For the ENV results, difficult access and general rural are combined and indigenous rural areas are shown separately.

24.   Administrative data from the Ministry of Education show that at the province level also, areas with high primary school repetition rates are not favored in terms of preschool programs. As can be seen in Table 3, the two provinces with the highest repetition rates, Darien and Bocas del Toro, are precisely those with the lowest rate of preschool enrollment. In short, areas with lower repetition rates are receiving more preschool investment than other areas. Some of the potential benefit of preschool spending on decreasing repetition rates is being lost.

Table 3: Repetition Rates in Primary and Enrollment Rates in Preschool, by Province

Province	Repetition Rates[1]: Primary	Net Enrollment: Preschool
San Blas	15.8	. . .
Darien	22.1	39.9
Bocas del Toro	17.1	31.1
Veraguas	13.1	51.7
Chiriqui	10.9	41.5
Cocle	7.8	49.0
Herrera	9.6	59.5
Colon	10.5	49.8
Los Santos	6.7	55.0
Panama	7.4	42.7
Total	10.2	45.5

... Not available.
[1] Refers only to Public School.
Source: Ministry of Education, Statistics Department.

(ii)   Poverty

25.   Preschool programs in Panama are not well targeted to the poor either, even though poorer children might benefit more from such programs than their non-poor counterparts. Data from the 1997 ENV were used to calculate the preschool attendance rates among the extreme poor, the poor and the non-poor.[22] As shown in Graph 3, pre-school attendance is rare among those in extreme poverty: only six percent of children aged 3-5 who live in extreme poverty are enrolled in a preschool program of any sort.   Among all poor (including the extreme poor) enrollment rates are still low at just over twelve percent. In fact, it is only among the non-poor that pre-school enrollment is at all common, with slightly more than one-third attending a preschool program.

Graph 3: Poverty and Pre-School Enrollment

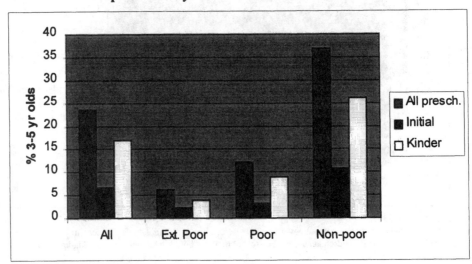

Source: ENV 1997, MIPPE.

---

[22] Poverty is defined as having a per capita consumption below the poverty line of B/905 per year and extreme poverty as having per capita consumption below the extreme line of B/519 per year.

26.   Another important feature of the distribution of pre-school attendance mentioned above (Graph 2) is that attendance in pre-primary programs is heavily skewed to urban dwellers. As can be seen in the Graph, urban poverty is significantly lower than poverty in both rural areas and indigenous areas.   If preschool is heavily skewed to urban areas, and urban areas are significantly less poor than other areas in the country, it is not, perhaps, surprising that the highest levels of attendance are among the non-poor.

27.   Figures from 1992, which plot preschool enrollment against a Basic Needs Index confirm these findings (see Table 4).   If all provinces are ranked according to a basic needs index,[23] the poorest provinces do not have the highest rates of pre-school enrollment. In fact, the second and third poorest provinces have the lowest pre-school enrollment rates in the country.

Table 4: Enrollment Rates and Basic Needs Index by Province, 1992

Province	Basic Needs Index[1]	Net Enrollment
San Blas	19.1	. . .
Darien	29.9	39.9
Bocas del Toro	47.3	31.1
Veraguas	52.3	51.7
Chiriqui	67.9	41.5
Cocle	71.8	49.0
Herrera	80.1	59.5
Colon	84.8	49.8
Los Santos	85.7	55.0
Panama	94.9	42.7
Total	. . .	45.5

Source: World Bank, 1996.
1/ This is a Basic Needs Index (called the Poverty Index) where the lowest score represents the lowest level of welfare or the highest level of need.
... Not available.

28.   A final point on the targeting of preschool programs by poverty is the importance of public spending on preschool attendance.   As can be seen in Graph 4, without   public   spending,   preschool opportunities would not exist for extremely poor children and even among all poor children it would be minimal. Thus, the government's decisions about where and how to invest in preschool have a significant impact on the welfare of poor children and their educational opportunities.

---

[23] The MIPPE poverty map is based on an index of the following characteristics: Housing which includes the percent of households with running water, sanitary services and electricity, and crowding; education which is based on the percent of children ages 5-15 who are not in school, the percent of persons over age 10 who are illiterate and those with less than three years of primary school; and, third, health indicators of infant mortality rate, percent of first grade students with stunting and the percent of births not attended by medical personnel.

Graph 4: Source of Preschool Programs by Poverty Group

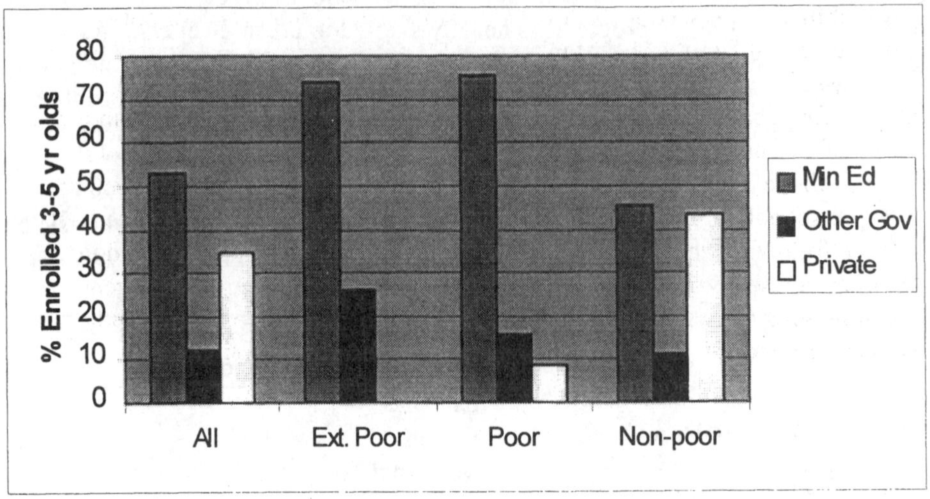

Source: ENV 1997, author's calculations

29.   Overall, pre-school education is being largely consumed by the non-poor and urban children. Even though the non-poor use the private sector more that the poor the majority of public spending on preschool education benefits the non-poor.   Both from an equity and an efficiency perspective, the present use of preschool resources may diminish the benefits that could be accrued from public preschool spending.   Greater targeting of resources to areas of the country with higher repetition rates and to poor and disadvantaged children will, all else being equal, increase the impact of preschool programs in the country.

IV.   DETERMINANTS OF PRE-SCHOOL ATTENDANCE

30.   The above analysis has shown that preschool enrollment rates are lowest among the very children who could most benefit from preschool programs. Clearly an argument can be made for redistributing the existing resources.   But, while redistributing the public expenditures in preschool could solve a significant portion of the problem, the fact that preschool education is mandatory, but not compulsory, implies that the head of the household makes decisions about their children's enrollment that are also affecting the overall enrollment rates.   In order to fully understand present patterns of preschool attendance it is, therefore, necessary to understand the factors which affect households' decisions concerning preschool enrollment.

31.   The standard model of household behavior indicates that a child will be enrolled in school up to the point where the households' marginal returns from this educational investment equals the marginal return to other uses of household resources.[24] This is the standard concept applied to decisions to enroll at higher levels of schooling but is relevant to the preschool decision making process also.

32.   It is assumed that the factor that most affects enrollment decisions is the presence or absence of pre-school programs, i.e. the physical availability of the supply.   Households may be located in an area not served by any preschool program or so distant from them that the opportunity and transport costs associated with using the program may be greater than the rate of return accruing to the household from participation. Clearly, this lack of facilities will keep enrollment levels low. This is especially important in Panama where the number of facilities is small nationally, and where the distribution of such facilities is biased towards urban areas.

---

[24] Paqueo, 1981.

33.   Thus, to analyze the overall determinants of preschool enrollment, it is important to take into account the availability of preschool facilities.   Unfortunately, the ENV did not collect information on the presence of pre-school facilities near the households in the sample.   Due to this lack of information, it is not possible to assess the determinants of preschool enrollment at a national level. Instead, the analysis is carried out only for urban children. Given the prevalence of pre-schools in urban areas, it is assumed, for the purposes of the present analysis, that some pre-school opportunity exists for all children in all urban areas.   To the extent that this assumption is incorrect, and it may well be that in poorer neighborhoods pre-school in less prevalent in spite of specific programs targeted at these areas, the conclusions of the following analysis will suffer from omitted variable bias.   In addition, as the analysis only includes urban households, the results may not be applicable to rural or indigenous areas. Thus, the findings of the following analysis should be used with caution and serve more to indicate areas of further investigation than for concrete policy decisions.

(i)   Data

34.   The data come from the ENV and include 446 children ages three to five living in urban areas for whom complete information exists.   As can be found in Table 5, of these children, 36.3 percent attend some type of preschool program, be it initial education or kindergarten.   Most children live in households with other very young children (on average households have 1.8 children under the age of six) and with additional primary school age children.   Only 7.3 percent of children live in households without their mothers present but more than one quarter lives in households without a father. Education levels for mothers and fathers are fairly similar.   Most children live in homes with access to electricity and which are of solid construction materials.

Table 5: Characteristics of Urban, Pre-School Age Children

Variable	Mean	Std. Dev.
In pre-school	0.363	0.482
PC Consumption (Balboas/10)	18.13	14.60
Mother completed primary	0.116	0.320
Mother incomplete secondary	0.368	0.483
Mother complete secondary or more	0.460	0.499
Father completed primary	0.103	0.304
Father incomplete secondary	0.357	0.480
Father complete secondary or more	0.456	0.499
Metropolitan region	0.754	0.431
Occidental region	0.145	0.352
Center	0.101	0.301
Male	0.460	0.499
Years of Age	4.019	0.822
No. Primary age children in hhld	0.819	0.978
No. Children under 6 in hhld	1.813	1.088
Mother absent	0.073	0.261
Mother works	0.477	0.500
Electricity	0.981	0.136
Cement or wood walls	0.977	0.150
Primary School in Community	0.683	0.466
Father Absent	0.261	0.439

Source: ENV 1997.

Note: Contains data on children ages 3-5 living in urban areas, N=446

(ii)   Model

35.   A probit model is used to estimate attendance at the preschool level where the dependent variable takes on the value of one (1) if the child is enrolled in either an initial education program or a kindergarten program and zero otherwise. Although, in theory, initial education and kindergarten are not exactly the same and the programs' goals vary (and hence participation would be affected by different factors), in practice there are not clear distinctions among the programs as far as content and goals are concerned. For this reason it was decided to include both attendance in initial education and kindergarten programs.

36.   The probability of a child attending a preschool program is a function of individual characteristics, household characteristics and characteristics of the area where the child resides. The individual characteristics included are age and gender. It is expected that attendance will increase with age as more programs are available for older children than for younger ones. While gender affects attendance in other levels of schooling (for example, in much of Latin America, females are more likely than males to attend high school) it is not clear, a priori, what impact, if any, it will have on preschool enrollments.

37.   Household characteristics included are income (and wealth), parental education and presence in the household as well as the number of other young children in the household. Income, proxied here by per capita household consumption, is expected to have a positive impact on preschool enrollment due to the costs associated with preschool. Two variables that attempt to look at the quality of the housing, electricity and materials of walls are also included. It is expected that, the greater the wealth of the household, the higher the probability of attendance.

38.   As noted, parental education, which has been shown to affect both the probability of attending school at other levels as well as overall educational attainment[25] is included. Education levels of mothers and fathers are included separately as dummy variables for completed primary schooling, some secondary, or completed secondary or higher. The omitted variable is mother (father) with less than a complete primary education.

39.   The presence or absence of a parent in the household is also included as well as whether or not the mother works. The absence of the mother and/or the fact that the mother works is expected to increase the probability of preschool attendance as it increases the costs of childcare. It is not clear what the effect of father's absence will be. On the one hand, it may increase the probability of preschool attendance as it may be highly correlated with the mother's labor force status; single mothers are more likely to be economically active. On the other hand, to the extent that the lack of a father decreases the resources available to the household, this absence may decrease preschool attendance. In Nicaragua, the absence of a father did increase the probability of preschool participation.[26]

40.   The number of other preschool and primary age children in the household is expected to decrease preschool attendance. The presence of additional children increases the reservation wage of mothers, thereby lowering their participation rate.[27] By decreasing employment among mothers, it is expected that this will lower the probability of preschool attendance.

41.   The community in which a child resides is expected to play an important role in the probability of attendance. Preschool programs are not evenly distributed in the country and some programs are only found in specific areas. Two dummy variables are used for region, the first takes on the value of one (1) if the child lives in the Western region and zero otherwise and the second which takes on the value of one (1) if the child resides in the Metropolitan region. The central region is the omitted variable.[28]

42.   Finally, a further characteristic of the community in which the child lives that may affect preschool attendance is whether or not there is a primary school in the community. The presence of primary school is expected to increase participation by two means. First, preprimary programs are often held in primary schools;[29] the presence of a primary school may capture much of the access to preschool programs. Second, there may be a perception of higher value to preschool programs in a location where primary school is a more viable option.

---

[25] Cameron and Heckman, 1993; Manski et al, 1992.
[26] Scott, 1994.
[27] Psacharopoulos and Tzannatos, 1992.
[28] Note that the eastern region is not included in the analysis as there were no urban households sampled from that region.
[29] World Bank, 1995.

(iii)   Results

43.   The results of the probit equation can be found in Table 6. As expected, age is an important determinant of preschool attendance. The impact is quite marked as can be seen in Table 7. Simulations of the probability of attendance of a child age three is only 4.1 percent, whereas, all else held equal, a five-year old would have a 70 percent chance of attendance. The impact of gender on participation, however, is insignificant.

Table 6: Probit Estimates of Pre-school Enrollment

Variable	Coefficient	t-ratio	Partial Derivative
Constant	−5.215	−5.172	−1.757
PC Consumption (Balboas/100)	0.031	4.336	0.010
Mother completed primary	0.843	1.586	0.284
Mother incomplete secondary	1.205	2.397	0.406
Mother complete secondary or more	1.144	2.243	0.385
Father completed primary	−0.413	−1.033	−0.139
Father incomplete secondary	−0.156	−0.439	−.053
Father complete secondary or more	0.031	0.087	0.011
Metropolitan region	−0.756	−3.067	−0.255
Occidental region	−0.682	−2.181	−0.230
Male	−0.154	−0.990	−0.052
Years of Age	1.139	10.825	0.384
No. Primary age children in hhld	−0.233	−2.648	−0.079
No. Children under 6 in hhld	−0.095	−1.261	−.032
Mother absent	0.601	2.095	0.203
Mother works	0.305	1.910	0.103
Electricity	−0.585	−0.943	−0.197
Cement or wood walls	−0.036	−0.053	−0.012
Father Absent	−0.134	−0.731	−0.045
Primary School in Community	0.108	0.644	0.036
Log Likelihood = -189.004	N = 446		

44.   Per capita consumption also is an important determinant of preschool enrollment. As shown in Table 7, children living in households with per capita consumption of 50 balboas per month have only a 16.3 percent probability of attending preschool. In contrast, a child in a household with consumption at 300 balboas has a probability of 41.3 percent. And, for the highest consumption groups, the probability of attendance is over 90 percent. Neither of the other variables associated with household wealth was significant, perhaps because of low variation.

Table 7: Predicted Probability of Preschool Enrollment

Characteristic	Estimated Probability
Of Child:	
Years of Age	
Three years	4.1
Four years	27.3
Five years	70.4
Of Household	
Consumption Level:	
50 balboas	16.3
300 balboas	41.3
550 balboas	70.7
800 balboas	90.5
Region	
Metropolitan	25.2
Occidental	27.6
Central	53.5
Primary Aged Children	
None	34.8
One	26.6
Three	19.6
Five	6.0
Of Parents	
Mother's Education	
Less than secondary	5.0
Incomplete Secondary	32.9
Compl. Sec./ Higher	30.7
Mother in Household	
Absent	49.0
Present	26.6
Mother's labor Status	
Not working	23.4
Works	33.7

45.   As expected, parental education affects preschool attendance but only the education of the mother and only once this level of education is greater than primary school. For a child with a mother whose educational level is less than secondary, the probability of attendance is very low, 5 percent. If that same child had a mother with incomplete secondary at least, the probability of participation would increase to 32.9 percent. Note that father's education has no impact on whether or not a child attends preschool.

46.   Additionally, the father's presence or absence is not a determinant of enrollment. In contrast, the mother's presence lowers the probability of enrollment, as does a non-working mother. This indicates that preschool, in addition to education, serves an important daycare function for households.

47.   Finally the presence of primary school aged children in the household decreases the probability of attendance but the presence of additional preschool age children does not. It is not clear why this is the case. If the issue were the increase in the reservation wage of having multiple young children in the household it would be expected that both pre-school and primary age children would decrease

participation. It may be that, unlike pre-school age children who must be cared for, primary-aged children can care for themselves at some point and, more importantly, take over some of the daycare functions for younger children. The net effect of this would be to free mothers' labor force participation.

V. CONCLUSIONS AND RECOMMENDATIONS

48. The trends in overall participation in preschool in Panama are positive in that enrollment levels are increasing. But coverage is limited and lags behind other countries in the region. Equally important, if not more so, the present distribution of preschool resources, in both the public and the private sector, benefits primarily non-poor, urban children. While government spending is more targeted than the private sector, non-poor children still benefit more from public preschool spending than poor. By not targeting the poor and those children at a greater risk of repetition or drop out in primary school, the present distribution of preschool programs limits the impact that existing preschool investments could have on national education levels and welfare.

49. An effort to increase preschool opportunities for poor and non-urban children is needed. There are several ways to do this. As this paper has shown, a redistribution of the resources presently devoted to preschool education toward poorer children and areas and school districts with high repetition rates could increase the overall impact on both education and, perhaps, health status of children. However, given the present low levels of coverage, a simple redistribution would probably not be adequate to increase participation in preschool greatly. An increase in resources will probably be required, but more information is needed on the tradeoffs between different levels of schooling and what impact increasing preschool spending will have on spending for other levels of education.

50. Other ways to increase the preschool opportunities of poor and non-urban children are to adopt alternative methods of preschool provision. Reliance on formal kindergartens may make it impossible to reach all children due to the geographic distribution of primary schools, the relatively disperse population in various parts of the country and the costs of such preschool. In contrast, the community-based programs are both less expensive than traditional kindergarten and are targeted to children in rural and indigenous areas. The large *Madre a Madre* program, which, instead of setting up formal pre-school programs, trains mothers, is an innovative effort to promote child development in areas where population density prohibits more standard programs. These appear to be an important alternative to traditional models and, as such, are an experiment that should be studied carefully. The other type of preschool, workplace-based programs, may or may not serve to target poorer children. It is necessary to determine the types of workplaces most likely to have such programs and whether their employees could be classified as poor. It may be that the poor work primarily in the informal sector where such workplace-based programs are unavailable.

51. As the findings on the determinants of preschool enrollment for urban children showed, there are other ways in which the government can increase preschool participation. Household consumption is positively correlated to preschool enrollment. Thus, efforts to decrease costs are critical. This can be done by increasing the number of preschool places and thus lowering the transportation and opportunity costs to the household of obtaining preschool services or by focusing on other fees and costs associated with preschool attendance. Labor market and other educational policies will also affect preschool enrollment as mothers' labor force participation and education are important determinants of their children's enrollment. Family planning policies could also increase enrollment as households with more children are less likely to enroll their children in preschool.

52. The findings of the present analysis are, at best, partial. The lack of national information on the impact of the different types of preschool, and whether certain groups of children stand to benefit more from preschool attendance than others, limits the ability of the government to make sound decisions on the proper investments in preschool in the country. While many decisions can be made on the basis of

existing data, studies of the impact of preschool education need to be carried out with specific attention being paid to the benefits of different types of preschool alternatives. Information on the health, cognitive and socialization impacts of preschool as well as later impacts on repetition rates in primary school, combined with detailed cost information, would allow the government to assess the adequacy of its present programs and to invest in the most effective programs.

References Cited

Berrueta-Clement, John R., Lawrence J. Schweinhart and David P. Weikart. 1983. "Lasting Effects of preschool education on children from low-income families in the United States", in Preventing School Failure: the relationship between preschool and primary education, proceedings of a workshop on preschool research held in Bogota, Colombia, 26-29 May 1981, International Development Research Centre, Ottawa, Ontario.

Cameron, Stephen V. and James J. Heckman. 1993. "Determinants of Young Male Schooling and Training Choices", National Bureau of Economic Research, Working Paper No. 4327.

Cochrane, Susan and Dean T. Jamison. 1981. "The Determinants and Consequence of Educational Achievement in the Rural Chiang Mai Valley", Discussion paper no. 81-61, Population and Human Resources Division, World Bank, Washington, D.C.

Currie, Janet and Duncan Thomas. 1993. "Does Head Start Make a Difference?". National Bureau of Economic Research, Working Paper No. 4406.

Currie, Janet and Duncan Thomas. 1996. "Does Head Start Help Hispanic Children?". National Bureau of Economic Research, Working Paper No. 5805.

Filp, Johanna and Sebastian Donoso, Cecilia Cardemil, Eleonor Dieguez, Jaime Torres and Ernesto Schiefelbein. 1983. "Relationship between preprimary and grade one primary education in state schools in Chile" in Preventing School Failure: the relationship between preschool and primary education, proceedings of a workshop on preschool research held in Bogota, Colombia, 26-29 May 1981, International Development Research Centre, Ottawa, Ontario.

Manski, Charles F., Gary D. Sandefur, Sara McLanahan and Daniel Powers. 1992. "Alternative Estimates of the Effect of Family Structure During Adolescence on High School Graduation Rates", Journal of the American Statistical Association, Vol. 87. No. 417: 25-37.

Meyers, Robert G. and Rachelle Hertenberg. 1987. "The Eleven Who Survive: Toward a Re-examination of Early Childhood Development Program Options and Costs", Discussion Paper, Education and Training Series No. EDT69, World Bank, Washington, D.C.

Ministerio de Planificación y Política Económica, Dirección de Políticas Sociales. 1998. "Encuesta de niveles de vida: documentación básica", Panama City, Panama.

Paqueo, Vicente B. 1981 "A Household Production Model of School Enrollment: A Probit Analysis of the 1978 Bicol Multipurpose Survey Data". Discussion paper No. 81-30, Population and Human Resources Division, World Bank, Washington, D.C.

Pozner, Pilar. 1983. "Relationship between preschool education and first grade in Argentina", in Preventing School Failure: the relationship between preschool and primary education, proceedings of a workshop on preschool research held in Bogota, Colombia, 26-29 May 1981, International Development Research Centre, Ottawa, Ontario.

Prakasha, Veda. 1983. "Our Future is in Our Children: the Case for Early Childhood Care and Education", Digest No. 1, UNESCO/UNICEF Co-operative Project, Paris.

Psacharopoulos, George and Ana Maria Arriagada. 1989. "The Determinants of Early Age Human Capital Formation: Evidence from Brazil", Economic Development and Cultural Change, vol. 37, 1989: 683-708.

Psacharopoulos, George and Zafiris Tzannatos. 1992. Women's Employment and Pay in Latin America, vol. I and II, Regional and Sectoral Studies, The World Bank, Washington, D.C.

Psacharopoulos, George and Ying Chu Ng. 1992. "Earnings and Education in Latin America: Assessing Priorities for Schooling Investments", Policy Research Working Papers Series, No. 1067, Technical Department, Latin America and the Caribbean, The World Bank, Washington, D.C.

Psacharopoulos, George. 1993. " Returns to Investment in Education: A Global Update", Policy Research Working Papers Series, No. 1067, Office of the Director, Latin America and the Caribbean, The World Bank, Washington, D.C.

Raudenbush, Stephen W., Somsri Kidchanapanish, and Sang Jin Kang. 1991. "The Effects of Preprimary Access and Quality on Educational Achievement in Thailand", in Comparative Education Review, Vol. 35, No. 2: 255-273

Scott, Kinnon. 1994. "The Determinants of Educational Attainment in Nicaragua". Background paper for Nicaragua Poverty Assessment, Latin American and the Caribbean, Region II, Human Resources, World Bank, Washington, D.C., unprocessed.

World Bank. 1995. "Panama: Issues in Basic Education", Report No. 13701-PAN, Country Department II, Human Resources Operations Division, Latin America and the Caribbean Regional Office.

World Bank, 1996. "Staff Appraisal Report: The Republic of Panama, Basic Education Project", Report No. 15109-PAN, Country Department II, Human Resources Operations Division, Latin America and the Caribbean Regional Office.

Zigler, Edward and Susan Muenchow. 1992. Head Start: the Inside Story of America's Most Successful Educational Experiment, BasicBooks, New York.

Annex 1
Household Expenditures on Preschool Education

Table A1:
Frequency of expenditures and average expenditures on preschool education, by type of education
(percent or balboas)

Category	Private	Public	Total
Had any expenditure (percent) [1]	100.0	95.9	97.3
Average annual expenditure (balboas)[2]	751.3	157.8	367.6

[1] Refers to all children ages 3-5 in preschool, expenditures include fees (annual and monthly), uniforms, books and other school supplies and transport.
[2] Refers to all children ages 3-5 in preschool who had some expenditures; expenditures include fees (annual and monthly), uniforms, books and other school supplies and transport.
Source: ENV, 1997.

Table A2:
Frequency of expenditures and average expenditures on preschool education, by poverty status
(percent or balboas)

Category	Poor	Non-Poor	Total
Had any expenditure (percent) [1]	92.1	99.1	97.3
Average annual expenditure (balboas)[2]	88.0	460.4	367.6

[1] Refers to all children ages 3-5 in preschool, expenditures include fees (annual and monthly), uniforms, books and other school supplies and transport.
[2] Refers to all children ages 3-5 in preschool who had some expenditures; expenditures include fees (annual and monthly), uniforms, books and other school supplies and transport.
Source: ENV, 1997.

Annex 14 – The Returns to Education

Kathy Lindert, October 9, 1998

Methodology

1.   The private and social returns to education can be calculated using a short-cut method developed by Psacharapoulos (1995).[1] **The private returns** obtained from obtaining an extra level of education can be estimated as follows:

$$(1) \text{ Private rate of return} = (Y_2 - Y_1)/(S * (Y_1 + C_p))$$

The term Y_2 refers to the mean monthly labor earnings at the higher level of education and Y_1 the mean labor earnings at the lower level of education. The number of years spent in school to obtain the higher level of education is denoted by "S." The term C_p is the average private monthly expenditures on education (available from the LSMS survey).[2] Thus Y_2-Y_1 is the earnings differential between the two levels of education (the private benefits of education). The term $Y_1 + C_p$ represents the cost of education, including the student's foregone earnings (the mean monthly earnings at the lower level of education during the period in school) plus his or her direct costs (C_p).

2.   **The social returns** to education should ideally take into account (i) the social benefits of education; and (ii) the social (public) costs of education (for those in public school). The social benefits of education generally arise from externalities coming from having a more literate workforce, from sharing ideas (whose value is not captured by the parties involved), and from the contribution to the functioning of civil society. Most of these externalities are associated with basic literacy -- and hence primary education.[3] As they are difficult to quantify, this analysis takes into account the social (public) costs of education, and simply notes that the social returns to primary education are probably underestimated. The "social" rate of return to education can thus be estimated as follows:

$$(2) \text{ Social rate of return} = (Y_2 - Y_1)/(S * (Y_1 + C_p + C_g))$$

where C_g is the monthly direct (public) cost of the higher level of (public) education. Since the costs are higher in a social rate of return calculation relative to the private rate of return, social returns are lower than private returns (though again, these calculations neglect the social benefits described above). The difference between the private and social rates reflects the degree of public subsidization of education.

Data

3.   Data on the mean labor earnings by level of education can be obtained from the LSMS. These are presented in Table A14.1. Note that while men earn significantly more each month than women regardless of education, this does not hold on an hourly basis due to the fact that women work fewer hours per month than men (at the *first* job). The returns to education analysis uses mean *monthly* earnings for several reasons. First, a practical reason: much of the data on household spending on education is collected on a monthly or yearly basis (it's easier to convert yearly education costs to monthly figures

---

[1] The "Full method" which discounts the actual net age-earnings profiles is the most appropriate method of estimating the returns to education because it takes into account the most important part of the early earning history of the individual. The private rate of return to educational investment in such a case can be estimated by finding the rate of discount that equalizes the stream of discounted benefits to the stream of costs at a given point in time. However, it requires more comprehensive data on age-educational earnings for constructing a "well behaved" (non-intersecting) age-earnings profiles.

[2] The private expenditures are converted from annual spending in Section 4 of the LSMS using a factor of 8.5 months per school year. In this analysis, we assume that it takes six years to complete primary and secondary education (S=6) and five years to complete university (S=5).

[3] Hammer (January 22, 1996).

than to hourly figures). Second, the use of monthly earnings captures the returns to education both in terms of hourly earnings and in terms of the opportunities for working (hours worked).[4]

Table A14.1 – Mean Labor Earnings by Education Level						
	Mean Hourly Earnings			Mean Monthly Earnings		
Balboas	Male	Female	All	Male	Female	All
No Education	1.0	1.2	1.1	113	66	101
Primary	1.4	1.5	1.4	186	132	173
Secondary	2.5	2.4	2.5	401	318	372
Higher	5.3	4.4	4.8	1094	686	887
Source: Panama LSMS 1997. Earnings include all income from labor (first job): gross wages, payments in kind from employment (food, transport, clothing, housing), benefits (including the 13th month benefit), and labor earnings from self-employment. Monthly earnings reflect actual number of hours worked. Hourly earnings were converted from monthly figures using hours worked.						

4.   Data on household (private) spending can also be obtained from the LSMS. The analysis of returns to education uses the *average* household spending on education per student for those who were enrolled in school (in public or private school). These data are presented in Table A14.2 (first column).

Table A14.2 – Annual Household Spending on Education			
Balboas	Average for All	Public Schools	Private Schools
Primary	198	106	973
Secondary	395	253	987
Higher	488	294	1150
Source: Panama LSMS 1997. Figures on a per student basis. One school year = 8.5 months. Averaged over those in school. 90% of primary school students are enrolled in public schools. 81% of secondary school students are enrolled in public schools. 80% of higher education students are enrolled in public schools.			

5.   Data on public spending on education were obtained from the *Dirección de Presupuesto de la Nación* in MIPPE. These are presented in Table A14.3 below.[5] Comparing per capita public spending with household spending reveals the subsidies to public education. The subsidy rates are 78 percent for primary and secondary school, and 84 percent for superior education.[6]

Results

6.   The private and social returns to education are presented in Table A14.4 below. The returns to education are higher for men at the secondary and higher levels, but interestingly higher for women at the primary level (compared with no education). Higher education generates larger private returns than primary or secondary for both men and women. Secondary education yields higher social returns for women, however, reflecting the substantial public costs of higher education, which are apparently not offset by women's earnings at this level (both due to relatively lower hourly earnings and shorter hours worked per month, see Table A14.1 above).

---

[4] The examined the impact of unemployment on the returns to education, since unemployment rates vary by level of education. The overall returns, however, did not vary significantly whether or not full employment was assumed.

[5] For calculating social returns in equation 2, public spending on education is pro-rated by the share of students who attend public school.

[6] Subsidy rates calculated as: Public Spending / Total Costs of public education, where Total Costs = public spending + household spending on public education (all in per student basis).

Table A14.3 – Public Spending on Education, 1997	
Primary & Pre-Primary School	
Direct Public Spending, B./1000 (1)	124,536
Administrative Spending, B./1000 (2)	16,348
Total Annual Public Spending, B./1000	140,884
Number of Students (3)	376,350
Total Annual Public Spending Per Student, B./	374
Total Monthly Public Spending Per Student, B./	44
Secondary School	
Direct Public Spending, B./1000 (1)	151,751
Administrative Spending, B./1000 (2)	11,457
Total Annual Public Spending, B./1000	163,208
Number of Students (3)	187,090
Total Annual Public Spending Per Student, B./	872
Total Monthly Public Spending Per Student, B./	102
Superior Education	
Direct Public Spending, B./1000 (1)	104,411
Administrative Spending, B./1000 (2)	42,109
Total Annual Public Spending, B./1000	146,520
Number of Students (3)	68,391
Total Annual Public Spending Per Student, B./	2,142
Total Monthly Public Spending Per Student, B./	251

(1) Direct public spending figures from MIPPE: Dirección de Presupuesto de la Nación
(2) Administrative public spending figures from MIPPE: Dirección de Presupuesto de la Nación. Administrative spending by MINEDUC calculated as pro-rated allocation between primary and secondary according to their shares of MINEDUC spending. Administrative spending by the Inst. para. Formac. y Aprov. de Rec. Humanos calculated as pro-rated allocation between primary, secondary and higher education according to their shares of spending.
(3) Student enrollment figures from Contraloria and MINEDUC.
Annual figures converted to monthly using a factor of 8.5 months per school year.

Table A14.4 – Private and Social Returns to Education (Percent)			
	Male	Female	Total
Private Returns			
Primary Education (vs. no education)	8.9	12.3	9.7
Secondary Education (vs. primary education)	15.4	17.4	15.1
Higher Education (vs. secondary education)	30.2	19.6	24.0
Social Returns			
Primary Education (vs. no education)	6.9	8.5	7.3
Secondary Education (vs. primary education)	11.4	11.9	11.0
Higher Education (vs. secondary education)	17.5	10.6	13.6

Annex 15 - Patterns of Health Care Use and the Incidence of Public Health Spending in Panama

Kinnon Scott and Roberto Gonzalez[1]

I.   Introduction

1.   Access to adequate health care is critical for maintaining health levels and, hence, for overall welfare. In Panama, as in any country, individuals spend private resources to obtain health care while, at the same time, the government spends a significant share of its budget on the provision of various, public, health care services. While it is clear who benefits from private spending on health care--the individual making the expenditure--, the beneficiaries of public health care spending are not as easily identified. Administrative records may provide information on the number of persons using the public health system, but these records are not designed to provide detailed information on the characteristics of the persons using the health system.

2.   The purpose of the present paper is start to answer the question of who, in Panama, benefits from public spending on health care. The two questions of primary interest are whether public health care spending is regressive or progressive (i.e. do the poor benefit more or less than the non-poor from such spending) and whether there are geographic differences in the distribution of benefits. To identify the beneficiaries of the health system requires detailed information on: (i) the patterns of use of public health care by the population and; (ii) the costs to the government of providing such health care services.   An excellent source of data exists for the former, the Panama 1997 Living Standards Measurement Study Survey (Encuesta Niveles de Vida, ENV). No data are, however, available for the latter. To make up for this lack of data, various scenarios are presented illustrating the impact of different cost structures on the distribution of public spending.

3.   The paper is organized in the following way.   A brief discussion of the importance of analyzing the incidence of public health spending is provided in Section II.   Section III contains details on the population's patterns of health care use for all types of health care.   The distribution of public spending is discussed in the fourth section and the results of the analysis presented.   Tentative conclusions and recommendations are contained in the final section.

II.   Importance of Identifying the Incidence of Public Health Spending

4.   Public spending on health represents a substantial commitment on the part of the government of Panama. In 1996, government spending on health care in Panama was 7.2 percent of gross domestic product (GDP) and 12.3 percent of all government spending. In addition, health care spending took up one-third of all spending on the social sectors.   Present levels of health spending represent a significant increase in the importance of health spending in the national budget. In 1980, health care spending was only 5.5 percent of GDP and 10.4 percent of all government spending.

5.   Present and past investment in health care by the government, as well as the private sector, have created a fairly extensive health care system.   If access is defined as living within one hour of a health care facility, the World Health Organization estimates that slightly more than 80 percent of the population

---

[1] The authors are from the World Bank and the Ministry of Planning and Economic Policy of Panama (MIPPE), respectively.   The paper is a result of a collaborative effort among MIPPE, the Ministry of Health of Panama and the World Bank. The authors would like to thank Lic. Rosa Elena de De la Cruz, Eudemia Pérez, Edith Kowalcyk and Maria Christina de Pastór from the MIPPE, and Drs. Pedro Contreras and Gloriella Gordón from the Ministry of Health for their inputs.

has access to health care in Panama. But this still leaves just under 20 percent of the population relatively remote from health care. Data from the recent household survey, ENV, show that for those who were sick and did not obtain care, cost and distance were key factors (see Table 1). The problem is worse among the poorer groups and among those living outside of urban areas.

Table 1: Reasons for Not Seeking Needed Medical Care

	Quintile 1	Quintile 2	Quintile 3	Quintile 4	Quintile 5	Urban	Rural	Indigen.	Total
Mild Case	34.6	59.9	73.9	78.4	74.3	72.6	56.0	30.4	62.3
Cost/Distance[1]	55.5	25.1	12.4	4.9	3.3	7.1	34.7	56.1	22.4
Quality	2.6	1.3	2.6	3.5	2.1	2.7	1.9	1.4	2.2
Other	8.2	13.7	11.1	13.2	20.3	19.7	7.5	12.1	13.1

Source: ENV, 1997, MIPPE, authors' calculations.
[1]It is difficult to separate cost from distance: the responses included here are: (i) facility too far; (ii) no money for transport, and (iii) service is costly.
Note: Includes all persons who reported an illness or injury in the four weeks prior to the survey but who did not obtain medical care.

6. In short, in spite of extensive investment in health care by the government, and the private health care system, access to affordable health care is not universal in the country. The cost of care and the distances involved in obtaining health care limit the possibilities of some part of the population to make use of health services. More importantly, those with the most limited access are those who are the poorest. It is assumed that much of the government investment in health has benefited poor and remote groups, more so than the private system. Even so, the investment has not been enough to completely cover the population.

7. One way to improve the levels of access to affordable health care is to move resources away from those who can afford to purchase care and towards those unable to do so. By determining who actually benefits from public spending on health, as well as from what types of health care spending, this paper can provide some insights on effective ways to do this. Different types of targeting mechanisms, such as means testing and sliding scale fees under cost recovery programs or by type of health care facility or even by geographic area, may all be useful in increasing coverage.

III.   USE OF HEALTH CARE SERVICES BY THE POPULATION

IIIa.   Data Source

8. Data on the use of health care come from the national survey on living conditions (ENV), that was carried out by the Ministry of Planning and Economic Policy in Panama (MIPPE)[2]. This survey of approximately 5000 households has several characteristics that make it especially useful for analyzing the incidence of health spending. First and foremost, the ENV collected detailed information on the use of health care services of the population. All individuals in the sampled households were asked about illness or injury in the month prior to the interview, whether any health care was obtained and, if so, where and from whom such care was obtained. Health services used are identified by type (public or private), level (hospital, health center, or health post) and by personnel who attended the patient (doctor, nurse, healer and the like).[3]

---

[2] For more information on the ENV, please see the Basic Information document produced by MIPPE.
[3] Information on other details, such as distance to health care, costs of care, average waiting time and the like were also collected but are not included here

9.   In addition to the detailed information on the use of health care services, the ENV collected the necessary data for determining the welfare level of all households and individuals. Based on per capita consumption, all persons and households can be ranked according to welfare (or poverty), from poorest to richest.[4] Thus it is possible to look at the use of health care services among groups with different levels of welfare. For the purpose of the present paper, consumption quintiles have been formed, with the poorest 20 percent of the population making up the first quintile.

10.   A further advantage of the ENV is that it is the only household survey in Panama that has a probability based sample design that includes the entire population. For financial and logistical reasons, all other surveys in the country exclude two geographical areas: difficult access rural areas and indigenous areas. The ENV includes all of these geographic areas and, thus, permits extrapolation to the national population and comparisons of poverty and health care use across geographic regions.

11.   The ENV does have some limitations, however. First, data on sickness and illness are self-reported. It has been found that, typically, the non-poor self-report more illness and injury than the poor. As the questionnaire uses the question on illness as a filter for further questions on the use of health care this could lead to an underestimation of health care usage among the poor. It seems reasonable, however, that, if a person sought health care, he or she would respond positively to the question about having been sick or injured. Thus, it is doubtful that this will affect the analysis.

12.   The second difficulty with the data is that information on preventive health care were not collected for all individuals. Only if an illness or injury in the reference period were not recorded was a person asked if preventive health care had been obtained. This questionnaire feature may lead to an underestimation of the total use of health care in the country. Unfortunately, no other data source exists that provides an indication of use patterns for preventive health care. Thus it is not possible to know if the underestimation of health service use is systematic, or whether the underestimation is greater for one group than another, or in one region or for one type of facility. This limitation of the data should be kept in mind when evaluating the results of the present analysis.

13.   Finally, a large share of the population is affiliated with the social security system and is thus eligible for services under the polyclinics and hospitals of the social security institute. The social security health system is neither completely public nor completely private. It relies on revenues from both private contributors and from the national budget (both in the form of employer contributions and direct transfers). Thus the system is a mixture of public and private financing. In the questionnaire, individuals were asked if they used a public or private hospital. After discussions with the Ministry of Planning and Ministry of Health staff, it was determined that respondents would consider the social security institute to be a public service and respond accordingly. Thus, use of public health services may be slightly overstated. As the Social Security Institute hospitals function primarily in large urban areas, this will result in the overestimation of the use of public health services in urban areas and, as social security affiliation is also found more among the non-poor (see Table 2), this will also tend to overestimate the non-poor's use of public health care.

Table 2: Affiliation in Social Security

	Quintile 1	Quintile 2	Quintile 3	Quintile 4	Quintile 5	Urban	Rural	Indigen.	Total
Affiliated	13.1	38.7	51.5	60.2	59.9	57.0	32.2	14.9	44.6

Source: ENV, 1997 MIPPE, authors' calculations.
Note: Refers to affiliation in the 'Caja de Seguro Social'.

---

[4] Please refer to the Poverty Profile for Panama, a part of the Poverty Assessment, for detailed information on how poverty is measured and the consumption aggregate constructed.

IIIb.   Patterns of Health Care Service Use

14.   In the four weeks prior to the survey, slightly more than one-third of the population report having had an illness or injury of some sort (see Table 3). For those under age five, this increases to more than half, with the vast majority of ailments among children under five being diarrhea and respiratory diseases. Typical patterns of underreporting of illness among the poor (or over-reporting among the rich) appear weaker in Panama than in other countries. Thus, the assumption that the filter question about illness having little effect on the analysis seems to be valid.

Table 3: Incidence of Illness or Injury

	Quintile 1	Quintile 2	Quintile 3	Quintile 4	Quintile 5	Urban	Rural	Indigen.	Total
All persons	33.3	36.4	34.9	36.9	34.4	35.2	36.1	31.0	35.2
Under five									
All illness	52.8	56.0	61.2	59.4	51.9	58.2	53.8	54.5	56.0
Diarrhea	25.0	23.4	22.1	15.0	14.7	18.4	20.6	36.9	21.5
Respirat.	40.3	42.2	41.8	45.7	36.9	43.7	40.7	35.4	41.5
Both.	49.8	51.1	54.5	53.3	43.5	52.4	48.4	52.3	50.8

Source: ENV, 1997 MIPPE, authors' calculations.
Note: Refers to self-reported illness or injury.

IIIb-1: Use of Health Care for Children under Five

15.   As can be seen in Table 4, the patterns of health care use for cases of diarrhea or respiratory ailments among children under five, are quite different between poorer and less poor children and among the different regions of the country. Children in higher quintiles are more likely to have consulted medical personnel while children in lower quintiles were more likely to be treated by their parents or other relatives in the home. Among children who were treated outside of the home, doctors were the most common type of health care professional consulted. This is especially true for children in top quintile: almost all of these children visited a doctor. For children in the bottom quintile, in contrast, nurses, health assistants, promoters and healers were consulted by almost one-third of those seen outside the home.

Table 4: Use of Health Services for Children Under Five
(percent)

	Quintile 1	Quintile 2	Quintile 3	Quintile 4	Quintile 5	Urban	Rural	Indig.	Total
Personnel Consult									
Doctor	34.3	61.9	69.5	70.9	80.0	69.3	55.2	20.9	57.9
Nurse, Assist.	11.1	3.6	1.8	2.1	0.0	1.9	5.1	16.9	5.0
Pharm. , Healer	4.6	1.1	0.9	1.3	1.5	0.7	2.4	7.4	2.2
Relative	50.0	33.4	27.9	25.7	18.5	28.1	37.1	54.4	34.9
Facility Used									
Pub. Hospital	15.2	19.7	34.8	31.6	26.3	33.5	16.5	6.8	23.6
Priv. Hospital	0.4	5.8	10.7	23.1	39.7	16.1	7.5	0.0	10.8
Center, Post[1]	28.9	39.1	23.9	14.7	6.5	18.4	35.1	30.6	26.3
Priv. Practice	1.0	0.3	1.5	2.6	5.1	2.0	1.2	0.4	1.5
Home, other	54.6	35.2	29.2	28.0	22.5	30.0	39.7	62.2	37.8

Source: ENV, 1997 MIPPE, authors' calculations.
Note: Refers to the percent of children under age five who reported some illness or injury.
[1]Includes health centers, sub-centers and health posts.

16.   Differences in the use of health care are also apparent geographically. Urban children were the most likely to have been taken to a doctor while children living in rural and indigenous areas were more likely to have been treated at home.   In both rural and indigenous areas, even among those children treated outside the home, less consultations with doctors were made.

17.   The use of health care facilities also varies. Children in the lower quintiles were more likely to use health centers, sub-centers and health posts than any other type of facility. This pattern is reversed among the higher quintiles with public and private hospitals being used more extensively by these groups. Geographic difference also exist, as would be expected. Hospitals are usually urban and health sub-centers and posts are found in rural areas. As can be seen in the Table, urban children are taken to hospitals while in rural and indigenous areas health centers and the like are the type of facility used most often.

IIIb-2:   Use of Health Care among Those Five and Older[5]

18.   Overall, for those five and older, the level of use of health care among the ill and injured is slightly greater than for infants and toddlers. Of those sick or injured under five, 34.9 percent were treated only by relatives while of those five and older, 29.3 percent did not seek medical care outside of their family (see Tables 4 and 5).   This may well reflect the greater complexity of diseases and treatments that would be suffered by the older group compared to the fairly straightforward nature of treating cases, unless unusually severe, of diarrhea and basic respiratory ailments among small children. As can be seen in Table 5, there is a greater use of hospitals for all consumption groups among this older group. And, for those in the top quintiles, there is a greater use of health personnel overall, with 44.4 percent of those in the bottom quintile not seeking care outside the home compared to only 12.4 of those in the top quintile.

---

[5] Note that this section refers to all those five years and older as well as children under five who had an illness or injury that was not diarrhea or respiratory.

Table 5: Use of Health Services for Persons Five
Years and Older
(percent)

	Quintile 1	Quintile 2	Quintile 3	Quintile 4	Quintile 5	Urban	Rural	Indig.	Total
Personnel Consult									
Doctor	39.9	56.9	71.8	79.5	87.7	72.1	61.8	22.8	64.7
Nurse, Assist.	12.9	3.4	4.1	3.7	0.0	2.9	4.4	26.5	5.0
Pharm. , Healer	2.9	1.6	0.0	0.0	0.0	0.9	1.4	0.0	1.0
Relative	33.7	29.7	17.4	12.0	7.0	18.2	25.7	27.0	21.8
Self-medicated	3.9	7.0	6.8	2.6	3.5	5.1	5.0	5.5	5.1
Did nothing	6.8	1.3	0.0	2.0	1.9	0.9	1.8	18.2	2.4
Facility Used[1]									
Pub. Hospital	38.7	40.9	47.5	51.3	31.6	49.0	36.5	25.4	43.1
Priv. Hospital	3.6	13.5	8.0	31.9	51.1	27.8	12.6	0.0	20.7
Center, Post[2]	47.4	34.6	42.3	12.3	7.8	17.6	40.3	74.6	28.8
Priv. Practice	5.1	0.0	2.2	4.4	9.5	3.4	4.5	0.0	3.7
Home, other	5.1	10.9	0.0	0.0	0.0	2.3	6.0	0.0	3.6

Source: ENV, 1997 MIPPE, authors' calculations.
Note: Includes all persons five years old and up reporating any illness or injury as well as any illnesses or injuries of under five year olds that are not diarrhea or respiratory.
1/ Percent of all those who sought care, i.e. those who reported consulting a doctor, nurse, health assistance, pharmacist or healer.
2/ Includes health centers, sub-centers and health posts.

19.   Although overall levels of health care use are slightly higher for those over five, many of the same patterns of use found for small children are found among this general population. Persons in higher quintiles are more likely to use hospitals than health centers. Among the highest quintile, private hospitals are more commonly used than public ones, although for all other quintiles public hospital use is more common. Note also that it is among the highest quintile that other private care is used the most.

20.   Geographic differences reflect the location of health care facilities. Hospitals are used most among the urban population, less in rural areas and least in indigenous areas. In indigenous areas, three-quarters of all care is obtained in health centers, posts or sub-centers. In urban areas, in contrast, only 17.6 percent of all visits to health personnel took place in such health centers.

IIIb-3: *Maternity Related Health Care*

21.   For woman ages 15-49, use of health services for prenatal care and for giving birth is high but unevenly distributed. The ENV data show that, of all women in this age group who had been pregnant in the five years previous to the survey, 43.9 percent had attended prenatal visits.[6]   These visits started, on average, by the third month of pregnancy, and women made, on average, over six visits. Thus, for those women who take advantage of prenatal care services, the frequency of visits is quite high. But this represents less than half of all women who are pregnant: more than the majority of all pregnant women do not use prenatal controls.

---

[6] These figures for overall use of prenatal care appear to be quite low compared to Ministry of Health estimates. There is nothing in the sample design or field work of the survey that would explain such a discrepancy. Further work to reconcile these data sources is clearly needed. The results of this section should be taken with caution until such work is done.

Table 6: Use of Prenatal Control Health Care
(percent and mean)

	Quintile 1	Quintile 2	Quintile 3	Quintile 4	Quintile 5	Urban	Rural	Indig.	Total
Prenatal Control	48.1	53.2	44.6	38.7	35.8	42.6	48.5	31.6	43.9
Month 1st control	3.3	2.8	2.3	2.3	1.9	2.4	2.8	2.9	2.6
Number of visits	5.2	6.4	6.8	7.0	8.0	7.0	6.2	5.1	6.6

Source: ENV, 1997 MIPPE, authors' calculations.
Note: Table refers to the percentage of women, ages 15-49, who were pregnant in the five years previous to the survey, who visited medical personnel for prenatal controls. For the average month in which such controls were begun and for the average number of such visits, the percentage refers to those women who used prenatal health care visits.

22.   For those who visited health care providers for prenatal controls, the most common source of care was doctor care at public hospitals or health centers. Woman in the lower quintiles, and in rural and indigenous areas, were more likely to visit health centers and sub-centers while those women in the top quintile used private care but mostly in hospitals and not at private practices. Only in indigenous areas and among the lowest quintile were any significant number of prenatal controls carried out by medical personnel below the level of doctor.

Table 7: Use of Health Services for Prenatal Controls
(percent)

	Quintile 1	Quintile 2	Quintile 3	Quintile 4	Quintile 5	Urban	Rural	Indig.	Total
Personnel Consult									
Doctor	74.5	92.0	93.1	94.4	96.9	95.3	86.4	58.2	90.1
Nurse, Assist.	20.3	5.1	4.2	3.2	0.3	2.1	10.5	30.6	6.6
Healer, Midwife[1]	5.2	2.9	2.7	2.3	2.8	2.6	3.1	11.2	3.3
Facility Used									
Pub. Hospital	31.3	29.8	36.9	30.0	24.3	31.9	30.5	19.8	30.8
Priv. Hospital	2.3	8.6	14.9	32.7	55.4	28.7	11.9	0.7	21.0
Center, Post[2]	62.8	61.0	45.2	33.3	15.6	36.2	55.5	71.9	45.3
Priv. Practice	0.8	0.3	2.0	3.2	4.8	2.7	1.3	0.0	2.0
Home, other	2.7	0.4	0.9	0.8	0.0	0.5	0.7	7.6	0.9

Source: ENV, 1997 MIPPE, authors' calculations.
Note: Refers to all women ages 15 to 49 who were pregnant in the five years prior to the survey interview, for multiple pregnancies, the data refer to the most recent pregnancy.
[1] Includes traditional midwives, healers, and others.
[2] Includes health centers, sub-centers and health posts.

23.   Among pregnant women, with the exception of those in the lowest quintile and/or those living in indigenous areas, the patterns of use of health care personnel for births is very similar. Doctors attend the vast majority of all births, even in rural areas (although this is a bit lower than in urban areas). But, only one quarter of births in indigenous areas were attended by doctors: having only family members in attendance was the most common situation (44.8 percent of all births). Among the births to women in the lowest quintile, the use of doctors was lower than for all other quintiles at just over 50 percent. After doctors, relatives are the next most common type of person to attend births for women in this quintile followed by midwives and nurses.

Table 8: Use of Health Services for Births
(percent)

	Quintile 1	Quintile 2	Quintile 3	Quintile 4	Quintile 5	Urban	Rural	Indigen	Total
Personnel Consult									
Doctor	50.6	89.9	94.0	95.2	97.4	95.2	80.6	24.5	82.1
Nurse, Assist.	8.7	4.0	2.4	2.9	1.6	2.8	6.2	6.4	4.4
Midwife	13.7	2.2	1.8	0.0	1.0	0.6	5.4	21.4	4.7
Relatives, other	26.9	3.9	1.8	1.8	0.0	1.4	5.9	44.8	8.8
Facility Used									
Pub. Hospital	50.0	87.3	90.6	83.1	57.7	81.9	76.1	22.6	73.3
Priv. Hospital	0.5	2.2	3.2	12.7	39.7	14.8	2.9	0.4	8.7
Center, Post[1]	6.9	4.0	3.6	2.8	0.5	1.5	6.3	8.7	4.0
Priv. Practice	0.0	0.4	0.0	0.0	1.0	0.3	0.3	0.0	0.2
Home, other	42.6	6.0	2.5	1.4	1.0	1.6	14.3	68.4	13.6

Source: ENV, 1997 MIPPE, authors' calculations.
Note: Refers to all woman ages 15-49 who gave birth within the five years previous to the survey.
[1]Includes health centers, sub-centers and health posts.

24.   The vast majority of women give birth in hospitals, again, with the exception of the women in the lowest quintile and the women living in indigenous areas.   Public hospitals account for the bulk of all births. Only among the top two quintiles and urban dwellers are private hospitals used. As would be expected, given the patterns of use of medical personnel among women giving birth who are in the bottom quintile or living in indigenous areas, many of these births take place at home. In fact, in indigenous areas, more than two-thirds of all births take place at home.

IIIc.   *Summary of Health Use Patterns*

25.   There are very clear patterns of health care use by welfare level and by geographic area, patterns which play a large role in the determination of who benefits from public spending. First, the poorest people, those in the bottom consumption quintile, use health care services less than other groups.   This means that much of the public expenditures on health care are going to the less poor and the non-poor. Second, in spite of the fact that those in the top quintile are more likely to use private health care than any other group, a substantial share of health cared received by the top quintile comes from public sector spending.   Finally, the geographical distribution of health care is very important. Urban dwellers are more likely to use hospitals and doctor provided health care. In rural and indigenous areas, more care is obtained from nurses and other type of personnel and services are provided in health centers, sub-centers or posts instead of hospitals. Because of the correlation between poverty and geographic location, urban populations use more health services overall.

IV.   Incidence of Public Health Care Spending

IVa.   *Value of Health Care Services Provided*

26.   In addition to needing data on the use of health services, determining the incidence of health spending requires a value to be placed on the health services received. This is both philosophically and practically difficult to do. In the first place, it requires that a value can be placed on human life or on a given level of health. Of course, the impact of the health care on this health level would also need to be established. Clearly, this is not a straightforward task, nor is it one where consensus will be easily reached.

27.   The second difficulty in determining the value of the benefits received is that not all benefits of health care are direct. An individual who never seeks medical care, who receives no direct benefits from the health care system, can still receive indirect benefits. Take for example the case of immunizations. The fact that other people are immunized, that the level of vaccination is high in a country, benefits an individual even if he or she is not vaccinated as it lowers the risk of disease.

28.   To avoid the problems of trying to determine the value of human life, the value of health care to the individual is set at the cost to the government of providing that service. While not addressing the issue of indirect benefits, this method at least has the advantage of being clear and non controversial.[7] To implement this valuation of health care, data on the average cost of health care services by level, by provider, and by location is needed. In the absence of more detailed information, the budget for each service level, divided by the total number of visits to this level is the minimum information needed. Any ability to disaggregate costs per type of visit and per personnel seen would improve the quality and precision of the analysis. For example, the ENV asks explicitly about outpatient curative care, outpatient preventive care, the use of prenatal controls, birth attendance and inpatient hospital stays although no information is collected on the illness itself. Thus, the cost to provide each of the mentioned services, averaged for all illnesses etc., is the most detail that can be usefully included in the analysis.

29.   At present it is not possible to determine the cost to the government of providing specific health care services: the administrative records do not allow this type of analysis. While this information will be available in the future-- two studies are presently underway to provide some estimation of such costs-- for the present analysis, costs per service have had to be assumed.[8] No effort has been made to guess at what actual costs in the sector might be or how expensive one type of health treatment is relative to another type. Instead, all types of treatments have been analyzed separately.[9] The only exception is for outpatient curative and preventive visits. These two types of visits are analyzed together with the value of a preventive care visit being estimated at half of the cost of a curative care visit, on average.[10]   Note also, when determining the difference in costs of a normal, vaginal birth to a cesarean, the costs were calculated with the cesearan being three times that of the normal birth, due to the longer hospitalization required by the latter.

30.   Relative prices are also important between or among types of health service facilities. Given the different patterns of health facility use in the population, if the hospital provided care is more expensive than care provided in other types of facilities, this will have an important impact on how public spending on health is distributed. To address this issue, three different scenarios were created. In the first, it is assumed that there is no difference in the cost of providing services through hospitals and health centers, sub-centers, or health posts. The second scenario is based on the assumption that it costs twice as much to provide health services through a hospital as it does through the other facilities. And the third scenario assumes that the price differential is three times. While no one knows, at present, what the actual difference in price is, by including these three scenarios, it is at least possible to determine what impact these price differences would have on the distribution of health spending.

31.   It is important to note that the analysis of incidence is based on data on the use of public services: in addition to a lack of data on the cost to the Government of providing these services, the analysis does not take into account household payments for these services. Ideally, the analysis would be based on the

---

[7] This assumption is reasonable when looking at the distribution of the benefits within a sector, i.e., health. It is less reasonable if one were trying to look at total social spending: comparing a year of education with a visit to a hospital, even if they cost the same to provide, becomes more conceptually ambiguous.

[8] Since the analysis takes place only within the sector, the absolute value of the service is unimportant; no attempt is made to compare health care benefits to education benefits or any other social benefits. For that type of analysis, accurate data on the costs of providing services in the different sectors would be required.

[9] The fact that neither actual absolute nor relative prices are used means that no assessment can be made of the total distribution of public health care spending. To do this would require, at least, information on relative prices.

[10] Note that prenatal care visits, while also preventive, are not included here but are analyzed separately.

total unit value of these services and would then analyze the incidence of public subsidies to these services (which represents only a fraction of the total cost of the services), separating out payments by households. Because these data are not available, the analysis indicates the incidence of the *use* of public services, rather than the incidence of public spending on these services.[11]

IVb. *Distribution of Spending*

32.   For general curative and preventive care, prenatal care and births, the costs of providing these services are estimated and matched with the use patterns seen in Section III. For each type of health care, the three scenarios illustrating the impact on the distribution of health care spending due to service provider are presented. Results are presented by welfare groups (consumption quintiles of the population) and by regional breakdowns.

IVa-1. *Curative and General Preventive*[12]

33.   If public health care spending were evenly distributed, the bottom twenty percent of the population should receive twenty percent of public health benefits. As can be seen in the Graph 1: Panel a, this is not the case for curative and general preventive care. The bottom quintile of the population receives less than 15 percent of the benefit from public spending on health in these categories. Note however, that the top quintile does not receive its 'fair' share either; all of the three middle quintiles receive more than twenty percent each. This observed distribution is, largely, a result of the fact that those in the bottom quintile use less health care overall than the other groups in the population and, at the other extreme, that those in the richest quintile substitute private health care for a portion of public care.

34.   Note, however, that if one were to look at benefits received by service provider, the poorest quintile relies much more heavily on public heath centers, posts and sub-centers than it does on the public hospitals. In fact, of all services provided by health centers, posts and sub-centers, the bottom quintile receives more than the twenty percent a perfectly equitable distribution would dictate. But, they receive significantly less than the twenty percent of services provided by public hospitals (8.6 percent). This pattern of using different types of health care providers within the public sector, leads to further inequities in the incidence of public health care spending. As shown in Panel b, if the provision of health care through hospitals costs more than through health centers, sub-centers and posts, a very plausible assumption and one supported by findings in other countries, then the incidence of public health care spending is further skewed away from the poor. The graph shows, that, the greater the gap in the cost of service provision between these two types of facility, the less equitable the distribution of public health care spending.

---

[11] Indeed, the LSMS reveals that 72% of non-poor households pay something (B./>0) for services (as compared with 61% of the poor).
[12] General preventive does not include prenatal care visits.

Graph 1: Incidence of Public Spending by Population Quintile

Panel a: Cost of Providing Services through Hospitals = Cost by Centers

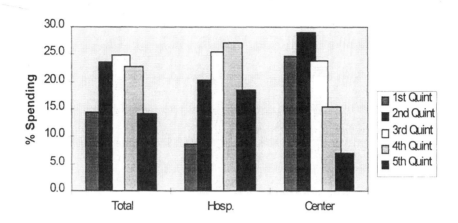

Panel b: Impact on Distribution as Costs of Providing Services through Hospitals Increase Relative to Health Centers, Sub-centers and Posts

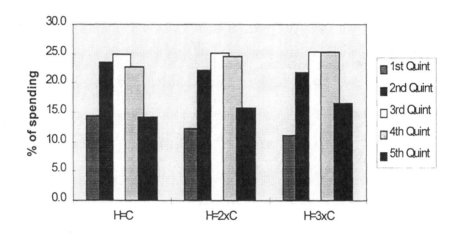

Source: Panama, ENV, 1997, authors' calculations.
Note: H stands for Hospital provided care, C stands for Health Centers, Sub-Centers and Posts, the first column refers to the distribution of public spending if hospital provided care cost the same as Health Center provided care. The second and third groups of bars show what this distribution would be if Hospital costs were two times and three times those of health centers.

35.   Inequities in the incidence of public health care spending on curative and general preventive health care are also apparent across geographic regions.   As shown in Graph 2; Panel A,   urban areas receive a bit more than what their share of the population would warrant as do the rural areas although the difference is probably not statistically significant.   In contrast, indigenous areas receive less than the share which corresponds to their population. This is true especially for hospital provided care.

Graph 2: Incidence of Public Spending by Region

Panel a: Cost of Providing Services through Hospitals = Cost by Centers

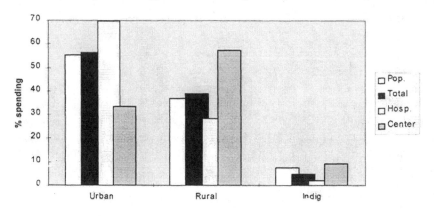

Panel b: Impact on Distribution as Costs of Providing Services through Hospitals Increase Relative to Health Centers, Sub-centers and Posts

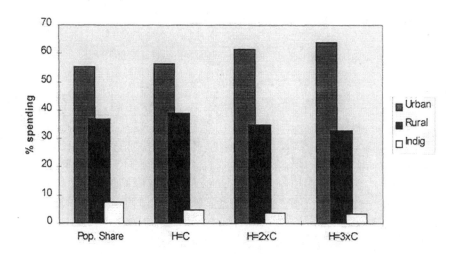

Source: Panama, ENV, 1997, authors' calculations.
Note: H stands for Hospital provided care, C stands for Health Centers, Sub-Centers and Posts, the first column refers to the distribution of public spending if hospital provided care cost the same as Health Center provided care. The second and third groups of bars show what this distribution would be if Hospital costs were two times and three times those of health centers.

36.   While urban and rural (non-indigenous) populations receive a share of total public health spending proportionate to their share of the national population, significant differences in the sources of health care exist. In urban areas, the share of services coming from hospitals is way in excess of the population share while, in rural areas, the opposite is true. Thus, if the assumption that health care services cost the same to provide, regardless of the type of facility, is relaxed, then the incidence of health care spending becomes quite skewed. As can be seen in Panel b of Graph 2, if hospital provided care is much more costly, urban populations receive more of the total benefit of public health spending and the rural populations then would be receiving less than the amount they should based on their population size. The existing shortfall in indigenous areas would increase.

37.   In short, the results of this analysis of curative and general preventive care show that the benefit of public health care spending is not evenly distributed, either across welfare groups or across geographic areas.   The actual distribution, of course relies on how accurate the assumptions on relative costs of preventive and curative care are.   Just as significantly, if not more so, is the impact that the cost of service provision by type of health facility has.   The more expensive hospital provided care is, relative to that provided by health centers, posts and sub-centers, the less the poorest groups and those in rural and indigenous areas receive the benefits of public spending on health.

IVa-2. Maternal Health Care

38.   The incidence of health spending on maternal care shows some differences relative to that of curative and general preventive care.   For prenatal care, the population in the bottom three consumption quintiles all receive more than twenty percent each of health care spending (see Graph 3; Panel a).   This is due to the fact that women in upper quintiles use more private health care services as well as to the fact that family sizes among the lowest quintile are much larger than among the higher ones.   Thus, more women in lower quintiles use maternity-related health care than among the highest quintiles.   As shown in Panel b of Graph 3, even if hospital provided prenatal care is three times that of care provided elsewhere, the lowest three quintiles still benefit more from this type of public spending.

Graph 3: Incidence of Public Spending on Prenatal Care by Population Quintile

Panel a: Cost of Providing Services through Hospitals = Cost by Centers

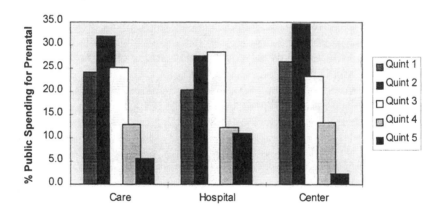

Panel b: Impact on Distribution as Costs of Providing Services through Hospitals IncreaseRelative to Health Centers, Sub-centers and Posts

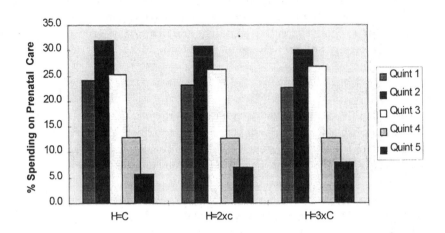

Source: Panama, ENV, 1997, authors' calculations
Note: H stands for Hospital provided care, C stands for Health Centers, Sub-Centers and Posts, the first group of bars refers to the distribution of public spending if hospital provided care cost the same as Health Center provided care. The second and third groups of bars show what this distribution would be if Hospital costs were two times and three times those of health centers.

39.   Unlike the case of curative and general preventive care, urban populations receive slightly less than their share (based on population) of public health care spending on prenatal care while rural areas get slightly more. (See Graph 4.)   In indigenous areas the proportion is equal to that of the population living in these areas: the only type of public health spending that fills this condition.   Again, though, the difference in where people obtain health care by geographic area makes the relative costs of service provision important for the overall incidence of health spending.   As shown in Panel b of Graph 4, if hospital provided services were three times the cost of other facilities' services, then urban areas would be receiving slightly more than their share of prenatal spending and indigenous areas would be receiving less.

Graph 4: Incidence of Public Spending on Prenatal Care by Region

Panel a: Cost of Providing Services through Hospitals = Cost by Centers

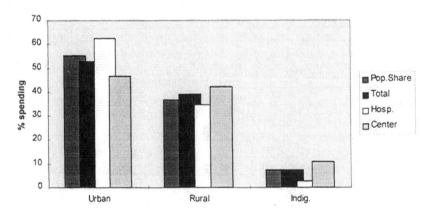

Panel b: Impact on Distribution as Costs of Providing Services through Hospitals Increase Relative to Health Centers, Sub-centers and Posts

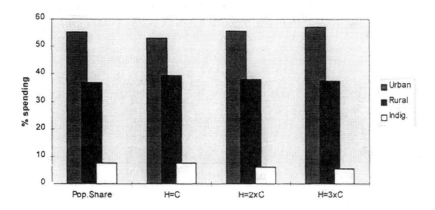

Source: Panama, ENV, 1997, authors' calculations
Note: H stands for Hospital provided care, C stands for Health Centers, Sub-Centers and Posts, the first group of bars shows the population share by region. The second group of bars refers to the distribution of public spending if hospital provided care cost the same as Health Center provided care. The third and fourth groups of bars show what this distribution would be if Hospital costs were two times and three times those of health centers.

40.   The final type of health care service examined here is that of births. As for prenatal care, the incidence of public spending for medical attendance to births is also greater among the lower quintiles than it is for general curative and preventive care. The lowest quintile receives almost exactly its share while the second and third quintiles receive much more than their population driven share. As shown in Graph 5, Panel A, the extremely low use of non-hospital facilities for giving birth, among all population groups, seen in the previous section, leads to little difference in the incidence of benefits based on the prices of services. Similar results can be seen on regional breakdown (Panel b).

Graph 5: Incidence of Public Spending for Birth

Panel a: By population quintile
Impact on Distribution as Costs of Providing Services through
Hospitals Increase Relative to Health Centers, Sub-centers and Posts

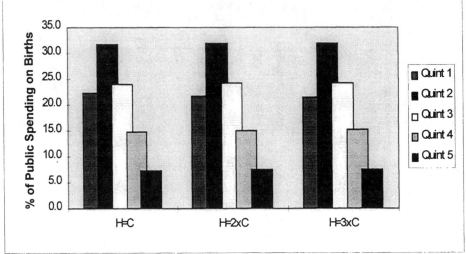

Note: H stands for Hospital provided care, C stands for Health Centers, Sub-Centers and Posts; the first group of bars refers to the distribution of public spending if hospital provided care cost the same as Health Center provided care. The second and third groups of bars show what this distribution would be if Hospital costs were two times and three times those of health centers

Panel b: By region
Impact on Distribution as Costs of Providing Services through
Hospitals Increase Relative to Health Centers, Sub-centers and Posts

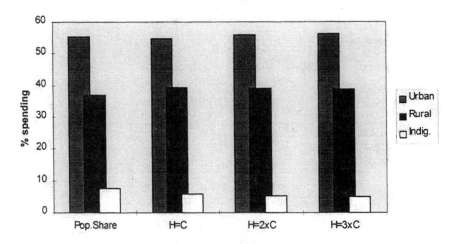

Source: Panama, ENV, 1997, authors' calculations
Note: H stands for Hospital provided care, C stands for Health Centers, Sub-Centers and Posts, the first group of bars shows the population share by region. The second group of bars refers to the distribution of public spending if hospital provided care cost the same as Health Center provided care. The third and fourth groups of bars show what this distribution would be if Hospital costs were two times and three times those of health centers.

41. In summary, health care spending by the public sector on maternity-related care benefits the poorer groups more than other types of care. In part this is a function of the fact that poorer women are more likely to have children than less poor women. And, it also reflects the fact that the richer women

are more likely to seek private health care. Only in indigenous areas are health care benefits for maternity not received in an amount proportional to the share of the population living in such areas.

V. Conclusions

42.   Obviously, many of the findings in this study must be taken as indicative of what the true incidence of health care spending in the country might be. Nevertheless, the extensive data on the use of health care, information that can be related to both the welfare status of the person using the care and the geographic location of the person, supports the following three conclusions:

- The poorest and the richest quintiles are those who benefit the least from public spending on health care. For those in the richest quintile, this is due to a voluntary substitution of private health care for public care. For the poorest, however, this is due to low levels of health care use in general, regardless of the type.

- Health care spending on general curative care is regressive while spending on maternity related care is more progressive. It is not possible to determine whether health care spending in total is regressive or progressive due to the problems with the data.

- Hospital based care is used more by the non-poor populations and those in urban areas. Thus spending on hospital based care is likely to be regressive. The health centers, posts and sub-centers are used more by poorer groups and, thus, spending on these facilities benefits the poor more.

43.   These tentative findings suggest ways in which present government spending on health care can be used to increase coverage of the population. At present, even though the population in the highest consumption quintile use significant amounts of private health care, this group still benefits from public spending on health.   As the poorest groups in the country are suffering from a shortage of affordable health care, the argument can be made that public resources, presently benefiting the non-poor, be targeted to the poor.

44.   While sliding scale fee systems and means testing within health care facilities are important mechanisms for targeting resources, they are also quite costly to administer.   An alternative, or at least, complementary mechanism, could be to target by geographic area and by type of health care facility. Given the distribution of the population, the correlation of poverty and geographic area, as well as the distribution of health care facilities in the country, resources invested in non-hospital based services will have more of an impact on the poor than similar resources devoted to hospital provided care.

Annex 16 – The Distributional Incidence of School Feeding Programs

Kathy Lindert
March 23, 1999

MAIN CONCLUSIONS

1.   Panamanian children currently benefit from two national school-feeding programs: an early-morning snack sponsored by the Ministry of Education and a school lunch program supported by the Social Fund (FES).   Community members, parents and teachers are heavily involved in the implementation of the schemes, which appears to have greatly contributed to their success.   Both programs contain a degree of self-targeting by virtue of their use of public schools as a vehicle for channeling transfers to the poor (wealthier children tend to enroll in private schools).   The FES school lunch program is even further geographically targeted through its use of poverty and nutrition indicators to select eligible school districts.   Both programs appear to have had a slight impact on reducing the share of the population living below the poverty line.   There is also a likely impact on educational attainment, as the in-kind transfers generated by the program are tied to school attendance.   An upcoming impact evaluation study by the GOP and the Bank will attempt to measure this impact.

POVERTY & ECONOMIC CONTEXT

2.   Despite Panama's relatively high per capita income (B./3,080 in 1997), inequality[1] is high and more than one million Panamanians (37 percent of the population) live in poverty and half a million (19% of the population) live in extreme poverty.[2] *Half* of all children under twelve live in poverty due to higher fertility rates among poor families.

3.   Poverty is largely concentrated in the countryside.   Although less than half the population lives in rural areas, some three-quarters of the poor and 91 percent of the extreme poor reside in the countryside. Close to two-thirds of rural residents fall below the full poverty line and 40 percent live in extreme poverty.

4.   Poverty in indigenous areas can only be described as abysmal.   Over 95 percent of indigenous residents (close to 200,000 people) fall below the full poverty line.   Roughly 86 percent live in extreme poverty.   Only five percent do *not* live in poverty.   Although indigenous areas account for less than eight percent of the national population, one-fifth of the poor and one-third of the extreme poor in Panama live in these areas.

5.   Poverty is lower in urban areas, though a significant share of city-dwellers live just above the poverty line and could be considered "vulnerable."   Roughly 15 percent of the urban population falls below the full poverty line, accounting for one quarter of Panama's poor.   Nonetheless, survey data reveal a significant clustering of the urban population just above the poverty line indicating the presence of a substantial "vulnerable" group of city dwellers.

6.   Malnutrition is highly correlated with poverty in Panama.   About 85 percent of malnourished children in Panama are poor.[3]   Over one quarter of poor children under five and one-third of those living in extreme poverty are malnourished compared with only five percent of non-poor children.   The

---

[1] See Annex 10 of the Poverty Assessment.
[2] These findings are based on a full poverty line of B/.905 per person per year and an extreme poverty line of B/.519 per person per year (See Annex 2 of the Poverty Assessment.
[3] Overall, 16% of all children under age 5 are malnourished in Panama (about 50,000 children).

incidence of malnutrition mimics the geographic distribution of poverty, with higher malnutrition rates in rural and indigenous areas.

PANAMA'S SOCIAL SAFETY NET

7.   Although Panama does not have a comprehensive safety net, considerable resources have been mobilized for social assistance programs. An estimated one percent of GDP is currently allocated to social programs, most of which have been strengthened since the early 1990s. These programs rightly address key poverty issues, including (i) cash and food-based transfers (mainly school feeding programs)[4] designed to alleviate economic barriers to school enrollment by the poor; (ii) programs to respond to community requests for basic and social infrastructure, such as the emergency social fund (FES) and a local investment program (PROINLO); and (iii) a number of small pilot programs designed to provide tailored assistance to meet the needs of key vulnerable groups (housing assistance for low income families, NGO-executed social programs for street children, poor elderly, poor women and youths, indigenous groups, and Afro-Panamanians, and targeted nutrition interventions for malnourished women and children).

SCHOOL FEEDING PROGRAMS: DESIGN ISSUES

Objectives & Benefits

8.   School feeding programs constitute the largest social assistance transfer programs in Panama, and began in the 1950s (Law No. 57 dated December 19, 1951, under which the school lunch program was instituted). Currently, there are two main school feeding programs in Panama: an early-morning snack program run by the Ministry of Education (MINEDUC) and a lunch program run by the Social Emergency Fund (FES).[5] These programs carry the dual objectives of improving the nutritional status of primary and pre-primary school-aged children and boosting school performance.[6] They also generate an income transfer to the families of the beneficiaries, as they relieve these households of the burden of providing these meals to the beneficiaries.

9.   The Ministry of Education's use of a snack (or light lunch) program began in 1987, providing school children with a nutritional mixture (*crema*), evaporated milk and sugar. Currently, two types of interventions are used. The first consists of a nutritional mixture enriched with corn, incorporating the milk and sugar, and fortified with 10 vitamins and 6 minerals. In the poorest districts, the snack also includes nutritionally enriched crackers. The second type of intervention provides whole liquid milk and a nutritionally fortified cracker. The milk began being distributed in official primary schools in 1991, and the cracker in 1992. In 1997, 69 percent of those matriculated in primary school received the nutritionally enriched mixture (*crema*).

10.   The *lunch program* (*almuerzo*) was initiated in 1991 by the FES, with the collaboration of the Ministry of Education, and consists of a lunch made from rice, beans, and oil.[7] Each ration provides not less than 20 percent of each recipient's daily recommended calorie and protein intake.[8]

---

[4] These compensatory education transfer programs mainly include school feeding programs, but also include a recently piloted "balboa per day" cash transfer program tied to school attendance (being piloted in Barú).

[5] There are a number of other locally-run school feeding schemes (run by churches, municipalities, NGOs, etc.) in various parts of the country.

[6] The food is legally destined only for children and must be consumed on the school premises. To avoid leakages to other individuals, the rules governing the programs state that students are not allowed to take any portion of their daily rations home with them under any circumstances.

[7] The content of the lunch fits well with local dietary patterns, and adjustments have been made to take into account differences in these patterns (e.g., indigenous children are served rations with a slightly lower content of cooking oil to better accommodate their traditional diets).

Targeting Mechanisms

11.   Both programs are self-targeted to a certain degree through the public school system (see below). Nonetheless, the MINEDUC *snack program* (milk and crackers) is becoming explicitly universal. Though it was initially geographically targeted to the "poorest" districts, a June 1995 law mandates an expansion of the program to cover the entire pre-school and primary school population.[9]

12.   In contrast, the FES *lunch program* is explicitly geographically targeted using pre-determined poverty, malnutrition, and education indicators.[10] Using these criteria, the program is targeted to primary and pre-school children in the poorest districts (with an emphasis on rural and indigenous areas).

Administration and Community Participation

13.   Although the FES and Ministry of Education administer the programs, implementation involves a high degree of community participation, which appears to have contributed greatly to their success.[11] Teachers and school directors are involved in program administration at the local level and in the mobilization of community involvement. Parents rotate participation in preparing food, and maintaining school gardens. Program meetings are also held regularly in recipient communities.

14.   Administration of the programs is relatively simple. Information on the reception of the food is reported on a regular basis to the central level. Direct distribution of food is always costly, but attempts have been made to keep these costs down.[12] The food is delivered to schools in the district (*cabacera*), which then distribute pro-rated amounts to satellite schools in the surrounding areas. The timely delivery of food has been hampered in remote areas (for example in certain parts of Bocas del Toro); food for these schools is distributed via helicopter on an irregular basis at a high cost. A number of possibilities for reducing distribution costs for the school feeding programs are being considered (Box A16.1), including the option of providing schools with funds to buy food directly on local markets (as has been done for the purchase of sports equipment in Panama's secondary schools, for example).

Box A16.1 – Decentralizing School Feeding Programs in Remote Areas: the Potential of Block Grants

Both the MINEDUC Snack Program and the FES Lunch Program suffer inefficiencies in the physical delivery of food to remote areas. Before the start of the next school year, both programs should design more cost-effective mechanisms for transferring resources to these communities (which have high incidences of poverty and malnutrition). Some options:

♦ **Government delivery is costly.** In some instances, the food has had to be delivered via helicopter (at a cost of B./800 per hour per helicopter!), horses, or boats.

♦ **Community pick-up is costly and ineffective.** One option that has been tried involves requiring communities to pick up the food themselves at satellite delivery points (the cost remains, but is borne by the communities). This has not been effective, however, and there are numerous reports of the food being left to waste.

♦ **Block grants are a promising alternative.** An alternative involves the decentralization of food purchases to the communities themselves. The Government could transfer funds as block grants directly to the communities, who would then purchase the food locally (according to pre-advised nutritional criteria consistent with local food supplies). A cost-benefit analysis suggests that, with proper monitoring and mechanisms for accountability, this would be by far the most cost-effective option.

---

[8] An analysis of the reported content of each ration reveals that it provides much more than that (645 calories and 16 grams of protein per beneficiary per day, representing about 37% of caloric requirements and 51% of the recommended protein intake for the age cohort).

[9] Ley 35 del 6 de julio 1995.

[10] The FES lunch program was initially geographically targeted according to a composite index of basic needs, as well as malnutrition and educational indicators. As the program is expanded, newly eligible districts are selected on the basis of a new poverty map constructed using data from the LSMS and the National Census. Indicators of educational attainment and malnutrition are used at the *corregimiento* level to obtain a more disaggregated degree of targeting.

[11] The program documents for both programs emphasize community participation, even stating that they will not take on a paternalistic nature from the central Government.

[12] Though cost data are not disaggregated for distribution costs.

THE COST OF SCHOOL FEEDING PROGRAMS

15.   **Fiscal Outlays.** The overall fiscal outlays on the school feeding programs are quite small. In 1997, the MINEDUC snack program cost about B./8.4 million, or 0.1 percent of GDP and 0.4 percent of total Government spending. The FES lunch program cost about B./986 thousand in 1997, which represented 0.01 percent of GDP and 0.04 percent of total Government spending.

16.   **Unit Subsidies.** Government outlays subsidize the delivery of free food up to the wholesale level, since communities are responsible for the delivery and preparation of the food beyond that point (see above for discussion of implementation arrangements). With 372,000[13] beneficiaries of the MINEDUC program in 1997, the official unit subsidy per beneficiary was approximately B./23 per year. With a total number of beneficiaries of the FES program of 47,007[14] in 1997, the official unit subsidy per beneficiary was approximately B./21 per year. The actual value of the rations received by the students is higher. In fact, self-reported values from the LSMS averaged B./72 for the snacks and B./172 for the lunches. The difference between the self-reported values and the actual per unit subsidies comes from the value added of preparation, storage, and transportation from the wholesale level to the point of consumption as well as the addition of other ingredients by parents and communities in the case of the lunches.

17.   There are substantial differences in the unit subsidy of the different food items delivered to the children (Table A16.1). As compared with other programs in Latin America, the MINEDUC program is fairly expensive and the FES lunch program is average in terms of their subsidy cost per 1000 calories transferred. Among snack items, the enriched *crema* is by far the cheapest in terms of its subsidy cost per ration and per 1000 calories and 100 grams of protein delivered. Milk is the most expensive in terms of subsidy cost per ration and per 1000 calories transferred (though, due to its higher protein content, it is a slightly more efficient way to deliver protein than the cookie). The milk is twice as costly as the *crema*. Eliminating milk from the program and substituting crema instead could substantially reduce program costs. This conflicts with Law No. 35 which states that all school children (regardless of poverty status) have the right to a free daily serving of milk, which seems to have strong backing from the milk processing and packaging lobby in Panama.[15] The protein- and calorie-packed lunch (made of beans, rice and vegetable oil) appears to be quite cost efficient.

18.   **Administrative and Targeting Costs.** A recent evaluation of the MINEDUC program indicates that administration and supervision costs represent about ten percent of the total costs of the snack program; likewise, the FES reports that administration absorbed nine percent of total outlays for the lunch program. With respect to the cost of targeting the programs, it is unlikely that the self-selection mechanism used in both programs (via the public school system) entails any direct costs (and rather generates savings of not providing the transfers to wealthier students in private schools). The geographic targeting mechanism used in the FES scheme is also likely to be quite cheap, covering only the cost of data collection on poverty and malnutrition indicators (which were already available from the census and malnutrition surveys).

---

[13] MINEDUC reports that 114,733 students received milk and cookies in 1997 and 257,267 received crema, for a total number of beneficiaries of 372,000 that year. However, under 250,000 pre-primary and primary school students reported receiving the snacks in the LSMS. Official figures are based on enrollment and do not take into account desertion during the school year, students who opt not to consume the snack, or leakages of the snacks (due to delivery failures, etc.).

[14] The program has since expanded substantially and is expected to reach over double this figure in 1999. Some 75,000 pre-school and primary students report receiving free lunches at school in the LSMS (1997). This higher figure likely comes from participation in other local lunch programs.

[15] Indeed, the Central America and Caribbean branch of Tetra Pak S.A., the company responsible for packaging the free milk, highlights its role in the program in its own company advertising (see "Tetra Bridge," a company brochure, May 1997).

Table A16.1 - Unit Costs of School Feeding Subsidies					
		Calories		Protein (grams)	
	Subsidy per rationᵃ	Per Ration	Subsidy Cost Per 1000 cal./day	Per Ration	Subsidy Cost per 100 g./day
Milk	B./0.21	159	B./1.33	8.1	B./2.62
Crema	B./0.09	161	B./0.55	4.0	B./2.22
Cookie	B./0.13	150	B./0.84	2.2	B./5.70
Lunch (FES)	B./0.13	645	B./0.20	16.3	B./0.80
Other programs in LAC: (a)			US$=B./		
Range	n.a.	n.a.	0.03-0.84	n.a.	n.a.
Mean	n.a.	n.a.	0.17	n.a.	n.a.
Median	n.a.	n.a.	0.24	n.a.	n.a.

Sources: MINEDUC, FES. MINEDUC reports that milk was distributed 160 days, the crema 140 days and the cookie 92 days in 1997. FES reports that the lunches were received 160 days. b\The calorie and protein content of the lunch was calculated from data on rations contained in "FES: Programa Nacional de Nutrición Escolar, October 1995" (Anexo 2) and calorie/protein composition coefficients from INCAP. (a) Comparison figures for LAC programs taken from del Rosso (1998).

DISTRIBUTIONAL INCIDENCE OF SCHOOL FEEDING PROGRAMS

19.   **Main Conclusions.** Data from the 1997 Living Standards Measurement Survey shows that both programs are self-targeted through their use of the public primary school system and benefit the poor more than the non-poor. The lunch program is much better targeted than the MINEDUC snack, however, which should come as no surprise, given that the FES lunch program is explicitly geographically targeted (as discussed above).

20.   **Self-Targeting via Public Schools.** The targeting of school feeding to poor children depends to some extent on the degree to which they enroll in school, particularly public school as the food supplements are distributed virtually exclusively at public schools. Most children, including poor children, attend primary school in Panama (see Table A16.2). Moreover, most poor children attend public school at the primary level, whereas a higher share of wealthier children enroll in private school. As such, channeling transfers through public primary schools guarantees a certain degree of self-targeting. Pre-primary school does not appear to be as efficient a vehicle for channeling transfers to the poor, however, given that a much smaller share of poor children actually enroll in school at this level (Table A16.2).[16] Pre-primary enrollment is particularly low among children in indigenous areas (the poorest areas in Panama).

---

[16] Children of pre-primary age, however, *do* constitute important targets for nutrition-related interventions as children under 5 tend to be the most at risk for nutritional deficiencies.

Table A16.2 – The Target Population: Distribution of Children and Enrollment by Poverty Group and Area							
	Extr. Poor[a]	All Poor[a]	Non-Poor	TOTAL	Urban	Rural	Indig.
Pre-Primary School							
Age Cohort (population)							
Group as % of children aged 3-5	30%	53%	47%	100%	46%	42%	12%
Enrollment							
Gross Enrollment Rate	10%	16%	42%	29%	41%	20%	10%
Group as % of total enrolled	10%	30%	70%	100%	66%	29%	4%
Public vs. Private School							
Enrolled in public school/total enrolled	98%	92%	59%	69%	59%	88%	100%
Group as % of public school enrollment	14%	40%	60%	100%	56%	38%	6%
Primary School							
Age Cohort (population)							
% of children aged 6-11	27%	49%	51%	100%	49%	40%	11%
Enrollment							
Gross Enrollment Rate	113%	112%	102%	107%	103%	110%	114%
Group as % of total enrolled	29%	51%	49%	100%	47%	41%	12%
Public vs. Private School							
Enrolled in public school/total enrolled	99%	99%	79%	89%	80%	97%	98%
Group as % of public school enrollment	32%	56%	44%	100%	42%	45%	13%
Both Pre-Primary and Primary							
Age Cohort (population)							
% of children aged 3-11	28%	50%	50%	100%	48%	41%	11%
Enrollment							
Gross Enrollment Rate	78%	80%	84%	82%	84%	80%	79%
Group as % of total enrolled	27%	49%	51%	100%	49%	40%	11%
Public vs. Private School							
Enrolled in public school/total enrolled	99%	98%	76%	87%	77%	96%	98%
Group as % of public school enrollment	30%	55%	45%	100%	43%	44%	13%

Source: Panama LSMS 1997. (a) All poor includes extreme poor.

21. **The MINEDUC Snack Program.**[17] In terms of coverage of the target group, the MINEDUC snack program reaches a respectable two-thirds of poor and extreme poor *primary* students (Figure A16.1, Table A16.3). Moreover, since access to primary school is virtually universal in Panama, the program reaches the majority of poor primary-school aged children. In contrast, while a substantial share of poor *pre-*

Figure A16.1

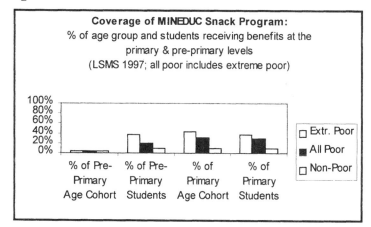

primary students also receive the snacks, the program reaches only a small share of the age cohort since very few children (particularly poor children) attend primary school (see Table A16.3 and Figure A16.1).

22. With regards to the target incidence of the program, the distribution of benefits[18] is slightly self-targeted and parallels the progressivity of enrollment in public school (since the snacks are distributed

---

[17] The LSMS asked whether or not students had received free snacks at school without specifying whether or not these snacks were provided by MINEDUC. As such the data could capture other local free snack benefits, although the MINEDUC program is the largest snack program in Panama.

[18] This analysis assumes a constant transfer per student of B./23 per year (not the self-reported values of the program from the LSMS).

exclusively through public schools). Poor children in *primary* school received more benefits than the non-poor, reflecting the fact that a substantial share of wealthier children attend private primary school (see Figure A16.2). At the *pre-primary level,* the program disproportionately benefits the non-poor, with a comparatively low share of benefits going to the poor and extreme poor.

23.   In terms of coverage, the MINEDUC snack program does not appear to possess any strong regional biases (owing largely to the virtual universality of primary school access in Panama, see Tables A16.2 and 16.3). A **Figure A16.2** slightly higher share of children aged 3-11 in rural areas received the school snacks (Table A16.3). The distribution of beneficiaries strongly reflects the geographic distribution of the population: while 46 percent of beneficiaries reside in urban areas, 48 percent of children aged 3-11 live in urban areas; likewise, while

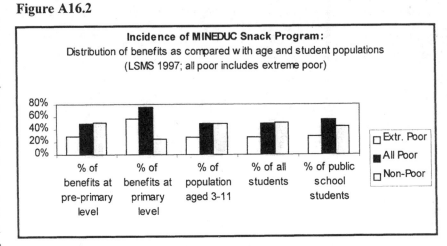

10 percent of beneficiaries reside in indigenous areas, 11 percent of the age cohort live in these areas. The remaining 44 percent of beneficiaries and 41 percent of the age cohort reside in non-indigenous rural areas.

Table A16.3 – Distributional Incidence of the MINEDUC[a] School Snack Program, by Poverty Group and Area							
	Extr. Poor[b]	All Poor[b]	Non-Poor	TOTAL	Urban	Rural	Indig.
Pre-Primary School							
Coverage (Recipients)							
Recipients as % of those enrolled	63%	70%	41%	50%	44%	59%	69%
Recipients as % of age cohort	6%	12%	17%	14%	18%	12%	7%
Target Incidence (Dist. of benefits)							
% of total benefits (incidence)	13%	42%	58%	100%	59%	35%	6%
Primary School							
Coverage (Recipients)							
Recipients as % of those enrolled	66%	69%	60%	64%	61%	70%	58%
Recipients as % of age cohort	74%	77%	61%	69%	63%	77%	65%
Target Incidence (Dist. of benefits)							
% of total benefits (incidence)	30%	54%	46%	100%	44%	45%	11%
Both Pre-Primary & Primary							
Coverage (Recipients)							
Recipients as % of those enrolled	66%	69%	57%	63%	58%	69%	58%
Recipients as % of age cohort	51%	55%	47%	51%	49%	55%	46%
Target Incidence (Dist. of benefits)							
% of total benefits (incidence)	28%	53%	47%	100%	46%	44%	10%
Source: Panama LSMS 1997. (a) The LSMS asked whether or not students had received free snacks at school without specifying whether or not these snacks were provided by MINEDUC. As such the data could capture other local free snack benefits, although the MINEDUC program is the largest snack program in Panama. (b) All poor includes extreme poor.							

24. **The FES School Lunch Program.**[19] In terms of <u>coverage</u>, the FES school lunch program is smaller than the MINEDUC snack program. Just under one fifth of all pre-primary and primary school students receive free lunches at school (Table A16.4). At both levels, the FES program reaches a larger share of the poor than the non-poor (even at the pre-primary level, which tends to be poorly targeted).

25. With regards to the <u>distributional incidence</u> of benefits,[20] the FES school lunch program is remarkably well targeted, particularly at the primary level (Figure A16.4). Over half of the benefits of the program accrue to children living in extreme poverty, compared with only one quarter for the non-poor (Table A16.4). This impressive result reflects not only the self-targeted effect of channeling transfers through public schools but also the explicit use of poverty, education and malnutrition indicators to geographically target the program.

Figure A16.3

Coverage of FES Lunch Program:
% of age group and students receiving benefits at the primary & pre-primary levels
(LSMS 1997; all poor includes extreme poor)

26. In terms of geographic distribution, the FES school lunch program is clearly oriented towards indigenous and non-indigenous rural areas (Table A16.4). Over half of indigenous children aged 3-11 received the school lunches, compared with 15 percent and just four percent of their counterparts in non-indigenous and rural areas respectively. While 41 percent of

Figure A16.4

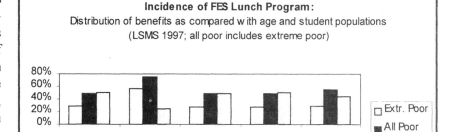

Incidence of FES Lunch Program:
Distribution of benefits as compared with age and student populations
(LSMS 1997; all poor includes extreme poor)

beneficiaries live in indigenous areas, only twelve percent of children aged 3-11 reside in these areas. The converse is true for urban areas: while 14 percent of beneficiaries are urban, close to half of all children aged 3-11 reside in urban areas. The remaining 44 percent of beneficiaries and 42 percent of the age cohort live in non-indigenous rural areas. The bias of the FES school lunch program to indigenous and rural areas clearly reflects the explicit geographic targeting of the program according to indicators of malnutrition: a higher share of indigenous and non-indigenous rural children are malnourished compared with those in urban areas.

---

[19] The LSMS asked whether or not students had received free lunches at school without specifying whether or not these lunches were provided by the FES. As such the data could capture other local free lunch benefits, although the FES program is the largest lunch program in Panama.

[20] This analysis assumes a constant transfer per student of B./21 per year (not the self-reported values of the program from the LSMS).

Table A16.4 – Distributional Incidence of the FES[a] School Lunch Program, by Poverty Group and Area							
	Extr. Poor[b]	All Poor[b]	Non-Poor	TOTAL	Urban	Rural	Indig.
Pre-Primary School							
Coverage (Recipients)							
Recipients as % of those enrolled	37%	20%	9%	13%	7%	17%	62%
Recipients as % of age cohort	4%	3%	4%	4%	3%	3%	6%
Target Incidence (Dist. of benefits)							
% of total benefits (incidence)	30%	49%	51%	100%	38%	40%	21%
Primary School							
Coverage (Recipients)							
Recipients as % of those enrolled	38%	29%	10%	19%	6%	21%	67%
Recipients as % of age cohort	43%	32%	10%	21%	6%	23%	76%
Target Incidence (Dist. of benefits)							
% of total benefits (incidence)	57%	76%	24%	100%	38%	44%	41%
Both Pre-Primary & Primary							
Coverage (Recipients)							
Recipients as % of those enrolled	38%	28%	10%	19%	6%	21%	67%
Recipients as % of age cohort	30%	23%	8%	15%	5%	17%	53%
Target Incidence (Dist. of benefits)							
% of total benefits (incidence)	55%	74%	26%	100%	16%	44%	40%

Source: Panama LSMS 1997. (a) The LSMS asked whether or not students had received free lunches at school without specifying whether or not the FES provided these lunches. As such the data could capture other local free lunch benefits, although the FES program is the largest lunch program in Panama. (b) All poor includes extreme poor.

IMPACT OF SCHOOL FEEDING PROGRAMS ON POVERTY, NUTRITION, EDUCATION

27.   Depending on the circumstances, school feeding programs have the potential to (i) alleviate poverty by providing an in-kind transfer to the poor; (ii) reduce malnutrition; and (iii) provide incentives for improved educational enrollment, attendance, and performance.

Impact on Poverty Alleviation

28.   The provision of free food serves as an in-kind income transfer to those who receive it. This transfer can alleviate poverty (or the severity of poverty) if it is received by those below the poverty line. As discussed above, the average cash value of the *government subsidies* was B./23 and B./21 on the snacks and lunches respectively in 1997. In terms of relative importance, these transfers represent just over one percent of average annual total consumption per capita. The average self-reported value of the *entire rations* was B./72 for the snack and B./172 for the lunch, or four percent and nine percent of average annual total consumption respectively. The subsidies and rations were more important to the poor in terms of their relative importance, conferring a larger share of total consumption of the poor than the non-poor (Table A16.5).

29.   Simulations using the LSMS reveal that these transfers do indeed have an impact on poverty. If the both rations were eliminated, the share of the population below the poverty line would increase by over one percentage point, from 37.3 percent to 38.6 percent (or about 35,000 additional poor people). The effect would be slightly larger for the snack program than the lunch program due to the wider existing coverage of the snack program.[21] Of course, in addition to an increase in the number of people living below the poverty line, beneficiaries already living in poverty would be worse off from an elimination of either program.

---

[21] Poverty would rise from 37.3% to 38.3% if the snack program were eliminated and 37.6% if the lunch program were eliminated (LSMS simulations).

Table A16.5 – Relative Importance of School Feeding Programs, by Poverty Group				
	Extr. Poor[a]	All Poor[a]	Non-Poor	TOTAL
School Snacks (MINEDUC)				
Value of Government Transfers (Subsidies)				
Annual Value	B./23	B./23	B./23	B./23
Share of Total Consumption	7.5%	4.5%	0.9%	1.3%
Average Value over Entire Population	B./3.4	B./3.3	B./1.7	B./2.3
Share of Total Consumption	1.1%	0.6%	0.1%	0.1%
Self-Reported Value of Rations				
Annual Value	B./65	B./69	B./74	B./72
Share of Total Consumption	21.1%	13.7%	2.8%	3.9%
Average Value over Entire Population	B./9.6	B./9.8	B./5.4	B./7.1
Share of Total Consumption	3.1%	1.9%	0.2%	0.4%
School Lunches (FES)				
Value of Government Transfers (Subsidies)				
Annual Value	B./21	B./21	B./21	B./21
Share of Total Consumption	6.8%	4.2%	0.8%	1.2%
Average Value over Entire Population	B./1.8	B./1.2	B./0.3	B./0.6
Share of Total Consumption	0.6%	0.2%	0.0%	0.0%
Self-Reported Value of Rations				
Annual Value	B./190	B./185	B./126	B./172
Share of Total Consumption	61.9%	36.6%	4.8%	9.4%
Average Value over Entire Population	B./16.4	B./10.8	B./1.6	B./5.1
Share of Total Consumption	5.4%	2.1%	0.1%	0.3%
Source: Panama LSMS 1997. (a) All poor includes extreme poor.				

Nutritional Impact

30.   Improving malnutrition is also a common objective of school feeding programs, including those in Panama. The impact of such programs on nutritional status (as measured by anthropometric indicators such as height or weight for age) depends on several factors, including: (i) the pre-program nutritional status of the beneficiaries (i.e., whether or not the beneficiaries were malnourished without the program); and (ii) the extent to which the food provided at school is additional or whether is simply substitutes for food that would have otherwise been provided by the household (substitution effect). Although data are not available to assess the nutritional impact of Panama's school feeding programs, evaluations of programs in other countries have not found an impact on nutritional status among school children.[22]

Educational Impact

31.   By channeling food rations through the school system, school feeding programs have the potential to improve educational attainment by (i) inducing parents to enroll their children in school and keeping them in school longer (lowering the drop-out rate); (ii) encouraging regular attendance (reducing absenteeism); (iii) helping raise the learning capacity and cognitive function of school children by alleviating short-term hunger, which in turn should help improve attention and concentration; (iv) addressing specific nutrient deficiencies that directly affect cognition (particularly iodine and iron), depending on the content of the rations; and (v) increasing community involvement in schools through program participation.[23]   By improving educational attendance, these transfers have the potential to reduce poverty in the long run (thus adding an investment dimension to otherwise short-term poverty alleviation assistance).

[22] Del Rosso (1998). The exception is a pilot scheme in Lombok Indonesia, which found that a combined packaged of food and anthelminthic treatment improved anthropometric indicators in participating children.

[23] Indeed, evaluations of school feeding programs in the United States and Jamaica found significant impacts of these schemes on achievement tests and attendance. Del Rosso (1998).

32.   Evidence from the LSMS suggests that the linking of transfers to school attendance – such as the provision of food rations in the school feeding programs – indeed addresses a critical poverty problem in Panama. Indeed, the direct costs of schooling (including formal and informal fees, transportation, books, materials, etc.), which represent twelve percent of the poverty line, constitute the most frequently cited obstacle to school enrollment.[24] Providing an in-kind income transfer at school can help reduce the economic barriers to school attendance among the poor and enrollment among the indigenous (since enrollment among other groups is already quite high). It would likely also have an impact on increasing attendance (reducing absenteeism) for all groups.

33.   The GOP and the World Bank are currently working together to develop a methodology for evaluating the impact of Panama's school feeding programs on educational enrollment, attendance, and repetition rates. The evaluation should be completed during the 1999 school year, providing more concrete evidence on the educational impact of school feeding programs.

MAIN ISSUES & LESSONS LEARNED

34.   The above analysis highlights a number of important issues and lessons-learned associated with school feeding programs:

- **Targeting.** Channeling transfers through the public school system can generate a certain degree of self-targeting when wealthier children tend to enroll in private schools. In Panama, both the MINEDUC and the FES programs have benefited from this self-targeting. Geographic targeting according to poverty, malnutrition and education indicators can substantially improve targeting: the FES program is much better targeted to the poor (particularly the extreme poor in traditionally-excluded indigenous areas) due to the use of these indicators. The MINEDUC program should reconsider its decision to expand to cover *all* primary and pre-primary school children, and should instead attempt to improve geographic targeting through the use of nutritional indicators and an improved poverty map.

- **Coverage of the Poor.** The ability of school feeding programs to reach the poor depends on the access of the poor to the education system. Public primary schools appear to be better vehicles for reaching the poor than pre-primary schools: the poor in Panama have virtually universal access to primary education, whereas a much smaller share attend pre-primary school. (However, pre-primary school-aged children tend to be more nutritionally at risk than primary-aged children).

- **Poverty Impact.** The school feeding programs have generated in-kind income transfers that are of considerable importance to poor recipients. An elimination of these schemes would result in a slight increase in the share of the population living in poverty and a worsening of living conditions among beneficiaries already living below the poverty line.

- **Educational Impact.** The linking of these transfers to school attendance probably creates an investment-effect in long-term poverty reduction via improvements in educational attainment. A joint GOP-World Bank evaluation of this potential impact is planned for the 1999 academic year.

- **Program Design: Community Participation.** The participation of local communities, parents and teachers seems to have contributed greatly to the success of the programs.

---

[24] See Chapter 2 of the Main Poverty Assessment Report.

- **Recommended Reforms: Possible Ways to Cut Costs.** There are three ways in which Panama's school feeding programs can be improved to cut costs:

  a) The MINEDUC program should abandon plans to become universal and instead improve geographic targeting to the poor (see above);

  b) The MINEDUC snack program should consider eliminating milk and replacing it with the enriched *crema*, as the cream is much cheaper in terms of its unit costs and the cost of nutritional benefits transferred (see above); and

  c) Both programs should consider allocating financial grants to individual schools so as to allow the schools to purchase local food directly, thereby avoiding apparently higher distribution costs associated with direct delivery of food to these schools (particularly in remote areas).

REFERENCES

Del Rosso, Joy. 1998 "School Feeding Programs: Food for Education." World Bank. Draft.

Fondo de Emergencia Social. October 1995. "Programa Nacional de Nutrición Escolar." Plus various memos and tables through official communication.

INCAP. March 1998 Evaluación del Programa de Merienda Escolar del Ministerio de Educación.

Ministerio de Planificación y Política Económica, Dirección de Políticas Sociales. 1997. The Living Standards Measurement Survey (LSMS/ENV).

Ministerio de Educación. 1996. "Repuesta del Sector Educativo a la Problematica Alimentaria-Nutricional." Plus various tables through official communication.

Rokx, Claudia. May 1997. Panama Social Fund School Feeding Component: Back-to-Office Report. The World Bank.

The World Bank and the Ministerio de Economia y Finanzas. 1999. The Panama Poverty Assessment.

Annex 17 – Distributional Incidence of the Maternal-Infant Supplemental Feeding Program

Kathy Lindert
March 29, 1999

1.   With the support of the World Bank's Rural Health Project, the Ministry of Health (MINSA) has introduced a Maternal-Infant Supplemental Feeding Program (*Programa de Alimentación Complementaria*, PAC). This program is being phased in over the period from 1995-99 and will ultimately cover close to 30 districts. It is part of the Government's National Food and Nutrition Program (PRONAN) for 1992-2000 which seeks to reduce chronic malnutrition rates by half in children under five by the year 2000.

DESCRIPTION OF THE PROGRAM

2.   **Food Rations and Micronutrients.** The program involves distributing food rations, which consist of an enriched, pre-cooked instant meal made from a mixture of extruded rice and beans, supplemented by milk and micronutrients.[1] The meal does not require cooking, but is instead made into an instant porridge by adding water. Access to safe water is thus essential. The daily rations provide 15 percent and 22 percent of recommended daily calorie and protein intake respectively by pregnant and lactating mothers; 41 and 71 percent for infants 6-11 months; 32 and 69 percent for children 12-23 months; and 25 and 55 percent for children 24-59 months.

3.   **Distribution.** The rations are distributed by health posts to eligible women and children living in the vicinity and at the community/village level with the assistance of community health workers. Rations are delivered on a monthly basis (bi-monthly to remote areas) and the supplements are accompanied by nutrition education messages. Micronutrient supplements are also distributed twice a year (with supplements for vitamin A, iron and folic acid, and iodine).

4.   **Target Mechanisms.** The program is targeted to malnourished children aged six months (after weaning) to five years and to pregnant and breast-feeding women. The program maintains clear eligibility and exit criteria according to anthropometric indicators as follows:

- **Children** aged 6-60 months are eligible if they are at least two standard deviations below the norm for their weight-for-age (underweight) and have failed to register any weight gain between two successive controls (each two months apart). They remain eligible for program rations until they either resume a normal weight gain or their weight increases to within one standard deviation of the norm.
- **Pregnant women** are eligible if they are at least two standard deviations below the norm of weight for height given the stage of their pregnancy (severely underweight), or below normal weight and have failed to gain weight between two successive pre-natal controls. Severely underweight women can remain enrolled in the program until the sixth month after childbirth; the other women can continue to receive rations until childbirth.

5.   The program is also self-targeted to a certain degree by (a) the distribution of the rations via health posts (centers, sub-centers), which the poor tend to use whereas the non-poor tend to frequent private practices and health clinics;[2] and (b) the rather bland tasting nature of the instant meal. Screening is carried out by regular MINSA staff or by community health workers during regular checkups and on community health days. The program is combined with health monitoring and interventions; prior to allocating the rations, the health workers verify that the beneficiary is up-to-date on health controls.

---

[1] Each eligible recipient receives a monthly allocation of six pounds of this enriched meal, which is packaged in one pound plastic bags for easy use and storage.
[2] See Annex 15 of the Poverty Assessment.

6.   **Program Costs.** The program cost about B./850,000 in 1997, or 0.01 percent of GDP. Official estimates put the total number of beneficiaries at 13,755, yielding a per beneficiary cost of B./62.

THE DISTRIBUTIONAL INCIDENCE OF THE PAC

7.   **LSMS Data.** The LSMS collected data on the receipt of free food distributed by MINSA via health posts, centers, and sub-centers; these data provide an indication as to the number and distribution of beneficiaries of the PAC Program. The data were collected for children under six (aged 0-5). Data on program participation by women are not available.

8.   **Total Overall Coverage.** Close to 16,000 children aged five and under were reported in the LSMS as having received free food from MINSA. This represents about six percent of the total population of children in that age group.

9.   **Distribution of Beneficiaries by Poverty Group.**[3] In terms of coverage of the program by poverty group, a larger share of poor and extreme poor children receive MINSA food rations than non-poor children (Table A17.1). In terms of the distribution of all beneficiaries, the program appears to be quite well targeted with respect to poverty group: 82 percent of all beneficiaries are poor (65 percent live in extreme poverty), with the remaining 18 percent who are not poor. This compares with the overall distribution of the population of kids under age six in which 53 percent are poor (30 percent living in extreme poverty) and 47 percent are not poor.

10.   **Distribution of Beneficiaries by Nutritional Status.** In terms of coverage of malnourished children, the program delivers free rations to ten percent of children suffering from any form of malnutrition[4] (as compared with four percent of children who are not malnourished). With regards to the distribution of beneficiaries, about half are malnourished and about half are not.

11.   **Distribution of Beneficiaries by Geographic Area.** MINSA's food ration program reaches a larger share of indigenous and rural children than urban children. Some 14 percent of indigenous children and eight percent of rural children receive the free rations via the health system, as compared with only two percent of urban children. A disproportionate share of the total number of beneficiaries live in rural and indigenous areas: one third of total beneficiaries are indigenous and over half are rural, as compared with their respective population shares of twelve percent for all indigenous children and forty percent for rural children (Table A17.1). This pattern matches the higher concentration of malnourished (and poor) children in rural and indigenous areas than in Panama's cities.

---

[3] These findings are based on a full poverty line of B./95 per person per year and an extreme poverty line of B./519 per person per year (See Annex 2 of the Poverty Assessment.

[4] That is, children with z-scores that are more than two standard deviations of the reference point for any of the three anthropometric measures (height for age, weight for age, weight for height).

Table A17.1 – Coverage and Distribution of MINSA's Supplemental Feeding Program (percent)			
	COVERAGE	DISTRIBUTION	
	Beneficiaries as % of all children < age 6	Group as share of total beneficiaries	Group as share of total population of kids < 6
By Poverty Group			
Extreme Poor (a)	12	65	30
All Poor (a)	9	82	53
Non-Poor	2	18	47
By Nutritional Status (b)			
Not Malnourished	4	52	75
Malnourished	10	48	25
By Geographic Area			
Urban	2	15	48
Rural	8	55	40
Indigenous	14	29	12
Source: Panama LSMS 1997. (a) All poor includes extreme poor. (b) Any form of malnutrition (i.e., children are malnourished if their z-scores are more than two standard deviations below the reference point for any of the three anthropometric indicators: height-for-age, weight-for-age, weight-for-height).			

Annex 18 - Community Organization, Values and Social Capital in Panama

Maria-Valéria Junho Pena (LCSES)
Hector Lindo-Fuentes (Consultant)[1]

OBJECTIVES, DATA SOURCES AND DEFINITIONS

A. Objectives

1.   As increasingly more is expected from civil society and from the marketplace, community-based-organizations are being recognized as a privileged stakeholder to motivate the poor to seek solutions to their social and economic problems. This report deals with how communities organizations have been organized to promote community development in Panama.

2.   Specifically, the objectives of the report are to understand : (a) how rural non-indigenous communities, rural indigenous communities, and urban communities build their sense of identity; (b) some of the conditions that favor, and some of the conditions that discourage, the development of community organizations; (c) the communities' *perceptions* of changes in their living conditions - whether they feel conditions have improved, worsened, or stayed the same during their recent past; (d) the relationship between community organization, social capital and the *perceived* changes in living conditions among the three mentioned different types of communities; and (e) the relationship between social capital and poverty.

B. Data Sources

3.   This report draws on two main sources of data: (a) a Living Standards Measurement Survey (LSMS) conducted from June to September 1997; and (b) in-depth interviews from qualitative focus group discussions carried out in a Social Capital Qualitative Survey (SCQS) in November 1997. The LSMS includes a household questionnaire, which covers 4,945 households (21,427 individuals), and a community questionnaire covering 436 communities.[2] Although the LSMS household survey is nationally representative of the Panamanian population, the community questionnaire is only representative of the communities in the sample.[3] Likewise, although the SCQS is representative only of the sixteen communities included in the sample (a subset of those covered by the LSMS community questionnaire), it provides insights on how and why communities organize, and how these networks contribute to improving living conditions.

---

[1] Dra. Enriqueta Davis Villalba also contributed to this report through her participation in the focus group interviews for the Social Capital Qualitatitive Survey and her subsequent report 'Informe Sobre la Pobreza en Panama: Componente de Capital Social" on indigenous communities. The authors would like to thank Lic. Rosa Elena deDe la Cruz, Dra. Enriqueta Davis and Dr. Carlos Becerra for their participation in the Social Capital Qualitative Survey and their support to the elaboration of the focus groupguildelines. In addition, the authors would like to thank Enriqueta Davis and Carlos Sobrado for their inputs into the report. The authors would like to thankEnriqueta Davis, Caroline Moser, Kinnon Scott, and William Partridge for their comments on an earlier draft. Finally, the authors are grateful to Kathy Lindert, Task Manager of the Panama Poverty Assessment, who read, commented and contributed to the design of the Social Capital Qualitative Survey and to preliminary versions of this report. Finally, the authors would like to thank the World Bank's Strategic Compact and the Swiss Agency for Development and Cooperation for financial support.

[2] The LSMS community interviews were conducted in a "focus-group" type manner, sometimes coupled with interviews with single representatives of the communities).

[3] Moreover, community questionnaires were not implemented for 70 communities in the survey (covering 11 percent of the total sample of individuals). Due to conceptual difficulties in distinguishing community boundaries in an urban setting under an LSMS framework, the majority of these communities with "missing data" are urban (67 out of 70), and most of these are in Panama City (51 out of 67). Thus 30 percent of the urban population in the sample was not covered by the community questionnaire.

C. Concepts of Community

4.   **In Theory.** As societies are born out of the interactions between individuals, the most important need they have is related to the conditions in which collectivities as units perform social functions.[4] A "community" is a type of collectivity whose notion was classically opposed to that of "society." "Community" is typically characterized by its organic solidarity, with a division of labor that is simple (frequently by gender and age), and a stratification system based on ascription (such as kinship), rather than on achievement. On the other hand, "society" is characterized by an elaborate division of labor, a multitude of social roles, and social mobility based on performance. As Max Weber described it: "community" is the opposite of conflict (what paradoxically, in order to avoid transgression, may take them to extreme violence), while 'society" signifies compromise among conflicting interests.[5]

5.   **In Practice.** For practical purposes, the concept of "community" used in the LSMS and SCQS (and consequently in this study) is largely a geographic notion that is closer to the common idea of "neighborhood" than to the classic concept of community described above. An analysis of these data reveal that some of these "neighborhoods" possess characteristics that make them similar to the ideal type of "community" described above, while others have characteristics similar to the classic definition of society. Indeed, as discussed in more detail below, the classic concept of "community" in Panama proves to be a more accurate description of some of the rural and indigenous localities,[6] whereas the concept of "society" appears to be a more fitting description for many of the urban (and some rural) neighborhoods in the sample.

D. Concepts of Social Capital

6.   **In Theory.** Social capital is commonly understood as "features of social organization such as trust, norms, and networks, that can improve the efficiency of society by facilitating coordinated actions."[7] Certain forms of association, but not all of them, constitute social capital because they are they are instrumental in the generation of wealth by facilitating coordinated actions.

7.   Some of the key ingredients of social capital are trust, norms of reciprocity, and networks of civic engagement. **First**, trust. By functioning in associations, people learn the value of cooperation, but cooperation is possible only when people trust each other. Membership in certain associations is often linked to personal reputation, therefore, belonging to them is a hallmark of being trustworthy. Moreover, sometimes belonging to one association creates opportunities for participating in another, and thus trust becomes transitive. The greater the number of associations participating in a given network, the more people can work with each other without having to constantly check their backgrounds. In order words, the transaction costs decrease. **Second**, the development of norms allows personal trust to become social trust. To sustain cooperation, trust has to be stable and predictable; for that reason, norms are developed. Norms are not only internalized through a process of socialization, but are also enforced through mechanisms which establish sanctions and third-party enforcement for violations. The existence of widely accepted norms makes behavior predictable, again lowering transaction costs and making cooperation possible. **Finally**, the existence of a dense network of associations makes it possible to generalize those norms.

---

[4] "Subject both to the more general values of the system and to the norm regulating the behavior of the relevant differentiated types of units within the system, the normative culture of a collective defines and regulates a concrete system of coordinated activity that can at any given time be characterized by the commitments of specifically designated persons, and which can be understood as a specific system of collective goals in a specific situation." In Talcott Parsons, **Sociological Theory and Modern Society** (1967) (New York: The Free Press), p.10.

[5] Max Weber (1964) **Economia Y Sociedad** (Mexico: Fondo de Cultura Económica.)

[6] Communities and households in the LSMS (and consequently SCQS) are classified according to geographic areas, which include: "urban," "rural" (non-indigenous), and "indigenous."

[7] Robert D. Putnam (1963) **Making Democracy Work: Civil Tradition in Modern Italy** (Princeton: Princeton University Press) p. 167. That is, not all organizations constitute social capital, they have to have specific characteristics that improve the efficiency of society.

8.   **In Practice.** The Panama LSMS allows us to measure some of the ingredients of social capital, including: (i) the frequency of community interaction and organization as an element of trust in each other and of trust in the results of these interactions; and (ii) the density of networks of associations. The other dimension -- norms -- is captured in the SCQS.

9.   Using the **LSMS community questionnaire**, social capital is measured by a composite <u>Social Capital Index</u> encompassing the following questions[8]: (a) Is there in this community a committee or any other forms of organization to solve the problems of its inhabitants? (b) During the last five years, did members of this community participate in volunteer work to maintain or improve civil works in the community? (c) What is the extent to which members of this community participate in solving school problems? (d) What is the extent to which members of this community participate in solving health center problems? (e) What is the extent to which members of this community participate in solving problems pertaining to the organization of the community? (f) What is the extent to which members of this community participate in solving problems of access roads (*caminos de acceso)*? (g) What is the extent to which members of this community participate in solving problems with roads (*carreteras)*? (h) What is the extent to which members of this community participate in solving water and garbage-collection problems?[9]

10.   The Social Capital Index (SCI) varies from 0-8 where zero means negative answers to all the questions and 8 means positive answers to all the questions. Communities with SCI scores ranging from 0-2.5 are classified as having low social capital. Those with scores ranging from 3-5.5 are considered to have medium social capital. And those with scores ranging from 6-8 are classified as having high social capital.

11.   The **LSMS household questionnaire** also contains questions about the participation of household members in a variety of community organizations (*juntas comunales, locales o cívicas, concejos municipales*, cooperatives, committees, and indigenous associations). While these data only measure one dimension of social capital, they have the important advantages of (i) being gathered in the nationally representative household survey; and (ii) hence being linked to other household information (including poverty status). This report thus examines LSMS data on social capital from both the household and the community questionnaires.

12.   Using the quantitative Social Capital Index from the LSMS, 16 communities were selected for inclusion in the **SCQS focus group discussions**. They were selected from those scoring among the top and the bottom according to this index, while guaranteeing sufficient representation of communities in indigenous, rural non-indigenous, and urban areas. (See Appendix for details).

13.   In the SCQS, various aspects of social capital were explored, including: (a) the communities' social organization, horizontal and vertical connections, local system of decision-making, existing leadership and the extent of their influence; (b) the reasons why some communities are able to create social capital, others are not; (c) the conditions for, and constraints to, trust and what mechanisms provoke solidarity; (d) the basis for solidarity (interests, division of labor, tradition, etc.); (f) the relationship between social capital and gender; (g) mobilizing issues and their priorities; (h) perceptions of the role of government versus the community with respecting to promoting community development;

---

[8] The correlation coefficients between each of the above questions and the index showed it to be internally consistent.

[9] Composed by these questions, the Social Capital Index (SCI) has the advantage of presuming neither that social capital is equivalent to civic culture in the Almond and Verba tradition nor that social capital would mean the willingness to subordinate private interests to broader community goals, as in the Durkheim tradition. The peril of understanding social capital as civil culture is the trap of ethnocentrism (the indicators used by Almond and Verba led to the inexorable conclusion that Great Britain and the United States score the highest in civil culture). The peril of the Durkheim tradition is to be led to the opposite: by making trust equivalent to social capital, the latter can only be found where mechanical solidarity prevails. Gabriel A. Almond and Sidney Verba (1963) **The Civic Culture: Political Attitudes and Democracy in Five Nations** (Princeton: Princeton University Press); Emile Durkheim (1968) **La División du Travail Social** (Paris: P.U.F.).

and (i) the main differences regarding social capital building between indigenous and rural non-indigenous and urban communities.

Box A18.1 – Indigenous Communities in Panama and in the SCQS

The indigenous population in Panama is about 200,000, distributed among five different groups (in order of population size): the Ngobe-Buglé (or Guaymí sabanero), the Kunas or Tules, the Emberá-Waunana, the Teribe, and the Bokota. Although indigenous people live in all of Panama's provinces, indigenous groups have historically been concentrated in certain regions. In their greatest majority, the Ngobe-buglé live in the province of Boca de Toro, Chiriquí and Veraguas; the Kunas live primarily in the Comarca of San Blas and in Maduga (in the province of Panama); the Emberá and the Waunana live in the provinces of Darién and Panama; the Bokotas primarily reside in the provinces of Bocas del Toro and Veraguas; and the Teribe in the province of Bocas de Toro.

In the SCQS, four communities belonging to the Waunana, Kuna and Ngobe groups were visited. All the three groups live in rural areas, and agriculture is their main economic activity. Productivity is low due to inappropriate technology and lack of financing; the environment is degraded, and access to markets is almost non-existent. Labor is organized by sex and age, with all members of the family, and sometimes from other families, cooperating.

Sources: Enriqueta Davis, 1997; Panama SCQS 1997.

ORGANIZATION OF THE REPORT

14.   This report is organized in two broad parts. **Part I** explores the LSMS and SCQS with respect to the nature of communities: (a) how they identify themselves; (b) how they organize themselves; (c) their mobilizing issues; (d) how they perceive recent changes in their living standards; and (e) how communities relate to the external world. **Part II** explores the nature of communities' social capital, examining (a) trends in social capital by type of communities (urban, rural, indigenous); (c) social capital and internal community relations (including horizontal relations, gender, leadership, and norms); (c) the relationship between social capital and poverty, education, and perceived living standards; and (d) the relationship between social capital and external assistance.

PART I: COMMUNITIES

A. How Communities Identify Themselves

15.   The results of the LSMS community questionnaire reveal that space *does indeed constitute* an important element in creating a sense of community identity, thereby generating support for the adoption of a "geographic" definition of community in the implementation of this survey. In fact, the LSMS shows that, in spatial terms, the communities in the sample have been relatively stable overtime, with 88 percent reporting having existed for more than twenty years and only 2.1 percent been formed less than ten years ago. As expected, a higher share of rural and indigenous communities in the sample report longer stability, with 93 percent and 98 percent existing for longer than twenty years respectively. A higher frequency of urban communities, on the other hand, have been formed more recently (though the majority are older), with 20 percent having been formed less than twenty years ago (Table A18.1).

Table A18.1 - Age of Communities by Type (%)				
Age	Urban	Rural	Indigenous	Total
< 10 years	2%	2%	2%	2%
10-20 years	18%	5%	0%	10%
> 20 years	80%	93%	98%	88%
Total Sample	180	216	40	436
Source: Panama LSMS 1997, Community Questionnaire				

16.   In general, a sense of identity is pervasive among most of the communities surveyed in the SCQS, but the glue that holds their members together varied particularly across types of communities (urban, rural, indigenous). Sometimes, this glue is weak and almost invisible; in others, cohesion has almost the thickness of a "thing" alluded by Durkeim as a characteristic of the "social fact."[10]

17.   The SCQS confirms the findings of the LSMS regarding the coupling of community identity with a pride of *place* in all three types of communities (urban, rural, indigenous). One rural community in the sample, for example, maintains a park as a unifying element in the community. In an indigenous community in the Kuna islands, teams of women sweep the streets and keep them clean. In an urban community members make special efforts to maintain the mausoleum of a parish priest revered for his good works and performing of "miracles:" the lawn is kept green and free of weeds and the hedges are neatly trimmed.

18.   In rural and urban communities in the SCQS sample, interests and aspirations regarding the future, and the efforts needed to realize them, are important elements underpinning their sense of community identity. For example, members of one urban community indicated that "we are identified by the fact that we all want to get ahead." And, in another, "our characteristic is the interest in struggling and helping others... selflessness to help and give back to the community." The SCQS found this same sense of engagement in collective efforts to be a unifying theme in rural communities: "unity produces results" and "selfish communities never prosper."

19.   In contrast, in indigenous communities in the SCQS, community identity is much more related with a sense of pride and culture than with ideas about a specific agenda. For example, in the Kuna communities visited in the SCQS, although manifested differently from island to island, this sense of pride is the most salient trait when they talk about who they are. In one island they are proud of "their language and culture," and of being "the first purveyors of Western culture in the "Comarca." The office of their Sahila (chief) was presided by the portrait of the first Kuna to bring schools to the region. In another island community, they emphasize their defense against assaults to their traditions and are proud of the "revolution that we made in 1925 when colonial authorities tried to destroy our traditions" (he was referring to the Tule Revolution). Their meeting was presided by the portrait of Nugalipte, a leader of the confrontation. Among the Ngobe communities visited in the SCQS, a similar pride in their culture exists with more explicit connection to their ability to hold together as a community: "we are proud of our language, our customs," "we work in an organized fashion, we fight and have pride."

B. How Communities Organize Themselves

20.   Organizations within communities are in part determined by institutional frameworks established by the government. In Panama, municipalities have "Juntas Comunales" with representatives from each district (*corregimiento*), and "Juntas Locales" at the level of each community. In addition, public schools have parent's organizations (Asociaciones de padres de familia) and health centers have health committees (Juntas de salud). Communities in Panama also report a number of organizations that are not affiliated with state institutions, such as church groups, sports clubs, and ad-hoc committees designed to deal with community problems (see Box A18.2 for examples). Many government social programs in Panama, such as PROINLO, FES and Municipios Siglo XXI, rely on the existence of local organizations to function.

---

[10] Emile Durkeim (1956) **Les Regles de la Méthode Sociologique**: (Paris, P.U.F.)

21.   The existence of state-sponsored organizations does not necessarily imply that the community is organized, since the latter is embedded in culture.   Groups such as parent's organizations or health committees can be either empty shells or part of lively networks of associations.

22.   The LSMS community survey reveals that there is a sharp contrast between urban and rural (indigenous and non-indigenous rural) communities in the sample in terms of the existence of community organizations. Some 75 percent and 80 percent of non-indigenous rural and indigenous communities in the LSMS sample affirm having some sort of community organization, as compared with just half of urban communities in the sample (see Table A18.2).[11]

Box A18.2 - Examples of Committees in a Kuna Island Community
Street sweeping committee
Storage committee
Hotel committee
Aqueduct committee
Tax committee
Pier committee
Sports committee
Festivities committee
Comptrollers committee
And when asked if they get tired of too many committee meetings, a young man answered "But we don't have enough."
Source: Panama SCQS 1997

Table A18.2 - Existence of Community Organization by Type of Community				
Community organization	Urban	Rural	Indigenous	Total
Existence of organization	51%	75%	81%	66%
No community organization	49%	25%	19%	34%
Total	100%	100%	100%	100%
Source: Panama LSMS 1997, Community Questionnaire				

23.   Results of the LSMS household questionnaire confirm these geographic patterns of participation at the household level.   As shown in Table A18.3 below, indigenous households participate in organizations much more than their urban counterparts. Over 40 percent of indigenous households report participating in some type of community organization, compared with only 28 percent and 30 percent of urban and rural households respectively.   Indigenous residents mainly participate in local associations, followed by committees and cooperatives. The main forms of participation for non-indigenous rural residents are local committees and cooperatives, followed by *juntas communales*.   Interestingly, cooperatives, which tend to generate more private benefits from participation (since they generally support private productive or consumption activities) than the other more "public good" forms of community organizations, were the only significantly frequent form of participation among urban residents.

Table A18.3 - Household Participation in Various Organizations by Geographic Area % of Households Reporting at Least One Member Participating				
	Urban	Rural	Indigenous	Total
Junta Communal	6%	11%	7%	8%
Concejo Municipal	1%	1%	2%	1%
Committees	5%	14%	14%	9%
Local Associations	1%	0%	24%	2%
Cooperatives	22%	13%	14%	17%
Any of Above	28%	30%	41%	30%
Mean # of Above[a]	0.34	0.39	0.61	0.34
Source: Panama LSMS 1997, household questionnaire (note: nationally representative sample) a\Mean # of types of groups (junta, concejo, committee, local association, cooperative) in which at least one household member participates.				

---

[11] As shown in Table 11 below, the existence of community organizations does not necessarily lead to people being engaged with them.

C. Why Communities Organize Themselves: Some Mobilizing Issues

24.   As manifested in answers to open-ended questions in the community questionnaire of the LSMS and in the focus groups for the SCQS, priorities are consistent across communities: transport and roads, employment, potable water, health, housing, sewerage and sanitation, communal spaces, etc.   The priorities normally change depending on which of those services is already provided. For example, as shown in Table A18.4, indigenous communities in the LSMS dedicate a more intense participation (much) to schools, health centers and local roads than their urban counterparts, possible reflecting the relative lack of these services in indigenous areas.   This may be partly one of the reasons why communities located in major urban areas tend to have lower levels of organization since basic services are already in place.

Table A18.4 - Mobilizing Issues for Community Participation by Type of Community				
Participation	Urban	Rural	Indigenous	Total
In schools				
No	28%	15%	14%	20%
Little	44%	40%	35%	41%
Much	28%	17%	51%	39%
Total	100%	100%	100%	100%
In health				
No	70%	67%	38%	66%
Little	23%	16%	30%	20%
Much	7%	17%	32%	39%
Total	100%	100%	100%	100%
In community organizations				
No	29%	10%	5%	18%
Little	51%	51%	46%	50%
Much	20%	39%	49%	32%
Total	100%	100%	100%	100%
In local roads				
No	61%	17%	19%	32%
Little	32%	44%	46%	39%
Much	17%	39%	35%	29%
Total	100%	100%	100%	100%
In roads				
No	55%	23%	51%	39%
Little	29%	45%	32%	37%
Much	16%	32%	16%	24%
Total	100%	100%	100%	100%
In water and garbage				
No	32%	18%	35%	25%
Little	41%	34%	32%	37%
Much	27%	48%	32%	38%
Total	100%	100%	100%	100%
Source: 1997 Panama LSMS, Community Questionnaire				

25.   Other important issues such as public order, employment or major environmental problems can have a high priority but people realize that they it is beyond their possibilities to address them, no matter how organized they may be.   Although communities in the LSMS and in the SCQS stress alcoholism, drugs, and robberies as some of their most impeding problems, they do not seem to mobilize themselves around these issues.   More, a certain degree of robbery, violence, drug consumption in general, and alcoholism in particular, seems to be acceptable, if not with tolerance, at least as inevitable.

26.   In the LSMS, communities were asked whether they organize to address specific issues, including: schools, health centers, in the organization of the community, access roads (*caminos de acceso*), roads (*carreteras*), and water and garbage collection. Of these specific issues, schools, water and garbage were considered as the most mobilizing. Overall, 38 of the communities in the sample indicate strong community participation in improving schools, with the same proportion affirming participation in solving water and garbage issues. Health by far is the least mobilizing issue concerning communities: 66 percent of the communities in the sample indicate no participation in solving problems of local health center. Indigenous communities in the sample also reported more participation than urban and rural communities in solving problems pertaining to schools, health centers and the community *per se*, while indigenous and rural communities reported a similarly high degree of participation in the solution of problems of local roads. In contrast, urban communities report consistently less community participation in the solving of these problems. (Table A18.4).

D. Communities' Perceptions of Recent Changes in Living Standards

27.   The LSMS community questionnaire includes a variety of questions about the communities' *perceptions* of changes in their living standards over the past five years,[11] both in terms of their "overall" living standards (*condiciones de vida o de bienestar*) and in terms of specific aspects of their living standards, including perceived changes in the delivery of street lighting, access to safe water, sewer services, garbage collection, and housing.

28.   **Perceptions of Changes in Overall Well-Being.** Overall, the record of communities perceiving worse, constant, and improved living conditions is a pretty even split: about one third for each category (see Table A18.5). The impressions are markedly different by geographic area, however. Interestingly, community perceptions of changes in living standards contradict the profile of poverty as measured by annual consumption. As discussed in detail in other parts of the Poverty Assessment, poverty as measured by consumption is *much* higher among residents of indigenous areas (95 percent of all indigenous residents), than non-indigenous rural areas (63 percent of rural residents) and urban areas (16 percent of city-dwellers). This profile of poverty is consistent with differences in access to basic services across the different geographic areas (see Box A18.3 and other chapters of the Poverty Assessment).

Table A18.5 - Perceived Changes in Well-Being by Type of Community				
Percent of Communities Interviewed in LSMS in Each Geographic Area				
Well-Being	*Urban*	*Rural*	*Indigenous*	*Total*
Worse	41%	31%	14%	34%
Same	28%	31%	54%	32%
Better	30%	38%	32%	34%
Total	100%	100%	100%	100%
Source: Panama LSMS 1997, community questionnaire				

---

[11] Specifically, the questionnaire asks if conditions have worsened, stayed the same, or improved.

Box A18.3 - Community Access to Basic Services in Panama
Overall, three fifths of Panamanian communities sampled in the LSMS do not have a sewer system; more than half do not have any form of garbage recollection; one fourth do not have street lighting; more than one tenth do not have access to a close source of potable water. Urban communities are much better off than indigenous and rural communities in terms of access to services: only 2 percent do not have street lightening; only 2,5 percent do not have access to safe water; and 75 percent have garbage collection. Access to sewer systems is clearly a case in which, although with a much higher access than rural and indigenous communities, the urban are also insufficiently covered (44 percent). In general, among indigenous communities, the lack of access to these services is still worse than among non-indigenous rural communities, and is often dismal: 95 percent do not have access to a sewer system; 84 percent receive no garbage collection; 81 percent do not have street lighting; and 43 percent do not have access to a close source of potable water.
Source: Panama LSMS 1997, community questionnaire

29.   In contrast, however, indigenous communities in the LSMS sample were much less pessimistic about their perceptions of recent changes in living standards than their non-indigenous rural and urban counterparts. Only 14 percent of indigenous communities in the LSMS sample perceive a worsening of conditions over the past five years, as compared with 41 percent for urban communities and 31 percent for rural communities in the sample (see Table A18.5). The more positive outlook among indigenous communities was also found among communities sampled in the SCQS (see Box A18.4).

30.   **Perceptions of Changes in the Delivery of Specific Basic Services.** Despite the more negative perceptions of changes in overall living standards, the urban communities were more optimistic than their indigenous and non-indigenous rural counterparts in their assessment of changes in the delivery of specific services over the past five years. Table A18.6 reveals that there is a stronger feeling among urban communities

Box A18.4 - Positive Perceptions of Change in an Indigenous Community
The positive perceptions of changes in living standards among indigenous communities are evident in these remarks made during one of the focus group discussions in the SCQS:
"Before, we had no town, the children no schools"   "We had poverty before"   "We didn't know whether our products were cheap or expensive"   "We lived like wild animals"   "Now we live in towns, community. One realizes (the advantages). Living far away from each other is too much work."
Source: Panama 1997 SCQS

that the situation regarding street lighting, water, sewer services, and garbage collection has improved during the last five years. Housing is the exception: although progress is recognized by 70 percent of all communities in the sample, the perception of improvement seems to be stronger among rural communities and there is a higher frequency of perception of a worsening of housing conditions among urban communities (see Table A18.6).

31.   A composite index of the communities' perceptions of changes in street lighting, access to water, sewer services, garbage collection and housing was constructed for the communities in the LSMS sample (with scores of positive, neutral, or negative).[12] This index reveals that about two-fifths of communities in the LSMS sample feel positive, perceiving better conditions for these basic services than five years ago, while about one quarter of communities believe that these basic services have worsened (see Table A18.7). That the majority of communities are urban in the LSMS sample in part reflects this relative overall optimism. Indeed, the absolute majority of urban communities in the sample presents a positive evaluation of changes in these services. This does not hold true for indigenous and rural communities in the sample. Among the former, less than one fifth believe they are better off with respect to the provision

---

[12] The change index encompasses five questions which asked how communities evaluate changes (better, worse, equal) in the previous five years with regard to housing, water, sewer service, garbage collection. The index varies from 0-4, where zero means the situation has worsened in all dimensions and four means the situation has improved in all dimensions. Those with a score of 0-1 were considered as having a poor evaluation of recent changes in these services, those scoring 2 as having a medium evaluation, and those scoring 3-4 as having a positive evaluation of recent changes in these services. All questions were shown to be highly correlated to the index.

of these services, while more than two-fifths perceive a worsening of service delivery; among the latter, the proportion of rural communities that evaluate an improvement in conditions (30 percent) is roughly the same as those perceiving a worsening in conditions pertaining to basic services (29 percent).

32.   A comparison of the communities' perceptions of changes in overall well-being (Table A18.4) and their evaluation of changes in specific aspects of well-being (composite index of perceptions of changes in housing, street lighting, water, sewerage, and garbage collection in Table A18.7) reveals a quite dissimilar pattern in attitudes towards recent changes. For the entire sample of communities, the general perception of a worsening of overall living conditions is stronger than the negative perceptions of changes in the composite index of services. In other words, although there is a smaller frequency of negative feelings regarding changes in specific aspects of life (composite index of services), a higher share of communities perceive a worsening of overall well-being.

Table A18.6 - Perceived Changes in Delivery of Basic Services and Housing by Type of Community
Percent of Communities Interviewed in LSMS in Each Geographic Area

Perceived changes in:	Urban	Rural	Indigenous	Total
Street Lighting				
Don't have service	2%	39%	81%	25%
Worsened	21%	13%	5%	16%
Stayed the same	39%	14%	8%	27%
Improved	38%	33%	5%	32%
Total	100%	100%	100%	100%
Access to Safe Water				
Don't have service	2%	23%	43%	16%
Worsened	27%	20%	24%	23%
Stayed the same	39%	20%	22%	29%
Improved	32%	37%	11%	33%
Total	100%	100%	100%	100%
Sewer Services				
Don't have service	44%	96%	94%	74%
Worsened	17%	1%	3%	8%
Stayed the same	32%	2%	3%	15%
Improved	7%	1%	0%	3%
Total	100%	100%	100%	100%
Garbage Collection				
Don't have service	17%	80%	84%	54%
Worsened	30%	4%	8%	15%
Stayed the same	23%	6%	5%	13%
Improved	30%	10%	3%	18%
Total	100%	100%	100%	100%
Housing				
Worsened	17%	6%	5%	10%
Stayed the same	14%	20%	49%	20%
Improved	70%	74%	46%	70%
Total	100%	100%	100%	100%

Source: Panama LSMS 1997, community questionnaire

Table A18.7 - Composite Index of Perceived Changes in Services by Type of Community				
Percent of Communities Interviewed in LSMS in Each Geographic Area				
Composite Index	Urban	Rural	Indigenous	Total
Negative	17%	30%	43%	25%
Neutral	28%	41%	38%	36%
Positive	55%	29%	19%	39%
Total	100%	100%	100%	100%

Source: Panama LSMS 1997, community questionnaire. The composite index is an unweighted index of community perceptions of changes in the following services over the past five years: street lighting, access to safe water, sewer services, garbage collection and housing. A negative score reflects a lack of access to the service and/or community perceptions that the service has worsened over the past five years. A neutral score reflects community perceptions that the conditions of service have remained the same. And a positive score reflects community perceptions that conditions have improved.

33.   This dissimilarity is particularly striking when comparing urban and indigenous communities. Urban communities in the sample tended to be 24 percentage points more pessimistic about changes in their general well-being than when evaluating the set of specific community services (composite index of housing, water, street lighting, sewer systems, and garbage collection), as shown in Table A18.8 (which compares Tables 6 and 7). Likewise, a higher share of urban communities provided a positive evaluation of changes in specific services over the past five years (55 percent in Table A18.7) than those who perceived an improvement of overall living conditions (30 percent in Table A18.5). In contrast, the opposite pattern is seen among indigenous communities in the sample. The feeling that overall well-being has improved is more widespread (32 percent in Table A18.4) than the communities' evaluation of changes in specific services (19 percent for the composite index in Table A18.7).

Table A18.8 - Paradox of Perceptions: Comparison of Community Perceptions of Changes in Overall Well-Being (from Table A18.5) and Perceptions of Changes in Changes in Basic Services (from Table A18.7)				
Attitudes towards change	Urban	Rural	Indigenous	Total
Worse	24	1	-29	9
Same	0	-10	16	-4
Better	-25	9	13	-5

Source: 1997 Panama LSMS, community questionnaire. The Table indicates the % of communities in sample perceiving X change in overall well-being - % of communities perceiving X change in composite index of basic services over past five years, by geographic area. E.g.,: urban communities in the sample tended to be 24 percentage points more pessimistic about changes in their overall well-being than when evaluating changes in the composite index of basic services.

Box A18.5 - Pessimism in an Urban Community: A Matter of Pride
One urban community in the SCQS focus group discussions offers a striking example of community members' pride in revealing how bad conditions are. Considering it as an honorable mission, the members went out of their way to point out the deterioration of their physical surroundings. At the end of the focus group meeting, they insisted on visiting some of the worst examples, even though it was already dark and the local police commander, feeling that the neighborhood was not a wholesome environment, had sent three policemen with bullet-proof vests to escort the World Bank consultants. The community members wanted us to see old houses that were in a state of complete disrepair, noting "it's a danger for the children...when the house fell down the other day because of the rains, people knew way before that it was going to fall down but no one did anything until it fell."

Source: Panama SCQS 1997.

34.   There are a number of possible explanations for this discrepancy and the paradox that those who are empirically better off feel less privileged than those who are worse off. **First,** although statistically coherent, the equal weighting of the different components of the composite index of services might not

match the relative importance the community members actually attach to each component. **Second,** measures of consumption and the delivery basic services do not capture all aspects of well-being. Community perceptions of overall well-being are not direct and matter-of-fact, and are probably based on a number of other factors (such as safety, empowerment, social interactions, etc.). **Third,** the demonstration effect is stronger in urban communities than in more remote rural and indigenous communities; no matter how much urban communities have improved in specific aspects of life, the proximity to wealthier populations provokes a gap between achievement and expectations, thereby increasing disappointment. With relative deprivation, this would not hold true for indigenous communities, whose aspirations, in spite of the dismal absolute poverty in which they live, might be lower given their isolation and absence of an external group of reference, which would allow comparison.[13]

E. Communities' Relations with the External World: Isolation and Distrust

35.   Results from the LSMS community questionnaire suggest a general feeling of estrangement from the government, politicians and the outside world.[14] More than two thirds of the communities in the sample do not perceive the government as supporting them. Over 70 percent indicate they do not perceive the politicians as supporters. Only ten percent affirm having received support by any NGO. Two exceptions to this overall perception of lack of support are worthy of note: churches and schools are recognized by about half of the communities as giving them support.

36.   Overall, urban and rural communities in the sample report more support than indigenous communities. A higher frequency of communities reporting support from politicians -- but not from the Government -- is a distinct feature of urban communities in the LSMS sample, which may suggest traditional clientelism relations in these areas (see Table A18.9). This type of relation is also apparent in the focus group meetings: one urban community for example reported that their library building was provided "by the legislator," and also that a man "from Switzerland" offered to provide funds for a retirement home for which the architectural plans would be designed by a relative of a Representative.

---

[13] It is worth noting that, as discussed in Box A18.3, some indigenous communities in the SCQS compared themselves with their historical past, feeling better because they do not live "like wild animals" anymore.

[14] The LSMS community questionnaire asks the communities: "Which persons or institutions help in the organization of the community? (a) the Government; (b) politicians; (c) the church; (d) schools/teachers; (e) ONGs?; (f) the community.

Table A18.9 - Institutions Supporting Communities by Type of Community				
Percent of communities in sample each geographic area indicating support from various institutions				
Support	Urban	Rural	Indigenous	Total
From the Government				
yes	22%	41%	20%	33%
no	78%	59%	80%	67%
From politicians				
yes	43%	23%	17%	29%
no	57%	77%	83%	71%
From churches				
yes	48%	52%	50%	51%
no	52%	48%	50%	49%
From NGOs				
yes	9%	11%	10%	10%
no	91%	89%	90%	90%
From schools				
yes	19%	54%	60%	43%
no	81%	46%	40%	57%
Source: 1997 Panama LSMS, community questionnaire.				

37.   The Government does not appear to be associated with the services it provides. The communities in the SCQS focus group interviews frequently expressed the idea that the Government is not run in their best interest and that "they do not care about us." In general, their relations with the Government seem mediated by a certain level of politicization and clientelism, with the perception that the provision of government services and public work is highly politicized.

38.   The mistrust of the government was expressed in three different ways in the SCQS. **First,** there is a strong presumption that the Government is not responsive. A variety of different stories raised during the SCQS focus group interviews reveal the general feeling. In one urban community, members stated that "three years ago we asked for telephone lines" and nothing was done. In another urban community with housing problems, it was felt that "they had no interlocutor or authority to provide solutions." For members of a rural community, it was necessary to insist to obtain government services: "one has to be like a water drop." Or, "... much talk and writing and nothing is resolved ... they write a report and one doesn't know whether it ends up in the waste basket." And "It is difficult [to deal with the Government] ... one has to fight with them ... one always has to go to Panama [City]." The indigenous communities were no exception in this attitude: "We have gone to Panama [City] and there are no answers ... they always say 'tomorrow' ... the Indian people have always been deceived. We have asked for the support of the legislator and she has not responded." They expressed that projects are "less accountable when there is no Indian person working on them. One does not know how [projects] are managed and sometimes they have a car in the project and claim that they do not have funds." **Second**, the SCQS reveals perceptions that when the government does something, it does them for the wrong reasons. Perceptions of Government officials' approach as being manipulative is widespread, particularly among indigenous communities in the sample: "only when elections are near [is the presence of government is felt.] There is a political season ... they all come ... we do not believe in them." "When election time comes they 'roar' and always say that they will give and then do not return." Or: "[the legislator] may come when the political time [elections] comes." And **third,** the mistrust of Government emerges from perceptions raised in the SCQS that the Government is synonymous of divisiveness. A number of complaints that the Government transfers problems to the communities were raised in the focus group discussions: "Some

things are not done because there are political rivalries between "regidor" and "legislador." Or: "If we receive government support we end up having a commitment to them."[15]

39.   Given the high degree of basic service provision in urban areas, the frustration voiced by urban communities in the SCQS sample suggests that these communities have come to expect that problems are to be solved by the Government rather than community organizations. In some cases, services are readily available nearby, though not necessarily located in the community itself; however, some communities did not concern themselves with learning about government programs to obtain these services. On the other hand, almost always there is a clear perception of what is beyond their organizational possibilities. An urban community in the SCQS describes an environmental problem caused by a slaughterhouse and explained that that the community, as a small group of poor people, has no leverage against a very wealthy company owned by powerful people. When trying to do something on their own they were ineffective and realized that the problem was beyond their reach. In another urban community the solution of their sewage problem is part of a much wider project at the district level which has a budget of US$2 million. The road to access a rural area had an equally high price tag.

40.   The focus group discussions in the SCQS suggest that the presence of religious associations is not necessarily an element of cohesion, even when efforts are made to organize members. Some of the discussions revealed that Christian sects have occasionally become divisive issues among indigenous communities. In one Kuna island community, for example, part of the community refuses to recognize the "Asambleas de Dios," with their congress "not wanting any more churches" because the proliferation of churches is seen as fragmenting the community into "small units." In one urban community, a priest tried to organize people to solve their housing problems but with very mixed results. In that community, the only real gathering place is the parish where organizational meetings are held every two weeks. Even though meetings are supposed to be for the whole community, invitations are made during mass which means that most participants are Catholic. Attendance is not good. A similar case was observed in a town where they added a generational dimension, "only we support [the church] ... children do not support this old people." If the community is divided, those divisions are reflected in church organizations. In one community the perception is that there are two parishes, one for poor people and one for rich people. Pews in the affluent parish are numbered and a humble black participant in the focus group said that the parish priest had asked him to leave, while the professional participants of the group made expressions of disbelief. In that community, boy scouts are organized by Adventists and girl scouts by Catholics.

PART II: COMMUNITY ORGANIZATION AND SOCIAL CAPITAL

A. Social Capital by Type of Community: Urban, Rural, and Indigenous

41.   As measured by the Social Capital Index, indigenous and rural communities have higher social capital than urban communities in the LSMS community sample (see Table A18.10), reflecting more and more active networks of associations in these communities. Only 15 percent of urban communities in the sample had high levels of social capital, compared with about one-third of rural and indigenous communities; close to one half of the urban communities had low social capital, versus only 11 percent and 16 percent in rural and indigenous communities respectively (see Table A18.10).

---

[15] Yet, despite all the complaints, the presence of government programs is felt everywhere. Public primary schools and health centers are accessible even in the most distant places. Rural communities reported receiving support from the Ministry of Agriculture and "food for work" programs. FES has road projects. Programs exist to improve roads during weekends. The Ministry of Health is present with health centers or, if not, with medical visits or vaccination campaigns.

Table A18.10 - Social Capital Index by Type of Community				
Percent of Communities in LSMS Sample in Each Area by Social Capital Index				
Social Capital Index	Urban	Rural	Indigenous	Total
Low	45%	11%	16%	26%
Medium	40%	54%	51%	48%
High	15%	35%	32%	26%
Total	100%	100%	100%	100%

Source: Panama LSMS 1997, community questionnaire. The Social Capital Index (SCI) is a composite index of scores on eight different questions in the LSMS community questionnaire about community participation and organization, as described in more detail above and in Lindo-Fuentes (1997). Communities with SCI scores ranging from 0-2.5 are classified as having "Low" social capital. Those with scores ranging from 3-5.5 are considered as having "Medium" social capital. And those with scores ranging from 6-8 are classified as having "High" social capital.

42.   The higher frequency of household participation in community groups among indigenous residents revealed in the LSMS *household* survey corroborates these geographic trends in social capital. As shown in Table A18.3 above, indigenous households participate in twice as many types of community groups (*juntas locales, concejos municipales,* committees, local associations, cooperatives) their urban counterparts. Moreover, as discussed above, while indigenous and non-indigenous households mainly participate in "public good" type of social organizations (such as committees, *juntas comunales*, local associations), urban residents primarily join cooperatives, which tend to offer more private production and/or consumption benefits.

43.   The SCQS also confirmed this pattern of social capital by type of community, finding particularly high networks of associations among indigenous communities with high SCI scores. Historically, indigenous groups have developed community organization as a solution for confronting economic, social and political challenges. Lacking physical capital, and with more difficult access to the institutional resources that build human capital, without the spacious social experience that is behind the sentiment of citizenship, social capital became their capital. Social capital essentially became a "homeward" solution among indigenous communities, organized through face-to-face interactions. In the indigenous community Puerto Lara in the state of Darién, for example, a women's organization was formed in 1994, a parent association exists, a health committee organize meetings and work on issues such as sanitation and the environment, and a water committee was founded. A community house has also been constructed.

Box A18.6 - An Example of the Usefulness of Social Capital in Rural Panama
An example of the usefulness of network associations can be found in the rural town of La Laguna in Panama, where a variety of committees lend money to each other. The constant interaction of members of the community in a variety of associations has created an atmosphere of trust that makes this lending possible. The same community has norms of reciprocity. When the time came to decide on priorities for a PROINLO project, the inhabitants of La Laguna supported a project that benefited a neighboring community. They did this knowing that, when they need support for a future project, they can expect reciprocity. The economic benefits of this are obvious. The scarce PROINLO funds can be assigned more efficiently to priority projects rather than being co-opted by narrow interests.
Source: Panama SCQS 1997.

44.   The Kuna in particular have a long tradition of organization and a thick associational networks. On one Kuna island visited in the SCQS, community members meet every day and hold a traditional congress Fridays and Mondays. In their daily meetings, they discuss issues related to the work that everyone owes to the community: airstrip maintenance, house construction, road maintenance, unloading boats. On another island, the community has ordinary meetings once a month and extraordinary meetings when the Sahila goes to the congress or to other islands so that he can give a report to the rest of the community. Smaller groups meet more often, with women getting together to discuss sweeping the

streets. Another group meets weekly to discuss commerce and solve social or economic problems and activities to promote development. Another example is the housing committee (*junta de construcción de la casa*), which builds about four houses every three months with about eight people on the committee. Women have a group to prepare for the traditional party held when a girl reaches puberty. They help the family whose "fiesta" will take place. In the indigenous community of San Ignacio de Tupile, there are as many as eight different community organizations covering issues such as schools, cleaning of local roads, nutrition, and water.

45.   Likewise, in the Waunana community visited in the SCQS, they hold bi-monthly general meetings where every sub-group also meets and reports to the general meeting. They discuss the aqueduct, the road, the school's parents' association, and the health center. Among the Ngobe communities in the sample, there is great receptivity to organizing, but more variation in actual levels of organization.

46.   The existence of community organizations does not guarantee the presence of social capital: in some urban communities, social capital was low despite the presence of community associations. In one inner-city community interviewed in the SCQS, for example, a meeting was called to discuss repairs of a building with forty-two apartments, but only eight people attended. A children's sports club was organized by a self-appointed leader without a shred of community support. The same neighborhood has a health committee and a parent's group, but they are perceived as politicized instruments, with the essential element of trust absent. In another urban community, they have a sports club but games end up in fights because of excessive alcohol consumption. Liquor was prohibited, but the members of the club say that if beer and liquor are not sold there is no money to pay the referee. The same community also has a Bingo group that organizes games to finance Christmas parties, but people fight over money. The health committee was appointed by the Ministry of Health and is not active, and the Junta Local does not meet. In another urban community in the SCQS, an ecological organization was formed after a problem with a garbage dump site. About 3000 people attended the initial meetings, but the community had clear class divisions and had lost steam. The ecological group is now a small NGO dominated by professionals. There is also a sports group for youngsters directed by a self-appointed leader with no community support.

B. Social Capital and Internal Community Relations

47.   **Horizontal Connections Among Communities.** The SCQS found that horizontal connections are stronger among those communities which scored higher on the Social Capital Index in the LSMS. These horizontal connections manifest themselves either through different organizations in the same community cooperating with each other, or through the establishment of links with groups in neighboring communities.

48.   The SCQS found that horizontal connections are strongest among indigenous communities, where the Kunas have designed a blueprint which is imitated by others. The most important horizontal connection are the "congresos" of Kuna communities. One such congress had taken place the day before the SCQS focus groups were conducted and one of the Sahilas informed us that they had discussed a wide range of problems: drugs, abandonment of children, problems at the border with Colombia, relations with international aid organization. In addition to the horizontal connections common to all Kuna, each group takes specific initiatives in this regard. In one group, meetings are held with six neighboring Kuna communities to solve common problems. In another, they get together with their neighbors for traditional chants that reinforce their identity. Their chants "talk about work in the fields ... chants give advice to the community." Every three weeks, they meet in a different place to chant. The Waunana and the Ngobe also meet with other communities and have "congresos," a practice based on the organization of the Kuna and encouraged by the Panamanian Government starting with the Primer Congreso Nacional Indígena

(First National Indigenous Conference) of 1969. The Ngobe, having weaker organization within their own community, presented fewer examples of horizontal connections during the SCQS discussions. The last "congreso" that one community had attended took place in 1994 and the other community had never attended one. As they themselves put it "we have to organize ourselves first".

49.   In rural and urban communities some horizontal connections are prompted by the institutional framework established by the Panamanian Government. The most salient example of this are the activities of PROINLO (Proyecto de Inversión Local). PROINLO is a local investment program administered by MIPPE that was established in 1994.[16] The program assigns $25,000 to each district (*corregimiento*) for a community project. In theory, the district's Representante organizes a meeting with the main local organizations to identify a project to be financed with PROINLO funds. In rural communities with a high level of associational life, the system works as planned. In one of the communities visited during the SCQS, the meeting had taken place the previous weekend and they had decided to use the funds to build an access road to a neighboring hamlet that belongs to the same corregimiento. "The entire town attended" the meeting, and men and women participated. "Everyone agreed [on the project]," there were outsiders who "congratulated us for not being selfish." In another town a similar process was followed and they decided to use the money to buy an ambulance. They cooperate with neighboring communities to organize medical visits.

50.   **Gender Roles and Social Capital.** The SCQS reveals that gender roles are assigned early in life, usually in the conventional way: in urban communities in the sample, girls "stay at home, do homework, watch TV, and do house work, the wash, sweep floors" while boys are allowed to go to the sports fields. The situation is not very different in rural communities, where girls help their mothers sweeping floors and working in the vegetable garden. Later in life, in rural communities men do "work," going to the fields and clearing with machete and the like. Women's cooking is not considered work. Women participate in the harvest but not in sowing the seeds. In one rural community and one Ngobe community in the SCQS, mention was made of single parents who are male. Among the Kuna, the care of elderly people is the specific responsibility of their daughters.

51.   The LSMS community questionnaire reveals that gender equity -- if not present in social life -- is generally found in community participation in Panama. Of those with some degree of participation, communities report fairly equal participation by men and women overall (see Table A18.11). However, a higher share of communities with low social capital report more participation by women, while men were reported to be more likely to participate in communities with high social capital.

---

[16] As discussed in other Chapters of the Poverty Assessment.

Table A18.11 - Gender Equity in Community Participation by Social Capital Index
Percent of Communities with Various Scores on the Social Capital Index

| Reported Participation | Social Capital Index | | | |
	Low	Medium	High	Total
Any Participation by Members:				
Someone participates	38%	15%	44%	32%
No one participates	62%	85%	66%	68%
Total	100%	100%	100%	100%
Participation by Gender:[a]				
Only men participate	7%	19%	21%	17%
Only women participate	22%	19%	10%	17%
Both sexes participate	70%	62%	69%	65%
Total	100%	100%	100%	100%

Source: Panama LSMS 1997, community questionnaire; question 8.14: "who usually participates more in the solution of community problems: (a) males; (b) females; (c) equal for males and females; and (d) no one participates. The Social Capital Index (SCI) is a composite index of scores on eight different questions in the LSMS community questionnaire about community participation and organization, as described in more detail above and in Lindo-Fuentes (1997). Communities with SCI scores ranging from 0-2.5 are classified as having "Low" social capital. Those with scores ranging from 3-5.5 are considered as having "Medium" social capital. And those with scores ranging from 6-8 are classified as having "High" social capital. a\Of those who participate (excludes share of communities who report NO participation).

52.   The SCQS shows that the early definition of gender roles does not preclude later participation in community life, but does help to define the character of that participation. On one hand, the domestic role assigned to women still keeps many at home which, in one urban community in the SCQS, meant that "they have more time [to participate in the community while] men work." In certain activities in particular, such as parents' associations, the participation of women is more active. In one rural community visited in the SCQS, although women participate, "men say what has to be done." Women's participation by doing the cooking is very frequent in school lunch programs, while men repair roads or when a medical visit takes place. It became clear that even if it is not openly acknowledged, women participate in community meetings by defining problems and offering solutions.

Box A18.7 - Low Social Capital, Gender Roles and Social Decline: Drugs and Premature Sex

The discussion of gender roles in an SCQS focus group interview in an urban community with a very low Social Capital Index offered a sad example of what can happen to girls when all norms have been abandoned. In this community, "girls who are twelve or thirteen years old are already women. Drug dealers give them money, they see that they have developed breasts...they offer them money, invite them to lunch and buy them new shoes....15- and 16-year old girls lure the younger ones who sometimes [spontaneously] offer themselves to older men." Participants in the focus group meeting explained how the result of this process was that young girls end up as mistresses of drug dealers or as prostitutes. Boys run drugs.

Source: Panama SCQS 1997

---

53.   The SCQS suggests that in indigenous communities, as elsewhere, the role of women in the community seems to be in the process of redefinition (see Box A18.8). In one Kuna community, for example, the Sahila designated a woman to participate in the focus group, in her words, "the Sahilas never invite women, but this third Sahila invited me because he knows that I am active ... We have the same rights as men, we have the right to speak ... Sometimes when we are in meetings with men and women men don't want to pay attention to what we say ... The rules of the Congresos are different, they favor men ... Some women [don't participate] they are afraid of making mistakes ... they need to educate themselves." In this community, the participation of women has had results that go much beyond being a mere supporting role. A group of women insisted on the need for a dining room for children in a meeting with the Sahila. The project got off the ground with the support of a group of Spaniards who were visiting and who contributed US$800. The food is provided by the government and the dining room is run by women.

Box A18.8 - Indigenous Communities: Redefining Gender Roles in the Community
In one Kuna island community visited in the SCQS, the President of the *Junta Local* is a woman. She has similar authority as the Sahila and can impose sanctions. She is also a *Nelegua* (traditional Medicine woman) and is involved in the program "Madre-Maestra." When there are land disputes, the *Reglamento* indicates that the *Junta Local* makes decisions, the Sahila said "If there is a problem they come to me, and I send them to the *Señora Presidente de la Junta*." Even her body language in the SCQS focus group meeting was similar to that of the Sahila: every participant of the focus group spoke in Spanish and looked at the interviewers directly in the eye. However, although both the Sahila and the Presidente know Spanish, they chose to speak in their own language. Every time they spoke they both turned their faces and their entire bodies away from the interviewers, waiting regally for the translators to do their job.
In one Waunana community visited in the SCQS, the women's group is under the leadership of a very charismatic woman and has promoted the construction of an exhibit space for their crafts. Following her leadership, men cooperated with their labor in the construction of an open structure with a straw roof. The woman leader had seen in the *Comarca* how women can organize (the community visited by the SCQS was outside the *Comarca*). She had also been invited by an NGO to a seminar in Panama City (presumably about women's organizations).
Source: Panama SCQS 1997.

54.   **Leadership and Social Capital.** The SCQS reveals that in communities with a high Social Capital Index, community leaders are often identified by their effectiveness. A number of characteristics emerged from the focus group discussions as requirements for an effective leader: (a) take initiative; (b) to be honest; (c) to be democratic; and (d) to be open to participation. In one urban community visited in the SCQS, leaders are known "through struggle and honesty," and they had to show initiative; in another, leaders were required "to be dynamic, to work, to be charismatic, not to look over his shoulder (meaning not to feel superior), to have support." In a rural community, leaders had to show "initiative....belief in the organization...[and be] active;" in another, community members noted that he/she had to be "willing to work ... if something has to be done that he/she does it." In an indigenous community in the SCQS focus group discussions, participants said that leadership has to be very active: "the community gets together and sees how the leadership works." In these communities, focus-group participants commonly declared that the leadership is not monopolized by the same individuals, but that there is a rotation "so that everyone learns and knows how to continue ahead," as was expressed in a rural community. In one urban community, the very interaction of the focus group showed how the natural leader, a very charismatic and active woman, avoided any monopoly of the conversation and encouraged others to participate and to share the leadership. Another feature of leadership in these communities was the willingness to listen and consult. This feature was most developed among the Kuna where it was demanded by the community. In one Kuna island community, Sahilas are elected for a four year period and the people carefully watch their performance: "The Sahilas sometimes make unilateral decisions ... if they do something wrong they are removed ... they have to consult." The Kuna have multiple leadership that constitutes a system of checks and balances: in one island they said that "the *Reglamento Junta* also has power, it makes sure that people abide by the *Reglamento*." On another island, the president of the *Junta Local* was a woman who has similar authority to the Sahila and can impose sanctions.

55.   A difficulty selecting leadership was revealed to be a characteristic of communities with a low Social Capital Index in the SCQS. Active and well-intentioned people do exist in these communities, but no one seems interested in following anyone for a common purpose. For example, in one urban community, two self-appointed leaders try to organize sports activities for youngsters. They enjoy respect but not support. A woman organizes activities for the day of San Miguel and for the International Day of the Children. She makes bags with candy and gives refreshments. Sometimes she gets help, sometimes not. Another community that was hopelessly divided between old and new (and often illegal) residents were not able to arrive at any decision and had serious difficulties in identifying the names of even informal leaders. In that community, the parish priest seems to have influence over Catholics, but his interventions in the focus group discussion seemed to suggest that he has a rather vertical relation with his parishioners (more by temperament than by ideological posture). Later in the discussion, someone declared "the community has no voice." "Here there are no leaders," was the expression used

elsewhere. In that community, there is a hard-working man who has taken it upon himself to organize activities for children and a group of Alcoholic Anonymous. The members of the local elite do not pay attention to him.

56.   **Role of Norms and Enforcement.** In all the communities where focus group discussions in the SCQS were held it was clear that decisions were reached by simple majority. In general, people would raise their hands in community meetings to vote to approve whatever issue had been discussed. The Waunana offered the variation of applauding instead of raising hands.

57.   In communities with a higher Social Capital Index, an effort is made to seek consensus "one reaches consensus according to the priority of the problem." When that is the case, "when the time to work comes, all participate," as was expressed in one urban community. This method is reinforced by success: in a rural community they explained that when there are disagreements and people "see results," they change their minds. Some communities go still a step further: to ensure consensus the leadership engages in frequent consultations, whether informally or through frequent general meetings. The informal method was simply stated in an urban locality where "the community is consulted," to resolve differences. A more scripted process is followed by the Kuna who have frequent meetings (some thought that they are never enough) and where the leaders who fail to consult lose legitimacy.

Box A18.9 - Efforts to Update Norms

The SCQS reveals a constant effort to update norms, and preoccupations when they seem to weaken. In one indigenous island community, the Sahila worried that norms were not being transmitted to the next generation: "parents do not offer guidance," "young men do not go to the fields [to work] ... they want to dive all day long." (The Sahila considered that only agricultural activities constituted "work;" fishing and diving, although lucrative, were not considered work, neither was the work performed by women). Enforcement was felt as necessary to remind everyone of the norms: in the week prior to the focus group interview, a man had beaten his wife had been hand-cuffed to the flag-pole overnight "so that other men would see that one's wife ought not to be beaten." Men who failed to perform work obligations in the community were fined five Balboas, "so that the union that comes from work is not lost." Drinking is supposed to be limited to Friday, Saturday, and Sunday, but the *Reglamento* is not always applied.

A similar effort to create internal norms and establish enforcement mechanisms was observed n rural communities in the SCQS. In one community, those who did not attend the meetings of the school's parents' association were fined five Balboas: "they had all agreed that they had to attend meetings or if not, they had to pay the fine." Similar fines were found in other rural communities. Enforcement is not necessary where there is a widespread perception of the benefits of the project at hand. In this same community, focus-group participants told how "there was no problem with the aqueduct and it was not necessary to impose fines because everyone agreed that water is important and they all worked." They are concerned about the dangers of alcohol consumption and have imposed regulations. "Here, we do not produce beer or alcohol...we ought to be vigilant about those who want to hurt the community... in the community, we should not allow the bad vices coming from outside ... it is better if we make the 'chicha' (an alcoholic beverage made from fermented corn) that we make here." The use of common space is also regulated by explicit of implicit norms. In this community, where the need of land for cultivation is large, a large space is considered common, it was part of the land donated by the Representative for the community to get together as a nucleated settlement. The piece of land has been considered common from the start and no one has challenged its use.

Source: Panama SCQS 1997

---

58.   Some decisions are obviated by the adoption of generally accepted norms. The elaboration of internal norms is part of having high social capital. There are certain things, like community work, that are expected of people, that constitute a behavioral code. To reinforce that code, finally, enforcement mechanisms are put in place. In one Kuna island community visited in the SCQS, when women do not sweep the streets they have to pay a fine, if they refuse to do so they are reported to the "*fiscalía,*" where a kind of a jury sentences them to forced work (20 extra days) if the fine is not paid in 48 hours. People who do not attend *Junta Local* meetings pay a fine of five Balboas. Everyone seems to be aware of the

specifics of the *Reglamento*, a legal document in existence since 1948 but modified by the community. The *Reglamento* mandates decisions by majority.[17]

59.   Where social capital is low it is difficult to enforce the most basic norms, even when the benefits to the community seem clear. In one community in the SCQS, the local *junta* lent money to residents to install electricity in their homes and no one repaid the loan. In another urban community, the common space, the Casa de la Juventud (House of Youth), was controlled by the legislator, it was fenced in and seldom used, and people had to pay to use it for parties. If there are problems between neighbors, the arbiter is supposed to be the *Representante* or the *Regidor* "but we do not trust." Disciplining a neighbor's child was not a good idea in this community: "one tries to call attention [to children who engage in acts of vandalism] and is confronted with profanity." In another community, there are no norm enforcers that could be trusted, "the police should not patrol because they are corrupted" presumably by bribe offers from drug dealers. The lack of trust hinders the organization of activities: "respect is lost, if someone wants to do something ... always someone steals the money." In that same community, focus-group participants explained that children are at the edge of violence "they do not say hello, do not respect, they want to beat you up."

60.   The SCQS found that, in general, the enforcement of norms is more likely to come from the community itself when it is isolated. Third-party enforcement is more frequent in urban areas. "The government should impose fines," they would say. The tendency to rely on third-party enforcement is also a characteristic of low-social-capital groups.

C. Social Capital, Poverty, Education, and Living Conditions

61.   **Social Capital and Poverty.** The LSMS suggests that social capital is the asset of the poor. Table A18.12 shows that a disproportionate share of individuals living in communities with low social capital are non-poor: while the non-poor account for 58 percent[18] of the population, they represent about three quarters of those living in communities with a low Social Capital Index. In contrast, the poor and the extreme poor account for a disproportionate share of those living in communities with high social capital: although the poor (including the extreme poor) represent 42 percent of the population (for which community data are available), they account for 54 percent of those living in communities with a high Social Capital Index.

62.   Likewise, Table A18.13 shows that the poorer quintiles represent a higher share of those living in communities with high Social Capital. Among those in the poorest quintile, the proportion of those living in communities with high social capital is more than double the share living in communities with low social capital. The reverse is true for the highest quintile: the proportion living in communities with low social capital is almost three times higher than the share living in communities with high social capital. Figure 1 (and Table A18.13) highlights the fact that the upper quintiles represent the majority of those living in communities with low social capital, while individuals in the poorest quintiles account for a higher proportion of those in communities with high social capital.

63.   The LSMS household questionnaire reveals that the poor tend to participate more in community committees and associations than the non-poor, whereas wealthier households tend to participate in

---

[17] Francis Fukuyama establishes a strong link between social capital, trust and norms. To him "social capital is a capability that arises from the prevalence of trust in a society or in certain parts of it." By trust he means "the expectation that arises within a community of regular, honest, and cooperative behavior, based on commonly shared norms, on the part of other members of the community." Francis Fukuyama,*Trust* (New York: The Free Press, 1995) p. 26. Many of the norms discussed in this report are directly linked to people's ability to cooperate with each other and function in organizations. In this report the importance of norms of honesty is exemplified by negative cases.

[18] Note that these results cover those individuals and households in the LSMS for which community data are available (as discussed above). Hence the distribution of the population by poverty group for those with community data available differs from the distribution of the entire population by poverty group.

cooperatives. The poor are 1.5 times more likely to join local committees and four times more likely to participate in local associations than the non-poor. In contrast, wealthier households were close to three times more likely to join cooperatives than the poor. These patterns seems to suggest that the poor see more benefits of participating in "public good" type community organizations, whereas the rich tend to enter into more production-oriented "private good" type unions such as cooperatives.

Table A18.12 - Social Capital and Poverty: By Poverty Group
% of people living in communities with low, medium, high Social Capital Indices[a] by poverty group

	Low SCI	Med.SCI	High SCI	Total
Poverty Groups[b] by Social Capital				
Extreme Poor	16%	51%	33%	100%
All Poor	19%	50%	31%	100%
Non-Poor	35%	46%	19%	100%
Total	28%	48%	24%	100%
Social Capital by Poverty Group[b]				
Extreme Poor	14%	26%	34%	24%
All Poor	27%	44%	54%	42%
Non-Poor	73%	56%	46%	58%
Total	100%	100%	100%	100%

Source: Panama LSMS 1997, household questionnaire (education data) and community questionnaire (social capital index). a\The Social Capital Index (SCI) is a composite index of scores on eight different questions in the LSMS community questionnaire about community participation and organization, as described in more detail above and in Lindo-Fuentes (1997). Communities with SCI scores ranging from 0-2.5 are classified as having "Low" social capital. Those with scores ranging from 3-5.5 are considered as having "Medium" social capital. And those with scores ranging from 6-8 are classified as having "High" social capital. b\The extreme poor include all people with total per capita consumption less than $470 per year for whom community questionnaire data were available. The all poor category includes all people with total per capita consumption less than $726 per year (including the extreme poor) for whom community questionnaire data were available. The non-poor category includes all people with total per capita consumption more than $726 per year for whom community questionnaire data were available. Note that the "all poor" and the "non-poor" categories add up to 100% (since the all poor category includes the extreme poor).

Table A18.13 - Social Capital and Poverty: By Quintile
% of people living in communities with low, medium, high Social Capital Indices[a] by quintile

	Low SCI	Med.SCI	High SCI	Total
Quintiles[b] by Social Capital				
Quintile 1	16%	51%	33%	100%
Quintile 2	21%	50%	29%	100%
Quintile 3	30%	49%	21%	100%
Quintile 4	36%	47%	18%	100%
Quintile 5	45%	38%	17%	100%
Total	28%	48%	24%	100%
Social Capital by Quintile[b]				
Quintile 1	13%	24%	31%	23%
Quintile 2	16%	23%	26%	22%
Quintile 3	23%	22%	19%	21%
Quintile 4	24%	19%	14%	19%
Quintile 5	23%	12%	10%	15%
Total	100%	100%	100%	100%

Source: Panama LSMS 1997, household questionnaire (education data) and community questionnaire (social capital index). a\The Social Capital Index (SCI) is a composite index of scores on eight different questions in the LSMS community questionnaire about community participation and organization, as described in more detail above and in Lindo-Fuentes (1997). Communities with SCI scores ranging from 0-2.5 are classified as having "Low" social capital. Those with scores ranging from 3-5.5 are considered as having "Medium" social capital. And those with scores ranging from 6-8 are classified as having "High" social capital. b\Quintiles of individuals for whom LSMS community data were available as ranked by total per capita annual consumption.

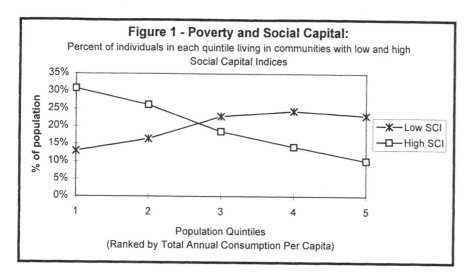

Figure 1 - Poverty and Social Capital:
Percent of individuals in each quintile living in communities with low and high Social Capital Indices

64.	Given the geographic distribution of poverty in Panama, with indigenous and non-indigenous rural residents contributing to three-fourths of national poverty and virtually all indigenous residents being poor, it is difficult to distinguish geographic and cultural determinants of social capital from economic and poverty-related factors. Clearly, the higher degree of social capital among the poor in Panama is partly driven by the fact that the indigenous and non-indigenous populations, who have higher social capital, are also the poorest. Indeed, poor non-indigenous rural residents account for 64 percent of poor individuals living in communities with a high Social Capital Residents and poor indigenous residents account for twenty percent. *Within* urban areas, the poor account for a slightly higher share of those living in communities with high social capital: although the poor represent about 19 percent of the population (for whom LSMS community data are available), they account for 30 percent of the population living in communities with a high Social Capital Index. *Within* rural and indigenous communities, where the majority of the population is poor, the correlation between poverty and social capital is weak, with the distribution of the population by poverty group for those living in communities with high social capital virtually matching the distribution of the overall population by poverty group.

65.	**Social Capital and Education.** Table A18.14 suggests a relationship between social capital and education. A disproportionate share of households whose head or companion have secondary or superior education live in communities with a low Social Capital Index. Conversely, a disproportionate share of households whose head or companion have primary or no formal education live in communities with a high Social Capital Index.

66.	The LSMS household questionnaire also suggests a correlation between education and the type of organization in which households participate. Households whose head or companion have a secondary or superior education are much more likely to join cooperatives, which tend to offer "private" production-related economic benefits, whereas those with only a primary or no formal education tend to participate in "public-good" type organizations, such as community committees and local associations.

67.	**Social Capital and Perceived Changes in Living Standards.** The LSMS community questionnaire suggests a positive association between social capital and community perceptions of recent changes in their overall well-being among rural and indigenous communities. Table A18.15 reveals that, among rural and indigenous communities, the higher the social capital, the more communities feel their well-being has been enhanced. This correlation is not present among urban communities.

Table A18.14 - Social Capital and Education

% of individuals living in communities with low, medium and high social capital, by level of education

Maximum Level of Education[b]	Social Capital Index[a]			
	Low	Medium	High	Total
Superior	24%	12%	8%	15%
Secondary	46%	35%	31%	37%
Primary	26%	42%	49%	39%
None	4%	11%	12%	9%
Total	100%	100%	100%	100%

Source: Panama LSMS 1997, household questionnaire (education data) and community questionnaire (social capital index). a\ The Social Capital Index (SCI) is a composite index of scores on eight different questions in the LSMS community questionnaire about community participation and organization, as described in more detail above and in Lindo-Fuentes (1997). Communities with SCI scores ranging from 0-2.5 are classified as having "Low" social capital. Those with scores ranging from 3-5.5 are considered as having "Medium" social capital. And those with scores ranging from 6-8 are classified as having "High" social capital. _b\Maximum level of education of reported household head or companion.

Table A18.15 - Social Capital and Perceived Changes in Overall Well-Being

Percent of Communities

Communities by SCI	Perceived Changes in Well-Being over the Past Five Years			
	Negative	Neutral	Positive	Total
Urban Communities				
Low SCI	42%	29%	29%	100%
Medium SCI	34%	34%	32%	100%
High SCI	58%	11%	31%	100%
Rural Communities				
Low SCI	43%	48%	9%	100%
Medium SCI	32%	28%	40%	100%
High SCI	25%	30%	45%	100%
Indigenous Communities				
Low SCI	17%	83%	0%	100%
Medium SCI	5%	58%	37%	100%
High SCI	25%	33%	42%	100%
All Communities in Sample				
Low SCI	41%	36%	23%	100%
Medium SCI	30%	23%	37%	100%
High SCI	33%	33%	41%	100%

Source: Panama LSMS 1997, community questionnaire. The Social Capital Index (SCI) is a composite index of scores on eight different questions in the LSMS community questionnaire about community participation and organization, as described in more detail above and in Lindo-Fuentes (1997). Communities with SCI scores ranging from 0-2.5 are classified as having "Low" social capital. Those with scores ranging from 3-5.5 are considered as having "Medium" social capital. And those with scores ranging from 6-8 are classified as having "High" social capital.

D. Social Capital and External Assistance

68.   The results of the LSMS community questionnaire suggest a fairly strong correlation between social capital and external assistance regardless of geographic type of community. Table A18.16 shows that communities with a high Social Capital Index report a higher frequency of assistance from of assistance from the Government and NGOs. Overall, communities with high social capital are close to four times more likely to receive Government assistance and two times more likely to receive NGO assistance than those with low social capital. This correlation is observed in all three geographic areas, and is particularly strong in rural and indigenous areas. Although the direction of causality is not established, this pattern suggests that social capital is a significant factor in communities' ability to leverage assistance. Box A18.10 paints a picture of how important social capital can be to indigenous communities in terms of gaining access to water.

Table A18.16 - Social Capital and External Existence
Percent of Communities with low, medium, and high Social Capital Indices Reporting External Assistance

| Communities Reporting Assistance | Social Capital Index | | | |
	Low	Medium	High	Total
Urban Communities				
From Government	19%	46%	35%	100%
From NGOs	24%	56%	20%	100%
All Communities (aid or not)	45%	40%	15%	100%
Rural Communities				
From Government	5%	56%	39%	100%
From NGOs	5%	63%	32%	100%
All Communities (aid or not)	11%	54%	35%	100%
Indigenous Communities				
From Government	0%	50%	50%	100%
From NGOs	0%	50%	50%	100%
All Communities (aid or not)	16%	51%	32%	100%
All Communities in Sample				
From Government	10%	52%	38%	100%
From NGOs	15%	57%	28%	100%
All Communities (aid or not)	26%	48%	26%	100%

Source: Panama LSMS 1997, community questionnaire. The Social Capital Index (SCI) is a composite index of scores on eight different questions in the LSMS community questionnaire about community participation and organization, as described in more detail above and in Lindo-Fuentes (1997). Communities with SCI scores ranging from 0-2.5 are classified as having "Low" social capital. Those with scores ranging from 3-5.5 are considered as having "Medium" social capital. And those with scores ranging from 6-8 are classified as having "High" social capital.

Box A18.10 - The Difference Social Capital Can Make Among Indigenous Communities: Access to Water
Percent of Communities in LSMS Sample

Access to Water:	Low SCI	High SCI
None	50%	25%
Have access	50%	75%

Source: Panama LSMS 1997, community questionnaire. The Social Capital Index (SCI) is a composite index of scores on eight different questions in the LSMS community questionnaire about community participation and organization, as described in more detail above and in Lindo-Fuentes (1997). Communities with SCI scores ranging from 0-2.5 are classified as having "Low" social capital. Those with scores ranging from 3-5.5 are considered as having "Medium" social capital. And those with scores ranging from 6-8 are classified as having "High" social capital.

PART III: CONCLUSIONS AND IMPLICATIONS

69. **Conclusions.** Given the geographic distribution of poverty in Panama, with indigenous and non-indigenous rural residents accounting for three-fourths of national poverty and virtually all indigenous residents being poor, it is difficult to distinguish geographic and cultural determinants of social capital from economic and poverty-related factors. In quantitative terms, the higher degree of social capital among the poor in Panama is partly driven by the fact that the indigenous and non-indigenous rural populations, who have higher social capital, are also the poorest.

70. However, the SCQS provides new insights on what could be seen as a mere relationship between poverty and solidarity. Cohesion can only exist when a sense of identity prevails. Identity can be built in many different ways. Among the indigenous communities in the SCQS, its principal element is the sharing of a common history, a common culture, a common pride in the past, in sum the sharing of a common passion. Among the urban communities analyzed (but also among many of the rural

communities in the SCQS), identity is based on the sharing of some needs and the sharing of an agenda on how to answer them, in sum, on the sharing of common interests. As the past is more resilient than the future, and as passions are more lasting than interests, indigenous communities tend to be not only more stable overtime, but more cohesive than urban and many rural communities.

71.   Cohesion, although not sufficient for development, can be a source of happiness. The LSMS and SCQS indicates that indigenous communities have a more positive outlook about their situation than urban and non-indigenous rural communities, despite the fact that they have a higher incidence of poverty. As they feel they are their history, the changes that history provokes are seen as improvements, even when schools are worse, water is more scarce, garbage is simply not collected, etc. Among non-indigenous rural communities, but particularly among urban communities, the future is an agenda to be implemented and the past an agenda that was not implemented accordingly. Frustration is almost endemic to this situation that equates happiness to comfort: as soon as a definable need is supplied, another one takes it place. The Government, seen as the greatest urban supplier, is for this reason viewed as the major agent leading to frustration. Hence urban communities rate the Government unfavorably, as they do for their recent past, which is perceived negatively despite the fact that the urban situation has been recognized as improving for specific issues (e.g., schools, health, water, sanitation, etc.).

72.   Social capital is not revealed by either the LSMS or the SCQS as having a major role to play in the urban communities analyzed. This might be explained because they perceive the Government as responsible for bringing about change and realizing their interests.   Conversely, in indigenous communities visited by the LSMS and the SCQS, social capital, after all an indicator of cohesion, is related to a positive view about what history is bringing about.

73.   Any community, no matter how poor or how bad the living conditions are, if provided with the adequate outside support, can improve itself through its own efforts, in an enabling environment. Poverty among the indigenous, even when social capital is high, is dismal. The fact that they are cohesive and proud of being so is an asset for the implementation of social policies addressed to them. But they need these social policies and a more active presence of government working *with* them.

74.   On the other hand, in a context of fiscal constraints with rising expectations, the capacity of governments to plan, finance and manage all that is necessary in urban development needs to be balanced with an increasing capacity of governance by urban communities related to their own community development. Frustration, pessimism and a lack of ownership of urban development were found to be common sentiments in the SCQS and the LSMS, despite the relatively better level of public services and lower poverty. The Government should seek to work more closely with communities, building on their first-hand understanding of local needs and the surrounding social reality. Community leaders should be identified and trained as partners to carry out programs, and links between communities, donors and the private sector should be facilitated to implement these programs.

75.   **Recommendations for the Bank.** The indigenous communities possess strong social capital and community organizations but are scarcely reached by development programs. The Bank should thus support efforts of the Government to bring services to these communities, but in a manner in which the development agenda would be defined and implemented in partnership with community organizations. For urban communities, which are poorly organized but have more access to public services, the Bank should support efforts to create and strengthen urban community organizations, empowering them to promote community development in a collaborative way with the Government.

Annex 19 – Poverty and Female Headed Households in Panama: Summary of Findings[1]

Nobuhiko Fuwa, April 26, 1999

1.   It is commonly believed that households headed by females tend to be poorer or more vulnerable than those headed by males, due to potential discrimination (in wages or employment opportunities for example) and a general absence of support.[2] As such, female-headed households (FHH) are viewed as deserving of special policy attention, via targeted interventions. This paper seeks to empirically examine the extent to which FHH are over-represented among the poor[3] population in Panama using data from the Living Standards Measurement Survey (LSMS, 1997).

DEFINITIONS OF HOUSEHOLD HEADSHIP

2.   **Self-Reported Definition of Headship.** One well-known problem with headship analysis is the fact that the typical survey definition of household headship (i.e., self-reported headship without any clear *a priori* definition) was created for the purposes of survey implementation and not for analytical purposes. That is to say, the main purpose of they typical survey definition of headship is to account for all household members and to avoid double counting during survey interviews by assigning a reference person (the "household head") against whom all the relationships among household members are identified.

3.   While this self-reported definition is useful for survey purposes, problems could arise when such a definition is applied for analytical purposes. Generally, different *uses* of the concept of household headship require different *definitions* of headship altogether. Alternative operational definitions of household headship typically include definitions based on household demographics and those based on economic contributions (Figure A19.1).

4.   **Demographic Definitions of Headship.** A common alternative definition, typically used in analysis of census data, classifies households without an adult male as "potentially female-headed" (cases G, H, and I in Figure A19.1). Because of the potential heterogeneity among the self-reported FHH, a common practice is to distinguish between *de facto* and *de jure* FHHs. *De facto* FHHs are those where the self-declared male head is absent for a large proportion, usually at least half, of the time (cases D, E, F in Figure A19.1). *De jure* FHHs are those where the self-reported female head does not have any legal or common-law union male partner (cases G, H, and I in Figure A19.1). Often, *de facto* FHHs may be supported by the male partners who are migrant workers but still play a role in decision making and in income contribution (cases D and F). On the other hand, *de jure* FHHs are headed by widows, by unmarried women, or by those who are separated or divorced.

5.   **Economic Definitions of Headship.** One main reason why FHHs are claimed to be worthy of special policy attention is that such households are at greater economic disadvantage due to a "triple burden:" (1) the "head" of FHHs is often a single income earner (rather than one of two earners); (2) the income earner being female faces various potential disadvantages in the labor market and in other productive activities (such as access to credit); and (3) the time pressure on the female head is acute due to the dual responsibilities of earning income and maintaining the household (e.g., child care). This view has led to a dissatisfaction with the demographic deinitions of female headship. There are a number of alternative economic definitions of headship depending on the various ways of measuring economic contribution to the household. One approach is to use measures of incomes earned by individual

---

[1] This is a summary version of the findings of this study with select Tables and Figures. A full version of the paper is available upon request, either from Nobu Fuwa at fuwa@midori.h.chiba-u.ac.jp or from Kathy Lindert at KLINDERT@WORLDBANK.ORG

[2] It is important to note that, since female headship analysis primarily focuses on the household level, rather than the individual level, it cannot be viewed as a proxy for analyzing the living conditions of poor*women* or as providing complete treatment of "gender and poverty" issues (which largely consist of intra-household and individual-level issues).

[3] For a discussion of poverty lines and the classification of poor or non-poor, see Annex 2 of the Poverty Assessment.

members; examples include: (i) the "cash head" or "major earner," where the household head is defined as the largest cash income earner (contributing 50% or more of household earnings); and (ii) the "major income contributor," where the female head contributes 50% or more of income from all sources (including non labor income). Another approach is to measure the contribution to household maintenance by the hours of labor time devoted by individual members ("working head").

6. **Shares of FHHs in Panama by Alternative Definitions.** Table A19.1 presents data from the LSMS to demonstrate the extent to which different definitions of FHHs identify sets of households as female headed:

- **Self-reported FHHs** represent roughly one quarter (24%) of all households, with a higher share in urban areas.

- Of these, *de jure* **FHHs** (no male partner) account for 84% of all self-reported FHHs nationwide, with a higher share in urban areas and a very low share in indigenous areas. There are very few *de facto* **FHHs** (male partner exists but is absent).

- With respect to pure demographic definitions, nationwide, about 20% of all households have no adult male (i.e., there is no working age male present in the household). As a subset of these, 80% of these (16% of all households) are **"potential female-headed,"** defined as those FHHs where there is no working age male *and* there is at least one working age female member.

- Using the **"working head"** economic definition of headship, where the head is the member who contributed more than 50% of total hours worked by all members, yields a figure of 16% of all households nationwide being headed by "working female heads."

POVERTY AND HOUSEHOLD HEADSHIP

7. The extent to which FHHs are over- (or under-) represented among the poor for the above definitions of headship was examined using a number of different techniques:

- Head-count poverty ratios using per capita consumption as a measure of welfare (and for the definition of the poverty line), see Table A19.2;[4]

- Head-count poverty ratios using a consumption measure of welfare that takes into account adult equivalence scales (since household consumption may be spread across household members unevenly, with, for example, children consuming less than adults);

- Head-count poverty ratios using a consumption measure of welfare that takes into account economies of scale in consumption (whereby the cost of additional household members is smaller than that of the first member);

- Alternative poverty measures such as the poverty gap and poverty severity indices (FGT measures of poverty) (Table A19.3);

- Stochastic dominance tests to examine whether or not the share of FHHs in poverty is higher (or lower) than the share of MHHs in poverty regardless of the level of the poverty line that is used; and

- Multi-variate analysis of poverty (Table A19.4).

8. The results of this analysis can be summarized as follows:[5]

- **Overall, female-headed households are not more poor.** FHHs are not systematically over-represented among the poor in Panama. This conclusion holds *regardless* of the definition of

---

[4] See Annex 2 of the Poverty Assessment.
[5] Detailed results are available upon request in the full draft of this paper, either from Nobu Fuwa at fuwa@midori.h.chiba-u.ac.jp or from Kathy Lindert at KLINDERT@WORLDBANK.ORG

headship that is used (self-reported, demographic, economic) or the technique for measuring poverty that is adopted. Generally, the evidence supporting the poverty of FHHs tends to be much weaker when the economic "working head" definition of headship is used rather than with self-reported definitions. Indeed, in many respects, "working" FHHs are found to be consistently better off than "working" MHHs.

- **Some sub-groups of female-headed households are more poor.** In **urban areas**, the poverty rate among FHHs with unmarried partners (*unida*) is significantly higher than that of MHHs with unmarried partners, although such households represent a very minor share (2% of all households). In **indigenous areas**, self-reported FHHs headed by divorced women and widows appear to be particularly more disadvantaged than similar households headed by males. Again, these represent a very small share of the total population. In general, the evidence of higher poverty among FHHs appears to be weakest in **rural areas**.

- **FHH should not be used as a criterion for designing poverty targeted policy interventions** given the lack of a systematic relationship between female headship and poverty.

CHARACTERISTICS OF FEMALE HEADED HOUSEHOLDS

9.   The characteristics of female household heads and their households also shed light on their living standards and the potential inter-generational transmission of vulnerability (Tables A19.5-14). An analysis of these characteristics using data from the LSMS reveals the following patterns:

- **Household Size and Dependency.** FHHs tend to be smaller and have fewer children, except those with male partners. The only exception is reported female household heads with unmarried partners (*unidas*) who tend to have higher fertility. Correlations between female headship and the dependency ratio, however, do not appear generally strong, except for some sub-categories of self-reported FHHs in urban areas (which tend to have higher dependency ratios). Multi-variate analysis indicates that most of the observed association between female headship and *lower* poverty is largely due to the smaller household size of FHHs rather than female headship *per se*: once household size (and other characteristics) are controlled for, female headship has no independent association with per capita household consumption (positive or negative).

- **Dependence on Transfer Income.** FHHs (mainly those without male partners) tend to depend more heavily on transfer income than MHHs, especially in urban areas, indicating the potential of their vulnerability. In indigenous areas, however, dependence on transfers is uniformly high regardless of the gender of the household head.

- **Age of Household Head.** Female heads are generally older than male heads, except for married female heads and "working" female heads.

- **Education of Household Head.** Self-reported female heads tend to have lower levels of education, especially in indigenous areas (there are some exceptions among sub-groups). Generally, "working" female heads are better educated than heads in other households. Some (but not all) categories of female heads may face "double day" duty: self-reported FHHs without male partners tend to work significantly fewer labor hours in economic activities than other heads, while this is not the case with the "working" female heads. This appears consistent with the possibility that household maintenance activities are indeed a binding constraint on their labor supply in economic activities.

- **Education of Children in FHHs.** One way of inferring the potential likelihood of inter-generational transmission of disadvantages is the association between female headship and school enrollment of children in FHHs. At the primary school level, there is a positive correlation between female headship and school enrollment, though this effect is weaker when other factors are taken into account. This correlation suggests that older children (commonly girls) are not being used as substitutes for working women's time in terms of covering household responsibilities.

- **Triple burden of FHHs?** As discussed above, there is a common belief that FHHs are at a greater economic disadvantage due to the triple burden of (1) potential labor market discrimination against women, (2) dual responsibilities of income generation and household maintenance, and (3) the role of the female head as the single earner (rather than joint). With respect to the first "burden," labor-market analysis[6] of the LSMS does not find that women face discrimination in terms of wages but potentially face limited employment opportunities. Women also tend to have higher educational endowments than men, though there are some exceptions (such as self-reported heads, as discussed above). Regarding the second time "burden" on female heads of income generation *and* household maintenance, there is some evidence that household responsibilities are indeed the binding constraint on female labor force participation (see above). The third "burden" (the possibly higher dependency burden) appears least compelling among FHHs in Panama. FHHs have fewer children and smaller total household size and dependency ratios are commonly lower among FHHs. Furthermore, the cases *positive* bivariate correlation between female headship and *lower* poverty disappear once household size is accounted for in the context of multi-variate regression. This suggests that many sub-categories of self-reported FHHs are indeed *better off* than MHHs *despite* the female heads' possibly lower earnings capacities and the "double day" time burden on female heads because their dependency burden is often *lower* than that of MHHs (in contrast with the "triple burden" view).

CONCLUSIONS

10. Female-headed households are not systematically poorer than male-headed households in Panama. In fact, FHHs defined in terms of economic definitions of headship are found to be generally better off than non-female headed households. At the same time, however, disadvantages of some categories of FHHs are largely an urban phenomena. In particular, FHHs with unmarried partners are particularly disadvantaged, though the number of such households is small. These households register higher rates of poverty, lower levels of the heads' education, higher dependency ratios, longer working hours of the female head, and lower school enrollment ratios of children, particularly girls. Another disadvantaged group of FHHs is those headed by widows in indigenous areas. There is little indication of over-representation of FHHs among the poor in rural areas. Female headship should not be used as an indicator for targeting anti-poverty programs, at least in these areas.

---

[6] See Annex 11 of the Poverty Assessment.

Figure A19.1 - Alternative Definitions of Household Headship

		Demographic			
		adult male and adult female Present	only adult female currently present		only adult male currently present
			male partner temporarily absent[1]	no male partner[2]	
economic contribution	male main(sole) contributor	A	D	G	J
	female main(sole) contributor	B	E	H	K
	both male and female contribute	C	F	I	L

[1]. This category includes households where the female 'head' has a steady partner (legal husband or common union partner) who are temporarily absent due to temporary labor migration or other mainly occupational reasons (military, seaman, track driver, etc.).

[2]. This category includes female 'head' who is single (never married), divorced/separated, or widowed.

Table A19.1 - Shares of Female Headed Households by Alternative Definitions

	Nationwide	urban	rural	indigenous
Total household	100.00%	100.00%	100.00%	100.00%
A) Self-Reported Female Headed	23.68%	28.62%	17.07%	14.97%
A)-1. Reported de jure FHH	19.89%	24.34%	14.40%	8.27%
A)-1.a. Reported de jure FHH: divorce/sepa	7.30%	9.15%	4.81%	4.18%
A)-1.b. Reported de jure FHH: widow only	5.89%	6.21%	5.88%	2.06%
A)-1.c. Reported de jure FHH: single o.ly	6.70%	8.98%	3.72%	2.03%
A)-2. Reported de facto FHH	1.78%	1.93%	1.27%	3.99%
A)-3. Reported FHH: unida only	2.34%	2.60%	1.69%	4.38%
A)-4. Reported FHH: casada only	1.45%	1.68%	0.97%	2.33%
B) Potential FHH	12.77%	15.79%	8.72%	7.40%
C) No Adult Male	20.33%	21.88%	19.44%	8.19%
D) Female working head	16.44%	20.98%	10.30%	8.87%
E) Core FHH [C+D]	7.51%	10.03%	4.12%	3.11%

Table A19.2 - Head-count Poverty Ratios of Female Headed Households by Alternative Headship Definitions
(Per capita household consumption: no economies of scale, no adult equivalence adjustment)

	Nation wide			Urban			Rural			Indigenous		
	FHH	nonFHH	t stat.	FHH	nonFHH	t stat.	FHH	nonFHH	t stat.	FHH	nonFHH	t stat.
1 Reported female headed	0.202	0.298	-5.651	0.103	0.100	0.156	0.383	0.485	-3.332	0.907	0.908	-0.010
2 Reported dejure	0.182	0.299	-7.283	0.087	0.106	-1.33	0.377	0.483	-3.460	0.936	0.905	0.625
3 Reported defacto	0.256	0.276	-0.388	0.131	0.101	0.619	0.345	0.469	-1.525	0.785	0.913	-1.108
4 Reported fhh: unida	0.385*	0.273	2.154	0.258*	0.097	2.721	0.510	0.467	0.428	0.948	0.906	0.805
5 Reported fhh: casada	0.180	0.277	-2.150	0.093	0.102	-0.179	0.251	0.470	-2.438	0.730	0.912	-1.235
6 Reported fhh: div/sepa	0.188	0.282	-4.125	0.092	0.102	-0.513	0.382	0.472	-1.732	1.000*	0.904	4.109
7 Reported fhh: widow	0.191	0.281	-3.605	0.071	0.103	-1.398	0.352	0.475	-2.786	1.000*	0.906	4.082
8 Reported fhh: single	0.166	0.283	-4.555	0.093	0.102	0.377	0.408	0.470	-1.078	0.739	0.911	-1.026
9 Potential fhh	0.160	0.292	-7.065	0.071	0.107	-2.163	0.346	0.479	-3.345	0.782	0.918	-1.819
10 No adult male	0.167	0.303	-8.257	0.061	0.113	-3.281	0.321	0.503	-6.098	0.803	0.917	-1.651
11 Female working head	0.141	0.301	-8.846	0.069	0.110	-2.327	0.301	0.487	-5.163	0.799	0.918	-1.821
12 Core fhh	0.113	0.288	-8.208	0.062	0.106	-2.310	0.256	0.477	-4.068	0.655	0.916	-2.220

Table A19.3 - Alternative Poverty Measures of Female Headed Households by Alternative Headship Definitions

Nation wide

	Head Count		Poverty Gap*		P2**		P Sen***	
	FHH	nonFHH	FHH	nonFHH	FHH	nonFHH	FHH	nonFHH
1 reported female headed	0.202	**0.298**	0.073	**0.123**	0.039	**0.069**	0.102	**0.166**
2 reported dejure	0.182	**0.299**	0.064	**0.123**	0.033	**0.069**	0.089	**0.166**
3 reported defacto	0.256	**0.276**	**0.112**	0.111	**0.065**	0.062	0.149	**0.151**
4 reported fhh: unida	**0.385**	0.273	**0.154**	0.110	**0.084**	0.062	**0.207**	0.149
5 reported fhh: casada	0.180	**0.277**	0.079	**0.112**	0.043	**0.062**	0.101	**0.151**
6 reported fhh: div/sepa	0.188	**0.282**	0.069	**0.114**	0.038	**0.064**	0.097	**0.155**
7 reported fhh: widow	0.191	**0.281**	0.067	**0.114**	0.036	**0.064**	0.094	**0.154**
8 reported fhh: single	0.166	**0.283**	0.055	**0.115**	0.026	**0.065**	0.076	**0.156**
9 potential fhh	0.160	**0.292**	0.059	**0.119**	0.031	**0.067**	0.081	**0.161**
10 no adult male	0.167	**0.303**	0.061	**0.124**	0.031	**0.070**	0.083	**0.168**
11 female working head	0.141	**0.302**	0.046	**0.124**	0.022	**0.070**	0.064	**0.168**
12 core fhh	0.113	**0.288**	0.035	**0.117**	0.017	**0.066**	0.049	**0.159**

POV5.LOG

Urban areas

	Head Count		Poverty Gap*		P2**		P Sen***	
	FHH	nonFHH	FHH	nonFHH	FHH	nonFHH	FHH	NonFHH
1 reported female headed	**0.103**	0.101	**0.028**	0.023	**0.012**	0.008	**0.040**	0.033
2 reported dejure	0.087	**0.106**	0.022	**0.025**	0.009	**0.009**	0.032	**0.036**
3 reported defacto	**0.131**	0.101	**0.037**	0.024	**0.013**	0.009	**0.047**	0.035
4 reported fhh: unida	**0.258**	0.097	**0.084**	0.023	**0.036**	0.009	**0.111**	0.033
5 reported fhh: casada	0.093	**0.102**	**0.029**	0.025	**0.010**	0.009	0.033	**0.035**
6 reported fhh: div/sepa	0.093	**0.102**	**0.029**	0.025	**0.010**	0.009	0.033	**0.035**
7 reported fhh: widow	0.071	**0.103**	0.019	**0.025**	0.007	**0.009**	0.025	**0.035**
8 reported fhh: single	**0.093**	0.102	**0.026**	0.025	**0.011**	0.009	**0.037**	0.035
9 potential fhh	0.071	**0.107**	0.019	**0.026**	0.008	0.009	0.027	**0.036**
10 no adult male	0.061	**0.113**	0.016	**0.027**	0.007	**0.010**	0.024	**0.038**
11 female working head	0.069	**0.110**	0.015	**0.027**	0.005	**0.010**	0.021	**0.039**
12 core fhh	0.062	**0.106**	0.011	**0.026**	0.004	**0.010**	0.017	**0.037**

Table A19.3 (continued)

Rural areas

	Head Count		Poverty Gap*		P2**		P Sen***	
	FHH	nonFHH	FHH	nonFHH	FHH	nonFHH	FHH	nonFHH
1 reported female headed	0.383	**0.485**	0.132	**0.195**	0.065	**0.104**	0.182	**0.259**
2 reported dejure	0.377	**0.483**	0.132	**0.193**	0.066	**0.103**	0.181	**0.257**
3 reported defacto	0.345	**0.469**	0.129	**0.185**	0.067	**0.098**	0.174	**0.247**
4 reported fhh: unida	**0.510**	0.467	0.161	**0.185**	0.076	**0.098**	0.224	**0.246**
5 reported fhh: casada	0.251	**0.470**	0.094	**0.185**	0.043	**0.098**	0.116	**0.247**
6 reported fhh: div/sepa	0.382	**0.472**	0.141	**0.186**	0.069	**0.099**	0.187	**0.249**
7 reported fhh: widow	0.352	**0.475**	0.119	**0.188**	0.061	**0.099**	0.168	**0.251**
8 reported fhh: single	0.408	**0.470**	0.140	**0.186**	0.068	**0.098**	0.191	**0.248**
9 potential fhh	0.346	**0.479**	0.127	**0.190**	0.062	**0.100**	0.169	**0.253**
10 no adult male	0.321	**0.503**	0.115	**0.201**	0.057	**0.107**	0.156	**0.267**
11 female working head	0.301	**0.487**	0.098	**0.194**	0.045	**0.103**	0.134	**0.259**
12 core fhh	0.256	**0.477**	0.092	**0.188**	0.043	**0.100**	0.120	**0.251**

POVS.LOG

Indigenous areas

	Head Count		Poverty Gap*		P2**		P Sen***	
	FHH	nonFHH	FHH	NonFHH	FHH	nonFHH	FHH	NonFHH
1 reported female headed	0.907	**0.908**	**0.616**	0.604	**0.448**	0.438	0.703	0.703
2 reported dejure	**0.936**	0.905	**0.635**	0.603	**0.466**	0.437	**0.732**	0.700
3 reported defacto	0.785	**0.913**	0.526	**0.609**	0.375	**0.442**	0.592	**0.707**
4 reported fhh: unida	**0.948**	0.905	**0.648**	0.604	**0.464**	0.439	**0.726**	0.702
5 reported fhh: casada	0.730	**0.912**	0.486	**0.608**	0.351	**0.442**	0.545	**0.706**
6 reported fhh: div/sepa	**1.000**	0.904	**0.706**	0.601	**0.542**	0.435	**0.808**	0.698
7 reported fhh: widow	**1.000**	0.906	**0.704**	0.604	**0.532**	0.438	**0.806**	0.700
8 reported fhh: single	0.739	**0.911**	0.419	**0.609**	0.242	**0.444**	0.451	**0.707**
9 potential fhh	0.782	**0.918**	0.495	**0.614**	0.353	**0.447**	0.588	**0.712**
10 no adult male	0.803	**0.917**	0.503	**0.615**	0.354	**0.447**	0.598	**0.712**
11 female working head	0.799	**0.918**	0.470	**0.619**	0.314	**0.452**	0.566	**0.715**
12 core fhh	0.655	**0.916**	0.378	**0.613**	0.274	**0.445**	0.482	**0.710**

*poverty gap (P1), P2, and P Sen are defined, respectively, as: $P1 = \frac{1}{N}\sum_{i=1}^{N}\left(1 - \frac{x_i}{z}\right)1(x_i \leq z)$, $P2 = \frac{1}{N}\sum_{i=1}^{N}\left(1 - \frac{x_i}{z}\right)^2 1(x_i \leq z)$, and $Psen = P0\gamma^P + P1\left(1 - \gamma^P\right)$,

where x_i is the per capita household expenditures for household i; z if the amount of per capita household expenditure at the poverty line, '$1(x_i \leq z)$' takes the value 1 if $x_i \leq z$ holds and 0 otherwise, P0 is the headcount poverty ratio, and γ^P is the Gini coefficient of inequality among the poor.

Table A19.4 - Estimated coefficients on female headship dummy in the per capita household expenditure determination regression* (t statistics in parentheses)

Headship category	Nationwide		Urban only		Rural only		Indigenous only	
	Without household size	With household size	Without household size	With household size	Without household size	With household size	Without household size	With household size
reported FHH	0.0668 (2.54)	-0.1019 (-4.03)	-0.0120 (-1.24)	-0.1719 (-6.10)	0.1038 (2.33)	-0.0566(-1.32)	0.0403 (0.37)	-0.1165 (-1.10)
reported dejure	0.0926 (3.27)	-0.1082 (-3.94)	0.0077 (0.24)	-0.1835 (-6.09)	0.1222 (2.53)	-0.0701(-1.50)	0.0353 (0.27)	-0.1523 (-1.19)
reported defacto	0.1047 (1.50)	-0.0091 (-0.14)	0.1858 (2.26)	0.1009 (1.34)	0.0444 (0.36)	-0.0809(-0.69)	0.1841 (0.97)	0.0231 (0.12)
reported fhh: unida	-0.0604 (-1.004)	-0.0449 (-0.80)	-0.1395 (-2.03)	-0.1104 (-1.75)	0.0005 (0.01)	0.0219 (0.21)	0.0729 (0.44)	0.0421 (0.27)
reported fhh: casada	-0.0122 (-0.15)	-0.0075 (-0.80)	0.0674 (0.75)	0.0929 (1.13)	-0.0004 (-0.03)	-0.0120(-0.09)	-0.0844 (-0.33)	-0.1590 (-0.66)
reported fhh: div/sepa	0.0582 (1.54)	-0.0593 (-1.67)	-0.0438 (-1.08)	-0.1472 (-3.94)	0.1455 (2.14)	0.0180 (0.28)	-0.1106 (-0.65)	-0.2099 (-1.30)
reported fhh: widow	0.1036 (2.32)	-0.0448 (-1.07)	0.0808 (1.52)	-0.0420 (-0.86)	0.1031 (1.55)	-0.0662(-1.05)	0.1527 (0.63)	-0.1765 (-0.77)
reported fhh: single	0.0375 (0.92)	-0.1052 (-2.73)	0.0103 (0.24)	-0.1230 (-3.09)	-0.0139 (-0.18)	-0.1008(-1.41)	0.5415 (2.14)	0.1266 (0.51)
potential fhh	0.2202 (6.52)	-0.0438 (-1.32)	0.1970 (5.11)	-0.0567 (-1.51)	0.1730 (3.10)	-0.0484(-0.89)	0.4044 (2.60)	-0.0287 (-0.18)
no adult male	0.3046 (9.35)	-0.1105 (-3.17)	0.2911 (7.59)	-0.0926 (-2.29)	0.2850 (5.58)	-0.1165(-2.14)	0.4350 (2.85)	-0.0069 (-0.04)
female working head	0.3320 (4.68)	0.0214 (0.79)	0.0548 (1.72)	-0.0483 (-1.62)	0.1617 (3.20)	0.0537 (1.14)	0.3158 (2.46)	0.1776 (1.47)
core fhh	0.2340 (5.46)	-0.0604 (-1.46)	0.1687 (3.67)	-0.0876 (-1.97)	0.2442 (3.11)	-0.0275(-0.32)	0.4708 (2.08)	-0.1071 (-0.48)

hhreg3_log

*Dependent variable is: logarithm of per capita household expenditure; control variables, in addition to female headship dummy, included are: age of household head and its squared, years of schooling of household head, agricultural land owned, logarithm of household size, share of household members by sex and age groups (female 0-4, male 0-4, female 5-9, male 5-9, female 10-14, male 10-14, female 15-54, male 15-54 and female 54-), and regional dummies. More detailed regression results are found in Appendix Table 3.

Table A19.5 - Age of Household Head by Alternative Headship Definitions

	Nation wide			Urban			Rural			Indigenous		
	FHH	nonFHH	t stat.	FHH	nonFHH	t stat.	FHH	nonFHH	t stat.	FHH	nonFHH	t stat.
1 reported female headed	52.20	47.56	7.99	50.90	47.09	5.17	56.18	48.69	8.37	47.08	43.86	1.89
2 reported dejure	53.62	47.43	9.85	51.91	46.98	6.22	58.39	48.55	10.70	50.10	43.82	1.95
3 reported defacto	43.26	48.76	-3.05	42.16	48.30	-2.39	47.13	50.00	-1.20	40.00	44.52	-2.05
4 reported fhh: unida	41.30	48.84	-5.76	40.67	48.38	-4.55	42.03	50.10	-3.11	43.70	44.37	-0.37
5 reported fhh: casada	50.38	48.64	0.95	52.08	48.11	1.62	48.11	49.98	-0.67	42.73	44.38	-0.52
6 reported fhh: div/sepa	50.44	48.52	2.36	49.83	48.01	1.80	52.31	49.85	1.73	49.71	44.11	2.03
7 reported fhh: widow	65.89	47.59	20.94	65.76	47.01	15.51	66.36	48.94	14.27	60.12	44.01	2.24
8 reported fhh: single	46.30	48.83	-2.45	44.45	48.54	-3.40	53.64	49.82	2.20	40.76	44.42	-0.75
9 potential fhh	52.26	48.14	4.29	50.30	47.78	2.13	57.77	49.22	6.31	52.55	43.69	2.92
10 no adult male	59.83	45.81	17.57	56.67	45.80	9.87	65.63	46.18	23.55	55.28	43.37	3.29
11 female working head	38.95	40.33	-2.40	38.91	39.48	-0.79	39.36	42.13	-2.30	36.32	35.29	0.42
12 core fhh	38.61	40.22	-2.19	38.26	39.49	-1.39	39.99	41.93	-1.09	37.68	35.30	0.53

NOINC.LOG

Table A19.6 - Literacy Rate of Female Household Head by Alternative Headship Definitions

	Nation wide			Urban			Rural			Indigenous		
	FHH	nonFHH	t stat.	FHH	nonFHH	t stat.	FHH	nonFHH	t stat.	FHH	nonFHH	t stat.
1 reported female headed	0.890	0.896	-0.54	0.965	0.971	-0.75	0.770	0.832	-2.30	0.181	0.603	-8.15
2 reported dejure	0.892	0.895	-0.19	0.968	0.969	-0.23	0.751	0.834	-2.81	0.098	0.580	-9.01
3 reported defacto	0.870	0.895	-0.67	0.949	0.969	-0.68	0.821	0.891	1.19	0.341	0.548	-1.79
4 reported fhh: unida	0.856	0.895	-1.24	0.932	0.970	-1.31	0.877	0.821	1.06	0.234	0.554	-2.79
5 reported fhh: casada	0.904	0.894	0.26	0.977	0.969	0.33	0.866	1.821	0.44	0.378	1.544	-1.23
6 reported fhh: div/sepa	0.889	0.895	-0.28	0.954	0.971	-1.01	0.788	0.823	-0.79	0.067	0.561	-7.33
7 reported fhh: widow	0.847	0.897	-2.42	0.963	0.969	-0.47	0.692	0.830	-3.30	0.00	0.552	-13.39
8 reported fhh: single	0.936	0.891	3.41	0.985	0.967	2.00	0.796	0.823	-0.59	0.261	0.546	-1.79
9 potential fhh	0.913	0.891	1.85	0.971	0.969	0.33	0.808	0.823	-0.43	0.355	0.555	-2.00
10 no adult male	0.863	0.902	-3.36	0.963	0.971	-0.93	0.716	0.847	-5.44	0.321	0.560	-2.61
11 female working head	0.960	0.904	6.10	0.981	0.975	0.78	0.937	0.841	4.11	0.565	0.629	-0.82
12 core fhh	0.947	0.890	4.26	0.976	0.968	0.75	0.876	0.819	1.22	0.516	0.541	-0.17

NOINC.LOG

Table A19.7 - Total Years of Schooling of Household Head by Alternative Headship Definitions

	Nation wide			Urban			Rural			Indigenous		
	FHH	nonFHH	t stat.	FHH	nonFHH	t stat.	FHH	nonFHH	t stat.	FHH	nonFHH	t stat.
1 reported female headed	8.119	7.846	1.27	9.623	10.162	-2.16	4.842	5.342	-2.11	2.114	3.260	-1.54
2 reported dejure	8.224	7.832	1.67	9.852	10.058	-0.77	4.454	5.391	-3.58	0.838	3.292	-5.03
3 reported defacto	7.656	7.915	-0.55	8.617	10.034	-2.56	6.470	5.241	1.73	5.016	3.007	1.01
4 reported fhh: unida	7.172	7.928	-1.87	7.952	10.061	-4.45	6.865	5.229	2.23	2.448	3.117	-0.63
5 reported fhh: casada	8.189	7.906	0.55	8.851	10.027	-1.89	7.052	5.239	2.17	6.027	3.017	1.31
6 reported fhh: div/sepa	8.369	7.874	1.49	9.933	10.015	-0.22	4.570	5.291	-1.89	0.401	3.206	-6.05
7 reported fhh: widow	6.304	8.012	-5.01	8.114	10.133	-4.50	3.595	5.360	-5.37	0.000	3.153	-8.79
8 reported fhh: single	9.756	7.778	5.59	10.971	9.911	2.72	5.662	5.241	0.93	2.593	3.098	-0.32
9 potential fhh	8.913	7.763	4.71	10.362	9.940	1.56	5.414	5.241	0.47	3.485	3.056	0.30
10 no adult male	7.535	8.007	-2.08	9.635	10.112	-1.73	4.091	5.538	-6.49	3.147	3.082	0.05
11 female working head	10.279	8.152	10.32	11.026	10.313	3.02	8.461	5.718	8.32	5.064	3.793	1.31
12 core fhh	10.426	8.347	6.53	11.077	10.395	1.94	8.308	5.903	3.99	6.738	3.915	1.43

NOINC.LOG

Table A19.8 - Hours of Work of Household Heads by Alternative Headship Definitions

	Nation wide			Urban			Rural			Indigenous		
	FHH	nonFHH	t stat.	FHH	nonFHH	t stat.	FHH	nonFHH	t stat.	FHH	nonFHH	t stat.
1 reported female headed	34.15	44.19	-9.67	33.44	45.37	-7.35	31.25	43.91	-7.75	26.68	34.10	-1.20
2 reported dejure	33.49	43.88	-9.68	34.98	44.96	-7.36	30.00	43.73	-7.88	27.30	33.99	-1.37
3 reported defacto	28.94	42.04	-4.96	26.99	42.83	-4.59	34.27	41.85	-1.77	27.10	33.70	-0.95
4 reported fhh: unida	38.08	41.91	-1.56	39.06	42.62	-1.13	39.62	41.79	-0.46	26.06	33.78	-1.47
5 reported fhh: casada	36.84	41.89	-1.45	36.60	42.63	-1.38	35.06	41.82	-1.13	44.95	33.16	0.71
6 reported fhh: div/sepa	34.75	42.37	-4.45	36.33	43.15	-3.54	31.27	42.28	-3.12	23.67	33.86	-1.70
7 reported fhh: widow	30.56	42.52	-6.86	32.41	43.20	-4.50	27.53	42.34	-6.11	30.23	33.51	-0.28
8 reported fhh: single	34.68	42.33	-4.67	35.37	43.23	-3.81	32.27	42.12	-4.43	31.82	33.47	-0.23
9 potential fhh	30.08	43.53	-11.64	30.83	44.72	-9.51	28.23	43.04	-7.42	27.67	33.90	-1.59
10 no adult male	23.29	46.54	-25.64	23.82	47.77	-18.93	22.18	46.47	-19.26	26.56	34.05	-2.14
11 female working head	43.64	41.46	2.37	43.20	42.35	0.78	45.36	41.33	2.18	40.42	32.76	1.25
12 core fhh	39.26	42.02	-2.56	40.07	42.80	-2.19	36.88	41.96	-1.95	31.96	33.49	-0.31

NOINC.LOG

Table A19.9 - Number of Children of Female Headed Households by Alternative Headship Definitions

	Nation wide			Urban			Rural			Indigenous		
	FHH	nonFHH	t stat.	FHH	nonFHH	t stat.	FHH	nonFHH	t stat.	FHH	nonFHH	t stat.
1 reported female headed	1.03	1.46	-7.97	0.97	1.20	-3.42	1.02	1.56	-6.11	2.37	3.53	-3.74
2 reported dejure	0.92	1.47	-10.18	0.89	1.21	-4.85	1.57	0.88	-8.29	2.47	3.44	-1.95
3 reported defacto	1.48	1.36	0.68	1.44	1.13	1.53	1.41	1.47	-0.17	1.86	3.42	-3.00
4 reported fhh: unida	1.90	1.35	3.28	1.65	1.12	2.73	2.19	1.46	2.11	2.80	3.39	-1.36
5 reported fhh: casada	1.09	1.37	-1.82	1.06	1.13	-0.43	1.16	1.47	-1.00	1.19	3.41	-3.81
6 reported fhh: div/sepa	1.14	1.38	-2.82	1.09	1.14	-0.49	1.17	1.48	-2.80	2.51	3.40	-1.72
7 reported fhh: widow	0.70	1.40	-9.18	0.64	1.17	-5.18	0.66	1.52	-8.58	3.56	3.36	0.14
8 reported fhh: single	0.87	1.40	-5.83	0.87	1.16	-2.69	0.85	1.49	-4.71	1.30	3.40	-3.29
9 potential fhh	1.05	1.41	-5.21	0.99	1.16	-2.05	1.13	1.50	-3.05	1.92	3.47	-3.86
10 no adult male	0.70	1.53	-14.80	0.73	1.25	-7.34	0.59	1.68	-11.97	1.84	3.50	-4.56
11 female working head	1.13	1.41	-4.80	1.02	1.16	-2.17	1.30	1.49	-1.70	2.70	3.42	-2.12
12 core fhh	1.01	1.39	-4.34	0.95	1.15	-2.02	1.18	1.48	-1.93	1.60	3.42	-3.39

NOINC.LOG

Table A19.10 - Household size of Female Headed Households by Alternative Headship Definitions

	Nation wide			Urban			Rural			Indigenous		
	FHH	nonFHH	t stat.	FHH	nonFHH	t stat.	FHH	nonFHH	t stat.	FHH	nonFHH	t stat.
1 reported female headed	3.61	4.38	-8.57	3.55	4.20	-5.43	3.54	4.29	-6.44	5.52	7.03	-2.96
2 reported dejure	3.41	4.39	-11.47	3.38	4.22	-7.59	3.33	4.30	-7.92	5.46	6.91	-2.24
3 reported defacto	3.95	4.20	-0.93	3.94	4.02	-0.19	3.67	4.17	-1.16	4.66	6.89	-2.78
4 reported fhh: unida	4.92	4.18	2.75	4.62	4.00	2.05	5.23	4.14	1.75	6.26	6.83	-0.81
5 reported fhh: casada	4.22	4.20	0.07	3.38	4.01	0.98	3.75	4.16	-1.35	4.32	6.86	-2.62
6 reported fhh: div/sepa	3.72	4.24	-4.20	3.67	4.05	-2.52	3.63	4.19	-2.73	5.96	6.84	-1.61
7 reported fhh: widow	3.25	4.26	-7.08	3.29	4.06	-4.03	3.02	4.23	-6.24	7.00	6.80	0.11
8 reported fhh: single	3.20	4.27	-7.23	3.15	4.10	-5.27	3.43	4.19	-3.60	2.86	6.89	-4.87
9 potential fhh	3.18	4.35	-12.77	3.11	4.18	-9.23	3.29	4.24	-6.59	3.97	7.03	-5.69
10 no adult male	2.54	4.62	-26.28	2.65	4.40	-17.66	2.29	4.61	-17.78	3.85	7.07	-6.64
11 female working head	3.68	4.30	-7.22	3.54	4.14	-5.82	3.87	4.19	-2.00	5.84	6.90	-1.73
12 core fhh	3.07	4.29	-10.221	3.02	4.12	-7.72	3.27	4.20	-4.750	4.08	6.92	-5.466

NOINC.LOG

Table A19.11 - Dependency Ratio of Female Headed Households by Alternative Headship Definitions

	Nation wide			Urban			Rural			Indigenous		
	FHH	nonFHH	t stat.	FHH	nonFHH	t stat.	FHH	nonFHH	t stat.	FHH	nonFHH	t stat.
1 reported female headed	0.484	**0.548**	-2.12	**0.479**	0.450	0.78	0.465	**0.606**	-2.94	0.784	**1.116**	-3.26
2 reported dejure	0.443	**0.555**	-3.47	0.448	**0.461**	-0.32	0.398	**0.613**	-4.75	0.899	**1.082**	-1.04
3 reported defacto	**0.845**	0.527	2.67	**0.848**	0.450	2.78	**0.927**	0.578	1.24	0.622	**1.085**	-2.69
4 reported fhh: unida	**0.834**	0.525	3.36	**0.806**	0.449	3.05	**0.900**	0.577	1.76	0.835	**1.077**	-1.62
5 reported fhh: casada	0.479	**0.533**	-0.59	0.417	**0.459**	-0.55	0.707	0.581	0.43	0.281	**1.085**	-6.89
6 reported fhh: div/sepa	**0.594**	0.528	1.18	**0.586**	0.445	1.95	0.575	**0.583**	-0.11	0.975	**1.071**	-0.40
7 reported fhh: widow	0.249	**0.550**	-9.70	0.207	**0.475**	-7.89	0.289	**0.600**	-5.35	0.904	**1.070**	-0.42
8 reported fhh: single	0.450	**0.539**	-1.71	**0.474**	0.456	0.27	0.342	**0.591**	-4.26	0.739	**1.074**	-1.10
9 potential fhh	**0.647**	0.516	2.88	**0.636**	0.425	3.73	**0.654**	0.575	0.99	0.891	**1.081**	-1.21
10 no adult male	0.437	**0.557**	-3.45	**0.471**	0.454	0.37	0.354	**0.637**	-5.62	0.855	**1.086**	-1.68
11 female working head	**0.534**	0.532	0.04	**0.501**	0.446	1.55	**0.594**	0.581	0.21	0.922	**1.081**	-1.91
12 core fhh	**0.634**	0.524	2.06	**0.605**	0.442	2.72	**0.711**	0.577	1.15	0.980	**1.069**	-0.31

NOINC.LOG

Table A19.12 - Dependence on Transfer Income of Female Headed Households by Alternative Headship Definitions

	Nation wide			Urban			Rural			Indigenous		
	FHH	nonFHH	t stat.	FHH	nonFHH	t stat.	FHH	nonFHH	t stat.	FHH	nonFHH	t stat.
1 reported female headed	**0.124**	0.076	5.81	**0.104**	0.047	7.10	**0.152**	0.087	3.67	**0.363**	0.303	0.91
2 reported dejure	**0.121**	0.079	4.59	**0.104**	0.050	5.76	**0.157**	0.088	3.33	0.266	**0.316**	-0.84
3 reported defacto	**0.191**	0.086	3.78	**0.150**	0.061	3.43	**0.181**	0.097	1.64	**0.463**	0.306	1.56
4 reported fhh: unida	**0.146**	0.086	2.87	**0.129**	0.061	3.06	0.082	**0.098**	-0.56	**0.467**	0.305	1.26
5 reported fhh: casada	**0.133**	0.087	1.63	**0.068**	0.063	0.28	**0.192**	0.097	1.58	**0.514**	0.307	2.38
6 reported fhh: div/sepa	**0.102**	0.086	1.25	**0.086**	0.061	1.76	**0.129**	0.096	1.62	0.265	**0.314**	-0.68
7 reported fhh: widow	**0.140**	0.084	3.39	**0.116**	0.059	4.30	**0.172**	0.093	2.10	0.303	**0.312**	-0.08
8 reported fhh: single	**0.126**	0.085	2.57	**0.113**	0.058	3.37	**0.169**	0.095	1.62	0.231	**0.313**	-0.77
9 potential fhh	**0.121**	0.083	3.66	**0.110**	0.054	4.74	**0.136**	0.094	1.89	0.278	**0.315**	-0.50
10 no adult male	**0.135**	0.075	6.35	**0.113**	0.049	6.18	**0.164**	0.082	4.69	**0.315**	0.311	0.04
11 female working head	0.086	**0.088**	-0.18	**0.079**	0.059	2.90	0.088	**0.099**	-0.87	0.291	**0.314**	-0.24
12 core fhh	**0.102**	0.086	1.48	**0.100**	0.059	3.41	**0.100**	0.098	0.13	0.211	**0.315**	-1.47

NOINC.LOG

Table A19.13 - School Enrollment Ratios of Children by Alternative Headship Definitions: Primary school age (Boys age 6-12)

	Nation wide			Urban			Rural			Indigenous		
	FHH	nonFHH	t stat.	FHH	nonFHH	t stat.	FHH	nonFHH	t stat.	FHH	nonFHH	t stat.
1 reported female headed	0.981	0.946	3.43	0.985	0.975	0.70	1.000	0.942	6.00	0.884	0.839	0.78
2 reported dejure	0.982	0.948	3.15	0.986	0.975	0.73	1.000	0.944	5.95	0.829	0.846	-0.25
3 reported defacto	0.957	0.953	0.14	0.956	0.978	-0.51	1.000	0.948	5.92	0.890	0.843	0.40
4 reported fhh: unida	0.969	0.952	0.72	0.969	0.978	-0.26	1.000	0.947	5.94	0.923	0.840	0.92
5 reported fhh: casada	1.000	0.952	7.37	1.000	0.977	2.73	1.000	0.948	5.93	1.000	0.843	4.66
6 reported fhh: div/sepa	0.970	0.951	1.01	0.971	0.978	-0.32	1.000	0.947	5.92	0.896	0.843	0.62
7 reported fhh: widow	0.979	0.952	1.68	1.000	0.977	2.73	1.000	0.947	5.95	0.500	0.849	-1.48
8 reported fhh: single	1.000	0.950	7.40	1.000	0.976	2.74	1.000	0.947	5.91	1.000	0.843	4.60
9 potential fhh	0.975	0.950	1.97	0.990	0.976	1.02	0.976	0.946	1.27	0.71	0.849	-0.66
10 no adult male	0.977	0.949	2.23	0.990	0.975	1.06	0.979	0.945	1.70	0.789	0.848	-0.54
11 female working head	0.979	0.948	2.75	0.983	0.976	0.50	0.979	0.945	2.04	0.914	0.839	1.05
12 core fhh	0.978	0.951	1.77	0.984	0.977	0.35	1.000	0.946	5.94	0.700	0.848	-0.80

NOINC.LOG

(Girls age 6-12)

	Nation wide			Urban			Rural			Indigenous		
	FHH	nonFHH	t stat.	FHH	nonFHH	t stat.	FHH	nonFHH	t stat.	FHH	nonFHH	t stat.
1 reported female headed	0.971	0.960	0.95	0.983	0.992	-0.80	0.963	0.950	0.56	0.863	0.856	0.13
2 reported dejure	0.974	0.960	1.27	0.991	0.989	0.33	0.962	0.951	0.41	0.761	0.864	-1.33
3 reported defacto	0.938	0.962	-0.53	0.935	0.991	-0.89	0.908	0.952	-0.54	1.000	0.854	5.00
4 reported fhh: unida	0.942	0.962	-0.59	0.923	0.992	-1.29	0.959	0.952	0.19	1.000	0.852	5.01
5 reported fhh: casada	1.000	0.961	7.94	1.000	0.990	2.61	1.000	0.952	5.67	1.000	0.856	5.01
6 reported fhh: div/sepa	0.986	0.960	2.19	1.000	0.989	2.60	1.000	0.949	5.72	0.703	0.862	-1.04
7 reported fhh: widow	0.939	0.963	-0.69	1.000	0.989	2.60	0.898	0.954	-0.78	0.750	0.860	-0.61
8 reported fhh: single	0.982	0.961	1.65	0.978	0.991	-0.94	1.000	0.951	5.69	1.000	0.856	4.94
9 potential fhh	0.975	0.960	0.96	0.977	0.992	-0.81	0.979	0.949	1.22	0.891	0.856	0.35
10 no adult male	0.975	0.960	1.07	0.978	0.992	-0.80	0.980	0.949	1.37	0.891	0.856	0.35
11 female working head	0.980	0.959	2.38	0.984	0.991	-0.76	0.991	0.948	3.07	0.871	0.856	0.22
12 core fhh	0.980	0.961	1.34	0.974	0.991	-0.96	1.000	0.950	5.63	1.000	0.856	4.99

NOINC.LOG

Table A19.14 - School Enrollment Ratios of Children by Alternative Headship Definitions: Secondary school age (Boys age 13-18)

	Nation wide			Urban			Rural			Indigenous		
	FHH	nonFHH	t stat.	FHH	nonFHH	t stat.	FHH	nonFHH	t stat.	FHH	nonFHH	t stat.
1 reported female headed	0.730	0.676	1.64	0.857	0.854	0.10	0.471	0.530	-0.84	0.401	0.435	-0.26
2 reported dejure	0.728	0.679	1.37	0.867	0.852	0.40	0.440	0.532	-1.34	0.336	0.439	-0.72
3 reported defacto	0.780	0.685	1.04	0.864	0.855	0.10	0.534	0.521	0.05	0.222	0.434	-1.11
4 reported fhh: unida	0.665	0.688	-0.30	0.713	0.861	-1.54	0.598	0.519	0.60	0.543	0.427	0.48
5 reported fhh: casada	0.874	0.684	2.92	1.000	0.852	8.93	0.545	0.521	0.12	0.444	0.431	0.04
6 reported fhh: div/sepa	0.725	0.684	0.85	0.853	0.856	-0.05	0.513	0.522	-0.08	0.336	0.437	-0.68
7 reported fhh: widow	0.759	0.684	0.17	0.933	0.851	1.75	0.276	0.527	-1.91	0.500	0.430	0.20
8 reported fhh: single	0.708	0.686	0.39	0.857	0.835	-0.37	0.424	0.524	-0.91	0.000	0.433	-9.03
9 potential fhh	0.825	0.682	2.40	0.919	0.852	1.17	0.548	0.520	0.18	1.000	0.417	11.84
10 no adult male	0.833	0.680	2.78	0.921	0.852	1.23	0.640	0.516	1.07	1.000	0.413	11.64
11 female working head	0.853	0.658	6.44	0.894	0.846	1.41	0.790	0.491	5.15	0.579	0.419	1.24
12 core fhh	0.931	0.682	4.80	1.000	0.851	8.90	0.727	0.518	1.20	1.000	0.424	11.71

NOINC.LOG

(Girls age 13-18)

	Nation wide			Urban			Rural			Indigenous		
	FHH	nonFHH	t stat.	FHH	nonFHH	t stat.	FHH	nonFHH	t stat.	FHH	nonFHH	t stat.
1 reported female headed	0.730	0.728	0.04	0.800	0.850	-1.30	0.660	0.650	0.18	0.337	0.332	0.04
2 reported dejure	0.749	0.724	0.77	0.827	0.840	-0.33	0.648	0.652	-0.08	0.207	0.348	-0.23
3 reported defacto	0.535	0.732	-1.67	0.495	0.841	-2.11	0.630	0.652	-0.12	0.500	0.325	0.60
4 reported fhh: unida	0.663	0.731	-0.78	0.669	0.842	-1.68	0.804	0.648	0.85	0.354	0.332	0.12
5 reported fhh: casada	0.561	0.730	-1.13	0.502	0.839	-1.33	0.506	0.653	-0.63	0.737	0.320	1.62
6 reported fhh: div/sepa	0.704	0.731	-0.51	0.774	0.843	-1.07	0.654	0.651	0.03	0.115	0.345	-1.86
7 reported fhh: widow	0.721	0.729	-0.13	0.805	0.838	-0.40	0.686	0.650	0.34	0.167	0.339	-1.23
8 reported fhh: single	0.827	0.722	2.42	0.895	0.830	1.61	0.590	0.654	-0.49	0.611	0.329	0.86
9 potential fhh	0.834	0.710	3.78	0.901	0.821	2.44	0.682	0.648	0.47	0.500	0.326	0.76
10 no adult male	0.836	0.709	3.97	0.904	0.820	2.62	0.690	0.646	0.61	0.500	0.326	0.76
11 female working head	0.809	0.710	3.18	0.901	0.816	2.65	0.641	0.653	-0.18	0.314	0.335	-0.14
12 core fhh	0.852	0.716	3.71	0.913	0.825	2.48	0.676	0.650	0.28	0.440	0.331	0.36

NOINC.LOG

Distributors of World Bank Group Publications

Prices and credit terms vary from country to country. Consult your local distributor before placing an order.

ARGENTINA
World Publications SA
Av. Cordoba 1877
1120 Ciudad de Buenos Aires
Tel: (54 11) 4815-8156
Fax: (54 11) 4815-8156
E-mail: wpbooks@infovia.com.ar

AUSTRALIA, FIJI, PAPUA NEW GUINEA, SOLOMON ISLANDS, VANUATU, AND SAMOA
D.A. Information Services
648 Whitehorse Road
Mitcham 3132, Victoria
Tel: (61) 3 9210 7777
Fax: (61) 3 9210 7788
E-mail: service@dadirect.com.au
URL: http://www.dadirect.com.au

AUSTRIA
Gerold and Co.
Weihburggasse 26
A-1011 Wien
Tel: (43 1) 512-47-31-0
Fax: (43 1) 512-47-31-29
URL: http://www.gerold.co/at.online

BANGLADESH
Micro Industries Development
Assistance Society (MIDAS)
House 5, Road 16
Dhanmondi R/Area
Dhaka 1209
Tel: (880 2) 326427
Fax: (880 2) 811188

BELGIUM
Jean De Lannoy
Av. du Roi 202
1060 Brussels
Tel: (32 2) 538-5169
Fax: (32 2) 538-0841

BRAZIL
Publicacões Tecnicas Internacionais Ltda.
Rua Peixoto Gomide, 209
01409 Sao Paulo, SP.
Tel: (55 11) 259-6644
Fax: (55 11) 258-6990
E-mail: postmaster@pti.uol.br
URL: http://www.uol.br

CANADA
Renouf Publishing Co. Ltd.
5369 Canotek Road
Ottawa, Ontario K1J 9J3
Tel: (613) 745-2665
Fax: (613) 745-7660
E-mail: order.dept@renoufbooks.com
URL: http:// www.renoufbooks.com

CHINA
China Financial & Economic
Publishing House
8, Da Fo Si Dong Jie
Beijing
Tel: (86 10) 6401-7365
Fax: (86 10) 6401-7365

China Book Import Centre
P.O. Box 2825
Beijing

Chinese Corporation for Promotion of Humanities
52, You Fang Hu Tong,
Xuan Nei Da Jie
Beijing
Tel: (86 10) 660 72 494
Fax: (86 10) 660 72 494

COLOMBIA
Infoenlace Ltda.
Carrera 6 No. 51-21
Apartado Aereo 34270
Santafé de Bogotá, D.C.
Tel: (57 1) 285-2798
Fax: (57 1) 285-2798

COTE D'IVOIRE
Center d'Edition et de Diffusion
Africaines (CEDA)
04 B.P. 541
Abidjan 04
Tel: (225) 24 6510; 24 6511
Fax: (225) 25 0567

CYPRUS
Center for Applied Research
Cyprus College
6, Diogenes Street, Engomi
P.O. Box 2006
Nicosia
Tel: (357 2) 59-0730
Fax: (357 2) 66-2051

CZECH REPUBLIC
USIS, NIS Prodejna
Havelkova 22
130 00 Prague 3
Tel: (420 2) 2423 1486
Fax: (420 2) 2423 1114
URL: http://www.nis.cz/

DENMARK
SamfundsLitteratur
Rosenoerns Allé 11
DK-1970 Frederiksberg C
Tel: (45 35) 351942
Fax: (45 35) 357822
URL: http://www.sl.cbs.dk

ECUADOR
Libri Mundi
Libreria Internacional
P.O. Box 17-01-3029
Juan Leon Mera 851
Quito
Tel: (593 2) 521-606; (593 2) 544-185
Fax: (593 2) 504-209
E-mail: librimu1@librimundi.com.ec
E-mail: librimu2@librimundi.com.ec

CODEU
Ruiz de Castilla 763, Edif. Expocolor
Primer piso, Of. #2
Quito
Tel/Fax: (593 2) 507-383; 253-091
E-mail: codeu@impsat.net.ec

EGYPT, ARAB REPUBLIC OF
Al Ahram Distribution Agency
Al Galaa Street
Cairo
Tel: (20 2) 578-6083
Fax: (20 2) 578-6833

The Middle East Observer
41, Sherif Street
Cairo
Tel: (20 2) 393-9732
Fax: (20 2) 393-9732

FINLAND
Akateeminen Kirjakauppa
P.O. Box 128
FIN-00101 Helsinki
Tel: (358 0) 121 4418
Fax: (358 0) 121-4435
E-mail: akatilaus@stockmann.fi
URL: http://www.akateeminen.com

FRANCE
Editions Eska; DBJ
48, rue Gay Lussac
75005 Paris
Tel: (33-1) 55-42-73-08
Fax: (33-1) 43-29-91-67

GERMANY
UNO-Verlag
Poppelsdorfer Allee 55
53115 Bonn
Tel: (49 228) 949020
Fax: (49 228) 217492
URL: http://www.uno-verlag.de
E-mail: unoverlag@aol.com

GHANA
Epp Books Services
P.O. Box 44
TUC
Accra
Tel: 223 21 778843
Fax: 223 21 779099

GREECE
Papastiriou S.A.
35, Stournara Str.
106 82 Athens
Tel: (30 1) 364-1826
Fax: (30 1) 364-8254

HAITI
Culture Diffusion
5, Rue Capois
C.P. 257
Port-au-Prince
Tel: (509) 23 9260
Fax: (509) 23 4858

HONG KONG, CHINA; MACAO
Asia 2000 Ltd.
Sales & Circulation Department
302 Seabird House
22-28 Wyndham Street, Central
Hong Kong, China
Tel: (852) 2530-1409
Fax: (852) 2526-1107
E-mail: sales@asia2000.com.hk
URL: http://www.asia2000.com.hk

HUNGARY
Euro Info Service
Margitszgeti Europa Haz
H-1138 Budapest
Tel: (36 1) 350 80 24, 350 80 25
Fax: (36 1) 350 90 32
E-mail: euroinfo@mail.matav.hu

INDIA
Allied Publishers Ltd.
751 Mount Road
Madras - 600 002
Tel: (91 44) 852-3938
Fax: (91 44) 852-0649

INDONESIA
Pt. Indira Limited
Jalan Borobudur 20
P.O. Box 181
Jakarta 10320
Tel: (62 21) 390-4290
Fax: (62 21) 390-4289

IRAN
Ketab Sara Co. Publishers
Khaled Eslamboli Ave., 6th Street
Delafrooz Alley No. 8
P.O. Box 15745-733
Tehran 15117
Tel: (98 21) 8717819; 8716104
Fax: (98 21) 8712479
E-mail: ketab-sara@neda.net.ir

Kowkab Publishers
P.O. Box 19575-511
Tehran
Tel: (98 21) 258-3723
Fax: (98 21) 258-3723

IRELAND
Government Supplies Agency
Oifig an tSoláthair
4-5 Harcourt Road
Dublin 2
Tel: (353 1) 661-3111
Fax: (353 1) 475-2670

ISRAEL
Yozmot Literature Ltd.
P.O. Box 56055
3 Yohanan Hasandlar Street
Tel Aviv 61560
Tel: (972 3) 5285-397
Fax: (972 3) 5285-397

R.O.Y. International
PO Box 13056
Tel Aviv 61130
Tel: (972 3) 649 9469
Fax: (972 3) 648 6039
E-mail: royil@netvision.net.il
URL: http://www.royint.co.il

Palestinian Authority/Middle East
Index Information Services
P.O.B. 19502 Jerusalem
Tel: (972 2) 6271219
Fax: (972 2) 6271634

ITALY, LIBERIA
Licosa Commissionaria Sansoni SPA
Via Duca Di Calabria, 1/1
Casella Postale 552
50125 Firenze
Tel: (39 55) 645-415
Fax: (39 55) 641-257
E-mail: licosa@ftbcc.it
URL: http://www.ftbcc.it/licosa

JAMAICA
Ian Randle Publishers Ltd.
206 Old Hope Road, Kingston 6
Tel: 876-927-2085
Fax: 876-977-0243
E-mail: irpl@colis.com

JAPAN
Eastern Book Service
3-13 Hongo 3-chome, Bunkyo-ku
Tokyo 113
Tel: (81 3) 3818-0861
Fax: (81 3) 3818-0864
E-mail: orders@svt-ebs.co.jp
URL: http://www.bekkoame.or.jp/~svt-ebs

KENYA
Africa Book Service (E.A.) Ltd.
Quaran House, Mfangano Street
P.O. Box 45245
Nairobi
Tel: (254 2) 223 641
Fax: (254 2) 330 272

Legacy Books
Loita House
Mezzanine 1
P.O. Box 68077
Nairobi
Tel: (254) 2-330853, 221426
Fax: (254) 2-330854, 561654
E-mail: Legacy@form-net.com

KOREA, REPUBLIC OF
Dayang Books Trading Co.
International Division
783-20, Pangba Bon-Dong,
Socho-ku
Seoul
Tel: (82 2) 536-9555
Fax: (82 2) 536-0025
E-mail: seamap@chollian.net

Eulyoo Publishing Co., Ltd.
46-1, Susong-Dong
Jongro-Gu
Seoul
Tel: (82 2) 734-3515
Fax: (82 2) 732-9154

LEBANON
Librairie du Liban
P.O. Box 11-9232
Beirut
Tel: (961 9) 217 944
Fax: (961 9) 217 434
E-mail: hsayegh@librairie-du-liban.com.lb
URL: http://www.librairie-du-liban.com.lb

MALAYSIA
University of Malaya Cooperative
Bookshop, Limited
P.O. Box 1127
Jalan Pantai Baru
59700 Kuala Lumpur
Tel: (60 3) 756-5000
Fax: (60 3) 755-4424
E-mail: umkoop@tm.net.my

MEXICO
INFOTEC
Av. San Fernando No. 37
Col. Toriello Guerra
14050 Mexico, D.F.
Tel: (52 5) 624-2800
Fax: (52 5) 624-2822
E-mail: infotec@rtn.net.mx
URL: http://rtn.net.mx

Mundi-Prensa Mexico S.A. de C.V.
c/Rio Panuco, 141-Colonia
Cuauhtemoc
06500 Mexico, D.F.
Tel: (52 5) 533-5658
Fax: (52 5) 514-6799

NEPAL
Everest Media International Services
(P.) Ltd.
GPO Box 5443
Kathmandu
Tel: (977 1) 416 026
Fax: (977 1) 224 431

NETHERLANDS
De Lindeboom/Internationale
Publicaties b.v.-
P.O. Box 202, 7480 AE Haaksbergen
Tel: (31 53) 574-0004
Fax: (31 53) 572-9296
E-mail: lindeboo@worldonline.nl
URL: http://www.worldonline.nl/~lindeboo

NEW ZEALAND
EBSCO NZ Ltd.
Private Mail Bag 99914
New Market
Auckland
Tel: (64 9) 524-8119
Fax: (64 9) 524-8067

Oasis Official
P.O. Box 3627
Wellington
Tel: (64 4) 499 1551
Fax: (64 4) 499 1972
E-mail: oasis@actrix.gen.nz
URL: http://www.oasisbooks.co.nz/

NIGERIA
University Press Limited
Three Crowns Building Jericho
Private Mail Bag 5095
Ibadan
Tel: (234 22) 41-1356
Fax: (234 22) 41-2056

PAKISTAN
Mirza Book Agency
65, Shahrah-e-Quaid-e-Azam
Lahore 54000
Tel: (92 42) 735 3601
Fax: (92 42) 576 3714

Oxford University Press
5 Bangalore Town
Sharae Faisal
PO Box 13033
Karachi-75350
Tel: (92 21) 446307
Fax: (92 21) 4547640
E-mail: ouppak@TheOffice.net

Pak Book Corporation
Aziz Chambers 21, Queen's Road
Lahore
Tel: (92 42) 636 3222; 636 0885
Fax: (92 42) 636 2328
E-mail: pbc@brain.net.pk

PERU
Editorial Desarrollo SA
Apartado 3824, Ica 242 OF. 106
Lima 1
Tel: (51 14) 285380
Fax: (51 14) 286628

PHILIPPINES
International Booksource Center Inc.
1127-A Antipolo St, Barangay,
Venezuela
Makati City
Tel: (63 2) 896 6501; 6505; 6507
Fax: (63 2) 896 1741

POLAND
International Publishing Service
Ul. Piekna 31/37
00-677 Warzawa
Tel: (48 2) 628-6089
Fax: (48 2) 621-7255
E-mail: books%ips@ikp.atm.com.pl
URL: http://www.ipscg.waw.pl/ips/export

PORTUGAL
Livraria Portugal
Apartado 2681, Rua Do Carm
o 70-74
1200 Lisbon
Tel: (1) 347-4982
Fax: (1) 347-0264

ROMANIA
Compani De Librarii Bucuresti S.A.
Str. Lipscani no. 26, sector 3
Bucharest
Tel: (40 1) 313 9645
Fax: (40 1) 312 4000

RUSSIAN FEDERATION
Isdatelstvo <Ves Mir>
9a, Kolpachniy Pereulok
Moscow 101831
Tel: (7 095) 917 87 49
Fax: (7 095) 917 92 59
ozimarin@glasnet.ru

SINGAPORE; TAIWAN, CHINA MYANMAR; BRUNEI
Hemisphere Publication Services
41 Kallang Pudding Road #04-03
Golden Wheel Building
Singapore 349316
Tel: (65) 741-5166
Fax: (65) 742-9356
E-mail: ashgate@asianconnect.com

SLOVENIA
Gospodarski vestnik Publishing
Group
Dunajska cesta 5
1000 Ljubljana
Tel: (386 61) 133 83 47; 132 12 30
Fax: (386 61) 133 80 30
E-mail: repansekj@gvestnik.si

SOUTH AFRICA, BOTSWANA
For single titles:
Oxford University Press Southern
Africa
Vasco Boulevard, Goodwood
P.O. Box 12119, N1 City 7463
Cape Town
Tel: (27 21) 595 4400
Fax: (27 21) 595 4430
E-mail: oxford@oup.co.za

For subscription orders:
International Subscription Service
P.O. Box 41095
Craighall
Johannesburg 2024
Tel: (27 11) 880-1448
Fax: (27 11) 880-6248
E-mail: iss@is.co.za

SPAIN
Mundi-Prensa Libros, S.A.
Castello 37
28001 Madrid
Tel: (34 91) 4 363700
Fax: (34 91) 5 753998
E-mail: libreria@mundiprensa.es
URL: http://www.mundiprensa.com/

Mundi-Prensa Barcelona
Consell de Cent, 391
08009 Barcelona
Tel: (34 3) 488-3492
Fax: (34 3) 487-7659
E-mail: barcelona@mundiprensa.es

SRI LANKA, THE MALDIVES
Lake House Bookshop
100, Sir Chittampalam Gardiner
Mawatha
Colombo 2
Tel: (94 1) 32105
Fax: (04 1) 432104
E-mail: LHL@sri.lanka.net

SWEDEN
Wennergren-Williams AB
P. O. Box 1305
S-171 25 Solna
Tel: (46 8) 705-97-50
Fax: (46 8) 27-00-71
E-mail: mail@wwi.se

SWITZERLAND
Librairie Payot Service Institutionnel
C(tm)tes-de-Montbenon 30
1002 Lausanne
Tel: (41 21) 341-3229
Fax: (41 21) 341-3235

ADECO Van Diermen
EditionsTechniques
Ch. de Lacuez 41
CH1807 Blonay
Tel: (41 21) 943 2673
Fax: (41 21) 943 3605

THAILAND
Central Books Distribution
306 Silom Road
Bangkok 10500
Tel: (66 2) 2336930-9
Fax: (66 2) 237-8321

TRINIDAD & TOBAGO AND THE CARRIBBEAN
Systematics Studies Ltd.
St. Augustine Shopping Center
Eastern Main Road, St. Augustine
Trinidad & Tobago, West Indies
Tel: (868) 645-8466
Fax: (868) 645-8467
E-mail: tobe@trinidad.net

UGANDA
Gustro Ltd.
PO Box 9997, Madhvani Building
Plot 16/4 Jinja Rd.
Kampala
Tel: (256 41) 251 467
Fax: (256 41) 251 468
E-mail: gus@swiftuganda.com

UNITED KINGDOM
Microinfo Ltd.
P.O. Box 3, Omega Park, Alton,
Hampshire GU34 2PG
England
Tel: (44 1420) 86848
Fax: (44 1420) 89889
E-mail: wbank@microinfo.co.uk
URL: http://www.microinfo.co.uk

The Stationery Office
51 Nine Elms Lane
London SW8 5DR
Tel: (44 171) 873-8400
Fax: (44 171) 873-8242
URL: http://www.the-stationery-office.co.uk/

VENEZUELA
Tecni-Ciencia Libros, S.A.
Centro Cuidad Comercial Tamanco
Nivel C2, Caracas
Tel: (58 2) 959 5547; 5035; 0016
Fax: (58 2) 959 5636

ZAMBIA
University Bookshop, University of
Zambia
Great East Road Campus
P.O. Box 32379
Lusaka
Tel: (260 1) 252 576
Fax: (260 1) 253 952

ZIMBABWE
Academic and Baobab Books (Pvt.)
Ltd.
4 Conald Road, Graniteside
P.O. Box 567
Harare
Tel: 263 4 755035
Fax: 263 4 781913